Phil Edmonston

LEMON-AID

2011

NEW CARS and TRUCKS

DUNDURN PRESS

TORONTO

Editing: Andrea Battiston, Caroline Hardy
Design: Jack Steiner
Printer: Webcom

1 2 3 4 5   14 13 12 11 10

 Conseil des Arts du Canada   Canada Council for the Arts    Canadä    ONTARIO ARTS COUNCIL CONSEIL DES ARTS DE L'ONTARIO

We acknowledge the support of the **Canada Council for the Arts** and the **Ontario Arts Council** for our publishing program.
We also acknowledge the financial support of the **Government of Canada** through the **Canada Book Fund** and
Livres Canada Books, and the **Government of Ontario** through the **Ontario Book Publishers Tax Credit program**,
and the **Ontario Media Development Corporation**.

Printed and bound in Canada.
www.dundurn.com

Dundurn Press
3 Church Street, Suite 500
Toronto, Ontario, Canada
M5E 1M2

Gazelle Book Services Limited
White Cross Mills
High Town, Lancaster, England
LA1 4XS

Dundurn Press
2250 Military Road
Tonawanda, NY
U.S.A. 14150

FSC   **Mixed Sources**
Product group from well-managed
forests, and other controlled sources
www.fsc.org Cert no. SW-COC-002358
© 1996 Forest Stewardship Council

CONTENTS

Squeezing the Most Out of *Lemon-Aid*

Read Part One before visiting the dealer. You will learn about the elements that make a vehicle a good buy, from the standpoint of price, safety, reliability, performance, and fuel-economy. Tips for negotiating the contract are also a must-read. Part Two outlines the best way to get a refund when things go wrong. Your rights and the dealer's obligations are spelled out in detail, and we provide a sample claim letter that you can copy to get action fast. A summary of little-known secret warranties and winning court cases completes your legal arsenal. Part Three and Appendix I describe the best and worst buys for the past two model years and predict how the 2011 models will perform. Appendix II lists 20 easy ways to save fuel, and Appendix III serves up a specially culled list of informative and amusing websites. Appendix IV gives you some tips on buying a vehicle in the States, and Appendix V includes some of the latest secret warranties and confidential service bulletins. Finally, the model index at the back of the book groups models by rating and allows you to go straight to our discussion of a particular model.

Appendix I

MINI-REVIEWS AND PREVIEWS 480

Appendix II

Appendix III

Appendix IV

Appendix V

KEY DOCUMENTS

Lemon-Aid is a feisty owner's manual that has no equal anywhere. We don't want you stuck with a lemon, or to wind up paying for repairs that are the automaker's fault and are covered by secret "goodwill" warranties. That's why we are the only book that includes many hard-to-find, confidential, and little-known documents that automakers don't want you to see.

In short, we know you can't win what you can't prove.

The following charts, documents, and service bulletins are included so that you can stand your ground and be treated fairly. Photocopy and circulate whichever document will prove helpful in your dealings with automakers, dealers, service managers, insurance companies, or government agencies. Remember, most of the summarized service bulletins outline repairs or replacements that should be done for free.

Part One

GOOD BUYS AND GOODBYES

Part Two

THE ART OF COMPLAINING

Part Three

MAKING THE RIGHT CHOICE

AMERICAN VEHICLES

Appendix III

INTERNET INFO

Appendix V

SECRET WARRANTIES AND CONFIDENTIAL SERVICE BULLETINS

GRAND THEFT AUTOMAKER

Help! Toyota has been hijacked by pirates! (That's why their trucks are rust-cankered, their brakes fail, and their cars accelerate on their own, right?)

"We Were Hijacked by Pirates"

Toyota doesn't want me to speak out, but I can't stand it anymore and somebody has to tell it like it is. The root cause of their problems is that the company was hijacked, some years ago, by anti-family, financially oriented pirates.

JIM PRESS
FORMER PRESIDENT OF TOYOTA USA
THE DETROIT NEWS
FEBRUARY 24, 2010

"Our Reputation Is Horrible"

Let's face it: Our reputation as an industry is horrible. In the U.S. we are viewed for the most part as a slow, dimwitted industry that is typically unresponsive to consumer and environmental needs. If that weren't bad enough, our executives are criticized for lavish compensation, abundant perks and unnecessary entitlements.

JOHN KRAFCIK
ACTING CEO OF HYUNDAI NORTH AMERICA
CHICAGO AUTO SHOW SPEECH
FEBRUARY 11, 2009

Press and Krafcik know what they're talking about. Unfortunately, most auto columnists shut their eyes and ignored this bigger story.

Former Toyota president Jim Press was a top executive for 36 years and the only American member of the company's 30-member board of directors. He made the startling accusation quoted above in an email press release he sent to *The Detroit News* on February 24, 2010—the same day Toyota President Akido Toyoda testified before the U.S. Congress.

Toyoda told the House Oversight Committee that he was only recently made aware of the automaker's sudden, unintended acceleration and brake failures. He refused to comment on Press's accusation, and both men have since faded into the auto underbrush, where they will stay until the class action lawyers come a-calling.

In 2007, Hyundai chairman Chung Mong-koo was convicted of embezzling over $100 million of Hyundai's money and was slapped with a three-year jail sentence. However, that sentence was suspended because Chung was considered by the authorities to be too important to the Korean economy and the future of Hyundai to go to prison. Instead, the court ordered that he donate $1.1 billion of his personal assets to society and perform community service.

In 2009, Chrysler and GM were also considered too big to fail and were both rewarded for their deception and incompetence with almost $100 billion in U.S. and Canadian bailouts. Then, to add insult to injury, GM's Chairman Ed Whitacre aired a misleading TV commercial in April of 2010 where he bragged:

> We have repaid our government loan—in full, with interest—five years ahead of the original schedule.

Then he went on to say:

> Before I started this job I admit I had some doubts. [pause] Probably a lot like you.

Independent auto journalists from the website *The Truth About Cars* (*www.thetruth aboutcars.com*) took Whitacre to task:

> *What* doubts? Did you think GM cars were crap? Crap how? Unreliable? Uncomfortable? Badly built? What? And why "probably"? That's an admission wrapped in a denial shrouded in mystery. Whitacre's vague statement is so Old GM: wishy-washy and vague whilst trying (and failing) to be genuine and sincere.

The truth is that the U.S., Canadian, and Ontario governments provided loans of $8.4 billion and took equity stakes in the new company. But GM had posted losses of $4.3 billion in the latter half of 2009 after it had been bailed out by $52 billion of taxpayer money. *The Washington Post* reported that "a majority of the $52 billion" was "converted into a 61 percent government ownership stake." GM repaid $7.1 billion "ahead of schedule" only because Washington extended the due date. And with what did GM pay the cash debt? The company used its TARP bailout fund held in escrow to repay the bailout loan.

Says the April 28, 2010, edition of the *New Hampshire Union Leader*:

> GM's new ad is identical to those over-the-top Burger King ads. Both are shamelessly selling Whoppers.

And what of the other bailout money GM got? The Congressional Budget Office says taxpayers will likely lose more than $30 billion of it.

A decade ago, *Lemon-Aid* predicted the bankruptcy of Chrysler and GM, so it was no surprise to us when, in June 2009, GM threw in the towel and followed Chrysler into bankruptcy.

The Chrysler and GM bankruptcies were promoted as deft, pre-packaged administrative moves that saved American automobile industry jobs. The truth is that bankruptcy allowed both companies to tear up their dealer franchise contracts (without justification and with little compensation), steal the money owed to their suppliers and customers, and funnel part of the taxpayer-supplied largesse to their Chinese-based factories.

Ford saw the downturn coming and burned through less cash than GM and Chrysler after getting its unions to agree to a pay cut. Ford also borrowed almost $32 billion earlier when market conditions were more favourable and used some of this money to upgrade its aging fleet of small and mid-size cars and crossover vehicles. These moves gave Ford enough reserves to buy time as it awaited the arrival of its popular European-built Fiesta and prepared a lineup of new and revamped 2010 models. In retrospect, Ford made all the right moves. It was the only one of the Detroit Three automakers that didn't take government bailout money.

The only downside to importing the 2011 Fiesta is that Ford has never had a successful European transplant in North America (remember the Cortina, Merkur, Land Rover, and Jaguar models?).

Good Buys in Bad Times

Bad news for Detroit is good news for car buyers. New- and used-car prices have plummeted. Recently built large trucks and SUVs now cost less than half their original list prices because of soaring fuel costs that have abated but are headed up again.

Smart car buyers should be patient as vehicle prices fall during the winter months and unsold vehicles pile up on dealers' lots. Now through to the summer of 2011 is the best time to buy a new 2010 or 2011 car or truck, if you're careful and follow *Lemon-Aid*'s tips in Part One for buying a cheap, reliable, and recession-proof car.

Depreciation Dominoes

Resale values have gone for a vertiginous ride during the economic recession and the auto industry restructuring we have seen over the past two years. As the Canadian dollar flies higher toward parity with the American greenback and many new-car prices sink lower, Canadian shoppers are in the driver's seat to get fully-loaded new vehicles discounted by about 20 percent. Cash and increased access to credit makes price haggling a breeze.

Both new and used car prices are trending downward. This includes the high-performance Ford Focus and Mazda3 GT (above), as well as trucks, SUVs, and minivans.

Used SUV prices are even more of a bargain. For example, an all-equipped 2006 Yukon Denali (rated Average) that sold for $63,645 can now be bought for less than $20,000 and won't likely depreciate more than a couple of thousand dollars more per year. At the other end of the choices available, let's look at the depreciation-induced savings given by two popular sporty small cars, one a Ford, the other a Mazda.

A fairly reliable 2006 Ford Focus ZX5 SES four-door hatchback that listed new for $21,800 can now be picked up for $8,500. A comparable, slower-depreciating 2006 Mazda3 Sport GT hatchback, sold new for $21,695, would cost $12,000, or $3,500 more than the lesser-known (but more easily found) Ford. Incidentally, I have used the 2006 model year as an example of a good year to buy most cars, vans, SUVs, and trucks because it was a watershed year for across-the-board safety and quality improvements.

Residual values for most small cars, SUVs, and trucks are expected to fall even further in the new year as the 2011 Fiesta and Mazda2 hit the streets, Hyundai sells new $20,000 Santa Fes, and Toyota's safety problems continue. Larger cars and full-sized vehicles will also lose value rapidly as fuel prices continue to rise.

Interestingly, cars and trucks that are currently coming off three- and five-year leases have added to the savings possible when buying used. Dealers gave these vehicles inordinately high buy-back residual values, resulting in owners dumping the cars at the end of their lease and buying something else more affordable. This has created a glut of reliable, overpriced, low-mileage vehicles that will be massively discounted. And these price cuts will be sweetened through the summer of 2011.

Theft by Freight

Lemon-Aid has always cautioned new-car buyers against paying transportation and PDI (pre-delivery inspection) fees or suggested they be whittled down by about half. This advice worked a few decades ago when the costs were first announced, coming in at about $500. Now, the charges have ballooned to $1,400–$2,000.

Chrysler Canada has a neat trick where their 2010 Ontario-dealer Caravan ads say "SAVE THE $1,400 FREIGHT" and then, in very small print, they add that dealers may charge up to $1,098 in administration/pre-delivery fees and up to $1,298 for optional anti-theft/safety products. In other words, your $1,400 "freight savings" may wind up costing you $2,396. Incidentally, the small print also says that only 1,000 vehicles are eligible and that the freight savings only apply to minivans bought during May 2010 in Ontario.

VEHICLE PRICING IS NOW EASIER TO UNDERSTAND BECAUSE ALL OUR PRICES INCLUDE FREIGHT, PDI AND MANDATORY GOVERNMENT LEVIES.
Prices do not include applicable taxes and PPSA. Consumers may be required to pay up to $599 for Dealer fees.***

Hmmm...GM Canada also includes the freight charge in the manufacturer's suggested retail price (MSRP) and only mentions $599 in extra dealer fees.

Volvo's Downgrade

Because a number of automakers will be gone this year and others will be gobbled up by bigger manufacturers (VW buying Suzuki, Tata owning Jaguar and Land Rover, and Spyker's buyout of Saab, for example), we have downgraded our ratings for many new-car models in this year's *Lemon-Aid* until we see how reliability, pricing, and servicing are impacted.

Volvos were excellent buys that turned sour after Ford bought the company.

Take Volvo, for instance. *Lemon-Aid* once recommended Volvo as a safe and reliable, though dealer-dependent, car. However, we lowered our rating when the company was sold to Ford in 1999 for $6.45 billion U.S. Shortly thereafter, our quality fears were confirmed when reports of poor reliability and mediocre servicing started boiling up from *Lemon-Aid* readers and various consumer groups.

Apparently, many of the best long-time Volvo dealers have closed up shop because of Ford's maladministration of the brand, lack of quality control, and spotty servicing support. Dealer morale also hit rock-bottom as dealers learned that Ford was quietly shopping around the brand to the Chinese. With a weakened dealer network and only disheartened dealers remaining, the Volvo brand continued to sell cars. However, the Chinese uncertainty is beginning to take its toll.

If the accepted bid by Zhejiang Geely Holding Co. is approved by the Chinese authorities, the marketing, quality, and servicing will fall under Chinese control. That's a scary thought, judging by the poor-quality, uncrashworthy vehicles China has built in the past (the Brilliance, among others). That's why this year's *Lemon-Aid* will not recommend Volvo vehicles, in spite of protests from Volvo Canada's president.

A LETTER FROM VOLVO

3/10/10

Dear Mr. Edmonston,

During your guest appearance on CityTV Toronto's Breakfast Television in the morning of March 1, you incorrectly informed viewers that the Volvo brand would "perhaps" be shut down.

The Canadian public looks to you as an important resource on the automotive industry and to provide them with reliable information. At no point has any official from Ford or Volvo said the future of the Volvo brand is in doubt. As a result, your statement is a clear error and damaging to the image of the company.

I request that you provide a retraction for your next appearance on CityTV to ensure the Canadian public has accurate information about the Volvo brand.

Regards,

Jeff Pugliese, President & CEO Volvo Cars of Canada Corp.

PHIL'S RESPONSE

Thank you, Jeffrey, for your email relative to my negative remarks concerning Volvo.

Here we will have to agree to disagree. I do believe that Volvo, as we know it, will possibly shut down in the near future, particularly in view of its likely acquisition by Chinese interests.

Furthermore, despite having long been a booster of some Volvos, I recognize that its dumping by Ford and eventual purchase by the Chinese will hurt the company deeply. That the Chinese have absolutely no North American auto marketing, building, or experience, and a history of dreadful, even toxic, quality control, only makes me sad for Volvo, which has gone from being a "pioneer" in auto safety to an "orphan" in the automotive sense.

Of course, I have said the same and been right in my prediction about the eventual demise of American Motors (yes, I have been reviewing the auto industry for over 40 years), Renault, Hummer, Saab, and Saturn.

My advice to you is to make sure your pension benefits are carried over to the subsequent Volvo buyer.

Of course, I express these opinions under the "free comment" protection of our Canadian Supreme Court as stated in *Grant v. Torstar* and *Quan v. Cusson.*

Best of luck in the future,

Phil
Lemon-Aid

Lemon-Aid 2011

This year's *Lemon-Aid* sees the North American auto industry still in chaos, but slowly getting back on its feet. Many automakers and dealers on both sides of our border are shutting their doors, while others are doing anything to make a buck—cutting some prices to the bone, sometimes scamming customers into thinking $1,500 "freight" fees have been dropped when they haven't, or scrambling to find new partners to buy their factories and dealerships. With all of these changes coming about so quickly and many more to be expected, auto shoppers are understandably confused as to what are the best buys in Canada. Furthermore, consumers want to know which vehicles will likely cost more and which ones will cost less as we go into 2011.

Lemon-Aid has the answers to these questions and many others. This year's guide is current up to the last few months, easier to read, and more content-rich as Detroit's sales crawl out of the basement. It also rates more new cars, SUVs, trucks, and vans than ever before, taking into account the possibility that warranties and resale values may change dramatically on some models and that servicing and parts supplies may be problematic on others.

You'll find descriptions of the best and worst vehicles for seniors, tips on getting dealers to bid for your business, and reasons why hybrids, electrically powered, or diesel-equipped cars may not be as "green" as they claim. Also, we will compare fuel economy using both miles to the gallon and litres per 100 kilometres.

As always, we'll suggest which vehicles are the safest, most reliable, and cheapest to fuel, service, and insure—without breaking your budget or getting snagged when dealers or automakers close their doors. And, for when things go terribly wrong, we include sample complaint letters, negotiation tips, and the jurisprudence needed to help you get your money back.

GM's new Volt electric car. The Volt is no more a solution to our energy dependence than was the ethanol bandwagon. In 2009, the Presidential Task Force on the Auto Industry warned: "While the Chevy Volt holds promise, it is currently projected to be much more expensive than its gasoline-fueled peers and will likely need substantial reductions in manufacturing cost in order to become commercially viable." *Lemon-Aid* knows that "reductions in cost" means government subsidies, which in turn mean taxpayer payouts.

Lemon-Aid cannot recommend the 2011 Jeep Grand Cherokee. First, we need to know if the drivetrain, electrical system, brakes, and AC components are more reliable than before and if servicing support is adequate.

This year's guide also combines test results with owner feedback to provide a critical comparison of 2010 and 2011 vehicles. In Appendix I, "Mini-Reviews and Previews," we rate vehicles that have been on the market for only a short time or are sold in small numbers.

If new features are "more show than go," or improvements and additional safety features don't justify the higher costs of newer models (like run-flat tires), we say so, and suggest you buy a less-loaded, safer, more reliable, cheaper alternative. Front, offset, side, rear, and rollover crash test results are also included, along with an exhaustive list of useful and useless accessories and optional safety features. We show how much profit dealers make on each vehicle, and what should be considered a fair price. We are also watching cross-border prices carefully, as we have done in the past. We know new-car prices in the States will tumble more quickly as inventory piles up there, and we expect to see new cars and trucks discounted by at least 30 percent across the border when compared with vehicles sold in Canada.

Above all, *Lemon-Aid* is still the comprehensive, practical owner's manual you know and trust. We don't want you to get stuck with a lemon or wind up with a car that can't be serviced. We don't think you should pay for repairs that are the automaker's fault and are covered by secret "goodwill" warranties. We show you how to get an automaker or government refund for your repairs by exposing many hard-to-find, confidential, and little-known service bulletins and memos that automakers don't want you to see.

In short, as we celebrate more than 40 years of *Lemon-Aid*, this edition drives into the 2011 model year still blowing the whistle on the auto industry's "Dark Side," where unsafe vehicles, dealer and automaker thievery, and deceptive practices are the norm—not the exception.

Phil Edmonston
November 2010

Part One
GOOD BUYS AND GOODBYES

"Orphan" cars will soon flood the auto-market landscape.

Asia Rules

If you want satisfaction, buy from Japan. Nearly every category is topped by a sensible, well put-together piece of Japanese metal, and nearly every category sees a badly built, unreliable European banger at the bottom.... Of our top 20 models, 15 are built by Japanese manufacturers, while 11 of the bottom 20 are French. Build quality and customer care apparently remain major problems for the French PSA group, with Citroens and Peugeots scoring abysmally in just about every category but handling.... German manufacturers, once the epitome of solid reliability, remain on the slide, although last year's most dismal duffer, the moribund Mercedes M-Class, is displaced by no fewer than four fragile French marques.... At least the traditional whipping boys, the Italians, show varied success, with a couple of positives in there. Fiat remains off the pace....

BBC'S TOP GEAR
NOVEMBER 1, 2005

"Only" 10 Percent of Chryslers are Lemons

Out of 100 vehicles, we're apt to build 10 that are as good as any that Toyota has ever built, 80 that are okay and 10 that cause repeat problems for our customers.

ROBERT LUTZ
FORMER PRESIDENT, CHRYSLER U.S.
CHRYSLER TIMES
JULY 17, 1995

Detroit's Second Chance

Detroit is now earning more profit while selling far fewer vehicles.

For the first quarter of 2010, Ford, GM, and Chrysler earned pre-tax profits of $2.1 billion, $1.3 billion, and $1.4 million, respectively. Yet GM's revenues were only three-fourths of what they were when GM lost a bundle in the money-losing first quarter of 2008. In other words, the leaner Detroit automakers can now make a profit at an annual selling rate of 11.5 million vehicles, instead of the minimal annual rate of about 16 million three years ago.

Ford and GM Revival

Two other facts emerge from these first-quarter results. First, the most profit was earned by Ford and GM, two companies that aren't headed by an "auto guy." GM Chairman Ed Whitacre Jr. is the former chairman of AT&T, and Ford's CEO Alan Mulally, the man at the helm of America's last remaining independent car company, was hired away from Boeing in 2006. Secondly, the most money was earned by Ford, the only one of the Detroit Three not to take a government bailout from Washington, Ottawa, and Ontario.

In a desperate effort to cut costs, a lot of makes have been culled from the Detroit herd within the last few years, much to the relief of *Lemon-Aid* staff who said their

Jaguar's 2011 XF ($61,800 CDN in Canada; $53,000 U.S. in the States). Jaguar hopes that its offer of free maintenance will revive its sales in 2011. *Lemon-Aid* believes dropping the price in Canada by $15,000 would be a better idea.

purchase was a huge mistake in the first place. Those divisions that weren't shut down this year (Pontiac, Mercury, and Saturn) were sold to other auto manufacturers for barely one-third what they originally cost to acquire (Jaguar, Land Rover, Saab, and Volvo).

Ford ended three years of staggering losses in 2009 as Chrysler and GM slid into bankruptcy. Since Mulally's arrival three years ago, Ford has cut its North American workforce by 47 percent and is now rolling out a fuel-efficient product mix that earned the automaker a $2.7 billion profit last year.

Mulally engineered Ford's revival by borrowing heavily when rates were low. The company got $23 billion worth of loans in late 2006 before credit markets froze, and put up all major assets, including its name, as collateral to build a cash cushion to withstand losses while developing new models.

The U.S.-based *Automotive Lease Guide* says Ford posted the largest increase of any automaker in its Perceived Quality Study between fall 2009 and spring 2010.

Honda was number one, while Toyota fell from first place to sixth, largely due to its recall of almost 9 million vehicles early this year due to unintended acceleration, hybrid brake failures, and pickup truck corrosion.

Ford's higher scores mean higher residual values for its vehicles. For example, its average car resale value was up by $2,400 U.S. from 2009 to 2010. Market watchers attribute the higher resale values and quality perception to Ford's refusing government handouts, *Consumer Reports*' higher quality ratings, and the allure of new products like the 2011 Fiesta and the redesigned Focus, Fusion, and Taurus models.

Ford recently shuttered Mercury after selling Jaguar, Land Rover, and Aston Martin to Tata Motors, an Indian automaker that builds the world's cheapest car, the Nano. Tata says Jaguar and Land Rover manufacturing will be subcontracted out to China. Thus two British icons, which became Ford "trophy cars," were snapped up by Tata and then shipped off to China. Esperanto, old chap?

Tata sells the $2,160 (U.S.) Nano (top) alongside the 2011 Range Rover ($79,275 in the States; $93,800 in Canada).

GM could now stand for "Government Motors" following its Chapter 11 bankruptcy filing and partial ownership by the U.S. and Canadian governments and the United Auto Workers (UAW). True, GM had a tougher time getting rid of its non-performing divisions during its 2009 bankruptcy, and Opal's future is still up in the air, but by capriciously firing 1,200 dealers General Motors poured sugar into its own gas tank. Nevertheless, the company either dropped or sold Hummer, Pontiac, Saab, Saturn, and Vauxhall. Furthermore, GMC, the automaker's upscale Chevrolet truck division, is expected to be axed or converted into GM's only truck brand.

Quo Vadis, Chrysler?

GM's extensive restructuring goals make Chrysler's roll of the dice with a Fiat partnership look extremely risky and short-sighted. With Chrysler hitching its wagon (and minivan) to Fiat, it will be like two drunks propping each other up on the street corner, waiting for the reworked Jeep Grand Cherokee to give them a lift.

What we have with Chrysler and Fiat is two automakers known for making crappy cars combining into one huge company to make more crappy cars and SUVs. Fiat's econoboxes are frugal—and feeble. They won't come on the market before late next year, if then. North American mechanics have no idea how to repair Fiats, and their parts supply has always been problematic. Few shoppers will risk their money on a Chrysler-Fiat combo, and it's even less likely that Chrysler's large-

CHRISIS-LER

platform factories in Canada will build many of these cars—no matter what the two companies promise.

Chrysler is no longer a viable entity, no matter whom it's partnered with. (Remember, not even Mercedes could afford to support Chrysler's cash burn, and it recently dumped its 19 percent stake in the company.) Furthermore, Chrysler's lack of product before the 2012 model year means the company will have to survive another year with only a revamped Jeep Grand Cherokee and 2010 leftovers. Investors, workers, and the Canadian and U.S. governments shouldn't have put a penny into the Chrysler bailout. Crafty Fiat didn't risk one lira on Chrysler, and will probably still get 35 percent of the restructured company.

2010 AND 2011 HITS AND MISSES

HITS

1. Chrysler PT Cruiser and Jeep Wrangler
2. Ford Edge, Escape, Escape Hybrid, Flex, Focus, Fusion, Fusion Hybrid, and Mustang
3. GM Acadia, Camaro, Enclave, Equinox, Terrain, Traverse, Express, Savana, Tahoe, and Yukon
4. Honda (all models)
5. Hyundai (all models)
6. Infiniti (all models)
7. Lincoln MKZ and Town Car
8. Mazda3, Mazda5, Mazda6, B-Series, Miata, and Tribute
9. Nissan Frontier, Leaf, Rogue, Sentra, and X-Trail
10. Suzuki SX4
11. Subaru Legacy and Forester

MISSES

1. Chrysler (all models except the PT Cruiser and Wrangler)
2. Ford's "orphans": Aston Martin, Jaguar, Land Rover, and Volvo
3. GM's "orphans": Hummer, Pontiac, Saab, and Saturn
4. GM Canyon, Colorado, and Volt
5. Honda Insight
6. Nissan Quest
7. Smart ForTwo
8. Suzuki Equator
9. Toyota (all models, due to quality and safety problems)
10. Volkswagen Routan

Jeep's entry-level Wrangler model has always been a top-seller for Chrysler, mainly because of its off-roading prowess. Four-door Wranglers are back-ordered for months.

Nissan's poorly designed, glitch-prone 2010 Quest proves that Japan *can* make bad minivans. The revised 2011 version will no longer be built in the U.S.

Recession-Proof Buys

Bad news for automakers is good news for car buyers. Three-year-old large trucks and SUVs now cost less than half their original list prices because of higher fuel costs and poor sales. Most vehicle prices have remained stable for 2011, though many new vehicles are selling at huge discounts, with low-interest financing and leases.

10 tips for big savings

Here are 10 ways you can save money by purchasing a recession-proof vehicle from a dependable dealer as you ride out this economic downturn amid mass bankruptcies and changing automaker alliances:

1. Buy a new or used vehicle that is relatively uncomplicated, is easy to service, and has been sold in large numbers over a decade or so. This will ensure that independent garages can provide service and parts, because many parts suppliers and dealers will have shut their doors.
2. Look for a vehicle that's finishing its model run. But steer clear of models that were axed because of poor reliability or mediocre performance, like GM's front-drive minivans.
3. Stay away from European cars, vans, and complicated SUVs. Dealership networks are weak, parts are inordinately expensive and hard to find, and few garages will invest in the expensive equipment needed to service complicated emissions and fuel-delivery systems. The old axiom that there is a right way, a wrong way, and a European way to troubleshoot a car still holds true.
4. Don't buy a hybrid, electric, or diesel model. They are complicated to service and dealer-dependent, and they don't provide the fuel economy or savings they hype. Furthermore, with gas still comparatively cheap, there really is no imperative to complicate your life with a complex piece of machinery. Diesel complexity comes from emissions regulations passed last year requiring the use of cleaner-burning engines and hard-to-service fuel systems, as well as frequent urea fill-ups.
5. Don't buy most Chrysler or Dodge models, with the exception of a well-inspected Jeep Wrangler or Liberty or a minivan, which are the best of the bad. Chrysler is the weakest of the Detroit Three, and, except for the reworked 2011 Grand Cherokee, most prices will fall dramatically in the late fall. Be careful, though. Most of the Chrysler lineup has a sad history of serious safety- and performance-related defects, and its automatic transmissions, brakes, and air conditioners are particularly troublesome. As for the new Grand Cherokee refinements, it's too early to tell if Chrysler has improved the vehicle's quality.
6. Don't buy GM or Chrysler front-drive models or vehicles made in China. As a rule, they are less reliable than the rear-drives and have poorly performing powertrains and brakes. Furthermore, crash test ratings for many China-made vehicles are listed as "Poor," and their assembly quality is neanderthal, at best. Start shopping for a GM car or truck in the first quarter of 2011, when the auto show hoopla has died down and prices are lowest.

7. Consider Ford—the automaker has offered more reliable and better-performing buys since it started cutting costs and selling off large chunks of the company several years ago. The added cash was invested in new models and better quality control that has made some Not Recommended models (such as the 2000–04 Focus) into Above Average (2005–10 Focus) or better buys.

8. Don't buy from dual dealerships. Parts inventories at many dealerships may have been depleted due to slow sales, and qualified mechanics may be in short supply. The represented auto companies see the dealerships as less than loyal and will cut them little slack in vehicle deliveries and warranty assistance.

9. Don't buy any vehicle that has been stored longer than three months; the Transport Canada–required date-of-manufacture plate will give you the month and year the car left the factory. Don't buy any vehicle that requires an extended warranty due to a reputation for past failures. It is likely warranties will be worthless when companies merge or shut down. And, as cash gets scarce, automakers and dealers will find more reasons to deny warranty coverage as they try to cover their payrolls instead.

10. Use your credit card for the down payment, and put down as little money as possible. Use credit instead of cash to pay for repairs and maintenance charges. If you want to cancel a sales contract or work order, it's easier to do with a credit card than with cash.

Whom Can You Trust?

No one. Not even *Lemon-Aid*. Check facts out with several other independent sources. On the Internet, there's always *www.thetruthaboutcars.com*, *www.jalopnik.com*, and *www.safercar.gov*. Here's what the NHTSA complaint website looks like—pay particular attention to the tabs running down the left side of the page.

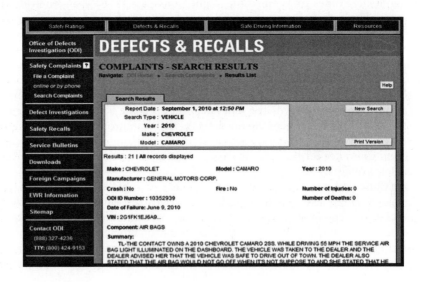

NHTSA is useful when dealer service managers lie and say your problem isn't safety-related or isn't a common failure. For example, here is what another Camaro owner says about the 2010's sudden stalling problem:

> Traveling westbound on Interstate 80 from Reno to San Francisco [going] 55–65 mph [90–105 km/h], without warning my 2010 Camaro had 100% loss of all power and operating functions; out of control down the mountain during heavy traffic I was able to stop the vehicle by jamming into the guardrail, trapping myself in the car. Nothing worked... no OnStar... I called my daughter in Reno and told her to send help... I was in shock. I had no clue what happened or why... but after the traffic slowed down, I exited the vehicle, still no help or response. Car started with limited abilities at 25 mph [40 km/h]; was advised that is was okay to drive back to Reno and "bring it on in" at my convenience. Nothing was done. The car was ready before the shuttle got back to the shop. The service men shrugged it off and told me to watch for the warning signs; I can't have any serious problems because they haven't had any electrical problems with these cars across the board?! I had no warning signs... I am lucky that I was not killed and did not kill anybody with my imaginary car problems. [Second] incident all systems went crazy: extreme heat coming from the dash, no heat turned on, false readings, all warning lights and gauges went off, power locks [didn't] work, no more auto start. I requested service with no response for five days. I left a very expressive message for [the] fleet manager and service department finally responded. Bad service... rude. I paid over $300 for car rental; GM picked up 1 day. They concluded again nothing was wrong with car. Malfunction was caused by snow and cold weather (not acceptable because it wasn't driven in snow). [Third] time driving with kids on the freeway in Reno... guess what? No power!! Was advised once again that I could drive it on in the next business day. Well, I learned the GM secret: Let her sit and she'll reset. I will not be able to live with the consequences of a death caused by a $50,000 time bomb. Dream car not worth a life or the fear of what might happen every time you start it.

Publications you can trust are *Consumer Reports* and the British Consumers Association's *Which?* In Canada, the *Toronto Star*'s long-time consumer columnist Ellen Roseman is a tough advocate for consumer rights who often scoops the motoring press in exposing scams and defects.

The *Toronto Star*'s Saturday "Wheels" section has come a long way during the past three decades. It no longer relies so much on auto industry "puff pieces", gobs of free press junkets, and oodles of free product "souvenirs" to garnish automaker press conferences. Originally an apologist for the automakers with "kissy-kissy" car reviews and a weekly "say nothing" column from the president of the Toronto Automobile Dealers Association (TADA), "Wheels" has been improved by its increased use of young freelance journalists and female writers. Yes—female writers! They sweat the details more, are less likely to be intimidated by Oshawa and Oakville "suits," and take into account (when necessary) what families need in terms of vehicle performance.

I particularly like the practical articles written by Mark Toljagic (such as "If the warranty runs out, who ya gonna call?"—an article about good places to repair

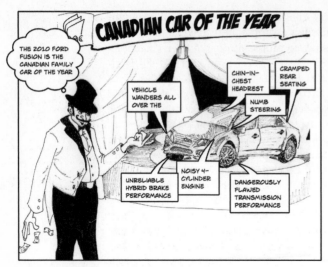

Sadly, automakers have had to "pay to play" the Car of the Year game.

Hondas, Saabs, and Volvos in Toronto, which can be found at *www.wheels.ca/Article Category/ article/784979*) and independent-minded Jil McIntosh, an antique car and hot rod hobbyist with knowledge of custom cars and restored vehicles (such as "Prius-like Lexus hardly worth premium," which can be found at *www.wheels. ca/Hybrid/article/785978*).

An example of the "Wheels" section's new tough reporting style is John LeBlanc's May 15, 2010, exposé of the Automobile Journalists Association of Canada (AJAC) and that group's annual Canadian Car of the Year (CCOTY) awards.

In a large header, John asks a simple question: "Should Automakers Pay for Awards?"

His article begins by rehashing the *Wall Street Journal*'s report blasting *Consumers Digest* magazine (not to be confused with *Consumer Reports*) for asking automakers to pay them $35,000 for the right to advertise that they've received *CD*'s "Best Buy" rating, and $25,000 for each lower rating ("Auto Awards Clouded by Fees," *Wall Street Journal*, May 10, 2010).

Wikipedia, the free online encyclopedia, gives this take on *Consumers Digest* at *en.wikipedia.org/wiki/Consumers_Digest*:

> Founded in 1960 and published by Consumers Digest Communications, LLC, *Consumers Digest* is an American for-profit magazine that allows companies to use its reviews for marketing purposes for a fee. Many car makers have financial ties to the publication. The magazine chose 15 General Motors vehicles for its 2010 "Best Buy" awards—and then GM paid the magazine for the right to mention those awards. According to *Consumers Digest*, the magazine awards its *Consumers Digest* Best Buy seal to products its staff judges to be of the best quality for the most reasonable price.
>
> The magazine charges a $35,000 annual fee for use of its green and gold *Consumers Digest* Best Buy seal. Some of the brands that have licensed the seal include Cal Spas hot tubs, Bridgestone Tires, Brinks Home Security, Multi-Pure Drinking Water Systems, McKleinUSA Business Cases and Mercury Automobiles.... The magazine is sold at newsstands only and does not reveal its sales figures. In 2001, when it ceased subscription distribution, it listed 700,000 subscribers....

The publication has no connection to the *Consumer Reports* magazine published by Consumers Union (which, unlike *Consumers Digest*, is an independent non-profit organization). It also has no relationship to the defunct *Consumers Digest* published by the pioneering Consumers' Research, Inc., 1910–1983, from which Consumers Union sprang.

But how's this for an example of Canadian car columnists' ingenuity: LeBlanc discovered that AJAC doesn't charge a fee for publicizing its 56 or so annual vehicle ratings (hurray!). Instead, AJAC demands that the automakers simply pay the Association $6,900 for each of the 56 vehicles tested, after supplying the vehicle *gratis*.

Writes LeBlanc:

> Although AJAC says on its site the purpose of its event is to "provide consumers with sound, comparative information on vehicles that are new to the market," not all "new" cars are evaluated.... Brands like Aston Martin, Bentley, Chrysler Group, Ferrari, Maserati, Maybach, Lamborghini, Lotus and Rolls-Royce did not participate at all.
>
> So, the question is: Should there be a clear separation of church (automotive award organizers) and state (automaker PR departments) when it comes to automotive awards?

Lemon-Aid says the real question to ask should be this one: If you take bribes (money, trips, computers, clothes, etc.) from companies to extol their products, are you a journalist or a whore?

We first answered that question in the 1995 edition of *Lemon-Aid* when we denounced the AJAC and car columnists for taking money from the industry whose cars they were testing:

> When automakers fail to buy a magazine's loyalty with free test cars, trips, and advertising deals, they are not above using blackmail to "goose" the advertising department into bringing the editorial people into line. Toyota boycotted *Road & Track* for almost a year and a half when *R & T*'s February 1991 issue failed to include any Toyota model in its listing of the "10 Best Cars of the World." Former *Car and Driver* publisher David E. Davis Jr. felt GM's sting, as well, when the carmaker pulled all its ads from his *Automobile* magazine after he criticized the company. A subsequent GM memo said pulling the ads was a way of repaying Davis with "our undying neglect."
>
> The ubiquitous H. Ross Perot, a former GM Board member and one-time candidate for the American presidency, unleashed scathing criticism of GM mismanagement in a 1988 *Fortune* story. As a result, GM pulled the magazine off its media list for an eight-page as insert. *Fortune* didn't flinch, but few Canadian publications could have withstood the loss of that many advertising dollars. Take the *Montreal Gazette*, a paper for which I once wrote a consumer column. In a May 18, 1991, story on Chrysler's call for trade restraints on Japanese imports, the *Gazette* rightfully suggested that

Chrysler Canada President Yves Landry was a hypocrite for supporting import quotas. The story pointed out that Chrysler, part owner of Mitsubishi, is a large-scale importer of Japanese-made vehicles sold under Chrysler's name as the Colt, Eagle Laser, and Talon. Chrysler claimed the story was unfair and yanked all of its advertising from the paper.

Car columnists claim their integrity is not for sale, but there is no doubt that it can be rented. CTV's *W5* news magazine confirmed this fact when it ran an exposé last January [1994] that showed Canadian car columnists and broadcasters ripping off automakers by demanding $3,000 corporate membership fees to join their Automotive Journalists Association—individual membership being $100.

Travel junkets, public relations, and advertising contracts all sweetened the honey pot that the press people licked. One enterprising writer for a large Toronto newspaper and owner of his own travel agency sold junkets to drivers who wanted to test-drive free cars with him in Europe.

Following the CTV broadcast, the *Toronto Star* required its car columnists to indicate in a footnote to their articles if their information came from a travel junket or if a manufacturer-supplied vehicle was used. Incidentally, General Motors pulled out of the Canadian Car of the Year competition held shortly after the CTV broadcast.

The "Wheels" article alleges that AJAC is possibly charging automakers 56 times $6,900 annually, or $386,400, not counting the 125 or so individual journalist memberships at $320 each, $3,000 corporate dues, $935 associate corporate dues, and $175 affiliate dues. That's a lot of gas money, and it certainly merits investigation as to where the money goes, who pays what, how elections are carried out, and what family relationships the directors and employees have with the auto writers.

I assume everything is on the up and up with AJAC, but when dealing with the auto industry and its apologists, keep in mind that their credibility is only a notch or so above British Petroleum (BP) in Louisiana.

For an exceptionally well-written and thoroughly researched update on "Wheels" junkets and more, go to Joe Clark's personal blog at *blog.fawny.org/2008/05/18/wheels-ethics*.

Auto-Criticism? No Way!

Auto companies are no different from apple vendors: Some of their stock is fresh, and some of it is rotten. All automakers and dealers have one goal in common, and that's to convince buyers that they're getting the safest, most reliable, and best vehicle money can buy—even if it's not true. GM doesn't want to hear about its 1995–2004 history of V6 engine intake manifold gasket failures or its 2005–07 Corvette roofs flying off. Ford won't admit that most of its lineup has been plagued by premature engine and automatic transmission burnouts from the early '90s

2010 CANADIAN CAR OF THE YEAR WINNERS

Canadian Car of the Year: Volkswagen Golf GTI
Canadian Utility Vehicle of the Year: Subaru Outback
Best New Small Car (under $21,000): Mazda3
Best New Small Car (over $21,000): Mazda3 Sport
Best New Family Car (under $30,000): Volkswagen Golf Wagon TDI
Best New Family Car (over $30,000): Ford Taurus
Best New Luxury Car (over $50,000): BMW 335d Sedan
Best New Prestige Car: Porsche Panamera
Best New Sports/Performance Car (under $50,000): Volkswagen Golf GTI
Best New Sports/Performance Car (over $50,000): Audi S4
Best New Convertible: Audi S5 Cabriolet
Best New SUV/CUV (under $35,000): Subaru Outback
Best New SUV/CUV ($35,000–$60,000): Volkswagen Touareg TDI Clean Diesel
Best New SUV/CUV (over $60,000): Lexus RX450h
Best New Technology: Audi Drive Select
Best New Green Technology: Ford Next Generation Hybrid System and Smartgauge
Best New Design: BMW 335d Sedan

Interesting that the VW/Audi group got the top score in seven out of the 17 rankings and that the Volkswagen Golf GTI snagged the top ranking, 2010 Canadian Car of the Year. Honda, Hyundai, Mercedes, Nissan, and Toyota were nowhere to be found. Could it be that they balked at paying the $6,900 "testing" fee?

through 2005. And Chrysler hypes its Hemi engines while denying that its automatic transmissions, which equip most of its lineup, are failure prone.

After nearly 40 years writing *Lemon-Aid*, I know that car manufacturers run from the truth and look upon independent critics with hostile suspicion. That's why independent car critics have such a difficult time rating new and used vehicles without selling out to the car industry.

Yet the road to "auto-censorship" is so subtle that few writers or broadcasters can resist compromising their integrity: The kids need private schooling; the mortgage must be paid. The smooth-talking executive car pimps are always there to say how much the company admires your work, but then they tell your editor or program director how much better your stories would be with more "balance."

According to the *New York Times*, "General Motors recalled 22,000 Corvettes because the roof might fly off, and what do you think kicked the company into action? Complaints on the National Highway Traffic Safety Administration Web site from owners? Was it the safety agency itself, worried about the complaints? Concerns raised by the Federal Aviation Administration? Nope. It was the Japanese Ministry of Land Infrastructure and Transport, unhappy about the problem on imported Corvettes."

And then these hustlers invite you on their trips to Asia and Europe, where they give you geishas, hats, jackets, laptop computers, specially prepared vehicles, and interviews with the top brass. They even sponsor annual journalism awards to make sure their coterie of friendly scribes spouts the party line.

Auto shows promote a herd mentality where truth is the first casualty.

Here are the dismal facts published in 2006 by the authors of *Branding Iron: Branding Lessons from the Meltdown of the U.S. Auto Industry*:

The headlines offer a simplistic interpretation. They say that legacy costs, poor cost control, ill-advised investments in other automakers and in undistinguished products, all of which are serious issues, caused the trouble.

That's wrong. Or, worse, incomplete and myopic. It's the same kind of myopia that created the problem in the first place. Like many a crisis, this one has been brewing for decades. And the cost-cutting quick fixes proposed by many industry experts won't solve it. Why not? Because it's not the root cause. What is killing U.S. automakers is their inability to attract growing numbers of customers to its numerous brands, many of which seem almost irrelevant today.

Other Trustworthy Sources

The government lies to us about fuel economy and airbag dangers. Automakers lie to us about the reliability and "real" prices of their products. Car dealers routinely charge us for services covered by "goodwill" extended warranties and put pricing information in such small print in newspapers that no one can read it. And many car journalists lie to us when they say that they're unbiased, aren't intimidated by their editors and automaker reps, and can't be, ahem…bribed.

Most investigative stories done on the auto industry in Canada (such as exposés on secret car warranties, dangerous airbags, and car company shenanigans) have been written by business columnists, freelancers, or "action line" troubleshooters rather than by reporters on the auto beat. This is because most auto beat reporters are regularly beaten into submission by myopic editors and greedy publishers who don't give them the time or the encouragement to do hard-hitting investigative exposés. In fact, it's quite impressive that we do have a small cadre of reporters who won't be cowed. Links to some of the best Canadian and American sites can be found in Appendix III.

Canada also has a number of auto experts and consumer advocates who aren't afraid to take on the auto industry and follow good stories, no matter where they lead. Here are some of my favourites:

- Jeremy Cato and Michael Vaughan are two of Canada's best-known automotive and business journalists. This duo is the epitome of auto journalism and business reporting excellence because they ask the tough questions automakers hate to answer.
- Mohamed Bouchama, president of Car Help Canada, shakes up the auto industry by rating new and used cars, providing legal advice, and teaching consumers the art of complaining on *AutoShop* every Sunday evening on Toronto's CP24.
- I have known and respected the *Toronto Star*'s Ellen Roseman for more than 30 years. She is one of Canada's foremost consumer advocates and business columnists, and never pulls back from an important story—no matter how loudly advertisers squeal. She teaches, does TV and radio, and maintains a blog to give her readers current information on all types of consumer issues.
- Phil Bailey is a Lachine, Quebec, garage owner with almost five decades of experience with European, Japanese, and American cars. In his insightful comments on the car industry, he's as skillful with his pen as he is with a wrench, and he's got the everyday garage experience that make him and Toronto CFRB broadcaster Alan Gelman such unimpeachable auto industry critics.

These reporters and consumer advocates represent the exception, not the rule. Even the most ardent reporters frequently have to jump through hoops to get their stories out, simply because their editors or station managers have bought into many of the fraudulent practices so common to the auto industry. Haranguing staff for more "balance" is the pretext du jour for squelching hard-hitting stories that implicate dealers and automakers. News editors don't want truth; they want copy and comfort. They'll spend weeks sifting through Prime Minister Stephen Harper's trash bins looking for conflicts of interest while ignoring the auto industry scams threaded throughout their own advertisers' ads and commercials.

Want proof? Try to decipher the fine print in *The Globe and Mail*'s or the *Toronto Star*'s new car ads, or better yet, tell me what the fine print scrolled at breakneck speeds on television car commercials really says. Where is the investigative reporter who will submit these ads to an optometrists' group to confirm that the message is unreadable?

Think about this: Dealers posing as private parties and selling used cars from residences ("curbsiders") are periodically exposed by dealer associations and "crusading" auto journalists. Yet these scam artists place dozens or more ads every week in the classified sections of local newspapers that employ these same muckraking reporters. The same phone numbers and billing addresses reappear in the ads, sometimes days after the scam has been featured in local news reports. The ad order-takers know who these crooks are. News editors know that their own papers are promoting these scammers. Why isn't there an ad exposé by reporters working for these papers? Why don't they publish the fact that it's mostly new-vehicle dealers who supply curbsiders with their cars? That's what I'd call balanced reporting.

Two of my favourite auto journalists, Dan Neil, automotive writer for the liberal *Los Angeles Times*, and Robert Farago, a long-time columnist, auto critic, and creator of *The Truth About Cars* (a British-based website), were both punished for writing the truth.

Neil's paper was hit with a $10 million (U.S.) loss after General Motors and its dealers pulled their ads in response to his sharp criticism of GM for a series of poor management decisions that lead to the flop of its 2005 G6 model:

> GM is a morass of a business case, but one thing seems clear enough, and Lutz's mistake was to state the obvious and then recant: The company's multiplicity of divisions and models is turning into a circular firing squad, someone's head ought to roll, and the most likely candidate would be the luminous white noggin of Lutz. [The G6] is not an awful car. It's entirely adequate. But plainly, adequate is not nearly enough.
>
> *LOS ANGELES TIMES*
> APRIL 6, 2005

The *Times* stood by Neil, a Pulitzer Prize–winning automobile columnist. GM's ads eventually returned after a hiatus of several months.

Farago didn't fare as well. In late August 2005, he was canned and stayed canned. His column was permanently axed, without explanation, by the uber-liberal *San Francisco Chronicle* after his criticism of Subaru's Tribeca, an SUV wannabe that never will be:

> I'm not sure if the *Chronicle* removed my description of the SUV's front end as a "flying vagina" (the editors ignored my request for a copy of the published review), but even without it my analysis of the B9 was not bound to please its manufacturer.
>
> In fact, the Subaru B9 Tribeca is both subjectively (to the best of my knowledge and experience) and empirically a dreadful machine that besmirches the reputation of its manufacturer. Sure, the B9 handles well. The review pointed this out. But to suggest that it's an SUV worthy of its manufacturer's hype ("The end of the SUV as we know it" and "The ideal balance of power and refinement") is to become a co-conspirator in Subaru's attempts to mislead the public.
>
> And here's the thing: I believe the media in general, and newspapers in particular, have an obligation to tell the truth about cars. You know all those puff pieces that fill up the odd blank spot in every single automotive section in this great country of ours? … And that's why so many car enthusiasts have turned to the web. Other than Dan Neil at the *Los Angeles Times*, there are no print journalists ready, willing and able to directly challenge the auto manufacturers' influence with the plain, unvarnished truth (including the writers found in the happy clappy buff books). Car lovers yearn for the truth about cars. Sites like *www.jalopnik.com* are dedicated to providing it. And that's why the mainstream press' cozy little Boys' Club is doomed.

The American "Car of the Year" Scam

Once you've established a budget and selected some vehicles that interest you, the next step is to ascertain which ones have high safety and reliability ratings. Be wary of the "Car of the Year" ratings found in enthusiast magazines and on most websites; their supposedly independent tests are a lot of baloney. Mark Toljagic and Frank Williams, two freelance Canadian auto journalists published in the *Toronto Star*'s "Wheels" section, agree. Williams says:

> You'd be forgiven for thinking COTY awards are little more than a gift to car advertisers, who provide a self-appointed number of "elite" journalists with priority access to press cars, and then co-promote a new product with an old publication. It's certainly an excellent excuse for carmakers like Renault (Alliance), Chevrolet (Citation), Plymouth (RIP, Volare) and Ford (Probe) to sell cars by touting their COTY award like they'd won the Nobel Prize.

> If not pissing off your paymasters is the priority, it is perhaps significant that *Car and Driver's* 2006 "10 Best" awards considered 52 cars in new categories, including "Best Luxury Sports Car," "Best Sports Coupe," "Best Roadster," "Best Sports Car" and "Best Muscle Car." Perhaps *C&D* hopes persnickety pistonheads will spend so much time debating which car belongs in what category they'll be too tired to dispute the winners.

Doggedly independent, Toljagic penned the following observations about press junkets from a lakeside château in Salzburg, Austria, where all expenses were paid by Lexus:

> Waves of automotive writers from the U.S., Canada, Europe and Asia were treated to business-class flights, their own luxury suites, gourmet meals, a cigar lounge and an evening at the Fortress Restaurant overlooking Mozart's hometown of Salzburg. While there are economies of scale to be realized in conducting one global event, it still doesn't come cheap. Toyota estimates the cost to fly each journalist to be about $10,000. Airline points are major currency for freelancers. Auto companies assign the points to the writer, so it's easy to rack up impressive totals that can be used at vacation time.

Imagine: *Car and Driver* rated the Ford Focus as a "Best Buy" during its first three model years, while government and consumer groups decried the car's dozen or so recall campaigns and the huge number of owners' safety and reliability complaints.

There are dozens of organizations and magazines that rate cars for everything from their overall reliability and frequency of repairs (J.D. Power and *Consumer Reports*) to their crashworthiness and appeal to owners (NHTSA, IIHS, and Strategic Vision's Total Quality Survey (TQS)). These ratings don't always match.

Getting Reliable Info

Funny, as soon as they hear that you're shopping for a new car, all your relatives, co-workers, and friends want to tell you what to buy.

After a while, you'll get so many conflicting opinions that it'll seem as if any choice you make will be wrong. Before making your decision, remember that you should invest a month of research into your $15,000–$30,000 new-car-buying project. This includes two weeks for basic research and another two weeks to actually bargain with dealers to get the right price and equipment. The following sources provide a variety of useful information that will help you ferret out what vehicle best suits your needs and budget.

Auto shows

Auto shows are held from January through March across Canada, starting in Montreal and ending in Vancouver. Although you can't buy or drive a car at the show, you can easily compare prices and the interior and exterior styling of different vehicles. In fact, show officials estimate that about 20 percent of auto show visitors are actively seeking info for an upcoming new-car purchase. Interestingly, while the shows are open, dealer traffic nosedives, making for much more generous deals in showrooms. Business usually picks up following the auto shows.

Online services

Anyone with access to the Internet can now obtain useful information about the auto industry in a matter of minutes at little or no cost. Simply go to a search engine like Google and type in a few keywords to find thousands of relevant sites. An extensive listing of informative and helpful auto information websites can be found in Appendix III.

 ### Shopping on the Internet

The key word here is "shopping," because *Consumer Reports* magazine has found that barely 2 percent of Internet surfers actually buy a new or used car online. Yet over 80 percent of buyers admit to using the Internet to get prices and specifications before visiting the dealership. Apparently, few buyers want to purchase a new or used vehicle without first seeing what's offered and knowing all money paid will be accounted for.

New-vehicle shopping through automaker and independent websites is a quick and easy way to compare prices and model specifications, but you will have to be careful. Many so-called independent sites are merely fronts for dealers and automakers, tailoring their information to steer you into their showroom or convince you to buy a certain brand of car.

Shoppers now have access to information they once were routinely denied or had trouble finding, such as dealers' price markups and incentive programs, the book value for trade-ins, and considerable safety data. Canadian shoppers can get Canadian invoice prices and specs by contacting the Automobile Protection Agency (APA) by phone or fax, or online by visiting *www.canadiandriver.com*.

Other advantages to online shopping? Some dealers offer a lower price to online shoppers; the entire transaction, including financing, can be done on the Internet; and buyers don't have to haggle—they merely post their best offers electronically to a number of dealers in their area code (for more convenient servicing of the vehicle) and then await counteroffers. But here are three caveats: (1) You will have to go to a dealer to finalize the contract, and be preyed upon by the financing and insurance (F&I) sales agents; (2) as far as bargains are concerned, *Consumer Reports* says its test shoppers obtained lower prices more frequently by visiting the dealer's showroom and concluding the sale there; and (3) only one-third of online dealers respond to customer queries.

Auto Quality Rankings

Consumer groups and non-profit auto associations like APA and Car Help Canada (see Appendix III) are your best bets for the least biased auto ratings for Canadians. They're not perfect, though, so it's a good idea to consult both groups and look for ratings that agree with each other.

Consumer Reports (CR) is an American publication that once had a tenuous affiliation with the Consumers' Association of Canada. Its ratings, extrapolated from Consumers Union's annual U.S. member survey, don't quite mirror the Canadian experience. Components that are particularly vulnerable to our harsh climate usually don't perform as well as the *CR* reliability ratings indicate, and poor servicing caused by a weak dealer body in Canada can make some service-dependent vehicles a nightmare to own here, whereas the American experience may be less problematic.

Based on more than one million responses from subscribers to *Consumer Reports* and *ConsumerReports.org*, *CR*'s annual auto reliability findings are impressively comprehensive, though they may not always be correct. Statisticians agree that *CR*'s sampling method leaves some room for error, but, with a few notable exceptions, the ratings are fair, conservative, and consistent guidelines for buying a reliable vehicle. Not so for child safety seats. A January 2007 *CR* report said that 10 out of 12 seats it tested failed disastrously at impact speeds of 56–61 km/h. NHTSA checked *CR*'s findings and discovered that the side-impact speeds actually exceeded 112 km/h. *CR* admitted it made a mistake.

My only criticism of the *CR* auto ratings is that many Asian models, like ones by Toyota and Honda, are not as harshly scrutinized as their American counterparts, yet service bulletins and extended "goodwill" warranties have shown for years that they also have serious engine, transmission, brake, and electrical problems.

Consumer Reports confirmed this anomaly in its April 2006 edition, where it admitted that Asian vehicle quality improvement has "slowed" since 2002—one incredible understatement when one considers that Toyota especially has been coasting on its reputation for quality since the mid-'90s. Toyota owner reports of sudden unintended acceleration incidents started to climb in 2002.

When and Where to Buy

When to Buy

This year, new-car sales and prices will likely go in opposite directions. Sales figures will go higher as automakers, principally Chrysler, Ford, Honda, Nissan, and Toyota, throw out millions of dollars in consumer rebates and dealer sales incentives to drive prices downward. Shoppers who can wait until the summer or early fall of 2011 can double-dip from additional automakers' dealer incentive and buyer rebate programs—which can mean thousands of dollars in additional savings. Remember, too, that vehicles made between March and August offer the most factory upgrades and fewer factory-related glitches.

Allow yourself at least two weeks to finalize a deal if you aren't trading in your vehicle, or longer if you sell your vehicle privately. Visit the showroom at the end of the month, just before closing, when the salesperson will want to make that one last sale to meet the month's quota. If sales have been terrible, the sales manager may be willing to do some extra negotiating in order to boost sales staff morale.

Where to Buy

If all you care about is getting a low price, shopping in auto-factory towns will get you the cheapest vehicles because assembly-line workers buy heavily discounted cars in order to "flip" them. Large towns have more of a selection, and dealers offer a variety of payment plans that will likely suit your budget.

Good dealers aren't always the ones with the lowest prices, though. Buying from someone who you know gives honest and reliable service is just as important as getting a good deal. Check a dealer's honesty and reliability by talking with motorists who drive vehicles purchased from that dealer (identified by the nameplate on the vehicle's trunk). If these customers have been treated fairly, they'll be glad to recommend their dealer. You can also ascertain the quality of new-vehicle preparation and servicing by renting one of the dealer's vehicles for a weekend, or by getting your trade-in serviced.

How can you tell which dealers are the most honest and competent? Well, judging from the thousands of reports I receive each year, dealerships in small suburban and rural communities are fairer than big-city dealers because they're more vulnerable to negative word-of-mouth testimonials and to poor sales—when their vehicles aren't selling, good service picks up the slack. Their prices may also be more competitive, but don't count on it. Unfortunately, as part of their bankruptcy restructuring, Chrysler and General Motors closed down many dealerships in suburban and rural areas because the dealers couldn't generate sufficient sales volume to meet the automakers' profit targets.

Dealers that sell more than one manufacturer's product line present special problems. Their overhead can be quite high, and the cancellation of a dual dealership by an automaker in favour of setting up an exclusive franchise elsewhere is an ever-present threat. Parts availability may also be a problem because dealers with two separate vehicle lines must split their inventory and may, therefore, have an inadequate supply on hand.

The quality of new-vehicle service is directly linked to the number and competence of dealerships within the network. If the network is weak, parts are likely to be unavailable, repair costs can go through the roof, and the skill level of the mechanics may be subpar, since better mechanics command higher salaries. Among foreign manufacturers, Asian automakers have the best overall dealer representation across Canada, except for Mitsubishi and Kia.

Kia's dealer network is weak but growing, through strong sales after having been left by its former owner, Hyundai, to fend on its own for many years. Mitsubishi, on the other hand, is floundering, despite having a good array of quality products. Its major problem is that Canadian dealers piggybacked their sales outlets on bankrupt Chrysler franchises.

European automaker profits are expected to grow throughout 2011 as higher fuel prices and the quest for better highway performance drives shoppers to European imports like the BMW 1 series, the Ford Fiesta, and the Mazda2. Servicing, however, will continue to be problematic, inasmuch as many good mechanics left the business during the 2008–09 economic downturn.

Despite these drawbacks, you can always get better treatment by going to dealerships that are accredited by auto clubs such as the Canadian Automobile Association (CAA) or consumer groups like the Automobile Protection Association (APA) or Car Help Canada. Auto club accreditation is no ironclad guarantee that a dealership will exhibit courteous, honest, or competent business practices; however, if you're insulted, cheated, or given bad service by one of their recommended garages (look for the accreditation symbol in a dealer's phone book ads, on the Internet, or on their shop windows), the accrediting club is one more place to take your complaint to apply additional mediation pressure. And, as you'll see in Part Two, plaintiffs have won substantial refunds by pleading that an auto club is legally responsible for the actions of a garage it recommends.

Automobile Brokers and Vehicle-Buying Services

Brokers are independent agents who act as intermediaries to find the new or used vehicle you want at a price below what you'd normally pay. They have their

Rolodex of contacts, speak the sales lingo, know all of the angles and scams, and can generally cut through the bull to find a fair price—usually within days. Their services may cost a few hundred dollars, but you may save a few thousand. Additionally, you save the stress and hassle associated with the dealership experience, which for many people is like a trip to the dentist.

Brokers get new vehicles through dealers, while used vehicles may come from dealers, auctions, private sellers, and leasing companies. The broker's job is to find a vehicle that meets a client's expressed needs and then to negotiate its purchase (or lease) on behalf of that client. The majority of brokers tend to deal exclusively in new vehicles, with a small percentage dealing in both new and used vehicles. Ancillary services vary among brokers and may include such things as comparative vehicle analysis and price research.

The cost of hiring a broker can be charged either as a flat fee of a few hundred dollars or as a percentage of the value of the vehicle (usually 1–2 percent). The flat fee is usually best because it encourages the broker to keep the selling price low. Reputable brokers are not beholden to any particular dealership or make, and they'll disclose their flat fee up front or tell you the percentage amount they'll charge on a specific vehicle.

 ### Finding the right broker

Good brokers are hard to find, particularly in western Canada. Buyers who are looking for a broker should first ask friends and acquaintances if they can recommend one. Word-of-mouth referrals are often the best because people won't refer others to a service with which they were dissatisfied. Your local credit union or the regional CAA office is a good place to get a broker referral. For instance, Alterna Savings recommends a car-buying service called Dealfinder.

Dealfinder

For most buyers, going into a dealer showroom to negotiate a fair price is intimidating and confusing. Numbers are thrown at you, promises are made and broken, and after getting the "lowest price possible," you realize your neighbour paid a couple thousand dollars less for the same vehicle.

No wonder smart consumers are turning away from the "showroom shakedown" and letting professional buyers, like Ottawa-based Dealfinder Inc. (*www.dealfinder. ca*), separate the steak from the sizzle and real prices from "come-ons." In fact, simply by dealing with the dealership directly, Dealfinder can automatically save you the $200+ sales agent's commission before negotiations even begin.

For a $159 (plus tax) flat fee, Dealfinder acts as a price consultant after you have chosen the vehicle you want. The agency then shops dealers for the new car or truck of your choice in any geographic area you indicate. It gets no kickbacks from retailers or manufacturers, and if you can negotiate and document a lower price than Dealfinder gets, the fee will be refunded. What's more, you're under no obligation to buy the vehicle they recommend, since there is absolutely no collusion between Dealfinder and any manufacturer or dealership.

Dealfinder is a small operation that has been run by Bob Prest for over 17 years. He knows the ins and outs of automobile price negotiation and has an impressive list of clients, including some of Canada's better-known credit unions. His reputation is spread by word-of-mouth recommendations and the occasional media report. He can be reached by phone at 1-800-331-2044, or by email at *dealfinder@magma.ca*.

Buying a New Car, Truck, SUV, or Van

I remember in the '70s, American Motors gave away free TVs with each new car purchase, just before shutting its doors. In the past decade, GM gave away free Dell computers and VW hawked free guitars with its cars. The Detroit Three auto-makers continue to build poor-quality cars and trucks, although there appears to be some improvement over the past three years, mainly by Ford. The gap between Asian and American automobile quality has narrowed; however, this may reflect only a lowered benchmark following recent Honda, Nissan, and Toyota power-train, electrical system, and body fit glitches. Nevertheless, Japanese makes and Ford continue to dominate J.D. Power and Associates' dependability surveys, while other American and European makes are mostly ranked below the industry average.

Toyota has done extraordinarily well, even in light of its sudden unintended acceleration and brake failure safety problems that resulted in a $16.5 million government-imposed fine this year and $10 billion spent in recall campaigns and investigations. The company still has a cash reserve of almost $20 billion. Plus, they had never sold as many vehicles worldwide as they have since the safety investigations and class-actions were announced. This confirms that most buyers are more concerned with price and reliability—not safety.

Step 1: Keep it Simple

First, keep in mind that you are going to spend much more money than you may have anticipated—almost $31,000 for the average vehicle transaction, according to Dennis DesRosiers, a Toronto-based auto consultant. This is because of the many hidden fees, like freight charges and so-called administrative costs, that are added to the bottom line. But, with cut-throat discounts and armed with tips from this guide, you can bring that amount down to less than $25,000.

According to the Canadian Automobile Association (CAA), the average household owns two vehicles, which are each driven about 20,000 km annually and cost an average of $800 a year for maintenance; DesRosiers estimates $1,100.

Also, the CAA says in its *2009 Driving Costs* brochure that the annual cost of driving a 2009 Chevrolet Cobalt LT works out to $6,516 per year, or $17.85 a day, when factoring in insurance costs, licensing fees, depreciation, and financing. The cost rises to $23.63 per day when a 2009 Dodge Grand Caravan SE is used as a comparison vehicle.

Keep in mind that it's practically impossible to buy a bare-bones car or truck because automakers cram them with costly, non-essential performance and convenience features in order to maximize their profits. Nevertheless, money-wasting gadgets like electronic navigation and sophisticated entertainment systems can easily be passed up with little impact on safety or convenience. Full-torso side curtain airbags and electronic stability control, however, are important safety options that are well worth the extra expense.

Our driving needs are influenced by where we live, our lifestyles, and our ages (see pages 45–48 for a discussion of vehicles best suited to mature drivers). The ideal car should be crashworthy and easy to drive, have minimal high-tech features to distract and annoy, and not cost much to maintain.

In the city, a small wagon or hatchback is more practical and less expensive than a mid-sized car like the Honda Accord or Toyota Camry. Furthermore, have you seen the newer Civic and Elantra? What once were small cars are now quite large, relatively fuel-efficient, and equipped with more horsepower than you'll ever likely need. Nevertheless, if you're going to be doing a lot of highway driving, transporting small groups of people, or loading up on accessories, a medium-sized sedan, wagon, or small sport-utility could be the best choice for price, comfort, and reliability.

Don't let spikes in fuel prices stampede you into buying a vehicle unsuitable to your driving needs. If you travel less than 20,000 km per year, mostly in the city, choose a small car or SUV equipped with a 4-cylinder engine that produces about 140 hp to get the best fuel economy without sacrificing performance. Anything more powerful is just a waste. Extensive highway driving, however, demands the cruising performance, extra power for additional accessories, and durability of a larger, 6-cylinder engine. Believe me, fuel savings will be the last thing on your mind if you buy an underpowered vehicle.

Be especially wary of the towing capabilities bandied about by automakers. They routinely exaggerate towing capability and seldom mention the need for expensive optional equipment, or that the top safe towing speed may be only 72 km/h (45 mph), as is the case with some minivans. Generally, 3.0L to 3.8L V6 engines will safely accommodate most towing needs. The 4-cylinder engines may handle light loads, but will likely offer a white-knuckle experience when merging with highway traffic or travelling over hilly terrain.

Remember, you may have to change your driving habits to accommodate the type of vehicle you purchase. Front-drive braking is quite different from braking with a rear-drive, and braking efficiency on ABS-equipped vehicles is compromised if you pump the brakes. Also, rear-drive vans handle like trucks, and you may scrub the right rear tire during sharp right-hand turns until you get the hang of making wider turns. Limited rear visibility is another problem with larger vans, forcing drivers to carefully survey side and rear traffic before changing lanes or merging.

Step 2: Be Realistic... If You Can't, Bring Along Someone Who Can

Before paying big bucks, you should know what your real needs are and how much you can afford to spend.

Don't confuse styling with needs (do you have a bucket bottom to conform to those bucket seats?) or trendy with essential (will a cheaper Mazda5 mini-minivan suit you as well as, or better than, a mid-sized car?). Visiting the showroom with your spouse, a level-headed relative, or a sensible friend will help you steer a truer course through all the non-essential options you'll be offered.

Oftentimes, getting a female perspective can be really helpful. Women don't generally receive the same welcome at auto showrooms as men do, but that's because they make the salesmen (yes, usually less than 10 percent of the sales staff are women) work too hard to make a sale. Most sales agents admit that female shoppers are far more knowledgeable about what they want and more patient in negotiating the contract's details than men, who tend to be mesmerized by many of the techno-toys available and often skip over the fine print and bluff their way through the negotiations.

In increasing numbers, women have discovered that minivans, SUVs, and small pickups are more versatile than passenger cars and station wagons. And, having spotted a profitable trend, automakers are offering increased versatility combined with unconventional styling in so-called "crossover" vehicles. These blended cars are part sedan and part station wagon, with a touch of sport-utility added for function and fun. For example, the 2011 Ford Flex is a smaller, sporty crossover vehicle that looks like a miniature SUV. First launched as a 2009 model, the Flex comes in an entry-level SE trim line that brings down the starting price, and its fuel-frugal EcoBoost engine uses turbochargers to give the power of a V8 with the fuel savings of a V6.

Women ask the important questions. Men, take your mother, wife, or sister along next time!

The Ford Flex.

Step 3: What Can I Afford?

Determine how much money you can spend, and then decide which vehicles in that price range interest you. Have several models in mind so that the overpriced one won't tempt you too much. As your benchmarks, use the ratings, alternative models, estimated purchase costs, and residual value figures shown in Part Three of this guide. Remember, logic and prudence are the first casualties of showroom hype, so carefully consider what you actually need and how these things will fit into your budget before comparing models and prices at a dealership. Write down your first, second, and third choices relative to each model and the equipment offered. Browse the automaker websites both in Canada and in the States, and consult *www.canadiandriver.com* for the Canadian manufacturer's suggested retail price (MSRP), promotions, and package discounts. Look for special low prices that may apply only to Internet-generated referrals. Once you get a good idea of the price variations, get out the fax machine or PC at home or work (a company letterhead is always impressive) and then make the dealers bid against each other (see page 88). Call the lowest-bidding dealership, ask for an appointment to be assured of getting a sales agent's complete attention, and take along the downloaded info from the automaker's website to avoid arguments.

Sometimes a cheaper "twin" will fit the bill. Twins are nameplates made by different auto manufacturers, or by different divisions of the same company, that are virtually identical in body design and mechanical components, like the Chevrolet Cobalt and Pontiac Pursuit or the Chrysler Avenger and Dodge Sebring.

 Let's look at the savings possible with "twinned" Chrysler minivans. A 2006 Grand Caravan SXT that was originally listed for $35,735 is now worth about $7,500. An upscale 2006 Town & Country Limited that performs similarly to the Grand Caravan, with just a few additional gizmos, first sold for $47,905 and is now worth about $13,500. Where once almost $12,000 separated the two minivans, the price difference is now only $6,000—and you can expect the gap to close to almost nil over the next few years. Did the little extras really justify the Town & Country's higher price, or make it a better buy than the Grand Caravan? Obviously, the marketplace thinks not.

The Buick Enclave (left), Chevrolet Traverse (centre), and GMC Acadia (right) are all quite similar midsize SUVs that are reasonably reliable and well-appointed. The downside: poor fuel economy, and a sticker price for the Enclave that's easily 20 percent higher than its worth. Consider the cheaper Chevrolet Traverse, GMC Acadia, or a remaindered 2009 Saturn Outlook.

And don't get taken in by the "Buy Canadian!" chanting from Chrysler, Ford, General Motors, and the Canadian Auto Workers. It's pure hokum. While Detroit-based automakers are beating their chests over the need to buy American, they buy Japanese and South Korean companies and then market the foreign imports from Asian factories as their own. This practice has resulted in bastardized nameplates whose parentage isn't always easy to nail down. For example, is the Aveo a Chevy or a Daewoo? (For the record, it's a Daewoo, and not that reliable, to boot.)

Vehicles that are produced through co-ventures between Detroit automakers and Asian manufacturers have better quality control than vehicles manufactured by companies that were bought outright, and this looks like one of the factors that may save the American auto industry. For example, Toyota and Pontiac churned out identical Matrix and Vibe compacts in Ontario and the United States; however, the cheaper, Ontario-built Matrix has the better reputation for quality. On the other hand, Jaguar and Volvo quality have stagnated or declined since Ford bought the companies, and GM-owned Saab hasn't done much better. As for Daimler's takeover of Chrysler, what innovative, high-quality products did we see as a result? Very little.

Sometimes choosing a higher trim line that packages many options as standard features will cost you less when you take all the features into account separately. It's hard to compare these bundled prices with the manufacturer's base price and added options, though. All of the separate prices are inflated and must be negotiated downward individually, while fully equipped vehicles don't allow for options to be deleted or priced separately. Furthermore, many of the bundled options are superfluous, and you probably wouldn't have chosen them to begin with.

Minivans, for example, often come in two versions: a base commercial (or cargo) version and a more luxurious model for private use. The commercial version doesn't have as many bells and whistles, but it's more likely to be in stock and will probably cost much less. And if you're planning to convert it, there's a wide choice of independent customizers that will likely do a better—and less expensive—job than the dealer. Of course, you will want a written guarantee from the dealer or customizer, or sometimes both, that no changes will invalidate the manufacturer's

warranty. Also, look on the lot for a low-mileage (less than 10,000 km) current-year demonstrator that is carried over unchanged as a 2010 version. You will get an end-of-model-year rebate, a lower price for the extra mileage, and sundry other sales incentives that apply. Remember, if the vehicle has been registered to another company or individual, it is not a demo and should be considered used and be discounted accordingly (by at least 25 percent). You will also want to carry out a CarProof VIN search and get a complete printout of the vehicle's service history.

Owning a GM front-drive minivan is akin to owning beachfront property in Louisiana.

Leasing without Losing

Why Leasing Costs More

There are many reasons why leasing is a bad idea. It's often touted as an alternative used to make high-cost vehicles more affordable, but for most people, it's really more expensive than buying outright. Lessees usually pay the full MSRP on a vehicle loaded with costly options, plus hidden fees and interest charges that wouldn't be included if the vehicle was purchased instead of leased. Researchers have found that some fully loaded entry-level cars leased with high interest rates and deceptive "special fees" could cost more than what some luxury models would cost to buy. A useful website that takes the mystery out of leasing is *www.federal-reserve.gov/pubs/leasing* (Keys to Vehicle Leasing), run by the U.S. Federal Reserve Board. It goes into incredible detail comparing leasing versus buying, and has a handy dictionary of the terms you're most likely to encounter.

Decoding "Lease-Talk"

Take a close look at the small print found in most leasing ads. Pay particular attention to words relating to the model year, condition of the vehicle ("demonstration" or "used"), equipment, warranty, interest rate, buy-back amount, down payment, security payment, monthly payment, transportation and preparation charges, administration fees ("acquisition" and "disposal" fees), insurance premiums, number of free kilometres, and excess-kilometre charges.

Leasing Advantages

Leasing in Canada once made up almost 35 percent of all motor vehicle sales transactions because of then-rising interest rates and prices. Now, hard-to-find credit and the economic recession have driven leasing down to about 20 percent of all auto transactions. Detroit automakers have backed away from leases, leaving the market to the Asians and Europeans. But leasing is still a fairly popular option, leading to 60-month leases and a proliferation of leasing deals on luxury models. Insiders say that almost all vehicles costing $60,000 or more are leased vehicles.

Experts agree: If you must lease, keep your costs to a minimum by leasing for the shortest time possible, by assuming the unexpired portion of an existing lease, and by making sure that the lease is close-ended (meaning that you walk away from the vehicle when the lease period ends)—an option used by 75 percent of lessees, according to the CAA.

Leasing does have a few advantages, though. First, it saves some of your capital, which you can invest to get a return greater than the leasing interest charges. Second, if you are taking a chance on a new model that hasn't been proven, you know that yours can be dumped at the dealer when the lease expires.

But taking a chance on an unproven model raises several questions: What are you doing choosing such a risky venture in the first place? And will you have the patience to wait in the service bay while your luxury lemon waits for parts or a mechanic who's ahead of the learning curve?

Some Precautions and an Alternative

On both new and used purchases and leases, be wary of unjustified hidden costs, like a $495 "administrative" or "disposal" fee, an "acquisition" charge, or boosted transport and freight costs that can collectively add several thousand dollars to a vehicle's retail price. Also, look at the lease transfer fee charged by the leasing company, the dealer, or both. This fee can vary considerably. For example, Ford Credit, GMAC Financial Services, and BMW Financial Services charge $175, $450, and $1,500, respectively. Ford and BMW dealers can also impose a transfer fee.

Instead of leasing, consider purchasing used. Look for a three- to five-year-old off-lease vehicle with 60,000–100,000 km on the clock and some of the original warranty left. Such a vehicle will be just as reliable for less than half the cost of one bought new or leased. Parts will be easier to find, independent servicing should be a breeze, insurance premiums will come down from the stratosphere, and your financial risk will be lessened considerably if you end up with a lemon.

Breaking a Lease

Not an easy thing to do, and you may wind up paying $3,000–$8,000 in cancellation fees.

The last thing you want to do is stop your payments, especially if you've leased a lemon: The dealer can easily sue you for the remaining money owed, and you will have to pay the legal fees for both sides. You won't be able to prove the vehicle was defective or unreliable, because it will have been seized after the lease payments stopped. So there you are, without the vehicle to make your proof and on the receiving end of a costly lawsuit.

There are several ways a lease can be broken. First, you can ask for free Canadian Motor Vehicle Arbitration Plan (CAMVAP) arbitration (see page 128) if you believe you have leased a lemon. A second recourse, if there's a huge debt remaining, is to send a lawyer's letter cancelling the contract by putting the leasing agency and automaker on notice that the vehicle is unacceptable. This should lead to some negotiation. If this fails, inspect the vehicle, have it legally tendered back to the dealer, and then sue for what you owe plus your inconvenience and assorted sundry expenses. You can use the small claims court on your own if the amount in litigation is less than the court's claim limit.

The leasing agency or dealer may claim extra money when the lease expires, because the vehicle may miss some original equipment or show "unreasonable" wear and tear (dings, paint problems, and excessive tire wear are the most common reasons for extra charges). Prevent this from happening by having the vehicle inspected by an independent retailer and taking pictures of the vehicle prior to returning it.

Buying the Right Car or Truck

Front-Drives

Front-drives direct engine power to the front wheels, which pull the vehicle forward while the rear wheels simply support the rear. The biggest benefit of front-drives is foul-weather traction. With the engine and transmission up front, there's lots of extra weight pressing down on the front-drive wheels, increasing tire grip in snow and on wet pavement. But when you drive up a steep hill, or tow a boat or trailer, the weight shifts and you lose the traction advantage.

Although I recommend a number of front-drive vehicles in this guide, I don't like them as much as rear-drives. Granted, front-drives provide a bit more interior room (no transmission hump), more car-like handling, and better fuel economy than do rear-drives, but damage from potholes and fender-benders is usually more extensive, and maintenance costs (especially premature suspension, tire, and brake wear) are much higher than with rear-drives.

Rear-Drives

Rear-drives direct engine power to the rear wheels, which push the vehicle forward. The front wheels steer and also support the front of the vehicle. With the

engine up front, the transmission in the middle, and the drive axle in the rear, there's plenty of room for larger and more durable drivetrain components. This makes for less crash damage, lower maintenance costs, and higher towing capacities than with front-drives.

On the downside, rear-drives don't have as much weight over the front wheels as do the front-drives, and therefore, they can't provide as much traction on wet or icy roads and tend to fishtail unless they're equipped with an expensive traction-control system.

Ford's 2011 rear-drive Mustang comes with a much-needed 305 hp 305 V6 engine that will reignite the Camaro-Mustang battle.

Four-Wheel Drive (4×4)

Four-wheel drive (4×4) directs engine power through a transfer case to all four wheels, which pull and push the vehicle forward, giving you twice as much traction. On most models, the vehicle reverts to rear-drive when four-wheel drive isn't engaged. The large transfer-case housing makes the vehicle sit higher, giving you additional ground clearance.

Keep in mind that extended driving over dry pavement with 4×4 engaged will cause the driveline to bind and result in serious damage. Some buyers are turning instead to rear-drive pickups equipped with winches and large, deep-lugged rear tires.

Many 4×4 customers driving SUVs set on truck platforms have been turned off by the typically rough and noisy driveline, a tendency for the vehicle to tip over when cornering at moderate speeds, vague or truck-like handling, high repair costs, and poor fuel economy.

All-Wheel Drive (AWD)

Essentially, this is four-wheel drive that's on all the time. Used mostly in sedans and minivans, AWD never needs to be deactivated when running over dry pavement and doesn't require the heavy transfer case that raises ground clearance and cuts fuel economy. AWD-equipped vehicles aren't recommended for off-roading because of their lower ground clearance and fragile driveline parts, which aren't as rugged as 4×4 components. But anyhow, you shouldn't be off-roading in a car or minivan in the first place.

Subaru's Forester combines reliability, roominess, and full-time all-wheel drive in a versatile, crashworthy small SUV.

Safety and Comfort

Do You Feel Comfortable in the Vehicle?

The advantages of many sports cars and minivans quickly pale in direct proportion to your tolerance for a harsh ride, noise, a claustrophobic interior, and limited visibility. Minivan owners often have to deal with a high step-up, a cold interior, lots of buffeting from wind and passing trucks, and poor rear visibility. With these drawbacks, many buyers find that after falling in love with the showroom image, they end up hating their purchase—all the more reason to test drive your choice over a period of several days to get a real feel for its positive and negative characteristics.

 Check to see if the vehicle's interior is user-friendly. For example, can you reach the sound system and AC controls without straining or taking your eyes off the road? Are the controls just as easy to operate by feel as by sight? What about dash glare onto the front windshield, and headlight aim and brightness? Can you drive with the window or sunroof open and not be subjected to an ear-splitting roar? Do rear-seat passengers have to be contortionists to enter or exit, as is the case with many two-door vehicles?

To answer these questions, you need to drive the vehicle over a period of time to test how well it responds to the diversity of your driving needs, without having some impatient sales agent yapping in your ear. If this isn't possible, you may find out too late that the handling is less responsive than you'd wanted.

You can conduct the following showroom tests: Adjust the seat to a comfortable setting, buckle up, and settle in. Can you sit 25 cm away from the steering wheel and still reach the accelerator and brake pedals? When you look out the windshield and use the rear- and side-view mirrors, do you detect any serious blind spots? Will optional mirrors give you an unobstructed view? Does the seat feel comfortable enough for long trips? Can you reach important controls without moving your back from the seatback? If not, shop for something that better suits your needs.

Which Safety Features Are Best?

Automakers have loaded 2010–11 models with features that wouldn't have been imagined several decades ago, because safety devices appeal to families and some, like airbags, can be marked up by 500 percent. Yet some safety innovations, such as anti-lock brake systems (ABS) and adaptive cruise control (ACC), don't deliver the safety payoffs promised by automakers and may create additional dangers. For example, anti-lock breaks often fail and are expensive to maintain, while adaptive cruise control may slow the vehicle down when passing another car on the highway. Some of the more-effective safety features are head-protecting side airbags, electronic stability control (ESC), adjustable brake and accelerator pedals, standard integrated child safety seats, seat belt pretensioners, adjustable head restraints, and sophisticated navigation and communication systems.

Seat belts provide the best means of reducing the severity of injury arising from both low- and high-speed frontal collisions. In order to be effective, though, seat belts must be adjusted properly and feel comfortably tight without undue slack. Owners often complain that seat belts don't retract enough for a snug fit, are too tight, chafe the neck, or don't fit children properly. Some automakers have corrected these problems with adjustable shoulder-belt anchors that allow both tall and short drivers to raise or lower the belt for a snug, more comfortable fit. Another important seat belt innovation is the pretensioner (not found on all seat belts), a device that automatically tightens the safety belt in the event of a crash.

Crashworthiness

A vehicle with a high crash protection rating is a lifesaver. In fact, crashworthiness is the one safety improvement over the past 40 years that everyone agrees has paid off handsomely without presenting any additional risks to drivers or passengers.

By surrounding occupants with a protective cocoon and deflecting crash forces away from the interior, auto engineers have successfully created safer vehicles without increasing vehicle size or cost. And purchasing a vehicle with the idea that you'll be involved in an accident someday is not unreasonable. According to IIHS, the average car will likely have two accidents before ending up as scrap, and it's twice as likely to be in a severe front-impact crash as a side-impact crash.

Since some vehicles are more crashworthy than others, and since size doesn't always guarantee crash safety, it's important to buy a vehicle that gives you the best protection from frontal, frontal offset, side, and rear collisions while keeping its rollover and roof-collapse potential to a minimum.

Two Washington-based agencies monitor how vehicle design affects crash safety: the National Highway Traffic Safety Administration (NHTSA) and the Insurance Institute for Highway Safety (IIHS). Crash information from these two groups doesn't always correspond because tests and testing methods vary. NHTSA's crash tests performed on 2011 models are much tougher than the tests previously performed, resulting in dropped star ratings for many vehicles. For example, in the first batch of 30 cars tested this fall, only the BMW 5 Series and Hyundai Sonata kept their five-star safety ratings. Two surprising losers were the Toyota Camry, which went from five stars to three, and the Nissan Versa, which earned an overall rating of only two stars while the previous model had earned four stars.

NHTSA crash-test results for 1990–2011 vehicles and tires are available at *www.safercar.gov/Safety+Ratings*. Information relating to safety complaints, recalls, defect investigations, and service bulletins can be found at *www.safercar.gov/Vehicle+Owners*. IIHS results may be found at *www.iihs.org/ratings*.

Don't get taken in by the five-star crash rating hoopla touted by automakers. There isn't any one vehicle that can claim a prize for being the safest. Vehicles that do well in NHTSA side and front crash tests may not do very well in IIHS offset crash tests, or may have poorly designed head restraints that can increase the severity of neck injuries. Or a vehicle may have a high number of airbag failures, such as the bags deploying when they shouldn't or not deploying when they should.

Before making a final decision on the vehicle you want, look up its crashworthiness and overall safety profile in Part Three.

Cars versus trucks

Occupants of large vehicles have fewer severe injury claims than do occupants of small vehicles. This was proven conclusively in a 1996 NHTSA study that showed that collisions between light trucks or vans and small cars resulted in car occupants having an 81 percent higher fatality rate than the occupants of the light trucks or vans did.

Vehicle weight offers the most protection in two-vehicle crashes. In a head-on crash, for example, the heavier vehicle drives the lighter one backward, which decreases forces inside the heavy vehicle and increases forces in the lighter one. All heavy vehicles, even poorly designed ones, offer this advantage in two-vehicle collisions. However, they may not offer good protection in single-vehicle crashes.

Crash test figures show that SUVs, vans, and trucks also offer more protection to adult occupants than do passenger cars in most crashes because their higher set-up allows them to ride over other vehicles (Ford's 2002 4×4 Explorer lowered its bumper height to prevent this hazard). Conversely, because of their high centre of gravity, easily overloaded tires, and unforgiving suspensions, these vehicles have a disproportionate number of single-vehicle rollovers, which are far deadlier than frontal or side collisions. In the case of the early Ford Explorer, Bridgestone/ Firestone CEO John Lampe testified in August 2001 that 42 of the 43 rollovers involving Ford Explorers in Venezuela were on competitors' tires—shifting the rollover blame to the Explorer's design and crashworthiness.

Interestingly, a vehicle's past crashworthiness rating doesn't always guarantee that subsequent model years will be just as safe or safer. Take Ford's Escort as an example. It earned five stars for front-passenger collision protection in 1991 and then earned fewer stars every year thereafter, until the model was discontinued in 2002. The Dodge Caravan is another example. It was given five stars for driver-side protection in 2000, but has earned four stars ever since.

Rollovers

Although rollovers represent only 3 percent of crashes (out of 10,000 annual U.S. road accidents), they cause one-third of all traffic deaths from what are usually single-vehicle accidents.

Rollovers occur less frequently with passenger cars and minivans than with SUVs, trucks, and full-sized vans (especially the 15-passenger variety). That's why electronic vehicle stability systems aren't as important a safety feature on passenger cars as on minivans, vans, pickups, and SUVs.

More Safety Considerations

Unfortunately, there will never be enough easy safety solutions to protect us from ourselves. According to NHTSA's figures, seat belts prevented 75,000 deaths between 2004 and 2008, while over 40 percent of passengers killed in accidents in 2007 were not wearing seat belts. NHTSA has also discovered that kids wear their seat belt 87 percent of the time if their parents do, and that 60 percent of children killed on the roads in 2005 were not wearing a seat belt.

Although there has been a dramatic reduction in automobile accident fatalities and injuries over the past three decades, safety experts feel that additional safety features will henceforth pay small dividends, and they expect the highway death and injury rate to start trending upward. They say it's time to target the driver.

NHTSA believes that we could cut automobile accident fatalities by half through 100 percent seat belt use and the elimination of drunk driving. The entirely preventable epidemic of drunk driving is responsible for 33.8 percent of motor vehicle fatalities in Canada, according to a 2002 Transport Canada study (*www. tc.gc.ca/media/documents/roadsafety/tp11759e_2000.pdf*).

This means that safety programs that concentrate primarily on motor vehicle standards won't be as effective as measures that target both the driver and the vehicle—such as more-sophisticated "black box" data recorders; more-stringent licensing requirements, including graduated licensing and de-licensing programs directed at teens and seniors; and stricter law enforcement.

Incidentally, police studies have shown that there's an important side benefit to arresting traffic-safety scofflaws: They often net dangerous career criminals or seriously impaired drivers before they have the chance to harm others. Apparently, sociopaths and substance abusers don't care which laws they break.

Beware of unsafe designs

Although it sounds hard to believe, automakers will deliberately manufacture a vehicle that will kill or maim simply because, in the long run, it costs less to stonewall complaints and pay off victims than to make a safer vehicle. I learned this lesson after listening to the court testimony of GM engineers—who deliberately placed fire-prone "sidesaddle" gas tanks in millions of pickups to save $3 per vehicle—and after reading the court transcripts of *Grimshaw v. Ford* (fire-prone Pintos) from 1981. Reporter Anthony Prince wrote the following assessment of Ford's indifference in an article titled "Lessons of the Ford/Firestone scandal: Profit motive turns consumers into road kill," *People's Tribune* (Online Edition); Vol. 26, No. 11, November 2000:

> Rejecting safety designs costing between only $1.80 and $15.30 per Pinto, Ford had calculated the damages it would likely pay in wrongful death and injury cases and pocketed the difference. In a cold and calculating "costs/benefits" analysis, Ford projected that the Pinto would probably cause 180 burn deaths, 180 serious burn injuries, [and] 2,100 burned vehicles each year. Also, Ford estimated civil suits of $200,000 per death, $67,000 per injury, [and] $700 per vehicle for a grand total of $49.5 million. The costs for installing safety features would cost approximately $137 million per year. As a result, the Pinto became a moving target, its unguarded fuel tank subject to rupture by exposed differential bolts shoved into it by rear-end collisions at speeds of as little as 21 miles per hour [34 km/h]. Spewing gasoline into the passenger compartment, the car and its passengers became engulfed in a raging inferno.

And here are more recent examples of corporate greed triumphing over public safety: Pre-1997 airbag designs that maim or kill women, children, and seniors; anti-lock brake systems that don't brake; flimsy front seats and seatbacks; the absence of rear head restraints; and fire-prone GM pickup fuel tanks and Ford cruise-control deactivation switches. Two other examples of hazardous engineering designs that put profit ahead of safety are failure-prone Chrysler, Ford, and GM minivan sliding doors and automatic transmissions that suddenly shift into Neutral, allowing the vehicle to roll away when parked on an incline or causing it to break down in traffic.

Active safety

Advocates of active safety stress that accidents are caused by the proverbial "nut behind the wheel" and believe that safe driving can be best taught through schools or private driving courses. Active safety components are generally those mechanical systems—such as anti-lock brake systems (ABS), high-performance tires, and traction control—that may help a driver to avoid accidents if they're skillful and mature.

I am not a fan of ABS. The systems are often ineffective, failure-prone, and expensive to service. Yet they are an essential part of most systems' electronic stability control (ESC), which is a proven lifesaver. Essentially, ABS prevents a vehicle's wheels from locking when the brakes are applied in an emergency situation, thus reducing skidding and the loss of directional control. When braking on wet or dry roads, your stopping distance will be about the same as with conventional braking systems. But in gravel, slush, or snow, your stopping distance will be greater.

The theory of active safety has several drawbacks. First, a recent study of seriously injured drivers at the Shock Trauma Center in Maryland showed that 51 percent of the sample tested positive for illegal drugs while 34 percent tested positive for alcohol (*www.druggeddriving.org/ddp.html*). Drivers who are under the influence of alcohol or drugs cause about 40 percent of all fatal accidents. All the high-performance options and specialized driving courses in the world will not provide much protection from impaired drivers who draw a bead on your vehicle. And, because active safety components get a lot of use—you're likely to need anti-lock brakes 99 times more often than you'll need an airbag—they have to be well designed and well maintained to remain effective. Finally, consider that independent studies show that safe driving taught to young drivers doesn't necessarily reduce the number of driving-related deaths and injuries (*Lancet*, July 2001; 1978 DeKalb County, Georgia, Study):

> The DeKalb Study compared the accident records of 9,000 teens that had taken driver education in the county's high schools with 9,000 teens that had no formal driver training. The final results showed no significant difference between the two groups. In other words, DeKalb County, Georgia, paid a large amount of money for absolutely no value.

Passive safety

Passive safety assumes that you will be involved in life-threatening situations and should be either warned in time to avoid a collision or automatically protected from rolling over, losing traction, or bearing the brunt of collision forces. Head-protecting side airbags, electronic stability control, brake override systems, daytime running lights, and a centre-mounted third brake light are four passive safety features that have paid off handsomely in reduced injuries and lives saved.

Passive safety features also assume that some accidents aren't avoidable and that, when those accidents occur, vehicles should provide as much protection as possible to drivers, passengers, and other vehicles that may be struck—without depending on the driver's reactions. Passive safety components that have consistently been proven to reduce vehicular deaths and injuries are seat belts, laminated windshields, and vehicle structures that enhance crashworthiness by absorbing or deflecting crash forces away from the vehicle's occupants.

Safety Features That Kill

In the late '60s, Washington forced automakers to include essential safety features like collapsing steering columns and safety windshields in their cars. As the years have passed, the number of mandatory safety features increased to include seat belts, airbags, and crashworthy construction. These improvements met with public approval until quite recently, when reports of deaths and injuries caused by ABS and airbag failures showed that defective components and poor engineering negated the potential life-saving benefits associated with having these devices.

For example, one out of every five ongoing NHTSA defect investigations concerns inadvertent airbag deployment, deactivation of the front passenger airbag, failure of the airbag to deploy, or injuries suffered when the bag did go off. In fact, airbags are the agency's single-largest cause of current investigations, exceeding even the full range of brake problems, which runs second.

Side Airbags—Good and Bad

Side and side curtain airbags are designed to protect drivers and passengers in rollovers and side-impact crashes, which are estimated to account for almost one-third of vehicular deaths. They have also been shown to help keep unbelted occupants from being ejected in rollovers. Head-protecting side airbags can reduce serious crash injuries by 45 percent. Side airbags without head protection reduce injuries by only 10 percent. Ideally, you want a side airbag system that protects both the torso and head.

Because side airbags aren't required by federal regulation in Canada or the States, neither government has developed any tests to measure their safety for children or small adults. Indeed, new side-protection rules went into effect in September 2009, giving automakers four years to comply with a new government-imposed "performance standard."

There's a downside to increased side airbag protection: Sit properly in your seat, or face serious injury from the deploying side airbag. Preliminary safety studies show that side airbags may be deadly to children or to any occupant sitting too close to the airbag, resting his or her head on the side pillar, or holding onto the roof-mounted assist handle. Research carried out in 1998 by safety researchers (Anil Khadikar of Biodynamics Engineering Inc. and Lonney Pauls of Springwater Micro Data Systems, *Assessment of Injury Protection Performance of Side Impact Airbags*) shows there are four hazards that pertain to most airbag systems:

1. Inadvertent airbag firing (short circuits, faulty hardware or software)
2. Unnecessary airbag firing (sometimes the opposite-side airbag will fire; the airbag may deploy when a low-speed side-swipe wouldn't have endangered occupant safety)
3. A small child, say, a three-year-old, restrained in a booster seat could be seriously injured
4. Out-of-position restrained occupants could be seriously injured

The researchers conclude with the following observation: "Even properly restrained vehicle occupants can have their upper or lower extremities in harm's way in the path of an exploding [side] airbag."

The 1998 study and dozens of other scientific papers confirm that small or tall restrained drivers face death or severe injury from frontal and side airbag deployments for the simple reason that they are outside of the norm of the 5'8", 180-pound, male test dummy. These studies also debunk the safety merits of anti-lock brakes, so it's no surprise they go unheralded by Transport Canada and other government and private safety groups.

And don't forget NHTSA's side airbag warning issued on October 14, 1999:

> Side impact airbags can provide significant supplemental safety benefits to adults in side impact crashes. However, children who are seated in close proximity to a side airbag may be at risk of serious or fatal injury, especially if the child's head, neck, or chest is in close proximity to the airbag at the time of deployment.

Protecting yourself

Because not all airbags function, or malfunction, the same way, *Lemon-Aid* has done an exhaustive analysis of U.S. and Canadian recalls, crash data, and owner complaints to determine which vehicles and which model years use airbags that may seriously injure occupants or deploy inadvertently. That data can be found in Part Three's model ratings.

 Additionally, you should take the following steps to reduce the danger from airbag deployment:

• Buy a vehicle with head-protecting side curtain airbags for front and rear passengers.

- Make sure that seat belts are buckled and all head restraints are properly adjusted (to about ear level).
- Choose vehicles with head restraints that are rated "Good" by IIHS (see Part Three).
- Insist that passengers who are frail or short or who have recently had surgery sit in the back and properly position themselves away from side airbags.
- Ensure that the driver's seat can be adjusted for height and has tracks with sufficient rearward travel to allow short drivers to remain at a safe distance (over 25 cm) away from the bag's deployment and still be able to reach the accelerator and brake.
- Consider buying pedal extensions to keep you at a safe distance away from a deploying airbag if you are short-statured.

Top 20 Safety Defects

The U.S. federal government's online safety complaints database contains well over 100,000 entries, going back to vehicles made in the late '70s. Although the database was originally intended to record only incidents of component failures that relate to safety, you will find every problem imaginable dutifully recorded by clerks working for NHTSA.

A perusal of the listed complaints shows that some safety-related failures occur more frequently than others and often affect one manufacturer more than another. Here is a summary of the most commonly reported failures:

1. Sudden unintended acceleration
2. ABS total brake failure; wheel lock-up
3. Airbags not deploying when they should, or deploying when they shouldn't
4. Tire-tread separation
5. Electrical or fuel-system fires
6. Sudden stalling
7. Sudden electrical failures
8. Transmission failing to engage, or suddenly disengaging
9. Transmission jumping from Park to Reverse or Neutral; vehicle rolling away when parked
10. Steering or suspension failures
11. Seat belt failures
12. Collapsing seatbacks
13. Defective sliding door, door locks, and latches
14. Poor headlight illumination; glare
15. Dash reflecting onto windshield
16. Hood flying up
17. Wheel falling away
18. Steering wheel lifting off
19. Transmission lever pulling out
20. Exploding windshields

Vehicles for Older Drivers

Drivers over 80 are the fastest-growing segment of the driving population. According to Candrive, the Canadian Driving Research Initiative for Vehicular Safety in the Elderly, there are currently about 3 million senior drivers in Canada, and their numbers are expected to double by 2040. A quarter of Canadians 85 and older now have a driver's licence, and 105 licences have been issued to centenarians in Ontario and Manitoba alone. By 2030, it's estimated that there will be roughly 15,000 centenarians driving in Canada—approximately three times as many as there are today. Husbands do the bulk of family driving, which usually involves short trips (11–17 km per day, on average) for medical appointments and visits to family, friends, and shopping malls. This puts older women, who tend to outlive their husbands, in a serious bind because of their lack of driving experience—particularly in rural areas, where driving is a necessity rather than a choice.

I'm 66, so I know that older drivers, like most other drivers, want cars that are reliable, relatively inexpensive, and fuel efficient. Additionally, we require vehicles that compensate for some of the physical challenges associated with aging (I'm getting fatter, slower, and much more taciturn, I'm told) and provide protection for accidents more common with mature drivers (side impacts, for example). Furthermore, as drivers get older, they find that the very act of getting into a car (sitting down while moving sideways, without bumping their heads or twisting their necks) demands considerable acrobatic skill. And don't even ask about reaching up and over for the shoulder belt!

Access and Comfort for Older Drivers

I've been told that some drivers with arthritic hands have to insert a pencil into their key ring to twist the key in the ignition. Make sure your ignition lock doesn't require that much effort. Power locks and windows are a must, especially if the vehicle will be operated with hand controls. A remote keyless entry will allow entry without having to twist a key in the door lock. A vehicle equipped with a buttonless shifter will be less difficult to activate for arthritis sufferers and drivers with limited upper-body mobility. Cruise control can be helpful for those with lower-body mobility challenges.

Get a vehicle that's easy to enter and exit. Check for door openings that are wide enough to get into and out of easily, both for you and for any wheelchairs or scooters that may need to be loaded. Make sure the door catches when opened on a slight incline so that it doesn't close as you are exiting. If necessary, your trunk or rear cargo area should have a low liftover and room to stow your wheelchair or scooter. Bench seats are preferable because they're roomier and easier to access; getting a power-adjustable driver's seat with memory is also a good idea. Make sure the seat is comfortable and has plenty of side bolstering.

Forget minivans, unless you invest in a step-up, choose one with an easily reached inside-grip handle, and don't mind bumping the left-side steering-column stalk with your knee each time you slide into the driver's seat. Incidentally, General Motors' 2009 minivans offered a Sit-N-Lift option: a motorized, rotating lift-and-lower passenger seat that's accessed through the middle door and can be taken out when not needed.

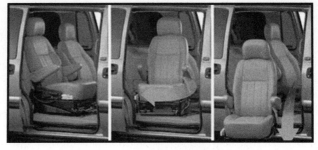

GM has dropped its front-drive minivans that used this versatile feature; but the mechanism is still available from GM suppliers.

Drivers with limited mobility, or those who are recovering from hip surgery, give kudos to the Cadillac Escalade SUV and GM Venture/ Montana minivans; Toyota's Echo, Yaris, Matrix, and Avalon; and small SUVs such as the Honda CR-V, Hyundai Tucson, and Toyota RAV4. Of this group, only the recently discontinued GM minivans give me cause for concern, because of their poor reliability.

Incidentally, NHTSA warns drivers with physical disabilities against the use of special steering-control devices on airbag-equipped vehicles.

Safety Features for Older Drivers

The driver's seat should be mounted high enough to give a commanding view of the road (with slower reaction times, seniors need earlier warnings). Driver's seats must offer enough rearward travel to attenuate the force of an exploding airbag, which can be particularly hazardous to older or small-statured occupants, children, or anyone recovering from surgery. Adjustable gas and brake pedals are a must for short-legged drivers.

And while we're discussing airbags, remember that they are calibrated to explode during low-speed collisions (at less than 10 km/h) and that reports of injuries caused by their deployment are commonplace. Therefore, always put at least 25 cm between your upper torso and the steering wheel.

Look for handles near the door frame that can be gripped for support when entering or leaving the vehicle, bright dashboard gauges that can be seen in sunlight, and instruments with large-sized controls.

Remote-controlled mirrors are a must, along with adjustable, unobtrusive head restraints and a non-reflective front windshield (many drivers put a cloth on the dash-top to cut the distraction). Make sure that the brake and accelerator pedals aren't mounted too close together.

As far as safety features are concerned, a superior crashworthiness rating is essential, as well as torso- and head-protecting side airbags, since most intersection collisions involving mature drivers occur when drivers are making a turn into oncoming traffic. The extra head protection can make a critical difference in side impacts. For example, Toyota's 2004 RAV4 with $680 head-protecting side airbags earned a "Best Pick" designation from the Insurance Institute for Highway Safety (IIHS). When tested without the head protection, it received a "Poor" rating in the side test.

Don't be overly impressed by anti-lock brakes, since their proper operation (no tapping on the brakes) runs counter to everything you have been taught, plus they aren't that reliable. Look for headlights that give you a comfortable view at night, as well as easily seen and heard dash-mounted turn signal indicators. Ensure that the vehicle's knobs and switches are large and easy to identify. Having an easily accessed, full-sized spare tire and a user-friendly lug wrench and jack stand is also important.

Other Buying Considerations

When "New" Isn't New

Nothing will cause you to lose money more quickly than buying a new car that's older than advertised, has previously been sold and then taken back, has accident damage, or has had the odometer disconnected or turned back.

Even if the vehicle hasn't been used, it may have been left outdoors for a considerable length of time, causing the deterioration of rubber components, premature body and chassis rusting, or severe rusting of internal mechanical parts, which leads to brake malfunction, fuel line contamination, hard starting, and stalling.

You can check a vehicle's age by looking at the date-of-manufacture plate usually found on the driver-side door pillar. If the date of manufacture is 7/10 or earlier, your vehicle was probably one of the last 2010 models made before the September changeover to the 2011s. Redesigned vehicles or those new to the market are exceptions to this rule. They may arrive at dealerships in early spring or mid-summer and are considered to be next year's models. They also depreciate more quickly owing to their earlier launching, but this difference narrows over time. For 2011, GM plans to change the model-year of its full-sized pickups in July (two months earlier than before).

Sometimes a vehicle can be too new and cost you more in maintenance because its redesign glitches haven't yet been worked out. As Honda's North American manufacturing chief, Koki Hirashima, so ably put it, carryover models generally have fewer problems than vehicles that have been significantly reworked or just introduced to the market. Newly redesigned vehicles get quality scores that are, on average, 2 percent worse than vehicles that have been around for a while, says J.D. Power. Some surprising poor performers are the Jaguar X-Type, Nissan Altima and Quest, and Toyota Corolla and Tundra.

Because they were the first off the assembly line for that model year, most vehicles assembled between September and February are called "first-series" cars. "Second-series" vehicles, made between March and August, incorporate more assembly-line fixes and are better built than the earlier models, which may depend on ineffective "field fixes" to mask problems until the warranty expires. Second-series vehicles will sell for the same price or less, but they will be a far better buy because of their assembly-line upgrades and more generous rebates. Service bulletins for Chrysler's new Caliber and Charger; GM's Solstice, Torrent, and Sky roadsters; and the Ford Fusion, Zephyr, and Milan show these vehicles all had serious quality shortcomings during their first year on the market. It usually takes a couple of years for the factory to get most of the quality glitches corrected.

There's also the very real possibility that the new vehicle you've just purchased was damaged while being shipped to the dealer and was later fixed in the service bay during the pre-delivery inspection. It's estimated that this happens to about 10 percent of all new vehicles. Although there's no specific Canadian legislation allowing buyers of vehicles damaged in transit to cancel their contracts, B.C. legislation says that dealers must disclose damages of $2,000 or more. In a more general sense, Canadian common-law jurisprudence does allow for cancellation or compensation whenever the delivered product differs markedly from what the buyer expected to receive. Ontario's revised *Consumer Protection Act* is particularly hard-nosed in prohibiting this kind of misrepresentation.

Fuel Economy Follies

Poor gas mileage is one of the top complaints among owners of new cars and minivans. Drivers say gas mileage is seldom as high as it's hyped to be; in fact, it's likely to be 10–20 percent less than advertised with most vehicles. (Gas mileage, measured in mpg, is the opposite of metric fuel consumption, measured in L/100 km. In other words, you want gas mileage to be high and consumption to be low.) *Consumer Reports* magazine estimates that 90 percent of vehicles sold don't get the gas mileage advertised, and their reporters target hybrids built by Honda and Toyota as the worst offenders. (Incidentally, Honda dropped its Insight hybrid for three years and has just returned its much-improved 2010 version to the market.)

Why such a contradiction between promise and performance?

It's simple: Automakers cheat on their tests. They submit their own test results to the government after testing under optimum conditions. Transport Canada then publishes these self-serving "cooked" figures as its own research. One Ford service bulletin is remarkably frank in discounting the validity of these tests:

> Very few people will drive in a way that is identical to the EPA [sanctioned] tests. These [fuel economy] numbers are the result of test procedures that were originally developed to test emissions, not fuel economy.

FUEL ECONOMY CONVERSION TABLE

L/100 KM	MPG (U.S.)	L/100 KM	MPG (U.S.)	L/100 KM	MPG (U.S.)
5.2	45	7.1	33	11.2	21
5.3	44	7.4	32	11.8	20
5.5	43	7.6	31	12.4	19
5.6	42	7.8	30	13.1	18
5.7	41	8.1	29	13.8	17
5.9	40	8.4	28	14.7	16
6.0	39	8.7	27	15.7	15
6.2	38	9.0	26	16.8	14
6.4	37	9.4	25	18.1	13
6.5	36	9.8	24	19.6	12
6.7	35	10.2	23	21.4	11
6.9	34	10.7	22	23.5	10

Stephen Akehurst, a senior manager at Natural Resources Canada, which tests vehicles and publishes the annual *Fuel Consumption Guide*, admits that his lab tests vehicles under ideal conditions. He says that actual driving may burn about 25 percent more fuel than what the government tests show. Too bad we never see this fact hyped in the automakers' fuel economy ads.

Some examples: One of the biggest gas-guzzlers tested, the Lincoln Aviator, burned 44 percent more than the *Fuel Consumption Guide*'s estimate. A Nissan Quest burned twice as much fuel as was advertised in the *Guide*. Only the Hyundai Elantra did well. It burned a full litre less than predicted by the guys in the white lab coats.

Although good fuel economy is important, it's hardly worth a harsh ride, excessive highway noise, side-wind buffeting, anemic acceleration, and a cramped interior. You may end up with much worse gas mileage than advertised and a vehicle that's underpowered for your needs.

If you never quite got the hang of metric fuel economy measurements, use the approximate fuel conversion table above to establish how many miles to a U.S. gallon of gas your vehicle provides.

 ## "Miracle" Fuels

The lure of cheap, "clean" fuel has never been stronger, and the misrepresentations as to the advantages of different fuels have never been greater. Take a look at the following list of flavour-of-the-month alternate fuels that have been proposed by politicians and businesses, and consider that, except for diesel, not a single other alternate fuel is economically viable.

Ethanol and flex-fuel vehicles (FFVs)

Ethanol is the trendy "fuel of the year" for automakers, oil companies, and politicians who have their heads stuck up their tailpipes. All three groups recite the mantra that increased ethanol use will cut fuel costs, make us less dependent on foreign oil sources (goodbye, Big Oil; hello, Big Corn), and create a cleaner environment. Unfortunately, this is simply not true—it's reminiscent of the misguided embrace of the 1997 Kyoto Accord by governments who promised they would be effective in cutting emissions that lead to global warming. Ironically, research now shows signatories to the Accord produce more emissions than non-signatories.

FFVs are all the rage with the Detroit Three, and they're being promoted over hybrids and diesel engines because the switchover is less costly for automakers. They only have to modify the fuel-delivery system on their vehicles and then lobby the federal government to pay billions of dollars for new pipelines, tankers, and gas stations. Millions of their vehicles are already on the market and can run on a mixture of 85 percent ethanol and 15 percent gasoline (called E85), but oil companies limit the supply of ethanol available because charging high gasoline prices is more profitable. Furthermore, governments won't pony up the billions of dollars needed to construct new ethanol pipelines (at an estimated cost of $1.6 million per kilometre for 322,000 km) and to convert filling stations (at an estimated cost of $240,000 per new tank and pump) just to provide real competition for gas-selling stations. At the moment, most E85 FFVs are gasoline-powered because ethanol retailers can't be found (only 608 out of 168,987 filling stations sell ethanol in the States; there are only a couple in Canada that do). Yet the automakers get important tax credits because they have converted much of their production to run on ethanol fuel (in theory), though most of the vehicles stay on a pure gasoline diet.

Brazil, a huge ethanol producer since the late '70s, doesn't need a pipeline because most of its sugar cane fields are located where they can distill and market the resulting ethanol, thereby forgoing expensive transportation costs. In North America, most of the corn and other ethanol-producing crops are found in the U.S. Midwest and Central and Western Canada, far away from major population areas.

Indeed, ethanol is smokeless, burns cleaner, and (theoretically) leads to less engine maintenance. Plus, you can drink it (diluted, or with a chaser).

But will the increased use of ethanol make North America much less dependent on gasoline? No way—not if you do the math: About 4 billion gallons of ethanol are produced annually in the States, but they burn an average of 140 billion gallons of gasoline each year.

Accepting that ethanol filling stations are practically nonexistent and are expected to stay that way, here are some other jaw-dropping facts that ensure ethanol won't be the fuel of the future: The fuel costs almost as much as gasoline in some places (unless you distill it yourself); gas mileage *drops* by up to 30 percent when ethanol is used; cold-weather performance is mediocre; and the product is highly corrosive, with a particular fondness for snacking on plastic and rubber components.

Hybrids

You have to be quite stupid to plunk down about $27,800 for a hybrid like the Toyota Prius in the hope of saving gas, money, and the environment. Canadian auto columnist John LeBlanc (*www.straight-six.com/blog*) calls the Toyota Prius "one of the worst cars" of the decade (*autos.ca.msn.com/editors-picks/gallery. aspx?cp-documentid=23127790&page=8*):

> With the '04 Prius, you had the pleasure of paying about twice as much as a sub-compact that got similar fuel savings. But it was slow, handled like a shopping cart, had a steering wheel that may as well be made out of sandstone for all the feel it transmitted, didn't achieve anywhere near its rated fuel consumption in adverse driving conditions and is costly to repair out of warranty. If it wasn't for the Prius, we wouldn't have rubber band continuously-variable-transmissions or the word "hyper-miling." Think about that. The Prius is THE car for people who loathe cars. Me? I love cars. Therein I loathe the Prius.

As practical as the promise of ethanol fuel for everybody seemed to be at first, hybrids use a pie-in-the-sky alternative fuel system that requires expensive and complex electronic and mechanical components to achieve the same fuel economy that a bare-bones Honda Civic can achieve for about two-thirds the cost of the Prius—and without polluting the environment with exotic toxic metals leached from battery packs and powertrain components.

Consumer Reports tested six pairs of vehicles, with each pair including a conventional vehicle and the equivalent hybrid model, and published the astounding results in its April 2006 edition. *CR* found that in each category of car, truck, and

---

ESTIMATED COSTS FOR 2006 GASOLINE-FUELED VEHICLES VS. HYBRIDS

Over a 5-year period, the smallest estimated U.S.–dollar operating cost difference was between the two Honda Civics ($3,700), followed by Toyota's Corolla and Prius ($5,250). The biggest gap between two similar models was registered by the gasoline-powered Toyota Highlander SUV and its hybrid version ($13,300 U.S.), with the Lexus RX330 and RX400h posting a $13,100-higher cost for the hybrid version. The first two figures are the manufacturers' suggested retail prices.

	GASOLINE	HYBRID	HIGHER OPERATING COST
Ford Escape SUV	$22,818	$29,140	$ 8,350
Honda Accord EX	$25,862	$31,540	$10,250
Honda Civic	$18,444	$22,400	$ 3,750
Lexus RX330/RX400h	$37,960	$46,755	$13,100
Toyota Highlander	$32,650	$39,835	$13,300
Toyota Corolla/Prius	$16,607	$22,305	$ 5,250

Source: *Consumer Reports*, April 2006

SUV, the extra cost for the hybrid version was unacceptably *higher* than the cost of the same vehicle equipped with a conventional propulsion system.

Other disadvantages of hybrids are their mechanical and electronic complexities; dependence on specialized dealers for basic servicing; high depreciation rates and insurance costs; overblown fuel-efficiency numbers (owners report getting 40 percent less mileage than promised); and the $3,000 cost to replace their battery packs.

Finally, consider this: Hybrid vehicles like the Toyota Prius use rare-earth minerals such as lanthanum, scandium, and yttrium mixed oxides and aluminas (which are used in almost all automotive emissions control systems). Neodymium is another rare element needed for the lightweight permanent magnets that power hybrid motors. It's a radioactive substance found almost exclusively in China, which has begun restricting its sale for domestic use and slapped on heavy export duties. Furthermore, the mining and refining of these rare minerals has had a devastating effect on China's environment—something North American "green" advocates overlook.

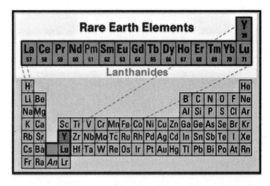

Rare earth elements are really not that rare (they take up 17 slots on the periodic table), but they're so named because few of them exist in a pure form naturally. Mining and processing these elements is both expensive and toxic to workers.

Western nations simply cannot afford to mine and refine neodymium within their borders due to the enormous environmental toxicity that mining it produces. In a sense, China is not cornering the neodymium market using their mineral reserves, but rather their willingness to sacrifice their environment and expose their populace to a higher cancer rate. In the end, North American motorists may trade a dependence on Middle Eastern oil for a troubling dependence on Chinese-sourced neodymium that's poisoning the Chinese people in the process.

Diesels

Diesel fuel is cleaner these days and far more fuel-efficient than ever before. Among the alternative fuels tested by independent researchers, diesel comes closest to the estimated fuel economy figures. It's also widely available and requires neither a steep learning curve in the service bay nor exotic replacement parts. Additionally, unlike hybrids, diesel-equipped vehicles are reasonably priced and hold their value quite well.

As with the changeover to unleaded gasoline two decades ago, owners of diesel-equipped Detroit-made vehicles can expect horrendously expensive maintenance costs, considerable repair downtime, and the worsening of the diesel's poor reliability trend, which was seen over the past decade with Ford's Powerstroke and

Sheesh, it seemed like a simple solution at the time.

General Motors' Duramax. Additionally, many of the 2010 and 2011 diesel engines (Ford excepted) now require that owners regularly fill up with urea—an unexpected extra expense and annoyance.

To pee or not to pee? Recent model diesels, like the Mercedes' Bluetec, inject a urea solution—known as AdBlue—into the exhaust to reduces nitrous oxide (NOx) emissions. Audi, BMW, VW, and the Detroit Three also use urea injection under different names.

A yearly urea refill can be expected since the urea tank contains roughly 8 gallons (U.S.), which is good for about 19,300 kilometres (12,000 miles) of standard operation. Generally, automakers will add the urea solution at every scheduled maintenance visit.

Mercedes-Benz Blutec diesels will not run if the urea tank doesn't contain a certain amount. If the tank reaches one gallon, the car notifies the driver. It does so again with only 20 starts remaining. To reset the system, at least two gallons of AdBlue—or four half-gallon bottles, at $7.75 each—must be added. Not a lot to clean the environment, you say? Read on.

Consumer Reports was charged an outrageous $317 to put 7.5 gallons of AdBlue in its Mercedes GL320 test car at $32/gallon for the fluid, even though 7.5 gallons would only cost $116.25 in half-gallon bottles elsewhere. So, what can you do if your car or truck is urea-immobilized, there is no dealership around, or you refuse to pay through the nose for a simple fill-up?

That brings us back to our original question: "To pee or not to pee?"

Don't pee, at least not into the urea tank. Yes, human urine contains 2 to 4 percent urea, but modern diesels won't use your pee because it's too diluted and full of other substance like salts, toxins, bile pigments, hormones, and up to 95 percent water. AdBlue, TDI, and other urea products have a concentration of 32.5 percent urea mixed with deionized water. If you put anything else in the urea tank, your car or truck won't start.

Fuel economy misrepresentation

So if you can't make a gas-saving product that pours into your fuel tank or attaches to the fuel or air lines, you have to use that old standby and, well, lie. Hell, if automakers and government fuel-efficiency advocates can do it, why not dealers?

Fuel economy misrepresentation is actionable, and there is Canadian jurisprudence that allows for a contract's cancellation if the gas-mileage figures are false (see Part Two). Most people, however, simply keep the car they bought and live with the fact that they were fooled.

There are a few choices you can make that will lower fuel consumption. First off, choose a smaller version of the vehicle style you are interested in buying. Secondly, choose a manual transmission or an automatic with a fuel-saving Fifth or Sixth gear. Thirdly, an engine with a cylinder-deactivation feature or variable valve timing will increase fuel economy by 8 and 3 percent, respectively.

Excessive Maintenance Fees

Maintenance inspections and replacement parts represent hidden costs that are usually exaggerated by dealers and automakers to increase their profits on vehicles that either rarely require fixing or are sold in insufficient numbers to support a service bay.

Alan Gelman, a well-known Toronto garage owner and former host of CFRB radio's *Car Talk*, warns drivers:

> There are actually two maintenance schedules handed out by car companies and dealers. The dealer inspection sheets often call for far more extensive and expensive routine maintenance checks than what's listed in the owner's manual. Most of those checks are padding; smart owners will stick with the essential checks listed in the manual and have them done by cheaper, independent garages.

Getting routine work done at independent facilities will cost about one-third to one-half the price usually charged by dealers. Just be sure to follow the automaker's suggested schedule so no warranty claim can be tied to botched servicing. Additionally, an inexpensive ALLDATA service bulletin subscription (see Appendix III) will keep you current as to your vehicle's factory defects, required check-ups, and recalls; tell you what's covered by little-known "goodwill" warranties; and save you valuable time and money when troubleshooting common problems.

Choosing a Reliable, Cheap Vehicle

Overall vehicle safety and body fit and finish on both domestic and imported vehicles are better today than they were three decades ago. Premature rusting is less of a problem, and reliability is improving. Repairs to electronic systems and powertrains, however, are outrageously expensive and complicated. Owners of cars and trucks made by GM, Ford, and Chrysler still report serious engine and automatic transmission deficiencies, often during the vehicle's first year in service. Other common defects include electrical system failures caused by faulty computer modules; malfunctioning ABS systems; brake rotor warpage; early pad wearout; failure-prone air conditioning and automatic transmissions; and faulty engine head gaskets, intake manifolds, fuel systems, suspensions, and steering assemblies.

Nothing shows the poor quality control of the Detroit Three automakers as much as the poor fit and finish of body panels. Next time you're stuck in traffic, look at the trunk lid or rear hatch alignment of the vehicle in front of you. Chances are, if it's a Detroit-bred model, the trunk or hatch will be so misaligned that there will be a large gap on one side. Then look at most Asian products: Usually, you will see perfectly aligned trunks and hatches without any large gaps on either side.

That, in a nutshell, is Detroit's problem.

Detroit's "Good" Products

Don't get the impression that Detroit automakers can't make reasonably good vehicles, though. Chrysler's PT Cruiser and the Jeep Wrangler are good values; Ford's Mustang, Crown Victoria, Grand Marquis, and its much-improved 2004–11 Focus carry little risk; GM's full-sized rear-drive vans are good buys; and the Acadia, Enclave, Equinox, Terrain, and Traverse SUVs also perform well, though long-term reliability is still unproven.

General Motors' products are quite a mixed bag: Its full-sized vans and SUVs, small cars, and joint ventures with Toyota and Suzuki have all done well, but its recent mid-sized family cars (think Malibu and Impala) are mediocre, at best—and its just-discontinued, bargain-basement minivans are poison.

Most studies done by consumer groups and private firms show that, in spite of improvements attempted over the past two decades, vehicles made by Chrysler, GM, and (to a lesser extent) Ford still don't measure up to Japanese and some South Korean products, such as Hyundai's, in terms of quality and technology. This is particularly evident in SUVs and minivans, where Honda and Toyota have long retained the highest reliability and dependability ratings, despite a handful of missteps with powertrain durability.

Chrysler

Chrysler's bailout, bankruptcy, and betrothal to Fiat is like giving a transfusion to an Italian corpse. In effect, Washington has forced the merger of the world's two worst automakers into one giant piece of *guano*.

Don't buy a Chrysler unless it's a Jeep Wrangler or a well-inspected Ram pickup with a manual transmission and a diesel engine. That's it. All the other products are failure-prone and costly to maintain, though the minivans are the best of a bad lot.

Ford

Ford sold off most of its assets and borrowed billions of dollars just before the recession hit. The fact that it didn't go bankrupt means that Ford not only has kept its own loyal customers and critical rural dealers but is also well poised to poach Toyota, Chrysler, and GM sales.

"Oh, we ain't got a barrel of money..."

Ford's management is less dysfunctional than what we see at Chrysler and GM. Moreover, the company has improved its quality control during the past several years and brought out popular new products like the Edge and Fusion. Lincoln's reliable and profitable Town Car will likely remain for a few more years as Ford's only rear-drive Lincoln, due to its popularity with seniors and fleet managers.

What not to buy from Ford? The new Explorer, scheduled to be launched as a 2011 or 2012 model. It was glitch-prone when first launched in 1990 and will likely be troublesome during the first year as a revamped model. Also, you want to steer clear of any Ford imported from Europe or China. Remember that piece of trash called the Ford Cortina, or the mishmash of letters and numbers called the Merkur XR4Ti?

General Motors

First the flowers, then the flower pot. GM has actual cash flow coming into the company rather than going downstream, and eight divisions have been whittled down to a more manageable four (it has sold Saab and Hummer, and Saturn and Pontiac have been successfully shut down). On the other hand, the company's terminated dealers are clogging the courts with hundreds of lawsuits seeking compensation for the arbitrariness of GM's action; the company still owes the Canadian and American governments almost $50 billion; the expected Initial Public Offering of GM stock (which is needed to repay the billions in bailout funds) is flying into a careening, skeptical Wall Street crowd; and GM's money-losing Opel is floundering now that Germany gave all of its bailout money to Greece.

GM has lost its customer and dealer base thanks to its willy-nilly closing of dealerships in many rural areas and shutting down or divesting itself of four divisions. Notwithstanding GM's termination notices sent to dealers, the company has privately extended settlement offers of as much as $1 million to reinstate almost 700 of the 1,160 dealers who threatened to challenge the automaker's action through arbitration.

Major quality deficiencies still affect most of its lineup, notably American-built front-drives and imported pickups. Owners cite unreliable powertrains, poor braking performance, electrical problems, and subpar fit and finish as the main offenders.

The company's increased reliance on factories in China to build economy cars for North America is pretty scary. Imagine: Not only are North Americans' bailout funds being used to create jobs in China, but we also will have the dubious pleasure of driving some of the worst-made automobiles in the world, imported from the country that sold us lead-laced-paint-coated kids' toys and poisoned pet food ingredients. Move over, Fiat! Here come Chery's economy and Brilliance's "brilliant" crashworthiness. (Don't just take my word that these are bad cars— watch the crash videos.)

An interesting conclusion relative to Chinese manufacturing, according to several independent studies—like those done by Christensen Associates, Inc. (*www. camcinc.com/library/SoYou'reBuyingFromChina.pdf*) and by Paul Midler in *Poorly Made in China: An Insider's Account of the Tactics Behind China's Production Game* (John Wiley & Sons, 2009)—is that safety and quality are trumped by price. Your car has no brakes? No problem. We'll give you a 10 percent discount and shoot the factory foreman.

Asian Automakers

Almost all of the Asian automakers make exceptionally good cars and weathered the poor 2009 sales year better than most. The only exceptions are Mitsubishi, Suzuki, and Kia; the first two automakers were crippled by an almost nonexistent dealer network (Mitsu dualed with Chrysler for some time under the Colt label),

A 2011 loser: Kia's Sorento... proof-positive that not all that is Asian is top-quality.

while Suzuki had little product and an equally weak dealer body. Earlier this year, though, Volkswagen bought a 20 percent interest in Suzuki, a move that may strengthen Suzuki's dealer presence. Kia has done quite well this past year, selling what are mostly subpar products. As for Hyundai, its parent company (which once had a similarly poor quality reputation), it has failed to correct the numerous factory-related defects that plague most of its Kia models.

Don't buy into the myth that parts for imports are overpriced or hard to find. It's actually easier to find parts for Japanese and South Korean vehicles than for domestic ones because of the large number of units produced, the presence of hundreds of independent suppliers, the ease with which relatively simple parts can be interchanged among different models, and the large reservoir of used parts available. When a part is hard to find, the annual *Mitchell* manuals are useful guides to substitute parts that can be used for many different models. They're available in some libraries, most auto parts stores, and practically all junkyards.

Sadly, customer relations have been the Japanese automakers' Achilles' heels. Dealers are spoiled rotten by decades of easy sales and have developed a "take it or leave it" showroom attitude, which is often accompanied by a woeful ignorance of their own model lineups. This was once a frequent complaint of Honda and Toyota shoppers, though recent APA undercover surveys show a big improvement among Toyota dealers.

A 2011 winner: The rear-drive Hyundai Genesis comes with a 3.8L 290 hp V6 or an optional 4.6L 375 hp V8.

Where attitudes have gotten worse is in the service bay, where periodic maintenance visits and warranty claims end up costing more than expected. Well-known factory-related defects (Honda engine oil leaks and Toyota engine and tranny problems) are corrected under extended warranties, but you always have the feeling you owe the "family."

There's no problem with discourteous or ill-informed South Korean automakers. Instead, poor quality has been their bugaboo. Yet, like Honda's and Toyota's recoveries following start-up quality glitches, Hyundai (South Korea's biggest automaker) has made

The Kia Sedona has everything to attract minivan buyers, except dependability.

considerable progress in bringing quality up almost to Toyota's and Honda's level.

Up to the mid-'90s, South Korean vehicles were merely cheap, poor-quality knock-offs of their Japanese counterparts. They would start to fall apart after their third year because of subpar body construction, unreliable automatic transmission and electrical components, and parts suppliers who put low prices ahead of reliability and durability. This was particularly evident with Hyundai's Pony, Stellar, Excel, and early Sonata models. During the past several years, though, Hyundai's product lineup has been extended and refined, and quality is no longer a worry. In fact, Hyundai's 2011 upscale Genesis is a top-performing $38,999 (watch out for the $1,760 freight fee) luxury sedan that's recommended by *Consumer Reports* and

Lemon-Aid. Also, Hyundai's comprehensive base warranty protects owners from most of the more-expensive breakdowns that may occur.

Hyundais are easily repaired by independent garages, and their rapid depreciation doesn't mean much; they cost so little initially, and entry-level buyers are known to keep their cars longer than most, thereby easily amortizing the higher depreciation rate.

Kia, a struggling, low-quality, small South Korean compact automaker bought by Hyundai in October 1998, has come a long way. At first, it languished under Hyundai's "benign neglect," as Hyundai spent most of its resources on its own cars and SUVs. But, during the past few years, Hyundai has worked hard to improve Kia reliability and fit and finish by using more Hyundai parts in each Kia redesign and by improving quality control on the assembly line. Kia's Rondo and Sportage are the models with the fewest quality problems, while the Optima, Sedona, and Sorento are riddled with drivetrain, electrical, brake, and fuel system defects, in addition to poor fit and finish.

European Models

Lemon-Aid doesn't recommend many European cars; there are way too many with serious and expensive quality and servicing problems. Heck, even the Germans have abandoned their own products. For example, a 2002 J.D. Power survey of 15,000 German car owners found that German drivers are happiest at the wheel of a Japanese Lexus. This survey included compact and luxury cars as well as off-roaders. Toyota won first place on quality, reliability, and owner satisfaction, while Nissan's Maxima headed the luxury class standings. BMW was the first choice among European offerings.

For those who feel the German survey was a fluke, there's also a 2003 study of 34,000 car owners with vehicles up to eight years old, published by Britain's Consumers' Association. It found that less than half of British owners would recommend a British-made Rover or Vauxhall to a friend. The most highly rated cars in the study were the Japanese Subaru, Isuzu, and Lexus: Over 85 percent of drivers would recommend them.

And there's more. In 2005, Britain's Warranty Direct, a third-party warranty provider, checked the cost of repairs and reliability of 250 of the most popular models sold in the British Isles. It found the Honda Accord to be the most reliable and the Fiat Punto to be the least reliable in its survey (are you listening, Chrysler?). Overall, Asian cars fared best in reliability and cost of repair ratings.

Honda was the brand least likely to require repairs, with Mazda, Toyota, Subaru, Nissan, Mitsubishi, and Lexus all top-ranking. Smart, Mini, and Porsche were the only European nameplates in the top 10.

Another poor performer was Land Rover. It recorded a horrendous warranty claim rate of 47 percent in an average year. This was followed up by Renault and Saab, both with a 38 percent chance of requiring a repair in an average year, while Jeep scored similarly low on the reliability index. Other reliability "bottom feeders" were Audi, Volvo, Chrysler, and Mercedes-Benz.

Jag's a drag: The XK8 has a breakdown rate of 62 percent, says Britain's 2005 Warranty Direct survey.

Mercedes not "world-class"

Here's another surprise: Although it builds some of the most expensive cars and SUVs in the world, Mercedes' quality isn't always first-class. After stumbling badly when it first launched its rushed-to-production American-made SUV for the 1998 model year, the automaker sent out many urgent service bulletins that sought to correct a surprisingly large number of production deficiencies affecting its entire lineup, including C-Class and, to a lesser extent, E-Class models.

Mercedes executives admit that the company's cars and SUVs have serious quality shortcomings, and have vowed to correct them. But such a turnaround is complicated by M-B's huge financial losses from Chrysler and Smart. The "oh, so cute" Smart division has lost billions and doesn't compare with the more-refined and safer Asian competition.

While Mercedes sorts through its woes, shoppers who can't resist having a German nameplate should buy a VW Jetta (not the cheapened base version), or a BMW 3 Series or 5 Series and take special courses to learn how to manage the cars' iDrive multifunctional cockpit controller.

Volkswagen's quality isn't quite as bad as Mercedes', and its sales have been on the upswing. True, VW has always been early on the scene with great concepts, but their ideas have often been accompanied by poor execution and a weak servicing network. With its failure-prone and under-serviced Eurovan and Camper, the company hasn't been a serious minivan player since the late '60s, and VW's Rabbit and Golf small cars were resounding duds. Even the company's forays into luxury cruisers have been met with underwhelming enthusiasm and general derision.

But not all the news is bad. For 2010–11, VW's small cars and diesel-equipped models will continue to be strong sellers. Resale values are strong, and prices will be even more competitive.

Nevertheless, with European models, your service options are limited and customer-relations staffers can be particularly insensitive and arrogant. You can count on lots of aggravation and expense because of the unacceptably slow distribution of parts and their high markups. Because these companies have a quasi-monopoly on replacement parts, there are few independent suppliers you can turn to for help. And auto wreckers, the last-chance repository for inexpensive car parts, are unlikely to carry European parts for vehicles that are either more than three years old or manufactured in small numbers.

These vehicles also age badly. The weakest areas remain the drivetrains, electronic control modules, electrical and fuel systems, brakes, accessories (including the sound system and AC), and body components.

Cutting Costs

Watch the Warranty

There's a big difference between warranty promise and warranty performance. Most automakers offer bumper-to-bumper warranties that are good for at least the first 3 years/60,000 km, and most models get powertrain coverage up to 5 years/100,000 km, although Mitsubishi offers a 5-year/100,000 km base warranty and a 10-year/160,000 km powertrain warranty. It's also becoming an industry standard for car companies to pay for roadside assistance, a loaner car, or hotel accommodations if your vehicle breaks down while you're away from home and it's still under warranty. This assistance may be for as long as 5 years, without any kilometre restriction. *Lemon-Aid* readers report few problems with these ancillary warranty benefits.

Don't buy more warranty than you need

As part of its bailout program for the auto industry, Ottawa has given Detroit automakers millions of dollars to pay for warranty claims on most 2009–11 models, but some vehicles purchased before March 2008 may not be included in the government payout. This means that there will be no government warranty backup for those vehicles if the well goes dry.

If you pick a vehicle rated Recommended by *Lemon-Aid*, the manufacturer's warranty won't be that important and you won't need to spend money on additional warranty protection. On those vehicles that have a history of engine and transmission breakdowns, but the selling price is too good to turn down, budget about $1,500 for an extended powertrain warranty backed by an insurance policy. If the vehicle has a sorry repair history, you will likely need a $2,000 comprehensive warranty. But first ask yourself this question: "Why am I buying a vehicle that's so poorly made that I need to spend several thousand dollars to protect myself until the warranty company grows tired of seeing my face?"

Just like the weight-loss product ads you see on TV, what you see isn't always what you get. For example, bumper-to-bumper coverage usually excludes stereo components, brake pads, clutch plates, and many other expensive parts. And automakers will pull every trick in the book to make you pay for their factory screw-ups. These tricks include blaming your driving or your vehicle's poor maintenance, penalizing you for using an independent garage or the wrong fuel, or simply stating that the problem is "normal" and it's really you who is out of whack.

Part Two has all the answers to the above lame excuses. There, you will find plenty of court decisions and sample claim letters that will make automakers and their dealers think twice about rejecting your claim.

Don't pay for repairs covered by "secret" warranties

Automobile manufacturers are reluctant to publicize their secret warranty programs because they feel that such publicity would weaken consumer confidence in their products and increase their legal liability. The closest they come to an admission is to send out a "goodwill policy," "special policy," or "product update" service bulletin intended for dealers' eyes only. These bulletins admit liability and propose free repairs for defects that include faulty paint, air conditioning malfunctions, and engine and transmission failures.

If you're refused compensation, keep in mind that secret warranty extensions are, first and foremost, an admission of manufacturing negligence. You can usually find them in technical service bulletins (TSBs) that are sent daily to dealers by automakers. Your bottom-line position should be to accept a pro rata adjustment from the manufacturer, whereby you, the dealer, and the automaker each accept a third of the repair costs. If polite negotiations fail, challenge the refusal in court on the grounds that you should not be penalized for failing to make a reimbursement claim under a secret warranty that you never knew existed!

Service bulletins are written by automakers in "mechanic speak" because service managers relate better to them that way. They're great guides for warranty inspections (especially the final one), and they're useful in helping you decide when it's best to trade in your car. Manufacturers can't weasel out of their obligations by claiming that they never wrote such a bulletin.

If your vehicle is out of warranty, show these bulletins to less-expensive, independent garage mechanics so they can quickly find the trouble and order the most recent upgraded part, ensuring that you don't replace one defective component with another.

Canadian service managers and automakers may deny at first that the bulletins even exist, or they may shrug their shoulders and say that they apply only in the States. However, when they're shown a copy, they usually find the appropriate Canadian part number or bulletin in their files. The problems and solutions don't change from one side of the border to another. Imagine American and Canadian tourists' cars being towed across the border because each country's technical service bulletins were different. Mechanical fixes do differ in cases where, for example, a bulletin is for California only, or it relates to a safety or emissions component used only in the States. But these instances are rare, indeed. What is quite gratifying is to see some automakers, like Honda, candidly admit in their bulletins that "goodwill" repair refunds are available. What a shame other automakers aren't as forthcoming!

The best way to get bulletin-related repairs carried out is to visit the dealer's service bay and to attach the specific ALLDATA-supplied service bulletin covering your vehicle's problems to a work order.

Getting your vehicle's service bulletins

Free summaries of automotive recalls and technical service bulletins listed by year, make, model, and engine can be found at the ALLDATA (*www.alldata.com/ TSB*) and NHTSA (*www.safercar.gov*) websites. But, like the NHTSA summaries, ALLDATA's summaries are so short and cryptic that they're of limited use. You can download the complete contents of all the bulletins applicable to your vehicle from ALLDATA at *www.alldatadiy.com* if you pay the $26.95 (U.S.) annual subscription fee. Many bulletins offering "secret warranty" coverage are reproduced in Part Three and Appendix V.

Trim Insurance Costs

Insurance premiums can average between $900 and $2,000 per year, depending on the type of vehicle you own, your personal statistics and driving habits, and whether you can obtain coverage under your family policy.

There are some general rules to follow when looking for insurance savings. For example, vehicles older than five years do not necessarily need collision coverage, and you may not need loss-of-use coverage or a rental car. Other factors that should be considered are as follows:

- A low damageability rating and an average theft history can reduce rates by 10–15 percent. These rankings can be checked at *www.ibc.ca/en/Car_Insurance/ Buying_a_New_Car/HCMU.asp*. Don't be surprised, though, if there appears to be no rhyme or reason for the disparity in the ratings of similar vehicles. Insurance statistics aren't as scientific as insurers pretend—they often charge whatever the market will bear.
- When you phone for quotes, make sure you have your serial number in hand. Many factors—such as the make of the car, the number of doors, if there's a sports package, and the insurer's experience with the car—can affect the quote. And be honest, or you'll find your claim denied, the policy cancelled, or your premium cost boosted.
- Where you live and work also determine how much you pay. In the past, auto insurance rates have been 25–40 percent lower in London, Ontario, than in downtown Toronto because there are fewer cars in London and fewer

kilometres to drive to work. Similar disparities are found in B.C. and Alberta.

- Taking a driver-training course can save you thousands of premium dollars.
- You may be able to include your home or apartment insurance as part of a premium package that's eligible for additional discounts.

InsuranceHotline.com, based in Ontario but with quotes for other provinces, says that it pays to shop around for cheap auto insurance rates. The group has found that the same insurance policy could vary in cost by a whopping 400 percent. For example, a 41-year-old married female driving a 2002 Honda Accord and a 41-year-old married male driving a 1998 Dodge Caravan, both with unblemished driving records, should pay no more than $1,880, but some companies surveyed asked as much as $7,515.

"Hidden" Costs

Depreciation

No one wants to be stuck with a relatively new vehicle that can't be sold for a fair price. And, with job uncertainty and pensions threatened, one's vehicle may be the only place where you have some equity to tide you over through the rough spots. That's something you should think twice about when buying a Pontiac, Saab, Saturn, or Hummer: resale value (or lack thereof). The same caveat applies to other "orphans" abandoned by Chrysler and Ford. The only model that breaks this rule is the Mercury Marquis, rated Recommended despite Ford's intention to take it off the market next year when it closes down Mercury in North America.

Depreciation is the biggest—and most often ignored—expense that you encounter when you trade in your vehicle or when an accident forces you to buy another vehicle before the depreciated loss can be amortized. Most new cars depreciate a whopping 30–45 percent during the first two years of ownership. For 2010 models, expect prices to tumble by about 15 percent.

The best way to use depreciation rates to your advantage is to choose a vehicle listed as being both reliable and economical to own and then keep it for 10 years or more. Generally, by choosing a lower-depreciating vehicle—such as one that keeps at least half its value over four years—you are storing up equity that will give you a bigger down payment and fewer loan costs with your next purchase.

 ### Gas Pains

With gas prices once again headed toward the $1.00 a litre mark, motorists are scratching their heads trying to find easy ways to cut gas consumption. Here are three simple suggestions (and 20 more tips are found in Appendix II):

1. Buy a used compact car for half its original price. Savings on taxes, freight fees, and depreciation: about $15,000.

2. Find low-cost fuel referrals on the Internet (*www. gasbuddy.com*). You can save about 15 cents a litre.
3. Keep your vehicle properly tuned for a 10 percent savings from improved fuel economy.

Gas-saving gadgets and government mileage figures? Don't trust 'em. Ottawa hoodwinks us with gas mileage figures that are impossible to achieve.

The government's *Fuel Consumption Guide* is a work of fiction intended to make automakers, bureaucrats, and environmentalists feel "green" and empowered. Ordinary drivers will feel suckered.

More dirt on diesels

The only reasons to buy a diesel-equipped vehicle are for their potential to deliver outstanding fuel economy and for their much lower maintenance and repair costs when compared with similar-sized vehicles powered by gasoline engines. Unfortunately, independent data suggests that both claims by automakers may be false.

Let's examine the fuel-savings issue first. In theory, when compared with gasoline powerplants, diesel engines are up to 30 percent more efficient in a light vehicle and up to 70 percent cheaper to run in a heavy-duty towing and hauling truck or SUV. They become more efficient as the engine load increases, whereas gasoline engines become less so. This is the main reason diesels are best used where the driving cycle includes a lot of city driving—slow speeds, heavy loads, frequent stops, and long idling times. At full throttle, both engines are essentially equal from a fuel-efficiency standpoint. The gasoline engine, however, leaves the diesel in the dust when it comes to high-speed performance.

On the downside, fleet administrators and owners report that diesel fuel economy in real driving situations is much less than what's advertised—a complaint also voiced by owners of hybrids. Many owners say that their diesel-run rigs get about 30 percent less mileage than what the manufacturer promised.

Also undercutting fuel-savings claims is the fact that, in some regions, the increased cost of diesel fuel—because of high taxes and oil company greed, some say—makes it more expensive than regular fuel.

The diesel engine's reputation for superior reliability may have been true in the past, but no longer. This fact is easily confirmed if you cross-reference owner complaints with confidential automaker service bulletins and independent industry polling results put out by J.D. Power and others, a task done for you in Part Three's ratings section.

Many owners of diesel-equipped vehicles are frustrated by chronic breakdowns, excessive repair costs, and poor road performance. It's practically axiomatic that bad injectors have plagued Ford Power Stroke, GM Duramax engines, and (to a lesser extent) Dodge Cummins diesels.

In the past, defective injectors were often replaced at the owner's expense and at a cost of thousands of dollars. Now, GM and Ford are using "secret warranty" programs to cover replacement costs long after the base warranty has expired (11–13 years). Chrysler has been more recalcitrant in making payouts, apparently because fewer vehicles may be involved and costs can be quite high (expensive lift pumps and injectors may be faulty).

Hybrid cars

Automakers are offering hybrid vehicles like the Toyota Prius and Honda Civic and Accord Hybrids that use an engine/electric motor for maximum fuel economy and low emissions while providing the driving range of a comparable small car. Yet this latest iteration of the electric car still has serious drawbacks, which may drive away even the most green-minded buyers:

- Real-world fuel consumption may be 20 percent higher than advertised.
- Cold weather can cut fuel economy by almost 10 percent.
- AC and other options can increase fuel consumption even more.
- Electrical systems can deliver a life-threatening 275–500 volts if tampered with through incompetent servicing or during an emergency rescue.
- Battery packs can cost up to $3,000 (U.S.), and fuel savings equal the hybrid's extra costs only after about 20,000 km of use.
- Hybrids cost more to insure, and they depreciate just as much as non-hybrid vehicles that don't have expensive battery packs to replace.
- Hybrids make you a captive customer where travel is dependent on available service facilities.

If you find the limitations of an electric hybrid too daunting, why not simply buy a more fuel-efficient small car? Here are some environmentally friendly cars recommended by Toronto-based Environmental Defence Canada (*www.environmentaldefence.ca*) and by *Lemon-Aid*:

- Ford Focus
- Honda Civic and Fit
- Hyundai Accent and Tucson
- Mazda3 and Mazda5
- Nissan Sentra and Versa (although the Versa received a two-star crash rating)
- Toyota Corolla and Yaris
- VW Golf/Jetta TDI

Test for "Real" Performance

Take the phrase "car-like handling" with a large grain of salt. A van isn't supposed to handle like a car. Since many rear-drive models are built on a modified truck chassis and use steering and suspension components from their truck divisions, they tend to handle more like trucks than cars, in spite of automakers' claims to the contrary. Also, what you see isn't necessarily what you get when you buy or lease a new sport-utility, van, or pickup, because these vehicles seldom come with enough standard features to fully exploit their versatility. Additional expensive options are usually a prerequisite to make them safe and comfortable to drive or capable of towing heavy loads. Consequently, the term "multipurpose" is a misnomer unless you are prepared to spend extra dollars to outfit your car or minivan. Even fully equipped, these vehicles don't always provide the performance touted by automakers.

Rust Protection

Most vehicles built today are much less rust-prone than they were several decades ago, thanks to more-durable body panels and better designs. When rusting occurs now, it's usually caused by excessive environmental stress (road salt, etc.), a poor paint job, or the use of new metal panels that create galvanic corrosion or promote early paint peeling—the latter two causes being ones that are excluded from most rustproofing warranties.

Invest in undercoating, and remember that the best rustproofing protection is to park the vehicle in a dry, unheated garage or under an outside carport and then wash it every few weeks. Never bring it in and out of a heated garage during the winter months, since it is most prone to rust when temperatures are just a bit above freezing; keep it especially clean and dry during that time. If you live in an area where roads are heavily salted in winter, or in a coastal region, have your vehicle's undercoating sprayed annually.

Annual undercoating, which costs around $150, will usually do as good a job as rustproofing. It will protect vital suspension and chassis components, make the vehicle ride more quietly, and allow you to ask a higher price at trade-in time. The only downside, which can be checked by asking for references, is that the undercoating may give off an unpleasant odour for months, and it may drip, soiling your driveway.

Whether you are rustproofing the entire vehicle or just undercoating key areas, make sure to include the rocker panels (make a small mark inside the door panels on the plastic hole plugs to make sure that they were removed and that the inside was actually sprayed), the rear hatch's bottom edge, the tailgate, and the wheel-wells. It's also a smart idea to stay at the garage while some of the work is being done to see that the overspray is cleaned up and all areas have been covered.

Surviving the Options Jungle

The best options for your buck are a 5- or 6-speed automatic transmission, an anti-theft immobilizer, air conditioning, a premium sound system, and higher-quality tires—features that may bring back one-third to half their value come trade-in time. Rustproofing can also make cars easier to sell in some provinces where there's lots of salt on the roads in the winter, but paint protection and seat sealants are a waste of money. Most option packages can be cut by 20 percent, while extended warranties are overpriced by about 75 percent.

Dealers make more than three times as much profit selling options as they do selling most cars (50 percent profit versus 15 percent profit). No wonder their eyes light up when you start perusing their options list. If you must have some options, compare prices with independent retailers and buy where the price is lowest and the warranty is the most comprehensive. Buy as few options as possible from the dealer, since you'll get faster service, more comprehensive guarantees, and lower prices from independent suppliers. Remember, extravagantly equipped vehicles hurt your pocketbook in three ways: They cost more to begin with but return only a fraction of what they cost when the car is resold; they drive up maintenance costs; and they often consume extra fuel.

A heavy-duty battery and suspension, and perhaps an upgraded sound system, will generally suffice for American-made vehicles; most imports already come well equipped. An engine block heater with a timer isn't a bad idea, either. It's an inexpensive investment that ensures winter starting and reduces fuel consumption by allowing you to start out with a semi-warm engine.

When ordering parts, remember that purchases from American outlets can be slapped with a small customs duty if the part isn't made in the United States. And then you'll pay the inevitable GST or HST levied on the part's cost and customs duty. Finally, your freight carrier may charge a $15–$20 brokerage fee for representing you at the border.

Smart Options

The problem with options is that you often can't refuse them. Dealers sell very few bare-bones cars and minivans, and they option-pack each vehicle with features that can't be removed. You'll be forced to dicker over the total cost of what you are offered, whether you need the extras or not. So it isn't a case of "yes" or "no," but more a decision of "at what cost?"

Adjustable Pedals and Extensions

This device moves the brake and accelerator pedals forward or backward about 10 cm (4 in.) to accommodate short-statured drivers and protect them from airbag-induced injuries.

If the manufacturer of your vehicle doesn't offer optional power-adjustable pedals, there are several companies selling inexpensive pedal extensions by mail order through the Internet; for example, go to HDS Specialty Vehicles' website at *hdsmn. stores.yahoo.net*. If you live in Toronto or London, Ontario, check out Kino Mobility (*www.kinomobility.com*).

Adjustable Steering Wheel

This option allows easier access to the driver's seat and permits a more-comfortable driving position. It's particularly useful if more than one person will drive the vehicle.

Air Conditioning

AC systems are far more reliable than they were a decade ago, and they have a lifespan of five to seven years. Sure, replacement and repair costs can hit $1,000, but that's very little when amortized over an eight- to 10-year period. AC also makes your car easier to resell.

Does AC waste or conserve fuel when a vehicle is driven at highway speeds? Edmunds, a popular automotive information website, conducted fuel-efficiency tests and concluded that there wasn't that much difference between open or closed windows, a finding confirmed by *Consumer Reports*. See *www.edmunds.com/ advice/fueleconomy/articles/106842/article.html*:

> While the A/C compressor does pull power from the engine wasting some gas, the effect appears to be fairly minimal in modern cars. And putting the windows down tends to increase drag on most cars, canceling out any measurable gain from turning the A/C off. But this depends on the model you're driving. When we opened the sunroof in our SUV, the mileage did decrease even with the A/C off. Still, in our experience, it's not worth the argument because you won't save a lot of gas either way. So just do what's comfortable.

AC provides extra comfort, reduces wind noise (from not having to roll down the windows), and improves window defogging. Factory-installed units are best, however, because you'll get a longer warranty and improve your chances that everything was installed properly.

Anti-Theft Systems

You'd be a fool not to buy an anti-theft system, including a lockable fuel cap, for your much-coveted-by-thieves Japanese compact or sports car. Auto break-ins and thefts cost Canadians more than $400 million annually, meaning that there's a one in 130 chance that your vehicle will be stolen but only a 60 percent chance that you'll ever get it back.

Since amateurs are responsible for stealing most vehicles, the best theft deterrent is a visible device that complicates the job while immobilizing the vehicle and sounding an alarm. For less than $150, you can install both a steering-wheel lock and a hidden remote-controlled ignition disabler. Satellite tracking systems like GM's OnStar feature are also very effective.

Battery (Heavy-Duty)

The best battery for northern climates is the optional heavy-duty type offered by many manufacturers for about $100. It's a worthwhile purchase, especially for vehicles equipped with lots of electric options. Most standard batteries last only two winters; heavy-duty batteries give you an extra year or two for about 20 percent more than the price of a standard battery.

Make sure your new vehicle comes with a fresh battery—one manufactured less than six months earlier. Batteries are stamped with a date code, either on the battery's case or on an attached label. The vital information is usually in the first two characters—a letter and a numeral. Most codes start with a letter indicating the month: A for January, B for February, and so forth. The numeral denotes the year: Say, 0 for 2000. For example, "B3" stands for February 2003.

Don't order an optional battery with cold cranking amps (CCA) below the one specified for your vehicle, or one rated 200 amps or more above the specified rating. It's a waste of money to go too high. Also, buy a battery with the longest reserve capacity you can find; a longer capacity can make the difference between driving to safety and paying for an expensive tow.

Replacement batteries are very competitively priced and easy to find. Sears' DieHard batteries usually get *Consumer Reports'* top ratings. A useful link for finding the right battery with the most CCA for your car and year is *www.autobatteries.com/basics/selecting.asp.*

Central Locking Control

Costing around $200, this option is most useful for families with small children, car-poolers, or drivers of minivans who can't easily slide across the seat to lock the other doors.

Child Safety Seat (Integrated)

Integrated safety seats are designed to accommodate any child more than one year old or weighing over 9 kg (20 lb.). Since the safety seat is permanently integrated into the seatback, the fuss of installing and removing the safety seat and finding someplace to store it vanishes. When not in use, it quickly folds out of sight, becoming part of the seatback. Two other safety benefits: You know that the seat has been properly installed, and your child gets used to having his or her "special" seat in back, where it's usually safest to sit.

Electronic Stability Control (ESC)

The latest IIHS studies conclude that as many as 10,000 fatal crashes could be prevented if all vehicles were equipped with ESC. Its June 2006 report concluded that stability control is second only to seat belts in saving lives because it reduces the risk of fatal single-vehicle rollovers by 80 percent and the chance of having other kinds of fatal collisions by 43 percent.

Electronic stability control was first used by Mercedes-Benz and BMW on the S-Class and 7 Series models in 1995 and then was featured on GM's 1997 Cadillacs and Corvettes. It helps prevent the loss of control in turns, on slippery roads, or when you must make a sudden steering correction. The system applies the brakes to individual wheels or cuts back the engine power when sensors find the vehicle is beginning to spin or skid. It's particularly useful in maintaining stability with SUVs, but it's less useful with passenger coupes and sedans.

It's worrisome that there won't be any federal standard governing the performance of these systems before 2012, considering that not all electronic stability control systems work as they should. In tests carried out by *Consumer Reports* on 2003 models, the stability control system used in the Mitsubishi Montero was rated "unacceptable," BMW's X5 3.0i system provided poor emergency handling, and Acura's MDX and Subaru's Outback VDC stability systems left much to be desired.

Engines (Cylinder Deactivation)

Choose the most powerful 6- or 8-cylinder engine available if you're going to be doing a lot of highway driving, if you plan to carry a full passenger load and luggage on a regular basis, or if you intend to load up the vehicle with convenience features like air conditioning. Keep in mind that minivans, SUVs, and trucks with 6-cylinder or larger engines are easier to resell and retain their value the longest. For example, Honda's '96 Odyssey minivan was a sales dud in spite of its bulletproof reliability, mainly because buyers didn't want a minivan with an underpowered 4-cylinder powerplant. Some people buy underpowered vehicles in the mistaken belief that increased fuel economy is a good trade-off for decreased engine performance. It isn't. That's why there's so much interest in peppy 4-cylinders hooked to 5- or 6-speed transmissions and in larger engines with a "cylinder deactivation" feature.

In fact, cylinder deactivation is one feature that appears more promising than most other fuel-saving add-ons. For example, *AutoWeek* magazine found the overweight Jeep Commander equipped with a "Multiple Displacement System" still managed a respectable 13.8 L/100 km (17 mpg) on the highway in tests published in its March 2006 edition.

Honda employs a similar method, which cuts fuel consumption by 20 percent on the Odyssey. It runs on all six cylinders when accelerating, and on three cylinders when cruising. So far, there have been neither reliability nor performance complaints.

Engine and Transmission Cooling System (Heavy-Duty)

This relatively inexpensive option provides extra cooling for the transmission and engine. It can extend the life of these components by preventing overheating when heavy towing is required. It's a must-have feature for large cars made by Chrysler, Ford, or General Motors.

Extended Warranties

A smart buy if the dealer will discount the price by 50 percent and you're able to purchase the extra powertrain coverage only. However, you are throwing away $1,500–$2,000 if you buy an extended warranty for cars, vans, or trucks rated Recommended in *Lemon-Aid* or for vehicles sold by automakers that have written "goodwill" warranties covering engine and transmission failures. If you can get a great price for a vehicle rated just Average or Above Average but want protection from costly repair bills, patronize garages that offer lifetime warranties on parts listed in this guide as being failure-prone, such as powertrains, exhaust systems, and brakes.

Buy an extended warranty only as a last resort, and make sure you know what it covers and for how long. Budget $1,000 after dealer discounting for the powertrain warranty. Incidentally, auto industry insiders say the average markup on these warranties varies from 50 to 65 percent, which seems almost reasonable when you consider that appliance warranties are marked up from 40 to 80 percent.

Flat-Folding Rear Seats

Fold-down rear seats give sedans and coupes additional room to carry long or bulky items. Split-folding rear seats are the most useful because they allow you to carry another passenger in the rear with one of the seats folded.

Keyless Entry (Remote)

This safety and convenience option saves you from fiddling with your key in a dark parking lot, or taking off a glove in cold weather to unlock or lock the vehicle. Try to get a keyless entry system combined with anti-theft measures such as an ignition kill switch or some other disabler. Incidentally, many automakers no longer make vehicles with an outside key lock on the passenger's side.

 Paint Colour

Choosing a popular colour can make your vehicle easier to sell at a good price. DesRosiers Automotive Consultants say that blue is the preferred colour overall, but green and silver are also popular with Canadians. Manheim auctioneers say that green-coloured vehicles brought in 97.9 of the average auction price, while silver ones sold at a premium 105.5 percent. Remember that certain colours require particular care.

Black (and other dark colours): These paints are most susceptible to sun damage because of their heavy absorption of ultraviolet rays.

Pearl-toned colours: These paints are the most difficult to work with. If the paint needs to be retouched, it must be matched to look right from both the front- and side-angle views.

Red: This colour also shows sun damage, so keep your car in a garage or shady spot whenever possible.

White: Although grime looks terrible on a white car, white is the easiest colour to care for. But the colour is also very popular with car thieves, because white vehicles can be easily repainted another colour.

Power-Assisted Sliding Doors, Mirrors, Windows, and Seats

Merely a convenience feature with cars, power-assisted windows and doors are a necessity with minivans—crawling across the front seat a few times to roll up the passenger-side window or to lock the doors will quickly convince you of their value. Power mirrors are convenient on vehicles that have a number of drivers, or on minivans. Power seats with memory are particularly useful, too, if more than one person drives a vehicle. Automatic window and seat controls currently have few reliability problems, and they're fairly inexpensive to install, troubleshoot, and repair. As a safety precaution, make sure the window control has to be lifted. This will ensure no child is strangled from pressing against the switch. Power-sliding doors on minivans are even more of a danger. They are failure-prone on all makes and shouldn't be purchased by families with children.

Side Airbags

A worthwhile feature if you are the right size and properly seated, side airbags are presently overpriced and aren't very effective unless both the head and upper torso are protected. Side airbags are often featured as a $700 add-on to the sticker price, but you would be wise to bargain aggressively.

Stow 'n Go Seating

Pioneered by Chrysler in its minivans, Stow 'n Go seating allows the second- and third-row seats to be folded into, not onto, the floor. Folding the seats is a one-hand operation, and the head restraints don't need to be removed. Pop the spring-loaded seats back up, and there's an in-floor storage bin under each seat. One caveat: These seats sacrifice comfort for versatility. But check them out.

Suspension (Heavy-Duty)

Always a good idea, this inexpensive option pays for itself by providing better handling, allowing additional ride comfort (though a bit on the firm side), and extending shock life by an extra year or two.

Tires

There are three rules to remember when purchasing tires. First, neither brand nor price is a reliable gauge of performance, quality, or durability. Second, the cheapest prices are offered by tire discounters like Tire Rack (*www.tirerack.com*), and Discount Tire Direct (*www.discounttiredirect.com*), and their Canadian equivalents like Canadian Tire and TireTrends (*www.tiretrends.com/index.php3*). Third, choosing a tire recommended by the automaker may not be in your best interest, since traction and long tread life are often sacrificed for a softer ride and maximum EPA mileage ratings. And lastly, don't buy any new tire that's more than two years old (you can check the date of manufacture on the side wall of the tire), since the rubber compound may have deteriorated because of poor handling and improper storage (like being stored near electrical motors).

Two types of tires are generally available: all-season and performance. "Touring" is just a fancier name for all-season tires. All-season radial tires cost from $90 to $150 per tire. They're a compromise since, according to Transport Canada, they won't get you through winter with the same margin of safety as snow tires will and they don't provide the same durability on dry surfaces as do regular summer tires. In areas with low to moderate snowfall, however, these tires are adequate as long as they're not pushed beyond their limits.

Mud or snow tires provide the best traction on snowy surfaces, but traction on wet roads is actually decreased. Treadwear is also accelerated by the use of softer rubber compounds. Beware of using wide tires for winter driving; 70-series or wider give poor traction and tend to float over snow.

Remember, too, that buying slightly larger wheels and tires may improve handling—but there's a limit. For example, many cars come with 16-inch original equipment (OE) tires supplied by the carmaker. Moving up to a slightly larger size, say a 17-inch wheel, could improve your dry and wet grip handling. Getting any larger wheels can have serious downsides, though, like making the vehicle harder to control, providing less steering feedback, making the car more subject to hydroplaning ("floating" over wet surfaces), and causing SUVs and pickups to roll over more easily.

Don't over-inflate tires to lower their rolling resistance for better fuel economy. The trade-off is a harsher ride and increased risk of a blowout when passing over uneven terrain. Excessive tire pressure may also distort the tread, reducing contact with the road and increasing wear in the centre of the tread. Under-inflation is a far more common occurrence. Experts agree that tire life decreases by 10 percent for every 10 percent the tire is under-inflated, sometimes through lack of maintenance or due to the perception that an under-inflated tire improves traction. Actually, an under-inflated tire makes for worse traction. It breaks traction more easily than a tire that is properly inflated, causing skidding, pulling to the side when braking, excessive wheelspin when accelerating, and tire failure due to overheating.

Spare tires

Be wary of space-saver spare tires. They often can't match the promised mileage, and they seriously degrade steering control. Furthermore, they are usually stored in spaces inside the trunk that won't hold a normal-sized tire. The location of the stored spare can also have safety implications. Watch out for spares stowed under the chassis or mounted on the rear hatch. Frequently, the attaching cables and bolts rust out or freeze, so the spare falls off or becomes next to impossible to use when you need it.

Self-sealing and run-flat tires

Today, there are two technologies available to help maintain vehicle mobility when a tire is punctured: self-sealing and self-supporting/run-flat tires.

Self-sealing: Ideal if you drive long distances. Punctures from nails, bolts, or screws up to 3/16 of an inch in diameter are fixed instantly and permanently with a sealant. A low air-pressure warning system isn't required. Expert testers say a punctured self-sealing tire can maintain air pressure for up to 200 km—even in freezing conditions. The Uniroyal Tiger Paw NailGard ($85–$140, depending on the size) is the overall winner in a side-by-side test conducted by Tire Rack (*www. tirerack.com*).

Self-supporting/run-flat: Priced from $175 to $350 per tire, 25 to 50 percent more than the price of comparable premium tires, Goodyear's Extended Mobility Tire (EMT) run-flat tires were first offered as an option on the 1994 Chevrolet Corvette and then became standard on the 1997 model. These tires reinforce the side wall so it can carry the weight of the car for 90 km, or about an hour's driving time, even after all air pressure has been lost. You won't feel the tire go flat; you must depend on a $250–$300 optional tire-pressure monitor to warn you before the side wall collapses and you begin riding on your rim. Also, not all vehicles can adapt to run-flat tires; you may need to upgrade your rims. Experts say run-flats will give your car a harder ride, and you'll likely notice more interior tire and road noise. The car might also track differently. The Sienna's standard Dunlop run-flat tires have a terrible reputation for premature wear. At 25,000 km, one owner complained that her Sienna needed a new set at $200 each. You can expect a backlog of over a month to get a replacement. Goodyear and Pirelli run-flat tires have been on the market for some time now, and they seem to perform adequately.

RECOMMENDED TIRES

ALL-SEASON T-SPEED (ALL SEASON, EXCEPT WINTER)
Michelin HydroEdge
Michelin Energy Saver A/S
Hankook Optimo H727
Pirelli P4 Four Seasons
Goodyear Assurance TripleTred
Pirelli Cinturato P5
Cooper GFE

PERFORMANCE ALL-SEASON H-SPEED
Michelin Primacy MXV4*
Falken Ziex ZE912
Nokian WR G2*
Yokohama Avid H4s
Kumho Solus KH16*
Continental ContiProContact
Michelin Pilot Exalto A/S

PERFORMANCE ALL-SEASON V-SPEED
Michelin Pilot Exalto A/S*
Firestone Firehawk GTv
Bridgestone Turanza Serenity
Dunlop Signature*
Toyo Versado LX
General Altimax HP

ALL-SEASON UHP
Falken Ziex ZE912
Nitto Neo Gen ZR
Yokohama Advan S4
Falken Ziex ZE512
General Exclaim UHP
Continental ContiExtremeContact*

SUMMER UHP
Michelin Pilot Sport P52
Pirelli P-Zero
BF Goodtich G-force TA
Bridgestone Potenza RE 050
Michelin Pilot Exalto PE2
Continental ContiSportConract 3
Dunlop SP Sport Maxx
Goodyear Eagle F1 GS-D3

WINTER PERFORMANCE
Continental ContiWinterContact TS810
Bridgestone Blizzak LM-25
Nokian WR All Weather Plus

WINTER
Michelin X-Ice X12**
General Altimax Arctic**

Nokian Hakkapelitta 5**
Michelin Primacy Alpin PA3
Nokian Hakkapelitta R
Continental ExtremeWinterContact
Bridgestone Blizzak WS60
Pirelli Sottozero 210 H
Dunlop Graspic DS-2
Hankook Winter Pike

WINTER (LIGHT TRUCKS)
Michelin Latitude X-Ice
Bridgestone Blizzak DM-Z3

ALL-SEASON (TRUCKS)
General Grabber HTS
Continental CrossContact LX
Kumho Road Venture Apt KL51
Cooper Discoverer CTS
Michelin LTX M/S
Yokohama Geolander H/T-S GO51

4X4 (TRUCKS)
Pirelli Scorpion ATR***
Yokohama Geolander
Bridgestone Dueler A/T Revo
Michelin LTXA/T 2
Toyo Open Country

*Includes winter driving. **A best performer in severe winters. ***Pirelli has just introduced its Scorpion Verde "green" all-season tire (for crossovers, SUVs, and light trucks) to Canada. Consumer comments have been positive from a performance perspective, inasmuch as it's too early to judge the tire's durability.

NOT RECOMMENDED TIRES

ALL-SEASON T-SPEED RATED
Firestone FR710
Uniroyal Tiger Paw Tour SR
Yokohama Avid Touring S
Dunlop SP60
Falken Sincera SN828
Bridgestone Turanza EL400
Yokohama Avid T4
Cooper Lifeliner GS
Sumitomo HTR T4?

PERFORMANCE ALL-SEASON H-SPEED
Fuzion HRi

Hankook Optimo H418
Pirelli P6 Four Seasons
Goodyear Assurance Fuel Max
General Altimax HP
Cooper CS4 Touring
Falken Ziex ZE512

PERFORMANCE ALL-SEASON V-SPEED
Fuzion VR1
Hankook Optimo H418
Pirelli P6 Four Seasons
Kumho Ectsa LX Platinum
Goodyear Eagle ResponsEdge

Bridgestone Potenza GO19 Grid

ALL-SEASON UHP
Hankook Ventus V4 ES H105
Avon Tech M550 A/S
Cooper Zeon Sport A/S
Toyo Proxes 4
Bridgestone Potenza RE960
Pirelli P-Zero Nero
Sumitomo HTR+*

SUMMER UHP
Pirelli P-Zero Rosso
Nitto NT 555 Extreme ZR

Nitto Invo	Firestone Winterforce	Nitto Dura Grappler
Avon Tech M500	Goodyear Ultra Grip Ice	Toyo Open Country H/T
Pirelli P-Zero Nero	Yokohama Ice Guard IG20	Goodyear Fortera
WINTER PERFORMANCE	**WINTER (LIGHT TRUCKS)**	**4X4 (TRUCKS)**
Dunlop SP Winter Sport M3	Winterforce M+S	General Grabber AT 2
Pirelli Winter 210	Cooper Discoverer M&S	Goodyear Wrangler
Hankook Icebear W300	**ALL-SEASON (TRUCKS)**	Dayton Timberline AT II
Michelin Pilot Alpin PA2	Falken Ziex S/TZ-04	Kelly Safari Trek
WINTER	BF Goodrich Rugged Trail	Fuzion XTi
Hankook Icebear W300	Uniroyal Laredo Cross Country	
Cooper Weather-Master	Dunlop Grandtrek AT20	

*Includes winter driving.

"Green" tires

No, these tires aren't coloured differently; they're simply tires with a lower rolling resistance that have been proven (through independent tests) to save fuel, which saves you money and contributes to lower greenhouse gas emissions. In the above list of recommended tires, the Michelin's Energy Saver A/S ranked highest for fuel savings; the Cooper GFE also gave good fuel economy, but its overall performance was only average. The Department of Transportation says fuel savings can be substantial, depending on the tire, knocking down fuel consumption by 4 percent in city driving and 7 percent on the highway. *Consumer Reports* magazine pegs the annual savings at $100 per set. Lower rolling resistance tires may also produce less road noise and have a longer tread life.

Nitrogen air refills

The National Highway Traffic Safety Administration (NHTSA) has seen reduced aging of tires filled with nitrogen. Claims have also been made that nitrogen maintains inflation pressure better than air. Though the data technically does support that passenger car tires could benefit from being filled with nitrogen, tire manufacturers say that they already design tires to perform well with air inflation. And while nitrogen will do no harm, manufacturers say that they don't see the need to use nitrogen, which generally adds $5 or more per tire charge.

Consumer Reports says consumers can use nitrogen and might enjoy the slight improvement in air retention provided, but you can do just as well without paying an extra penny by performing regular inflation checks.

Which tires are best?

There is no independent Canadian agency that evaluates tire performance and durability. However, the U.S.-based NHTSA rates treadwear, traction, and resistance to sustained high temperatures; etches the ratings onto the side walls of all tires sold in the States and Canada; and regularly posts its findings on the Internet (*www.safercar.gov*). NHTSA also logs owner complaints relative to different brands. *Lemon-Aid* summarizes these complaints in the ratings of specific models in Part Three.

You can get more-recent complaint postings, service bulletins, and tire recall notices at the same government website, and check out independent owner performance ratings as compiled by Tire Rack, a large tire retailer, at *www.tirerack. com/tires/surveyresults/index.jsp.*

Traction Control

This option limits wheelspin when accelerating. It is most useful with rear-drive vehicles and provides surer traction in wet or icy conditions.

Trailer-Towing Equipment

Just because you need a vehicle with towing capability doesn't mean that you have to spend big bucks. But you should first determine what kind of vehicle you want to do the job and whether your tires will handle the extra burden. For most towing needs (up to 900 kg/2,000 lb.), a passenger car, small pickup, or minivan equipped with a 6-cylinder engine will work just as well as a full-sized pickup or van (and will cost much less). If you're pulling a trailer that weighs more than 900 kg, most passenger cars won't handle the load unless they've been specially outfitted according to the automaker's specifications. Pulling a heavier trailer (up to 1,800 kg/4,000 lb.) will likely require a large vehicle equipped with a V8 powerplant.

Automakers reserve the right to change limits whenever they feel like it, so make any sales promise about towing an integral part of your contract. A good rule of thumb is to reduce the promised tow rating by 20 percent. In assessing towing weight, factor in the cargo, passengers, and equipment of both the trailer and the towing vehicle. Keep in mind that five people and luggage add 450 kg (almost 1,000 lb.) to the load, and that a full 227L (60 gal.) water tank adds another 225 kg (almost 500 lb.). The manufacturer's gross vehicle weight rating (GVWR) takes into account the anticipated average cargo and supplies that your vehicle is likely to carry.

Automatic transmissions are fine for trailering, although there's a slight fuel penalty. Manual transmissions tend to have greater clutch wear caused by towing than do automatic transmissions. Both transmission choices are equally acceptable. Remember, the best compromise is to shift the automatic manually for maximum performance going uphill and to maintain control while not overheating the brakes when descending mountains.

Unibody vehicles (those without a separate frame) can handle most towing chores as long as their limits aren't exceeded. Front-drives aren't the best choice for pulling heavy loads in excess of 900 kg, since they lose some steering control and traction with all the weight concentrated in the rear.

Whatever vehicle you choose, keep in mind that the trailer hitch is crucial. It must have a tongue capacity of at least 10 percent of the trailer's weight; otherwise, it may be unsafe to use. Hitches are chosen according to the type of tow vehicle and, to a lesser extent, the weight of the load.

Most hitches are factory-installed, even though independents can install them more cheaply. Expect to pay about $200 for a simple boat hitch and a minimum of $600 for a fifth-wheel version.

Equalizer bars and extra cooling systems for the radiator, transmission, engine oil, and steering are prerequisites for towing anything heavier than 900 kg. Heavy-duty springs and brakes are a big help, too. Separate brakes for the trailer may be necessary to increase your vehicle's maximum towing capacity.

Transmissions

Despite its many advantages, the manual transmission is an endangered species in North America, where manuals equip only 8–10 percent of all new vehicles (mostly econocars, sports cars, and budget trucks), and that figure is slated to fall to 6 percent by 2012 as more vehicles adopt fuel-saving CVT transmissions, among other powertrain innovations. One theory on why the manual numbers keep falling: North American drivers are too busy with cell phones, text messaging, and cappuccinos to shift gears. Interestingly, European buyers opt for a manual transmission almost 90 percent of the time. (And they also drink cappuccinos, but usually not in 20 oz. paper takeout cups.)

Automakers are currently offering hybrid manumatic transmissions that provide the benefits of an automatic transmission while also giving the driver the NASCAR-styled fun of clutchless manual shifting. Or, if all you want is fuel savings, there are now 5- and 6-speed automatic models—and even 7- and 8-speed versions—that are fuel-sippers.

Some considerations: The brake pads on stick-shift vehicles tend to wear out less rapidly than those on automatics do; a transmission with five or more forward speeds is usually more fuel-efficient than one with three forward speeds (hardly seen anymore); and manual transmissions usually add a mile or two per gallon over automatics, although this isn't always the case, as *Consumer Reports* recently discovered. Their road tests found that the 2008 Toyota Yaris equipped with an automatic transmission got slightly better gas mileage than a Yaris powered by a manual tranny.

Unnecessary Options

All-Wheel Drive (AWD)

Mark Bilek, editorial director of *Consumer Guide*'s automotive website (*consumerguideauto.howstuffworks.com*), is a critic of AWD. He says AWD systems generally encourage drivers to go faster than they should in adverse conditions, which creates trouble stopping in emergencies. Automakers like AWD as "a marketing ploy to make more money," Bilek contends. My personal mechanic adds, "Four-wheel drive will only get you stuck deeper, farther from home."

Anti-Lock Brakes (ABS)

Like adaptive cruise control and backup warning devices, ABS is another safety feature that's fine in theory but mostly impractical under actual driving conditions. (If you want the highly recommended electronic stability control (ESC), you must use anti-lock brakes.) The system maintains directional stability by preventing the wheels from locking up. This will not reduce the stopping distance, however. In practice, ABS is said to make drivers overconfident. Many still pump the brakes and render them ineffective; total brake failure is common; and repairs are frequent, complicated, and expensive to perform.

Take the Toyota Yaris, for example. *Lemon-Aid* has learned from Canadian readers, American owners posting safety complaints on NHTSA's website, Toyota owner forums, and Toyota's own internal service bulletins that the 2007 and 2008 Yaris has serious ABS brake defects caused by faulty sensors.

Here's how T. D., a 2007 Yaris owner from Trenton, Ontario, describes the defect:

> Hi Phil. Toyota NEEDS an additional recall for ABS braking system on Yaris. Please help!
>
> Toyota appears to be ignoring a very large manufacturing problem that is directly affecting Toyota Yaris owners having to compromise their safety over the price of the repair of the housing unit/sensors/wires/harness (priced at over $1,200 per affected side). The problems appear to be within the sensor circuits, as the current housing units do not protect the circuits from the harsh Canadian winter exposure, therefore leading to corrosion of the wires and circuits and thereby leading to the replacement of the entire wheelbearing (sensor is built in the wheelbearing and cannot be replaced seperately).
>
> Thankfully, I found *www.yarisworld.com/forums/showthread.php?t=11533&high light=rear+sensor&page=11*, and multiple other additional threads located on the *yarisworld.com* site. I have been able to have my local mechanic provide a simple, inexpensive fix ($60) for my left rear sensor, however, my right rear sensor is too far gone and needs to be replaced, for which after-market parts do not exist as of yet.

I have contacted Toyota Canada, and they will provide $100 towards the repair if done by the dealership... I refuse to cooperate with the "steal-ership" any longer as they refused to admit this was a systemic/model problem and my local mechanic has gone above and beyond in researching this dilemma and repairing the flaw that has existed since I bought my car brand new.

Toyota is well aware of this problem, as evident with this release, *www.etimago.com/yaris/TSB/T-SB-0120-08%20%28ABS%20M.I.L.%20ON%20DTC%20C0210%20or%20C0215%29.pdf*. However, as it states, it is only for vehicles under warranty. I bought this car for the fuel mileage... I drive A LOT and am well over the 36,000-mile [58,000-kilometre] warranty, however, I have only had this car (bought brand new off the lot) for less then three years.

I have also filed a complaint with Transport Canada in regards to this safety issue, as most, according to the forum *yarisworld.com* (search "rear sensor" or "ABS brake and emergency light"), are choosing to ignore the warning lights and continue driving their vehicles without the ABS...which is fine, but there are reported cases on this site stating that the brakes are also "becoming soft" and are failing or "kicking on" at inappropriate times.

Please help. Toyota needs additional pressure to do anything, and I firmly believe there are consumers out there who won't think of looking up this mechanical issue online and researching the problem. Most will probably fix it and fork out the huge unnecessary expense. Others will not, and this poses a potential safety concern for themselves and the drivers around them on the roads.

NHTSA Yaris Brake Complaints

My ABS and brake warning lights came on at the same time on my 2008 Yaris Sedan. The manual states to contact the dealer immediately in this situation. The ABS is disabled in this situation. The problem was [that] a left rear wheel speed sensor shorted (code P0215). Due to excessive corrosion on the connection, the wiring harness was also replaced. The replaced parts were 89544-02070 (sensor, skid control) and 89516-52100 (wire, skid control). The car was less than a year old with 12,465 miles [20,000 kilometres] at the time. The amount of corrosion on the sensor and connecting wires on the Yaris point to a potential design issue. A car that is less than a year old should not have these issues.

•

The contact owns a 2008 Toyota Yaris. The contact stated that the brakes and the ABS lights remained illuminated on his vehicle continuously. The vehicle was not diagnosed by the dealer and he was not advised what caused the failure to occur. The VIN was unavailable. The failure mileage was 66,000 [106,200 kilometres].

•

I own a 2007 Toyota Yaris, purchased August 2006. The brake and ABS indicator lights started coming on intermittently in December 2009 (often when it was raining or snowing outside). My dealer said that this was caused by an issue with the right rear speed sensor, and shouldn't indicate any actual problems with the brakes. However, soon afterward (January 2010), I started experiencing brake problems—the brake pedal would shudder or vibrate occasionally, even when I was driving on a smooth surface at low speeds. Even pumping the breaks, I had trouble stopping and slid through a stop sign more than once. My dealer said this indicated that the ABS was kicking in when it shouldn't, and recommended a $600 replacement of the right rear speed sensor. I got this repair done, and the problem seems to be solved.

•

Thirteen months have passed and now I have a failure of the left rear wheel speed sensor to match the failed right rear wheel speed sensor that was replaced. The repair action will be to replace the sensor and wiring harness. Due to excessive corrosion, the dealer is recommending replacement of both the left and right rear wheel speed sensor wiring. This will be the third rear wheel speed sensor failure on two Yaris that I have had to deal with in 14 months. The cold weather and salt used on the roads during a snowy winter appear to wreak havoc on the connection between the wiring harness and the rear wheel speed sensor on the Yaris Sedans. A little internet research will lead you to the conclusion that this is a very common problem in Canada or anywhere salt is used on the roads in winter. Since this problem does not present itself on the Corolla in the same way, then there must be a design issue on the Yaris. A proper water/weather tight connection between the wiring harness and the rear wheel speed sensors would solve this issue. This is a safety issue as the intermittent connection causes erratic operation (if any) of the ABS on these models. I believe there is a TSB released on this subject, but no recall. Consumers (me) are footing the bill for this defect. Three times and counting.

•

My ABS and brake lights came on at the same time on my 2007 Yaris Sedan. The manual states to stop driving the car and contact the dealer immediately. The car is a daily commute car with 75,000 miles [120,700 kilometres] at the time. The problem was an internal failure of the right rear wheel speed sensor. The dealer replaced the sensor (part number 42450-52060/HUB & BRG ASSY R), and cleaned the corrosion from the wiring harness where it connects to the speed sensor. The total repair cost was over $650. The amount of corrosion on a car just over 2 years old on the rear ABS wheel speed sensors shows a potential design flaw in this part and how it is attached on the Yaris vehicle line. This failure disables the ABS system and causes erratic operation. On one occasion on the way to the dealer, while the ABS light was off, I had a brake anomaly. I applied the brakes at a parking lot stop sign at slow speed (~5 mph [~8 km/h]) and the ABS kicked in and I couldn't stop. The weather and street was dry. It took more than 25 feet [7.6 metres] to stop! The corrosion at this connection is causing intermittent operation of the ABS system, which is a safety concern.

•

A bad connector leading to the ABS speed sensor failed on our 2007 Toyota Yaris causing two warning lights to come on. Owners manual states to "stop immediately and contact Toyota dealer." ABS speed sensor was replaced at a cost of over $500 but in fact the problem is a corroded connector. Toyota and dealer stated that a technical

---

TOYOTA BRAKES—ABS LAMP ON/DTC'S C0210 OR C0215 SET

BULLETIN NO.: TSB-0120-08   DATE: JUNE 27, 2008

Brake Control/Dynamic Control System

MARKET: USA

Some 2007–08 model year Yaris vehicles may exhibit an ABS M.I.L. "ON" condition with either one or both of the following Diagnostic Trouble Codes (DTCs):

- C0210—Rear Speed Sensor RH Circuit
- C0215—Rear Speed Sensor LH Circuit

The sealing performance of the rear wheel speed sensor connectors has been improved to address this condition. Use the following repair procedure to diagnose and repair customer complaint vehicles.

APPLICABLE WARRANTY: This repair is covered under the Toyota Comprehensive Warranty. This warranty is in effect for 36 months or 36,000 miles [58,000 kilometres], whichever occurs first, from the vehicle's in-service date. Warranty application is limited to correction of a problem based upon a customer's specific complaint.

REPAIR PROCEDURE: If either C0210 or C0215 DTC codes are stored under ABS, inspect the rear speed sensor connectors and sensor pins for rust/corrosion. If rust/corrosion is found in the left rear and/or right rear speed sensor connector, disconnect the connector and replace the speed sensor wire harness. If rust/corrosion is also found on the terminals of the rear speed sensors, replace the speed sensors.

Is this free repair only to be provided when a customer complains about the charges?

service bulletin was issued regarding this problem. I was then told that because a "connector" not a "module" failed this problem [is] not subject to a recall. However, since the manual says to "stop immediately" which freaked out my wife this clearly is a safety problem. Also, it should not take $500 to replace a faulty connector. I found a chat-room online where it became clear that many others are having this problem.

•

I have a 2007 Toyota Yaris Sedan, with 71,000 miles [114,250 kilometres] on it. The ABS and brake lights come on for times up to 2 days before going out. Toyota released a TSB in June of 2008, acknowledging the problem, to correct the problem but failed to do anything unless the customer complained. The problem is corrosion of the contact points of the rear wheel speed sensors and wiring harness in northern weather areas where we use salt. The cost to the consumer is approximately $400 per side to fix if it happens after the 3-year/36,000 mile warranty. I think this is unacceptable. I called Toyota and basically got hung up on. Can you look into this problem? Our northern customers in Canada are also experiencing this problem.

•

Defective design on 2007 Yaris ABS harness/connectors causes it to become inoperative after corrosion sets in, mine happened after 2 years and around 68,000 miles [110,000 kilometres]. Replacement of harness and connectors is only a short term fix, according to the forums on *www.yarisworld.com*.

Cruise Control

Automakers provide this $250–$300 option, which is mainly a convenience feature, to motorists who use their vehicles for long periods of high-speed driving.

The constant rate of speed saves some fuel and lessens driver fatigue during long trips. Still, the system is particularly failure-prone and expensive to repair, can lead to driver inattention, and can make the vehicle hard to control on icy roadways. Malfunctioning cruise-control units are also one of the major causes of sudden acceleration incidents. At other times, cruise control can be very distracting, especially to inexperienced drivers who are unaccustomed to sudden speed fluctuations.

Adaptive cruise control is the latest evolution of this feature. It senses a vehicle ahead of you and then automatically downshifts, brakes, or cuts your vehicle's speed. This commonly occurs when passing another car or when a car passes you, and it can make for a harrowing experience...especially when you are in the passing lane.

Electronic Instrument Readout

If you've ever had trouble reading a digital watch face or resetting your VCR, you'll feel right at home with this electronic gizmo. Gauges are presented in a series of moving digital patterns that are confusing, distracting, and unreadable in direct sunlight. This system is often accompanied by a trip computer and vehicle monitor that determine fuel use and how many kilometres you can drive until the tank is empty, indicate average speed, and signal component failures. Figures are frequently in error or slow to catch up.

Fog Lights

A pain in the eyes for some, a pain in the wallet for others who have to pay the high bulb replacement costs. Fog lights aren't necessary for most drivers who have well-aimed original-equipment headlights on their vehicles.

Gas-Saving Gadgets and Fuel Additives

Ah, the search for the Holy Grail. Magic software and miracle hardware that will turn your gas-hungry Hummer into a fuel-frugal Prius when the right additive is poured into your fuel tank.

The accessory market has been flooded with hundreds of atomizers, magnets, and additives that purport to make vehicles less fuel-thirsty. However, tests on over 100 gadgets and fuel or crankcase additives carried out by the U.S. Environmental Protection Agency have found that only a handful produce an increase in fuel economy, and the increase is tiny. These gadgets include warning devices that tell the driver to ease up on the throttle or shift to a more fuel-frugal gear, hardware that reduces the engine power needed for belt-driven accessories, cylinder deactivation systems, and spoilers that channel airflow under the car. The use of any of these products is a quick way to lose warranty coverage and fail provincial emissions tests.

GPS Navigation Systems

This navigation aid links a Global Positioning System (GPS) satellite unit to the vehicle's cellular phone and electronics. Good GPS devices cost $125–$1,500 (U.S.) when bought from an independent retailer. As a dealer option, you will pay $1,000–$2,000 (U.S.). For a monthly fee, the unit connects drivers to live operators who will help them with driving directions, give repair or emergency assistance, or relay messages. If the airbag deploys or the car is stolen, satellite-transmitted signals are automatically sent from the vehicle to operators who will notify the proper authorities of the vehicle's location.

Many of the systems' functions can be performed by a cellular telephone, and the navigation screens may be obtrusive, distracting, washed out in sunlight, and hard to calibrate. A portable Garmin GPS unit is more user-friendly and much cheaper.

High-Intensity Headlights

These headlights are much brighter than standard headlights, and they cast a blue hue. Granted, they provide additional illumination of the roadway, but they are also annoying to other drivers, who will flash their lights—or give you the middle finger—thinking that your high beams are on. These lights are easily stolen and expensive to replace. Interestingly, European versions have a device to maintain the light's spread closer to the road so that other drivers aren't blinded.

ID Etching

This $150–$200 option is a scam. The government doesn't require it, and thieves and joyriders aren't deterred by the etchings. If you want to etch your windows for your own peace of mind, several private companies will sell you a $15–$30 kit that does an excellent job (try *www.autoetch.net*), or you can wait for your municipality or local police agency to conduct one of their periodic free VIN ID etching sessions in your area.

Paint and Fabric Protectors

Selling for $200–$300, these "sealants" add nothing to a vehicle's resale value. Although paint lustre may be temporarily heightened, this treatment is less effective and more costly than regular waxing, and it may also invalidate the manufacturer's guarantee at a time when the automaker will look for any pretext to deny your paint claim.

Auto fabric protection products are nothing more than variations of Scotchgard, which can be bought in aerosol cans for a few dollars—a much better deal than the $50–$75 charged by dealers.

Power-Assisted Minivan Sliding Doors

Not a good idea if you have children. These doors have a high failure rate, opening or closing for no apparent reason and injuring children caught between the door and post.

Reverse-Warning System

Selling for about $500 as part of an option package, this safety feature warns the driver of any objects in the rear when backing up. Although a sound idea in theory, in practice the device often fails to go off or sounds an alarm for no reason. Drivers eventually either disconnect or ignore it.

Rollover-Detection System

This feature makes use of sensors to determine if the vehicle has leaned beyond a safe angle. If so, the side airbags are automatically deployed and remain inflated to make sure occupants aren't injured or ejected in a rollover accident. This is a totally new system that has not yet been proven. It could have disastrous consequences if the sensor malfunctions, as has been the case with front and side airbag sensors over the past decade.

Rooftop Carrier

Although this inexpensive option provides additional baggage space and may allow you to meet all your driving needs with a smaller vehicle, a loaded roof rack can increase fuel consumption by as much as 18 percent. An empty rack can increase your gas bill by about 10 percent.

Rustproofing

Rustproofing is no longer necessary, since automakers have extended their own rust warranties. In fact, you have a greater chance of seeing your rustproofer go belly up than having your untreated vehicle ravaged by premature rusting. Even if the rustproofer stays in business, you're likely to get a song and dance about why the warranty won't cover so-called internal rusting, or why repairs will be delayed until the sheet metal is actually rusted through.

 Be wary of electronic rustproofing. Selling for $425 to $700, these electrical devices claim to inhibit vehicle corrosion by sending out a pulse current to the grounded body panels, protecting areas that conventional rust-inhibiting products can't reach. There is much debate as to whether these devices are worth the cost, or if they work at all.

Sunroof

Unless you live in a temperate region, the advantages of having a sunroof are far outweighed by the disadvantages. You aren't going to get better ventilation than a good AC system would provide, and a sunroof may grace your environment with painful booming wind noises, rattles, water leaks, and road dust accumulation. A sunroof increases gas consumption, reduces night vision because overhead highway lights shine through the roof opening, and can lose you several centimetres of headroom.

Tinted Glass

On the one hand, tinting jeopardizes safety by reducing your night vision. On the other hand, it does keep the interior cool in hot weather, reduces glare, and hides the car's contents from prying eyes. Factory applications are worth the extra cost, since cheaper aftermarket products (costing about $150) distort visibility and peel away after a few years. Some tinting done in the United States can run afoul of provincial highway codes that require more transparency.

Cutting the Price

Bidding by Fax or Email

Dealers are more receptive to fax and email bidding this year because showroom traffic has dwindled, thanks to the economic recession. The process is quite easy: Simply fax or email an invitation for bids to area dealerships, asking them to give their bottom-line price for a specific make and model. Be clear that all final bids must be sent within a week. When all the bids are received, the lowest bid is sent to the other dealers to give them a chance to beat that price. After a week of bidding, the lowest price gets your business. Incidentally, with the Canadian loonie headed to parity with the American dollar, try doing an Internet search for American prices and then using that lower figure to haggle with Canadian dealers.

UNITED STATES
2010 CHEVY TAHOE LTZ
$53,615 PRICE
$950 FREIGHT
$54,565

CANADA
2010 CHEVY TAHOE LTZ
$69,100 PRICE
$1,400 FREIGHT
$70,500

There is no justice when you compare Canadian and American car prices.

Dozens of *Lemon-Aid* readers have told me how this bidding approach has cut thousands of dollars from the advertised price and saved them from the degrading song-and-dance routine between the buyer, sales agent, and sales manager ("he said, she said, the sales manager said").

A *Lemon-Aid* reader sent in the following suggestions for buying by fax or email:

First, I'd like to thank you for writing the *Lemon-Aid* series of books, which I have used extensively in the fax-tendering purchase of my '99 Accord and '02 Elantra. I have written evidence from dealers that I saved a bare minimum of $700 on the Accord (but probably more) and a whopping $900 on the Elantra through the use of

SAMPLE FAX BID REQUEST

WITHOUT PREJUDICE

Date: _____

Dear Sir or Madam,

I will be purchasing a new 2011 Toyota Sienna or a new 2011 Honda Odyssey and am issuing a request for quotation to several dealerships. I am willing to travel to complete a deal.

The quoted price is to *include* my requested options as well as any applicable pre-delivery inspection, administration, documentation, freight, and delivery fees. I understand that tire tax, air conditioning tax, battery tax, and provincial and federal sales tax are extra and are not required on your quotation. The dealer may sell off the lot or order the vehicle.

Please complete the attached form and either fax or email it back to me before the deadline of *5:00 pm, April 14, 2010*. All respondents will be contacted after the deadline to confirm their bid. The winning bidder will then be contacted soon after to complete the transaction.

I will accept an alternate price quotation for a demonstration model with similar options, but this is not a mandatory requirement.

Please direct any questions via email to me at _____ and I will respond promptly. Alternately you may call me at my office at _____.

Sincerely,
Joe Buyer

fax-tendering, over and above any deals possible through Internet-tendering and/or showroom bargaining.

Based on my experience, I would suggest that in reference to the fax-tendering [or email-tendering] process, future *Lemon-Aid* editions emphasize:

- Casting a wide geographical net, as long as you're willing to pick the car up there. I faxed up to 50 dealerships, which helped tremendously in increasing the number of serious bidders. One car was bought locally in Ottawa, the other in Mississauga.
- Unless you don't care much about what car you end up with, be very specific about what you want. If you are looking at just one or two cars, which I recommend, specify trim level and all extended warranties and dealer-installed options in the fax letter. Otherwise, you'll end up with quotes comparing apples and oranges, and you won't get the best deal on options negotiated later. Also, specify that quotes should be signed. This helps out with errors in quoting.

- Dealerships are sloppy, there is a 25–30 percent error rate in quotes. Search for errors and get corrections, and confirm any of the quotes in serious contention over the phone.
- Phone to personally thank anyone who submits a quote for their time. Salespeople can't help themselves, they'll ask how they ranked, and often want to then beat the best quote you've got. This is much more productive than faxing back the most competitive quote (I know, I've tried that too).

Another reader, in British Columbia, was successful with this approach (the fax bid request they used appears on the previous page):

> I purchased your 2005 edition *SUVs, Vans, and Trucks* earlier this year from Chapters. Thanks for all the information that helped me decide to purchase a new Honda Odyssey EX-L for a super price from a good dealer. After completing my research (and vacillating for a few weeks) I ended up issuing a faxed "request for quotation" (RFQ) from several dealerships. I can tell you that some of them were not happy and tried to tell me that Honda Canada was clamping down on this activity. In the end, one dealership did not respond and one "closer" salesperson called to attempt to get me in their dealership so he could "assess my needs." I told him that my needs were spelled out very specifically in my request but he refused to give me a price. In the end, I received five quotations by phone, fax, and email. I purchased my van in Chilliwack for about $2,200 off list. It turned out that the salesperson just started selling cars two months ago and was very appreciative of my business. The whole deal was completed in half an hour. I was in full control but treated every respondent fairly. I did not play dealers off one another and went with the lowest first offer.

Getting a Fair Price

"We Sell Below Cost"

This is no longer a bait-and-switch scam. Many dealers who are going out of business are desperate to sell their inventory, sometimes for 40 percent below the

---

DEALER MARKUP

DEALER MARKUP (AMERICAN VEHICLES)		DEALER MARKUP (JAPANESE VEHICLES)	
Small cars:	10%–12%	Small cars:	10%%
Mid-sized cars:	13%–15%	Mid-sized cars:	11%–13%
Large cars:	16%–18%	Large cars:	15%
Sports cars:	15%–20%	Sports cars:	15%–20%
High-end sports cars:	20+%	High-end sports cars:	20+%
Luxury cars:	20+%	Luxury cars:	20+%
High-end luxury cars:	20+%	High-end luxury cars:	20+%
Minivans:	15%	Minivans:	12%–15%
High-end minivans:	16%–20%	High-end minivans:	15%–17%

MSRP. Assuming the vehicle's cost price was 20 percent under the MSRP, astute buyers are getting up to a 20 percent discount. The chart lists the profit margins for various vehicle categories, excluding freight, PDI, and administrative fees, which you should bargain down or not pay at all.

South Korean, Chrysler, and General Motors prices are the most negotiable, while Ford and Japanese and European vehicle prices are much firmer. In addition to the dealer's markup, some vehicles may also have a 3 percent carryover allowance paid out in a dealer incentive program. Finance contracts may also tack on a 2 percent dealer commission.

Holdback

Ever wonder how dealers who advertise vehicles for "a hundred dollars over invoice" can make a profit? They are counting mostly on the manufacturer's holdback.

In addition to the MSRP, the invoice price, dealer incentives, and customer rebates (available to Canadians at *www.apa.ca*), another key element in every dealer's profit margin is the manufacturer's holdback—the quarterly payouts dealers depend on when calculating gross profit.

The holdback was set up over 45 years ago by General Motors as a guaranteed profit for dealers tempted to bargain away their entire profit to make a sale. It usually represents 1–3 percent of the sticker price (MSRP) and is seldom given out by Asian or European automakers, which use dealer incentive programs instead. There are several free Internet sources for holdback information: The most recent and comprehensive are *www.edmunds.com* and *www.kbb.com*, two websites geared toward American buyers. Although there may be a difference in the holdback percentage between American automakers and their Canadian subsidiaries, it's usually not significant.

Some GM dealers maintain that they no longer get a holdback allowance. They are being disingenuous—the holdback may have been added to special sales "incentive" programs, which won't show up on the dealer's invoice. Options are the icing on the cake, with their average 35–65 percent markup.

Can You Get a Fair Price?

Yes, but you'll have to keep your wits about you and time your purchase well into the model year—usually in late winter or spring.

New-car negotiations aren't wrestling matches where you have to pin the sales agent's shoulders to the mat to win. If you feel that the overall price is fair, don't jeopardize the deal by refusing to budge. For example, if you've brought the contract price 10 percent or more below the MSRP and the dealer sticks you with a $200 "administrative fee" at the last moment, let it pass. You've saved money and the sales agent has saved face.

Of course, someone will always be around to tell you how he or she could have bought the vehicle for much less. Let that pass, too.

To come up with a fair price, subtract two-thirds of the dealer's markup from the MSRP and then trade the carryover and holdback allowance for a reduced delivery and transportation fee. Compute the options separately, and sell your trade-in privately. Buyers can more easily knock $4,000 off a $20,000 base price if they wait until Chrysler and GM hold their new year "fire" sales in early 2011 and ratchet up the competition. Remember, choose a vehicle that's in stock, and resist getting unnecessary options.

Beware of Financing and Insurance Traps

Once you and the dealer have settled on the vehicle's price, you aren't out of the woods yet. You'll be handed over to an F&I (financing and insurance) specialist, whose main goal is to convince you to buy additional financing, loan insurance, paint and seat cover protectors, rustproofing, and extended warranties. These items will be presented on a computer screen as costing only "a little bit more each month."

 Compare the dealer's insurance and financing charges with those from an independent agency that may offer better rates and better service. Often, the dealer gets a kickback for selling insurance and financing. And guess who pays for it? Additionally, remember that if the financing rate looks too good to be true, you're probably paying too much for the vehicle. The F&I closer's hard-sell approach will take all your willpower and patience to resist, but when he or she gives up, your trials are over.

Add-on charges are the dealer's last chance to stick it to you before the contract is signed. Dealer pre-delivery inspection (PDI) and transportation charges, "documentation" fees, and extra handling costs are ways that the dealer gets extra profits for nothing. Dealer preparation is often a once-over-lightly affair, with a car seldom getting more than a wash job and a couple of dollars' worth of gas in the tank. It's paid for by the factory in most cases, but when it's not, it should cost no more than 2 percent of the car's selling price. Reasonable transportation charges are acceptable, although dealers who claim that the manufacturer requires the payment often inflate them.

"No Haggle" Pricing Is "Price Fixing"

All dealers bargain. They hang out the "No dickering; one price only" sign simply as a means to discourage customers from asking for a better deal. Like parking lots and restaurants that claim they won't be responsible for lost or stolen property, they're bluffing. Still, you'd be surprised by how many people believe that if it's posted, it's non-negotiable.

No-haggle pricing is not only a deceptive practice, but it's also illegal under federal price-fixing statutes. Several *Lemon-Aid* readers say that some Honda dealers refuse to negotiate prices via email or fax or through third-party auto brokers because Honda Canada has threatened to yank their franchise if they do so. Following *Lemon-Aid*'s formal complaint, the feds opened a formal investigation of Honda's practice. They closed the probe six months later because the new *Competition Act* says that a price-fixing practice actually has to be proven as having affected the prices customers would have paid.

Lemon-Aid was luckier with a similar Toyota complaint. In June 2004, Toyota Canada abandoned its Access no-haggle price strategy sales system after settling out of court (for several millions of dollars) a price-fixing probe undertaken by the federal Competition Bureau at the behest of *Lemon-Aid*.

Now it seems that Hyundai Canada is threatening owners that it won't service vehicles under warranty in Canada that were bought in the States. *Lemon-Aid* believes this is price-fixing of the worst kind and will be calling for a Competition Tribunal Investigation of Hyundai in the coming months.

 ## Price Guidelines

When negotiating the price of a new vehicle, remember that there are several price guidelines and dealers use the one that will make them the most profit on each transaction. Two of the more-common prices quoted are the MSRP (what the automaker advertises as a fair price) and the dealer's invoice cost (which is supposed to indicate how much the dealer paid for the vehicle). Both price indicators leave considerable room for the dealer's profit margin, along with some extra padding in the form of inflated transportation and preparation charges. If you are presented with both figures, go with the MSRP, since it can be verified by calling the manufacturer. Any dealer can print up an invoice and swear to its veracity. If you want an invoice price from an independent source, contact *www. apa.ca* or *www.carhelpcanada.com*.

Buyers who live in rural areas or in western Canada are often faced with grossly inflated auto prices compared to those charged in major metropolitan areas. A good way to get a more-competitive price without buying out of province is to check online to see what prices are being charged in different urban areas. Show the dealer printouts that list selling prices, preparation charges, and transportation fees, and then ask for his or her price to come closer to the advertised prices.

Another tactic is to take a copy of a local competitor's car ad to a competing dealer selling the same brand and ask for a better price. Chances are they've already lost a few sales due to the ad and will work a little harder to match the deal; if not, they're almost certain to reveal the tricks in the competitor's promotion to make the sale.

Dealer Incentives and Customer Rebates

Sales incentives haven't changed much in the past 30 years. When vehicles are first introduced in the fall, they're generally overpriced; early in the new year, they'll sell for about 20–30 percent less. After a year, they may sell for less through a combination of dealer sales incentives (manufacturer-to-dealer), cash rebates (manufacturer-to-customer), zero percent interest financing (manufacturer's-finance-company-to-customer), and discounted prices (dealer-to-customer).

In most cases, the manufacturer's rebate is straightforward and mailed directly to the buyer from the automaker. There are other rebate programs that require a financial investment on the dealer's part, however, and these shared programs tempt dealers to offset losses by inflating the selling price or pocketing the manufacturer's rebate. Therefore, when the dealer participates in the rebate program, demand that the rebate be deducted from the MSRP, not from some inflated invoice price concocted by the dealer.

Some rebate ads will include the phrase "from dealer inventory only." So if your dealer doesn't have the vehicle in stock, you won't get the rebate.

Sometimes automakers will suddenly decide that a rebate no longer applies to a specific model, even though their ads continue to include it. When this happens, take all brochures and advertisements showing your eligibility for the rebate plan to provincial consumer protection officials. They can use false advertising statutes to force automakers to give rebates to every purchaser who was unjustly denied one.

If you are buying a heavily discounted vehicle, be wary of "option packaging" by dealers who push unwanted protection packages (rustproofing, paint sealants, and upholstery finishes) or who levy excessive charges for preparation, filing fees, loan guarantee insurance, and credit life insurance.

Rebates and Quality

Forget the old adage "You get what you pay for." Many reliable, top-performing vehicles come with rebates—especially considering that auto sales were down more than 40 percent for 2009. Rarely will Toyota and Honda offer more than $1,500 rebates, but Chrysler, Ford, and GM routinely hand out $5,000–$7,000 discounts and other sales incentives. The rest of the auto manufacturers fall somewhere in between. To come out ahead, you have to know how to play this rebate game by choosing quality first.

Customer and dealer incentives are frequently given out to stimulate sales of year-old models that are unpopular, scheduled to be redesigned, or headed for the axe. By carefully choosing which rebated model you buy, it's easy to realize important savings with little risk. For example, GM's $2,000 incentives are good deals when applied to its reasonably reliable compact cars (Aveo excepted) but not worth it when applied to the company's glitch-prone small trucks. Ford's Explorer and Expedition rebates ($4,000 plus) also aren't sufficient to offset the greater risk of factory-related defects afflicting these poor-quality models. Post-bankruptcy Chrysler's sizeable rebates can be a good deal only when applied to minivans and Jeeps like the Wrangler and Liberty, but they're not advisable as a reason to buy the company's less-reliable cars and SUVs. Chrysler's little Caliber econobox has been slammed by *Consumer Reports* for being underpowered, with a hard ride, poor handling, and a tacky interior. Not a good buy, no matter what rebates are given.

Prices Go Up; Prices Go Down

Generally, vehicles are priced according to what the market will bear and then are discounted as the competition heats up (Chrysler's larger rear-drive cars and its PT Cruiser and GM's SUVs are prime examples). This year, though, all vehicles are cheaper than ever due to historically bad sales seen in 2008–09. A vehicle's stylishness, scarcity, or general popularity doesn't count for much when unemployment is pandemic, credit is scarce, and many dealers are going bust with hundreds of unsold new vehicles in their inventories.

Cash is once again king, and the once overpriced and hard-to-find popular models are now heavily discounted, or have been dropped entirely, sending their resale values plummeting. For example, Chrysler's rear-drive Hemi-engine-equipped Magnum and 300 had prevailing market values about $1,000 higher than their suggested selling prices when launched in 2004. They were a unique entry in a hot market niche, and were in short supply. But all that doesn't matter any more. Sales of these models have dropped by more than 40 percent during the last four years, and new models are sold with 30–40 percent discounts.

This year, the best prices will come early in the first quarter of 2011 and will continue through the summer. This includes Ford's brand new 2011 Mustang, which will likely have had its first-year factory-related deficiencies corrected. On the other hand, if your choice has an unusually low sticker price, find out why it's so unpopular and then decide if the savings are worth it. Vehicles that don't sell because of the recession or their weird styling are no problem, but poor quality control (think Chrysler's cars and some Kias) can cost you big bucks.

 ## Leftovers

The 2010 leftovers are being picked clean as the 2011s arrive in September. They could be good buys, if you can amortize the first year's depreciation by keeping the vehicle for eight years or more. But if you're the kind of driver who trades every two or three years, you're likely to come out a loser by buying an end-of-the-season vehicle. The simple reason is that, as far as trade-ins are concerned, a leftover is a "used" vehicle that has depreciated at least 20 percent in its first year. The savings the dealer gives you may not equal that first year's depreciation (a cost you'll incur without getting any of the first year's driving benefits). If the dealer's discounted price matches or exceeds the 30 percent depreciation, you're getting a pretty good deal.

Ask the dealer for all work orders relating to the vehicle, including the PDI checklist, and make sure that the odometer readings follow in sequential order. Remember as well that most demonstrators should have less than 5,000 km on the ticker and that the original warranty has been reduced from the day the vehicle was first put on the road. Also, make sure the vehicle is relatively "fresh" (about three months old) and check for warranty damage. With demos, have the dealer extend the warranty or lower the price about $100 for each month of warranty that has expired. If the vehicle's file shows that it was registered to a leasing agency or any other third party, you're definitely buying a used vehicle disguised as a demo. You should walk away from the sale—you're dealing with a crook.

Cash versus Financing

Up until this year, car dealers preferred financing car sales instead of getting cash, because of the 1–2 percent kickbacks lenders gave them. This is less the case now, because fewer companies are lending money, and those that do are giving back very little to dealers and don't want to give loans for more than two-thirds of the purchase price. Dealers are scrambling for equity and will sell their vehicles for less than what they cost if the buyer pays cash. Cash is, once again, king.

If you aren't offered much of a discount for cash, financial planners say it can be smarter to finance the purchase of a new vehicle if a portion of the interest is tax-deductible. The cash that you free up can then be used to repay debts that aren't tax-deductible (mortgages or credit card debts, for example).

Rebates versus Low or Zero Percent Financing

Low-financing programs have the following disadvantages:

- Buyers must have exceptionally good credit.
- Shorter financing periods mean higher payments.
- Cash rebates are excluded.
- Only fully equipped or slow-selling models are eligible.
- Buyers pay full retail price.

The above stipulations can add thousands of dollars to your costs. Remember, to get the best price, first negotiate the price of the vehicle without disclosing whether you are paying cash or financing the purchase (say you haven't yet decided). Once you have a fair price, you can then take advantage of the financing.

Getting a Loan

Borrowers must be at least 18 years old (the age of majority), have a steady income, prove that they have discretionary income sufficient to make the loan payments, and be willing to guarantee the loan with additional collateral or with a parent or spouse as a co-signer.

Before applying for a loan, you should have established a good credit rating via a paid-off credit card and have a small savings account with your local bank, credit union, or trust company. Prepare a budget listing your assets and obligations. This will quickly show whether or not you can afford a car. Next, prearrange your loan with a phone call. This will protect you from much of the smoke-and-mirrors showroom shenanigans.

Incidentally, if you do get in over your head and require credit counselling, contact Credit Counselling Service (CCS), a not-for-profit organization located in many of Canada's major cities (*www.creditcanada.com*).

Hidden Loan Costs

The APA's undercover shoppers have found that most deceptive deals involve major banking institutions rather than automaker-owned companies.

In your quest for an auto loan, remember that the Internet offers help for people who need an auto loan and want quick approval, but don't want to face a banker. The Bank of Montreal (*www.bmo.com*), RBC (*www.rbc.com*), and other banks allow vehicle buyers to post loan applications on their websites. Loans are available to any web surfer, including those who aren't current BMO or RBC customers.

Be sure to call various financial institutions to find out the following:

- The annual percentage rate on the amount you want to borrow, and the duration of your repayment period
- The minimum down payment that the institution requires
- Whether taxes and licence fees are considered part of the overall cost and, thus, are covered by part of the loan
- Whether lower rates are available for different loan periods, or for a larger down payment
- Whether discounts are available to depositors, and if so, how long you must be a depositor before qualifying

When comparing loans, consider the annual rate and then calculate the total cost of the loan offer—that is, how much you'll pay above and beyond the total price of the vehicle.

Dealers may be able to finance your purchase at interest rates that are competitive with the banks' because of the rebates they get from the manufacturers and some lending institutions. Don't believe dealers that say they can borrow money at as much as five percentage points below the prime rate. Actually, they're jacking up the retail price to more than make up for the lower interest charges. Sometimes, instead of boosting the price, dealers reduce the amount they pay for the trade-in. In either case, the savings are illusory.

When dealing with banks, keep in mind that the traditional 36-month loan has now been stretched to 48 or 60 months. Longer payment terms make each month's payment more affordable, but over the long run, they increase the cost of the loan considerably. Therefore, take as short a term as possible.

Be wary of lending institutions that charge a "processing" or "document" fee ranging from $25 to $100. Sometimes consumers will be charged an extra 1–2 percent of the loan up front in order to cover servicing. This is similar to lending institutions adding "points" to mortgages, except that with auto loans, it's totally unjustified. In fact, dealers in the States are the object of several state lawsuits and class actions for inflating loan charges.

Some banks will cut the interest rate if you're a member of an automobile owners' association or if loan payments are automatically deducted from your chequing account. This latter proposal may be costly, however, if the chequing account charges exceed the interest-rate savings.

Loan Protection

Credit insurance guarantees that the vehicle loan will be paid if the borrower becomes disabled or dies. There are three basic types of insurance that can be written into an installment contract: credit life, accident and health, and comprehensive. Some car companies, like Hyundai, will make some of your loan payments if you become unemployed. Most bank and credit union loans are already covered by some kind of loan insurance, but dealers sell the protection separately at an extra cost to the borrower. For this service, the dealer gets a hefty 20 percent commission. The additional cost to the purchaser can be significant. The federal GST is applied to loan insurance, but RST may be exempted in some provinces.

Collecting on these types of policies isn't easy. There's no payment if your unemployment was due to your own conduct or if an illness is caused by some condition that existed prior to your taking out the insurance. Generally, credit insurance is unnecessary if you're in good health, you have no dependants, and your job is secure. Nevertheless, if you need to cancel your financial obligations, the same company that started up LeaseBusters now offers FinanceBusters (*www. financebusters.com*). They provide a similar service to a lease takeover, but for customers who have vehicle loans.

Personal loans from financial institutions (particularly credit unions) now offer lots of flexibility, like fixed or variable interest rates, a choice of loan terms, and no penalties for prepayment. Precise conditions depend on your personal credit rating.

Leasing contracts are less flexible. There's a penalty for any prepayment, and rates aren't necessarily competitive.

Financing Scam: "Your Financing Was Turned Down"

This may be true, now that credit has become more difficult to get. But watch out for the scam that begins after you have purchased a vehicle and left your trade-in with the dealer. A few days later, you are told that your loan was rejected and that you now must put down a larger down payment and accept a higher monthly payment. Of course, your trade-in has already been sold.

Protect yourself from this rip-off by getting a signed agreement that stipulates that financing has been approved and that monthly payments can't be readjusted. Tell the dealer that your trade-in cannot be sold until the deal has closed.

The Contract

How likely are you to be cheated when buying a new car or truck? APA staffers posing as buyers visited 42 dealerships in four Canadian cities in early 2002. Almost half the dealers they visited (45 percent) flunked their test, and (hold onto your cowboy hats) auto buyers in western Canada were especially vulnerable to dishonest dealers. Either dealer ads left out important information or vehicles in the ads weren't available or were selling at higher prices. Fees for paperwork and vehicle preparation were frequently excessive.

Now, eight years later, we know dealers are much more honest. Ahem…maybe.

The Devil's in the Details

Watch what you sign, since any document that requires your signature is a contract. Don't sign anything unless all the details are clear to you and all the blanks have been filled in. Don't accept any verbal promises that you're merely putting the vehicle on hold. And when you are presented with a contract, remember it doesn't have to include all the clauses found in the dealer's pre-printed form. You and the sales representative can agree to strike some clauses and add others.

When the sales agent asks for a deposit, make sure that it's listed on the contract as a deposit, try to keep it as small as possible (a couple hundred dollars at the most), and pay for it by credit card—in case the dealer goes belly up. If you decide to back out of the deal on a vehicle taken from stock, let the seller have the deposit as an incentive to cancel the contract (believe me, it's cheaper than hiring a lawyer and probably equal to the dealer's commission).

Scrutinize all references to the exact model (there's a heck of an upgrade from base to LX or Limited), prices, and delivery dates. Make sure you specify a delivery date in the contract that protects the price.

Contract Clauses You Need

You can put things on a more-equal footing by negotiating the inclusion of as many clauses as possible from the sample additional contract clauses found on the

---

ADDITIONAL CONTRACT CLAUSES

1. **Original contract:** This is the ONLY contract; i.e., it cannot be changed, retyped, or rewritten, without the specific agreement of both parties.
2. **Financing:** This agreement is subject to the purchaser obtaining financing at _____% or less within _____ days of the date below.
3. **"In-service" date and mileage:** To be based on the closing day, not the day the contract was executed, and will be submitted to the automaker for warranty and all other purposes. The dealership will have this date corrected by the automaker if it should become necessary.
4. **Delivery:** The vehicle is to be delivered by _____, failing which the contract is cancelled and the deposit will be refunded.
5. **Cancellation:**
   (a) The purchaser retains the right to cancel this agreement without penalty at any time before delivery of the vehicle by sending a notice in writing to the vendor.
   (b) Following delivery of the vehicle, the purchaser shall have two days to return the vehicle and cancel the agreement in writing, without penalty. After two days and before thirty-one days, the purchaser shall pay the dealer $25 a day as compensation for depreciation on the returned vehicle.
   (c) Cancellation of contract can be refused where the vehicle has been subjected to abuse, negligence or unauthorized modifications after delivery.
   (d) The purchaser is responsible for accident damage and traffic violations while in possession of the said vehicle.
6. **Protected price:** The vendor agrees not to alter the price of the new vehicle, the cost of preparation, or the cost of shipping.
7. **Trade-in:** The vendor agrees that the value attributed to the vehicle offered in trade shall not be reduced, unless it has been significantly modified or has suffered from unreasonable and accelerated deterioration since the signing of the agreement.
8. **Courtesy car:**
   (a) In the event the new vehicle is not delivered on the agreed-upon date, the vendor agrees to supply the purchaser with a courtesy car at no cost. If no courtesy vehicle is available, the vendor agrees to reimburse the purchaser the cost of renting a vehicle.
   (b) If the vehicle is off the road for more than two days for warranty repairs, the purchaser is entitled to a free courtesy vehicle for the duration of the repair period. If no courtesy vehicle is available, the vendor agrees to reimburse the purchaser the cost of renting a vehicle of equivalent or lesser value.
9. **Work orders:** The purchaser will receive duly completed copies of all work orders pertaining to the vehicle, including warranty repairs and the pre-delivery inspection (PDI).
10. **Dealer stickers:** The vendor will not affix any dealer advertising, in any form, on the vehicle.
11. **Fuel:** Vehicle will be delivered with a free full tank of gas.
12. **Excess mileage:** New vehicle will not be acceptable and the contract will be void if the odometer has more than 200 km at delivery/closing.
13. **Tires:** Original equipment Firestone or Bridgestone tires are not acceptable.

_____   _____   _____
     Date   Vendor's Signature   Buyer's Signature

previous page. To do this, write in a "Remarks" section on your contract and then add, "See attached clauses, which form part of this agreement." Then attach a photocopy of the "Additional Contract Clauses" and persuade the sales agent to initial as many of the clauses as possible. Although some clauses may be rejected, the inclusion of just a couple of them can have important legal ramifications later on if you want a full or partial refund.

"We Can't Do That"

Dealers and automakers facing bankruptcy can do almost anything to get your business. Don't take the dealer's word that "We're not allowed to do that"—heard most often in reference to reducing the PDI or transportation fee. Some dealers have been telling *Lemon-Aid* readers that they are "obligated" by the automaker to charge a set fee and could lose their franchise if they charge less. This is pure hogwash. No dealer has ever had their franchise licence revoked for cutting prices. Furthermore, the automakers clearly state that they don't set a bottom price, since doing so would violate Canada's *Competition Act*—that's why you always see them putting disclaimers in their ads saying the dealer can charge less.

The Pre-delivery Inspection

The best way to ensure that the PDI (written as "PDE" in some regions) will be done is to write in the sales contract that you'll be given a copy of the completed PDI sheet when the vehicle is delivered to you. Then, with the PDI sheet in hand, verify some of the items that were to be checked. If any items appear to have been missed, refuse delivery of the vehicle. Once you get home, check out the vehicle more thoroughly, and send a registered letter to the dealer if you discover any incomplete items from the PDI.

Selling Your Trade-In

When to Sell

Used cars are worth more than ever because new cars are suspect (in terms of price and insecurities about warranties being honoured and dealer/automaker backup). New prices are lower than ever before, and used prices are rising. This makes it hard for most owners to figure out when is the best time to buy another vehicle. It doesn't take a genius to figure out that the longer one keeps a vehicle, the less it costs to own.

If you're happy with your vehicle's styling and convenience features and it's safe and dependable, there's no reason to get rid of it. But when the cost of repairs becomes equal to or greater than the cost of payment for a new car, you need to consider trading it in. Shortly after your vehicle's fifth birthday (or whenever you start to think about trading it in), ask a mechanic to look at it to give you some idea of what repairs, replacement parts, or maintenance work it will need in the coming year. Find out if dealer service bulletins show that it will need extensive repairs in the near future (see Appendix III for how to order bulletins from ALLDATA). If it's going to require expensive repairs, you should trade the vehicle right away; if expensive work isn't predicted, you may want to keep it. Auto owners' associations provide a good yardstick. They figure that the annual cost of repairs and preventive maintenance for the average vehicle is about $800. If your vehicle is five years old and you haven't spent anywhere near $4,000 in maintenance, it would pay to invest in your old vehicle and continue using it for another few years.

Consider whether your vehicle can still be serviced easily. If it's no longer on the market, the parts supply is likely to dry up and independent mechanics will be reluctant to repair it.

Don't trade for fuel economy alone. Most fuel-efficient vehicles, such as front-drives, offset the savings through higher repair costs. Also, the more fuel-efficient vehicles may not be as comfortable to drive because of their excessive engine noise, lightweight construction, stiff suspension, and torque steer.

Reassess your needs. Has your family grown to the point that you need a new vehicle? Are you driving less? Are you taking fewer long trips? Let your car or minivan show its age, and pocket the savings if its deteriorating condition doesn't pose a safety hazard and isn't too embarrassing. If you're in sales and are constantly on the road, it makes sense to trade every few years—in that case, the vehicle's appearance and reliability become a prime consideration, particularly since the increased depreciation costs are mostly tax-deductible.

Getting the Most for Your Trade-In

Customers who are on guard against paying too much for a new vehicle often sell their trade-ins for too little. Before agreeing to any trade-in amount, read Part Three of *Lemon-Aid Used Cars and Trucks*. The guide will give your vehicle's dealer price and private selling price, and it offers a formula to figure out regional price fluctuations.

Now that you've nailed down your trade-in's approximate value, here are some tips on selling it with a minimum of stress:

- Never sign a new-vehicle sales contract unless your trade-in has been sold—you could end up with two vehicles.
- Negotiate the price from retail (dealer price) down to wholesale (private sales).

If you haven't sold your trade-in after two weekends, you might be trying to sell it at the wrong time of year or have it priced too high.

Make Money—Sell Privately

If you must sell your vehicle and want to make the most out of the deal, consider selling it yourself and putting the profits toward your next purchase. You'll likely come out hundreds of dollars ahead—buyers will pay more for your vehicle because they know cars sold by owners cost less. The most important thing to remember is that there's a large market for used vehicles in good condition in the $5,000–$7,000 range. Although most people prefer buying from individuals rather than from used-car lots, they may still be afraid that the vehicle is a lemon. By using the following suggestions, you should be able to sell your vehicle quite easily:

1. Know its value. Study dealers' newspaper ads and compare them with the prices listed in *Lemon-Aid*. Undercut the dealer's price by $300–$800, and be ready to bargain down another 10 percent for a serious buyer. Remember, prices can fluctuate wildly depending on which models are trendy, so watch the want ads carefully.

2. Enlist the aid of the salesperson who's selling you your new car. Offer him or her a few hundred dollars to find you a buyer. The fact that one sale hinges on the other, along with the prospect of making two commissions, may work wonders.

3. Post notices on bulletin boards at your office or local supermarkets, and place a "For Sale" sign in the window of the vehicle itself. Place a newspaper ad only as a last resort.

4. Don't give your address right away to a potential buyer responding to your ad. Instead, ask for the telephone number where you may call that person back.

5. Be wary of selling to friends or family members. Anything short of perfection, and you'll be eating Christmas dinner alone.

6. Don't touch the odometer. If you do, you may get a few hundred dollars more—and a criminal record.

7. Paint the vehicle. Some specialty shops charge only $300 and give a guarantee that's transferable to subsequent owners.

8. Make minor repairs. This includes a minor tune-up and patching up the exhaust. Again, if any repair warranty is transferable, use it as a selling point.

9. Clean the vehicle. Go to a reconditioning firm, or spend the weekend scrubbing the interior and exterior. First impressions are important. Clean the chrome, polish the body, and peel off old bumper stickers. Remove butts from the ashtrays and clean out the glove compartment. Make sure all tools and spare parts have been taken out of the trunk. Don't remove the radio or speakers—the gaping holes will lower the vehicle's worth much more than the cost of the sound equipment. Replace missing or broken dash knobs and window cranks.

10. Change the tires. Recaps are good buys.

11. Let the buyer examine the vehicle. Insist that it be inspected at an independent garage, and then accompany the prospective buyer to the garage. This gives you protection if the buyer claims you misrepresented the vehicle.

12. Don't mislead the buyer. If the vehicle was in an accident or some financing is

still to be paid, admit it. Any misleading statements may be used later against you in court. It's also advisable to have someone witness the actual transaction in case of a future dispute.

13. Keep important documents handy. Show prospective buyers the sales contract, repair orders, owner's manual, and all other documents that show how the vehicle has been maintained. Authenticate your claims about fuel consumption.

14. Write an effective ad, if you need to use one.

Selling to Dealers

Selling to a dealer means that you're likely to get 20 percent less than if you sold your vehicle privately, unless the dealer agrees to participate in an accommodation sale based on your buying a new vehicle from them. Most owners will gladly pay some penalty to the dealer, however, for the peace of mind that comes with knowing that their eventual buyer won't lay a claim against them. This assumes that the dealer hasn't been cheated by the owner—if the vehicle is stolen, isn't paid for, has had its odometer spun back (or forward to a lower setting), or is seriously defective, the buyer or dealer can sue the original owner for fraud. Sell to a dealer who sells the same make. He or she will give you more because it's easier to sell your trade-in to customers who are interested in only that make of vehicle.

Drawing Up the Contract

The province of Alberta has prepared a useful bill of sale applicable throughout Canada that can be accessed at *www.servicealberta.gov.ab.ca/pdf/mv/ BillOfSaleReg3126.pdf.* Your bill of sale should identify the vehicle (including the serial number) and include its price, whether a warranty applies, and the nature of the examination made by the buyer.

The buyer may ask you to put in a lower price than what was actually paid in order to reduce the sales tax. If you agree to this, don't be surprised when a Revenue Canada agent comes to your door. Although the purchaser is ultimately the responsible party, you're an accomplice in defrauding the government. Furthermore, if you turn to the courts for redress, your own conduct may be put on trial.

Summary

Purchasing a used vehicle and keeping it at least five years saves you the most money. It takes about eight years to realize similar depreciation savings when buying new. Giving the biggest down payment you can afford, using zero percent financing programs, and piling up as many kilometres and years as possible on your trade-in are the best ways to save money with new vehicles. Remember that safety is another consideration that depends largely on the type of vehicle you choose.

Buy Safe

Here are some safety features to look for:

1. High NHTSA and IIHS crashworthiness ratings for front, offset, and side collisions (pay particular attention to the side rating if you are a senior driver) and roof strength, plus a low rollover potential due to electronic stability control
2. Good-quality tires; be wary of "all-season" tires and Bridgestone/Firestone makes and follow *www.tirerack.com* consumer recommendations
3. Three-point seat belts with belt pretensioners and adjustable shoulder belt anchorages
4. Integrated child safety seats and seat anchors, safety door locks, and override window controls
5. Depowered dual airbags with a cut-off switch; side airbags with head protection; unobtrusive, effective head restraints that don't push your chin into your chest; and pedal extenders
6. Front driver's seat with plenty of rearward travel and a height adjuster
7. Good all-around visibility; a dash that doesn't reflect onto the windshield
8. An ergonomic interior with an efficient heating and ventilation system
9. Headlights that are adequate for night driving and don't blind oncoming traffic
10. Dash gauges that don't wash out in sunlight or produce windshield glare
11. Adjustable head restraints for all seating positions
12. Delaminated side-window glass
13. Easily accessed sound system and climate controls
14. Navigation systems that don't require a degree from MIT to calibrate
15. Manual sliding doors in vans (if children are being transported)

Buy Smart

1. Buy the vehicle you need and can afford, not the one someone else wants you to buy, or one loaded with options that you'll probably never use. Take your time. Price comparisons and test drives may take a month, but you'll get a better vehicle and price in the long run.
2. Buy in winter or later in the new year to double-dip from dealer incentives and customer rebate or low-cost financing programs.
3. Sell your trade-in privately.
4. Arrange financing before buying your vehicle.
5. Test drive your choice by renting it overnight or for several days.
6. Buy through the Internet or by fax, or use an auto broker if you're not confident in your own bargaining skills, you lack the time to haggle, or you want to avoid the "showroom shakedown."
7. Ask for at least a 25 percent discount off the MSRP, and cut PDI and freight charges by at least 50 percent. Insist on a specific delivery date written in the contract, as well as a protected price in case there's a price increase between

the time the contract is signed and when the vehicle is delivered. Also ask for a free tank of gas.

8. Order a minimum of options, and seek a 30–40 percent discount on the entire option list.
9. Put the vehicle's down payment on your credit card.
10. Avoid leasing. If you must lease, choose the shortest time possible, drive down the MSRP, and refuse to pay an "acquisition" or "disposal" fee.
11. Look at Japanese vehicles made in North America, co-ventures with American automakers, and rebadged imports. They often cost less than imports and are just as reliable. However, some European imports may not be as reliable as you might imagine—Mercedes' M-Class sport-utilities, for example. Get extra warranty protection from the automaker if you're buying a model that has a poorer-than-average repair history. Use auto club references to get honest, competent repairs at a reasonable price.

Now that you know how to get a recession-proof vehicle for the least amount of money, Part Two will show you how to get your money back if that "dream car" turns into a nightmare, or if the dealer goes bankrupt.

Part Two

THE ART OF COMPLAINING

Oh! Henry

Never complain. Never explain.

HENRY FORD III

Oh! John

Regulatory Agencies: In youth they are vigorous, aggressive, evangelistic and even intolerant. Later, they become mellow; and in old age—after some 10 or 15 years— they become, with some exceptions, either an arm of the industry they are regulating or senile.

JOHN KENNETH GALBRAITH
ECONOMIST
THE GREAT CRASH

Warranty Madness

Get ready for a tsunami of auto warranty complaints filed in small claims courts across the country as automakers, dealers, and third-party warranty providers are sued for the non-payment of their warranty liabilities. They will mostly hide behind bankruptcy protection and insist that customers were dealing with the "old" corporation, not the brand "new" Chrysler or General Motors entity. Think British Leyland in the '6os, American Motors a decade later, and Renault a few years after that. It doesn't matter that the Canadian government backed Chrysler's and GM's warranties with almost $200 million. GM's warranty payouts alone topped $4.5 billion (U.S.) in 2007, according to its Securities and Exchange Commission filings. Who will pony up the extra money? And how are we going to make quality "Job 1" when many autoworkers have lost that one job?

In a June 4, 2009, interview with *Globe and Mail* auto journalist Jeremy Cato, GM Canada's public affairs director, Stew Low, said that GM operations, warranty approvals, and quality control will continue unchanged, despite the company's Chapter 11 bankruptcy filing. Keep in mind, this is the same motor mouthpiece who two years ago swore to the *Globe* and to the *Toronto Star* that GM didn't have an intake manifold gasket design defect in a decade's worth of V6-engine-equipped cars, trucks, and minivans (1995–2004). Six months later, GM settled a Canadian class action lawsuit over the engines for tens of millions of dollars. Low never recanted.

I gave pro bono testimony for that case, and found some of the plaintiffs. I will always remember how GM's lawyers, engineers, PR flacks, and consultants (among them auto consultant Dennis DesRosiers) tried to make a silk purse out of a sow's ear. Hard feelings, Mr. Low? Yes, indeed. You lied. Why should anyone believe what you say today?

GM's Secret "Oil Spill"

Quality? Just take a look, Mr. Low, at the internal GM bulletin on the following page, sent to dealers a full five months after you assured the *Globe and Mail* that General Motors' quality had improved. Does eight years building engines with the same oil leak afflicting almost your entire lineup, including the 2010 models, signify progress in your eyes? And why would you do this to your relaunched and re-engineered 2010 Chevrolet Camaro?

Bankruptcy Means Never Having to Say You're Wrong

Chrysler's and GM's bankruptcies mean that their warranties technically no longer exist, consumer product liability lawsuits don't have deep-pocket defendants, dealers have lost franchise contracts, suppliers have lost purchasers, and many autoworkers have lost jobs and some of their pensions.

Runzheimer International consultants say that one out of every 10 American vehicles produced by the Detroit Three is a lemon; former Chrysler president Bob Lutz agrees with that figure. I would guess that owners of Chrysler and GM vehicles with broken down automatic transmissions and warped plastic engine intake manifold gaskets, or of Toyotas

GM's Corvette's may go "topless" at any time.

GM ENGINE OIL LEAKS FROM REAR COVER

BULLETIN NO.: 05-06-01-034J

DATE: NOVEMBER 12, 2009

5.3L, 5.7L, 6.0L, 6.2L, 7.0L—ENGINE OIL LEAK AT REAR COVER ASSEMBLY AREA (ENGINE BLOCK POROSITY RTV REPAIR PROCEDURE)

MODELS: 2004–07 Buick Rainier; 2008–09 Buick LaCrosse Super, Allure Super (Canada Only); 2005–10 Cadillac CTS-V; 2007–10 Cadillac Escalade, Escalade ESV, Escalade EXT; 2003–09 Chevrolet TrailBlazer; 2003–10 Chevrolet Corvette; 2004–06 Chevrolet SSR; 2005–10 Chevrolet Silverado, Silverado SS; 2006–07 Chevrolet Monte Carlo SS; 2006–09 Chevrolet TrailBlazer SS, Impala SS; 2007–10 Chevrolet Avalanche, Suburban, Tahoe; 2009–10 Chevrolet Colorado Pickup; 2010 Chevrolet Camaro; 2003–09 GMC Envoy; 2003–10 GMC Sierra; 2004–05 GMC Envoy XUV; 2007–10 GMC Yukon XL, Yukon Denali, Yukon XL Denali; 2009–10 GMC Canyon; 2004–06 Pontiac GTO; 2005–08 Pontiac Grand Prix GXP; 2008–09 Pontiac G8 GT; 2009 Pontiac G8 GXP; 2005–09 Saab 9-7X 5.3i; 2008–09 Saab 9-7X Aero; 2003–10 HUMMER H2; 2006–10 HUMMER H3 with 5.3L, 5.7L, 6.0L, 6.2L, 7.0L VORTEC(TM) GEN III or GEN IV V8 Engine (All Aluminum Block)

CONDITION: Some customers may comment on an engine oil leak.

CAUSE: Upon initial diagnosis, it may be determined that the leak is coming from the rear cover gasket. This condition may be caused by engine block porosity on the sealing surface. This issue pertains to aluminum block applications only.

with unreliable powertrains that hesitate then suddenly speed up when accelerating in traffic ("lag and lurch"), would put the lemon estimate much higher.

I've saved the most bizarre for last: Would you believe Corvettes may suddenly go "topless"? Yep! Just look at the GM service bulletin below; it warns 2005–06 model Corvette owners that their cars' roofs may break off and fly away.

GM PAINTED ROOF ADHESIVE SEPARATION

BULLETIN NO.: 05112C

DATE: JUNE 7, 2006

This program is in effect until March 31, 2007.

CONDITION: On certain 2005–06 Chevrolet Corvette vehicles, the painted roof panel may separate from its frame in some areas if it is exposed to stresses along with high temperature and humidity. The occupants of the vehicle may notice one or more of these symptoms: a snapping noise when driving over bumps, wind noise, poor roof panel fit, roof panel movement/bounce when a door or hatch is closed, or a water leak in the headliner.

CORRECTION: Dealers are to apply adhesive foam to ensure proper adhesion, or in a small number of vehicles, replace the roof panel.

GM WATER LEAKS INTO CAB PAST SUNROOF

BULLETIN NO.: 08-08-67-006A

DATE: OCTOBER 28, 2009

HEADLINER WET, WATER LEAK INTO CAB, WATER LEAK PAST SUNROOF GLASS WEATHERSTRIP/SEAL (INSPECT SUNROOF WEATHERSTRIP/SEAL AND REPLACE IF NECESSARY)

MODELS: 2007–10 Chevrolet Silverado Crew Cab Models; 2007–10 GMC Sierra Crew Cab Models with Sunroof (RPO CF5)

CONDITION: Some customers may comment on the headliner being wet or water leaking into the cab.

CAUSE: The sunroof glass weatherstrip/seal may not be completely water tight. The weatherstrip/seal may not be properly secured to the glass panel.

And, let's give GM truck owners equal time as they sing out "raindrops keep falling on my head," paying homage to another 2007–10 model goof confirmed by GM service bulletins (see previous page).

Four Ways to Get Your Money Back

If you've bought an unsafe vehicle or one that was misrepresented, or you've had to pay for repairs to correct factory-related defects, this section's for you. It's intended is to help you get your money back—without going to court or getting frazzled by a dealer's broken promises or "benign neglect." But if going to court is your only recourse, this section has the jurisprudence you'll need to cite in your complaint to get an out-of-court settlement or to win your case without spending a fortune on lawyers and research.

Remember the "money-back guarantee"? Well, that's long gone. Automakers are reluctant to offer any warranty that requires them to take back a defective car or minivan, because they know that there are a lot of lemons out there. Fortunately, our provincial consumer protection laws have filled the gap when the base warranty expires, so now any sales contract for a new or used vehicle can be cancelled—or free repairs can be ordered—in the following situations:

- Vehicle is unfit for the purpose for which it was purchased
- Vehicle was misrepresented
- Repairs are covered by a secret warranty or a "goodwill" warranty extension
- Vehicle hasn't been reasonably durable, considering how well it was maintained, the mileage driven, and the type of driving that was done (this is particularly applicable to engine, transmission, and paint defects)

The four legal concepts enumerated above can lead to the sales contract being cancelled, the purchase price being partially refunded, and/or damages being awarded. For example, if the seller says that a minivan can pull a 900 kg (2,000 lb.) trailer and you discover that it can barely tow half that weight or won't reach a reasonable speed while towing, you can cancel the contract for misrepresentation. The same principle applies to a seller's exaggerated claims concerning a vehicle's fuel economy or reliability, as well as to "demonstrators" that are, in fact, used cars with false (rolled-back) odometer readings. GM's and Chrysler's secret paint warranties and Ford's engine and transmission "goodwill" programs have all been successfully challenged in small claims court. And reasonable durability is an especially powerful legal argument that allows a judge to determine what the dealer and auto manufacturer will pay to correct a premature failure long after the original warranty has expired.

Unfair Contracts

Sales contracts aren't fair, nor are they meant to be. Dealers' and automakers' lawyers spend countless hours making sure their clients are well protected with ironclad contracts.

Called "standard form contracts," or "contracts of adhesion," these agreements are looked upon by judges with a great deal of skepticism. They know these are contracts in which you have little or no bargaining power, such as loan documents, insurance contracts, and automobile leases. So when a dispute arises over terms or language, provincial consumer protection statutes require that judges interpret these contracts in the way most favourable to the consumer.

"Hearsay" Not Allowed

It's essential that printed evidence and/or witnesses (relatives are not excluded) are available to confirm that a false representation actually occurred, that a part is failure-prone, or that its replacement is covered by a secret warranty. Stung by an increasing number of small claims court defeats, automakers are now asking small claims court judges to disallow evidence from *Lemon-Aid*, service bulletins, or memos on the pretext that such evidence is hearsay (not proven) unless confirmed by an independent mechanic or unless the document is recognized by the automaker's or dealer's representative at trial ("Is this a common problem? Do you recognize this service bulletin? Is there a case-by-case 'goodwill' plan covering this repair?"). This is why you should bring in an independent garage mechanic or body expert to buttress your allegations. Sometimes, though, the service manager or company representative will make key admissions if questioned closely by you, a court mediator, or the trial judge. That questioning can be particularly effective if you call for the exclusion of witnesses until they're called (let them mill around outside the courtroom wondering what their colleagues have said).

Automakers often blame owners for having pushed their vehicle beyond its limits. Therefore, when you seek to set aside the contract or get a repair reimbursed, it's essential that you get the testimony of an independent mechanic and his or her co-workers in order to prove that the vehicle's poor performance isn't caused by negligent maintenance or abusive driving.

It Should Have Lasted Longer!

The reasonable durability claim is your ace in the hole. It's probably the easiest allegation to prove, since all automakers have benchmarks as to how long body components, trim and finish, and mechanical and electronic parts should last (see the "Reasonable Part Durability" chart on page 122). Vehicles are expected to be reasonably durable and merchantable. What "reasonably durable" means depends on the price paid, the kilometres driven, the purchaser's driving habits, and how well the vehicle was maintained by the owner. Judges carefully weigh all these factors in awarding compensation or cancelling a sale.

Whatever the reason you use to get your money back, don't forget to conform to the "reasonable diligence" rule that requires you to file suit within a reasonable time after the vehicle's purchase or after you've discovered the defect. If there have been no negotiations with the dealer or automaker, this period cannot exceed a few months. If either the dealer or the automaker has been promising to correct the defects for some time, or has carried out repeated unsuccessful repairs, the delay for filing the lawsuit can be extended.

Refunds for Other Expenses

It's a lot easier to get the automaker to pay to replace a defective part than it is to obtain compensation for a missed day of work. Manufacturers seldom pay for consequential expenses like a ruined vacation, a vehicle not living up to its advertised hype, or an owner's mental distress, because they can't control the amount of the refund. Courts, however, are more generous, having ruled that all expenses (damages) flowing from a problem covered by a warranty or service bulletin are the manufacturer's or dealer's responsibility under both common law (which covers all provinces except Quebec) and Quebec civil law. Fortunately, when legal action is threatened—usually through small claims court—automakers quickly up their ante to include most of the owner's expenses because they know the courts will be more generous.

One precedent-setting judgment (cited in *Sharman v. Ford*, found on page 148) giving generous damages to a motorist fed up with his "lemon" Cadillac was rendered in 1999 by the British Columbia Supreme Court in *Wharton v. Tom Harris Chevrolet Oldsmobile Cadillac Ltd.* ([2002] B.C.J. No. 233, 2002 BCCA 78d). In that case, Justice Leggatt threw the book at GM and the dealer in awarding the following amounts:

(a) Hotel accommodations: $ 217.17
(b) Travel to effect repairs at 30 cents per kilometre: The plaintiff claims some 26 visits from his home in Ucluelet to Nanaimo. Some credit should be granted to the defendants since routine trips would have been required in any event. Therefore, the plaintiff is entitled to be compensated for mileage for 17 trips (approximately 400 km from Ucluelet to Nanaimo return) at 30 cents per kilometre.
                                       $2,040.00
TOTAL: $2,257.17

[20] The plaintiffs are entitled to non-pecuniary damages for loss of enjoyment of their luxury vehicle and for inconvenience in the sum of $5,000.

Warranties

It's really not that hard to get a refund if you take it one step at a time. Vehicle defects are covered by two warranties: the *expressed* warranty, which has a fixed time limit, and the *implied* (or *legal*) warranty, which is entirely up to a judge's discretion.

Expressed Warranties

The manufacturer's or dealer's warranty is an "expressed" promise that a vehicle will perform as represented and be reasonably reliable, subject to certain conditions. Regardless of the number of subsequent owners, this promise remains in force as long as the warranty's original time/kilometre limits haven't expired. The expressed warranty given by most sellers is often full of empty promises, and it allows the dealer and manufacturer to act as judge and jury when deciding whether a vehicle was misrepresented or is afflicted with defects they'll pay to correct. Rarely does it provide a money-back guarantee.

Some of the more familiar lame excuses used in denying expressed warranty claims are "You abused the car," "It was poorly maintained," "It's normal wear and tear," "It's rusting from the outside, not the inside," and "It passed the safety inspection." Ironically, the expressed warranty sometimes says that there is no warranty at all, or that the vehicle is sold "as is." And, when the warranty's clauses (or lack thereof) don't deter claimants, some dealers simply say that a verbal warranty or representation as to the vehicle's attributes is unenforceable.

Fortunately, these attempts to weasel out of the warranty and limit the seller's liability seldom make it through judicial review. Justice Searle put it this way in the *Chams* decision (see pages 150–156):

> Ford's warranty attempts to limit its liability to what it grants in the warranty. It is ancient law that one who attempts to limit his liability by, for example, excluding common law remedies, must clearly bring that limitation to the attention of the person who might lose those remedies. The evidence in this case is clear: The buyer of even a new car does not get a warranty booklet until after purchasing the car although he "would be" told the highlights sooner.

Implied Warranties

Thankfully, car owners get another kick at the can with the implied warranty ("of fitness"). As clearly stated in the unreported Saskatchewan decision *Maureen Frank v. General Motors of Canada Limited* (found exclusively in *Lemon-Aid* on page 139)—in which the judge declared that paint discoloration and peeling shouldn't occur within 11 years of the purchase of a vehicle—the implied warranty is an important legal principle. It's solidly supported by a large body of federal and provincial laws, regulations, and jurisprudence, and it protects you primarily from hidden dealer- or factory-related defects. But the concept also includes misrepresentation and a host of other scams.

This warranty also holds dealers to a higher standard of conduct than private sellers because, unlike private sellers, dealers are presumed to be aware of the defects present in the vehicles they sell. That way, they can't just pass the ball to the automaker or to the previous owner and then walk away from the dispute. For instance, in British Columbia, a new-car dealer is required to disclose damage requiring repairs costing more than 20 percent of the price (under the *Motor Dealer Act Regulations*).

- It establishes the concept of "reasonable durability" (see "How Long Should a Part or Repair Last?" on page 122), meaning that parts are expected to last for a reasonable period of time, as stated in jurisprudence, judged by independent mechanics, or expressed in extended warranties given by the automaker in the past (7–10 years/160,000 km for engines and transmissions).
- It covers the entire vehicle and can be applied for whatever period of time the judge decides.
- It can order that the vehicle be taken back, or that a major repair cost be refunded.
- It can help plaintiffs claim compensation for supplementary transportation, inconvenience, mental distress, missed work, screwed-up vacations, insurance paid while the vehicle was in the repair shop, repairs done by other mechanics, and exemplary (or punitive) damages in cases where the seller was a real weasel.
- It is frequently used by small claims court judges to give refunds to plaintiffs "in equity" (out of fairness) rather than through a strict interpretation of contract law.

Expressed and Implied Warranties: Fuel Economy Claims

Canadian courts are cracking down on lying dealers and deceptive sales practices, and the misrepresentation of fuel economy figures is squarely in the judiciary's sights. Ontario's *Consumer Protection Act, 2002* (*www.e-laws.gov.on.ca/html/statutes/english/elaws_statutes_02c30_e.htm*), for example, lets a vehicle buyer cancel a contract within one year of entering into an agreement if their dealer made a false, misleading, deceptive, or unconscionable representation. This includes using exaggeration, innuendo, or ambiguity as to a material fact or failing to state a material fact if such use or failure deceives or tends to deceive consumers.

This law means that new- or used-car dealers cannot make the excuse that they were fooled about the condition or performance of a vehicle, or that they were simply providing data supplied by the manufacturer. The law clearly states that both parties are jointly liable and that dealers are *presumed* to know the history, quality, and true performance of what they are selling.

Details like fuel economy *can* lead to a contract's cancellation if the dealer gives a higher-than-actual figure. In *Sidney v. 1011067 Ontario Inc. (c.o.b. Southside Motors)*, a precedent-setting case that was filed before Ontario's *Consumer Protection Act* was toughened in 2002, the buyer was awarded $11,424.51 plus prejudgment interest because of a false representation made by the defendant regarding fuel efficiency. The plaintiff claimed that the defendant advised him that the vehicle had a fuel efficiency of 800–900 km per tank of fuel when, in fact, the maximum efficiency was only 500 km per tank.

This consumer victory is particularly important as fuel prices soar and everyone from automakers to sellers of ineffective gas-saving gadgets make outlandishly false fuel economy claims. Not surprisingly, sellers try to use the expressed warranty to reject claims, while smart plaintiffs ignore the expressed warranty and argue for a refund under the implied warranty, instead.

Expressed and Implied Warranties: Tire Failures

Consumers have gained additional rights following Bridgestone/Firestone's massive tire recall in 2001. Because of the confusion and chaos surrounding Firestone's handling of the recall, Ford's 575 Canadian dealers stepped into the breach and replaced the tires with any equivalent tires dealers had in stock, no questions asked.

This is an important precedent that tears down the traditional liability wall separating tire manufacturers from automakers in product liability claims. In essence, whoever sells the product can now be held liable for damages. In the future, Canadian consumers will have an easier time holding the dealer, automaker, and tiremaker liable, not just for recalled products but also for any defect that affects the safety or reasonable durability of that product.

This is particularly true now that the Supreme Court of Canada (*Winnipeg Condominium v. Bird Construction* [1995] 1S.C.R.85) has ruled that defendants are liable in negligence for any designs that resulted in a risk to the public for safety or health. The Supreme Court reversed a long-standing policy and provided the public with a new cause of action that had not existed before in Canada. Prior to this Supreme Court ruling, companies dodged liability for falling bridges and crashing planes by warranty exclusion and "entire-agreement" contract clauses. In the *Winnipeg Condominium* case, the Supreme Court held that repairs made to prevent serious damage or accidents could be claimed from the designer or builder for the cost of repair in tort from any subsequent purchaser. Consumers with tire or other claims relating to the safety of their vehicles would be wise to insert the above court decision (with explanation) in their claim letter and then mail or fax it to the automaker's legal affairs or product liability department. A copy should also be deposited with the clerk of the small claims court, if you have to use that recourse.

Other Warrantable Items

Safety restraints, such as airbags and seat belts, have warranty coverage extended for the lifetime of the vehicle, following an agreement made between U.S. automakers and importers. In Canada, though, some automakers try to dodge this responsibility because they are incorporated as separate Canadian companies. That distinction didn't fly with B.C.'s Court of Appeal in the 2002 *Robson* decision (*www.courts.gov.bc.ca/jdb-txt/ca/02/03/2002bcca0354.htm*). In that class action petition, the court declared that both Canadian companies *and* their American counterparts can be held liable in Canada for deceptive acts that violate the provincial *Trade Practices Act* (in this case, Chrysler and GM paint delamination):

> At this stage, the plaintiffs are only required to demonstrate that they have a "good arguable case" against the American defendants. The threshold is low. A good arguable case requires only a serious question to be tried, one with some prospect of success: see *AG Armeno Mines, supra,* at para. 25 [*AG Armeno Mines and Minerals Inc. v. PT Pukuafu Indah* (2000), 77 B.C.L.R.(3d) 1 (C.A.)].

Aftermarket products and services—such as gas-saving gadgets, rustproofing, and paint protectors—can render the manufacturer's warranty invalid, so make sure you're in the clear before purchasing any optional equipment or services from an independent supplier.

DON'T BE SILLY. THAT'S CAUSED BY BIRD DROPPINGS!

INADEQUATE PRIMER CAUSED MY PAINT TO PEEL!

Paint delamination is a common defect that automakers often blame on everything from bird droppings to ultraviolet light—or they simply say the warranty has expired. The courts haven't been very receptive to these kinds of excuses.

How fairly a warranty is applied is more important than how long it remains in effect. Once you know the normal wear rate for a mechanical component or body part, you can demand proportional compensation when you get less than normal durability—no matter what the original warranty said.

Some dealers tell customers that they need to have original-equipment parts installed in order to maintain their warranty. A variation on this theme requires that routine servicing—including tune-ups and oil changes (with a certain brand of oil)—be done by the selling dealer, or the warranty is invalidated.

Nothing could be further from the truth. Canadian law stipulates that whoever issues a warranty cannot make that warranty conditional on the use of any specific brand of motor oil, oil filter, or any other component, unless it's provided to the customer free of charge.

Beware the Warranty Runaround

Sometimes dealers will do all sorts of minor repairs that don't correct the problem, and then, after the warranty runs out, they'll tell you that major repairs are needed. You can prevent this nasty surprise by repeatedly bringing your vehicle into the dealership before the warranty ends. During each visit, insist that a written work order include the specific nature of the problem as *you* see it and that the work order carry the notation that this is the second, third, or fourth time the same problem has been brought to the dealer's attention. Write it down yourself, if need be. This allows you to show a pattern of nonperformance by the dealer during the warranty period and establishes that it's a serious and chronic problem. When the warranty expires, you have the legal right to demand that it be extended on those items consistently reappearing on your handful of work orders. *Lowe v. Fairview Chrysler* (see page 156) is an excellent judgment that reinforces this important principle. In another lawsuit, *François Chong v. Marine Drive Imported Cars Ltd. and Honda Canada Inc.* (see page 164), a Honda owner forced Honda to fix his engine six times—until they got it right.

A retired GM service manager gave me another effective tactic to use when you're not sure that a dealer's warranty "repairs" will actually correct the problem for a reasonable period of time after the warranty expires. Here's what he says you should do:

> When you pick up the vehicle after the warranty repair has been done, hand the service manager a note to be put in your file that says you appreciate the warranty repair; however, you intend to return and ask for further warranty coverage if the problem reappears before a reasonable amount of time has elapsed even if the original warranty has expired. A copy of the same note should be sent to the automaker.... Keep your copy of the note in the glove compartment as cheap insurance against paying for a repair that wasn't fixed correctly the first time.

Extended (Supplementary) Warranties

You have to tread very carefully here. During Chrysler's and GM's bankruptcies, hundreds of small, independent supplementary warranty sellers invaded the marketplace. Their specialty: making automated "robo-calls" to pitch dubious auto warranties to scared owners. Asking to be put on a "do not call" list is not always effective, but threatening legal action helps. One fed-up owner of a 10-year-old vehicle writes (*www.complaintsboard.com/complaints/national-auto-warranty-service-c73231.htm*):

> I have no relationship with this company, but I'm about to send them a registered letter telling them that if they call me again I will bill them for my time and the use of my phone equipment for their marketing calls, and that their agreement to my terms will be signaled by their next call to my phone number. Failure to pay will result in a suit for collection in Maryland.

The manufacturer, the dealer, or an independent third party may sell supplementary warranties that provide extended coverage, and this coverage is automatically transferred when a vehicle is sold. They cost between $1,500 and $2,000 and should be purchased only if the vehicle you're buying has a reputation for being unreliable or expensive to service (see Part Three) or if you're reluctant to use the small claims courts when factory-related trouble arises. Don't let the dealer pressure you into deciding right away.

Dealers love to sell you extended warranties, whether you need them or not, because up to 60 percent of the warranty's cost represents dealer markup. Out of the remaining 40 percent comes the sponsor's administration costs and profit margin, calculated at another 15 percent. What's left to pay for repairs is a minuscule 25 percent of the original amount. The only reason that automakers and independent warranty companies haven't been busted for operating this Ponzi scheme is that only half of the vehicle buyers who purchase extended service contracts actually use them.

Those who do need help often find it difficult to collect a refund because independent companies frequently go out of business or limit the warranty's coverage through subsequent mailings. Provincial laws cover both situations. If the bankrupt warranty company's insurance policy won't cover your claim, take the dealer to small claims court and ask for the repair costs and a refund of the original warranty payment. Your argument for holding the dealer responsible is a simple one: By accepting a commission to act as an agent of the defunct company, the dealer also took on the obligations of that company. As for limiting the coverage after you have already bought the warranty policy, this practice is illegal and allows you to sue both the dealer and the warranty company for a refund of both the warranty and the repair costs.

Emissions-Control Warranties

These little-publicized warranties can save you big bucks if major engine or exhaust components fail prematurely. They come with all new vehicles and cover major components of the emissions-control system for up to 8 years/130,000 km, no matter how many times the vehicle is sold. Unfortunately, although owner's manuals vaguely mention the emissions warranty, most don't specify which parts are covered. The U.S. Environmental Protection Agency has intervened on several occasions, with hefty fines against Chrysler and Ford, and ruled that all major motor and fuel-system components are covered. These components include fuel metering, ignition spark advance, restart, evaporative emissions, positive crankcase ventilation (PCV), engine electronics (computer modules), and catalytic converter systems as well as parts like hoses, clamps, brackets, pipes, gaskets, belts, seals, and connectors. Canada, however, has no governmentally defined list, so it's up to each manufacturer and the small claims courts to decide which emissions-control components are covered.

Some of the confidential technical service bulletins listed in Part Three show parts failures that are covered under the emissions warranty (stinky exhausts caused by defective catalytic converters, for example), even though motorists are routinely charged for their replacement. Ford of Canada has issued one bulletin where owners of 2002–05 Ford Taurus and Sable models will get refunds for fuel gauge repairs under the emissions warranty. Faulty fuel gauges are a common problem with all automakers, with repairs costing $300–$500.

Make sure to get your emissions system checked out thoroughly by a dealer or an independent garage before the emissions warranty expires or before having the vehicle inspected by provincial emissions inspectors. In addition to ensuring that you'll pass provincial tests, this precaution could save you up to $1,000 if your catalytic converter and other emissions components are faulty.

Exposing "Secret" Warranties

Few vehicle owners know that secret warranties exist. The closest automakers come to an admission is sending out a "goodwill policy," "product improvement program," or "special policy" technical service bulletin (TSB) to dealers or first owners of record. Consequently, the only motorists who find out about these policies are the original owners who haven't moved or haven't leased their vehicles. The other motorists who get compensated for repairs are the ones who read *Lemon-Aid* each year, wave TSBs, and yell the loudest.

Remember, second owners and repairs done by independent garages are included in these secret warranty programs. Large, costly repairs, such as blown engines, burned transmissions, and peeling paint, are often covered.

Here are a few examples of the most comprehensive secret warranties that have come across my desk during the last several years.

All Years, All Models
Automatic transmissions

Problem: Faulty automatic transmissions that self-destruct, shift erratically, gear down to "limp home mode," are slow to shift in or out of Reverse, or are noisy. **Warranty coverage:** If you have the assistance of your dealer's service manager, expect an offer of 50–75 percent (about $2,500). File the case in small claims court, and a full refund will be offered up to 7 years/160,000 km. Acura, Honda, Hyundai, Lexus, and Toyota coverage varies between seven and eight years.

Brakes

Problem: Premature wearout of brake pads, calipers, and rotors. Produces excessive vibration, noise, and pulling to one side when braking. **Warranty coverage:** *Calipers and pads:* "Goodwill" settlements confirm that brake calipers and pads that fail to last 2 years/40,000 km will be replaced for 50 percent of the repair cost; components not lasting 1 year/20,000 km will be replaced for free. *Rotors:* If they last less than 3 years/60,000 km, they'll be replaced at half the price; replacement is free up to 2 years/40,000 km. *ABS brake sensors and electrical connections:* Should last for at least 5 years or 100,000 km.

Interestingly, early brake wearout, once mainly a Detroit failing, is now quite common with Asian makes, as well. Apparently, brake suppliers to all automakers are using cheaper calipers, pads, and rotors that can't handle the heat generated by normal braking on heavier passenger cars, trucks, and vans. Consequently, drivers find routine braking causes rotor warpage that produces excessive vibrations, shuddering, noise, and pulling to one side when braking.

Engines

Problem: At around 60,000–100,000 km, the engine may overheat, lose power, and burn extra fuel, or possibly self-destruct. Under the best of circumstances, the repair will take a day and cost about $800–$1,000. **Warranty coverage:** If you have the assistance of your dealer's service manager, expect a full refund up to 7 years/160,000 km, although initial offers will hover at about 50 percent of the costs. Ford Windstars and GM minivans are particularly afflicted with this defect. If you threaten small claims court action, cite the *Chams* decision (see pages 150–156).

No matter which automaker you're dealing with, filing your claim in small claims court always sweetens the company's settlement offer. Furthermore, you likely won't have to step inside a courtroom to get your refund, since most small claims court filings are settled at the pretrial mediation stage.

Exhaust systems

Problem: A nauseating "rotten-egg" exhaust smell permeates the interior. **Warranty coverage:** At first, owners are told they need a tune-up. And then they are told to change fuels and to wait a few months for the problem to correct itself. When this fails, the catalytic converter will likely be replaced and the power control module recalibrated. The replacement and recalibration is free up to 8 years under the emissions warranty.

Chrysler, Ford, General Motors, Honda, Hyundai, and Mazda

Paint

Problem: Faulty paint jobs that cause paint to turn white, peel off of horizontal panels, or produce thin white scratches. Mazda CX-9, Mazda3, Mazda5, and Mazda6 models are most affected (particularly the blue and black-cherry colours). **Warranty coverage:** Automakers will offer a free paint job or partial compensation up to six years with no mileage limitation. Thereafter, all these manufacturers offer 50–75 percent refunds on the small claims courthouse steps.

In *Frank v. GM*, the Saskatchewan small claims court set an 11-year benchmark for paint finishes, and three other Canadian small claims judgments have extended the benchmark to seven years, second owners, and pickups.

I wanted to let you and your readers know that the information you publish about Ford's paint failure problem is invaluable. Having read through your "how-to guide" on addressing this issue, I filed a suit against Ford for the "latent" paint defect. The day prior to our court date, I received a settlement offer by phone for 75 percent of what I was initially asking for.

This settlement was for a 9-year-old car. I truly believe that Ford hedges a bet that most people won't go to the extent of filing a lawsuit because they are intimidated or simply stop progress after they receive a firm no from Ford.

M.P.

How Long Should a Part or Repair Last?

How do you know when a part or service doesn't last as long as it should, and whether you should seek a full or partial refund? Sure, you have a gut feeling based on your use of the vehicle, how you maintained it, and the extent of work that was carried out on it. But you'll need more than emotion to win compensation from garages and automakers.

You can definitely get a refund if a repair or part lasts longer than its guarantee but not as long as is generally expected. But you'll have to show what the auto industry considers to be "reasonable durability." Automakers, mechanics, and the courts all have their own benchmarks as to what's a reasonable period of time or amount of mileage one should expect a part or adjustment to last. Consequently, I've prepared this table to show what most automakers consider to be reasonable durability, as expressed by their original and "goodwill" warranties.

Many of the guidelines on the following page were extrapolated from Chrysler and Ford payouts to thousands of dissatisfied customers over the past decade, in addition to Chrysler's original seven-year powertrain warranty (applicable from 1991–95 and reapplied from 2001–04). Other sources for this chart were the Ford and GM transmission warranties outlined in their secret warranties; Ford, GM, and Toyota engine "goodwill" programs laid out in their internal service bulletins; and court judgments where judges have given their own guidelines as to what is meant by "reasonable durability."

Safety features—with the exception of anti-lock brake systems (ABS)—generally have a lifetime warranty. Chrysler's 10-year "free-service" program, part of its 1993–99 ABS recall, can serve as a handy benchmark as to how long one can expect these components to last on more-recent models.

Airbags are a different matter. Those that are deployed in an accident—and the personal injury and interior damage their deployment will likely have caused—are covered by your accident insurance policy. However, if there is a sudden deployment for no apparent reason, the automaker and dealer should be held jointly responsible for all injuries and damages caused by the airbag. You can prove their liability by downloading data from your vehicle's data recorder. This will likely

REASONABLE PART DURABILITY

ACCESSORIES

Air conditioner	7 years
Cruise control	5 years/100,000 km
Power doors, windows	5 years
Radio	5 years

BODY

Paint (peeling)	7–11 years
Rust (perforations)	7–11 years
Rust (surface)	5 years
Water/wind/air leaks	5 years

BRAKE SYSTEM

Brake drum	120,000 km
Brake drum linings	35,000 km
Brake rotor	60,000 km
Brake calipers/pads	30,000 km
Master cylinder	100,000 km
Wheel cylinder	80,000 km

ENGINE AND DRIVETRAIN

CV joint	6 years/160,000 km
Differential	7 years/160,000 km
Engine (diesel)	15 years/350,000 km
Engine (gas)	7 years/160,000 km
Radiator	4 years/80,000 km
Transfer case	7 years/160,000 km
Transmission (auto.)	7 years/160,000 km
Transmission (man.)	10 years/250,000 km
Transmission oil cooler	5 years/100,000 km

EXHAUST SYSTEM

Catalytic converter	8–10 years/100,000 km or more
Muffler	2 years/40,000 km
Tailpipe	3 years/60,000 km

IGNITION SYSTEM

Cable set	60,000 km
Electronic module	5 years/80,000 km
Retiming	20,000 km
Spark plugs	20,000 km
Tune-up	20,000 km

"Black box" data can prove that the brakes, airbag, or another component failed.

lead to a more-generous settlement from the two parties and prevent your insurance premiums from being jacked up.

Use the manufacturer's emissions warranty as your primary guideline for the expected durability of high-tech electronic and mechanical pollution-control components, such as powertrain control modules (PCM) and catalytic converters. Look first at your owner's manual for an indication of which parts on your vehicle are covered. If you come up with few specifics, ask the auto manufacturer for a list of all components covered by the emissions warranty.

Recall Repairs

Vehicles are recalled for one of two reasons: Either they are unsafe or they don't conform to federal pollution-control regulations. Whatever the reason, recalls are a great way to get free repairs and keep your car safe—if you know which ones apply to you and you have the patience of Job.

A recall doesn't mean your vehicle will become a long-term problem. Most vehicles will undergo two or three recalls during their life cycle. Indeed, recalls happen in even the best automotive neighbourhoods, with manufacturers from Acura to Rolls-Royce subject to government-mandated recalls. Even quality-snob Toyota has sustained huge recalls on all of its models in the last couple of years, affecting some 10 million vehicles.

More than 390 million unsafe vehicles have been recalled by automakers for the free correction of safety-related defects since American recall legislation was passed in 1966 (a weaker Canadian law was enacted in 1971). During that time, NHTSA estimates that about 28 percent of the recalled vehicles never made it back to the dealership for repairs because owners were never informed, they just didn't consider the defect to be that hazardous, or they gave up waiting for corrective parts. Yet one study that estimated the effect of recalls on safety found that a 10 percent increase in the recall rate of a particular model will reduce the number of accidents involving that model by around 2 percent (*ms.cc.sunysb. edu/~hbenitezsilv/recall.pdf*).

The automaker has three options for correcting the defect: repair, replace, or refund. This probably means a trip to the dealer. However, in the case of a tire or child seat recall, you may mail in the defective item or go to the retailer that sold the product.

If you've moved, it's smart to pay a visit to your local dealer. Give the dealer your address to get a "report card" on which recalls, free service campaigns, and warranties apply to your vehicle. Simply give the service advisor the vehicle identification number (VIN)—found on your insurance card or on the dash, just below the windshield on the driver's side—and have the number run through the automaker's computer system. Ask for a computer printout of the vehicle's history (or have it faxed to you, if you're so equipped), and make sure you're listed in the automaker's computer as the new owner. This process ensures that you'll receive notices of warranty extensions and emissions and safety recalls.

There are limitations on automotive recalls. Vehicle manufacturers are not required to perform free recalls on vehicles that are more than 10 years old. Getting repairs when the automaker says you're too late often takes a small claims court filing. But these cases are easy to win and are usually settled out of court. U.S. recalls may be voluntary or ordered by the U.S. Department of Transportation, and they can be nationwide or regional. In Canada, all recalls are considered voluntary. Transport Canada can only order automakers to notify owners that their vehicles may be unsafe; it can't force them to correct the problem. Fortunately, most U.S.-ordered recalls are carried out in Canada, and when Transport Canada makes a defect determination on its own, automakers generally comply with an owner notification letter and a recall campaign.

Voluntary recall campaigns—frequently called "Special Service" or "Safety Improvement" campaigns—are a real problem. The government does not monitor the notification of owners; dealers and automakers routinely deny there's a recall, thereby dissuading most claimants; and the company's so-called fix, not authorized by any governing body, may not correct the hazard at all. Also, the voluntary recall may leave out many of the affected models or unreasonably exclude certain owners.

Wherever you live or drive, don't expect to be welcomed with open arms when your vehicle develops a safety- or emissions-related problem that's not yet part of a recall campaign. Automakers and dealers generally take a restrictive view of what constitutes a safety or emissions defect, and they frequently charge for repairs that should be free under federal safety or emissions legislation. To counter this tendency, look at the following list of typical defects that are clearly safety-related. If you experience similar problems to these, insist that the automaker fix them at no expense to yourself, including paying for a car rental:

- Airbag malfunctions
- Corrosion affecting the safe operation of the vehicle
- Disconnected or stuck accelerators
- Electrical shorts
- Faulty windshield wipers
- Fuel leaks
- Problems with original axles, driveshafts, seats, seat recliners, or defrosters
- Seat belt problems
- Stalling, or sudden acceleration
- Sudden steering or brake loss
- Suspension failures
- Trailer coupling failures

Regional recalls

Don't let any dealer refuse you recall repairs because of where you live. In order to cut recall costs, many automakers try to limit a recall to vehicles in a certain designated region. This practice doesn't make sense, since cars are mobile and an unsafe, rust-cankered steering unit can be found anywhere—not just in certain rust-belt provinces or American states.

In 2001, Ford attempted to limit its recall of faulty Firestone tires to five American states. Public ridicule of the company's proposal led to an extension of the recall throughout North America.

In July 2004, Ford announced a regional recall to install protective spring shields on almost one million 1999, 2000, and 2001 model-year Taurus and Sable sedans to correct defective front springs that can break and puncture a tire. As it did for Windstars and Aerostars recalled earlier for the same problem, Ford said it would send recall letters only to owners whose vehicles were registered in high-corrosion areas or where salt is used on roads. That limited recall was never challenged.

"Recall fatigue"

Safety experts agree that the sheer number of auto recalls has resulted in "recall fatigue," where affected owners ignore urgent calls to get corrective repairs. The increasing number of recalls (for example, recalls for Toyota's sudden acceleration problem, brake failures, and rust damaged suspension/steering systems) makes drivers immune to the message, leading them to believe that nothing bad will happen to them. However, if an item is relatively expensive or the perceived threat is immediate, consumers are more likely to seek recall assistance.

Car owners are particularly responsive. In one 2009 study carried out by the NHTSA, 73 percent of recalled autos and 45 percent of child car seats were taken in for recall corrections. Nevertheless, of the 10 million Toyotas recalled during 2010, barely half have been brought in and repaired.

 ### Safety Defect Information

If you wish to report a safety defect or want recall info, you may access Transport Canada's website at *www.tc.gc.ca/roadsafety/safevehicles/defectinvestigations/index.htm*. You can get recall information in French or English, as well as general information relating to road safety and importing a vehicle into Canada. Web surfers can now access the recall database for 1970 to current model-year vehicles, but unlike NHTSA's website, owner complaints aren't listed, defect investigations aren't disclosed, voluntary warranty extensions (secret warranties) aren't shown, and service bulletin summaries aren't provided. You can also call Transport Canada at 1-800-333-0510 to get additional information.

If you're not happy with Ottawa's treatment of your recall inquiry, try NHTSA's website at *www.safercar.gov*. It's more complete than Transport Canada's—NHTSA's database is updated daily and covers vehicles built since the '50s. You'll get immediate access to four essential database categories applicable to your vehicle and model year: the latest recalls, current and closed safety investigations, defects reported by other owners, and a brief summary of TSBs.

Four Steps to a Refund

Step 1: Informal Negotiations

Most vehicle owners won't take the steps outlined in the previous sections; instead, they'll try to settle things informally with a phone call. This tactic rarely works. Customer service agents (who recite policies but don't make them) will tell you the vehicle's warranty doesn't apply. This brush-off usually convinces 90 percent of complainers to drop their claims after some angry venting.

Nevertheless, don't take no for an answer. Contact someone higher up who has the authority to bend policies to satisfy your request. Speak in a calm, polite manner, and try not to polarize the issue. Talk about cooperating to solve the problem. Let a compromise emerge—don't come in with a hardline set of demands.

An independent estimate of the vehicle's defects and the cost of repairing them is essential if you want to convince the dealer that you're serious in your claim and that you stand a good chance of winning your case in court. Come prepared to use your estimate to challenge the dealer who agrees to pay half the repair costs and then tries to jack up the price 100 percent so that you wind up paying the whole shot.

Don't insist on getting the settlement offer in writing, but make sure that you're accompanied by a friend or relative who can confirm the offer in court if it isn't honoured. Be prepared to act upon the offer without delay so that if the dealer or automaker withdraws it, they won't be able to blame your hesitancy.

Dealer and service manager help

Service managers have more power than you may realize. They make the first determination of what work is covered under warranty or through post-warranty "goodwill" programs, and they're directly responsible to the dealer and manufacturer for their decisions. (Dealers hate manufacturer audits that force them to pay back questionable warranty decisions.) Service managers are paid to save the dealer and automaker money while mollifying irate clients—an almost impossible balancing act. Nevertheless, when a service manager agrees to extend warranty coverage, it's because you've raised solid issues that neither the dealer nor the automaker can ignore. All the more reason to present your argument in a confident, forthright manner with your vehicle's service history and *Lemon-Aid*'s "Reasonable Part Durability" chart (see page 122) on hand.

Also bring as many technical service bulletins and owner complaint printouts as you can find from websites like NHTSA's. It's not important that they apply directly to your problem; they establish parameters for giving out after-warranty assistance, or "goodwill." Don't use your salesperson as a runner, because the sales staff are generally quite distant from the service staff and usually have less pull than you do.

If the service manager can't or won't set things right, your next step is to convene a mini-summit with the service manager, the dealer principal, and the automaker's rep. By getting the automaker involved, you run less risk of having the dealer fob you off on the manufacturer, and you can often get an agreement where the dealer and automaker pay two-thirds of the repair costs.

Step 2: Send a Registered Letter, Fax, or Email

Don't worry; no one feels comfortable writing a complaint. But if you haven't sent a written claim letter, fax, or email, you haven't really complained—or at least that's the auto industry's mindset. Send the dealer and manufacturer a polite registered letter or fax that asks for compensation for repairs that have been done or need to be done, insurance costs during the vehicle's repair, towing charges, supplementary transportation costs like taxis and rented cars, and damages for your inconvenience (see the following sample complaint letter).

NEW-VEHICLE COMPLAINT LETTER/FAX/EMAIL

WITHOUT PREJUDICE

Date: _____

Name and address of dealer: _____

Name and address of manufacturer: _____

Please be advised that I am not satisfied with my _____ (indicate year, make, model, and serial number of vehicle). The vehicle was purchased on (indicate date) and currently indicates _____ km on the odometer. The vehicle presently exhibits the following defects:

    1. Premature rusting   3. Water leaks

    2. Paint peeling/discoloration   4. Other defects (explain)

(List previous attempts to repair the vehicle. Attach a copy of a report from an independent garage, showing cost of estimated repairs and confirming the manufacturer's responsibility.)

I hereby request that you correct these defects free of charge under the terms of the implied warranty provisions of provincial consumer protection statutes as applied in *Kravitz v. General Motors* (1979), I.S.C.R., and *Chabot v. Ford* (1983), 39 O.R. (2d).

If you do not correct the defects noted above to my satisfaction and within a reasonable length of time, I will be obliged to ask an independent garage to _____ (choose [a] estimate or [b] carry out) the repairs and claim the amount of $_____ (state the cost, if possible) by way of the courts without further notice or delay.

I have dealt with your company because of its competence and honesty. I close in the hope of hearing from you within five (5) days of receiving this letter, failing which I will exercise the alternatives available to me. Please govern yourself accordingly.

Sincerely,

(signed with telephone or fax number)

Specify five days (but allow 10 days) for either party to respond. If no satisfactory offer is made or your claim is ignored, file suit in small claims court. Make the manufacturer a party to the lawsuit, especially if an emissions warranty, a secret warranty extension, a safety recall campaign, or extensive chassis rusting is involved.

Step 3: Get the Government Involved

In this post-bankruptcy era, the federal government partially owns General Motors and Chrysler. That's why it's a good idea to send your local MP and the federal Minister of Industry a copy of your complaint. After all, the feds have given $185.3 million to automakers for warranty claims. It's in the government's interest to know if those claims are being paid. Plus, it won't hurt to have a discreet inquiry sent to the manufacturer by your MP or by someone in the Minister's office.

Step 4: Mediation and Arbitration

If the formality of a courtroom puts you off, or you're not sure that your claim is all that solid and don't want to pay the legal costs to find out, consider using mediation or arbitration offered by these groups: the Better Business Bureau (BBB), the Automobile Protection Association (APA), the Canadian Automobile Association (CAA), small claims court (mediation is often a prerequisite to going to trial), provincial and territorial government-run consumer mediation services, and the Canadian Motor Vehicle Arbitration Plan (CAMVAP):

> I just won my case with Chrysler Canada over my 2003 Ram SLT 44 quad cab truck. I've been having PCV valves freezing up (5 PCVs in 9,000 km). After one month in the shop, I went to CAMVAP to put in my claim, went to arbitration, and won. They have agreed to buy back my truck.

CAMVAP (1-800-207-0685; *www.camvap.ca*) is the best-known and most-efficient organization offering free arbitration. Decisions are usually reached within a few months. Awards are no longer confidential (thanks to pressure exerted by the Quebec government), and the stipulation that no appeals are allowed doesn't seem enforceable, as CAMVAP says on its own website:

> If you believe that the award or result of your hearing was improper because the arbitrator erred in law or erred in his or her assessment of the facts, then you may want to consider an appeal to the courts.

Getting Outside Help

Don't let poor preparation scuttle your case. Ask government or independent consumer protection agencies to evaluate how well prepared you are before going to your first hearing. Also, use the Internet and media sources to ferret out additional facts and to gather support (*www.lemonaidcars.com* is a good place to start).

Auto Industry Groups

Ontario consumers may file an online complaint with the Ontario Motor Vehicle Industry Council (OMVIC) at *www.omvic.on.ca/services/consumers/file_complaint_info.htm*. Sure, OMVIC is the dealer's self-defence lobby—made up of around

9,000 registered dealers and 20,000 registered salespeople—but it has the following mandate:

> [T]o maintain a fair, safe and informed marketplace in Ontario by protecting the rights of consumers, enhancing industry professionalism and ensuring fair, honest and open competition for registered motor vehicle dealers.

The way your complaint is handled will test the veracity of the above-stated goals.

Alberta has a similar self-regulating auto industry group, the Alberta Motor Vehicle Industry Council (AMVIC) (*www.amvic.org*). During 2004, 873 consumer files were opened with AMVIC and 844 were closed. Their investigators laid 403 charges under the *Fair Trading Act* and the Canadian *Criminal Code*. Court fines of $13,400 were levied under the *Fair Trading Act,* and the courts ordered $289,281 in restitution payments. Also, AMVIC obtained $1,687,180 by mediation in restitution for victims of unfair trade practices.

Classified Ads and Television Exposés

Put an ad in the local paper describing your plight, and ask for information from people who may have experienced a problem similar to your own. This approach alerts others to the potential problem, helps build a base for a class action or a group meeting with the automaker, and puts pressure on the local dealer and manufacturer to settle with you. Sometimes the paper's news desk will assign someone to cover your story after your ad is published, or you may gain attention by setting up a website.

Television producers and their researchers need articulate consumers with issues that are easily filmed and understood. If you want media coverage, you must summarize your complaint and have visual aids that will hold the viewer's interest (viewers should be able to understand the issues with the sound turned off). Paint delamination? Show your peeling car. Bought a "lemon" vehicle? Show your repair bills. Holding a demonstration? Make it a "lemon" parade: Target one of the largest dealers, give your group a nifty name, and then drive past the dealership in vehicles decorated with "lemon" signs.

Federal and Provincial Consumer Affairs

The wind left the sails of the consumer movement over two decades ago, leaving consumer agencies understaffed and unsupported by the government. Federal consumer protection is a government-created PR myth. Although the beefed-up *Competition Act* has some bite in regard to misleading advertising and a number of other illegal business practices, the government has been more reactive than proactive in applying the law. The *Act* also had some teeth pulled by an amendment that forces the government to prove in civil court that not only did price fixing occur, but that it also was successful in influencing prices. There is now a passive mindset among many pro-consumer government staffers throughout Canada who are tired of getting their heads kicked in by businesses, deadwood bosses, and budget cutters.

Nevertheless, you can lodge a formal complaint with the Competition Bureau if you encounter misleading advertising, odometer tampering, or price fixing. Use the online Enquiry/Complaint Form found at *www.competitionbureau.gc.ca*. Five years ago, an online complaint sent by *Lemon-Aid* made Toyota cease its Access price-fixing practices and pay out almost $2 million as a settlement fee. On the other hand, Ottawa just rejected *Lemon-Aid's* petition that Honda was fixing prices by warning dealers not to transact business with auto brokers. The threat to dealers was proven, but the proof that prices went up could not be made. Who could prove that? Interestingly, the recession has cured the problem. Hungry dealers will take business from any third party.

Consumer affairs offices can still help with investigation, mediation, and some litigation. Strong and effective consumer protection legislation has been left standing in most of the provinces, and resourceful consumers can use these laws in conjunction with media coverage to prod provincial consumer affairs offices into action. Furthermore, provincial bureaucrats aren't as well shielded from criticism as their federal counterparts. A call to your MPP or MLA, or to their executive assistants, can often get things rolling.

Invest in Protest

You can have fun and put additional pressure on a seller or garage by putting a "lemon" sign on your car and parking it in front of the dealer or garage, by creating a "lemon" website, or by forming a self-help group like the Chrysler Lemon Owners Group (CLOG) or the Ford Lemon Owners Group (FLOG). After forming your group, you can have the occasional parade of creatively decorated cars visit area dealerships as the local media are convened. Just remember to keep your remarks pithy and factual, don't interfere with traffic or customers, and remain peaceful.

One other piece of advice from this consumer advocate with more than 40 years of experience and hundreds of pickets and mass demonstrations under his belt: Keep a sense of humour, and never break off negotiations.

Finally, don't be scared off by threats that it's illegal to criticize a product or company. Unions, environmentalists, and consumer groups do it regularly (it's called "informational picketing"), and the Supreme Court of Canada in *R. v. Guinard* reaffirmed this right in February 2002. In that judgment, an insurance policyholder posted a sign on his barn claiming the Commerce Insurance Company was unfairly refusing his claim. The municipality of St-Hyacinthe, Quebec, told him to take the sign down. He refused, maintaining that he had the right to state his opinion. The Supreme Court agreed. This judgment means that consumer protests, signs, and websites that criticize the actions of corporations cannot be banned simply because they say unpleasant things.

Defamation and libel

Picketing a new car dealer or automobile manufacturer, having a "sit-in" at the local auto show, or placing an ad rounding up other "lemon" owners are all legitimate public-interest complaint tactics that get results—and lawsuits. However, the legal intimidation hanging over these actions is now a past threat thanks to recent ruling of our Supreme Court.

On December 2009, the Canadian Supreme Court rendered two judgments that make it much harder for plaintiffs to win cases alleging defamation or libel. The first decision overturned a lower court award of $1.5 million to a forestry executive who sued the *Toronto Star*. The *Star* alleged that he had used political connections to get approval for a golf course expansion (see *Grant v. Torstar Corp.*).

The Supreme Court struck down the judgment against the newspaper because it had failed to give adequate weight to the value of freedom of expression. The court announced a new defense of "responsible communication on matters of public interest." In the court's opinion, anyone (journalists, bloggers, unions, picketers, etc.) can avoid liability if they can show that the information they communicated—whether true or false—was of public interest and they tried their best to verify it.

In another case, also involving a major Canadian newspaper, a former Ontario police officer sued the *Ottawa Citizen* after it reported that he had misrepresented his search-and-rescue work at ground zero in New York City after the attacks of September 11, 2001. The Supreme Court reversed the $100,000 jury award because the judges felt the article was in the public interest (see *Quan v. Cusson*).

Typical Refund Scenarios

Sudden Acceleration, Chronic Stalling, and ABS and Airbag Failures

These kinds of failures are not that difficult to win in Canada under the doctrine of *res ipsa loquitur* ("the thing speaks for itself"), meaning, in negligence cases, that liability is shown by the failure itself. In a nutshell, the exact cause doesn't have to be pinpointed, and judges are free to award damages by weighing the "balance of probabilities" as to fault.

This advantage found in Canadian law was laid out succinctly in the July 1, 1998 issue of the *Journal of Small business Management* in its comparison of product liability laws on both sides of the border ("Effects of Product Liability Laws on Small Business" at *www.allbusiness.com/legal/laws-government-regulations/691847-1. html*):

> Although in theory the Canadian consumer must prove all of the elements of negligence (*Farro v. Nutone Electrical Ltd. 1990*; Ontario Law Reform Commission 1979; Thomas 1989), most Canadian courts allow injured consumers to use a procedural

aid known as *res ipsa loquitur* to prove their cases (*Nicholson v. John Deere Ltd. 1986*; *McMorran v. Dom. Stores Ltd. 1977*). Under *res ipsa loquitur*, plaintiffs must only prove that they were injured in a way that would not ordinarily occur without the defendant's negligence. It is then the responsibility of the defendant to prove that he was not negligent. As proving the negative is extremely difficult, this Canadian reversal of the burden of proof usually results in an outcome functionally equivalent to strict product liability (*Phillips v. Ford Motor Co. of Canada Ltd. 1971*; Murray 1988). This concept is reinforced by the principal that a Canadian manufacturer does not have the right to manufacture an inherently dangerous product when a method exists to manufacture that product without risk of harm. To do so subjects the manufacturer to liability even if the safer method is more expensive (*Nicholson v. John Deere Ltd. 1986*).

In *Jarvis v. Ford* (United States Second Circuit Court of Appeal, February 7, 2002), a judgment was rendered in favour of a driver who was injured when her six-day-old Ford Aerostar minivan suddenly accelerated as it was started and put into gear. What makes this decision unique is that the jury had no specific proof of a defect. The Court of Appeal agreed with the jury award, and Justice Sotomayor (now a Supreme Court Justice) gave these reasons for the Court's verdict:

...a product may be found to be defective without proof of the specific malfunction:

It may be inferred that the harm sustained by the plaintiff was caused by a product defect existing at the time of sale or distribution, without proof of a specific defect, when the incident that harmed the plaintiff:

(a) was of a kind that ordinarily occurs as a result of product defect; and

(b) was not, in the particular case, solely the result of causes other than product defect existing at the time of sale or distribution.

Restatement (Third) of Torts: Product Liability § 3 (1998). In comment c to this section, the Restatement notes:

[There is] no requirement that plaintiff prove what aspect of the product was defective. The inference of defect may be drawn under this Section without proof of the specific defect. Furthermore, quite apart from the question of what type of defect was involved, the plaintiff need not explain specifically what constituent part of the product failed. For example, if an inference of defect can be appropriately drawn in connection with the catastrophic failure of an airplane, the plaintiff need not establish whether the failure is attributable to fuel-tank explosion or engine malfunction...

The jury awarded Ms. Jarvis $24,568 in past medical insurance premiums, $340,338 in lost earnings, and $200,000 in pain and suffering. For future damages, the jury awarded $22,955 in medical insurance premiums, $648,944 in lost earnings, and $300,000 for pain and suffering.

Incidents of sudden acceleration or chronic stalling are quite common. However, they are often very difficult to diagnose, and individual cases can be treated very differently by federal safety agencies. Nevertheless, getting corroborative proof may be far easier in the future, now that the U.S. Department of Transportation under NHTSA will require that automakers install "black box" accident data recorders in all vehicles and give out their access codes to accident investigators. In fact, a number of impaired drivers have already been sent to jail in Canada based on black-box-accessed data.

Sudden acceleration is considered to be a safety-related problem—stalling, only sometimes. Never mind that a vehicle's sudden loss of power on a busy highway puts everyone's lives at risk. The same problem exists with engine and transmission powertrain failures, which are only occasionally considered to be safety-related. ABS and airbag failures, however, are universally considered to be life-threatening defects. If your vehicle manifests any of these conditions, here's what you need to do:

1. Get independent witnesses to confirm that the problem exists. Your primary tools include an independent mechanic's verification, passenger accounts, downloaded data from your vehicle's data recorder, and lots of Internet browsing using *www.lemonaidcars.com* and Google's search engine. Notify the dealer or manufacturer by fax, email, or registered letter that you consider the problem to be a factory-induced, safety-related defect. Make sure you address your correspondence to the manufacturer's product liability or legal affairs department. At the dealership's service bay, make sure that every work order clearly states the problem as well as the number of previous attempts to fix it. (You should end up with a few complaint letters and a handful of work orders confirming that this is an ongoing deficiency.) If the dealer won't give you a copy of the work order because the work is a warranty claim, ask for a copy of the order number "in case your estate wishes to file a claim, pursuant to an accident." (This wording will get the service manager's attention.) Leaving a paper trail is crucial for any claim you may have later on, because it shows your concern and persistence, and it clearly indicates that the dealer and manufacturer have had ample time to correct the defect.

2. Note on the work order that you expect the problem to be diagnosed and corrected under the emissions warranty or a "goodwill" program. It also wouldn't hurt to add the phrase on the work order or in your claim letters that "any deaths, injuries, or damage caused by the defect will be the dealer's and manufacturer's responsibility" because the work order (or letter, fax, or email) constitutes you putting them on "formal notice."

3. If the dealer does the necessary repairs at little or no cost to you, send a follow-up confirmation that you appreciate the "goodwill." Also, emphasize that you'll be back if the problem reappears—even if the warranty has expired—because the repair renews your warranty rights applicable to that defect. In other words, the warranty clock is set back to its original position. Understand that you won't likely get a copy of the repair bill, either, because dealers don't like to admit that there was a serious defect present and don't

feel that they owe you a copy of the work order if the repair was done *gratis*. You can, however, subpoena the complete vehicle file from the dealer and manufacturer (this costs about $50) if the case goes to small claims or a higher court. This request has produced many out-of-court settlements when the internal documents show extensive work was carried out to correct the problem.

4. If the problem persists, send a letter, fax, or email to the dealer and manufacturer saying so, look for ALLDATA service bulletins to confirm that your vehicle's defects are factory-related, and report the failure by contacting Transport Canada or NHTSA or by logging on to NHTSA's website. Also, you may want to involve the non-profit, Montreal-based Automobile Protection Association or the Nader-founded Center for Auto Safety in Washington, D.C. (*www.autosafety.org/auto-defects*) to get a lawyer referral and an information sheet covering the problem.

5. Now come two crucial questions: Repair the defect now or later? Use the dealer or an independent? Generally, it's smart to use an independent garage if you know the dealer isn't pushing for free corrective repairs from the manufacturer, if weeks or months have passed without any resolution of your claim, if the dealer keeps repeating that it's a maintenance item, and if you know an independent mechanic who will give you a detailed work order showing the defect is factory-related and not caused by poor maintenance. Don't mention that a court case may ensue, since this will scare the dickens out of your only independent witness. An added bonus is that the repair charges will be about half of what a dealer would demand. Incidentally, if the automaker later denies warranty "goodwill" because you used an independent repairer, use the argument that the defect's safety implications required emergency repairs, carried out by whoever could see you first.

6. Dashboard-mounted warning lights usually come on prior to airbags suddenly deploying, ABS brakes failing, or engine glitches causing the vehicle to stall out. (Sudden acceleration usually occurs without warning.) Automakers consider these lights to be critical safety warnings and generally advise drivers to immediately have their vehicle serviced to correct the problem when any of the warning lights come on (advice that can be found in the owner's manual). This fact bolsters the argument that your life was threatened, emergency repairs were required, and your request for another vehicle or a complete refund isn't out of line.

7. Sudden acceleration can have multiple causes, isn't easy to duplicate, and is often blamed on the driver mistaking the accelerator for the brakes or failing to perform proper maintenance. Yet NHTSA data shows that with the 1992–2000 Explorer, for example, a faulty cruise-control or PCV valve and poorly mounted pedals are the most likely causes of the Explorer's sudden acceleration. So how do you satisfy the burden of proof showing that the problem exists and it's the automaker's responsibility? Use the legal doctrine called "the balance of probabilities" by eliminating all of the possible dodges the dealer or manufacturer may employ. Show that proper maintenance has been carried out, you're a safe driver, and the incident occurs frequently and without warning.

8. If any of the above defects causes an accident, or if the airbag fails to deploy or you're injured by its deployment, ask your insurance company to have the vehicle towed to a neutral location and clearly state that neither the dealer nor the automaker should touch the vehicle until your insurance company and Transport Canada have completed their investigation. Also, get as many witnesses as possible and immediately go to the hospital for a check-up, even if you're feeling okay. You may be injured and not know it because the adrenalin coursing through your veins is masking your injuries. A hospital exam will easily confirm that your injuries are accident-related, which is essential evidence for court or for future settlement negotiations.

9. Peruse NHTSA's online accident and service bulletin database to find reports of other accidents caused by the same failure, bulletins that indicate part upgrades, current defect investigations, and reported failures that have resulted in recalls or closed investigations.

10. Don't let your insurance company bully you. Refuse to let them settle the case if you're sure the accident was caused by a mechanical failure. Even if an engineering analysis fails to directly implicate the manufacturer or dealer, you can always plead the aforementioned balance of probabilities. If the insurance company settles, your insurance premiums will soar and the manufacturer will get away with the perfect crime.

Toyota's "Throttle-Gate"

When you mess up, you should 'fess up—and in spite of all of Toyota's public apologies, the company still doesn't get it. As the internal Toyota service bulletin below clearly shows, the company knew in 2002 that its best-selling Camry model had an electronic glitch that made the 2002 and 2003 models suddenly accelerate.

TOYOTA ENGINE CONTROLS—LIGHT THROTTLE SURGING CONDITION

BULLETIN NO.: EG008-03   DATE: MAY 16, 2003

ECM CALIBRATION UPDATE: 1MZ-FE ENGINE SURGING
MODELS: 2003 Camry
INTRODUCTION: Some 2003 model year Camry vehicles equipped with the 1MZ-FE engine may exhibit a surging during light throttle input at speeds between 38–42 mph [61–68 km/h] with lock-up (LU) "ON."
THE ENGINE CONTROL MODULE: Powertrain Control Module/PCM calibration has been revised to correct this condition.
APPLICABLE VEHICLES: 2002 and 2003 model year Camry vehicles.

Neither Toyota CEO Akido Toyoda nor Toyota Canada Managing Director Stephen Beatty will confirm the authenticity of this bulletin and put an end to Toyota's deception.

In spite of all the bad publicity, Toyota still has almost $20 billion in cash reserves after allocating about $10 billion for the sudden acceleration, Prius brake failure, and small pickup corrosion recalls and investigations. Toyota, who covered up its knowledge of accidents and deaths linked to their vehicles' suddenly accelerating out of control, is now paying for its deception thanks to massive fines, a half-dozen ongoing government criminal and civil probes, and the filing of over three hundred lawsuits, many of which seek class action status for hundreds of thousands of plaintiffs.

Market forces are now wreaking havoc with Toyota's perceived quality. A U.S. *Consumer Reports* survey states that Toyota's brand loyalty rating has dropped by 13 per cent, knocking it from the top spot it held at the end of 2009.

Honda is in first place now, with 68 per cent of Honda owners described as "likely to purchase another Honda for their next new car." Second is Ford at 61 percent, followed by Toyota at 57 per cent. Toyota isn't doing poorly worldwide, however. It still made $1.2 billion in the first three months of 2010.

Although the Japanese automaker is giving out generous, never-before-seen purchase incentives to new-car buyers, Canadian shoppers aren't that impressed. For the first quarter of 2010, Toyota and Lexus dropped by 16.7 percent, far behind first-place Ford. Overall car sales in Canada improved by 4 percent.

"Lag and Lurch"

Toyota's sudden acceleration problems have been joined by another safety defect that delays acceleration from a stop and then suddenly shoots the car forward as the electronic sensors finally pick up the throttle command. This results in near rear-enders as the car appears to stall and then darts forward. Toyota has known about this "lag and lurch" safety hazard for well over a decade, and apparently it afflicts almost its entire fleet of vehicles.

Yaris Brake Failures

Affecting 2007 and 2008 entry-level Yaris models, this defect can lead to ABS brake failures (see page 84). Again, Toyota has known about the problem for years, yet it remains close-mouthed about whether the company will replace the brake sensors and correct the rusted-out electrical connections, or continue to make owners pay exorbitant fees to fix what is essentially Toyota's mistake.

Denial, Deception, and Deflection

At Congressional hearings last February, Toyota denied early knowledge of the sudden unintended acceleration problem affecting most of their lineup and rejected allegations that the defect was electronic, preferring to limit the problem to "creeping" floor mats and "sticky" accelerators.

They are denying these allegations to save their skins and their money. If any official admits to prior knowledge of the defect or electronic causes, they could be personally charged with criminal negligence and forced to recall their vehicles for a third "fix."

Nevertheless, some good has come from the decade-long fight to make Toyota accept responsibility for its negligence. For example:

- The U.S. government has proposed legislation to make all automakers recall suspect vehicles as soon as they are aware of a safety-related defect. A brake override system and black box recorders also have to be phased in next year on all vehicles, with the black box access codes shared. American automakers allow car owners to access the data to prove vehicle malfunctions; Toyota didn't up to now. Toyota had only one recorder reader in service in the States. Ottawa is likely to piggy-back similar legislation for Canadian car owners.
- The maximum NHTSA fine of $16.4 million dollars has been levied against Toyota because of its failure to promptly recall vehicles that could suddenly accelerate.
- Toyota/Lexus agreed to install brake override devices in all future vehicles.
- Transport Canada continues its investigation of Toyota's conduct and is collecting consumer and engineering input

What caused Toyota to backslide? Greed and arrogance, says its former North American president and top executive, Jim Press. Press, a top Toyota executive for 36 years and the only American member of the company's 30-member Board of Directors, told the *Detroit News* on February 24, 2010, that "the company was hijacked, some years ago, by anti-family, financially oriented pirates."

Buttressing Press's allegations, in the late '90s, Toyota owner complaints began to show more powertrain, fuel-delivery, brake, and suspension deficiencies than ever before. Toyota insiders told *Lemon-Aid* that Toyota's non-family executives wanted to quickly boost market share and profit, even if it meant quality and safety would suffer. The family tradition of quality, etc., was sidelined while family members took a backseat in the overall administration. This was confirmed by many Toyota documents subpoenaed by the U. S. Congress in early 2010.

Defective Tires

Tire companies are far easier to deal with than automobile manufacturers because, under the legal doctrine of *res ipsa loquitur*, tires aren't supposed to fail. When they do, smart claimants can use the *Robson v. General Motors B.C.* class action judgment to bring in the American corporation. You can also refer to the Supreme Court of Canada judgment *Winnipeg Condominium No. 36 v. Bird Construction Co. Ltd.* (1995; 1 S.C.R.85), which ruled that defendants are liable in negligence for any designs that result in a public safety or health risk. This decision reversed a long-standing policy and provided the public with a new cause of action that had not existed before in Canada.

No wonder tire and auto companies routinely avoid liability by imputing blame to someone or something else, like punctures, impact damage, overloading, over-inflating, or under-inflating.

If you have a tire failure that conceivably puts your life in peril, consider the 10 steps outlined previously in the "Sudden Acceleration, Chronic Stalling, and ABS and Airbag Failures" section, and add the following:

1. Access NHTSA on the Internet (see Appendix III) for current data about which tires are failure-prone and which companies are under investigation, conducting recalls, or carrying out "silent" recalls.
2. Keep the tire. If the tiremaker says an analysis must be done, permit only a portion of the tire to be taken away.
3. Plead the balance of probabilities, using friends and family to refute the tire company's contention that you caused the failure.
4. Ask for damages that are adequate to replace all the tires on your vehicle, including mounting costs.
5. Include in your damage claim any repairs needed to fix the body damage caused by the tire's failure.

Paint and Body Defects

The following settlement advice applies mainly to paint defects, but you can use these tips for any other vehicle defect that you believe is the automaker's or dealer's responsibility. If you aren't sure whether the problem is a factory-related deficiency or a maintenance fault, have it checked out by an independent garage or get a technical service bulletin summary for your vehicle. The summary may include specific bulletins relating to diagnosis and correction as well as information about ordering the upgraded parts needed to fix your problem.

Four good examples of favourable paint judgments are *Shields v. General Motors of Canada*, *Bentley v. Dave Wheaton Pontiac Buick GMC Ltd. and General Motors of Canada*, *Maureen Frank v. General Motors of Canada Limited*, and the most recent, *Dunlop v. Ford of Canada*.

In *Dunlop v. Ford of Canada* (No. 58475/04; Ontario Superior Court of Justice, Richmond Hill Small Claims Court; January 5, 2005; Deputy Judge M.J. Winer), the owner of a 1996 Lincoln Town Car that was purchased used in 1999 for $27,000 was awarded $4,091.64. Judge Winer cited the *Shields* decision (following) and gave these reasons for finding Ford of Canada liable:

> Evidence was given by the Plaintiff's witness, Terry Bonar, an experienced paint auto technician. He gave evidence that the [paint] delamination may be both a manufacturing defect and can be caused or [sped] up by atmospheric conditions. He also says that [the paint on] a car like this should last ten to 15 years, [or even for] the life of the vehicle.

It is my view that the presence of ultraviolet light is an environmental condition to which the vehicle is subject. If it cannot withstand this environmental condition, it is defective.

In *Shields v. General Motors of Canada* (No. 1398/96; Ontario Court, General Division, Oshawa Small Claims Court; July 24, 1997; Robert Zochodne, Deputy Judge), the owner of a 1991 Pontiac Grand Prix had purchased the vehicle used with over 100,000 km on its odometer. Beginning in 1995, the paint began to bubble and flake, and it eventually peeled off. Deputy Judge Zochodne awarded the plaintiff $1,205.72 and struck down every one of GM's arguments that the peeling paint was caused by acid rain, UV rays, or some other environmental factor. Here are some other important aspects of this 12-page judgment that GM didn't appeal:

1. The judge admitted many of the technical service bulletins referred to in *Lemon-Aid* as proof of GM's negligence.
2. Although the vehicle had 156,000 km on its odometer when the case went to court, GM still offered to pay 50 percent of the paint repairs if the plaintiff dropped his suit.
3. The judge ruled that the failure to protect the paint from the damaging effects of UV rays is akin to engineering a car that won't start in cold weather. In essence, vehicles must be built to withstand the rigours of the environment.
4. Here's an interesting twist: The original warranty covered defects that were present at the time it was in effect. The judge, taking statements found in the GM technical service bulletins, ruled that the UV problem was factory-related, existed during the warranty period, and, therefore, represented a latent defect that appeared once the warranty expired.
5. The subsequent purchaser was not prevented from making the warranty claim, even though the warranty had long since expired, from both time and mileage standpoints, and he was the second owner.

The small claims judgment in *Bentley v. Dave Wheaton Pontiac Buick GMC Ltd. and General Motors of Canada* (Victoria Registry No. 24779; British Columbia Small Claims Court; December 1, 1998; Judge Higinbotham) builds upon Ontario's *Shields v. General Motors of Canada* decision and cites other jurisprudence as to how long paint should last on a car. If you're wondering why Ford and Chrysler haven't been hit by similar judgments, remember that they usually settle out of court.

From *Maureen Frank v. General Motors of Canada Limited* (No. SC#12 (2001); Saskatchewan Provincial Court, Saskatoon, Saskatchewan; October 17, 2001; Provincial Court Judge H.G. Dirauf):

On June 23, 1997, the Plaintiff bought a 1996 Chevrolet Corsica from a General Motors dealership. At the time, the odometer showed 33,172 km. The vehicle still had some factory warranty. The car had been a lease car and had no previous accidents.

During June of 2000, the Plaintiff noticed that some of the paint was peeling off from the car and she took it to a General Motors dealership in Saskatoon and to the General Motors dealership in North Battleford where she purchased the car. While there were some discussions with the GM dealership about the peeling paint, nothing came of it and the Plaintiff now brings this action claiming the cost of a new paint job.

During 1999, the Plaintiff was involved in a minor collision causing damage to the left rear door. This damage was repaired. During this repair some scratches to the left front door previously done by vandals were also repaired.

The Plaintiff's witness, Frank Nemeth, is a qualified auto body repairman with some 26 years of experience. He testified that the peeling paint was a factory defect and that it was necessary to completely strip the car and repaint it. He diagnosed the cause of the peeling paint as a separation of the primer surface or colour coat from the electrocoat primer. In his opinion no primer surfacer was applied at all. He testified that once the peeling starts, it will continue. He has seen this problem on General Motors vehicles. The defect is called delamination.

Mr. Nemeth stated that a paint job should last at least 10 years. In my opinion, most people in Saskatchewan grow up with cars and are familiar with cars. I think it is common knowledge that the original paint on cars normally lasts in excess of 15 years and that rust becomes a problem before the paint fails. In any event, paint peeling off, as it did on the Plaintiff's vehicle, is not common. I find that the paint on a new car put on by the factory should last at least 15 years.

It is clear from the evidence of Frank Nemeth (independent body shop manager) that the delamination is a factory defect. His evidence was not seriously challenged. I find that the factory paint should not suffer a delamination defect for at least 15 years and that this factory defect breached the warranty that the paint was of acceptable quality and was durable for a reasonable period of time.

There will be judgment for the Plaintiff in the amount of $3,412.38 plus costs of $81.29.

Some of the important aspects of the *Frank* judgment are as follows:

1. The judge accepted that the automaker was responsible, even though the car had been bought used. The subsequent purchaser wasn't prevented from making the warranty claim, even though the warranty had long since expired, from both time and mileage standpoints, and she was the second owner.
2. The judge stressed that the provincial warranty can kick in when the automaker's warranty has expired or isn't applied.
3. By awarding full compensation to the plaintiff, the judge didn't feel that there was a significant "betterment" or improvement added to the car that would warrant reducing the amount of the award.
4. The judge decided that the paint delamination was a factory defect.
5. The judge also concluded that without this factory defect, a paint job should

last up to 15 years.

6. GM offered to pay $700 of the paint repairs if the plaintiff dropped the suit; the judge awarded five times that amount.

7. Maureen Frank won this case despite having to confront GM lawyer Ken Ready, who had considerable experience arguing other paint cases for GM and Chrysler.

Other paint and rust cases

Martin v. Honda Canada Inc. (March 17, 1986; Ontario Small Claims Court, Scarborough; Judge Sigurdson): The original owner of a 1981 Honda Civic sought compensation for the premature "bubbling, pitting, [and] cracking of the paint and rusting of the Civic after five years of ownership." Judge Sigurdson agreed with the owner and ordered Honda to pay the owner $1,163.95.

Thauberger v. Simon Fraser Sales and Mazda Motors (3 B.C.L.R., 193): This Mazda owner sued for damages caused by the premature rusting of his 1977 Mazda GLC. The court awarded him $1,000. Thauberger had also previously sued General Motors for a prematurely rusted Blazer truck and was awarded $1,000 in the same court. Both judges ruled that the defects couldn't be excluded from the automaker's expressed warranty or from the implied warranty granted by British Columbia's *Sale of Goods Act*.

Whittaker v. Ford Motor Company (1979) (24 O.R. (2d), 344): A new Ford developed serious corrosion problems despite having been rustproofed by the dealer. The court ruled that the dealer, not Ford, was liable for the damage for having sold the rustproofing product at the time of purchase. This is an important judgment to use when a rustproofer or paint protector goes out of business or refuses to pay a claim, because the decision holds the dealer jointly responsible.

See also:

- *Danson v. Chateau Ford* (1976) C.P. (Quebec Small Claims Court; No. 32-00001898-757; Judge Lande)
- *Doyle v. Vital Automotive Systems* (May 16, 1977; Ontario Small Claims Court, Toronto; Judge Turner)
- *Lacroix v. Ford* (April 1980; Ontario Small Claims Court, Toronto; Judge Tierney)
- *Marinovich v. Riverside Chrysler* (April 1, 1987; District Court of Ontario; No. 1030/85; Judge Stortini)

Using the Courts

When to Sue?

If the dealer you've been negotiating with agrees to make things right, give him or her a deadline for completing the repairs and then have an independent garage check them over. If no offer is made within 10 working days, file suit in court. Make the manufacturer a party to the lawsuit only if the original, unexpired warranty is still in place; if your claim falls under the emissions warranty, a TSB, a secret warranty extension, or a safety recall campaign; or if there is extensive chassis rusting caused by poor engineering.

Which Court?

Most claims can be handled without a lawyer in small claims court, especially now that courts' jurisdictions vary from $5,000 to $25,000. Still, it's up to you to decide what remedy to pursue—that is, whether you want a partial refund or a cancellation of the sale. To determine the refund amount, add the estimated cost of repairing the existing mechanical defects to the cost of prior repairs. Don't exaggerate your losses or claim for repairs that are considered to be routine maintenance. A suit for the cancellation of a sale involves practical problems. The court requires that the vehicle be "tendered," or taken back, to the seller at the time the lawsuit is filed. This leaves you without transportation for as long as the case continues, unless you purchase another vehicle in the interim. If you lose the case, you must then take back the old vehicle and pay the accumulated storage fees. You could go from having no vehicle to having two—one of which is a clunker!

Generally, if the cost of repairs or the sales contract amount falls within the small claims court limit (discussed later), file the case there to keep your costs to a minimum and to get a speedy hearing. Small claims court judgments aren't easily appealed, lawyers aren't necessary, filing fees are minimal (about $125), and cases are usually heard within a few months. In fact, your suit is almost always best argued in the provincial small claims court to keep costs and frustrations down and to get a quick resolution within a few months.

> Mr. Edmonston, I emailed you earlier in the year seeking help on my small claims case against Ford. I'm happy to report that I won my case and received a $1,900 settlement cheque from Ford in the mail yesterday! As you may recall I have a 1991 Explorer that has a significant paint peel problem.
>
> MARK G.

Here's another reason not to be greedy: If you claim more than the small claims court limit, you'll have to go to a higher court—where costs quickly add up, lawyers routinely demand 30 percent of your winnings or settlement, and delays of a few years or more are commonplace.

Small Claims Courts

Crooked automakers scurry away from small claims courts like cockroaches from bug spray, not because the courts can issue million-dollar judgments or force litigants to spend millions in legal fees (they can't), but because dealers and manufacturers don't want the bad publicity arising from the filings and eventual judgments. Other disincentives are that small claims courts can award sizeable sums to plaintiffs not represented by lawyers, and they make jurisprudence that other judges on the same bench are likely to follow.

For example, in *Dawe v. Courtesy Chrysler* (Dartmouth Nova Scotia Small Claims Court; SCCH #206825; July 30, 2004), Judge Patrick L Casey, Q.C., rendered an impressive 21-page decision citing key automobile product liability cases from the past 80 years, including *Donoghue*, *Kravitz*, and *Davis*. The court awarded $5,037 to the owner of a new 2001 Cummins engine–equipped Ram pickup with the following problems: It wandered all over the road; lost power, or jerked and bucked; shifted erratically; lost braking ability; bottomed out when passing over bumps; allowed water to leak into the cab; produced a burnt-wire and oil smell in the interior as the lights would dim; and produced a rear-end whine and wind noise around the doors and under the dash. Dawe had sold the vehicle and reduced his claim to meet the small claims threshold. Anyone with engine, transmission, or suspension problems or water leaking into the interior will find this judgment particularly useful.

Interestingly, "small claims" court is quickly becoming a misnomer, now that Alberta, Nova Scotia, British Columbia, Yukon, and (as of January 1, 2010) Ontario allow claims of up to $25,000 and other provinces permit $5,000–$20,000 filings. See the following table, and check your provincial or territorial court's website for specific rules and restrictions.

SMALL CLAIMS COURT LIMITS

PROVINCE/TERRITORY	CLAIM LIMIT	COURT WEBSITE
Alberta	$25,000	www.albertacourts.ab.ca
British Columbia	$25,000	www.courts.gov.bc.ca
Manitoba	$10,000	www.manitobacourts.mb.ca
New Brunswick	$ 6,000	www.gnb.ca/cour
Newfoundland and Labrador	$ 5,000	www.court.nl.ca
Northwest Territories	$10,000	www.nwtcourts.ca
Nova Scotia	$25,000	www.courts.ns.ca
Nunavut	$20,000	www.nucj.ca
Ontario	$25,000	www.ontariocourts.on.ca
Prince Edward Island	$ 8,000	www.gov.pe.ca/courts
Quebec	$ 7,000	www.justice.gouv.qc.ca
Saskatchewan	$20,000	www.sasklawcourts.ca
Yukon	$25,000	www.yukoncourts.ca

There are small claims courts in most counties of every province, and you can make a claim in the county where the problem happened or where the defendant lives and conducts business. Simply go to the small claims court office and ask for a claim form. Remember, you must identify the defendant correctly, which may require some help from the court clerk (look for other recent lawsuits naming the same party). Crooks often change their company's name to escape liability; for example, it would be impossible to sue Joe's Garage (1999) if your contract is with Joe's Garage, Inc. (1984).

At this point, it wouldn't hurt to hire a lawyer or a paralegal for a brief walk-through of small claims procedures to ensure that you've prepared your case properly and that you know what objections will likely be raised by the other side. If, instead, you'd like a lawyer to do all the work for you, there are a number of law firms around the country that specialize in small claims litigation. "Small claims" doesn't mean "small legal fees," though. In Toronto, some law offices charge a flat fee of $1,000 for a basic small claims lawsuit and trial.

Remember that you're entitled to bring to court any evidence relevant to your case, including written documents such as a bill of sale or receipt, contract, or letter. If your car has developed severe rust problems, bring a photograph (signed and dated by the photographer) to court. You may also have witnesses testify in court. It's important to discuss a witness's testimony prior to the court date. If a witness can't attend the court date, he or she can write a report and sign it for representation in court. This situation usually applies to an expert witness, such as an independent mechanic who has evaluated your car's problems.

If you lose your case in spite of all your preparation and research, some small claims court statutes allow cases to be retried, at a nominal cost, in exceptional circumstances. If a new witness has come forward, additional evidence has been discovered, or key documents (that were previously not available) have become accessible, apply for a retrial.

Alan MacDonald, a *Lemon-Aid* reader who won his case in small claims court, gives the following tips on beating Ford over a faulty automatic transmission:

> I want to thank you for the advice you provided in my dealings with the Ford Motor Company of Canada Limited and Highbury Ford Sales Limited regarding my 1994 Ford Taurus wagon and the problems with the automatic transmission (Taurus and Windstar transmissions are identical). I also wish to apologize for not sending you a copy of this judgment earlier...(*MacDonald v. Highbury Ford Sales Limited,* Ontario Superior Court of Justice in the Small Claims Court London, June 6, 2000, Court File #0001/00, Judge J.D. Searle).
>
> In 1999, after only 105,000 km, the automatic transmission went. I took the car to Highbury Ford to have it repaired. We paid $2,070 to have the transmission fixed, but protested and felt the transmission failed prematurely. We contacted Ford, but to no avail: Their reply was we were out of warranty, period. The transmission was so poorly repaired (and we went back to Highbury Ford several times) that we had to go to Mr. Transmission to have the transmission fixed again nine months later at a further $1,906.02.

It is at that point that I contacted you, and I was surprised, and somewhat speechless (which you noticed) when you personally called me to provide advice and encouragement. I am very grateful for your call. My observations with going through small claims court involved the following: I filed in January of 2000, the trial took place on June 1 and the judgment was issued June 6.

At pretrial, a representative of Ford (Ann Sroda) and a representative from Highbury Ford were present. I came with one binder for each of the defendants, the court and one for myself (each binder was about 3 inches thick, containing your reports on Ford Taurus automatic transmissions, ALLDATA Service Bulletins, Taurus Transmissions Victims (Bradley website), Center for Auto Safety (website), Read This Before Buying a Taurus (website), and the Ford Vent Page (website)).

The representative from Ford asked a lot of questions (I think she was trying to find out if I had read the contents of the information I was relying on). The Ford representative then offered a 50 percent settlement based on the initial transmission work done at Highbury Ford. The release allowed me to still sue Highbury Ford with regards to the necessity of going to Mr. Transmission because of the faulty repair done by the dealer. Highbury Ford displayed no interest in settling the case, and so I had to go to court.

For court, I prepared by issuing a summons to the manager at Mr. Transmission, who did the second transmission repair, as an expert witness. I was advised that unless you produce an expert witness you won't win in a car repair case in small claims court. Next, I went to the law school library in London and received a great deal of assistance in researching cases pertinent to car repairs. I was told that judgments in your home province (in my case Ontario) were binding on the court; that cases outside of the home province could be considered, but not binding, by the judge.

The cases I used for trial involved *Pelleray v. Heritage Ford Sales Ltd.*, Ontario Small Claims Court (Scarborough) SC7688/91 March 22, 1993; *Phillips et al. v. Ford Motor Co. of Canada Ltd. et al*, Ontario Reports 1970, 15th January 1970; *Gregorio v. Intrans-Corp.*, Ontario Court of Appeal, May 19, 1994; *Collier v. McMaster's Auto Sales*, New Brunswick Court of Queen's Bench, April 26, 1991; *Sigurdson v. Hillcrest Service & Acklands (1977)*, Saskatchewan Queen's Bench; *White v. Sweetland*, Newfoundland District Court, Judicial Centre of Gander, November 8, 1978; *Raiches Steel Works v. J. Clark & Son*, New Brunswick Supreme Court, March 7, 1977; *Mudge v. Corner Brook Garage Ltd.*, Newfoundland Supreme Court, July 17, 1975; *Sylvain v. Carroseries d'Automobiles Guy Inc. (1981)*, C.P. 333, Judge Page; [and] *Gagnon v. Ford Motor Company of Canada, Limited et Marineau Automobile Co. Ltée. (1974)*, C.S. 422–423.

In court, I had prepared the case, as indicated above, [and] had my expert witness and two other witnesses who had driven the vehicle (my wife and my 18-year-old son). As you can see by the judgment, we won our case and I was awarded $1,756.52, including pre-judgment interest and costs.

Key Court Decisions

The following Canadian and U.S. lawsuits and judgments cover typical problems that are likely to arise. Use them as leverage when negotiating a settlement or as a reference should your claim go to trial. Legal principles applying to Canadian and American law are similar; however, Quebec court decisions may be based on legal principles that don't apply outside that province. You can find a comprehensive listing of Canadian decisions from small claims courts all the way to the Supreme Court of Canada at *www.canlii.org* (Canadian Legal Information Institute).

Additional court judgments can be found in the legal reference section of your city's main public library or at a nearby university law library. Ask the librarian for help in choosing the legal phrases that best describe your claim.

LexisNexis (*global.lexisnexis.com/ca*) and FindLaw (*www.findlaw.com*) are two useful Internet sites for legal research. Their main drawback, though, is that you may need to subscribe or use a lawyer's subscription to access jurisprudence and other areas of the sites. However, there *is* a free online summary of class actions filed in Canada at *classactionsincanada.blogspot.com*. It's run by Ward Branch, one of the legal counsels in the Canada-wide $1.2 billion class action settled several years ago by General Motors for defective engine intake manifold gaskets.

 An excellent reference book that will give you plenty of tips on filing, pleading, and collecting your judgment is Justice Marvin A. Zuker's *Ontario Small Claims Court Practice 2010* (Carswell, 2009). Judge Zuker's annual publication is easily understood by non-lawyers and uses court decisions from across Canada to help you plead your case successfully in almost any Canadian court.

Product Liability

Almost three decades ago, before *Robson*, the Supreme Court of Canada in *Kravitz v. GM* clearly affirmed that automakers and their dealers are jointly liable for the replacement or repair of a vehicle if independent testimony shows that it is afflicted with factory-related defects that compromise its safety or performance. The existence of secret warranty extensions or technical service bulletins also help prove that the vehicle's problems are the automaker's responsibility. For example, in *Lowe v. Fairview Chrysler* (see page 156), technical service bulletins were instrumental in showing in 1989 that Chrysler had a history of automatic transmission failures similar to what we see in Ford and GM vehicles today.

In addition to replacing or repairing the vehicle, an automaker can also be held responsible for any damages arising from the defect (see *Wharton*, page 112). This means that loss of wages, supplementary transportation costs, and damages for personal inconvenience can be awarded. However, in the States, product liability damage awards often exceed millions of dollars, while Canadian courts are far less generous.

When a warranty claim is rejected on the pretext that you "altered" the vehicle, failed to carry out preventive maintenance, or drove abusively, manufacturers *must* prove to the court that there's a link between their allegation and the failure (see *Julien v. General Motors of Canada Ltd.* (1991), 116 N.B.R. (2d) 80).

Before settling any claim with GM or any other automaker, read the latest information from dissatisfied customers who've banded together and set up their own self-help websites (see Appendix III).

Implied Warranty (Reasonable Durability)

This is that powerful "other" warranty that they never tell you about. It applies during and after the expiration of the manufacturer's or dealer's expressed or written warranty and requires that a part or repair will last a "reasonable" period of time. Look at the "Reasonable Part Durability" chart on page 122 for some guidelines on what you should expect.

Judges usually apply the implied or legal warranty when the manufacturer's expressed warranty has expired and the vehicle's manufacturing defects remain uncorrected. The landmark Canadian decisions upholding implied warranties in auto claims have been *Donoghue v. Stevenson*, [1932] A.C. 562 (H.L.), and *General Motors Products of Canada Ltd. v. Kravitz*, [1979] 1 S.C.R. 790.

In *Donoghue*, the court had to determine if the manufacturer of a bottle of ginger beer owed a duty to a consumer who suffered injury as a result of finding a decomposed snail in the bottle after consuming part of the bottle's contents. Lord Atkin, in finding liability against the manufacturer, established the principle of negligence. His reasons have been followed and adopted in all the common-law countries:

> The rule that you are to love your neighbour becomes in law, you must not injure your neighbour; and the lawyer's question, who is my neighbour? receives a restricted reply. You must take reasonable care to avoid acts or omissions which you can reasonably foresee would be likely to injure your neighbour. Who, then, is my neighbour?
>
> The answer seems to be persons who are so closely and directly affected by my act that I ought reasonably to have them in contemplation as being so affected when I am directing my mind to the acts or omissions which are called in question.

Over 45 years later in Quebec, *Kravitz* said essentially the same thing. In that case, the court said the seller's warranty of quality was an accessory to the property and was transferred with it on successive sales. Accordingly, subsequent buyers could invoke the contractual warranty of quality against the manufacturer, even though they did not contract directly with it. This precedent is now codified in articles 1434, 1442, and 1730 of Quebec's *Civil Code* (see *Tardif v. Hyundai Motor America* at *www.canlii.org/fr/qc/qccs/doc/2004/2004canlii7992/2004canlii7992.html* for a full analysis of warranties, hidden defects, and misrepresentation relating to Hyundai's inability to be truthful about its horsepower ratings).

Minivan Doors (Windstar "Mental Distress")

In *Sharman v. Formula Ford Sales Limited, Ford Credit Limited, and Ford Motor Company of Canada Limited* (Ontario Superior Court of Justice; Oakville, Ontario; No. 17419/02SR; 2003/10/07), Justice Shepard awarded the owner of a 2000 Windstar $7,500 for mental distress resulting from the breach of the implied warranty of fitness plus $7,207 for breach of contract and breach of warranty. The problem with the Windstar was that its sliding door wasn't secure and leaked air and water after many attempts to repair it. The judge cited the *Wharton* decision as support for his award for mental distress:

> The plaintiff and his family have had three years of aggravation, inconvenience, worry, and concern about their safety and that of their children. Generally speaking, our contract law did not allow for compensation for what may be mental distress, but that may be changing. I am indebted to counsel for providing me with the decision of the British Columbia Court of Appeal in *Wharton v. Tom Harris Chevrolet Oldsmobile Cadillac Ltd.*, [2002] B.C.J. No. 233, 2002 BCCA 78. This decision was recently followed in *Tiavra v. Victoria Ford Alliance Ltd.*, [2003] B.C.J. No. 1957.

> In *Wharton*, the purchaser of a Cadillac Eldorado claimed damages against the dealer because the car's sound system emitted an annoying buzzing noise and the purchaser had to return the car to the dealer for repair numerous times over two-and-a-half years. The trial court awarded damages of $2,257.17 for breach of warranty with respect to the sound system, and $5,000 in non-pecuniary damages for loss of enjoyment of their luxury vehicle and for inconvenience, for a total award of $7,257.17....

> In the *Wharton* case, the respondent contracted for a "luxury" vehicle for pleasure use. It included a sound system that the appellant's service manager described as "high end." The respondent's husband described the purchase of the car in this way: "[W]e bought a luxury car that was supposed to give us a luxury ride and be a quiet vehicle, and we had nothing but difficulty with it from the very day it was delivered with this problem that nobody seemed to be able to fix. So basically we had a luxury product that gave us no luxury for the whole time that we had it."

> It is clear that an important object of the contract was to obtain a vehicle that was luxurious and a pleasure to operate. Furthermore, the buzzing noise was the cause of physical, in the sense of sensory, discomfort to the respondent and her husband. The trial judge found it inhibited listening to the sound system and was irritating in normal conversation. The respondent and her husband also bore the physical inconvenience of taking the vehicle to the appellant on numerous occasions for repairs.

> In my view, a defect in manufacture that goes to the safety of the vehicle deserves a modest increase. I would assess the plaintiff's damage for mental distress resulting from the breach of the implied warranty of fitness at $7,500.

Free Engine Repairs

In the following judgments, Ford was forced to reimburse the cost of engine head gasket repairs carried out under the implied warranty—long after the expressed warranty had expired.

Dufour v. Ford Canada Ltd. (April 10, 2001; Quebec Small Claims Court, Hull; No. 550-32-008335-009; Justice P. Chevalier): Ford was forced to reimburse the cost of engine head gasket repairs carried out on a 1996 Windstar 3.8L engine.

Schaffler v. Ford Motor Company Limited and Embrun Ford Sales Ltd. (Ontario Superior Court of Justice, L'Orignal Small Claims Court; Court File No. 59-2003; July 22, 2003; Justice Gerald Langlois): The plaintiff bought a used 1995 Windstar in 1998. The engine head gasket was repaired for free three years later under Ford's seven-year extended warranty. In 2002, at 109,600 km, the head gasket failed again, seriously damaging the engine. Ford refused a second repair.

Justice Langlois ruled that Ford's warranty extension bulletin listed signs and symptoms of the covered defect that were identical to the problems written on the second work order ("persistent and/or chronic engine overheating; heavy white smoke evident from the exhaust tailpipe; flashing 'low coolant' instrument-panel light even after coolant refill; and constant loss of engine coolant"). The judge concluded that the dealer knew of the problem well within the warranty period and was therefore negligent. The plaintiff was awarded $4,941 plus 5 percent interest. This award included $1,070 for two months' car rental.

John R. Reid and Laurie M. McCall v. Ford Motor Company of Canada (Superior Court of Justice, Ottawa Small Claims Court; Claim No. 02-SC-077344; July 11, 2003; Justice Tiernay): A 1996 Windstar bought used in 1997 experienced engine head gasket failure in October 2001 at 159,000 km. Judge Tiernay awarded the plaintiffs $4,145 for the following reasons:

> A Technical Service Bulletin dated June 28, 1999, was circulated to Ford dealers. It dealt specifically with "undetermined loss of coolant" and "engine oil contaminated with coolant" in the 1996–98 Windstar and five other models of Ford vehicles. I conclude that Ford owed a duty of care to the Plaintiff to equip this vehicle with a cylinder head gasket of sufficient sturdiness and durability that would function trouble-free for at least seven years, given normal driving and proper maintenance conditions. I find that Ford is answerable in damages for the consequences of its negligence.

Chams v. Ford Motor Company of Canada, Limited, and Courtesy Ford Lincoln Sales, Limited (Ontario Superior Court of Justice, Small Claims Court; London, Ontario; Claim No. 5868, Court File No. 103/04; November 22, 2004; Deputy Justice J.D. Searle):

Reasons for Judgment

1. J.D. SEARLE DEPUTY J.: The defendant Ford Motor Company of Canada, Limited, hereinafter referred to as "Ford" is a corporation based in Oakville, Ontario and is a manufacturer of motor vehicles. The defendant Courtesy Ford Lincoln Sales Limited, hereinafter referred to as "Courtesy" is a corporation which carries on the business of a Ford dealer in the city of London in the county of Middlesex.

2. Samir Chams resides in the city of London. In 1997 he purchased from Courtesy a low kilometerage 1995 Ford Windstar van with a 3.8 liter engine. By 1998 at the latest Ford was aware the head gaskets of such engines had a defect which could destroy the engine. In 2000 it offered to the plaintiff and other owners an "additional warranty" for this defect but limited the warranty to seven years from the date the vehicle first went into service or 160,000 kilometers, whichever came first. Upon receiving notice of the additional warranty in 2000 the plaintiff took his van to Courtesy but no problems were manifest. For the plaintiff the original warranty had expired by passage of time. The additional warranty expired on March 08, 2002 by passage of time.

3. On January 11, 2004, some 22 months after the additional warranty expired, the plaintiff's engine overheated and was destroyed within a matter of minutes. The van had only 80,000 kilometers on the odometer. In due course the engine was replaced at a cost of over $4,000.00 paid by the plaintiff. As the court understands the plaintiff's case he is suing outside the expired warranty. Against Ford he alleges manufacturing defect. Against Courtesy he alleges negligence in 2000 in not replacing the defective head gasket to avoid possible engine destruction or at least telling him that was an option at his own expense. He also invokes manufacturer's warranty.

4. Ford contends it has no responsibility beyond its warranty and the destruction of the engine was from a cause or causes other than the head gasket. The court finds the highly probable cause of destruction of the engine was failure of the head gasket. The allegation of alternate causes is speculation not supported by the evidence. Pure economic loss does not apply because there was damage to property. See also *Winnipeg Condominium Corporation No. 36 v. Bird Construction Co. Ltd.* [1995] 1 S.C.R. 85.

5. Courtesy contends it was not negligent: the additional warranty issued by Ford only applied to cases with manifest problems and to merely replace a head gasket at a cost to the customer of $1,200.00 to $1,400.00 in the absence of manifest problems did not make economic sense.

6. In the Nova Scotia case of *Ford v. Kenney* (2003, unreported) Boudreau J. of the Nova Scotia Supreme Court was hearing an appeal from a decision of the Small Claims Court Adjudicator. At page 5 of the oral reasons His Lordship said:

    > Ford Motor Company has the right to decide which vehicles they are going to provide repairs to and which vehicles they are not. That doesn't mean that they couldn't be successfully challenged by that on negligent proper negligent manufacturing evidence, but there was not that evidence in this case.

7. *Campbell v. Ford* is a judgment of the Nova Scotia Small Claims Court rendered on January 31, 2002 and not reported. The plaintiff's 1995 Ford Windstar van

was showing signs of head gasket problems and the head gasket was replaced at 168,000 [km] at the $1,600.00 expense of the plaintiff. At 207,000 kilometers the engine was destroyed. The engine was rebuilt or replaced at a much greater cost. In both instances the vehicle was beyond the kilometerage caps of both the original and additional warranties.

8. The Adjudicator dismissed the replacement of the head gasket as pure economic loss but said of the engine rebuilding or replacement:

> It is certainly arguable that if the head gasket failed and it was due to negligence of the designer/manufacturer and that failure in turn caused physical damage to the property of the Claimant, consequential damage to the engine itself, that may well be a recoverable head of damage and the basis for an action in negligence.

> The Adjudicator found there was insufficient admissible and reliable evidence to establish a causal connection between the gasket failure sought to be corrected at 168,000 kilometers and the destruction of the engine at 207,000 kilometers. The important point is that the Adjudicator was discussing the potential liability of Ford quite apart from its original or additional warranties.

9. *Beshara v. Barry* is an Ontario Small Claims Court judgment of Tierney J. with reasons released a few days before trial in the case at bar and not yet reported. The unrepresented plaintiff sued the president of Ford for the estimated cost of replacing an engine similar to the one in the case at bar. The action was dismissed because the failure occurred after the expiry of Ford's original and additional warranties and the negligence alleged was that of the repairer and not Ford. The repairer was not a party.

10. The foregoing cases were furnished to the court by the agent for Ford. In each case involving Ford that company was successful. The court did additional research.

11. In *Kozoriz v. Chrysler Canada Ltd.* [1992] O.J. No. 3937 the problem was a transaxle seal which failed at 16,000 kilometers. Thereafter there was frequent leaking and repair work. As the van neared the 80,000 kilometer warranty expiry the 80,000 kilometer inspection was done at a Chrysler dealership and no problem was found with the trans-axle seal or the transmission. A few days later in Iowa there was an expensive failure of these apparently related parts. Tierney J. of the Ontario Small Claims Court found both parts failed due to a nearly continuous leak of the seal since 16,000 kilometers.

12. Chrysler pleaded the failure occurred after the expiry of the 80,000 kilometer warranty. In part the warranty described itself as "[a] guarantee of the quality and engineering excellence." Judge Tierney found that to be equivalent to a warranty that the product was free of defect. He found the axle seal was defective almost immediately and failed after only 16,000 kilometers and the defect led to the transmission damage after the expiry of the warranty. At page 3:

Those damages occurred as a direct result of the manufacturer's breach of warranty. For that reason, it is my view that the amounts are recoverable as damages for breach of contract, even though the actual breakdown occurred after the warranty period had expired.

13. A similar case is *Shields v. General Motors of Canada Ltd.* [1997] O.J. No. 5434 (Ont. Sm. C.C.). A 1991 Pontiac with a three year warranty began losing an extensive amount of its paint in 1995. Zochodne, D.J. found the problem was a failure to ensure proper bonding when the vehicle was being painted originally. At page 6:

The defect, which I have found, that is the lack of primer surfacer, occurred at the time the vehicle was manufactured. At that point, however, the defect was latent. The defect became patent when the paint began to bubble, flake and then peel off the vehicle.

That being the case His Honour found the warranty must respond to the loss. Judgment was in favour of the plaintiff.

14. *Schaffler v. Ford Motor Co. of Canada and Embrum Ford Sales Ltd.* [2003] O.J. No. 3165 (Ont. Sm. C.C.) is yet another Ford Windstar case involving an engine identical to the one involved in the case at bar. On March 02 of 2000, August 06 of 2001 and October 16 of 2001 the plaintiff took the van to Embrum with problems involving coolant levels, one of the indicia of head gasket failure. On those dates the respective kilometerages were 59,850, 84,000 and 89,000. The additional warranty expired by passage of time on August 07, 2002. Two months later there was serious damage to the engine as a result of head gasket failure.

15. Deputy Judge Langlois found the dealer liable for failure to diagnose the head gasket problem and Ford liable on its additional warranty which had been invoked by the plaintiff within the additional warranty period although the major damage occurred after expiry of the warranty.

16. It is distressing to note that although Barry Holmes was able in the case at bar to produce cases from both Ontario and Nova Scotia when Ford was successful he produced none where Ford was not successful. That includes the *Schaffler* case of one year ago and in which he was Ford's representative. In the case at bar he was Ford's agent and only witness.

17. In the case at bar the plaintiff received notice in 2000 from Ford of a potential problem with the head gasket in his van. His response was to take the van to Courtesy and enquire what should he done about it. Although they are only estimates the van was 5.5 years from the original warranty start date and had traveled 49,000 kilometers. Courtesy took in the van and gave the plaintiff and his family a ride home. About one half hour later Courtesy called and said the van was ready to be picked up. There was no paperwork introduced at trial evidencing this occurrence and it is probable none exists. William Taylor was the service manager and a helpful and credible witness at trial. He was not surprised at the absence of paperwork and said by way of summary that "[w]e do not charge for conversation."

18. It is probable that what happened is this: the plaintiff took his van to Courtesy, did not have the Ford notice with him, told Courtesy he had received a notice about head gaskets, asked what should [be] done and got a ride home. Courtesy was readily able to identify the van by its vehicle identification number and pull up its file on the vehicle, including at least references to technical service bulletins and notices affecting the plaintiff's vehicle and others in its class.

19. Having received no report from the plaintiff nor made any observations themselves the Courtesy service people would not be aware of any of the mostly gross symptoms Ford said could trigger warranty work on the head gasket. According to Mr. Taylor Courtesy had done "a lot" of gasket-related work under the warranty program in 1999 and 2000. In the absence of reports or observations of at least one of the gross symptoms Courtesy would inspect the head gasket only if the customer paid. The court finds the absence of paperwork on this visit by the plaintiff makes it a near certainty there was no gasket inspection.

20. One of the four symptoms listed in the Ford notice received by the plaintiff in 2000 was "constant loss of coolant" and another was flashing of the "low coolant" sensor light. Neither the plaintiff nor his wife testified to the existence of either of these symptoms and Courtesy does not note, except perhaps informally on the back of a work order, whether coolant has been "topped up." The plaintiff's vehicle was well maintained and in otherwise good condition throughout with much of the servicing done at Courtesy and some oil changes at a large department store if Mrs. Chams was shopping there.

21. Based on what Courtesy knew at the time of this visit Mr. Taylor would not recommend changing the head gasket for two reasons: the cost would be $1,200.00 to $1,400.00 to head off a problem which was only potential and there is a risk of non-payment and alienation if the work is done and the customer starts contending it is warranty work. The mechanic who owns and operates the independent vehicle repair shop which eventually replaced the plaintiff's engine said that due to the problems which can arise from it he will not permit his shop to change a head gasket for the sole purpose of changing the head gasket.

22. Nothing more relevant to an engine problem happened until Sunday, January 11, 2004. The Chams family fueled the van and moved it a short distance to a car wash. While entering the wash the plaintiff noticed the engine temperature digital readout was climbing. It maximized after the wash when they were back on the street. Mr. Chams pulled into the next "Petro" or "petrol" station and looked under the hood but saw nothing awry. He drove about two blocks to his house where the engine would not restart.

23. He asked a friend knowledgeable about motor vehicles to come over. That person observed coolant coming from the exhaust and coolant mixed with oil under the hood. The van was towed to Courtesy that day or early the next.

24. The diagnosis was "coolant in cylinders, no start, no heat, intermittent hydraulic lock. No start due to coolant leak inside engine. Suspect head cracked." The recommendation was replacement of the engine with a rebuilt engine. The kilometerage was noted to be 80,671. The charge for the inspection was $79.00 plus tax, later voluntarily waived by Mr. Taylor in recognition of several members of the Chams family being good customers and, no doubt, because of the arising

of a warranty issue. Further, according to Mr. Chams he had urged a friend with a similar vehicle to his to go to the dealer in 2000 and the result was the replacement of the head gasket.

25. Courtesy advised Mr. and Mrs. Chams the problem was not covered by warranty. The occurrence was 22 months after the expiry of the additional warranty. Mr. and Mrs. Chams spent time unsuccessfully trying to get Ford and Courtesy to take responsibility for the problem. Either directly or indirectly the Chams had the van towed to Automotive Solutions. That is a London vehicle repair shop owned and operated by Mohamed Omar who employs two class "A" automotive mechanics in the shop and who himself is in the final stage of his apprenticeship. Mr. Omar testified.

26. The van was stored at Automotive Solutions for about three months until a rebuilt engine and ancillary equipment was purchased by Mr. Chams and installed by Automotive Solutions on and about May 01.

27. When he studied the engine of the Chams van, seemingly in the company of one of his licensed mechanics, Mr. Omar observed the engine appeared not to have been apart before. The head gasket was found to [be] "blown." Coolant was mixed with oil. The coolant had leaked into the inner part of the engine through the No. 1 cylinder where it could mix with the oil. Oil mixing with coolant can cause the head gasket to "blow." One purpose of the head gasket is to prevent coolant getting into the interior of the engine.

28. In the opinion of Mr. Omar if the head gasket failed in 2000 the vehicle could not be driven until 2004. Head gaskets in most cars do not fail by 80,000 kilometers. He was aware the 3.8 liter Ford engine had a head gasket problem and he has worked on "a few" with such a problem. He is not "100% sure" of the reason for the failure of the Chams engine.

29. William Taylor is the Courtesy service manager. Courtesy did "a lot" of head gasket related repairs to 3.8 liter engines in 1999 and 2000. He understands the problem is a head gasket wrongly configured or "too weak." He has not seen the Chams engine but testified that theoretically the damage could be caused by a defective head gasket, a cracked head or the timing cover.

30. Barry Holmes was Ford's agent and only witness. He is a licensed mechanic and is employed by Ford in its product liability department. His direct evidence was largely on the Ford warranty and there was little or no evidence by him on defect or otherwise the cause of the major engine damage. On cross examination he said he did not know the failure rate of the head gaskets in the affected 3.8 liter engines. On further examination he acknowledged it was possibly 85% but he was not sure and had not brought that information to court with him. The court does not accept that denial of knowledge. The court notes its comments above with respect to cherry picking of cases. Mr. Holmes is a Ford product liability employee. The figure of 85% figured in another case involving a Ford 3.8 liter engine. The case at bar is at least the third nearly identical case in which Mr. Holmes has been noted in the reasons for judgment as Ford's agent or witness or both. The court finds that Ford knows it has had a failure rate of at least 85% in this head gasket which is a component which can quickly destroy an engine if it fails. That makes it nearly a certainty that unless the offending gasket is replaced in time the engine will be destroyed by its failure.

31. As to warranty this court finds, as was found in the *Shields* case, (*supra*), the defect was in existence and known to the giver of the warranty not only during the period of the additional warranty but also during the period of the original warranty. Ford is therefore liable on its warranty.

32. As to negligence there can be no doubt the gasket has had a design or manufacturing defect which has existed since the time of design or manufacture. It is that defect which caused the destruction of the plaintiff's engine and made its replacement necessary.

33. Ford's warranty attempts to limit its liability to what it grants in the warranty. It is ancient law that one who attempts to limit his liability by, for example, excluding common law remedies, must clearly bring that limitation to the attention of the person who might lose those remedies. The evidence in this case is clear the buyer of even a new car does not get a warranty booklet until after purchasing the car although he "would be" told the highlights sooner.

34. Courtesy was not negligent nor in breach of any other obligation to the plaintiff. Ford would not entertain repairs under either of its warranties unless certain "symptoms" had become manifest before the work was done. The court has no doubt Mr. Chams would have declined if Courtesy had asked if he would pay $1,200.00 to $1,400.00 to replace the head gasket in 2000 when his vehicle was manifesting no problem. The action is therefore dismissed against Courtesy with costs of $375.00 payable by Ford. This court will leave the fancy dancing of Bullock orders and the like to the higher courts.

35. At trial the focus was understandably on liability with damages consigned to the periphery. The rebuilt engine and ancillary parts were obtained from a NAPA dealer. The net NAPA bill is $2,375.67 but to that must be added a down payment of $250.00 and from it must be deducted a core deposit of $300.00. The old core is still available for credit. The radiator and water pump are valid expenses in that they are essential to obtaining a NAPA warranty on the rebuilt engine.

36. One legitimate Automotive Solutions bill is for $776.25 for towing and storage. The other is for $1,383.45 for labour, fluids, minor parts and an alternator. Storage is acceptable, particularly when one notes the absence of a substitute vehicle claim or loss of use. The alternator could not be proved as related to the engine failure and so $126.50 will be deducted.

37. Damages are assessed at $4,358.87 and there will be judgment in that amount against Ford. That sum will attract interest pursuant to the provisions of the *Courts of Justice Act* from January 12, 2004. The Clerk is requested to make that calculation.

38. As to costs a sealed document has now been opened and found to be an October 18, 2004 offer by Ford to settle by waiving allowable costs which stood at $25.00 or $75.00 at the time of the offer.

39. The trial was scheduled for two days but was completed in one. Mr. Ferguson was helpful to the court, particularly by creating document briefs for all parties, thus collecting dozens of potential exhibits into a handful. The court agrees with Mr. Ferguson's contention that many of the [I]nternet printouts collected by or on behalf of the plaintiff and included in one of the briefs were nevertheless inadmissible. Mr. Dupuis as agent for the plaintiff put in his client's case in a

way that was economical in terms of trial time but nevertheless thorough and it underscores the need for reform of the law which does not currently permit the court to award a counsel fee with respect to agents even in substantial cases. The plaintiff shall have costs fixed at $200.00 against Ford.

General Motors Intake Manifold Gasket Class Action

A Canadian class action lawsuit was launched on April 24, 2006—with *Lemon-Aid*'s help—and sought $1.2 billion in damages to compensate owners of 1995–2004 GM vehicles with defective engine intake manifold gaskets. A year later, GM Canada settled out of court for an estimated $40 million.

Automatic Transmission Failures

Lowe v. Fairview Chrysler-Dodge Limited and Chrysler Canada Limited (May 14, 1996; Ontario Court (General Division), Burlington Small Claims Court; No. 1224/95): This judgment, in the plaintiff's favour, raises important legal principles relative to Chrysler.

- Internal dealer service bulletins are admissible in court to prove that a problem exists and certain parts should be checked out.
- If a problem is reported prior to a warranty's expiration, warranty coverage for the problematic component(s) is automatically carried over after the warranty ends.
- It's not up to the car owner to tell the dealer or automaker what the specific problem is.
- Repairs carried out by an independent garage can be refunded if the dealer or automaker unfairly refuses to apply the warranty.
- The dealer or automaker cannot dispute the cost of the independent repair if it fails to cross-examine the independent repairer.
- Auto owners can ask for and win compensation for their inconvenience, which in this judgment amounted to $150.
- Court awards quickly add up: Although the plaintiff was given $1,985.94, with the addition of court costs and prejudgment interest, plus costs of inconvenience fixed at $150, the final award amounted to $2,266.04.

New-Vehicle Defects

Bagnell's Cleaners v. Eastern Automobile Ltd. (1991) (111 N.S.R. (2nd), No. 51, 303 A.P.R., No. 51 (T.D.)): This Nova Scotia company found that the new van it purchased had serious engine, transmission, and radiator defects. The dealer pleaded unsuccessfully that the sales contract excluded all other warranties except for those contained in the contract. The court held that there was a fundamental breach of the implied warranty and that the van's performance differed substantially from what the purchaser had been led to expect. An exclusionary clause could not protect the seller, who failed to live up to a fundamental term of the contract.

Burridge v. City Motor (10 Nfld. & P.E.I.R.; No. 451): This Newfoundland resident complained repeatedly of his new car's defects during the warranty period, and he stated that he hadn't used his car for 204 days after spending almost $1,500 for repairs. The judge awarded all repair costs and cancelled the sale.

Davis v. Chrysler Canada Ltd. (1977) (26 N.S.R. (2nd), No. 410 (T.D.)): The owner of a new $28,000 diesel truck found that a faulty steering assembly prevented him from carrying on his business. The court ordered that the sale be cancelled and that $10,000 in monthly payments be reimbursed. There was insufficient evidence to award compensation for business losses.

Fox v. Wilson Motors and GM (February 9, 1989; Court of Queen's Bench, New Brunswick; No. F/C/308/87): A trucker's new tractor-trailer had repeated engine malfunctions. He was awarded damages for loss of income, excessive fuel consumption, and telephone charges under the provincial *Sale of Goods Act*.

Gibbons v. Trapp Motors Ltd. (1970) (9 D.L.R. (3rd), No. 742 (B.C.S.C.)): The court ordered the dealer to take back a new car that had numerous defects and required 32 hours of repairs. The refund was reduced by mileage driven.

Johnson v. Northway Chevrolet Oldsmobile (1993) (108 Sask. R., No. 138 (Q.B.)): The court ordered the dealer to take back a new car that had been brought in for repairs on 14 different occasions. Two years after the car's purchase, the buyer initiated a lawsuit for the purchase price and general damages. General damages were awarded.

Julien v. GM of Canada (1991) (116 N.B.R. (2nd), No. 80): The plaintiff's new diesel truck produced excessive engine noise. The dealer claimed that the problem was caused by the owner's engine alterations. The plaintiff was awarded the $5,000 cost of repairing the engine through an independent dealer.

Magna Management Ltd. v. Volkswagen Canada Inc. (May 27, 1988; Vancouver (B.C.C.A.); No. CA006037): This precedent-setting case allowed the plaintiff to keep his new $48,325 VW while awarding him $37,101—three years after the car was purchased. The problems were centred on poor engine performance. The jury accepted the plaintiff's view that the car was practically worthless with its inherent defects.

Maughan v. Silver's Garage Ltd. (Nova Scotia Supreme Court; 6 B.L.R., No. 303, N.S.C. (2nd), No. 278): The plaintiff leased a defective backhoe. The manufacturer had to reimburse the plaintiff's losses because the warranty wasn't honoured. The court rejected the manufacturer's contention that the contract's exclusion clause protected the company from lawsuits for damages resulting from a latent defect.

Murphy v. Penney Motors Ltd. (1979) (23 Nfld. & P.E.I.R.; No. 152, 61 A.P.R., No. 152 (Nfld. T.D.)): This Newfoundland trucker found that his vehicle's engine problems took his new trailer off the road for 129 days during a seven-month period. The judge awarded all repair costs, as well as compensation for business losses, and cancelled the sale.

Murray v. Sperry Rand Corp. (Ontario Supreme Court; 5 B.L.R., No. 284): The seller, dealer, and manufacturer were all held liable for breach of warranty when a forage harvester did not perform as advertised in the sales brochure or as promised by the sales agent. The plaintiff was given his money back and reimbursed for his economic loss, based on the amount his harvesting usually earned. The court held that the advertising was a warranty.

Oliver v. Courtesy Chrysler (1983) Ltd. (1992) (11 B.C.A.C., No. 169): This new car had numerous defects over a three-year period, which the dealer attempted to fix to no avail. The plaintiff put the car in storage and sued the dealer for the purchase price. The court ruled that the car wasn't roadworthy and that the plaintiff couldn't be blamed for putting it in storage rather than selling it and purchasing another vehicle. The purchase price was refunded, minus $1,500 for each year the plaintiff used the car.

Olshaski Farms Ltd. v. Skene Farm Equipment Ltd. (January 9, 1987; Alberta Court of Queen's Bench; 49 Alta. L.R. (2nd), No. 249): The plaintiff's Massey-Ferguson combine caught fire after the manufacturer had sent two notices to dealers informing them of a defect that could cause a fire. The judge ruled under the *Sale of Goods Act* that the balance of probabilities indicated that the manufacturing defect caused the fire, even though there wasn't any direct evidence proving that the defect existed.

Western Pacific Tank Lines Ltd. v. Brentwood Dodge (June 2, 1975; B.C.S.C., No. 30945-74; Judge Meredith): The court awarded the plaintiff $8,600 and cancelled the sale of a new Chrysler New Yorker with badly adjusted doors, water leaks into the interior, and electrical short circuits.

Leasing

Ford Motor Credit v. Bothwell (December 3, 1979; Ontario County Court (Middlesex); No. 9226-T; Judge Macnab): The defendant leased a 1977 Ford truck that had frequent engine problems, characterized by stalling and hard starting. After complaining for one year and driving 35,000 km (21,750 mi.), the defendant cancelled the lease. Ford Credit sued for the money owing on the lease. Judge Macnab cancelled the lease and ordered Ford Credit to repay 70 percent of the amount paid during the leasing period. Ford Credit was also ordered to refund repair costs, even though the corporation claimed that it should not be held responsible for Ford's failure to honour its warranty.

Schryvers v. Richport Ford Sales (May 18, 1993; B.C.S.C., No. C917060; Justice Tysoe): The court awarded $17,578.47, plus damages, to a couple who paid thousands of dollars more in unfair and hidden leasing charges than if they had simply purchased their Ford Explorer and Escort. The court found that this price difference constituted a deceptive, unconscionable act or practice, in contravention of the *Trade Practices Act*, R.S.B.C. 1979, c. 406.

Judge Tysoe concluded that the total of the general damages awarded to the Schryvers for both vehicles would be $11,578.47. He then proceeded to give the following reasons for awarding an additional $6,000 in punitive damages:

> Little wonder Richport Ford had a contest for the salesperson who could persuade the most customers to acquire their vehicles by way of a lease transaction. I consider the actions of Richport Ford to be sufficiently flagrant and high-handed to warrant an award of punitive damages.
>
> There must be a disincentive to suppliers in respect of intentionally deceptive trade practices. If no punitive damages are awarded for intentional violations of the legislation, suppliers will continue to conduct their businesses in a manner that involves deceptive trade practices because they will have nothing to lose. In this case I believe that the appropriate amount of punitive damages is the extra profit Richport Ford endeavoured to make as a result of its deceptive acts. I therefore award punitive damages against Richport Ford in the amount of $6,000.

Salvador v. Setay Motors/Queenstown Chev-Olds (Hamilton Small Claims Court; Case No. 1621/95): Robert Salvador was awarded $2,000 plus costs from Queenstown Leasing. The court found that the company should have tried harder to sell the leased vehicle, and at a higher price, when the "open lease" expired.

Incidentally, about 3,700 dealers in 39 American states paid between $3,500 and $8,000 each in 2004 to settle an investigation of allegations that they and Ford Motor Credit Co. overcharged customers who terminated their leases early.

See also:

- *Barber v. Inland Truck Sales* (11 D.L.R. (3rd), No. 469)
- *Canadian-Dominion Leasing v. Suburban Super Drug Ltd.* (1966) (56 D.L.R. (2nd), No. 43)
- *Neilson v. Atlantic Rentals Ltd.* (1974) (8 N.B.R. (2nd), No. 594)
- *Volvo Canada v. Fox* (December 13, 1979; New Brunswick Court of Queen's Bench; No. 1698/77/C; Judge Stevenson)
- *Western Tractor v. Dyck* (7 D.L.R. (3rd), No. 535)

Return of security deposit

Dealers routinely keep much of their lease customers' security deposits when their leases expire. However, that action can always be challenged in court. In the following claim, settled out of court, Ontario lawyer Harvey Goldstein forced GMAC and a GM dealer to refund his $525 security deposit:

1. The Plaintiff Claims:
   (A) Return of his security deposit of $525.00; and a finding that no amount is owing to the Defendants;
   (B) Alternatively, damages in the above amount;
   (C) Prejudgment interest on $525.00 at the rate of 2% per month (24% per annum) from June 22, 2005, to the date of this Claim, and thereafter on the date of payment or Judgment at the rate of 4% per annum, pursuant to Section 128 of the Courts of Justice Act, R.S.O. (1990) as amended;
   (D) Post-judgment interest at the post-judgment rate of interest, pursuant to Section 129 of the Courts of Justice Act, R. S. O. (1990) as amended;
   (E) His costs of this action;
   (F) Punitive damages in an amount to be determined; and
   (G) Such further and other relief as this Honorable Court deems just and proper.

• • •

4. On or about June 10, 2005, the Plaintiff advised the Defendant North York Chevrolet Oldsmobile Ltd. that he wanted it to inspect the said vehicle for chargeable damage prior to its return or that he be present when it was inspected after its return to the said Defendant.
5. The said Defendant advised that it had no control over the inspection process and that the Defendant GMAC Leaseco Limited would inspect the vehicle only after the lease expired, the vehicle was returned to the dealer and the Plaintiff was not present.
6. The Plaintiff sent an email on June 10, 2005 to the Defendant GMAC Leaseco Limited asking it for an inspection prior to the vehicle being returned.
7. The said Defendant did not respond to the request.
8. The Plaintiff called and spoke with a representative of the said Defendant on June 17, and wrote her a letter sent by fax the same day, again asking that an inspection be scheduled in his presence. The said Defendant did not respond to the letter.
9. On June 23, 2005, the Plaintiff again called the said Defendant. He was told that it had no record of the vehicle being returned to the dealership.
10. Shortly thereafter, the Plaintiff called the Defendant North York Chevrolet Oldsmobile Ltd. to enquire as to the status of his security deposit. The said Defendant advised that it had no record of the vehicle being returned to it.
11. Not having heard from either Defendant, the Plaintiff called the Defendant GMAC Leaseco Limited on July 15, 2005. He was advised that he owed the said Defendant $550.00, less the amount of the security deposit held by it. He was further advised that details of its claim to that amount could be found on the said Defendant's website. He was told that it did not inspect the said vehicle until July 7, 2005, 15 days after it was left in the dealership's service bay. He was told that the vehicle was at an auction and that he could not inspect the alleged damages for which the Defendants claimed compensation. He was advised that no adjustment would be made to their claim even though the vehicle was returned with 20,000.00 kilometers less than allowed by the lease agreement. Further, he was told that the alleged damages to the vehicle were not repaired prior to sending it to auction.

12. The Plaintiff denies that the vehicle required repairs claimed by the Defendants and puts them to the strict proof thereof.

13. The Plaintiff further claims that the process by which the Defendants seek to claim compensation from him is unfair, open to abuse and contrary to the principles of natural justice. The Defendants pay the fee of the alleged independent inspectors and deny the Plaintiff the opportunity to dispute the charges in any meaningful fashion. Further, its delay in inspecting the vehicle for 15 days, leaves open the question of when, if ever, the damages occurred.

Repairs: Faulty Diagnosis

Davies v. Alberta Motor Association (August 13, 1991; Alberta Provincial Court, Civil Division; No. P9090106097; Judge Moore): The plaintiff had a used 1985 Nissan Pulsar NX checked out by the AMA's Vehicle Inspection Service prior to buying it. The car passed with flying colours. A month later, the clutch was replaced, and then numerous electrical problems ensued. At that time, another garage discovered that the car had been involved in a major accident, had a bent frame and a leaking radiator, and was unsafe to drive. The court awarded the plaintiff $1,578.40 plus three years of interest. The judge held that the AMA set itself out as an expert and should have spotted the car's defects. The AMA's defence—that it was not responsible for errors—was thrown out. The court held that a disclaimer clause could not protect the association from a fundamental breach of contract.

False Advertising: Vehicle Not as Ordered

When you're buying a new vehicle, the seller can't misrepresent the vehicle through a lie or a failure to disclose important information. Anything that varies from what one would commonly expect or from the seller's representation must be disclosed prior to signing the contract. Typical scenarios are odometer turnbacks, accident damage, used or leased cars sold as new, new vehicles that are the wrong colour or the wrong model year, or vehicles that lack promised options or standard features.

Goldie v. Golden Ears Motors (1980) Ltd. (Port Coquitlam; June 27, 2000; British Columbia Small Claims Court; Case No. C08287; Justice Warren): In a well-written eight-page judgment, the court awarded plaintiff Goldie $5,000 for engine repairs on a 1990 Ford F-150 pickup in addition to $236 court costs. The dealer was found to have misrepresented the mileage and sold a used vehicle that didn't meet Section 8.01 of the provincial motor vehicle regulations (unsafe tires, defective exhaust, and headlights).

In rejecting the seller's defence that he disclosed all information "to the best of his knowledge and belief," as stipulated in the sales contract, Justice Warren stated the following:

> The words "to the best of your knowledge and belief" do not allow someone to be willfully blind to defects or to provide incorrect information. I find as a fact that the business made no effort to fulfill its duty to comply with the requirements of this form. The defendant has been reckless in its actions. More likely, it has actively deceived the claimant into entering into this contract. I find the conduct of the defendant has been reprehensible throughout the dealings with the claimant.

This judgment closes a loophole that sellers have used to justify their misrepresentation, and it allows for the cancellation of the sale and damages if the vehicle doesn't meet highway safety regulations.

Lister v. Scheilding (c.o.b. Kar-Lon Motors) [1983] (O.J. No. 907 (Co. Ct.)): Here, the plaintiff was entitled to rescind the contract because of the defendant's false representation. The defendant failed to state that the motor had been changed and was not the original motor.

MacDonald v. Equilease Co. Ltd. (January 18, 1979; Ontario Supreme Court; Judge O'Driscoll): The plaintiff leased a truck that was misrepresented as having an axle stronger than it really was. The court awarded the plaintiff damages for repairs and set aside the lease.

Seich v. Festival Ford Sales Ltd. (1978) (6 Alta. L.R. (2nd), No. 262): The plaintiff bought a used truck from the defendant after being assured that it had a new motor and transmission. It didn't, and the court awarded the plaintiff $6,400.

Bilodeau v. Sud Auto (Quebec Court of Appeal; No. 09-000751-73; Judge Tremblay): This appeals court cancelled the contract and held that a car can't be sold as new or as a demonstrator if it has ever been rented, leased, sold, or titled to anyone other than the dealer.

Chenel v. Bel Automobile (1981) Inc. (August 27, 1976; Quebec Superior Court (Quebec); Judge Desmeules): The plaintiff didn't receive Jacob brakes, essential to transporting sand in hilly regions, with his new Ford truck. The court awarded the plaintiff $27,000, representing the purchase price of the vehicle less the money he earned while using the truck.

Lasky v. Royal City Chrysler Plymouth (February 18, 1987; Ontario High Court of Justice; 59 O.R. (2nd), No. 323): The plaintiff bought a 4-cylinder 1983 Dodge 600 that had been represented by the salesman as being a 6-cylinder model. After putting 40,000 km on the vehicle over a 22-month period, the buyer was given her money back, without interest, under the provincial *Business Practices Act*.

Rourke v. Gilmore (January 16, 1928; *Ontario Weekly Notes*, Vol. XXXIII, p. 292): Before discovering that his new car was really used, the plaintiff drove it for over a year. For this reason, the contract couldn't be cancelled. However, the appeals court instead awarded damages for $500, which was quite a sum in 1928!

Insurance Liability

If you believe your insurance policy will protect you from liability when driving, like in an at-fault collision, you may be wrong. In "Deconstructing Automobile Insurance" (*papers.ssrn.com/sol3/papers.cfm?abstract_id=1262084*), Queen's University law professor Erik Knutson cited recent decisions by Canada's Supreme Court that he believes "significantly narrowed the scope of automobile coverage by restricting the once-expansive interpretive exercise to a more nuanced and categorical application":

> The Supreme Court's present approach to automobile insurance coverage fails to honour long-standing insurance law interpretation concepts and represents a results-driven process which puts principle by the wayside. The implications are serious and potentially far-reaching. In the end, the result may be less efficient, and ultimately less just, than the previous state of the law.

> The driving public cannot reliably predict when an accident is covered or not covered by automobile insurance. Neither can lawyers assisting accident victims or auto insurers. For example, if a driver operating a vehicle drops a child off to play and the child is seriously hurt crossing the street, is the child covered by first party no-fault automobile benefits from the driver's policy? Is the driver protected for his negligence by his third party liability automobile insurance policy, in the event the child sues the driver? Is any underinsured or uninsured automobile coverage available in the event of a shortfall in available compensation? Or is the child's loss not covered at all? The answer, according to the Supreme Court of Canada: it depends.

> The Court effectively created two interpretive tests for two types of insurance: a broad test for first party no-fault benefits and a narrower test for third party liability insurance. Despite the broadly worded coverage clause, the Court held that auto insurance coverage can only be triggered in the third party liability situation if the at-fault tortfeasor is at fault as a motorist. The Court's aim surely must have been to simplify the coverage question by restricting automobile coverage to standard two-vehicle auto collision situations and their corollaries. The shift to this default rule, from the previous default rule of pro-coverage as long as a vehicle is essentially in the factual matrix, surprisingly does not do anything to ameliorate the efficiency of the system. In fact, it makes the system more unpredictable.

Secret Warranty Claims

It's common practice for manufacturers to secretly extend their warranties to cover components with a high failure rate. Customers who complain vigorously get extended warranty compensation in the form of "goodwill" adjustments.

Tepei v. Uniroyal: Canadians injured by an American-manufactured tire can get compensation from American courts. (Contact the Vancouver, BC, law firm involved at *www.crossborderlaw.com*.) In this case, a Washington jury awarded $9.1 million (U.S.) in damages to the six Canadian plaintiffs—a 2004 verdict the *Vancouver Sun* reported was the largest judgment ever entered against an ICBC-insured driver for negligence (*www.crossborderlaw.com/PDF/CBL-Tepei-Verdict-040429.pdf*).

The jury found that the driver's negligence was the sole cause of the plaintiffs' injuries; nevertheless, the *Tepei v. Uniroyal* case shows that Canadian plaintiffs need a thorough knowledge of the laws on both sides of the border to maximize their recovery whenever United States law is implicated in litigation.

> The pre-trial legal maneuvering between the parties and Michelin over *forum non conveniens* and choice-of-law issues suggests that while U.S. corporate defendants will aggressively contest the efforts of Canadian plaintiffs to seek redress for injuries caused by defective American products, the American courts are generally open to such claims for relief.

> In Washington, as well as in the majority of states around the U.S. which have abandoned the *lex loci delecti* approach to choice-of-law issues, it is likely that a Canadian plaintiff who chooses to sue an American manufacturer in a state with some connection to the product in question would find the courts willing to entertain both jurisdiction over the case and the application of the American forum's products liability law—irrespective of where the injury to the plaintiff actually took place.

Indeed, many of the cases relied upon by Michelin in its attempt to suggest the place of the Tepei accident was "fortuitous" could be turned against a corporate defendant, supporting the argument that an injury occurring in Canada "could have occurred anywhere."

François Chong v. Marine Drive Imported Cars Ltd. and Honda Canada Inc. (May 17, 1994; British Columbia Provincial Small Claims Court; No. 92-06760; Judge C.L. Bagnall): Mr. Chong was the first owner of a 1983 Honda Accord with 134,000 km on the odometer. He had six engine camshafts replaced—four under Honda "goodwill" programs, one where he paid part of the repairs, and one via a small claims court judgment. (Please note that Honda's earlier engine problems and its arrogant attitude have since moderated a bit.)

In his ruling, Judge Bagnall agreed with Chong and ordered Honda and the dealer to each pay half of the $835.81 repair bill for the following reasons:

> The defendants assert that the warranty which was part of the contract for purchase of the car encompassed the entirety of their obligation to the claimant, and that it expired in February 1985. The replacements of the camshaft after that date were paid for wholly or in part by Honda as a "goodwill gesture." The time has come for these gestures to cease, according to the witness for Honda. As well, he pointed out

to me that the most recent replacement of the camshaft was paid for by Honda and that, therefore, the work would not be covered by Honda's usual warranty of 12 months from date of repair. Mr. Wall, who testified for Honda, told me there was no question that this situation with Mr. Chong's engine was an unusual state of affairs. He said that a camshaft properly maintained can last anywhere from 24,000 to 500,000 km. He could not offer any suggestion as to why the car keeps having this problem.

The claimant has convinced me that the problems he is having with rapid breakdown of camshafts in his car [are] due to a defect, which was present in the engine at the time that he purchased the car. The problem first arose during the warranty period and in my view has never been properly identified nor repaired.

Punitive Damages

Punitive damages (also known as "exemplary damages") allow the plaintiff to get compensation that exceeds his or her losses as a deterrent to those who carry out dishonest or negligent practices. These kinds of judgments, common in the U.S., sometimes reach hundreds of millions of dollars. Canadian courts, however, seldom award substantial punitive damages.

Nevertheless, there have been a few relatively recent cases where the Supreme Court of Canada has shocked the business establishment by levying huge exemplary damage awards. One such case was the *Whiten v. Pilot Insurance Co.* decision rendered in 2002. In this case, the plaintiff's home caught fire and burned to the ground, destroying all of the home's contents and killing three pet cats. Pilot Insurance made a single $5,000 payment for living expenses and covered the family's rent for a couple of months, and then cut off the rent payments without forewarning the family. The insurance claim went to trial, based on the respondent's allegation that the family had torched their own home, even though the local fire chief, the respondent's own expert investigator, and its initial expert all said there was no evidence whatsoever of arson. The original trial jury awarded the plaintiff compensatory damages and $1 million in punitive damages. Pilot Insurance fought this decision at the Court of Appeal, where the punitive damages award was reduced to $100,000. The case was then taken all the way to the Supreme Court, where the trial jury's unprecedented award of $1 million was restored:

> The jury's award of punitive damages, though high, was within rational limits. The respondent insurer's conduct towards the appellant was exceptionally reprehensible. It forced her to put at risk her only remaining asset (the $345,000 insurance claim) plus $320,000 in costs that she did not have. The denial of the claim was designed to force her to make an unfair settlement for less than she was entitled to. The conduct was planned and deliberate and continued for over two years, while the financial situation of the appellant grew increasingly desperate. The jury evidently believed that the respondent knew from the outset that its arson defence was contrived and unsustainable. Insurance contracts are sold by the insurance industry and purchased by members of the public for peace of mind. The more devastating the loss, the more

the insured may be at the financial mercy of the insurer, and the more difficult it may be to challenge a wrongful refusal to pay the claim.

Punitive damages are rarely awarded in Canadian courts against automakers. When they are given out, it's usually for sums less than $100,000. In *Prebushewski v. Dodge City Auto (1985) Ltd. and Chrysler Canada Ltd.*, the plaintiff got $25,000 in a judgment handed down in 2001 and confirmed by the Supreme Court in 2005. The plaintiff's 1996 Ram's running lights had shorted and caused her truck to burn to the ground, and Chrysler had refused her claim. The court basically said that aggrieved car owners may sue for much more than the depreciated value of what they bought under provincial consumer protection statutes. The Supreme Court reaffirmed the power of the lower courts to assess an additional financial penalty to punish automakers that treat their customers unfairly and ensure they don't repeat the offence.

Vlchek v. Koshel (1988; 44 C.C.L.T. 314, B.C.S.C., No. B842974): The plaintiff was seriously injured when she was thrown from a Honda all-terrain cycle on which she had been riding as a passenger. The court allowed for punitive damages because the manufacturer was well aware of the injuries likely to be caused by the cycle. Specifically, the court ruled that there is no firm and inflexible principle of law stipulating that punitive or exemplary damages must be denied unless the defendant's acts are specifically directed against the plaintiff. The court may apply punitive damages "where the defendant's conduct has been indiscriminate of focus, but reckless or malicious in its character. Intent to injure the plaintiff need not be present, so long as intent to do the injurious act can be shown."

See also:

- *Granek v. Reiter* (Ontario Court, General Division; No. 35/741)
- *Morrison v. Sharp* (Ontario Court, General Division; No. 43/548)
- *Schryvers v. Richport Ford Sales* (May 18, 1993; B.C.S.C., No. C917060; Judge Tysoe)
- *Varleg v. Angeloni* (B.C.S.C., No. 41/301)

Provincial business practices acts cover false, misleading, or deceptive representations and allow for punitive damages should the unfair practice toward the consumer amount to an unconscionable representation (see *Canadian Encyclopedic Digest (C.E.D.)*, Third Edition, s. 76, pages 140–145). And here are some specific cases to keep in mind:

- Exemplary damages are justified where compensatory damages are insufficient to deter and punish. See *Walker et al. v. CFTO Ltd. et al.* (1978; 59 O.R. (2nd), No. 104; Ontario C.A.).
- Exemplary damages can be awarded in cases where the defendant's conduct was "cavalier." See *Ronald Elwyn Lister Ltd. et al. v. Dayton Tire Canada Ltd.* (1985; 52 O.R. (2nd), No. 89; Ontario C.A.).
- The primary purpose of exemplary damages is to prevent the defendant and all others from doing similar wrongs. See *Fleming v. Spracklin* (1921).

- Disregard of the public's interest, lack of preventive measures, and a callous attitude all merit exemplary damages. See *Coughlin v. Kuntz* (1989; 2 C.C.L.T. (2nd); B.C.C.A.).
- Punitive damages can be awarded for mental distress. See *Ribeiro v. Canadian Imperial Bank of Commerce* (1992; Ontario Reports 13 (3rd)) and *Brown v. Waterloo Regional Board of Commissioners of Police* (1992; 37 O.R. (2nd)).

In the States, punitive damage awards have been particularly generous. Do you remember the Alabama fellow who won a multi-million-dollar award because his new BMW had been repainted before he bought it but the seller didn't tell him so? The case was *BMW of North America, Inc. v. Gore* (517 U.S. 559, 116 S. Ct. 1589; 1996). In this case, the U.S. Supreme Court cut the damages award and established standards for jury awards of punitive damages. Nevertheless, million-dollar awards are still quite common.

For example, an Oregon dealer learned that a $1 million punitive damages award wasn't excessive under *Gore* and under Oregon law. The Oregon Supreme Court determined that the standard it set forth in *Oberg v. Honda Motor Company* (888 P.2d 8; 1996), on remand from the Supreme Court, survived the Supreme Court's subsequent ruling in *Gore*. The court held that the jury's $1 million punitive damages award, 87 times larger than the plaintiff's compensatory damages in *Parrott v. Carr Chevrolet, Inc.* (2001 Ore. LEXIS 1; January 11, 2001), wasn't excessive. In that case, Mark Parrott sued Carr Chevrolet, Inc. over a used 1983 Chevrolet Suburban under Oregon's *Unlawful Trade Practices Act*. The jury awarded Parrott $11,496 in compensatory damages and $1 million in punitive damages because the dealer failed to disclose collision damage to a new buyer.

Now that you know how to get the best deal for less money while protecting your rights, take a look at Part Three to see which cars and trucks to pick and which ones to avoid.

Part Three

MAKING THE RIGHT CHOICE

Remember when Cadillacs were soft and pillowy and ambled around town in a kind of Vicodin haze? Remember when you felt like you needed to slip into supportive undergarments to drive one? Doesn't that seem a long time ago?

DAN NEIL
LOS ANGELES TIMES
SEPTEMBER 18, 2008

A man walks into a gas station and says, "How about a gas cap for my Yugo?" The attendant says, "Sounds like a fair trade to me."

UNKNOWN

All automakers build bad cars—some more often than others.

The trick is to know which models and years have the most problems. Like wine, vintage is important. For example, four decades ago, most Japanese small cars were underpowered rustbuckets; British cars were electrical system nightmares (joke: "Lucas is the Prince of Darkness and inadvertently invented the intermittent windshield washer."); the Italians used fuel systems that seldom held their "tune"; and the Germans made bizarre-behaving, hard-to-diagnose, and parts-challenged models that included VW's self-starting, fire-prone Rabbits (rain-water would run down the antenna mount and into the wiring). Since then, some automakers, like Ford, Honda, Hyundai, and Mazda, have gotten much better at building reliable, fuel-efficient vehicles—others, like Chrysler, Saab, and Volvo, have gotten worse.

Honda, for example, introduced the CVCC engine in 1975; it was fuel-efficient, produced low emissions, and didn't require a catalytic converter or unleaded fuel to meet emissions standards. Problem was it was prone to self-destruction and cost up to $5,000 to repair or replace. Quebec mechanics jokingly referred to the CVCC as the "ça va couter cher" engine. Honda heard the guffaws and dropped the CVCC in the early '80s. Today, its entire lineup is above reproach.

Toyota quality, on the other hand, has gone in the opposite direction. After coasting for over a decade on its high-quality reputation, Toyota's sudden unintended acceleration and brake problems have made buyers wary of its cars and trucks. *Lemon-Aid*, for instance, doesn't recommend any new Toyota unless it is equipped with a brake override system.

What Makes a Good Car or Truck?

The vehicle should first live up to the promises made by the manufacturer and dealer. It must be reasonably priced, provide safe highway performance, protect occupants in a crash, be fuel-efficient, and be capable of lasting 10–15 years; it should cost no more than about $800 a year to maintain; and it should provide you with a fair resale value a few years down the road. Parts should be affordable and easily available, and competent servicing shouldn't be hard to find.

And don't believe for one moment that the more you spend, the better the vehicle. For example, most Hondas are as good as more-expensive Acuras. The same is true of Toyota and Lexus. Even more surprising is that some luxury makes, like Jaguar, offer you a dressed-up Ford at a luxury-car price. The extra money buys you more features of dubious value and newer, unproven technology like rear-mounted video cameras and failure-prone electronic gadgetry.

In terms of road performance, at the very minimum, every vehicle must be able to merge safely onto a highway and have adequate passing power for two-lane roads. Steering feel and handling should inspire confidence. The suspension ought to provide a reasonably well-controlled ride on most road surfaces. Ideally, the passenger compartment will be roomy enough to accommodate passengers comfortably on extended trips. The noise level should not become tiresome or annoying. As a rule, handling and ride comfort are inversely proportional—good handling requires a stiff suspension, which pounds the kidneys, while a softer suspension that cushions those kidneys leaves you lacking in the handling department.

Lemon-Aid follows these five simple rules when rating new vehicles:

- We believe the best rating approach is to combine a driving test with an owners' survey of past models (only *Consumer Reports* and *Lemon-Aid* do this).
- Owner responses must come from a large owner pool (over a million responses from *CR* subscribers, for example). Anecdotal responses should then be cross-referenced, updated, and given depth and specificity through NHTSA's safety complaint prism. Responses must again be cross-referenced through automaker internal service bulletins to determine the extent of a defect over a specific model and model-year range and to alert owners to problems that are likely to occur.
- Rankings should be predicated upon important characteristics measured over a significant period of time, unlike "Car of the Year" contests or polls of owners who have just bought their car.
- Data must come from unimpeachable sources like *Consumer Reports*, *Which?*, ALLDATA, and NHTSA (crash and safety reports). There should be no conflicts of interest, such as advertising, consultant ties, or self-serving tests done under ideal conditions for an extra fee.
- Tested cars must be bought or rented, not borrowed from the car company, and serviced—not pampered as part of a journalists' fleet lent out for ranking purposes.

Responsible auto raters shouldn't hit up dealers or manufacturers for free test vehicles under any circumstances, but most auto columnists and some consumer groups compromise their integrity by doing so. Test vehicles should be rented or borrowed from an owner. I've adopted this practice from my early experience as a consumer reporter. Nissan asked me to test drive its new 1974 240Z—no strings attached. I took the car for a week, had it examined by an independent garage, spoke with satisfied and dissatisfied owners, and accessed internal service bulletins and government-logged owner safety complaints. The car's poor brake design apparently made it unsafe to drive, and I said so in my report. Nissan sued me for $2 million, fixed the brakes through a "product improvement campaign," and then dropped the lawsuit two years later. I was never offered another car.

Definitions of Terms

Key Facts

This year, we rate many more cars, trucks, and SUVs than ever before, and include previews of some 2012 models for readers planning to buy a new vehicle in mid-2011. We also include "miles per gallon" (mpg) in addition to our usual "litres per 100 kilometres" (L/km) in deference to our metric-challenged readers. More American prices are given this year as benchmarks for haggling successfully with Canadian dealers or when negotiating cross-border deals.

Prices: We list the manufacturer's suggested retail price (MSRP) range, in effect at press time and applicable to standard models. That price will likely drop during the year as customer rebates and manufacturer-to-dealer sales incentives kick in. Check the latest MSRP figure periodically on both sides of the border by accessing each manufacturer's website (like *www.honda.com* and *www.honda.ca*). Vehicles that aren't selling well usually carry the heftiest discounts and/or rebates; check the "Cost Analysis" section for a vehicle's predicted price negotiability.

Destination charges and the pre-delivery inspection (PDI) fee are quasi-fraudulent "back doors" into your wallet. Offer half of the indicated amount. Also, don't fall for the $99–$475 "administration fee" scam, unless the bottom-line price is so tempting that it won't make much difference. Sticking to your principles is one thing; losing an attractive deal is another.

Tow limit: Note that towing capacities differ depending on the kind of powertrain/suspension package or towing package you buy. And remember that there's a difference between how a vehicle is rated for cargo capacity or payload and how heavy a boat or trailer it can pull. Do not purchase any new vehicle without receiving very clear information from the dealer, in writing, about a vehicle's towing capacity and the kind of special equipment you'll need to meet your requirements. Ask the manufacturer of whatever it is you plan to tow (trailer, boat, etc.) what model and year would best meet your requirements to be certain you'll have what you need. Whichever model you choose, make sure to have the towing capacity and necessary equipment written into the contract.

Load capacity: This is defined as the safe combined weight of occupants and cargo (such as luggage). It is taken from the manufacturers' rating or from *Consumer Reports'* calculated safe load. Exceeding this maximum weight can adversely affect a vehicle's handling or make it unstable.

Ratings

We rate vehicles on a scale of one to five stars, with five stars as our top ranking. We use owner complaints, confidential technical service bulletins (TSBs), and test drives to ferret out serious factory-related defects, design deficiencies, and servicing glitches.

This guide emphasizes important new features that add to a vehicle's safety, reliability, road performance, and comfort, and points out those changes that are merely gadgets and styling revisions. Also noted are important improvements to be made in the future, or the dropping of a model line. In addition to its overall rating, each vehicle's strong and weak points are summarized.

Interestingly, some vehicles that are identical but marketed and serviced by different automakers may have different ratings. This variation occurs because servicing and after-warranty assistance may be better within one dealer network than another.

It takes about six months to acquire enough information for a fair-minded evaluation of a car's or truck's first year on the market, unless the vehicle has been available elsewhere under another name. Most new cars and trucks hit the market before all of the bugs have been worked out, so it would be irresponsible to recommend them before owner reports and internal service bulletins give them an "okay." Sadly, as we have seen with Toyota's acceleration problems and GM's poorly shifting transmission, it may take several years to correct some factory powertrain glitches.

Recommended: This rating indicates a "Best Buy," and it applies to many Asian models (Ford is also climbing in the rankings). "Recommended" vehicles usually combine a high level of crashworthiness with good road performance, few safety-related complaints, decent reliability, and a better-than-average resale value. Servicing is readily available, and parts are inexpensive and easy to find.

Above Average: Vehicles in this class are pretty good choices. They aren't perfect, but they're often more reasonably priced than their competition. Most vehicles in this category have quality construction, good durability, and plenty of safety features as standard equipment. On the downside, they may have expensive parts and servicing, too many safety-related complaints, or only satisfactory warranty performance—one or all of which may have disqualified them from the Recommended category.

Average: Some deficiencies or flaws make these good second choices. In many cases, certain components are prone to premature wear or breakdown or don't perform as well as the competition. An Average rating can also be attributed to such factors as substandard assembly quality, lack of a solid long-term reliability record, a substantial number of safety-related complaints, or a deficient parts and service network.

Below Average: This rating category denotes an unreliable or poorly performing vehicle that may also have a poor safety record. Getting an extended warranty is advised.

Not Recommended: Chances of having major breakdowns or safety-related failures are omnipresent. Inadequate road performance and poor dealer service, among other factors, can make owning one of these vehicles a traumatic and expensive experience, no matter how cheaply it's sold.

Vehicles that have not been on the road long enough to assess, or that are sold in such small numbers that owner feedback is insufficient, are either given a Not Recommended rating or left unrated.

Quality and reliability

Lemon-Aid bases its quality and reliability evaluations in the "Rating" and "Overview" sections on owner comments, confidential manufacturer service bulletins, and government reports from NHTSA safety complaint files. We also draw on the knowledge and expertise of professionals working in the automotive marketplace, including mechanics and fleet owners. The aim is to have a wide range of unbiased (and irrefutable) data on quality, reliability, durability, and ownership costs. Allowances are made for the number of vehicles sold versus the number of complaints, as well as for the seriousness of problems reported and the average number of problems reported by each owner.

Technical Service Bulletins (TSBs) give the most probable cause of factory-related defects on previous model years that will likely be carried over to the 2011

HONDA ENGINE OVERHEATS/LOSES COOLANT

BULLETIN NO.: 08-044   DATE: JULY 30, 2009

2006–08 Civic—ALL except GX, Hybrid, and Si

PROBLEM: Engine Overheats or Leaks Coolant. **SYMPTOM:** The engine leaks coolant and may overheat.

PROBABLE CAUSE: The engine block is cracking at the coolant passages. **CORRECTIVE ACTION:** Install a new engine block assembly.

IN WARRANTY: The normal warranty applies. **OUT OF WARRANTY:** Any repair performed after warranty expiration may be eligible for goodwill consideration by the District Parts and Service Manager or your Zone Office. You must request consideration, and get a decision, before starting work. **DIAGNOSIS:** Look for coolant leaking from cracks in the block at the points shown below. On the back side of the engine, remove the oil/air separator cover so you can check beneath it. Pressure-test the cooling system.

versions. TSBs are reliable sources of information because manufacturers depend on the dealer corrections outlined in their bulletins until a permanent, cost-effective engineering solution is found at the factory, which often takes several model years and lots of experimentation. Take, for example, these two service bulletins: Honda's shows that engine block cracks were carried over for three model years, while GM's bulletin covers many of its SUVs afflicted by fuel tank rustout over a six-year period. Both bulletins say that the automaker will pay to correct the problem—GM over a period of 10 years, and Honda for an indeterminate period under a "Goodwill" policy.

GM CAMPAIGN—FUEL TANK RESERVOIR CORROSION WARRANTY EXT.

BULLETIN NO.: 07076A   DATE: NOVEMBER 5, 2008

07076A—SPECIAL COVERAGE ADJUSTMENT—FUEL TANK MODULAR RESERVOIR ASSEMBLY CORROSION

2004 Buick Rainier

2002–04 Chevrolet TrailBlazer, TrailBlazer EXT

2002–04 GMC Envoy, Envoy XL

2004 GMC Envoy XUV

2002–04 Oldsmobile Bravada

On some 2004 model year Buick Rainier and GMC Envoy XUV; 2002–04 model year Chevrolet TrailBlazer, TrailBlazer EXT; GMC Envoy, Envoy XL; and Oldsmobile Bravada vehicles currently or previously registered in the corrosion areas shown above, the fuel tank modular reservoir assembly, which contains the fuel pump, may develop corrosion of the fuel feed/return pipes after an extended period of time. Severe corrosion may cause the formation of small perforations. These perforations may allow a small amount of fuel to accumulate in a recessed area outside of the fuel tank. If this were to occur, it would be accompanied by a fuel odor. If left uncorrected and the corrosion is allowed to progress, a fuel spray from the pipes may begin to occur.

SPECIAL COVERAGE ADJUSTMENT: This special coverage covers the condition described above for a period of 10 years or 120,000 miles (193,000 km), whichever occurs first, from the date the vehicle was originally placed in service, regardless of ownership. Dealers are to replace the fuel tank modular reservoir. The repairs will be made at no charge to the customer.

As you read through the ratings and manufacturers' confidential service bulletins, you'll quickly discover that most Japanese and South Korean manufacturers are far ahead of Chrysler and GM in terms of maintaining a high level of quality control in their vehicles. European makes are even worse performers, especially with VW/Audi's failure-prone DGS six-speed transmissions (see NHTSA's complaints page for the 2010 Volkswagen Jetta on the following page).

Safety features and crashworthiness

Some of the main features weighed are a model's crashworthiness scores and the availability of front and side airbags, effective head restraints, assisted stability and traction control, and front and rearward visibility.

Frontal and side crash protection figures are taken from the National Highway Traffic Safety Administration's (NHTSA) New Car Assessment Program. For the front crash test, vehicles are crashed into a fixed barrier, head-on, at 57 km/h

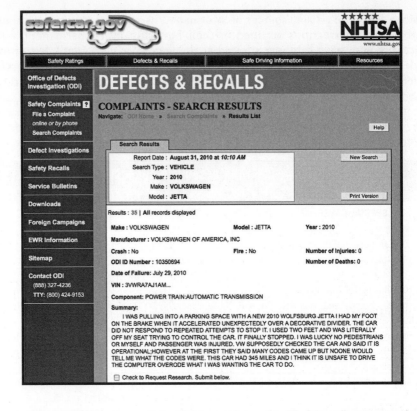

NHTSA road tests show the $47,900 (CDN) 2010 German-made, 12-passenger Sprinter 2500 Wagon has the highest propensity to roll over of all the 2010 vans on the market, earning just one out of a possible five stars. The second worst overall was the $38,299 (CDN) 2010 Ford E-350 15-passenger wagon (shown above), with a two-star rating (*www.safercar.gov*).

(35 mph). NHTSA uses star rankings to show the likelihood, expressed as a percentage, of belted occupants being seriously injured. The higher the number of stars, the greater the protection.

NHTSA's side crash test represents an intersection-type collision with a 1,368 kg (3,015 lb.) barrier moving at 62 km/h (38.5 mph) into a standing vehicle. The moving barrier is covered with material that has "give" to replicate the front of a car.

A vehicle's rollover resistance rating is an estimate of its risk of rolling over in a single-vehicle crash, not a prediction of the likelihood of a crash. The lowest-rated vehicles (one star) are at least four times more likely to roll over than the highest-rated vehicles (five stars) when involved in a single-vehicle crash.

In 2009, NHTSA upgraded the government safety standard governing roof crush resistance, a major factor in rollover accidents. The new rule requires that vehicles weighing 6,000 pounds or less must be able to withstand a force equal to three times their weight applied alternately to the left and right sides of the roof. However, vehicles weighing between 6,000 and 10,000 pounds need only withstand 1.5 times their own weight on the roof.

Safety advocates want the test improved. They say that gently applying weight to a vehicle's roof is not a proper way to test what happens when a speeding car rolls over, especially one that rolls over several times before coming to rest. NHTSA has argued that electronic stability control (due to be adopted universally in model-year 2013 vehicles) will, by preventing rollovers in the first place, save more lives than stronger roofs would.

The Insurance Institute for Highway Safety (IIHS) rates head-restraint and frontal, offset, and side crash protection as "Good," "Acceptable," "Marginal," or "Poor." In the Institute's 64 km/h (40 mph) offset test, 40 percent of the total width of each vehicle strikes a barrier on the driver's side. The barrier's deformable face is made of an aluminum honeycomb, which makes the forces in the test similar to those involved in a frontal offset crash between two vehicles of the same weight, each going just less than 64 km/h.

Though IIHS's 50 km/h (31 mph) side-impact test is carried out at a slower speed than NHTSA's side test, the barrier uses a front end shaped to simulate the typical front end of a pickup or SUV. The Institute also includes the degree of head injury in its ratings.

Last year, IIHS introduced its own roof-crush test that subjects a given roof to four times the vehicle's weight. This new test is now a factor in the IIHS's Top Safety Pick rating, along with evaluations of performance, front and side impacts, and seat/head restraints. For now, NHTSA's roof crush standard remains at three times the vehicle's weight—an improvement over the previous standard, but not as stringent as that suggested by IIHS.

Cost Analysis and Best Alternatives

Winter prices for the 2010 and 2011 models are much lower than last year's prices; Detroit automakers have ramped up generous discounts and rebates to move the millions of cars and trucks that are expected to fill dealer inventories by late summer. VW's 2011 Jetta Diesel TDI is returning as a slightly larger, less expensive offering. Leasing deals are also expected to pick up now that the American automakers have renewed their links with GMAC and other lenders.

Warranties

A manufacturer's warranty is a legal commitment. It promises that the vehicle will perform in the normal and customary manner for which it is designed. If a part

Wow, a savings of almost 50 percent!

malfunctions or fails (unless it's because of owner negligence or poor maintenance), the dealer must fix or replace the defective part or parts and then bill the automaker or warranty company for all of the part and labour costs. Warranties are an important factor in *Lemon-Aid*'s ratings. Unfortunately, it has been our experience that most automakers cheat on their warranty obligations and inflate the costs of scheduled maintenance work.

Most new-vehicle warranties fall into two categories: bumper-to-bumper, for a period of three to five years, and powertrain, for up to 5 years/100,000 km. Automakers sometimes charge an additional $50–$100 fee for repairs requested by purchasers of used vehicles with unexpired base warranties. For snowbirds, the federal and provincial governments can charge GST and sales tax on warranty and non-warranty repairs done south of the border—so beware. Also, keep in mind that some automakers, like Honda, may not honour your warranty if a vehicle is purchased in the States and registered in Canada.

A third kind of warranty, the 60-day "money-back" guarantee, is now offered with some GM vehicles. Although General Motors says few buyers have returned their purchase, owners report that it's not for lack of trying. Taxes, extra wear and tear charges, mileage limitations, and other hurdles usually prompt dissatisfied customers to choose another vehicle in the dealer's stock.

Cross-Border Warranty Restrictions

Cross-border sales still remain a viable alternative for buyers who want to save thousands of dollars on new and used top-end, fully equipped models. A couple of years ago, many automakers refused to honour warranties in Canada on vehicles bought in the U.S. and brought to Canada. That tactic didn't cut it with consumers, so this year buyers will find fewer warranty restrictions from a chastened auto industry.

Canada's non-profit Automobile Protection Association has drawn up the following list of companies and identified whether they have warranty restrictions on vehicles bought in the United States (check *www.apa.ca* for changes).

CROSS-BORDER WARRANTY POLICIES

ACURA/HONDA: No warranty coverage.

AUDI: Full warranty coverage.

BMW: Warranty coverage, but free scheduled service, standard in Canada, will not be offered. All modifications required to make cars conform to Canadian standards must be done by an authorized BMW dealer in Canada.

CHRYSLER CANADA: No warranty coverage.

FORD MOTOR COMPANY OF CANADA: Full warranty coverage.

GENERAL MOTORS OF CANADA: The owner of a new GM car imported from the U.S. must wait until the car is six months old before registering the warranty.

HYUNDAI CANADA: No warranty coverage.

INFINITI CANADA: The warranty applies with U.S. warranty limits of 4 years/60,000 miles bumper to bumper and 6 years/70,000 miles on the powertrain.

KIA CANADA: No warranty coverage.

MERCEDES BENZ: The car must be modified to meet Canadian specifications by a Mercedes-Benz Canada dealer and certified to ensure that standards are met. Mercedes-Benz Canada can then issue a Letter of Compliance and the same 4-year/80,000 km warranty that Canadian-market cars have. There is no corrosion warranty, and no extended warranty is available.

MITSUBISHI CANADA: No warranty coverage.

NISSAN: New U.S.-market Nissan cars must first be registered in the U.S. for the warranty to apply in Canada. If the car is sold by the Canadian purchaser within six months of the original purchase to another Canadian resident, the warranty becomes void.

SUBARU CANADA: Maybe yes, maybe no. The car must either be returned to the U.S. for warranty repairs, or the owner can have the car repaired by a Subaru dealer in Canada, pay for it in full, and submit the bill to Subaru U.S. for reimbursement. Keep in mind: This is basically a "gentlemen's agreement" and Subaru USA can change its policy at any time.

SUZUKI CANADA: Maybe yes, maybe no. Suzuki Canada will provide the equivalent warranty coverage for Suzuki vehicles that originate in the U.S., but the car has to be offered in Canada (the Suzuki Forenza and Reno won't be covered).

TOYOTA CANADA: Full warranty coverage.

VOLKSWAGEN CANADA: No warranty coverage.

VOLVO CANADA: Full warranty coverage.

AMERICAN VEHICLES

Bad Pants

I think of a Cadillac or a Lincoln as a car my Uncle Charlie, who's bald, smokes cigars, and wears bad pants, would drive.

KEVIN IRELAND
BUSINESS WEEK
DECEMBER 1, 1997

"Friendly Arrogance"

Chrysler was poorly run during its alignment with Daimler AG, and larded up with debt, hollowed out by years of mismanagement, Chrysler under (private equity firm) Cerberus never had a chance…GM's board of directors was utterly docile in the face of mounting evidence of a looming disaster, and former GM chairman and chief executive Rick Wagoner set a tone of "friendly arrogance" that permeated the company,

STEVE RATTNER
FORMER HEAD OF THE U.S. GOVERNMENT TASK FORCE THAT OVERSAW
THE RESTRUCTURING OF GENERAL MOTORS AND CHRYSLER
ASSOCIATED PRESS
OCTOBER 21, 2009

Yikes! After driving GM into bankruptcy and getting fired by Rattner, former GM CEO Rick Wagoner has joined the *Washington Post*'s Board of Directors. Insiders say the *Post* is just a few steps from bankruptcy. Hopefully, Wagoner won't do to the *Post* what he did to GM.

Last year's shakeout of the American auto industry left Ford as the only clear winner. Despite having just scrapped its Mercury division in the States, Ford has the best brand mix, a relatively satisfied dealer body, and great relations with its suppliers. GM, on the other hand, is more of a mixed bag. Its products have been relegated to four Detroit-based divisions instead of eight, and the company has decided to keep its Germany-based Opel operation after its calls for a bailout were spurned by Germany. Although GM's products are fewer, the company has a number of popular 2011 models like the Cruze, Equinox, Terrain, and Traverse. On the other hand, the automaker's dealer network is far from being as lean as GM said it must be; many dealers are forcing their way back into the network as a result of arbitration settlements, with hundreds of dealer lawsuits still to be litigated. Overall, GM dealers are restive and clamoring for more product and secure financing.

Chrysler is in similar straits. It has a sullen and litigious dealer body and the worst supplier relations imaginable. Its only new product this year is a revamped Jeep Grand Cherokee (the re-engineered 300 and Charger arrive in the spring of 2011).

The company's old model lineup will be at a serious disadvantage going into 2011, especially with the dropping of the compact PT Cruiser last July. Then, Ford's full 2011 lineup of popular cars, crossovers, SUVs, and trucks, and GM's popular SUVs and trucks will cut into Chrysler sales.

As for quality control, the Detroit automakers collectively beat imports in J.D. Power's June 2010 Initial Quality Study. Toyota's safety woes probably led to its ranking falling from 6th to 21st place. Anchoring the bottom rung of the quality ladder with the most defects: Land Rover, Mitsubishi, and Volkswagen.

Ford came out of the Power study as the top dog with the highest initial quality among all non-luxury brands. It moved to fifth place among all brands from eighth last year, breaking into the top five for the first time in the study's 24 years. The three Ford models that ranked highest within their respective categories were the Focus, Mustang, and Taurus.

J.D. Power and Associates 2010 Initial Quality Study℠ (IQS)

2010 Nameplate IQS Ranking
Problems per 100 Vehicles

Porsche	83
Acura	86
Mercedes-Benz	87
Lexus	88
Ford	93
Honda	95
Hyundai	102
Lincoln	106
Infiniti	107
Volvo	109
Industry Average	109
Ram	110
Audi	111
Cadillac	111
Chevrolet	111
Nissan	111
BMW	113
Mercury	113
Buick	114
Mazda	114
Scion	114
Toyota	117
Subaru	121
Chrysler	122
Suzuki	122
GMC	126
Kia	126
Jeep	129
Dodge	130
Jaguar	130
MINI	133
Volkswagen	135
Mitsubishi	146
Land Rover	170

Source: J.D. Power and Associates 2010 Initial Quality Study℠

Three-month ownership surveys aren't as telling as Power's three-year studies, though they do show which models will likely have more problems later on.

So what does the future hold for Chrysler, Ford, and General Motors?

Leaner, tougher times. GM will likely put all its trucks under the GMC label and consolidate Buick under the Chevrolet brand. We will have more supplier and dealer bankruptcies, more begging for handouts from Ottawa and Washington, and the busting up of different auto divisions to be sold to China, India, Europe, and various equity investors for 30 cents on the dollar (judging by the buyouts of Hummer, Jaguar, Saab, Land Rover, and Volvo). An industry that was riding high with 16 million cars sold annually will learn to make do with 11 million sold.

We will see many more fuel-efficient vehicles in the $10,000–$14,000 range in 2011—mostly co-productions with Asian and European automakers. The Asian link is a plus for reliability because many of the Asian platforms and components, like the Mazda6 parts found in Ford's Fusion, have been used and improved over many years and are much more dependable than their Detroit counterparts. In

Ford's Fusion looks good and performs well, but the Honda Accord gives better fuel economy and has a proven reliability record.

fact, *Consumer Reports* has given the Fusion high marks for safety and overall performance. But be careful; this isn't always the case. Chrysler's Mercedes hook-up and a number of other co-ventures with other countries' products didn't do very well. The the upcoming European-derived Ford Fiesta may have its own reliability and parts supply problems.

Another trend that will be obvious this year is the ever-increasing number of models that will employ hybrid powertrains. It's an innovation that has been used for years, most successfully in the Ford Escape and Toyota Prius, though their hybrid fuel-saving claims have more in common with Harry Potter than the Society of Automotive Engineers.

So, with the auto industry on its back and so many products to choose from, what should the prospective buyer of a Chrysler, Ford, or GM model do this year?

Be wary. Compacts will cost more and large cars will cost less as oil prices stay in the $80 U.S. per barrel range. Manufacturers will offer sweeter rebates and sales incentives as the 2011 summer months approach. Car shoppers can then get some good buys at ridiculously low prices while the industry is in turmoil; it'll be a buyer's market. On the other hand, some automakers and many dealers won't be around in the coming years to service or buy back the vehicle that today cost you so little. So buy a vehicle that's been around for awhile, has sold in large volume, and is recommended by *Lemon-Aid* as a "keeper"—one that'll last for a decade or two.

Chrysler

Bad Products

Perhaps with the exception of Ford in recent years, North American car companies have consistently put out such bad products they've commoditized themselves to a point where the only thing they can use to get us to buy their cars these days is deep discounts and government-engineered programs.... It's not surprising that the only real innovation in the automotive sector is coming from outsiders. Tesla offers an electric-powered sports car that will do 0 to 60 in 3.9 seconds. Toronto-based start-up ZENN Motor Co. provides a zero-emissions car with no noise.

JOHN WARRILLOW
GLOBE AND MAIL
MAY 5, 2010

Chrysler barely survived 2009, only staying alive thanks to an arranged marriage to Italy's Fiat. Aside from the fast-tracked Fiat 500, most fruits of this union won't reach dealer showrooms until 2012. In the meantime, Chrysler lost $3.78 billion during the almost seven-months of its post-bankruptcy existence last year and another $197 million during the first quarter of 2010. There's not a lot of time left for co-owner Fiat to turn the company around.

Chrysler isn't really "owned" by Fiat—at least not yet. The company's majority owner in the wake of bankruptcy continues to be a UAW health-care trust, with a 67.7 percent stake. The U.S. and Canadian governments combined hold a bit over 12 percent, and Fiat has the remaining 20 percent, acquired for "free" as part of the bankruptcy settlement after Fiat agreed to share technology and management.

This company has no new products, and what it does have, nobody wants. Of the three automakers we call "American," Chrysler has the farthest to go in improving performance, quality, and reliability. Granted, the company has beautifully styled cars like the 300 and high-performance models like the Viper; plus, its latest full-sized Ram 1500 pickup is noted for its impressive power and ride comfort. But reliability? Forget it. Quality? Forget that, too.

2009 CHRYSLER TOWN & COUNTRY 3.8L V6

All Technical Service Bulletins

NUMBER	DATE	TITLE
19-001-10	01/20/2010	Steering—Power Steering Return Line Fluid Leaks
08-017-09	10/27/2009	Body—Sliding Door Obstruction Detection Too Sensitive
14-001-09A	09/01/2009	Fuel System—Difficult Fuel Fill/Nozzle Shuts Off
05-004-09	08/20/2009	Brakes—Rear Brake Whirring Noise On Light Braking
24-003-09	07/29/2009	A/C—System Is Inoperative
23-020-09	07/03/2009	Body—Roof Rack Cross Bar Adjuster Seized/Corroded
23-016-09	05/19/2009	Body—Power Sliding Door Lower Hinge Grinding Noise
08-009-09	05/09/2009	Audio System—Distorted Sound When Playing An iPod
19-002-09	05/08/2009	Steering—Low Speed Squeaking Noises
08-007-09	04/10/2009	Instruments—"Blind Spot Not Available" Displayed
J01	03/10/2009	Recall—Electrical Connector Fire Hazard
08-003-09	02/13/2009	Audio System—Radio Inop. After Battery Disconnect
NHTSA09V046000	02/03/2009	Recall 09V046000: Electrical Connector Corrosion
08-001-09	01/06/2009	Interior—3rd Row Power Seat Latching Problems
08-037-08	12/19/2008	Interior—3rd Row Power Folding Seat Malfunctions
08-032-08	10/22/2008	Lighting—LED Turn Signal Indicator Serviceability
23-026-08	08/28/2008	Body—Rear Bumper Fascia Bulge/Bow or Bend

Chrysler minivans have improved, but they still have a long way to go.

Type in "automatic transmission failures" and Google throws up a picture of a Chrysler minivan (well, not really). All kidding aside, Chrysler has gone from a company noted for engineering innovation and strong, high-performance muscle cars to being known for ABS failures, AC malfunctions, and powertrains that fail after only a few years. Incidentally, Chrysler is coming out this year with a new Pentastar V6 engine; however, factory insiders say the engine has had a number of glitches that are keeping production low. Problems include faulty engine blocks and oil filter mounts and other defective parts.

More about Chrysler quality (or lack thereof). *Consumer Reports'* October 2009 edition says that two-thirds of Chrysler's models were below average and that the Chrysler Sebring convertible was the worst-rated car, with 2.8 times more problems than average. Other bottom-feeders: the Sebring/Avenger and Charger sedans, the Caliber hatchback, and the Liberty, Nitro, and Wrangler SUVs. *Consumer Reports* can't recommend any 2010 Chrysler model. Neither can *Lemon-Aid.*

The most apparent problem with Chrysler is its almost total dependence on trucks, SUVs, and minivans, aside from the few passenger cars it offers. And even the cars it does sell are huge, like the large, fuel-wasting Magnum, 300, and Charger. When gasoline was relatively cheap, big was profitable, but now cheaply made small cars are more in demand—and Chrysler is coming to the party late and with little to offer.

What about the 2011 models? Not a good idea. They are mostly warmed-over versions of the 2010s with some restyling and a new V6. Look, the Chrysler Corporation has enough problems meeting its payroll and paying suppliers. Warranty repairs and factory-related defect corrections are bound to take a back seat, especially with the new Jeep Grand Cherokee. Until Chrysler can show some stability and quality improvement, smart buyers should steer clear of the company's products this year. The only exceptions are the Jeep Wrangler and the minivan lineup—but only if you get an extended transmission warranty.

CALIBER   ★

bad buy

RATING: Not Recommended. **Strong points:** Expect a comfortable but firm ride; the CVT transmission usually "slips" into gear imperceptibly and can cut fuel consumption by about 5 percent; all-wheel drive works well; easy access to the interior; raised seating position is similar to a small SUV's; and rear seating space is adequate, though the Toyota Matrix is roomier. NHTSA gave the Caliber a five-star occupant protection rating in front and side collisions and four-star rollover resistance; rated "Good" in IIHS offset crash tests, but weak in others. Standard side-curtain airbags. **Weak points:** Engines lack reserve power for passing and merging, and are quite noisy; CVT sometimes jerks if, when slowing down, you hit the gas and then back off; handling is mediocre, at best; interior space is disappointing due to the excess door trim and wide centre console; not much room for cargo; the sloping rear windshield and large roof pillars limit rear visibility; lots of wind noise; the cheap-looking, plastic-dependent interior is fairly Spartan; subpar fit and finish; misaligned dashboard and centre panel; so-so fuel economy—the car's heft cuts into "real-world" gas mileage pretensions; and electronic stability control and traction control aren't available on all models. Rated "Marginal" in IIHS side-impact crash tests, despite the use of front and rear head curtain airbags. Head-restraint protection got a similarly low rating from the same insurance group. The AWD model is much more troublesome than the front-drive. **New for 2011:** Standard UConnect phone and Voice Command; supplemental side-curtain airbags.

> ## KEY FACTS
>
> **CANADIAN PRICE (VERY NEGOTIABLE):**
> *Value Package:* $13,995, *SE Plus:* $15,795, *SXT:* $17,645 **U.S. PRICE:** *Express:* $17,630, *Heat:* $18,845, *Mainstreet:* $18,810, *Rush/Uptown:* $20,745 **CANADIAN FREIGHT:** $1,350 **U.S. FREIGHT:** $750
> **POWERTRAIN (FRONT-DRIVE/AWD)**
> Engines: 2.0L 4-cyl. Turbo (158 hp) • 2.4L 4-cyl. Turbo (172 hp); Transmissions: 5-speed man. • CVT
> **DIMENSIONS/CAPACITY**
> Passengers: 2/3; Wheelbase: 104 in.; H: 60/L: 174/W: 69 in.; Headroom F/R: 5.5/4.0 in.; Legroom F/R: 41.5/26.0 in.; Cargo volume: 20 cu. ft.; Fuel tank: 51.5L/regular; Tow limit: 2,000 lb.; Load capacity: 865 lb.; Turning circle: 38 ft.; Ground clearance: 6.5 in.; Weight: 3,185 lb.

OVERVIEW: This is a bare-bones small car that doesn't cost much and gives you even less in return. From performance and quality perspectives, the Caliber is one of the least-reliable cars Chrysler makes. The 2011's added phone and side airbags are not enough to make this a desirable small car.

COST ANALYSIS: High fuel prices have kept the Caliber alive, with few leftover 2010s available. Look for discounts and rebates to drop 2011 prices by about 20 percent by early spring. **Best alternatives:** The Honda Civic and Fit, Mazda2 and Mazda3 hatchback, and Nissan Versa. **Options:** Consider the Security Group option package, which includes an anti-theft alarm (you may add an engine immobilizer), brake assist, and stability control for about $500. **Rebates:** $1,000–$2,000 rebates and discounts plus low-cost financing on all models. **Depreciation:** Faster than average. For example, an entry-level 2010 base Caliber that originally sold for $13,995 (plus $1,350 freight) is now worth about $9,500; a $19,145 2010 SXT's price has dropped to $13,400. **Insurance**

cost: Less than average. **Parts supply/cost:** Parts are reasonably priced and easily found. **Annual maintenance cost:** Average. **Warranty:** Bumper-to-bumper 3 years/60,000 km; powertrain 5 years/100,000 km; rust perforation 5 years/160,000 km. **Supplementary warranty:** Getting an extended powertrain warranty is a smart idea. **Highway/city fuel economy:** 7.3/9.0 L/100 km, 39/31 mpg.

OWNER-REPORTED PROBLEMS: Airbags fail to deploy:

> While driving at speeds of 50 mph [80 km/h], the vehicle crashed and the air bags did not deploy upon impact. There were three reported injuries and both the police and medical units arrived on scene. A police report was filed accordingly. The vehicle was towed to the vehicle rental company. The current and failure mileages were 3,000 miles [4,830 kilometres].

Poor positioning of the AC controls and four-way flasher; car vibrates excessively when underway with the rear windows down; and owners report a plethora of electrical short-circuits affecting all major components:

> While driving, the electric door locks will unlock and then lock themselves. This happens at any speed, in town or on freeways. Dealer has had car seven different times, and is unable to repair or even see the fault, although he has on different occasions found fault codes for stuck door lock switch.

CHALLENGER, CHARGER ★

bad buy

The Dodge Challenger.

RATING: Not Recommended. High fuel costs and Camaro/Mustang competition give both of these "high-performers" an uncertain future. **Strong points:** Styling, horsepower, and cachet. The 3.5L V6 has proven to be much more reliable than either of the two V8s, and it burns a lot less fuel. The Challenger was given five stars by NHTSA for front and side crashworthiness, and four stars for rollover resistance. The Charger earned five stars for frontal protection and four stars for rollover resistance. No testing was done for side-impact protection. IIHS rated the Charger "Good" for frontal offset protection. The Challenger has had fewer quality issues than the Charger, but it hasn't been on the market as long. **Weak points:** Stay away from the Charger's 2.7L V6; it's a dog that won't hunt. You will still get horrendous gas mileage due to the car's heft, even with the cylinder deactivation feature. Expect a stiff, jarring ride; overly assisted steering that requires constant correction; and marginal rear headroom. Stability control isn't available on all models. The Charger was rated "Poor" by IIHS for side-impact crashworthiness; head-restraint protection was rated "Marginal." Most quality complaints concern the automatic transmission, brakes, suspension, and climate system. **New for 2011:** The Challenger and Charger will get similar upgrades as those to the 300 series. We should see elegantly restyled exteriors and interiors; an all-new, supposedly fuel-efficient Pentastar 6-cylinder engine; an 8-speed automatic transmission; and rear cross-path and blind-spot monitoring systems.

OVERVIEW: Using the same platform and engines as the Chrysler 300, the Charger and Challenger combine a potent mixture of Hemi V8 power, rear drive, and an independent suspension supplied by Mercedes. Combined with the company's Multi-Displacement System (MDS), which shuts down half the cylinders under light load, the 5.7L Hemi engine produces more horsepower and slightly better fuel economy than previous engines. The downside is finding suitable Hemi engine repairs from a trimmed dealership network with limited parts inventories.

Although these cars are fun to drive and buy you entry into the high-performance "winner's circle," in the end, you will be the loser. High fuel, insurance, and depreciation costs will quickly thin out your wallet. Plus, the absence of a comprehensive seven-year or lifetime powertrain warranty is like performing a high-wire act without a net. Both of these cars will likely have a short shelf life, judging by the number of 300s and Magnums left over from last year, when fuel prices were much lower than they are now. Chrysler revived the Hemi name in 2002 with a 5.7L Hemi V8 engine used in its pickups and then extended it to the 300 Ram Wagon sedan—a winning combination that revived lagging pickup, sedan, and wagon sales. But that was when fuel was relatively cheap. For 2011, bigger is definitely not better.

PART THREE • AMERICAN VEHICLES

KEY FACTS

CANADIAN PRICE (VERY NEGOTIABLE): *Challenger SE:* $25,995, *Challenger SXT:* $27,695, *Challenger R/T:* $35,395, *Challenger R/T Classic:* $37,390, *Challenger SRT8:* $46,995, *Charger SE:* $29,095, *Charger SRT8:* $46,595 **U.S. PRICE:** *Challenger SE:* $23,695, *Challenger SE G Package:* $26,435, *Challenger R/T:* $31,610, *Challenger R/T J Package:* $33,415, *Challenger R/T Classic:* $34,940, *Challenger SRT8:* $43,680, *Charger SE:* $29,095, *Charger SRT8:* $46,595 **CANADIAN FREIGHT:** $1,400 **U.S. FREIGHT:** $750

POWERTRAIN (REAR-DRIVE/AWD)
Engines: 2.7L V6 (178 hp) • 3.5L V6 (250 hp) • 5.7L V8 (372–376 hp) • 6.1L V8 (425 hp); Transmissions: 4-speed auto. • 5-speed auto.; *Challenger:* 6-speed man.

DIMENSIONS/CAPACITY
Passengers: 2/3; Wheelbase: 116 in.; 120 in.; *Challenger:* H: 57/L: 198/W: 76 in., *Charger:* H: 58/L: 200/W: 75 in.; Headroom F/R: *Charger:* 2.5/ 2.0 in.; Legroom F/R: *Charger:* 41.5/ 28.0 in.; Cargo volume: 16 cu. ft.; Fuel tank: 68–72L/regular; Tow limit: *Challenger:* Not recommended, *Charger:* 1,000–2,000 lb.; Load capacity: 865 lb. est.; Turning circle: 41 ft.; Ground clearance: 4.5 in.; Weight: *Challenger:* 3,720–4,140 lb., *Charger:* 3,728–4,268 lb.

COST ANALYSIS: Look for discounts and rebates to drop prices by about 20 percent, thus putting pressure on leftover 2010 model year prices and sweetening 2011 model discounts early next year. The Challenger will continue with V6 and Hemi V8 engines to counter new threats from the Chevrolet Camaro and horsepower-boosted Ford Mustang V6. It's also the largest, roomiest, and heaviest entrant among these classic American sport coupes. But its lack of agility makes it more of a Clydesdale than a "pony car." **Best alternatives:** The Ford Five Hundred or Mustang, or Chevy's resurrected Camaro. **Options:** You'll want the 3.5L V6 engine for better all-around performance without much of a fuel penalty. Servicing will be easier and less expensive than with either of the Hemi engines. **Rebates:** $3,500–$7,000 rebates and discounts, plus zero percent financing by the spring of next year. **Depreciation:** Much faster than average. A 2007 Charger that sold for $28,370 is now worth about $9,500. The first-year 2009 SE Challenger's price has dropped from $24,995 to $19,500. **Insurance cost:** Higher than average. **Parts supply/cost:** Parts are not a problem due to the many different models using the same Chrysler 300 parts. Engine and body components are expensive and complex to troubleshoot; especially now that Chrysler has fewer dealers, parts suppliers, and skilled mechanics. **Annual maintenance cost:** Average; higher than average once the warranty expires. **Warranty:** Bumper-to-bumper 3 years/ 60,000 km; powertrain 5 years/100,000 km; rust perforation 5 years/160,000 km. **Supplementary warranty:** An extended powertrain warranty is a wise choice, since Chrysler is too cheap to provide Canadians with a lifetime powertrain warranty like the one offered in the States. **Highway/city fuel economy:** *Challenger 3.5L:* 8.0/11.8 L/100 km, 35/24 mpg. *Challenger 5.7L:* 8.2/13.8 L/100 km, 34/20 mpg. *Challenger 6.1L:* 9.2/15.6 L/100 km, 31/18 mpg. *Charger 2.7L:* 7.7/11.3 L/100 km, 37/25 mpg. *Charger 3.5L:* 8.1/12.2 L/100 km, 35/23 mpg. *Charger 5.7L:* 8.7/13.4 L/100 km, 32/21 mpg. *Charger 6.1L:* 10.6/16.0 L/100 km, 27/18 mpg.

OWNER-REPORTED PROBLEMS: *Challenger:* One vehicle shut off when the owner honked the horn and applied the brakes at the same time. The throttle sticks; vehicle loses power while under load, as in passing or going up hills as rpms race; and the rough-shifting automatic transmission causes the car to lose traction on wet roadways. *Charger:* Power distribution box under the hood caught fire and melted in one vehicle. When started, vehicle suddenly accelerated:

> The contact started the vehicle and while it was in the Park position, it suddenly accelerated and crashed into another vehicle which pushed that vehicle into another one.

Hard-shifting, shuddering automatic transmission; vehicle could be in Drive even though the shift lever indicates it is in Park; hazardous placement of the power accelerator toggle switch:

> Power accelerator and brake pedal movement system has a toggle switch on the driver's side seat that is easily caught by a jacket or a coat. This causes the accelerator pedal to move towards you while driving and in turn causes the vehicle to accelerate

faster because your foot is still on the accelerator. The toggle switch to move these pedals forward or back away from the driver needs to be relocated to the dash or inoperable when the vehicle is in the Drive position.

Plastic radiator cooling fan breaks apart, shattering the fan blades and fan shroud and destroying the radiator; when accelerating, a loud whistling sound can be heard; cruise control shuts off randomly; and the solid metal door handles can burn your hand in hot weather.

AVENGER, SEBRING ★

bad buy

The Chrysler Sebring.

RATING: Not Recommended. **Strong points:** Adequate V6 performance; comfortable ride; crisper handling, thanks to firmer springs and shocks and lower-profile 18-inch tires; plenty of interior room; a spacious trunk with wide-opening lid for easy loading and unloading; and few owner complaints on past models. The convertible is especially attractive because of its reasonable price and slow depreciation. *Avenger:* NHTSA awarded it five stars for frontal crashworthiness and four stars for rollover resistance. IIHS gave Avenger top marks ("Good") for frontal offset, side, and rear crash protection. *Sebring:* NHTSA gave it five stars for frontal and side crashworthiness; rollover resistance earned four stars. Like the Avenger, it also earned "Good" ratings from IIHS for frontal offset, side, and rear crash protection. *Sebring convertible:* NHTSA gave four stars for frontal and rear crashworthiness; side-impact occupant protection earned five stars. Front offset and side crashworthiness were deemed "Good" by the IIHS. **Weak points:** Mediocre, lethargic, and buzzy 4-cylinder engine; and just competent, not thrilling, V6 acceleration. The 4-speed automatic can't match the 5-speeds found in competing makes. Overly soft suspension and less-responsive handling on the

KEY FACTS

CANADIAN PRICE (VERY NEGOTIABLE):
Avenger SE: $22,995, *Avenger SXT:*
$24,795, *Avenger R/T:* $24,795,
Sebring LX: $23,995, *Sebring Touring*
2.7: $26,995, *Sebring Convertible LX:*
$30,665 **U.S. PRICE:** *Avenger SXT:*
$20,980, *Avenger Express:* $21,980,
Avenger R/T: $22,480, *Sebring Touring:*
$20,870, *Sebring Limited:* $22,865,
Sebring LX Convertible: $28,600, *Sebring*
Touring Convertible: $29,960, *Sebring*
Limited Convertible: $33,460 **CANADIAN**
FREIGHT: $1,400 **U.S. FREIGHT:** $750
POWERTRAIN (FRONT-DRIVE)
Engines: 2.4L 4-cyl. (173 hp) • 2.7L V6
(186 hp) • 3.5L V6 (235 hp) • 2.6L V6
(290 hp); Transmissions: 4-speed auto. •
6-speed manumatic
DIMENSIONS/CAPACITY
Passengers: 2/3; Wheelbase: 108.9 in.;
H: 59.0/L: 190.6/W: 71.2 in.; Headroom
F/R: 5.5/3.5 in.; Legroom F/R: 41/28 in.;
Cargo volume: 13.6 cu. ft.; Fuel tank:
64L/regular; Tow limit: *Sebring:* 1,000 lb.,
Avenger: 2,000 lb.; Load capacity:
Sebring: 825 lb., *Avenger:* 865 lb.;
Turning circle: *Sebring:* 40.5 ft., *Avenger:*
41.0 ft.; Ground clearance: *Sebring:*
5.0 in., *Avenger:* 5.5 in.; Weight: *Sebring:*
3,335 lb., *Avenger:* 3,550 lb.

4-cylinder and 2.7L V6-equipped models. Optional stability control. Five adults will feel cramped in seats that aren't sufficiently bolstered; and trunk space is limited. Owners complain that rainwater drains into the Avenger's trunk. *Sebring convertible:* Head-restraint protection rated "Marginal" by IIHS. **New for 2011:** *Avenger and Sebring:* By year's end, the Avenger and Sebring will get new styling, suspensions, and V6 and a 6-speed automatic tranny. Then around 2012 they will be turned into little Fiats (omigod!).

COST ANALYSIS: Look for discounts and rebates to drop prices by about 20 percent, thus putting pressure on 2011 model-year prices in early 2011. **Best alternatives:** The Honda Accord, Hyundai Elantra or Sonata, and Toyota Camry (only with the brake override feature). For convertible aficionados, consider the Mazda Miata. **Options:** You'll want the 3.5L V6 engine for better all-around performance without much of a fuel penalty. The wimpy 2.4L 4-banger also underwhelms the Caliber and Jeep Compass. **Rebates:** $3,000–$4,000 rebates and discounts plus zero percent financing. **Depreciation:** Mind-spinningly fast. A 2010 Sebring LX that sold for $24,000 is now worth about $16,500. The 2010 base Avenger? Not much better: Its price has gone from $22,995 to $16,000. **Insurance cost:** Average. **Parts supply/cost:** Parts are expected to be reasonably priced and easily found. **Annual maintenance cost:** Predicted to be average through the third year of ownership, and then a bit higher than average once the warranty expires. **Warranty:** Bumper-to-bumper 3 years/60,000 km; powertrain 5 years/100,000 km; rust perforation 5 years/160,000 km. **Supplementary warranty:** Getting an extended powertrain warranty is a smart idea. **Highway/city fuel economy:** *2.4L:* 6.6/9.7 L/100 km, 37/25 mpg. *3.5L:* 7.4/12.9 L/100 km, 35/23 mpg.

OWNER-REPORTED PROBLEMS: Side airbags fail to deploy; inaccurate fuel gauge readings make it easy to run out of gas; brakes fail when backing up; engine surges when brakes are applied; and tapping the brakes fails to disengage the cruise control.

300, 300C ★★

The Chrysler 300.

RATING: Below Average. These cars are scheduled to be dropped next year, if Chrysler doesn't drop first. **Strong points:** Plenty of power with the 3.5L V6; acceptable handling; a remarkably quiet and spacious interior; and a large trunk. The touring model gives a smoother, more-comfortable ride than does the 300C, which is the performance-oriented variant. **Weak points:** The base 2.7L V6 is no match for the car's weight. These cars are gas-guzzlers in spite of their engine cylinder deactivation feature. Hemi-equipped models are way overpriced and resale values have fallen considerably since 2005. Standard towing capability is less than one would expect from a rear-drive. Some of the electronics derived from Mercedes' luxury models have had serious reliability problems. The car's high waistline and tall doors make for a claustrophobia-inducing interior and limit outward visibility. Stability control isn't a standard feature on all models. **New for 2011:** Look for an elegantly restyled exterior and a plusher interior along with an all-new, supposedly fuel-efficient Pentastar 6-cylinder engine and a new 8-speed automatic transmission. New safety features will include rear cross-path and blind-spot monitoring systems.

KEY FACTS

CANADIAN PRICE (VERY NEGOTIABLE): *Touring:* $32,095, *Touring AWD:* $37,295, *C:* $46,745, *AWD:* $50,295, *SRT8:* $54,845 **U.S. PRICE:** *Touring:* $28,010, *Touring Plus:* $29,100, *Touring Signature:* $32,635, *300S:* $32,635, *C:* $46,745, *AWD:* $50,295, *SRT8:* $54,845 **CANADIAN FREIGHT:** $1,400 **U.S. FREIGHT:** $750

POWERTRAIN (REAR-DRIVE/AWD)

Engines: 2.7L V6 (178 hp) • 3.5L V6 (250 hp) • 5.7L V8 (359 hp) • 6.1L V8 (425 hp); Transmissions: 4-speed auto. • 5-speed auto. • 8-speed auto.

DIMENSIONS/CAPACITY (BASE)

Passengers: 2/3; Wheelbase: 120 in.; H: 58.4/L: 196.8/W: 74.1 in.; Headroom F/R: 4.5/2.5 in.; Legroom F/R: 43.0/30.5 in.; Cargo volume: 15.6 cu. ft.; Fuel tank: 68L/regular; Tow limit: 2,000 lb.; Load capacity: 865 lb.; Turning circle: 41 ft.; Ground clearance: 5.6 in.; Weight: *300:* 3,766 lb., *AWD:* 4,041 lb.

OVERVIEW: Front-drives are out and rear-drives are in—again—along with all-wheel drive and complicated Hemi V8 engines—all the ingredients for endless repair waits and extra expenses. The V8 is rather exceptional, in that it features Chrysler's Multi-Displacement System, which uses eight cylinders under load and then switches to 4-cylinder mode when cruising. This is unsettling, because the last time this was offered by an American automaker (Cadillac, in the '80s), owners found their cars running on four cylinders along freeways and then switching to eight cylinders in traffic. After a torrent of lawsuits, GM went back to a conventional powertrain set-up. So far, this has not been a problem with Chrysler.

COST ANALYSIS: Excess weight and large engines drive up fuel costs; consequently, resale values are dropping because buyers are shifting to smaller, more-economical sedans. **Best alternatives:** Ford's Crown Victoria or a used Grand Marquis are credible rear-drive alternatives. **Options:** Be wary of the new Pentastar V6 that will debut by year's end; first reports indicate it is likely to be troublesome during its first year on the market. Consider the SXT model with the 3.5L V6 and traction/stability control. **Rebates:** Expect $5,000–$6,000 discounts or rebates and low-interest financing programs by late winter. **Depreciation:** Higher than average. For example, a 2007 Chrysler 300C SRT8 equipped with a Hemi V8 sold new |for $51,170; today its resale value is barely $22,000. **Parts supply/cost:** Expect long delays and high costs. **Annual maintenance cost:** Higher than average. **Warranty:** Bumper-to-bumper 3 years/60,000 km; powertrain 5 years/100,000 km; rust perforation 5 years/160,000 km. **Supplementary warranty:** Get an extended powertrain warranty thrown into the deal. **Highway/city fuel economy:** *2.7L:* 7.7/11.3 L/100 km, 37/25 mpg. *3.5L:* 8.1/12.2 L/100 km, 35/23 mpg. *3.5L AWD:* 8.6/12.6 L/100 km, 33/22 mpg. *5.7L 300C (cylinder deactivation):* 8.0/13.5 L/100 km, 35/21 mpg. *5.7L AWD:* 8.7/13.4 L/100 km, 32/21 mpg. *6.1L:* 10.6/16.0 L/100 km, 27/18 mpg. Owners report that real-world fuel consumption with both engines, however, is far more than the above estimates.

OWNER-REPORTED PROBLEMS: One car caught on fire while parked and then exploded:

> My 2008 300 Touring was parked in a parking lot. The alarm started going off by itself. A fire started out of nowhere from under the hood. Then my car exploded from the front to the back through the exhaust pipe. I only had 6,100 or so miles [9,800 km] on my car.

Chronic electrical shorts and stalling; vehicle rolls backward when stopped for a light on an incline; automatic transmission clicking and banging into gear; transmission will suddenly slip into a lower gear; electronic stability control is ineffective on ice:

> I rented a Chrysler 300 over this past weekend. I want you to know that it was the scariest ride I've had in a while. Have you ever tested the electronic stability program on ice? It not only does not work, it is extremely dangerous. I had to drive about 600 miles [965 km] on icy and windy Wyoming roads which proved to be quite scary in the 300 with ESP.

CD player won't play a complete disc, and parts aren't available to repair the problem; steering knocks when turning; brakes drag and pulsate when stopping; horn won't sound if the car is not running or if it isn't hit in the right spot:

> Excessive effort is required to operate the horn. The driver must strike the horn pad cover with much stronger than typical force, and only in certain, very specific locations before the horn will sound. In a panic, a driver will likely not meet these location/force requirements and the horn will not sound, resulting in other drivers and pedestrians not receiving a warning.

Poorly performing Goodyear Integrity tires:

> Goodyear Integrity tires hydroplane every time it rains. I have already had one accident because I couldn't stop. I've run a red traffic light and I have experimented in a parking lot and hydroplaned at 15 mph [24 km/h].

Defective rack and pinion steering:

> The driver heard a grinding noise coming from the steering wheel when turning in either direction. The dealer stated that the noise was normal and would disappear once the tires were "broken in." The noise continued well over three months. The vehicle was taken to a different dealer and they stated that the rack and pinion steering was defective. They also stated that the part to repair the steering was unavailable.

PT CRUISER ★ ★

RATING: Below Average. The Cruiser was dropped in July 2010. Its resale value will plummet just like Oldsmobile, Saturn, and Pontiac models. **Strong points:** Excellent fuel economy (regular fuel); nimble handling around town; acceptable

KEY FACTS

CANADIAN PRICE (VERY NEGOTIABLE):
Classic: $20,500 **U.S. PRICE:** *Express:*
$17,630, *Heat:* $18,845 **CANADIAN**
FREIGHT: $1,400 **U.S. FREIGHT:** $750
POWERTRAIN (FRONT-DRIVE)
Engine: 2.4L 4-cyl. (150 hp);
Transmissions: 5-speed man.
• 4-speed auto.
DIMENSIONS/CAPACITY (BASE)
Passengers: 2/3; Wheelbase: 103 in.;
H: 63.0/L: 168.9/W: 67.1 in.; Headroom
F/R: 2.0/4.0 in.; Legroom F/R: 45.0/
28.0 in.; Cargo volume: 32 cu. ft.; Fuel
tank: 57L/regular; Tow limit: 1,000 lb.;
Load capacity: 865 lb.; Turning circle:
41 ft.; Ground clearance: 5.0 in.; Weight:
3,147 lb.

steering response, with good road feedback. Good braking; a versatile and spacious interior; many thoughtful interior amenities; and easy access. NHTSA awarded the PT Cruiser four stars for frontal, side, and rear crashworthiness; IIHS followed with its top "Good" rating for occupant protection in a frontal impact, but the car failed other tests. **Weak points:** The 150 hp 2.4L 4-cylinder engine is not very smooth-running when matched to the automatic transmission; it struggles when going uphill or merging with highway traffic. Going uphill or merging requires frequent downshifting and lots of patience—accelerating to 100 km/h takes about 9 seconds. The automatic transmission doesn't have much low-end torque, forcing early kickdown shifting and deft manipulation of the accelerator pedal. Rough downshifts; mediocre highway performance and handling; a firm ride; lots of engine, wind, and road noise; and limited rear visibility. Emergency handling is slow and sloppy. The turning diameter seems excessive for such a short vehicle. Hard cornering produces an unsteady, wobbly ride because of the car's height.

According to IIHS, the PT Cruiser isn't very crashworthy; it got a "Poor" rating in both the side and rear tests, and the organization blasted the vehicle's inability to protect occupants:

> In the side test, measures recorded on the driver dummy indicate that in a real-world crash of similar severity, rib fractures and internal organ injuries would be likely, along with a possible pelvic fracture. The rear passenger dummy's head contacted the C-pillar during the test because this car doesn't have rear-seat side airbags. Measures recorded on the dummy indicate that serious neck injuries and a fractured pelvis would be possible in a crash of this severity.

New for 2011: Nothing, as the Cruiser takes that last drive down the long Green Mile.

COST ANALYSIS: Since its debut as a year 2000 model, the Cruiser has been one of the best small cars Chrysler sells, which isn't saying a lot. Minus its turbocharged engine, the car loses much of its performance edge, but saves fuel and maintenance costs in the process. **Best alternatives:** Chevrolet HHR, Honda Civic, Hyundai Tucson, Kia Rondo, and Mazda3. **Options:** An anti-theft engine immobilizer would be a good idea. **Rebates:** Expect $2,000–$3,000 discounts or rebates by late winter. **Depreciation:** Faster than average. For example, the 2007 Classic sold for $20,940; now it's worth about $9,000 and will probably sell for much less than that when the model is dropped by year's end. **Parts supply/**

cost: No problem. **Annual maintenance cost:** Average. **Warranty:** Bumper-to-bumper 3 years/60,000 km; powertrain 5 years/100,000 km; rust perforation 5 years/160,000 km. **Supplementary warranty:** Get an extended powertrain warranty. **Highway/city fuel economy:** 7.5/9.8 L/100 km, 35/26 mpg.

OWNER-REPORTED PROBLEMS: Main complaint areas continue to be the automatic transmission, AC, and brakes. Airbags deploy for no reason or fail to deploy; gas pedal goes to the floor with no effect; vehicle suddenly shifts into First gear while cruising; headrests are too high, blocking vision; the instrument panel is hard to read; and water leaks into the interior. Other problems include sudden, unintended acceleration; sudden brake or steering lock-ups; extremely rough idling; high-speed engine surging; drivetrain whine; an annoying wind noise when driving with the rear window or sunroof open; moisture between the clearcoat and paint that turns the hood a chalky white colour; moisture accumulation in headlights; and sudden electrical shutdowns. The power windows may be hazardous to children:

> My 6-year-old stuck her head out the window... When she did, she accidentally kicked the power window button with her foot. The button was located near the floor in the backseat on the middle console. She rolled the window up on her own head and was stuck in the window. She only lived through the event because (1) her head was tilted at the time so the window rolled up on the side of her neck and not on her trachea; and (2) her 8-year-old sister in the back seat with her heard her screams and got her foot off the button and rolled the window back down. It was terrifying and painful and totally preventable. The button should be in a different place where it cannot be kicked or bumped so easily, and there should be a mechanism that allows the window to roll back down if it meets resistance.

GRAND CARAVAN, TOWN & COUNTRY ★★

The Dodge Grand Caravan.

KEY FACTS

CANADIAN PRICE (VERY NEGOTIABLE):
Grand Caravan: $20,945–$30,990, *Town & Country:* $32,745–$38,745 **U.S. PRICE:** *Grand Caravan:* $24,095–$29,195, *Town & Country:* $26,860–$33,595 **CANADIAN FREIGHT:** $1,400 **U.S. FREIGHT:** $750 **POWERTRAIN (FRONT-DRIVE)**
Engines: 3.3L V6 (180 hp) • 3.8L V6 (197 hp) • 4.0L V6 (251 hp) • 3.6L V6 (290 hp); Transmissions: 4-speed auto. • 6-speed auto.

DIMENSIONS/CAPACITY

Passengers: 2/2/3; Wheelbase: 121in.; H: 69/W: 77/L: 203 in.; Headroom F/R1/R2: *Grand Caravan:* 6/5/0 in., *Town & Country:* 3.5/4.5/0.0 in.; Legroom F/R1/R2: *Grand Caravan:* 41.0/30.5/27.0 in., *Town & Country:* 41/31/25 in.; Cargo volume: 61.5 cu. ft.; Fuel tank: 76L/regular; Tow limit: 3,800 lb.; Load capacity: 1,150 lb.; Turning circle: 41 ft.; Ground clearance: 5.0 in.; Weight: *Grand Caravan:* 4,600 lb., *Town & Country:* 4,755 lb.

RATING: Below Average, but this year's refinements may correct many of the past deficiencies, particularly the announced use of the new Pentastar V6 and an upgraded automatic transmission. It'll take a year to find out. And there is still the strong possibility that the minivan and Jeep divisions will be sold separately if Chrysler's Fiat gamble doesn't pay off; another reason to wait a year before jumping into the Chrysler pond. **Strong points:** Very reasonably priced and subject to deep discounting. Chrysler's top-of-the-line 4.0L engine is a better choice if you intend to do a lot of highway cruising—it's smooth and quiet with lots of much-needed low-end torque. The regular-sized minivans are the closest thing to a passenger car when it comes to ride and handling. The tight chassis and responsive steering provide a comfortable, no-surprise ride. Stiffer springs have greatly improved handling and comfort. Manoeuvring around town is easy. Excellent braking, lots of innovative convenience features, user-friendly instruments and controls, two side sliding doors, easy entry and exit, and plenty of interior room. Dual airbags include knee bolsters to prevent front occupants from sliding under the seat belts. Remote-controlled power door locks can be programmed to lock when the vehicle is put in gear. Chrysler has developed a mechanism that releases the power door locks and turns on the interior lights when the airbag is deployed. Both vehicles were given NHTSA's top five-star rating for frontal and side crashworthiness; rollover resistance earned four stars. **Weak points:** The new Pentastar V6 has been glitch-prone during early production this summer. The 41TE 4-speed automatic transmission with Overdrive shifts slowly and imprecisely. The transmission whines excessively. Power steering is vague and over-assisted as speed increases. Downshifting from the electronic gearbox provides practically no braking effect. Brake pedal feels mushy, and the brakes tend to heat up after repeated applications, causing a considerable loss of effectiveness (fade) and warping of the front discs. The ABS system has proved to be unreliable on older vans, and repair costs are astronomical. Mediocre handling with the extended versions, though the ride is smoother over bumps. A sad history of chronic powertrain, AC, ABS, and body defects that are exacerbated by the automaker's hard-nosed attitude in interpreting its after-warranty assistance obligations. Get used to a cacophony of rattles, squeals, moans, and groans caused by the vehicle's poor construction and subpar components. Fuel consumption is worse than advertised. **New for 2011:** The arrival of the new 290 horsepower Pentastar 3.6L V6 with a 6-speed automatic transmission; many interior upgrades; front seat active head restraints; and a slightly restyled exterior. A completely redesigned Caravan is due in 2014.

OVERVIEW: These versatile minivans return with a wide array of standard and optional features that include anti-lock brakes, child safety seats integrated into the seatbacks, flush-design door handles, and front windshield wiper and washer controls located on the steering-column lever for easier use. Childproof locks are standard. The Town & Country, a luxury version of the Caravan, comes equipped with the new Pentastar V6 and standard luxury features that make the vehicle more fashionable for upscale buyers.

COST ANALYSIS: Go for the more-refined 2011 model's second series made in the middle of 2011 or stay away until the 2012s arrive. This will allow the factory to work out any bugs found with the new V6 and automatic transmission. **Best alternatives:** Honda's Odyssey should be your first choice. The mini-minivan Mazda5 is also a good alternative because of its frugal 4-cylinder engine and wagon-like configuration. Full-sized GM rear-drive vans are also worth consideration. They are more affordable and practical buys if you intend to haul a full passenger load, do regular heavy hauling, are physically challenged, use lots of accessories, or take frequent motoring excursions. Don't splurge on a new luxury Chrysler minivan: Chrysler's upscale Town & Country may cost up to $10,000 more than a Grand Caravan, yet be worth only a few thousand dollars more after five years on the market. **Options:** As you increase body length, you lose manoeuvrability but gain ride comfort. The 3.8L V6 is a good choice for most city-driving situations; the Pentastar may be better, but it's too soon to tell. Try the 4.0L if you're planning on lots of highway travel or carrying four or more passengers. Since its introduction, it's been relatively trouble-free. The sliding side doors make it easy to load and unload children, install a child safety seat in the middle, or remove the rear seat. On the downside, the doors can expose kids to traffic and are a dangerous, failure-prone option. Child safety seats integrated into the rear seatbacks are convenient and reasonably priced, but Chrysler's versions have had a history of tightening up excessively or not tightening enough and allowing the child to slip out. Try the seat with your child before buying it. Other important features to consider are the optional defroster, power mirrors, power door locks, and power driver's seat (if you're shorter than 5'9" or expect to have different drivers using the minivan). You may wish to pass on the tinted windshields; they seriously reduce visibility. Ditch the failure-prone Goodyear original-equipment tires, and remember that a night drive is a prerequisite to check out headlight illumination, called inadequate by many. **Rebates:** The 2011 models will likely get $3,500 rebates or discounting plus zero percent financing throughout the year. **Depreciation:** Faster than average, especially for the Grand Caravan. Check this out: a $36,995 2010 Town & Country is now worth $28,000; a 2009 Grand Caravan that sold for $26,595 is now worth $14,000. **Insurance cost:** About average for a minivan. **Parts supply/cost:** Higher than average, especially for AC, transmission, and ABS components, which are covered under a number of "goodwill" warranty programs and several recall campaigns. **Annual maintenance cost:** Repair costs are average during the warranty period. **Warranty:** The base warranty is inadequate if you plan to keep your minivan for more than five years. Bumper-to-bumper 3 years/60,000 km; powertrain

5 years/100,000 km; rust perforation 5 years/160,000 km. **Supplementary warranty:** An extended powertrain warranty is a must-have. If buying the warranty separately, bargain it down to about one-third of the $2,000 asking price. Chrysler minivans can be expected to have some powertrain, electrical system, brake, suspension, AC, and body deficiencies similar to previous versions. Quality control has been below average since these vehicles were first launched more than 20 years ago and, surprisingly, got much worse after the 1990 model year introduced limp-prone transmissions. **Highway/city fuel economy:** *Grand Caravan 3.3L:* 8.4/12.6 L/100 km, 34/22 mpg. *4.0L:* 7.9/12.1 L/100 km, 36/23 mpg. *Town & Country 4.0L:* 7.9/12.2 L/100 km, 36/23 mpg.

OWNER-REPORTED PROBLEMS: Owners say powertrain and sliding-door failures make them afraid to drive these minivans. Their complaints also focus on electrical glitches, erratic AC performance, and early brake wear (see *forum.chryslerminivan. net*). In one NHTSA-logged complaint, the minivan, used as a hearse, was deemed unsafe to transport...dead bodies?

> All electrical equipment stopped working on the way home from the dealership. No gauges, no power windows or doors, no turn signals, no brake lights, no A/C, no radio. The only thing[s] working were the windshield wipers which came on by themselves and I could not shut them off. All the warning lights on the dash lit up. Made it home and called the dealership. Van has less than 100 miles [160 km] on it and already in for service. Called dealership Monday afternoon, they can't find any problems, must be the TIPM (Totally Integrated Power Module). They have ordered the part, but it is on backorder until who knows when. Van has been deemed unsafe to drive until repaired. Dealership provided me with a small sedan to drive until fixed, but this van was purchased by my funeral home to use for body transportation, stretchers, caskets, etc. Sedan is totally useless for my business.

The speed control feature automatically shifts transmission into low gear with a thud and high engine revs whenever the vehicle goes down an incline. At other times, the vehicle will lose all power until the ignition key is reinserted. Also, vehicle shuts down whenever both wheels pass over a pothole or speed bump. Other owners note the premature wearout of the cooling system, clutch, front suspension components, wheel bearings, air conditioning, and body parts (trim; weather stripping becomes loose and falls off; plastic pieces rattle and break easily). The front brakes need constant attention, if not to replace the pads or warped rotors after two years or 30,000 km, then to silence the excessive squeaks when braking. And don't expect engine compression to help with braking:

> As we have experienced to our horror on numerous occasions driving on the west coast (Vancouver Island), while trying to maintain vehicle control on a downhill stretch of paved road, this 4-speed electronic transmission system is incapable of providing any engine braking assistance whatsoever. The only alternative is to ride the brakes to maintain vehicle control.

SERVICE BULLETIN-REPORTED PROBLEMS: AC condenser road debris damage can be avoided by installing a condenser guard supplied by Chrysler (under warranty, of course). TSB #23-047-06 is very useful for determining when a cracked windshield should be replaced under warranty. Power liftgate failures can be easily corrected by recalibrating the power control module, says TSB #08-045-06. NHTSA has recorded numerous complaints of airbags deploying unexpectedly—when passing over a bump in the road or simply when turning the vehicle on—or failing to deploy in an accident. Owners who find the sliding door obstruction detection feature too sensitive need to reflash the electronic module.

POWER STEERING RETURN LINE FLUID LEAKS

BULLETIN NO.: 19-001-10   DATE: JANUARY 20, 2010

POWER STEERING RETURN LINES

OVERVIEW: This bulletin involves inspecting and if necessary removing and replacing the gear to cooler power steering return hose with a Kevlar braided return hose.

SYMPTOM/CONDITION: Customer may experience leaks in power steering return line, at cold start up in temperatures below –40°C (–40°F) and increased steering efforts or a noisy power steering pump.

RAM 1500, 2500, 3500 PICKUP   ★ ★ ★ ★

The Dodge Ram.

RATING: Above Average. **Strong points:** The crew cab model comes with a cargo bed that's longer than that of most of the competition, but not as huge as the Mega Cab; a Mega Cab/long bed configuration is also available on the Ram Heavy Duty models. The best engine choice, until the Pentastar V6 proves itself, is the 4.7L V8, with 310 horsepower and 330 pound-feet of torque; it's a good match for medium-duty work. The 2011 Ram 1500 remains the only full-size pickup with coil springs instead of leaf springs in conjunction with its solid rear axle. This produces exceptional ride comfort and chassis control over bumps. Compare the stability

KEY FACTS

CANADIAN PRICE (VERY NEGOTIABLE):
1500 ST V6 4×2: $21,270, *1500 ST V8 4×2:* $22,195, *1500 ST V8 4×2 SB:* $25,095, *1500 Quad ST V6 4×2:* $25,570, *1500 Quad ST V8 4×2:* $26,495, *1500 Quad ST V8 4×4:* $29,395, *1500 Crew ST 5.7 4×4:* $29,395, *2500 Reg ST 5.7 4×2:* $31,745, *2500 Reg ST 5.7 4×4:* $37,345, *2500 Crew ST 5.7 4×2:* $37,895, *2500 Crew ST 5.7 4×4:* $41,345, *3500 Crew ST SRW 4×2:* $50,715, *3500 Crew ST SRW 4×4:* $54,165 **U.S. PRICE:** *1500 ST V6 4×2:* $21,510, *1500 ST V8 4×4:* $25,965, *2500 Reg ST 5.7 4×2:* $28,165, *2500 Reg ST 5.7 4×4:* $31,140, *2500 Crew ST 5.7 4×2:* $31,415, *2500 Crew ST 5.7 4×4:* $34,810, *3500 Reg ST Diesel 4×2:* $35,630, *3500 Reg ST Diesel 4×4:* $38,545, *3500 Reg SLT Diesel 4×2:* $39,270, *3500 Reg SLT Diesel 4×4:* $42,440, *3500 ST Crew Diesel 4×2:* $39,200, *3500 ST Diesel 4×4:* $42,300, *3500 SLT Crew Diesel 4×2:* $44,435
CANADIAN FREIGHT: $1,400 **U.S. FREIGHT:** $750
POWERTRAIN (REAR-DRIVE/PART-TIME/ FULL-TIME AWD)
Engines: 3.7L V6 (215 hp) • 4.7L V8 (310 hp) • 5.7L V8 (390 hp) • 6.7L Diesel (Cummins); Transmissions: 4-speed auto. • 5-speed auto. • 6-speed man.
DIMENSIONS/CAPACITY (BASE)
Passengers: 3/2; Wheelbase: 141 in.; H: *1500:* 77, *2500:* 79/W: 80/L: 228 in.; Headroom F/R: 6/4 in.; Legroom F/R: *1500:* 40.5/25.0 in., *2500:* 40/26 in.; Cargo volume: N/A; Fuel tank: 132L/ regular; Tow limit: 5,655 lb.; Load capacity: *1500:* 1,120 lb., *2500:* 1,945 lb.; Turning circle: *1500:* 50 ft., *2500:* 51 ft.; Ground clearance: *1500:* 10.5 in., *2500:* 8.0 in.; Weight: *1500:* 5,655 lb., *2500:* 7,130 lb.

and ride with Toyota trucks and you will be impressed by Chrysler's better handling and more-comfortable ride. All 2011 Ram 1500s will return with standard safety features that include head-protecting curtain side airbags for both front and rear seating rows and an antiskid system that includes trailer-sway control. *2010 1500 four-door Regular Cab, 1500 four-door Crew Cab, and 1500 four-door Quad Cab:* NHTSA awarded five stars for frontal crashworthiness and four stars for rollover resistance. *2010 2500 Extended Cab 4×2 and 4×4:* These models earned four and three stars, respectively, for rollover resistance. *All 2010 1500 models:* IIHS gave frontal crash protection and head restraints a "Good" rating. On the emissions front: Ram 2500 and 3500 Heavy Duty pickups use a catalytic converter rather than urea to selectively trap NOx emissions. **Weak points:** The 3.7L V6 is a mediocre performer when compared with the Pentastar V6's potential, especially when hooked to a more-efficient 5-speed automatic. However, early production glitches rule out buying a Pentastar-equipped Ram until production changes by the summer of 2011 can offer a more-reliable powerplant. The fuel-thirsty Hemi V8 isn't a wise choice either. Its cylinder-deactivation feature is helpful, but not very. The Hemis are also complicated to service, and parts are often back-ordered. Full-time AWD and electronic stability control (ESC) are optional. Mediocre braking. If you are a short driver, you may not be able to see over the raised hood. *All 2010 1500 models:* IIHS gave side crash protection a "Marginal" rating. **New for 2011:** *Ram 1500:* The RAM 1500 was an all-new truck for the 2009 model year. New features that are carried on the 2011 models include an iPod connector, active head restraints, and an improved tire pressure monitoring system. *Ram 2500/3500:* The heavy-duty Ram gets a thorough going-over, including the addition of a crew cab. The styling follows that of the Ram 1500, but with a bigger, more-masculine look, while the interior is upgraded with new materials and amenities. A retuned suspension provides a more-comfortable ride. Engines are carryovers: the 5.7L Hemi V8 and the 6.7L Cummins turbodiesel. Fleet customers will be able to purchase a biodiesel-capable version of the Cummins engine that runs on B20 (20 percent biodiesel/80 percent petroleum diesel). Maximum

GVWR is up to 25,400 lb., while the Ram 2500 gained 2,000 lb. of trailer towing capacity with the 4.1 rear axle. *2011 Ram 2500/3500/4500/5500 Chassis cab:* The Ram 2500's tow rating increased on 2011 models from 20,000 to 22,000 lb. with the diesel and 4.1 axle ratio thanks to a beefier rear suspension and axle. Both the 2500 and 3500 have a standard EVIC (Electronic Vehicle Information Center), standard tire pressure monitoring, and standard trailer brake control on all but ST models.

OVERVIEW: These trucks were considerably improved in 2009, and so many have been sold over the years that their maintenance and support is practically bankruptcy-proof—with the exception of the Hemi engine and the automatic transmissions, which are the most problematic components.

Ram 2500 and 3500 models feature either the Hemi gas engine or the highly desirable Cummins diesel. As for power, Ford's new diesel has higher peak torque, but the Cummins is still the best choice for providing low-end torque.

COST ANALYSIS: Wait for the second-series 2011 Ram 1500 if you want to see whether the new V6 engine lives up to its hype. If you're inclined to stick with the V8s—including the problematic Hemi—then go for a 20 percent discounted 2010. The ideal combination is the diesel engine coupled to a manual transmission to dodge (pun intended) Chrysler's automatic transmission breakdowns. **Best alternatives:** Honda Ridgeline, Mazda B-Series, and Nissan Frontier. Ford's F-Series is the best Detroit alternative to the Ram. It was also redesigned at the same time as the Ram with a more-solid-feeling structure, larger cabs and cargo beds, as well as additional compartments and dividers. Ford F-Series trucks take a big step forward on the powertrain front for model-year 2011 with its introduction of the twin-turbocharged EcoBoost V6 and a strong new base V8 engine. Keep your fingers crossed that Ford's Powerstroke engine doesn't remain a "power-joke" due to sloppy manufacturing and crappy injectors. Leftover 2010 base Silverado and Sierra models aren't a smart buy despite what may be a bargain price. Their last redesign goes back to the 2007 model year. On the other hand, the 2011 Heavy Duty (HD) versions have just been redesigned and are much more refined than previous model years. Though they have a less accommodating, less comfortable crew cab, they're the only full-size pickups to offer a gas-electric hybrid model. **Rebates:** The 2010 and 2011 models will likely get $5,000 rebates or discounting plus zero percent financing throughout the year as higher fuel prices cut into the sales of the bigger rigs. **Depreciation:** Average, but much faster than average for the V8-equipped models. Diesels with manual transmissions hold their value best. **Insurance cost:** Average. **Parts supply/cost:** Higher than average, especially for Hemi engine, AC, transmission, and ABS components:

> I purchased the vehicle new and the first time I used the 4×4 auto the vehicle began to fail. It would stay in 4×4 for awhile then it would engage the 4×4 lock. I have had trouble getting it fixed because of a lack of supply of the required part. Also the windshield wipers went out and it was 2 weeks before they could get that part in. I have not had any luck with the customer support at Dodge at all.

Annual maintenance cost: Repair costs are average during the warranty period; however, this doesn't include lost wages or lost use of the truck due to long waits for back-ordered parts, which is a frequent complaint. **Warranty:** The base warranty is inadequate if you plan to keep your pickup for more than five years. Bumper-to-bumper 3 years/60,000 km; powertrain 5 years/100,000 km; rust perforation 5 years/160,000 km. **Supplementary warranty:** Consider buying an extended powertrain warranty. If buying the warranty separately, bargain it down to about one-third of the $2,000 asking price. **Highway/city fuel economy:** *3.7L V6:* 10.0/14.8 L/100 km, 28/19 mpg. *4.7L V8:* 10.0/15.6 L/100 km, 26/18 mpg. *5.7L V8 MDS:* 10.2/15.4 L/100 km, 28/18 mpg. *5.7L V8 4×4 MDS:* 10.8/16.2 L/100 km, 26/17 mpg.

OWNER-REPORTED PROBLEMS: Sudden unintended acceleration; gas pedal stuck to the floor; the airbag warning light comes on for no reason; two dealers could not get the airbag sensor replacement parts; the chrome trim ring around the console-mounted shifter reflects the sun into the driver's eyes; at 70 km/h, the truck shakes violently and veers out of lane when passing over small bumps; frequent front shock failures; excessive vibration:

> City of Ottawa has four (4) Dodge Ram 5500 units, bought in March 2010 with VIN numbers listed below, all have been plagued with steering problems which [cause them to drift] at speeds over 70 km/h and [are] difficult to control when facing consecutive small bumps—so much that in my test ride I was afraid I could end up in the opposite lane of traffic and cause a head-on collision. My personal concern is that if new or inexperienced drivers face such steering, it could cause accident, damage or even fatality if it goes unchecked. Unfortunately the dealerships (Southbank and Capital Dodge) seem to have very little knowledge of the root cause and no capacity to do real analysis and testing on these units. Chrysler Corporate has been contacted via 1-800 phone calls and fleet emails and files were opened on all our units but that has been the extent of their co-operation, and even the local service managers have not heard from Chrysler's engineering or the district service manager who usually tends to such calls.

Gas spews out of filler tube when filling up; wheel lug nuts sheared and wheel flew off truck; defective suspension front struts; sudden steering lockup; windshield wipers fall off because they no longer have a retention bolt.

SERVICE BULLETIN-REPORTED PROBLEMS: *2009–10 Ram 1500:* Vibration at highway speed (April 8, 2010, TSB: # 22-001-10); *2009–10, all models:* Hood creaking and squeaking (March 10, 2010, TSB: # 23-006-10).

RATING: Average. Called the "quintessential niche vehicle" by *www.edmonds.com*, the Wrangler is one of the most off-road-capable Jeeps ever made, but it falls short when driven on-road. What this fun-to-drive, competent off-roader gives in impressive performance is taken away by its overall lack of quality and poor reliability. Plus, its short wheelbase, loud and porous cabin, and mediocre highway performance makes this modern, entry-level CJ Jeep annoying at best as a daily commuter and outright uncomfortable as a road trip vehicle. But the Jeep cachet is fun if off-road thrills are your forte. That's why this is the only Jeep to own if Chrysler goes under. If Chrysler is broken up and sold piecemeal by Fiat, as *Lemon-Aid* predicts will happen, the popular minivans, Jeeps, and Rams will likely be spun off into new divisions with a host of new investors. **Strong points:** The Pentastar V6 and an upgraded transmission smooth out the powertrain's performance and the Wrangler remains an impressive off-roader. It comes

KEY FACTS

CANADIAN PRICE (FIRM): *2-door Sport:* $21,495, *2-door Sahara:* $28,495, *2-door Rubicon:* $31,495, *4-door Unlimited Rubicon:* $34,495 **U.S. PRICE:** *2-door Sport:* $21,915, *4-door Islander:* $25,220 **CANADIAN FREIGHT:** $1,400 **U.S. FREIGHT:** $750
POWERTRAIN (REAR-DRIVE/PART-TIME/ FULL-TIME AWD)
Engine: 3.6L V6 (290 hp); Transmissions: 6-speed man. • 4-speed auto.
DIMENSIONS/CAPACITY (BASE)
Passengers: 2/3; Wheelbase: 116 in.; H: 71/W: 74/L: 173 in.; Headroom F/R: 5.5/5.0 in.; Legroom F/R: 41/28 in.; Cargo volume: 34.5 cu. ft.; Fuel tank: 70L/regular; Tow limit: 3,500 lb.; Load capacity: 850 lb.; Turning circle: 43 ft.; Ground clearance: 8 in.; Weight: *Sport:* 3,849 lb., *Rubicon:* 4,165 lb.

with a roomy, plush cabin and a more-rigid frame that enhances handling; on the downside, it makes for a stiff ride. The front seat has plenty of headroom; the Unlimited models with four doors have 1.6 inches more legroom in the back. The Unlimited also has very generous cargo space. Safety features include stability control with rollover sensing, hill start assist, and anti-lock brakes. Front seat side airbags may be offered as an option. **Weak points:** These little SUVs are selling at their full list price and are not likely to be discounted by much as the year progresses. There is only a small amount of cargo room in the back of the two-door model; the previous V6 engine is coarse and underpowered, and the 6-speed manual transmission is anything but smooth. Handling is compromised by vague steering, a stiff ride, and low cornering limits (standard stability control is a plus), and violent shaking makes the vehicle practically uncontrollable ("Death Wobble") when passing over small bumps at cruising speeds:

> While driving my Jeep Wrangler at about 35–40 mph [56–64 km/h] over a rough spot on the road, I experienced horrible front end shake that I could not control until I pulled the car over. I'm very lucky there was nobody else in front or in back of me because I had no control of my vehicle. I looked into this online and have learned it's called the "Death Wobble" and it's happened to many other Jeep owners.

Owners report that the Wrangler's off-road prowess is compromised by poor original-equipment tires and thin body panels. Although there's not much you can do about the body panels, *www.tirerack.com* can give you invaluable, unbiased tips on the best and cheapest tires for the kind of driving you intend to do. Taller people may find that the legroom is limited in both the front and rear seats. Fuel economy? It isn't as good as advertised. **New for 2011:** A standard, more fuel-efficient 3.6L Pentastar V6, new interior and exterior, and Quadra-Coil suspension with regular, heavy-duty, or off-road tuning (depending on trim).

OVERVIEW: The Wrangler is the smallest and least expensive (we're talking bare-bones here) Jeep you can find. It's an iconic SUV that can easily handle open-air off-road driving anywhere you choose and still be presentable for Saturday night cruising downtown. How's this for versatility: The standard soft top can be folded down or the available hard top can be taken off. Then, if you want more adventure, the doors can be removed and the windshield folded down—in effect, creating many different vehicles out of one.

The two-door Wrangler is offered in Sport, Sahara, and Rubicon trim with standard four-wheel drive powered by a 290 hp 3.6L V6 engine, hooked to a standard 6-speed manual with Overdrive or an optional 4-speed automatic with Overdrive. Also standard is electronic stability control with roll control, traction control, brake assist, and hill hold control. The Rubicon offers equipment that off-road enthusiasts usually pick up from independent suppliers, like heavy-duty axles, front and rear electronic locking differentials, 32-inch BF Goodrich mud tires, a sway bar disconnect system, rock rails, and a heavy-duty transfer case with a 4:1 low-gear ratio. The available Freedom Top three-piece modular hardtop allows panels to be removed above the driver or passenger. Other options include

Dual Top Group, half doors, remote start system, front seat-mounted side airbags, and a multimedia infotainment system with 30-gigabyte hard drive and navigation system. The Unlimited is the first four-door Wrangler that carries five people and their luggage. It's the only four-door convertible available that offers rear-drive or four-wheel drive, making it equally at home on the trail or in the wilds of your local shopping mall's parking lot.

COST ANALYSIS: The 2011 models were substantially improved and are a better buy than any 2010 leftover. **Best alternatives:** Honda CR-V or Element, Hyundai Tucson, Kia Borrego, Nissan Xterra, Subaru Forester, and Toyota RAV4. But remember, none of these other models can follow the Wrangler off-road. In fact, with its new engine, the 2011 Jeep Wrangler could outperform them on-road. **Options:** The three-piece Freedom Top and the Sunrider Soft Top are nice touches, but beware of water and wind leaks (see below). Keep an eye out for the optional suspension system, which includes larger shock absorbers and heavy-duty springs. An aftermarket anti-theft system is also a plus. Ditch the Firestone tires. **Rebates:** The 2010 models are practically sold out, and they are expected to stay in short supply as fuel prices rise. Therefore, expect to buy a 2010 with a discount of no more than five percent on the higher-end models, if you are lucky. Four-door models are even harder to find, and they are selling at a premium with little haggling allowed. **Depreciation:** Faster than average, despite their overall popularity. A 2007 2-door X model that sold for $19,995 is worth barely $9,000 today. Even the much-in-demand 2010 four-door, entry-level Unlimited Sport version that originally retailed for $25,995 is now only fetching about $20,000— a $6,000 loss after barely 10 months. This is why you should hold onto your Wrangler until the depreciation losses have leveled off after five to eight years. **Insurance cost:** Higher than average. **Parts supply/cost:** Higher than average, especially for AC, transmission, and ABS components. **Annual maintenance cost:** Repair costs are average during the warranty period, but if Chrysler goes down for the count, these expenses become your responsibility. **Warranty:** Bumper-to-bumper 3 years/60,000 km; powertrain 5 years/100,000 km; rust perforation 5 years/160,000 km. **Supplementary warranty:** Get an extended powertrain warranty. Also, brake, powertrain, and exhaust system repairs should be carried out by agencies that provide extensive warranties on their work (lifetime). **Highway/city fuel economy:** *2010 3.8L V6 man.:* 10.6/13.9 L/100 km, 27/20 mpg. *2010 3.8L V6 auto.:* 10.5/14.4 L/100 km, 27/29 mpg.

OWNER-REPORTED PROBLEMS: Owners report frequent airbag failures, fuel-tank leaks, fuel-pump failures, malfunctioning fuel gauges, chronic engine stalling when accelerating or decelerating, front end torsion bar failures and fluid leaks, and clutch master and slave cylinder leaks and premature replacement. The 6-speed manual transmission sometimes pops out of gear; the automatic transmission slips erratically in and out of Second gear and leaks fluid; the power steering locks up; and there's excessive and premature brake wear, leading to brake failures. Other brake complaints concern the vehicle pulling to the left when braking; the rear brakes suddenly locking up while driving in the rain and approaching a stop sign;

and the vehicle going into open throttle position when the brakes are applied. There have also been many instances where drivers mistook the accelerator for the brake because the pedals are so close together. Body welds and seams are susceptible to premature rusting, and there have been frequent complaints about peeling paint and water leaks:

> Soft top leaks on both sides in the front. Seats getting stained and the carpet is starting to smell. Water stains on the doors, steering column, and down the dash.

> •

> Freedom top has leaked and stained my seats. Dealership just fixed it a month ago. Also, the Jeep was leaking oil, dealership just fixed the intake manifold gasket 3 weeks ago. It is scheduled to go back to dealership for this steering issue and it is rusting on both doors. Poor, poor quality.

WIND NOISE/WATER LEAK AT SOFT TOP HEADER	
BULLETIN NO.: 23-010-09	DATE: APRIL 17, 2009

SOFT TOP—WATER LEAK OR WIND LIKE SOUND AT HEADER
OVERVIEW: This bulletin involves replacing the header seal plate with a new design.
2007–09 Wrangler

WATER LEAK AT UPPER A-PILLAR DOOR SEALS	
BULLETIN NO.: 23-005-09	DATE: MARCH 24, 2009

SOFT TOP—WATER LEAK AT UPPER A-PILLAR DOOR SEAL TO DOOR RAIL INTERFACE
OVERVIEW: This bulletin involves the addition of foam to eliminate a possible water leak at the upper A-Pillar.
2007–09 Wrangler

The worst leaks occur at the bottom of the windshield frame. An easy way to check for this is to examine the underside of the frame to see if there's excessive rust. This has consistently been a problem area for Jeeps, hence all of the ads for aftermarket windshield frames. Watch for corroded windshield bracket bolts. The good news is that you can replace the windshield frame and all of the seals relatively cheaply. One failure that *can't* be repaired cheaply is a cracked windshield, another common Wrangler owner complaint.

SERVICE BULLETIN-REPORTED PROBLEMS: *2009–10 models:* Free installation of a chime device to warn when the transmission fluid is overheating (Customer Satisfaction Campaign: # J31, June, 2010); *2007–10 models:* Manual transmission pops out of gear (March 2, 2010, TSB: # 21-001-10).

bad buy

RATING: Not Recommended for two important reasons: Firstly, during the past decade the Grand Cherokee has been beset with chronic automatic transmission, brake system, and electrical system defects in addition to abysmally bad fit and finish. Take, for example, the fact that Jeep placed 27th out of 33 brands in J.D. Power and Associates' ranking of initial quality released in June 2010. Secondly, this year's extensively reworked model is an unknown; in the past, Chrysler models that had been revamped were more problematic than previous models. If Chrysler goes bankrupt, parts and servicing will be especially difficult to find.

Strong points: The 290 hp Pentastar V6 boosts power with 80 horses more than the previous 3.8L V6 engine. It features Variable Valve Timing (VVT), showing an increase of 33 percent in horsepower and 11 percent in torque over its predecessor, while also supposedly improving fuel economy up to 11 percent. Features on the base Cherokee include active front head restraints, 17-inch alloy wheels, dual-zone AC, passive keyless entry with push-button start, eight-way power driver's seat, 60/40 flat-folding rear seats, a front passenger seat that folds flat, fog lamps,

KEY FACTS

CANADIAN PRICE (FIRM, AT FIRST):
North Edition: $41,645, *SRT8:* $50,395, *Limited:* $54,645 **U.S. PRICE:** *North Edition:* $37,245, *SRT8:* $43,645, *Limited:* $47,895, *S Limited:* $50,645
CANADIAN FREIGHT: $1,400 **U.S. FREIGHT:** $750
POWERTRAIN (REAR-DRIVE/PART-TIME/ FULL-TIME AWD)
Engine: 3.6L V6 (280 hp) • 5.7L V8 (360 hp) • 2010 6.1L V8 (420 hp) Transmissions: 6-speed man. (2010 SRT8). • 5-speed auto.
DIMENSIONS/CAPACITY (BASE)
Passengers: 2/3; Wheelbase: 114.8 in.; H: 69.4/W: 84.8/L: 189.8 in.; Headroom F/R: N/A.; Legroom F/R: N/A.; Cargo volume: 36.3 cu. ft.; Fuel tank: 80L/ regular; Tow limit: 3,500–7,200 lb (the higher towing capacity applies to the 4×2 model).; Load capacity: 850 lb.; Turning circle: 37.1 ft.; Ground clearance: 11.1 in.; Weight: *Sport:* 3,849 lb., *Rubicon:* 4,165, lb.

CD/MP3 stereo, Sirius satellite radio, heated mirrors, tilt and telescopic steering column, automatic headlamps, a tire pressure monitor, and hill start assist. **Weak points:** Judging by initial orders, the new Grand Cherokee will likely sell at a premium during its first year on the market, but, as with the Chrysler PT Cruiser, cooler heads will prevail later on and the cost will go down by the summer of 2011. Another reason to wait until mid 2011 to buy the new Grand Cherokee: the Pentastar V6 engine has shown some quality glitches in production—not a good sign this early. Give Jeep time to work things out...if they can. Things that probably won't get fixed this model year: The V6 engine is a bit harsh at high rpms, there's excessive body roll with hard cornering, and the front seat cushions lack bolstering. **New for 2011:** The car has undergone a major redesign that includes a restyled, roomier interior (4 inches of extra legroom in the rear and 17 percent more cargo space than the previous version, which was last redesigned for the 2005 model year) and a more-sculpted exterior. It now comes with a larger fuel tank and a base fuel-efficient 3.6L V6 or an optional 5.7L Hemi V8. Both engines are coupled to a 5-speed automatic transmission. Newly available is a Selec-Terrain system that can be preset for Auto, Sport, Sand/Mud, Snow, and Rock. An optional Quadra-Lift air suspension raises or lowers the ride height. The Uconnect electronic feature on all models offers automatic crash notification, emergency calls, roadside assistance calls, remote door unlock, and stolen vehicle location assistance.

OVERVIEW: Nearly 18 years ago, Jeep created the premium SUV segment with the introduction of its upscale Grand Cherokee, then quickly lost sales momentum by falling behind in highway performance and quality control. Jeep sold about 300,000 Grand Cherokees in 1999 and roughly 50,300 in 2009. This year's upgrades seek to recapture the lost ground in a competitive field that Asians, GM, and Ford dominate.

Although the high-performance SRT8 model has been axed, Jeep has repowered its base model and used fuel-saving technology to provide more V6 and V8 power without sacrificing fuel economy.

The 2011 Grand Cherokee is built on a proven rear-drive unibody platform that the Mercedes-Benz ML has used for years; when combined with this year's new front and rear independent suspension systems, the result is enhanced on-road handling and comfort. Also, the stiffer body reduces noise, vibration, and harshness.

The reworked Grand Cherokee is also loaded with safety and security features that include standard electronic stability control (ESC) with Electronic Roll Mitigation, Hill-Start Assist, Trailer-Sway Control and available Hill-Descent Control; full-length side-curtain airbags to protect front and rear outboard passengers; seat-mounted side thorax airbags to enhance collision protection of the driver and front passenger; active head restraints that deploy in the event of a rear collision; an optional park assist system that detects stationary objects; a blind spot/rear cross-path detection system; adaptive cruise control that decreases a vehicle's preset cruise-control speed when closing in on another vehicle or when another vehicle pulls into same lane (this has been a failure-prone feature in the past); a Forward Collision Warning (FCW) system that detects when the vehicle may be approaching another vehicle too rapidly; and a remote starting feature.

COST ANALYSIS: OK. By now you know the 2011 model has been substantially improved, so don't waste your time or money on a cheaper 2010 version; however, don't buy until prices come down early next year. **Best alternatives:** Honda CR-V or Element, Hyundai Tucson, Subaru Forester, and Toyota RAV4 (only with the brake/accelerator override feature). Remember, none of these other models can follow the Grand Cherokee off-road, but they also won't be following it to the repair bay. **Options:** The optional Quadra-Lift air suspension that raises or lowers the ride height is complicated to troubleshoot and is useful only in special off-road environments. Ditch the Firestone and Bridgestone tires. **Rebates:** The 2011 models are seriously back-ordered, so wait until production picks up and rebates are sweetened during late winter or early spring. Also, it's axiomatic that redesigned models produced during the second half of the model year have fewer factory-related glitches. **Depreciation:** Traditionally, the Grand Cherokee loses its value more quickly than the Wrangler but not as rapidly as the Commander, which is essentially a stretched Grand Cherokee with cramped second- and third-row seating. A 2007 Laredo 4×4 Grand Cherokee that sold for $40,285 is now worth about $15,000. In comparison, a 2007 upscale Commander that sold for about $51,000 is now worth only $1,000 more ($16,000) than the same year's Grand Cherokee. **Insurance cost:** Higher than average. **Parts supply/cost:** Higher than average, especially for AC, transmission, and ABS components. **Annual maintenance cost:** Repair costs are average during the warranty period, but if Chrysler goes down for the count, these expenses become your responsibility. **Warranty:** Bumper-to-bumper 3 years/60,000 km; powertrain 5 years/100,000 km; rust perforation 5 years/160,000 km. **Supplementary warranty:** Get an extended powertrain warranty. Also, brake, powertrain, and exhaust system repairs should be carried out by agencies that provide extensive warranties on their work (lifetime). **Highway/city fuel economy:** 3.6L: 8.9/13.0 L/100 km, 32/22 mpg. 5.7L: 10.6/15.7 L/100 km, 27/18 mpg (thanks to the Multi-Displacement System (MDS) feature on the V8).

OWNER-REPORTED PROBLEMS: Most complaints centre on automatic transmission, electrical system, and fit and finish problems. Owners report frequent airbag failures, fuel-tank leaks, fuel-pump failures, malfunctioning fuel gauges, chronic engine stalling when accelerating or decelerating, front end torsion bar failures and fluid leaks, and clutch failures. The 6-speed manual transmission sometimes pops out of gear; the automatic transmission slips erratically in and out of Second gear and leaks fluid; the power steering locks up; and there's excessive and premature brake wear, leading to brake failures. Other brake complaints concern the vehicle pulling to the left when braking; the rear brakes suddenly locking up while driving in the rain and approaching a stop sign; and the vehicle going into open throttle position when the brakes are applied. There have also been many instances where drivers mistook the accelerator for the brake because the pedals are so close together. Body welds and seams are susceptible to premature rusting, and there have been frequent complaints about peeling paint and water leaks:

SERVICE BULLETIN-REPORTED PROBLEMS: 2009–10 *Grand Cherokees:* Inoperative tachometer or speedometer (September 29, 2010, TSB: # 08-28-00).

Ford

The Ford Mantra
Stand for something beyond profit. Rally your employees around a shared mission. Practice realistic optimism. Tell the truth without fear. These are Mulally's mantras and any CEO would do well to follow them.

> TONY SCHWARTZ
> APRIL 2, 2010
> *THE HARVARD BUSINESS REVIEW*

Ford Job 1: Get Me Out of Here!

For the past decade, Ford has had three ongoing problems that ended up almost bankrupting the company: bad products, bad quality, and bad management. Nevertheless, in a stunning reversal of fortunes, Ford has successfully corrected each one of these deficiencies in the short four-year period from 2006–10.

How did it happen that a kid from Boeing could call the shots and make Ford turn itself around in only four years? Ford's "non-auto" CEO, Alan Mulally, simply went back to the basics of quality car-building, seeking the biggest bang for the corporate buck while treating suppliers and customers with respect. Since Mulally came on board, the Escape SUV, Focus, Fusion, and F-Series pickups have picked up steam in new-vehicle sales and have won accolades for their quality control.

Ford has come the farthest of the Detroit Three in returning to its core business with very little government stimulus funding. Its recent models in particular have been more competitive from performance and reliability standpoints. In fact, most of its vehicles have scored Average or higher in *Consumer Reports'* reliability surveys. For example, Ford made considerable improvements to its F-Series pickups, the Ford Flex crossover (which looks ready to challenge the imports), and the freshened Fusion and Mercury Milan sedans (which combine good fuel economy with performance and quality). As far as hybrids go, the Fusion looks good, but the Escape Hybrid has proven itself since 2004 to be as good as or better than the Toyota Prius Hybrid.

This is not to say that most of Ford's models can match their Asian competition in terms of performance and reliability. They can't. A good example is the redesigned

Ford Taurus. It has more trunk space, highway performance has been cranked up several notches, and the interior is more user-friendly, with better-quality materials and more attention paid to ensuring a proper fit and finish. However, the car's interior feels closed in, visibility is limited, and there's not much rear-seat room. In effect, the car is "three steps forward and two steps back" after its revamping. The redesigned Hyundai Sonata, for example, gets it right, offering impressive fuel economy and a roomy interior. Not bad for a South Korean automaker that's a relative upstart when compared to Detroit-based automakers.

This isn't just a Taurus problem. Ford's other models are mostly mid-pack contenders as well. Some older models haven't been updated in years, and most of the company's SUVs (the Explorer, for example) lack refinement and style. The 2011 Explorer will become a more-competitive SUV by replacing its truck-like body-on-frame platform with a car-like unibody chassis. Just this one design change will improve handling, smooth out the ride, and provide better fuel economy. With any luck, powertrain "gear hunting" and intake manifold leaks won't reappear.

What Ford promises isn't always what it delivers.

Ford says it's closing its Mercury franchise in the States this year, 11 years after dropping Mercury in Canada (with the exception of the Grand Marquis and Marauder, which they continued to sell through Ford dealers). The Mountaineer, which was never sold in Canada, is also slated to be dropped in the States when the Mercury phase-out is complete. Of course, this move cuts the wasteful duplication of models, but it will also threaten Lincoln dealers who will no longer be paired with Mercury.

Can Ford's new Explorer transform a "lemon" into a "peach"? Not likely in just one model year. Wait for 2012.

Ford is also shifting its product mix to smaller vehicles that use more-reliable Japanese components and are assembled more cheaply in Mexico or offshore. Models like the Ford Fusion, Mercury Milan, and Lincoln Zephyr mid-sized cars, all based on the successful Mazda6, are built in Hermosillo, Mexico. Ford intends to extend this practice by copying European designs, importing some models directly from Europe, then transferring their production to North America. The next-generation Focus, for example, will be modelled after the highly rated European variant and will include a plug-in electric version. A small Fiesta four-door sedan/hatchback will be imported from Europe during the 2010 model year. By selling and building worldwide models that are virtually identical, Ford can keep production costs down and quickly get to market agile, fuel-efficient, and highway-proven vehicles that follow the marketplace's shifting trends.

Poor Quality

Ford has its own poor-quality woes, just like Chrysler and GM, as the service bulletin summary below clearly shows.

2009 FORD FOUR-WHEEL DRIVE F-150 V8

All Technical Service Bulletins

NUMBER	DATE	TITLE
09-26-8	01/04/2010	SYNC System—Software Update For Various Concerns
09-25-5	12/28/2009	Drivetrain—Rear Driveshaft Slip/Bump Condition
09-24-13	12/14/2009	Wipers/Washers—Rain Sensor Detached From Windshield
09-23-7	11/30/2009	Engine—Knocking Noise From R/H Cam Cover At Hot Idle
09-22-12	11/16/2009	Drivetrain—Shudder On Hard Acceleration
09-20-14	10/19/2009	A/T—Uncommanded TCC Lock Up On 1–2 Upshift
09-20-2	10/19/2009	Interior—Seat Cushion Cover Loose At Front Of Seat
09-18-13	09/21/2009	Steering—Steering Effort Varies On Left/Right Turns
09-18-8	09/21/2009	Body—Tailgate Applique Separating From Sheet Metal
09-17-6	09/07/2009	Body—Power Running Board Popping Noises
09-15-4	08/10/2009	Engine, A/T Controls—1–2 Shift Hesitation/DTC P0741
09-14-2	07/27/2009	Interior—Headliner Sags At rear Of Sunroof
09-14-3	07/27/2009	SYNC System—Functions Inoperative/DTCs Set
09-13-5	07/13/2009	SYNC System—Poor Cell Phone Sound Quality
09-11-1	06/15/2009	Instruments—Trans. Temperature Gauge Drops To Zero
09-11-8	06/15/2009	SYNC System—911 Assist VHR Software Upgrade
09-5-6	03/23/2009	Electrical—Trailer Brake Control Module DTC C2806
09-3-3	02/23/2009	A/T—4R75E Erratic Operation/Various DTCs Set
08-26-11	01/05/2009	A/C—No Communication With HVAC Control Module

Internal service bulletins are "smoking gun" indicators of vehicle reliability, durability, and quality control.

In the past decade, powertrain defects, faulty suspensions and steering components, and premature brake wear and brake failures were the primary concerns of Ford owners. The company's engine and automatic transmission deficiencies affected most of its products and have existed since the early '80s, judging by *Lemon-Aid* reader reports, NHTSA complaints, and confidential Ford internal documents and technical service bulletins. The quality of body components has traditionally remained far below Japanese and South Korean standards.

Over the past three decades, *Lemon-Aid* has warned a succession of Ford Canada presidents that quality control and management had to improve dramatically or sales and profits would plummet. The only Canadian president who ever listened and acted on hundreds of *Lemon-Aid*'s complaints relative to Taurus, Sable, and Windstar engine and transmission failures was Bobbie Gaunt. During her 1997–2000 tenure, Gaunt set up a special working group in Canada to extend Ford's warranty to compensate owners who were no longer covered by the original Ford warranty. Unfortunately, she never got the backing of Ford USA's CEO, Jacques Nasser, who refused to formally extend the warranty in Canada or apply it in the States. A year after Gaunt retired, Nasser was ousted as the head of Ford USA and received a compensation package worth $23 million as part of his 2001 pay and retirement; the company lost $5.5 billion in 2001—its worst performance since 1992. Nasser burned through money by investing in non-core businesses and by purchasing money-losing carmakers like Jaguar, Land Rover, and Volvo. It took Ford five years after Nasser's firing to begin its slow road to recovery, selling many of the businesses and auto companies Nasser had purchased. Ironically, Nasser's ineptitude forced Ford to trim costs and borrow money when loan rates were low, several years before GM and Chrysler headed for bankruptcy.

FOCUS ★★★★

RATING: Above Average. **Strong points:** Excellent handling and road-holding; a commanding view of the highway; plenty of interior space for occupants and cargo; well appointed for an entry-level vehicle; user-friendly control layout; improved quality control; and impressive fuel economy. Very reliable during the last five years, which is all the more surprising because the 2000–04 models were quintessential lemons. Standard ABS, stability and traction control, and side-curtain airbags. NHTSA gave the two-door 2010 Focus five stars for frontal crashworthiness, three stars for side protection, and four stars for rollover resistance. The four-door model was rated a bit differently: It got four stars for frontal crashworthiness, five stars for side protection, and three stars for rollover

KEY FACTS

CANADIAN PRICE (NEGOTIABLE): *Sedan S:* $14,499, *Sedan SE:* $17,699, *SES:* $20,399 **U.S. PRICE:** *Sedan S:* $16,290, *Sedan SE:* $17,110, *SES:* $18,799 **CANADIAN FREIGHT:** $1,350 **U.S. FREIGHT:** $725

POWERTRAIN (FRONT-DRIVE)

Engines: 2.0L DOHC 4 (140 hp) • 2.0L DOHC 4 (140 hp); Transmissions: 5-speed man. • 4-speed auto.

DIMENSIONS/CAPACITY

Passengers: 2/3; Wheelbase: 103 in.; H: 58.7/L: 175.1/W: 78.4 in.; Headroom F/R: 5.0/2.0 in.; Legroom F/R: 39.0/26.5 in.; Cargo volume: 14 cu. ft.; Fuel tank: 53L/regular; Tow limit: Not recommended; Load capacity: 825 lb.; Turning circle: 36 ft.; Ground clearance: 5.5 in.; Weight: 2,720 lb.

resistance. IIHS gave its top rating ("Good") for frontal offset and side crash protection. **Weak points:** Mediocre acceleration, excessive engine and road noise, and head-restraint/rear crash protection given only an "Average" rating. **New for 2011:** Mostly a carryover of the 2010 version. The spring 2011 model is sportier and more aerodynamic.

OVERVIEW: The 2011 Ford Focus will be a lame duck, though it's still a competent small car. It provides good mileage and a surprisingly supple ride for a competitive price. The four-door sedan is a better value for your dollar than the cramped two-door coupe that has been discontinued for 2011.

COST ANALYSIS: The Focus is for drivers who feel fuel economy is more important than sophisticated styling or performance. The car is still using the basic chassis/platform from its year 2000 model. The 2010 and 2011 aren't very different from each other; smart shoppers will wait for the more-refined 2012 model. **Best alternatives:** Honda Civic, Hyundai Accent or Elantra, Mazda2 and Mazda3, and Nissan Versa. **Options:** Ditch the original equipment Firestones. **Rebates:** $1,500 to $2,500. **Depreciation:** Average. **Insurance cost:** Average. **Parts supply/cost:** Average. **Annual maintenance cost:** Average. **Warranty:** Bumper-to-bumper 3 years/60,000 km; powertrain 5 years/100,000 km; rust perforation 5 years/unlimited km. **Supplementary warranty:** A good idea for the powertrain. **Highway/city fuel economy:** *Man.:* 5.6/8.5 L/100 km, 50/33 mpg. *Auto.:* 5.8/8.4 L/100 km, 49/34 mpg.

OWNER-REPORTED PROBLEMS: Not many problems reported, except for some engine stalling and surging; premature brake caliper and rotor replacements; early wearout of suspension components; electrical shorts; and a few fit and finish deficiencies. Head restraints also receive criticism for being angled downward too sharply, forcing the head to bend forward. Both wheels can lock up when the brakes are applied, or the car may accelerate when the brakes are applied.

SERVICE BULLETIN-REPORTED PROBLEMS: *2000–10 Ford Focus:* Excessive engine vibration at idle (April 5, 2010, TSB: # 10-05-11). The remedy for this problem is the removal of debris lodged in the rear engine roll restrictor and the installation of a service shield, if needed.

WARBLE TYPE NOISE ON ACCELERATION—FRONT DRIVE INTERMEDIATE SHAFT BEARING

2010 Focus

ISSUE: Some 2010 Focus vehicles equipped with an automatic transaxle and built between 10/1/2009–10/31/2009 may exhibit a warble (cyclical growling) type noise from the front of the vehicle while accelerating. This noise may be caused by the front drive intermediate shaft bearing rotating in the bearing support bracket

FUSION, MKZ ★★

The Ford Fusion.

RATING: Below Average. These practically identical mid-sized sedans are slightly smaller than the Ford Five Hundred and are set on a lengthened Mazda6 platform. **Strong points:** Very reasonably priced; good acceleration and fair handling; steering is tight, precise, and vibration-free; and Mazda's 4-cylinder and V6 engines are competent, thrifty, and dependable. Added rigidity and additional chassis tweaking have resulted in a car that will seat five passengers (four in comfort) and corner reasonably well. Standard four-wheel disc brakes do a good job stopping the car, with little fading after repeated stops. The Fusion/MKZ Hybrid uses an Atkinson-cycle version of the 2.5L engine, and its fuel economy estimates are better than the Toyota Camry and Nissan Altima hybrids. It can run on one or both of its power sources (to balance acceleration and fuel economy) and requires no plug-in charging. NHTSA gives the Fusion/MKZ and the Fusion/MKZ Hybrid five stars for front and side crashworthiness and four stars for rollover resistance; the AWD model earned five stars for rollover resistance. **Weak points:** A noisy 4-cylinder engine; dangerously flawed transmission performance; unreliable hybrid brake

KEY FACTS

CANADIAN PRICE (NEGOTIABLE): *Fusion S:* $21,499, *SE:* $22,799, *SEL:* $25,799, *SEL V6:* $28,799, *SEL V6 AWD:* $30,799, *Sport AWD:* $35,299, *Hybrid:* $31,999, *MKZ Front-drive:* $38,399, *AWD:* $42,199 **U.S. PRICE:** *Fusion S:* $19,695, *SE:* $21,225, *SEL:* $24,655, *SE V6:* $23,715, *MKZ Front-drive:* $34,225, *AWD:* $36,115 **CANADIAN FREIGHT:** $1,400 **U.S. FREIGHT:** $850 **POWERTRAIN (FRONT-DRIVE)** Engines: 2.5L 4-cyl. (175 hp) • 2.5L 4-cyl. hybrid (191 hp) • 3.0L V6 (240 hp) • 3.5L V6 (263 hp); Transmissions: 6-speed man. • 6-speed auto. • CVT **DIMENSIONS/CAPACITY (FUSION)** Passengers: 2/3; Wheelbase: 107 in.; H: 56.9/L: 190.6/W: 72.0 in.; Headroom F/R: 2.5/2.5 in.; Legroom F/R: 40.5/28.0 in.; Cargo volume: 16 cu. ft.; Fuel tank: 45L/regular; Tow limit: No towing; Load capacity: 850 lb.; Turning circle: 39 ft.; Ground clearance: 5.0 in.; Weight: 3,285 lb.

performance; and cramped rear seating. Vehicle wanders all over the road and head restraints are pure torture. Super-fast depreciation: A 2007 entry-level Fusion SE that sold new for $23,500 is now worth barely $9,500, while a $37,500 2007 Lincoln MKZ is now worth only $16,000. The Mercury Milan is not sold in Canada and will soon be dropped when the Mercury division is shut down in the States. **New for 2011:** The 2011 Fusion and Lincoln MKZ are mostly carryovers of the 2010 models, although the front-drive Lincoln MKZ gains a gas/electric hybrid model that pairs a 2.5L gasoline 4-cylinder engine with a battery-powered electric motor to produce a total of 191 horsepower. Hybrids get more safety and convenience features.

OVERVIEW: These four-door sedans offer four engine options: two 4-cylinders, one of which is a hybrid, and two V6s. The smaller engines can be coupled to either a 6-speed manual or a 6-speed automatic transmission; there's no choice with the V6, which comes with a 6-speed automatic. The 4-cylinder comes solely in front-drive; the 3.0L is available in front-drive or all-wheel drive, while the 3.5L is uniquely AWD. The hybrid variant is a spinoff of the Mazda6 and the Ford Escape Hybrid—two vehicles that have been recommended for years by *Lemon-Aid* for both their quality and performance.

So why are these cars so bad if they come from such good stock? The answer is that these relatively new cars have had less time on the market to detect and cure factory assembly and calibration glitches. As well, Ford has had little money and human resources to correct these deficiencies.

Also, why does *Consumer Reports* rate the Fusion, Milan, and MKZ Recommended while *Lemon-Aid* rates them as Below Average? *Lemon-Aid* gets tipped off early to the presence of safety- and performance-related defects by studying thousands of consumer complaints logged by NHTSA and then comparing these complaints to factory-generated confidential service bulletins sent weekly to auto dealerships. *Consumer Reports* drives the vehicle and publishes its member comments. No service bulletins or NHTSA-logged complaints are studied, nor are non-members polled.

COST ANALYSIS: The 2010 and 2011 models are essentially identical, so your best buy would be a 15 percent-discounted 2010 version for about $22,000. Used, a base Fusion would go for about $19,000. **Best alternatives:** Honda Accord, Hyundai Elantra or Tucson, Mazda6, Nissan Altima, and Toyota Camry (only if equipped with the brake override feature). **Options:** Pass on the leaky sunroof and original equipment Firestone/Bridgestone tires. **Rebates:** Don't expect much. The 2010 models are practically all gone. **Depreciation:** Much faster than average. A first-year base 2006 Fusion that sold for $23,000 is now worth only $9,000. **Insurance cost:** Average; the hybrid premium costs more than average. **Parts supply/cost:** Average. Hybrid parts costs are moderately expensive, but availability is no problem since parts are taken from the Mazda or Escape Hybrid bins. **Annual maintenance cost:** Repair costs have been average during the three-year warranty period. **Warranty:** Bumper-to-bumper 3 years/60,000 km; powertrain 5 years/100,000 km; rust perforation 5 years/160,000 km. **Supplementary warranty:** A good idea. Their first three years on the market have shown the Fusion and its brothers to be prone to serious automatic transmission failures, making an extended powertrain warranty worthwhile. **Highway/city fuel economy:** *2.5L:* 6.9/9.4 L/100 km, 41/30 mpg. *Auto.:* 6.9/9.4 L/100 km, 44/30 mpg. *3.0L:* 7.3/11.1 L/100 km, 29/35 mpg. *3.0L AWD:* 7.8/11.8 L/100 km, 36/24 mpg. *3.5L AWD:* 8.3/12.7 L/100 km, 34/22 mpg. *Hybrid:* 5.4/4.6 L/100 km, 52/61 mpg.

OWNER-REPORTED PROBLEMS: Knee airbag restricts brake pedal access:

> 2010 Fusion Hybrid. Foot space between the knee airbag housing and brake pedal is severely and dangerously restricted by the physical presence, bulk, and location of the knee airbag. This delays response for instant brake deployment for emergency deceleration. Vertical clearance is ~4" and is less if approached at an angle, swiveling on heel from accelerator to brake. Lifting foot with leg from hip bumps foot against airbag housing, stopping smooth transition to pedal with either foot. Foot then must slide horizontally into narrow space to engage brakes. Foot space is dangerously restricted.

Automatic transmission slams into gear or slips into Neutral:

> When driving the automatic transmission sometimes slips out of gear and goes to Neutral. This problem happens from 10–40 mph [16–64 km/h] at 0–50% throttle. Loss of power happens between 5–10 seconds and the engine rpm will increase to 7,000 rpm. Depressing the throttle allows the transmission to engage again with an abrupt and hard shift. Accelerating again after this is very slow and sluggish and it is believed that the car is in an upper gear. Almost caused a wreck that could have ended my life between two tractor trailers because of loss of power and failure to accelerate.

•

> Vehicle shifts unusually between Second and Third gear, and Third and Fourth gear. The condition is worse in wet and/or cold weather. On top of the regular malfunction of the gear shifting, on three separate occasions the vehicle has slammed between gears creating a "rear-end crash type feel" to the passengers inside the vehicle.

Sudden unintended acceleration:

While driving in extremely heavy traffic approximately between 3–4 mph [5–6 km/h], an unexpected increase of acceleration occurred. The contact applied pressure to the brake pedal and the vehicle continued to accelerate which caused the vehicle to crash into the preceding vehicle.

•

When the brake was depressed, the car accelerated until I depressed a second time—much harder. The consumer first began to notice [in August that] the vehicle would intermittently not start. He took the vehicle to the dealer, but they were unable to duplicate the problem. The consumer insisted there was a problem and eventually, they found a technical service bulletin that addressed the issue. The problem was attributed to radio frequency intermittently corrupting the crankshaft position sensor and a new ground strip was installed.

Door and hood latches fail, allowing the doors to fly open or the hood to fly up when underway:

The hood on my 2010 Ford Fusion Hybrid unlatches itself at interstate highway speed. The safety catch has successfully restrained the hood from flying open completely. There have been four incidents with three different drivers since the car was delivered.

Hybrid brakes fail and instrument cluster shorts out; instrument cluster readouts washed out by daylight; and poorly designed head restraints:

I just bought a 2010 Ford Fusion. I know now why they only allow you to test drive these cars around the block. The first time I drove it, I got a burning pain down my neck and a piercing headache. The headrest is a wedge with the greatest protrusion hitting the greatest protrusion of the back of your head. No adjustment of the seat or headrest helps. I tried to return the car immediately, but they refused. This weird angle puts your chin down on your chest and your sight line in a hazardous alignment. If there were a wreck, the angle would cause your neck to snap. Ford is aware of this, apparently, and has received many complaints, yet does nothing. People are resorting to turning the headrest around, which will not protect against whiplash, or having it bent in a vise, which could allow it to break in a collision. All the Fords now have this dangerous torture device, so you cannot change them. Help!

Windshields crack spontaneously; trunk takes too much effort to close and sometimes pops open when vehicle is underway; and excessive front-end drift/pull forces the driver to continually correct the steering:

This car will run off the road in a matter of seconds and is a considerable safety hazard. Ford's response to the problem is to instruct their dealers through an internal memo not to "attempt a repair for this problem."... I have driven two of these cars (one of which I own) and both do the same thing.

The 2008–10 Fusion, Milan, and MKZ may have sunroof leaks because of poor factory sealing. Hybrid brake failures are quite common, yet dealers are not always adept at correcting the defect, as this owner of a 2010 Hybrid relates:

> Brakes failed twice as above, slowed with parking brake, brakes okay after engine turn off and restart. Dealer called Ford. Ford authorized free rental car and provided a technician to assist dealer. Result: Replaced brake booster travel sensor, reprogrammed PCM powertrain control module with later version of the software. There is a tech service bulletin on this but my car did not show the codes the first 2 times I brought it in. On the third time the factory showed the dealer how to look for codes in a different manner.

Here is the service bulletin referred to above:

BRAKES, ENGINE CONTROLS—ABS/ESC LAMP ON

BULLETIN NO.: 09-22-11   DATE: NOVEMBER 16, 2009

CHANGE IN BRAKE PEDAL TRAVEL AND/OR ABS CONTROL/BRAKE WARNING LAMP

2010 Fusion; 2010 Milan

ISSUE: Some 2010 Fusion Hybrid and Milan Hybrid vehicles built on or before 10/17/2009 may experience electronic noise on the brake booster travel sensor. The customer may report an extended pedal travel of approximately 1 3/16 of an inch (30 mm). The system will remain in default mode throughout the key cycle. During the subsequent key cycle, if the system recognizes a properly operating Brake Booster Travel Sensor, brake by wire functionality will return.

ACTION: Replace the Brake Booster Travel sensor and reprogram both the Powertrain Control Module (PCM) and the ABS module to the latest calibration.

MUSTANG ★★★★★

KEY FACTS

CANADIAN PRICE (FIRM): *Coupe: $26,999, Convertible: $31,999, Coupe GT: $38,499, Convertible GT: $42,899* **U.S. PRICE:** *Coupe V6: $22,995, V6 Premium: 26,605, GT: $30,495, Shelby GT500: $49,495, V6 Convertible: $27,995, Premium V6 Convertible: $33,695, GT Premium Convertible: $38,695, Shelby GT500: $54,495*

CANADIAN FREIGHT: $1,350 **U.S. FREIGHT:** $850

POWERTRAIN (REAR-DRIVE)

Engines: 3.7L V6 (305 hp) • 4.6L V8 (315 hp) • 5.0L V8 (412 hp) • 5.4L V8 (550 hp); Transmissions: 6-speed man. • 6-speed auto.

DIMENSIONS/CAPACITY

Passengers: 2/2; Wheelbase: 107.1 in.; H: 55.6/L: 188.1/W: 73.9 in.; Headroom F/R: 5.0/1.0 in.; Legroom F/R: 40.5/23.5 in.; Cargo volume: 13.4 cu. ft.; Fuel tank: 60.1L/regular; Tow limit: 1,001 lb.; Load capacity: 720 lb.; Turning circle: 33.4 ft.; Ground clearance: 5.7 in.; Weight: 3,585 lb.

RATING: Recommended. Mustang has gone back to its muscle car roots while keeping prices in check. Unlike some of Ford's front-drives, few safety- or performance-related complaints have been lodged against the rear-drive Mustang. **Strong points:** Base models come equipped with a host of safety, luxury, and convenience features. Fast acceleration, and impressive handling, braking, and resale value. Better-than-average past crashworthiness, standard major safety features, and good overall reliability. **Weak points:** Insufficient rear-seat room, and all bets are off on the GT500 powertrain's long-term durability; Ford's dismal history with high-performance Yamaha-sourced engines would give Freddy Kruger nightmares, and aluminum engine components have had a high failure rate (warping and sealing problems) when used on other Detroit-built cars and trucks. **New for 2011:** The big news is Ford's huge horsepower boost on its base Mustang, turning up the heat from 210 hp to a sizzling 305 horses. ("Honest, officer, I was just following the Toyota up ahead that suddenly accelerated.") Incidentally, the 2011 GT500 ratchets performance up a few notches, too, with an all-new aluminum-block engine that produces 550 hp. Other goodies on the 2011 Mustangs: a new limited-clip differential, larger brakes (taken from the 2010 GT), electronic power steering, a retuned suspension, and stiffer rear anti-roll bars. Convertibles get less body flexing through the use of shock-tower braces. Another big change is fold-down rear head restraints to improve rear visibility. For parents, there's the MyKey system, which allows owners to limit the car's maximum speed and audio volume.

OVERVIEW: The perfect "back to the future" retro sports car, the Mustang's body panel creases reign supreme. And more than four decades after its debut, the original "pony car" still stands strong, both stylistically and in its highway performance. The Mustang offers a V6 or a V8 in the GT engines. Keep in mind, though, that the V6 is an entirely different, more-powerful powerplant than the 2010 version. Body assembly has also improved considerably.

The 2011 Mustang is undeniably a much better car than the 2010 version, even though the 2010 got some important improvements. *Shelby:* The Shelby GT500 got a power boost and other refinements last year—and again this year—to improve engine cooling and performance. Ford says its revamped transmission and final-drive gearing give better acceleration off the starting line with improved highway fuel economy. The GT500 comes in both coupe and convertible versions.

COST ANALYSIS: There are a few unsold 2010s available, but they are seriously outclassed by the vastly improved, more-powerful 2011 versions. Buying any model earlier than the 2010 would be cheating yourself out of some important standard safety and performance features. A word to the wise: Pounce on a relatively fresh Mustang built after March 2011 to make sure most of the redesign glitches have been debugged at the factory. Finally, this may be the ideal car to buy in the States; the price difference is $5,000 and availability shouldn't be a problem. **Best alternatives:** The resurrected Camaro. It wouldn't be a bad second choice, but consider this: The 2011 Mustang has about 250–300 fewer pounds than the V6 Camaro, plus it beats the Camaro in horsepower and fuel economy. Furthermore, confidential internal reports show that a high number of assembly-line deficiencies afflict the Camaro. Will "the Stang" suffer the same fate? Too early to tell. Forget about the Dodge Challenger. Its 250-hp engine and heavy body take it out of the running. **Options:** An anti-theft system (one that includes an engine immobilizer) and good tires recommended by *www.tirerack.com*. **Rebates:** $1,000 rebates, plus low-interest financing. **Depreciation:** Very slow. For example, a new $25,500 2010 base Mustang now costs almost $21,000 used. The convertibles fare even better: An entry-level 2010 that sold for $29,700 has a resale value of $26,500. Expect the boosted horsepower on the entry-level V6 engine (which rivals that of the GT V8) to send the GT's resale value plummeting. **Insurance cost:** Way higher than average. **Parts supply/cost:** Inexpensive and easily found among independent suppliers; some delays getting engine and body components. **Annual maintenance cost:** Lower than average: Most independent mechanics will be able to fix a Mustang. **Warranty:** Bumper-to-bumper 3 years/60,000 km; powertrain 5 years/100,000 km; rust perforation 5 years/unlimited km. **Supplementary warranty:** Not necessary. Put your money into handling options and theft protection. **Highway/city fuel economy:** Fuel consumption is cut considerably in the new 24-valve V6 from 11.7/7.6 L/100 km (24/37 mpg) city and highway to a frugal 11.1/6.9 (25/41). This places the Mustang a bit ahead of the Chevrolet Camaro and on par with the more-stylish Hyundai Genesis Coupe 3.8.

OWNER-REPORTED PROBLEMS: Airbags fail to deploy, and there are reports of the car suddenly accelerating. The automatic transmission, electrical system, and fit and finish remain primary weak spots. Body assembly quality is not up to the level of Japanese vehicles, but better than those built by the other Detroit-based automakers. Numerous complaints of convertible roof, door, and trunk water leaks, as well as side windows that leak when it rains. Owners also report that the engine surges when shifting from Third to Fourth gear; child safety seat tethers in the convertible may not be attached due to the interference from the power convertible top when it is lowered; the hood scoop will lift when the car is underway; there are windshield distortions; the side door window may shatter when the door is opened; premature wear of the Pirelli Zero Nero tires; and the hands-free phone doesn't work properly.

SERVICE BULLETIN-REPORTED PROBLEMS: Front-end creak and grunt; axle whine:

EXCESSIVE REAR DRIVE AXLE WHINE

BULLETIN NO.: 09-20-4   **DATE: OCTOBER 19, 2009**

2005–10 Mustang

ISSUE: Some 2005–10 Mustang vehicles may exhibit excessive axle whine noise.

ACTION: This condition may be corrected by installing tuned dampers on the rear axle assembly, if not already installed.

ESCAPE, TRIBUTE   ★★★★

The Ford Escape.

RATING: Above Average; points were taken away for the Escape's mediocre braking and reliability concerns. The Tribute is Mazda's version of the Escape, but without a hybrid variant. **Strong points:** Peppy V6 performance and a roomy interior that includes a large rear bench seat; lots of cargo space; improved braking; standard stability control; and a convenient Sync voice-control system. NHTSA gave the Escape and Escape Hybrid top marks (five stars) for front and side crashworthiness; three stars were awarded for rollover resistance. IIHS also gave its top rating ("Good") to the Escape for frontal offset, side, and rear crash protection (head-restraint effectiveness). **Weak points:** The 4-cylinder engine lacks grunt in the upper gear ranges; both the 4-banger and V6 are unusually noisy engines; handling is not precise and the ride is somewhat jarring and busy; a noisy interior; the folding second seat isn't very user-friendly; and fit and finish doesn't impress. **New for 2011:** Very little. This is the final model year for these two vehicles that date from the summer of 2000. Despite some engine and styling revisions, their basic engineering and design have remained very much the same since then. The 2012 Escape will share its platform with the 2012 Focus; it will be slightly smaller than today's model but should be roomier and have a smoother ride, thanks to a far-more-sophisticated suspension system.

OVERVIEW: This decade-old SUV is a good buy with its reasonable base price, standard cruise control, and standard anti-lock brakes, but it's in dire need of a redesign to create a roomier interior and improve ride and handling. The hybrid still uses a 4-cylinder powerplant, but a new engine processor installed on the 2010s allows the Escape to switch from electric to gasoline mode almost imperceptibly.

COST ANALYSIS: Most of the 2010s are gone, so you will have to shell out the extra bucks ($500–$1,000) and spring for a 2011 version. Actually, if you can afford to wait, don't buy this model year; instead, consider getting the completely redesigned 2012 version. **Best alternatives:** Honda CR-V, Kia Rondo, Mazda5, Subaru Forester, and Toyota Matrix (but only with the brake override option). **Options:** Nothing that is essential. **Depreciation:** Average. **Insurance cost:** Average. **Parts supply/cost:** Expensive and hard-to-get hybrid parts: A cooling pump cost $640 (U.S.). Reasonably priced parts for gasoline-powered models, but parts are frequently back-ordered. **Annual maintenance cost:** Average. **Warranty:** Bumper-to-bumper 3 years/60,000 km; powertrain 5 years/100,000 km; rust perforation 5 years/unlimited km. **Supplementary warranty:** Getting an extended powertrain warranty is a good idea. **Highway/city fuel economy:** 2.5L: 7.2/9.2 L/100 km, 39/21 mpg. *Auto.:* 7.0/9.4 L/100 km, 40/30 mpg. *2.5L AWD:* 7.7/10.4 L/100 km, 37/27 mpg. *3.0L V6:* 8.0/10.9 L/100 km, 35/26 mpg. *3.0L AWD:* 8.8/11.6 L/100 km, 32/24 mpg. *Hybrid:* 6.5/5.8 L/100 km, 43/49 mpg. *Hybrid AWD:* 7.4/7.0 L/100 km, 39/43 mpg.

OWNER-REPORTED PROBLEMS: Airbags deploy inadvertently; airbags fail to deploy when needed; the front passenger side wheel separates from the lower control arm; transmission loses Third gear (6-speed transmission) and goes into default Fifth gear as transmission fluid spews out through the dipstick, creating a fire hazard; transmission fluid leakage (possible causes: a faulty AC condenser hose or condenser; cost to replace: $750–$1,025 U.S.). The 2010 Escape had recall repairs done to the automatic transmission and the transmission still failed shortly thereafter. Sub-frame bolts missing:

> Four rear subframe bolts defective. Two front subframe bolts missing, two rear subframe bolts loose. Result: Rear wheels and axle were about to come off the vehicle

KEY FACTS

CANADIAN PRICE (NEGOTIABLE): *4x2:* $24,499, *3.0L:* $27,199, *4x4:* $27,999, *LTD 3.0:* $34,549, *Hybrid 4x2:* $34,899, **U.S. PRICE:** *4x2:* $21,020, *3.0L:* $27,199, *4x4:* $27,999, *LTD 3.0:* $34,549, *Hybrid 4x2:* $29,860, *4x4:* $37,299 **CANADIAN FREIGHT:** $1,350 **U.S. FREIGHT:** $850
POWERTRAIN (FRONT-DRIVE)
Engines: 2.5L 4-cyl. (171 hp) • 2.5L 4-cyl. hybrid (177 hp) • 3.0L V6 (240 hp); Transmissions: 5-speed man. • CVT • 6-speed auto.
DIMENSIONS/CAPACITY
Passengers: 2/3; Wheelbase: 103 in.; H: 70/L: 175/W: 70 in.; Headroom F/R: 3.0/4.0 in.; Legroom F/R: 40.5/28.0 in.; Cargo volume: 37.5 cu. ft.; Fuel tank: 61L/regular; Tow limit: 3,500 lb.; Load capacity: 1,000 lb.; Turning circle: 42 ft.; Ground clearance: 7.0 in.; Weight: 3,605 lb.

with my family in it. The rear subframe attaches to the main frame of the vehicle to keep the rear wheels on the car.

Oil filler tube is located directly above the exhaust manifold, creating a fire risk; cable lines fail, causing pedal to become inoperable; vehicle will not hold when stopped on an incline; sudden loss of braking ability or power steering; spontaneous windshield cracks and sunroof/side window shattering; distorted windshields:

> Windshield has a manufacturing defect that creates a heat shimmer like effect when looking through it. This causes a distortion during the day, but distortion increases at night or [in] rainy weather. Ford has replaced this once under warranty with another Ford windshield. New windshield has same defect.

One vehicle's parking brake failed, and the vehicle rolled backwards down a hill. Excessive glare from the instrument panel blinds driver. LED readout is washed out by sunlight. Tire jack won't raise the vehicle high enough to change the tire. *Hybrid:* Surprisingly for a vehicle that has such a complicated electrical system, there are just a handful of complaints concerning the hybrid version. One would normally expect to see, on average, 50 or so reports per model year. With the current model, owners report some brake failures.

SERVICE BULLETIN-REPORTED PROBLEMS: Harsh Fifth gear engagement on 2009–10 models. Front-end squeak/creak noise reduction tips on 2001–10 models.

EXPLORER, SPORT TRAC ★ ★ ★

The Ford Explorer.

RATING: *2011 Explorer:* Average with a second-series summer model to avoid the first-year redesign glitches. *2010 Explorer:* Below Average. *2010 Sport Trac:* Below Average; there won't be a 2011 version.

Strong points: Prices are set too high, but they can easily be haggled down on the less-refined 2010 Explorer and Sport Trac. The all-new unibody crossover 2011 Explorer won't arrive until year's end, but it's worth the wait. Standard stability control; average reliability with the V6 engine. NHTSA gave the Explorer five stars for frontal and side crashworthiness and three stars for rollover resistance, while IIHS scored frontal offset protection "Good" and side protection and head-restraint effectiveness "Acceptable." **Weak points:** The 2010 Explorer has a history of costly powertrain failures in addition to faulty brake, electrical system, and suspension components. You also get truck-like handling, a stiff ride, and poor fuel economy. The V8 engine is less reliable than the V6. **New for 2011:** Redesigned on a Taurus platform, with three-row seating and car-like fuel economy and performance, the Explorer goes from rear- to front-drive. Using a car-based crossover chassis, the new Explorer will perform much like the popular Ford Edge. Other changes include reduced ground clearance; no more V8; upgraded 4×4; a 3.5L V6; and 5 more inches of width.

2011 models will likely come with a naturally aspirated 3.5L V6, much like the Mustang's V6 and replacing Explorer's old 4.0L 6-banger. A 2.0L EcoBoost engine may also be used to deliver at least 25 mpg on the highway.

Still smarting from the Explorer's "rollover" reputation, Ford will introduce a Curve Control feature on its 2011 models to enhance directional stability. Explorer will also come with Terrain Management, a feature that instantly adapts to a variety of different road and driving conditions, such as snow, sand, mud, and hill descent.

OVERVIEW: This mid-sized SUV uses traditional body-on-frame, truck-type construction (this will change with the 2011 version). It offers rear-drive, all-wheel drive, or four-wheel drive that can be left engaged on dry pavement and has a low-range gear for off-roading. Trim levels include XLT, Eddie Bauer, and Limited. Available safety features include ABS, traction control, anti-skid system, side curtain airbags, and front side airbags. A third-row seat increases carrying capacity to seven passengers. Explorer's capless fuelling system allows owners to fill their

fuel tanks without having to remove a gas cap, and the optional Sync voice-activated cell phone and MP3 player control system is particularly useful.

Essentially an Explorer with a pickup bed, the Sport Trac debuted in 2001 as one of the first pickups with four full-sized doors, a comfortable four-passenger cabin, and a short cargo bed. Set on the Explorer's wheelbase, stretched by about 17 inches, it is offered with either a V6 or V8 engine and boasts a top towing capacity of 7,160 lbs. Its pluses and minuses mirror those of its brother, and defects affecting the one usually also affect the other. The Sport Trac is likely to be dropped in 2010.

COST ANALYSIS: In addition to the Explorer's many truck-based peers, numerous car-based crossover SUVs now occupy this price range; many of them are just as family-friendly, too, while offering more safety features, better fuel economy, and a more-refined cabin and powertrain. This is why it's best to steer clear of the Explorer until the redesigned 2011 model arrives at the end of 2010. The 2011 model will use a car-like unibody design to improve the ride, handling, and fuel economy. Plus, Ford's antiquated and problematic powertrain will be replaced by a more-refined system. Will it be less troublesome? Nobody's telling, but Ford's past redesigns have always been afflicted by numerous factory-related powertrain defects for the first couple of years. **Best alternatives:** Honda CR-V or Ridgeline, Hyundai Tucson or Santa Fe, and Toyota RAV4 (only with the brake override). **Options:** Be wary of the $1,700 Ironman Package. You are essentially getting larger tires, heated seats, a roof rack, and floor mats. **Rebates:** On the 2010s, look for $3,000 rebates, $2,000 discounts, and zero percent financing. 2011 Explorers will likely get 10 percent discounts and zero-interest financing by summer. **Depreciation:** Much faster than average. A 2009 base Explorer 4×4 that sold for $36,000 is now worth about $22,500. **Insurance cost:** Above average. **Parts supply/cost:** Parts are easy to find and are reasonably priced. **Annual maintenance cost:** Average while under warranty; higher than average thereafter, primarily because of powertrain breakdowns. **Warranty:** Bumper-to-bumper 3 years/60,000 km; powertrain 5 years/100,000 km; rust perforation 5 years/unlimited km. **Supplementary warranty:** Getting an extended powertrain warranty would be wise. **Highway/city fuel economy:** 4.0L: 11.0/16.2 L/100 km, 26/17 mpg; 4.6L: 10.4/15.5 L/100 km, 27/18 mpg; *Sport Trac 4.0L:* 10.8/15.9 L/100 km, 26/18 mpg; *Sport Trac 4.6L:* 9.8/14.4 L/100 km, 29/17 mpg; *4.0L 44:* 11.0/16.2 L/100 km, 26/17 mpg; *4.6L 44:* 10.4/15.5 L/100 km, 27/18 mpg.

OWNER-REPORTED PROBLEMS: Engine failures, automatic transmission failures, and fit and finish deficiencies. Owners continue to complain that the head restraints are literally a pain in the neck and can be dangerous if the airbags deploy:

The driver owns a 2009 Ford Explorer. Upon entering the vehicle, he noticed that the head rest pushes the driver's head towards the windshield due to its perpendicular design… If the air bag were to deploy, the driver could become seriously injured. The contact called the manufacturer and was informed that the vehicle was designed in that manner and no compensation would be provided.

SERVICE BULLETIN-REPORTED PROBLEMS: Engine knocking; harsh shifts; steering/suspension front-end click/pop; steering column noise on turns; underbody squeaks; hoot noise on light acceleration; front-end click/pop on bumps; exterior door handles hard to open, not flush; windows squeak/grind when operated.

F-150, F-250, F-350, F-450 PICKUP ★★★★

The Ford F-150.

RATING: Above Average. The F-150 has seen the best of times and the worst of times and is now coming out of a multi-year sales slump that almost forced Ford into bankruptcy. **Strong points:** Easily negotiated prices as fuel prices rise and truck prices fall. Handling is a breeze, although the ride is a bit stiff; a roomy cab with lots of convenient storage bins; a power-opening centre rear window; and a spring-assisted tailgate. NHTSA gave the 2010 F-150 five stars for front and side crashworthiness and four stars for rollover resistance. The F-250 wasn't tested. IIHS also gave the F-150 top marks ("Good") for frontal offset, side, and rear crashworthiness. **Weak points:** The powertrain is a bit rough and loud, and braking is just acceptable. Long-term reliability has yet to be determined. This is especially important because these trucks have disappointed owners after each redesign since the mid-'80s. **New for 2011:** Mostly more power and slight exterior restyling. Look for a new twin-turbo V6, the new EcoBoost engine, and a new Coyote V8 on most of the F-Series. The SVT Raptor gets a 6.2L 411 hp V8.

KEY FACTS

CANADIAN PRICE: *F-150 Regular:* $19,415, *F-150 Super Cab:* $23,947, *Super Crew Cab:* $31,129, *F-250 Regular:* $24,825, *Super Cab:* $27,491, *Crew Cab:* $28,781, *F-350 Regular:* $26,230, *Super Cab:* $28,466, *Crew Cab:* $29,928, *F-450 4×2:* $41,968, *F-450 4×4:* $45,064 **U.S. PRICE:** *F-150 XL:* $22,795; *STX:* $25,070; *XLT:* $25,265, *Lariat:* $33,765, *F-150 SVT Raptor:* $38,995, *King Ranch:* $40,865, *Platinum:* $42,885, *Harley Davidson:* $43,355 **CANADIAN FREIGHT:** $1,350 **U.S. FREIGHT:** $975

POWERTRAIN (REAR-DRIVE/PART-TIME 4×4/AWD)

Engines: 4.6L V8 (248 hp) • 4.6L V8 (292 hp) • 5.4L V8 (310 hp) 6.2L V8 (385 hp) • 6.4L V8 diesel (350 hp) • 6.7L V8 diesel (385 hp) • 6.8L V10 (362 hp) • 3.5L V6 (365 hp) • 3.7L V6 (302 hp) • 5.0L V8 (360 hp) • 6.2L V8 (411 hp); Transmissions: 4-speed auto. • 5-speed auto. • 6-speed auto. • 6-speed man.

DIMENSIONS/CAPACITY

Passengers: 2/1 up to 3/3; Wheelbase: 121 in.; H: 69/L: 201/W: 77 in.; Headroom F/R: 4.5/3.5 in.; Legroom F/R: 40.0/29.5 in.; Cargo volume: N/A; Fuel tank: 98.4L/regular, *Raptor:* 94L/regular, *Harley-Davidson:* 136L/regular; Tow limit: *F-150:* 5,400lb.; *F-250:* 12,500 lb.; Load capacity: 1,480–5,100 lb.; Turning circle: 48 ft.; Ground clearance: 8.5 in.; Weight: 5,620 lb.

The larger trucks will be led by the all-new Ford-engineered 6.7L Power Stroke V8 turbodiesel. The 2011 Ford F-150 SVT Raptor with an available all-new 6.2L V8 will produce 411 horsepower, making it the most powerful half-ton truck on the market today. Insiders say Ford is working on its first-ever mid-sized Ford pickup, reviving the F-100 name from a quarter-century ago. Built to 9/10ths scale, this next-generation mini-F-150 is expected to have a late-2010 release, a year ahead of the planned 2012 model redesign for the full-sized F-150. Fox Racing Shox internal-bypass shock absorbers, and 35-inch all-terrain tires on 17-inch wheels. The Raptor is 7 inches wider than the standard F-150 and is also styled differently.

OVERVIEW: The Ford F-Series ruled the roost for 30-odd years as the bestselling pickup in North America. Then Ford's house of cards came tumbling down. Abetted by lousy diesel engines; failure-prone powertrains, suspensions, and steering assemblies; and body construction that would make the Marquis de Sade proud, Ford began to lose market share a decade ago. It has never recovered. However, its 2009–11 models give hope that some of the worst design deficiencies have been corrected and that Ford is finally on the road to solvency.

COST ANALYSIS: Unless you're looking for a high-performance Raptor or are in dire need of an engine boost, look for a cheaper, leftover 2010 version (discount should be in the 10–15 percent realm). **Best alternatives:** GM's 2011 Silverado and Sierra HD series, Honda's Ridgeline, Nissan's Titan, GM Silverado and Sierra base models, and dead last Chrysler's Jurassic Ram with a Cummins diesel and more-reliable manual transmission. Some trucks that are ideal for lighter duties: Ford Ranger, Mazda B-Series, and Nissan Frontier or King Cab. **Options:** Take a pass on the Firestone/Bridgestone tires, heated seats, and Lariat Chrome package. **Rebates:** $3,000 rebates and low-cost financing on the larger trucks. **Depreciation:** Much faster than average. **Insurance cost:** Above average. **Parts supply/cost:** Reasonably priced parts are easy to find, mainly because many independent suppliers specialize in new and used F-Series parts. **Annual maintenance cost:** Average. **Warranty:** Bumper-to-bumper 3 years/60,000 km; powertrain

5 years/100,000 km; rust perforation 5 years/unlimited km. **Supplementary warranty:** Getting an extended bumper-to-bumper warranty is a good idea. **Highway/city fuel economy:** *4.6L V8:* 10.4/14.4 L/100 km, 27/20 mpg; *4.6L V8 6-speed:* 9.7/14.3 L/100 km, 29/20 mpg; *4.6L V8 4×4:* 10.2/14.9 L/100 km, 28/19 mpg; *5.4L V8 4×4:* 11.3/15.9 L/100 km, 25/18 mpg.

OWNER-REPORTED PROBLEMS: Fire ignited under the driver's door; a familiar litany of transmission and steering failures:

> F-150 Platinum Extended Cab. Steering is extremely stiff/spongy/hard to turn off-center. Must constantly fight side winds and road crowns. As if only 10% power-assisted. Dangerous as required constant attention to steering. Others who have driven it comment the same and will not drive truck again. Dealer claims it's "normal" for all Ford F-150s with no correction. Dangerous as when transferring to other vehicles with full power assist, one over-steers and quickness...is difficult to reacquaint. Driveline/transmission/etc. does not engage on inclines, slips and chatters into "full" engagement, shudders 1–3 times at stopping and starting. Ford dealer cannot locate problem...no repair attempted. Independent transmission repair firm says it's a drive line bind releasing...possibly a drive line misalignment at transmission output shaft spline, and/or loose engine/transmission mounts. Danger that transmission may disengage without warning at any time.

Sudden acceleration when merging; the gas pedal becomes stuck and the steering column locks up; when parked, automatic transmission won't hold the vehicle; early brake wearout; original equipment Goodyear Wrangler SRA tires may not be rated high enough for the vehicle, resulting in early tire failure (split right down the middle); during rainy conditions, the instrument panel lights fail to illuminate when they are needed because the sensor doesn't sense enough darkness to turn them on; at other times the readings are washed out by sunlight; headlights blind other drivers:

> The blue headlights are [a] problem for oncoming vehicles and should be outlawed as well as the little lights that are mounted below the headlights that come on when the headlights are on Dim. On the SUVs they are the worst. The ones that are on the Ford pickups and some of the Chevy pickups are as big as the headlight; in some cases brighter than the dim headlights and they blind oncoming vehicles and they too should be outlawed.

The SYNC computer system interferes with the backup camera transmission; the window regulator is faulty; and head restraints are uncomfortable and dangerous:

> Headrest forces driver's chin into the chest. Dealer stated that this is the new safety design. Headrests are non-adjustable. Also, they are very wide and, in conjunction with the frame post at the rear of the doors, create a blind spot on both sides of the pickup.
>
> •
>
> The truck owner stated that the driver's and passenger side headrests were not adjustable and constantly struck him in the back of the neck. The manufacturer

stated that this was a new design for safety. He was concerned that his neck could be seriously injured due to the air bags in the event of a crash.

Take note that Ford has a secret warranty extension covering fuel injector replacements on 2008 and 2009 F-250 through F-550 trucks equipped with a 6.4L diesel engine (Customer Satisfaction Program #09B08). Until March 31, 2010, Ford will replace, free of charge, injectors that have prematurely worn O-rings. After that date, only "emergency" repairs will be covered. This free repair also applies to subsequent owners.

SERVICE BULLETIN-REPORTED PROBLEMS: 2009–10 F-150s may experience a driveshaft slip/bump. The fix is given in TSB: #09-25-5, published December 12, 2009. Diagnosing and correction of engine knock:

KNOCKING NOISE FROM R/H CAM COVER AT HOT IDLE

BULLETIN NO.: 09-23-7   DATE: NOVEMBER 30, 2009

ENGINE KNOCKING NOISE AT HOT IDLE

2009–10 Expedition, F-150; 2009–10 Navigator

ISSUE: Some 2009–10 F-150 vehicles equipped with a 4.6L V8 or 5.4L V8 engine may exhibit a low-frequency knocking noise from the engine at hot idle. The noise is mostly heard from the right front wheel well area and/or the right hand engine cam cover. This noise may be generated from the RH variable camshaft timing (VCT) phaser assembly.

General Motors

Pay More, Get Less

Aside from new-for-2011 products (Cruze, Volt, Regal, and HD trucks), just about every other model has been totally left alone or decontented. I'm not listing instances where paint colors were the only changes, but some of this decontenting is just nuts.

www.blueovalforums.com/forums

This year, the model that stood out to me the most in terms of feature deletions was the Chevrolet Malibu. For 2011, the Malibu is losing its universal home remote and the LTZ model is losing its auto-dimming driver's side mirror. Granted, both instances are minor at best, but the devil is in the details when you're trying to make a comeback. Sadly, the poor Malibu has fallen victim to GM cost cutting every model year since its 2008 release. For 2009, the Malibu lost power-adjustable pedals and the front side markers that GM made a big deal out of at launch. 2010 was no different, when Malibu lost the beautiful electroluminescent LTZ instrument cluster and trunk cargo net. I am left wondering why anyone would bother with an LTZ; they have cut the most content from it, dwindling its advantage over LT models.

www.gminsidenews.com/forums

Desperate "Decontenting"

Having cut four of its eight brands (Pontiac, Saturn, Hummer, and Saab), thrown its dealers under its unsold buses, trucks, and cars, and spent billions of dollars on overseas factories in China, GM now says it has learned its lesson and is making reliable, best-in-class, content-rich vehicles.

I don't think so.

Aside from the new Daewoo Spark, Regal, Cruze, Volt, and HD pickups, there isn't much happening with the 2011 models. Most of the changes have to do with axed models like the Cobalt/G5, colour changes, and "decontenting" through option package deletions.

MALIBU DECONTENTING

MALIBU—FEATURES CUT

- Universal Home Remote (UG1)
- Auto-dimming feature (LTZ)
- Driver-side outside mirror (LTZ)
- Front door pull cup back-lighting (LS)
- 18" 5-spoke, bright finish aluminum wheels (NW5)—part of 2LT V6 Package
- 17" wheels with bright chrome (1LT)
- 3.5L V6 engine (LZ4/LZE)
- 4-speed automatic transmission (MN5)

MALIBU—NEW FEATURES:

- 17" ultra bright aluminum wheels (PFE)—standard on 1LT
- 18" Chrome-Tech aluminum wheels (QR2)—part of 2LT V6 Package

It appears that Chevrolet tends to bear the brunt of the feature whacking at GM every year. The Traverse is another product that has lost features since its 2009 launch. In 2010, the Traverse shed its projector beam headlamps (they were standard on LTZ), 110-volt power outlet (also standard on LTZ), the owner's manual pouch was deleted from all models and its power rear sunshade was replaced with a manual one. In the upcoming 2011 model year, the Traverse is giving up its power-folding mirrors with built-in turn signals. Yet again, it seems that the high end LTZ trim gets smacked by GM cost cutting.

www.gminsidenews.com/forums

This year, GM's model lineup will be more tightly positioned than ever before, again creating lots of overlap and brand dilution as GM seeks to sell thinly disguised Pontiacs through starving Buick-GMC dealers. Of course, this shoring up of Buick products is bound to hurt Cadillac, whose products will be seen as upscale Buicks with little Cadillac cachet.

Ironically, keeping Buick on life-support also means that the Impala, one of GM's least-competitive products, will stay around long after it should have been culled from the herd. Keeping the Impala without major upgrades weakens the Chevrolet brand and gives Ford's Taurus a boost. Until it has a modern full-sized ride in the lineup, Chevy's like a one-armed boxer—only packing half the punch. Chevy also needs a *good* alternative to the Malibu, like the recently discontinued, upscale Pontiac G8, which should have been carried over to Chevrolet.

Don't believe GM hype that the company has learned its lesson from over-dealering, overlapping models, rebadging (selling the same model under a different name), and keeping "dog" models around long after they've been rejected by the market. Product differentiation is still far off in the future, if it arrives at all.

Cruze

The 2011 Chevrolet Cruze will be built in Lordstown, Ohio, and is slotted to replace the poor-selling Chevrolet Cobalt and its Pontiac G5 twin as the leading homegrown compact car from GM. This may not be hard to do, since the Cobalt ranked a disappointing 24th out of 30 "affordable small cars" rated by *U.S. News and World Report*.

The Cruze is offered as a four-door sedan that comes with a fuel-frugal 138 hp 1.8L 4-cylinder engine. The Eco version uses a 138 hp turbocharged 1.4L 4-cylinder engine. A 6-speed manual transmission is standard on the LS and Eco; a 6-speed automatic is optional on those models, but comes standard on the LT and LTZ. Buyers get a wide choice of standard safety features that include ABS, traction control, an antiskid system, side curtain airbags, front and rear side airbags, and front knee airbags. The Eco models have ultra-low-rolling-resistance tires and other aerodynamic improvements designed to increase fuel economy.

European and Australian car columnists who have tested earlier local versions have mixed opinions. They praise the Cruze for its interior quality/space and modern styling, while criticizing the car's weight, wimpy engines, and mediocre handling; in any event, the 2011 Cruze will be a huge improvement on the Cobalt's cramped interior and antiquated look that turned off many buyers. Then again, drivers don't just want style or fuel economy; they want performance, too, which may stop the Cruze dead in its tracks if fuel costs stay reasonable enough for drivers to stick with less fuel-efficient vehicles.

Regal

The Opel-based Buick (Insignia) Regal will have to produce the increased sales that Buick dealers need to make up for the loss of Pontiac—and GM believes it will do just that, becoming Buick's best-selling model. Actual transaction prices for the 4-cylinder-only Regal are expected to be a few thousand dollars less than the LaCrosse. Though the Insignia has been well-received in Europe, the North American market will be a crap-shoot. The car will have to be positioned as sportier than the LaCrosse despite its only offering a 4-banger.

Volt

The Chevrolet Volt should be available at dealerships as part of GM's 2012 lineup. GM has planned to produce 10,000 units for 2012, with an MSRP of $43,000; GM will lose money on every one.

While paying lip service to hybrid engines, GM is gaining time and PR points by promoting the 2011 Volt electric car. Reminds me of a Hydro-Québec press conference 18 years ago when, with great fanfare, the Quebec utility boasted that it would corner the North American market for electrically powered vehicles. It never happened… and never will. GM's $40,000 (U.S.) Volt will endure the same fate. *Mais oui!*

You may get a jolt from the electric Volt. And isn't "green" just another marketing scam when cars are still being powered by dead dinosaurs?

Be skeptical of the fuel-savings figures that are bandied about. Nissan says that its 2011 Leaf EV achieves the equivalent of 0.6 L/100 km (367 mpg). Chevrolet says its Volt EV, also scheduled for a 2011 introduction, gets 1.0 L/100 km (230 mpg). For those of us wishing to go green and break our petroleum habit, these are tantalizing numbers. But the fuel economy figures are at best premature and at worst misleading.

The U.S. government's Environmental Protection Agency devises test procedures for determining miles per gallon. Their formula for testing electric vehicles, though, is still in draft form, so EV mileage numbers come from an equivalency calculation of gasoline and electrical energy content: an imperfect measure at best. In fact, it's not clear that mpg is the appropriate benchmark anymore. Will the Chevy Volt, which uses gasoline for its "extended-range EV" backup, actually go 230 miles for each gallon in its tank? And what's the meaning of 367 mpg when the Nissan Leaf doesn't use a gallon of gas to begin with?

Let's imagine it's early 2011 and I'm the proud owner of a Chevy Volt. A topped-up battery gives me the claimed 64 kilometres (40 miles) of pure EV range. After this, the gasoline engine takes over and drives the generator that powers electric propulsion. Will the average driver be satisfied with this limited and limiting arrangement? GM hasn't disclosed the fuel efficiency of this "series hybrid" operation in reaching its next plug-in. Furthermore, how many thousands of dollars will the battery packs cost to replace after eight years or so? And what is the environmental footprint of adding another vehicle to the car population, rather than recycling a used model? GM and Nissan are mum when asked these questions.

Spark

GM also plans to launch a Daewoo-bred Chevy econocar in late 2010 that should cost buyers less than half as much as the Volt. Called the Spark, it's a front-drive four-door hatchback that's a mini-Aveo, based on the old Matiz minicar sold around the world. GM picked up the Matiz when it formed GMDAT back in 2002 using the leftover rubble of Daewoo Motors.

Reviewers say that the Spark will have a difficult time competing with more-refined Asian and European models like the Mazda2 and the Ford Fiesta. Although it's seen as a politically correct offering to Washington and Ottawa politicos who want to see more fuel thrifty vehicles on the road, the Spark's downside is that Daewoo's products have a long history of being unreliable and not very durable. Also, Spark sales won't "spark" domestic employment on either side of the border. Instead, the jobs will flow to GM Daewoo Auto Technologies in South Korea.

Trucks and SUVs

General Motors' once-profitable truck and SUV division is in chaos as GM confronts stricter fuel-economy standards, new diesel-fuel NOx emissions rules that require regular urea fill-ups, gas price spikes that drive product planners batty, and a buying public that wants car-like handling and performance. Although the Tahoe, Yukon, Suburban, and Yukon XL will likely soldier on until at least 2013, the smaller, last-in-class Colorado and Canyon pickups will be discontinued in 2012.

GM's base 2011 pickups (1500 series) return unchanged; however, the 2500 and 3500 HD lineup will offer many new powertrain, suspension, and interior upgrades. These are major improvements that make these models more competitive with Ford's Super Duty lineup. Dodge trucks, on the other hand, are not as technologically sophisticated as GM's or Ford's. Ford's trucks will continue to have the high-tech edge since the improvements were made earlier and Ford has fixed many of the first-year production glitches, while GM's HD changes may open the door to major production glitches this year.

As buyers downsize from Detroit SUVs to CR-Vs, RAV4s, Foresters, and Tucsons, GM comes to the party a bit late; nevertheless, its 2011 Equinox and Terrain are credible competitors that are gaining market share from the downsized SUV boom. Unfortunately, despite the popularity of both vehicles, GM is still having difficulty explaining how consumers should choose between the two.

The GMC Terrain.

General Motors is still run by the same out-of-touch geezers who got it into trouble in the first place. Sure, Wagoner (the old prez) was kicked out at the U.S. government's urging, but is his replacement any different? Have you seen the ads where GM's new president walks the bustling GM hallways and stiffly extols the virtues of the company's 2010 lineup? The Cobalt? The Aveo? Pitiful. It's obvious he's not an auto man, no matter how much he puts on a Lee Iacocca front and brags about GM's products. All that's missing is him telling us to "Buy a car, and get a cheque."

GM is in much worse financial shape than Ford, but it won't likely be sold whole, as was the Chrysler group, or go bankrupt again, as some auto pundits predict. Instead, GM will be nibbled into nothing by Asian and European investors picking at its entrails. Asset-rich Toyota or Volkswagen may jump at the chance to pick up a restructured GM division for a third of its pre-recession value.

In the meantime, GM is desperately trying to stir up buyer enthusiasm and put some money in the till by focusing on its four remaining divisions (Buick, Cadillac, Chevrolet, and GMC) and increasing sales in Europe and China—two markets where its products are still popular and production costs are minimal. To further cut costs, the automaker dropped its infamously failure-prone front-drive minivans to make room for its popular (and *Lemon-Aid* recommended!) large SUVs that include the Buick Enclave, Chevrolet Traverse, and GMC Acadia.

Rather than rejuvenate Buick (an impossible task), GM needs to close it down and market through Chevrolet whatever Buicks sell best. Closing Pontiac and throwing money away on its Buick and Cadillac divisions is incredibly stupid, akin to the automaker buying Saab or paying a $2 billion penalty for reneging on its promise to buy Fiat.

And GM must stop lurching from discounts to rebates in an effort to "sell the deal" rather than selling its cars and trucks. Overpricing products in the fall and then cutting prices by 20 percent several months later doesn't build customer loyalty, it fosters customer anger and suspicion and tells shoppers that GM prices are a con. At first, only GM employees got rebates. Then it was close relatives, then third-cousin Billy Bob, then it was your first date (not first cousin, at least in Canada)…wink wink, nudge nudge.

How can GM build customer confidence in its pricing when everybody but you gets a special deal? Would you buy another GM after paying the high-end price—especially after learning that savvy buyers, cousins, and girlfriends got additional discounts that you didn't?

Warranties and Quality Control

I like GM's 60-day money-back guarantee, and you might, too (provided you drive no more than 4,000 km and keep up with your payments). A PR move? Of course it is. Still, it usually doesn't help boost sales for long. GM has done this in the past with Saturn and other vehicles that weren't very well made. Apparently, owners complain, but few go through the hassle of taking their car back. They just tell their friends never to buy another of the same model.

2009 CHEVY SILVERADO 1500 FOUR-WHEEL DRIVE 5.3L V8

All Technical Service Bulletins

NUMBER	DATE	TITLE
10-08-46-001	01/27/2010	Audio—Radio Does Not Mute Enough When Using OnStar
09-03-08-006B	01/12/2010	Suspension—Front End Creak/Clunk/Squeak Or Rattle
08-04-19-004A	01/06/2010	Drivetrain—Front Axle Vent Hose Routing
09-08-46-004A	12/17/2009	OnStar—Generation 8 Modules Inop./Battery Discharge
08-09-41-002E	12/07/2009	Restraints—Air Bag Lamp ON/Multiple TDCs Set
05-03-10-003E	12/04/2009	Wheels/Tires—Low Tire Pressure/Aluminum Wheels Leak
08-03-10-006B	12/04/2009	Wheels/Tires—Tire(s) Slowly Go Flat
09-08-68-001	11/14/2009	Engine Controls—Cruise Control Turns Off When Operated
05-06-01-034J	11/13/2009	Engine—Oil Leaks From Rear Cover
08-08-48-003C	11/10/2009	Body—Tapping/Clicking/Ticking Noise at Windshield Area
09-08-66-009	11/09/2009	Body—Tailgate Handle/Latch Binds/Hard To Open
00-03-10-006E	11/04/2009	Tires—Tire Radial Force Variation (RFV)
99-04-20-002F	11/03/2009	Drivetrain—Clunk Noise Shifting From PARK Into Gear
09-06-04-035A	11/03/2009	Engine Controls—Engine Stall On Deceleration When Hot
08-08-67-006A	10/28/2009	Body—Headliner Wet Water Leak Into Cab Past Sunroof
09184A	10/26/2009	Campaign—Possible Air-Bag Deployment/Service Light ON
06-08-64-001B	10/20/2009	Body—Side Window Chipping Information
05-03-08-002C	10/16/2009	Suspension—Shock Absorber/Strut Leakage Information
06-08-50-009D	10/06/2009	Restraints—Passenger Presence System Information
09-08-57-002A	09/28/2009	Body—General Sunroof Water Leak Diagnostic Guide
09-08-48-006	09/18/2009	Body—Stain/Film On Windshield Glass Perimeter
09-04-19-002	09/16/2009	Drivetrain—Excessive Effort When Shift 2HI to 4HI
08-08-52-001E	09/11/2009	Keyless Entry—Intermittent/Inoperative Remote
09-08-50-014	08/28/2009	Interior—Seat Memory Inoperative After Air Bag Deploys
08-07-30-021C	08/27/2009	Electrical—Multiple DTCs/Electrical Malfunction
04-08-50-006C	08/27/2009	Interior—Seat Cover Wrinkle/Crease/Burn Info
07-03-10-008B	08/13/2009	Tires—Slight/Mild Edge Feathering Information
09-04-21-003B	08/11/2009	Drivetrain—Clunk Noise at Stop Or From Launch
08-08-46-003C	08/07/2009	OnStar—Destination Download Incomplete/Intermittent
07-08-50-018E	08/05/2009	Interior—Lint Accumulation On Ebony Colored Seats
06-08-44-035C	08/04/2009	Entertainment System—DVD Screen Off After Ign. Cycle
09-01-38-004	07/31/2009	A/C—A/C Indicator Or Recirculation Indicator Flashing
08-08-61-005A	07/31/2009	Body—Front/Rear Fender Liners Warped/Wavy
07-08-46-002D	07/29/2009	Audio System—Noise When Using OnStar
07-06-01-016B	07/27/2009	Engine—Noise/Damage Oil Filter Application Importance
08-06-01-008A	07/27/2009	Engine—Drive Belt Misalignment Diagnostics
07-02-32-002H	07/08/2009	Steering—Fluid Leaks From The Steering Gear/Rack
09-08-50-011	06/26/2009	Body—Sticking/Binding Door Mounted Seat Switches
09-09-41-005	06/26/2009	Restraints—Air Bag Readiness Light On
05-08-51-008C	06/22/2009	Body—Bumps or Rust Colored Spots in Paint
08-07-30-020D	06/19/2009	A/T Controls—DTC P1825/P182E or P1915/MIL ON

08-06-03-008A	06/15/2009	Battery—Intermittent Drain Diagnostic Tips
99-01-39-004C	06/12/2009	A/C—Musty Odors Emitted From (HVAC) System
06-03-09-004B	06/04/2009	Suspension—Squeak Noise from Rear of Vehicle
09-08-64-023	06/03/2009	Body—Outside Door Handle Pulls Out of Base
03-03-09-002C	06/02/2009	Suspension—Rear Leaf Spring Slapping/Clunking Noise
09-08-110-013	06/02/2009	Interior—Sun Visor Fails to Stay In Up Position
03-08-48-006F	05/26/2009	A/C—Window Defroster Contact/Tab Repair Information
08-08-127-001A	05/26/2009	Park Assist System—Inoperative/Lamp ON/DTCs Set
09-06-05-004	05/20/2009	Exhaust System—Rattle/Thud Noise On Left Turns/Bumps
09-04-21-001	05/19/2009	Drivetrain—4 Wheel Drive Message/DTC C0387/C0569 Set
09-08-44-012	05/18/2009	Audio System—Radio Inoperative or No Display
07-09-40-001A	05/14/2009	Restraints/Interior—Front Seat Belt Twisted
02-08-44-007D	05/12/2009	OnStar—Negative Impact of Cloth/Vinyl Roofs
06-08-44-015B	05/12/2009	Audio System—Noise When Using Portable Playback Unit
07-08-42-006C	05/07/2009	Instruments—Bulb Outage Detection Restoration
09-03-09-001	05/06/2009	Suspension—Clunking Noise From Rear of Vehicle
09-08-42-003	05/05/2009	Lighting—Loose Front Fog Lamp
01-08-42-001G	05/04/2009	Lighting—Exterior Lamp Condensation Guidelines
09-05-22-003	04/29/2009	Brakes—Feel Grabby Or Touchy DTC C012E Reprogramming
09-05-22-003	04/29/2009	Brakes—Grabby/Touchy Or DTC C012E Stored
09-04-19-001	04/28/2009	Drivetrain—Whine or Click Type Noises From Front Axle
06-08-64-027G	04/28/2009	Mirrors—Driver's Door Mirror Glass Shakes/Flutters
09-08-66-007	04/28/2009	Liftgate—Close Actuator Motor Change
09-06-04-024	04/24/2009	Engine Controls—MIL ON/Multiple DTCs
09-08-64-015	04/24/2009	Body—Front or Rear Side Door Window Multiple Problems
09-08-63-004	04/23/2009	Body—High Pitched Squeak Noise At Left/Right A-Pillar
03-06-04-030G	04/22/2009	Fuel System—Driveability Issues/MIL/Multiple DTCs
09-07-30-004A	04/21/2009	A/T—Shift Flare/Harsh 2–3 Shifting
07-06-05-001F	04/20/2009	Exhaust System—Buzzing/Snapping/Popping Noises
09-08-66-004	04/20/2009	Body—Soft Tonneau Cover Appears Loose/Won't Latch
09-08-66-003	04/17/2009	Body—Tonneau Cover Fits Loose On Vehicle
08-08-50-001A	04/08/2009	Interior—Front Seat Cushion Cover Becomes Detached
09-08-47-001	04/07/2009	Body Controls—Unable to Reprogram Body Control Module
09-08-64-011	04/02/2009	Instruments—L/H Door Mirror Glass Distorted
08-02-35-004A	03/31/2009	Interior—Steering Wheel Cover Warped/Paint Peeling
09-08-43-001	03/25/2009	Electrical—Various Electrical Malfunction/Systems Inop.
09-08-48-002A	03/19/2009	Body—Marks/Stains on Windshield When Wet
07-08-66-003B	03/18/2009	Body—Accessory Toolbox Key Cylinder Won't Unlock
09-03-08-001A	03/17/2009	Suspension—Revised Front Lower Ball Joint Nut Torque
08-08-44-010F	03/09/2009	Navigation Radio—Diagnostic Tips
09-08-64-003	02/19/2009	Instruments—Outside Mirror Adjustment Information
09-09-40-001	02/17/2009	Restraints—Seat Belt Warning Lamp On/Buckling Issues
06-00-89-051C	02/11/2009	Locks—Key Code Security Rules And Information
08-09-41-009A	02/03/2009	Restraints—Information on DTC B0081 5A
02-08-98-002C	02/03/2009	Body—Hem Flange Rust Repair Information

08-08-44-030B	02/02/2009	Navigation Radio—Various Concerns/Issues
09-06-05-001	01/30/2009	Exhaust System—Sulfur Odor Explanation
01-07-30-036H	01/29/2009	A/T Control—DTC P0756 Diagnostic Tips
08-03-16-004A	01/29/2009	Tire Monitor System—Tire Pressure Light Stays ON
09-08-110-002	01/27/2009	Interior—Carpet Curling At Front Edge
01-06-01-011E	12/18/2008	Gasoline Engine—Oil Consumption Guidelines
07-03-10-013D	11/24/2008	Wheels/Tires—Vibration While Driving
08259A	11/06/2008	Campaign—Inoperative OnStar System
08-09-41-010	10/29/2008	Restraints—Air Bag Lamp ON/Multiple DTCs Set
08-06-03-009A	10/29/2008	Electrical—Reducing Intermittent Electrical Concerns
08313	10/03/2008	Campaign—XM Satellite Radio Receiver Replacement
08-07-300-042	09/30/2008	A/T—MIL ON/Various DTCs/Poor Driveability
00-00-89-027E	09/29/2008	Interior—Elimination Of Unwanted Odors
01-07-30-032E	09/29/2008	A/T—4T65E Fluid Leaking From A/T Vent
08-06-02-003	09/10/2008	Engine—Oil Leak At Oil Cooler Hose/Pipe Assembly
08-08-44-028	08/28/2008	Audio—Inadvertent Steering Wheel Button Activation
08-08-42-004	08/27/2008	Lighting—Dome/Reading Lamps Inoperative
08-08-110-013	08/18/2008	Interior—Wear Spots On Vinyl/Rubber Floor Covering
08-08-44-027	08/12/2008	Navigation Radio—Weak Or No GPS Signal Information
08-08-44-026	08/11/2008	Audio System—Refurbishing Radio Faceplates/Knobs
08-07-30-035	08/08/2008	A/T—Water Or Coolant Contamination Information
06-08-44-009A	08/04/2008	Electrical—Various Rear Door Electrical Malfunctions
06-08-44-034C	07/31/2008	Navigation Radio—Various Noises Explained
07-08-49-014A	07/30/2008	Parking Assist System—"Park Assist Off" Message on DIC
02-06-03-008D	07/21/2008	Charging System—Low Voltage Display/Battery Discharged
07-06-03-009A	07/21/2008	Charging System—Volt Meter Fluctuation Information
08-06-03-007	06/27/2008	Electrical—No Start/No Crank/Int. Electrical Operations
08-08-64-011	06/23/2008	Mirrors—Heated Mirror Defrosting Time
08-07-30-026	05/22/2008	A/T—Slight Vehicle Movement In Park At Start Up

This is ALLDATA's list of defect correction service bulletins for just one pickup. It's really quite simple: More quality means more sales. GM still doesn't get it.

Take a look at the preceding confidential service bulletin chart for 2009 Silverado and Sierra pickups. Many of these problems are carried over for three to five years. Not the sign of a company that sincerely believes in quality products.

GM's quality control needs serious improvement, and its recent bankruptcy has made that almost impossible. Unlike Ford, GM and Chrysler haven't made the supplier and production changes needed to improve quality enough to get buyers into its showrooms. GM's supplier base is decimated, employees are sullen, bankers are skeptical, dealers are afraid, and buyers are suspicious. Its engines and automatic transmissions still aren't as reliable or as durable as those of the Asian competition. Furthermore, GM brake and electronic components often fail prematurely and cost owners big bucks to diagnose and repair. The quality and assembly of body components remains far below Japanese and European standards.

GM's China Connection

As of November 2009, China is the biggest auto market in the world. No wonder GM, Ford, and Chrysler are staking out the country as both a production centre and a sales market for new products. For example, General Motors is seriously considering building a cheap compact car in China that could be sold worldwide for less than $10,000 (U.S.), as France's Renault has done with their popular $7,800 (U.S.) Logan model in Europe. That car is built by Romanian automaker Dacia, known in Canada for the failure-prone ARO SUV sold principally in Quebec during the mid '70s. If GM exports its Chinese-made cars to North America, forget about quality and expect American worker anger to explode. GM will have shot itself in the heart with a rice bullet.

The Chery QQ.

It is unlikely that exports from Chinese auto factories will pose much of a threat to GM or other North American automakers in the short run for a variety of reasons. Firstly, the Asian market prefers American cars. Additionally, most of the Chinese automakers are small and have to work overtime just to supply their domestic market with cars and parts. Furthermore, manufacturing costs are rising in China following unprecedented labour union victories that have raised the minimum autoworker wage by 30 percent. Finally, North American consumers aren't likely to buy cars made in China. They are rightfully distrustful of a country that exports poisoned pet food, sells lead-laced toys, and tries to rip off American automakers by selling their new car as a Chevy (changed to Chery after a flurry of lawyers' letters from GM).

AVEO ★★

KEY FACTS

CANADIAN PRICE (VERY NEGOTIABLE):
LS: $14,150, *LT:* $16,850, *LS Hatch:*
$13,950, *LT Hatch:* $16,650 **U.S. PRICE:**
LS: $11,965, *LT:* $14,100, *2LT:* $15,365
CANADIAN FREIGHT: $1,350 **U.S. FREIGHT:**
$975
POWERTRAIN (FRONT-DRIVE)
Engine: 1.6L 4-cyl. (108 hp);
Transmissions: 5-speed man. • 4-speed
auto.
DIMENSIONS/CAPACITY
Passengers: 2/3; Wheelbase: 97.6 in.;
H: 53.9/L: 169.7/W: 67.3 in., Headroom
F/R: 5.0/2.0 in..; Legroom F/R: 41/26 in.;
Maximum load: 860 lb.; Cargo volume:
12.4 cu. ft. Fuel tank: 45L/regular; Tow
limit: Not recommended; Turning circle:
35 ft.; Ground clearance: 5 in.; Weight:
2,557–2,579 lb.

RATING: Below Average. There is nothing particularly noteworthy with this GM/Daewoo product. **Strong points:** Cheap basic transportation and better-than-average occupant protection. Parts are plentiful and repairs aren't dealer-dependent. Good outward visibility, easy backseat access, and the hatchback storage area is easy to get to (though there is more room in the sedan's trunk). **Weak points:** Unimpressive fuel economy; mediocre handling degraded by vague steering and excessive body lean when cornering or braking; uncomfortable seats; and mediocre fit and finish. Depreciation is so rapid that a 2007 base model that sold for $13,000 is now worth only $5,500. Worse still is the car's poor reliability; almost every component has come up short. **New for 2011:** Nothing significant; a redesigned, non-functional optional spoiler and new colours.

OVERVIEW: The base price is quite reasonable; however, the Aveo doesn't give anywhere near the quality and fuel economy of most Asian automakers.

COST ANALYSIS: What you save on the purchase price you will lose paying for early repairs. Overall, it would be a better idea to buy next year's redesigned model, which will offer major performance upgrades for just a bit more money. **Best alternatives:** Honda Fit, Hyundai Accent, and Nissan Versa. **Options:** Anti-lock brakes with the engine immobilizer system. **Depreciation:** Average. **Insurance cost:** Average. **Parts supply/cost:** Parts aren't hard to find and are relatively inexpensive. **Annual maintenance cost:** Average. **Warranty:** Bumper-to-bumper 4 years/80,000 km; powertrain 5 years/160,000 km; rust perforation 6 years/160,000 km. **Supplementary warranty:** A good idea to get an extended powertrain warranty. **Highway/city fuel economy:** *Man.:* 5.7/7.6 L/100 km, 49/37 mpg. *Auto.:* 5.8/8.2 L/100 km, 49/34 mpg.

OWNER-REPORTED PROBLEMS: Engine and transmission malfunctions; early failures of the fuel system, suspension, electrical system, and climate control. Windshield wipers cannot clean the window; they are useless at highway speeds and the washer fluid sprays too low when the car is stopped:

> The dealer checked five or six similar cars on the lot and all of them have the same problem. Changed washer fluid and cleaned lines. Changed washer pump. Dealer does not believe replacing the nozzles with new ones from the factory will resolve the problem.

SERVICE BULLETIN-REPORTED PROBLEMS: Tires leak air or suddenly go flat; poor radio reception; radio does not mute when using OnStar.

MALIBU ★★★

RATING: Average. The Malibu's performance strengths are compromised by the car's so-so reliability. **Strong points:** Good V6 powertrain set-up. Well-appointed; provides a comfortable though firm ride; better-than-average handling thanks to an independent suspension that doesn't sacrifice solid handling for passenger comfort. Plenty of passenger and luggage space, and few squeaks and rattles. NHTSA gives the Malibu a five-star crashworthiness score for front and side protection and four stars for rollover resistance. Standard stability control. **Weak points:** The base 4-cylinder engine is barely adequate for highway driving with the automatic transmission and a full load. Hybrid version was dropped after the 2009 model-year. Rear head restraints block visibility. Expect lots of powertrain and brake problems. IIHS gives the Malibu a "Marginal" rating for head-restraint effectiveness. **New for 2011:** Nothing important.

KEY FACTS

CANADIAN PRICE (VERY NEGOTIABLE): *LS:* $23,995, *2LT:* $25,795, *LTZ:* $32,750 **U.S. PRICE:** *LS:* $21,825, *1LT:* $22,715, *2LT:* $25,175, *LTZ:* $26,955, **CANADIAN FREIGHT:** $1,350 **U.S. FREIGHT:** $720 **POWERTRAIN (FRONT-DRIVE)**
Engines: 2.4L 4-cyl. (169 hp) • 3.6L V6 (252 hp); Transmissions: 4-speed auto. • 6-speed auto.

DIMENSIONS/CAPACITY

Passengers: 2/3; Wheelbase: 112.3 in.; H: 57/L: 191.8/W: 70.3 in.; Headroom F/R: 4.0/2.0 in., 5.0/4.5 in.; Legroom F/R: 41.5/30.0 in.; Cargo volume: 15.1 cu. ft.; Fuel tank: 61L/regular; Tow limit: 1,000 lb.; Load capacity: 915 lb.; Turning circle: 42 ft.; Ground clearance: 5.0 ft.; Weight: 3,460 lb.

OVERVIEW: The Malibu is a popular front-drive, mid-sized sedan distinguished by its nice array of standard features. The base Malibu is "powered" (if you can call it that) by GM's wimpy 169 hp 2.4L 4-cylinder powerplant, found on many of its compact cars. Most buyers will be tempted to pay extra for the torquier and smoother 252 hp 3.6L V6.

The Malibu's styling is quite conservative and uncluttered. A fold-flat passenger seat and a 60/40-split rear folding bench seat maximize the interior room. Other useful standard amenities include a driver-seat power height adjuster; a telescoping steering column that also tilts; power windows, door locks, and outside mirrors; and power-adjustable brake and accelerator pedals (LS and LT).

COST ANALYSIS: The 6-speed automatic is worth the extra cost. Don't be tempted by any leftover 2009 Malibu Hybrids, says *New York Times* auto columnist Lawrence Ulrich (*www.nytimes.com/2009/06/21/automobiles/autoreviews/21malibu.html?partner=rss&emc=rss*):

> The Aura and Malibu are so-called mild hybrids, which makes them as authentic as supermarket salsa. To keep the price down, the Malibu forgoes the things that let full hybrids generate impressive mileage: a large electric motor that can propel the car with no help from the engine, a sizable battery pack and a continuously variable transmission to efficiently mix and match electric and gas power.

Best alternatives: The Honda Accord has more usable interior space, is super reliable, and has quicker and more-accurate steering; Hyundai's Elantra is cheaper and just as well put together; the Toyota Camry is plusher, though not as driver-oriented (make sure it carries the standard brake override feature). Other cars worth considering are the Mazda6 and Nissan Sentra. **Options:** The V6 and premium tires. **Rebates:** $3,500 rebates should kick in sometime during the new year. **Depreciation:** Average. **Insurance cost:** Higher than average. **Parts supply/cost:** Malibu uses generic GM parts that are usually easy to find and reasonably priced. However, since the company came out of bankruptcy, parts are often back-ordered for weeks at a time. **Annual maintenance cost:** Average. **Warranty:** 60-day money-back guarantee as long as you don't drive more than 4,000 km. Bumper-to-bumper 3 years/60,000 km; powertrain 5 years/160,000 km; rust perforation 6 years/160,000 km **Supplementary warranty:** An extended powertrain warranty would be a wise investment. **Highway/city fuel economy:** *2.4L:* 6.5/9.5 L/100 km, 43/30 mpg. *2.4L 6-speed:* 5.9/9.4 L/100 km, 48/30 mpg. *V6:* 7.8/12.2 L/100 km, 36/23 mpg.

OWNER-REPORTED PROBLEMS: At the top of the list are engine and transmission failures, electrical system glitches (door locks that open and close randomly, for example), the frequent replacement of brake and suspension components, AC malfunctions, and very poor fit and finish. Safety-related complaints include an engine compartment fire while the car was parked; airbags that deploy inadvertently or fail to deploy; and faulty airbag modules:

> I've had my 2010 Malibu just over 3 months. Air bag light continually lit up; took to dealership; I've waited over a week. They ordered 5 modules to replace safety air bag system; to replace they had to remove both front seats [and] cut the tracks of the seats out. They ordered new tracks and [have] to weld them back in the car. How safe is this car going to be at this point?

Park gear won't hold the vehicle parked on a hill; the 6-speed transmission hesitates before shifting; the vehicle has a tendency to wander to the left side of the road into oncoming traffic; door locks cannot be disabled to extricate an accident victim; sudden brake loss; premature warpage of the brake rotors; very loose steering; steering loss; sudden steering lock-up; chronic steering shimmy; frequent stalling for unexplained reasons; cruise control doesn't hold the set speed and may cause the car to suddenly accelerate with a wide-open throttle; original-equipment tires don't have gripping power and fail prematurely; severe glare from the dash onto the windshield; and inaccurate fuel gauges.

SERVICE BULLETIN-REPORTED PROBLEMS: Delayed shifting; drivetrain clunks; leaking aluminum wheels; and AC failures:

BULLETIN NO.: 09-01-38-005   **AC POOR COOLING PERFORMANCE**   **DATE: OCTOBER 9, 2009**

POOR A/C PERFORMANCE, COOLING FAN FUSE BLOWN (INSTALL REVISED FUSE AND WIRING)
2008–10 Chevrolet Malibu; 2006–10 Pontiac; G6 2007–10 Saturn Aura
CONDITION: Some customers may comment on poor A/C cooling performance. Technicians may find that the cooling fan fuse is blown.
CAUSE: High cooling fan start up loads may cause the 30-amp cooling fan fuse, located in the underhood fuse block, to blow. The lack of air flow through the A/C condenser, caused by the inoperative high-speed cooling fan, may affect the condenser's ability to dissipate heat.
CORRECTION: Install a heavier gauge power feed wire from the underhood fuse block to the cooling fan. After the wiring update is completed, replace the 30-amp cooling fan fuse with a 40-amp fuse.

Why in the heck did this fuse/wiring problem take five years to solve?

IMPALA, LACROSSE   ★★ / ★★★

The Chevrolet Impala.

KEY FACTS

CANADIAN PRICE (VERY NEGOTIABLE):
Impala LS: $27,320, *LTZ:* $30,565,
LaCrosse CX: $31,645, *CX V6:* $32,795,
CXL: $34,795, *AWD:* $38,245, *CXS:*
$40,795 **U.S. PRICE:** *Impala LS:* $24,290,
LTZ: $29, 930, *LaCrosse CX:* $26,245,
CX V6: $27,085, *CXL:* $29,645, *AWD:*
$31,820, *CXS:* $33,015 **CANADIAN
FREIGHT:** $1,350 **U.S. FREIGHT:** $750
POWERTRAIN (FRONT-DRIVE/AWD)
Engines: *Impala:* 3.5L V6 (207 hp) •
3.9L V6 (230 hp) • 5.3L V8 (303 hp),
LaCrosse: 2.4L 4-cyl. (182 hp) • 3.0L
V6 (255 hp) • 3.6L V6 (280 hp);
Transmissions: *Impala:* 4-speed auto.,
LaCrosse: 6-speed auto.
DIMENSIONS/CAPACITY
Passengers: 2/3; Wheelbase: *Impala:*
110.5 in., *LaCrosse:* 111.7 in.; *Impala:*
H: 58.7/L: 200.4/W: 72.9 in.; *LaCrosse:*
H: 58.9/L: 197.0/W: 73.1 in.; Headroom
F/R: 4.0/1.5 in.; Legroom F/R: *Impala:*
40.5/26 in.; Fuel tank: 64L/regular/
premium; Cargo volume: 16 cu. ft.; Tow
limit: 1,000 lb.; Load capacity: *Impala:*
945 lb., *LaCrosse:* 915 lb.; Turning circle:
Impala: 41.0 ft., *LaCrosse:* 38.8 ft.;
Ground clearance: *Impala:* 6.0 in.;
Weight: *Impala LS, LT:* 3,555 lb., *LTZ:*
3,649 lb., *LaCrosse CX:* 3,948 lb.

RATING: *Impala:* Below Average. *LaCrosse:* Average. **Strong points:** *Impala:* Comes with an array of standard features, provides a comfortable ride, and has an easily accessed interior, highlighted by a convenient flip-down centre console in the middle of the bench seats and rear seatbacks that fold flat, opening up cargo storage space. NHTSA gave the Impala a five-star crashworthiness rating for front and side protection and four stars for rollover resistance. *LaCrosse:* The 3.0L V6 provides smooth acceleration and works well with the 6-speed automatic transmission, though it could use more high-speed torque. Handling and ride are better than average, owing to recent suspension and steering refinements. For extended highway use, you'll find the 3.6L powerplant is better suited to your needs. Adequate rear legroom and a front bench seat. A much better reliability record than the Impala. The LaCrosse got five stars for front crash protection and four stars for rollover resistance; side protection with airbags merited three stars. Stability control is a standard LTZ feature. **Weak points:** *Impala:* The automatic 4-speed transmission is sometimes slow to downshift, and the Overdrive is clunky; this is a car that cries out for a 6-speed automatic gearbox. Rear seating is uncomfortable for three; bland styling; and obstructed rear visibility. Engine and transmission deficiencies have been commonplace. Subpar body construction, which puts the Impala on par with Chrysler's poor performers. Stability control isn't standard on the entry-level models. **New for 2011:** Nothing important.

OVERVIEW: GM's Impala is yesterday's sedan. With the V8 option gone, the car is overwhelmed by its unimpressive highway performance and overall lack of quality. The mid-level 3.9L V6 does offer cylinder deactivation, which improves fuel economy by shutting off half the engine's cylinders when they aren't needed.

The W-body 2006 Impala will soldier on until 2014 without any significant changes. It currently sells at about the same level as the Malibu, but its days are numbered. Everyone agrees that GM has given up on large front-drive sedans as a competitive volume product, and is relying instead on crossovers and downsized

SUVs to take up the slack. In the interim, the Impala will be GM's "ghost of Christmas past."

Worse still, anyone who wants a remotely competitive full-sized GM sedan will have to look at one of GM's luxury brands and dig much deeper into their wallet. Specifically, they will have to look at Buick or Cadillac's flagships, the LaCrosse or the XTS.

Last year, the mid-sized LaCrosse was completely restyled, and its four-wheel independent suspension was retuned to improve the ride and handling. CX and CXL models are powered by an all-new 255 hp 3.0L V6 hooked to a 6-speed automatic transmission; the CX has a 182 hp 2.4L 4-cylinder engine as its base powerplant. CX models come with front-drive, while the CXL's all-wheel drive is optional. The top-of-the-line CXS is now powered by a 280 hp 3.6L V6, 6-speed automatic, and front-drive. The available all-wheel-drive system employs a limited-slip differential to send torque to whichever wheel has more traction for better control on slippery roads.

COST ANALYSIS: 2010 Impala and LaCrosse models are discounted about 15 percent and are practically identical to the 2011s. **Best alternatives:** The more-reliable, better-performing Honda Accord, Mazda6, Hyundai Elantra, and Toyota Camry or Avalon (with brake override). Those wanting a bit more performance should consider the BMW 3 Series. More room and better performance can be had by purchasing a Hyundai Tucson or a Honda CR-V. **Options:** Pass on the Impala's rear spoiler, which obstructs rear visibility and is of doubtful utility. **Rebates:** *Impala:* The Impala is in a marketing segment that's steadily losing ground to Japanese entries. The longer you wait, the cheaper these cars will become. Look for a savings of at least $3,000 early in the new year. *LaCrosse:* Last year's redesign has created some buying buzz and has kept the price higher than it should be; this will pass and buyers can expect 2011 prices to be cut by at least 10 percent. **Depreciation:** *Impala:* Incredibly fast; a 2007 Impala LS that sold new for $25,230 is now worth only $11,500. *LaCrosse:* Again, depreciation is a big minus. A 2007 LaCrosse (which was called the Allure from 2005–09) CX that sold for $26,395 is now worth $12,000. **Insurance cost:** Higher than average. **Parts supply/cost:** Moderately priced parts that aren't hard to find. **Annual maintenance cost:** Higher than average. Independent garages can perform most non-emissions servicing; however, cylinder deactivation makes you a prisoner of GM dealer servicing. **Warranty:** 60-day money-back guarantee as long as you don't drive more than 4,000 km. Bumper-to-bumper 4 years/ 80,000 km; powertrain 5 years/160,000 km; rust perforation 6 years/160,000 km. **Supplementary warranty:** Essential, especially after the third year of ownership. Get an extended powertrain warranty to protect you from the usual GM engine and transmission problems. **Highway/city fuel economy:** *Impala sedan 3.5L:* 6.7/10.8 L/100 km, 42/28 mpg. *3.9L:* 7.4/12.0 L/100 km, 38/24 mpg. *LaCrosse 2.4L:* 6.6/10.9 L/100 km, 43/26 mpg. *3.0L FWD:* 7.7/12.7 L/100 km, 37/22 mpg. *AWD:* 8.0/13.3 L/100 km, 35/21 mpg. *3.6L:* 7.3/12.2 L/100 km, 39/23 mpg.

OWNER-REPORTED PROBLEMS: Electrical system failures. The airbag is disabled when a normal-sized occupant sits in the passenger seat. Front and rear brakes rust easily and wear out early, and the discs warp far too often. Shock absorbers and MacPherson struts wear out or leak prematurely. The power rack-and-pinion steering system degenerates quickly after three years and is characterized by chronic leaking. Poor body fit, particularly around the doors, leads to excessive wind noise and water leaking into the interior. *Impala:* Airbag failures; chronic stalling; engine sputters, hesitates; driver-side wheel falls off; vehicle jerks when passing over rough pavement; car rolls back at a stop; excessive front-end vibration; brake rotors on one vehicle had to be replaced at 7,500 km; popping sound on stopping, starting, and turning; left and right control-arm, lower control-arm, ball joint, and steering failures; and a poorly designed Reverse lighting feature. *LaCrosse:* Distracting mirror reflection; vehicle wanders all over the road; brake pad, caliper, and rotor failures.

SERVICE BULLETIN-REPORTED PROBLEMS: Clunk noise when shifting from Park into gear:

CLUNK NOISE SHIFTING FROM PARK	
BULLETIN NO.: 99-04-20-002F	DATE: NOVEMBER 2, 2009

INFORMATION ON DRIVELINE CLUNK NOISE WHEN SHIFTING BETWEEN PARK AND DRIVE, PARK AND REVERSE, OR DRIVE AND REVERSE

2010 and prior GM Passenger Cars and Light Duty Trucks (including Saturn); 2010 and prior HUMMER H2, H3; 2009 and prior Saab 9-7X

Some customers of vehicles equipped with automatic transmissions may comment that the vehicle exhibits a clunk noise when shifting between Park and Drive, Park and Reverse, or Drive and Reverse. Similarly, customers of vehicles equipped with automatic or manual transmissions may comment that the vehicle exhibits a clunk noise while driving when the accelerator is quickly depressed and then released.

NOTE: Compare this complaint vehicle to a like vehicle. If the results are the same, this is a normal condition.

Hmmm...let me see if I understand: If all of your vehicles "clunk" when shifting out of Park, it's "normal"? You've gotta be kidding.

LUCERNE ★★★★

RATING: Above Average. **Strong points:** A nice array of useful standard equipment at an affordable base price, but costs go up quickly as the options grow. Good V8 powertrain performance. The electronic 4-speed transmission works imperceptibly, but it exacts a high fuel penalty. Cruise control is much smoother without all those annoying downshifts we've learned to hate in GM cars. Handling is acceptably predictable, though a bit slow with variable-assist power steering. A comfortable ride and a plush interior; quiet running; plenty of passenger and cargo room. NHTSA gave the Lucerne its top five-star rating for front crash protection and rollover resistance; side crashworthiness scored four stars. IIHS says the car's frontal offset crash protection is "Good" and side protection is "Acceptable." **Weak points:** GM isn't serious with this model: Giving the "Super" version a powerful Cadillac Northstar-derived V8 and then hooking it to a rudimentary 4-speed automatic is worse than taking a shower in a raincoat. Acceleration isn't breathtaking with the base V6 either; at higher revs, torque falls off quickly. The V8 tends to fishtail when at full throttle. Power steering is a bit vague at highway speeds. Fuel-thirsty; poor-quality mechanical and body components; obstructed front and rear visibility; ponderous handling caused partly by a mediocre suspension and over-assisted steering; car fishtails at full throttle; and panic braking causes considerable nose-diving, which compromises handling. IIHS gives a "Marginal" rating for head-restraint effectiveness. **New for 2011:** Nothing significant.

OVERVIEW: Buick's Lucerne is a good idea gone nowhere; 2011 is its last model year.

It is a competent front-drive family car that replaced the LeSabre and Park Avenue in 2006. Though not a very fuel-efficient four-door sedan, its generous discounting will give you plenty of change in your pockets to buy the extra gas. Clean body lines and a large platform make for an aerodynamic, pleasing appearance and a roomy interior with more rear seatroom than the LaCrosse. The standard 3.9L V6 is rough-running and noisy when pushed. CXS models are powered by a high-performance V8, which offers much better low- and mid-range throttle response.

COST ANALYSIS: Get a 20 percent discount on the identical 2010 model. **Best alternatives:** Ford Taurus, Hyundai Genesis Coupe, and Lexus ES series. **Options:** Go for the more-powerful V8. **Rebates:** Look for big rebates and discounts of $4,000–$5,000+ as this car ends its days. **Depreciation:** Faster than average. **Insurance cost:** Higher than average. **Parts supply/cost:** Parts aren't hard to find, but they can be pricey. **Annual maintenance cost:** Average. **Warranty:** 60-day money-back guarantee as long as you don't drive more than

KEY FACTS

CANADIAN PRICE (VERY NEGOTIABLE): *CX:* $31,995, *CXL:* $34,995 **U.S. PRICE:** *CX-1:* $29,230, *CX-2:* $29,230, *CXL1:* $32,730 **CANADIAN FREIGHT:** $1,400 **U.S. FREIGHT:** $750
POWERTRAIN (FRONT-DRIVE)
Engines: 3.9L V6 (227 hp) • 4.6L V8 (292 hp); Transmission: 4-speed auto.
DIMENSIONS/CAPACITY
Passengers: 2/3; Wheelbase: 114.8 in.; H: 58/L: 203/W: 74 in.; Headroom F/R: 3.0/2.5 in.; Legroom F/R: 42.5/31.5 in.; Cargo volume: 17 cu. ft.; Fuel tank: 70L/ regular; Load capacity: 925 lb.; Tow limit: 1,000 lb.; Turning circle: 47 ft.; Ground clearance: 5.0 in.; Weight: 4,095 lb.

4,000 km. Bumper-to-bumper 4 years/80,000 km; powertrain 5 years/160,000 km; rust perforation 6 years/160,000 km. **Supplementary warranty:** An extended powertrain warranty will come in handy. **Highway/city fuel economy:** *3.9L V6: 7.4/12.0 L/100 km, 38/24 mpg. 4.6L V8: 8.7/13.8 L/100 km, 32/20 mpg.*

OWNER-REPORTED PROBLEMS: Below average quality. Owners single out the brakes, suspension, and fit and finish as the most troublesome areas. No airbag deployment; cruise control causes the vehicle to surge; steering linkage bolts detach, causing steering failure; speedometer and fuel gauges can't be read in daylight; the driver-side mirror doesn't give a clear view to the rear; side mirrors fog up; front pillars create a blind spot; and the fuel gauge gives inaccurate readings. Safety-related complaints logged by NHTSA include sudden unintended acceleration while parking; low-beam headlights that switch to high-beams and won't return to low; door stoppers that don't hold the door open on a moderate incline; and a navigation system that can't be seen when the gear shift is in Drive:

> You have to take your eyes off the road and turn your body towards center of car to see the directions for navigation and also to see dials on radio. Wrote a letter to CEO of GM in Jan. 2010. At first, they said it was [because of] my stature that I could not see navigation nor radio (am 4'9") and that if I wanted to rectify this situation, I would have to pay $800 for a different radio. Since then, I went to the dealer and had the car test driven by the service manager. I have a work order confirming this. Results: no one can see the navigation system in the drive position. Called GM—was angry, as they lied to me. They now admit that this is a problem.

SERVICE BULLETIN-REPORTED PROBLEMS: Drivetrain clunk noise; brake pulsations/noise; poor radio reception; shock absorber strut leakage; tires slowly go flat; and side window chipping.

CAMARO ★★★

RATING: Average going into its third year on the market. **Strong points:** Nicely styled, with a mixture of retro and modern touches. Impressive V6 and V8 acceleration with reasonable fuel economy and nice steering/handling.

NHTSA awarded the Camaro five stars for side crashworthiness and rollover resistance; four stars were given for frontal crash protection. **Weak points:** No headroom; if you are 6'2" or taller, your head will be constantly brushing up against the headliner; uncomfortable seats; rear seating is a "knees-to-chin" affair; not much cargo room; some of the gauges are mounted at shin-height on the console, where they can barely be seen; much of the interior trim looks and feels cheap; and owners report that fit and finish glitches are everywhere. Obstructed driver visibility. **New for 2011:** A convertible arrives in 2011.

OVERVIEW: The 2011 Chevrolet Camaro continues to breathe life into General Motors' iconic "pony car" high-performance two-door coupe; a two-door convertible version is due in March—without the Z28. This year, LS, 1LT, 2LT, 1SS, and 2SS models are offered with one of two engines: a V6 or a V8. The 3.6L V6 produces 304 hp. It's available on LS and LT versions. SS versions with a manual transmission are equipped with a 426 hp 6.2L V8. Automatic-equipped SS models get the same V8, but with "only" 400 hp and GM's Active Fuel Management cylinder deactivation. Available safety features include ABS, traction control, anti-skid system, front side airbags, and side curtain airbags.

KEY FACTS

CANADIAN PRICE (VERY NEGOTIABLE):
LS man.: $26,995, *LS auto.:* $28,175, *1LT man.:* $28,065, *2LT man.:* $32,300, *2LT auto.:* $33,465, *1SS man.:* $37,065, *1SS auto.:* $38,500, *2SS man.:* $41,430, *2SS auto.:* $43,120 **U.S. PRICE:** *LS man.:* $22,680, *1LT man.:* $23,880, *2LT man.:* $26,875, *1SS:* $30,995, *2SS:* $33,945
CANADIAN FREIGHT: $1,350 **U.S. FREIGHT:** $800
POWERTRAIN (FRONT-DRIVE)
Engines: 3.6L V6 (304 hp) • 6.2L V8 (426 hp); Transmissions: 6-speed manumatic
DIMENSIONS/CAPACITY
Passengers: 2/2; Wheelbase: 112.3 in.; H: 54.2/L: 190.4/W: 75.5 in.; Cargo volume: 11.3 cu. ft.; Fuel tank: 71.9L/ regular; Tow limit: No towing; Turning circle: 37.7 ft.; Weight: 3,769–3,849 lb.

COST ANALYSIS: Over 40,000 2010 model Camaros have been sold so far, which means dealers can ask for (and get) the full suggested retail price. Smart buyers will wait on the better-made and more reasonably priced 2011 models. The added competition of Ford's revamped 2011 V6 Mustang will also keep Camaro prices down. **Best alternatives:** The Ford Mustang and Hyundai Genesis Coupe. The base Camaro is no longer in the running against the 305 hp V6-equipped Mustang because Ford has tackled its suspension, braking, and steering problems, while the GM's Camaro has coasted for the last two years. When you compare V8s, the Mustang GT is the clear winner where price is concerned. Normally, the Dodge Challenger would also be a "challenger," but it doesn't have the power to compete. **Options:** Integrated child safety seats. The GPS navigation aids can be useful, but don't waste your money on the power sunroof, leather upholstery, or heated seats. **Rebates:** Rebates and discounts of only $1,000–$2,000 because both of these sports cars are "hot." **Depreciation:** Very slow. A 2010 base model that sold for $26,995 is now worth $23,500. Not much lost for a year's use. **Insurance cost:** Much higher than average. **Parts supply/cost:** Not easily found and quite costly. At present, dealers have a monopoly on parts and service. **Annual maintenance cost:** Higher than average; there's no competition. **Warranty:** 60-day money-back guarantee as long as you don't drive more than 4,000 km. Bumper-to-bumper 4 years/80,000 km; powertrain 5 years/160,000 km; rust perforation 6 years/ unlimited km. **Supplementary warranty:** An extended powertrain warranty is a good idea, considering that the Camaro is only going into its second year on the market. **Highway/city fuel economy:** *3.6L V6:* 6.8/12.3 L/100 km, 41/25 mpg. *Auto.:* 6.9/11.4 L/100 km, 42/23 mpg. *6.2L V8:* 8.2/13.2 L/100 km, 34/21 mpg. *Auto.:* 7.9/13.2 L/100 km, 36/21 mpg.

OWNER-REPORTED PROBLEMS: The cable running from the trunk-mounted battery may fray on the starter motor and ground out, causing a complete loss of power. Also, GM suspended shipments of the V8 engine- and manual transmission-equipped 2010 Camaro SSs while engineers looked into reports of failed output shafts.

Although the Camaro hasn't been on the road long enough to get reliable failure rates on its various components, one group of owners and Camaro enthusiasts at *www.camaro5. com/forums/index.php* prepared a table of defects seen with the most recently delivered 2010 models, which included the issues listed below. The group also points out those areas that require special scrutiny.

Loose bolts that hold fluid back causing leaks (example: on oil pan, tranny fluid). • Trunk locking mechanism (issues with opening w/o adding down pressure to top of trunk first and/or emergency release appears to be loose keeping the trunk from locking properly). • Trunk may not open with remote switch. • Loose plastic paneling around the 4-gauge cluster, launch control, cigarette power plug as well as loose left and right A-pillar trim, sill trim, and dash panel trim where doors and dash meet. • Uneven dash (driver's side is lower then passenger's side). • Loose spoiler (re-torque spoiler bolts). • Wiper transmission cable overheats creating a short circuit. • One headlight may be brighter than the other. • Mismatched paint or paint that is easily chipped. • Missing or peeling paint between trunk lid and spoiler (right rear section). • Loose rocker panel that peels off. • Faulty ambient door lighting. • Radiator leaks. • Hood release/latch won't unhook to open the hood. • Gap at base of OnStar antenna. • Incorrect speedometer readings; also keeps shutting off. • Transmission failure. • Clunking noise when changing gears. • Key sticks in the ignition. • Non-RS taillights installed on RS-equipped cars. • Faulty taillights. • Rocker panel misaligned with body and clipped incorrectly. • Look for misaligned body and door panels as well as the hood not centered. • Loose bumper. • Ambient lighting on driver's door should be as bright as the lighting on the passenger door. • Door gaps and poor alignment. • Door panel may be scratched from the seat belt. • Sometimes, only one door will unlock. • Side fenders may be misaligned (wheel cover well needs to be taken off and the fender bolt loosened). • Dirt/bubbles in rally stripes. • Shift knobs quickly wear out. • AC blows cold air intermittently. • Possible blockage in AC drainage and/or AC draining into the car instead of beneath it. • Check that USB drive and auxiliary port work. • Squeaky brakes. • Rims and tires may have been damaged in transport. • Check the locking mechanism of both doors. • Scraping sound when backing up. • Loose SS emblem on trunk. • Loose interior windshield trim. • GFX may be installed incorrectly and the front GFX lip may be loose. • Check that the front brake rotors are not worn. • Check that the hood latch handle retracts properly. • Look for scratches on the seats. • Check for oil cooler leaks. • Fuel gauge may give incorrect readings. • Driver's side roof light (the one with the toggle switch) may only work when it's toggled over to the passenger side. • Drive-shaft connection to the differential may crack when dropping the clutch. • Tachometer needle sticks. • Wiper motor wiring comes through bottom of the cowling-well in front of the driver. • Engine makes continuous clicking noise, beginning roughly 5 seconds after the engine starts. • Door sill plates may be wrinkled on the outside edges. • Trunk gasket at bottom of rear window may come off. • Loose weather stripping at back of the rear windows. • Driver's seat makes clicking noises when set all the way back.

SERVICE BULLETIN-REPORTED PROBLEMS: Engine moan/growl/groan/whine noise; drivetrain clunk noise or rear clicking sound; fuel system clicking or ticking; trunk lid binds; tires go flat; and rear bumper paint peeling.

CORVETTE ★★★

KEY FACTS

CANADIAN PRICE (VERY NEGOTIABLE):
Base Coupe: $67,050, *Convertible:*
$76,955, *Z06:* $95,620, *ZR1:* $128,515
U.S. PRICE: *Base Coupe:* $48,930,
Convertible: $53,580, *Z06:* $74,285,
ZR1: $106,880 **CANADIAN FREIGHT:**
$1,420 **U.S. FREIGHT:** $950
POWERTRAIN (REAR-DRIVE)
Engines: 6.2L V8 (430 hp) • 7.0L V8
(505 hp) • 6.2L V8 Supercharged
(638 hp); Transmissions: 6-speed man.
• 6-speed auto.

DIMENSIONS/CAPACITY
Passengers: 2; Wheelbase: 106 in.;
H: 49/L: 175/W: 73 in.; Headroom: 4 in.;
Legroom: 41 in.; Cargo volume: 11 cu. ft.;
Fuel tank: 68.1L/premium; Tow limit: Not
recommended; Load capacity: 390 lb.;
Turning circle: 42 ft.; Ground clearance:
4.5 in.; Weight: 3,280 lb.

RATING: Average; a brawny, bulky sport coupe that's slowly evolving into a more-refined machine. But quality control continues to be subpar, and safety-related transmission and body deficiencies are common. The Corvette does deliver high-performance thrills—along with suspension kickback, numb steering, and seats that need extra bolstering. Overall, get the quieter and less temperamental base Corvette; it delivers the same cachet for a lot less money. **Strong points:** Powerful and smooth powertrain that responds quickly to the throttle; the 6-speed gearbox performs well in all gear ranges and makes shifting smooth, with short throws and easy entry into all gears. Easy handling; enhanced side-slip angle control helps to prevent skidding and provides better traction control. No oversteer, wheel spinning, breakaway rear ends, or nasty surprises, thanks partly to standard electronic stability control. Better-than-average braking; the ABS-vented disc brakes are easy to modulate, and they're fade-free. The car has a relatively roomy interior, user-friendly instruments and controls, and lots of convenience features. There's a key-controlled lockout feature that discourages joy riding by cutting engine power in half. All Corvettes are also equipped with an impressively effective PassKey theft-deterrent system that uses a resistor pellet in the ignition to disable the starter and fuel system when the key code doesn't match the ignition lock. All models come with standard side airbags and revised interiors. Convertibles get a trunk spoiler, and cars equipped with manual transmissions get a Performance Traction Management (PTM) system that modulates the engine's torque output for fast starts. This feature also manages engine power when the driver floors the accelerator when coming out of a corner. **Weak points:** Vague steering; limited rear visibility; inadequate storage space; poor-quality powertrain; mediocre fit and finish; cabin amenities and materials that are not up to the competition's standards; and no crashworthiness or rollover data available from NHTSA or IIHS. The Corvette's sophisticated electronic and powertrain components have low tolerance for real-world conditions. The car is so low that its front air dam scrapes over the smallest rise in the road. Expect lots of visits to the dealer's repair bays. **New for 2011:** Nothing to write home about.

OVERVIEW: Standard models come with a 430 hp 6.0L V8 mated to a 6-speed manual or optional automatic transmission; keyless access with push-button start; large tires and wheels (18-inch front, 19-inch rear); HID xenon lighting; power hatch pull-down; heated seats; and an AM/FM/CD/MP3 player with seven speakers and in-dash six-CD changer.

Z06

Although not quite as fast as the Dodge Viper, this is the fastest model found in the Corvette lineup (0–100 km/h in 3.6–4.2 seconds). It's also the lightest Z06 yet, thanks to the magic of Detroit re-engineering. Instead of just adding iron and components to carry extra weight, GM has reinforced the rear axle and 6-speed clutch; installed coolers everywhere; adopted a dry-sump oil system to keep the engine well oiled when cornering; and added wider wheels and larger, heat-dissipating brakes. These improvements added about 50 kg of weight, which was trimmed by using cast-magnesium in the chassis structure and installing lighter carbon-fibre floorboards and front fenders. Net result: a monster 'Vette that is rated for 300+ km/h and weighs less than the base model.

To be honest, the Z06 chassis isn't very communicative to the driver, so the car doesn't inspire as much driving confidence as does the European competition, although it does feature standard stability control for when you get too frisky.

COST ANALYSIS: Go for a base model minus the Performance Traction Management (PTM) system and forego jackrabbit starts and high-speed cornering. Keep in mind that premium fuel and astronomical insurance rates will further drive up your operating costs. A word about the ZR1: It's like investing in Dell—don't! A 2010 model that sold new for $127,545 is now worth $102,000. **Best alternatives:** Other sporty models worth considering are the Ford GT or Shelby GT500 Mustang and the Porsche 911 or Boxster. The Nissan 370Z looks good on paper, but its quality problems carried over year after year make it a risky buy, much like Nissan's attractively styled Quest. **Options:** Remember, performance options rarely increase performance to the degree promised by the seller; the more performance options you buy, the less comfort you'll have, the more things can go wrong, and the more simple repairs can increase in complexity. Run-flat tires are not a good investment, either. They are hard to find and expensive. Forget about the head-up instrument display that projects speed and other data onto the windshield; it's annoyingly distracting and you'll end up turning it off. **Rebates:** The Corvette is so popular that GM normally doesn't have to offer rebates to boost sales, but there will be some discounting starting late in 2010 as fuel costs rise and sales return to the basement. **Depreciation:** Much faster than you would imagine and nowhere near the resale prices promised by salespeople. For example, an entry-level 2004 Corvette that sold for almost $70,000 new is now worth about $22,000. **Insurance cost:** Astronomical. **Parts supply/cost:** Parts are pricey and often back-ordered. **Annual maintenance cost:** Higher than average. **Warranty:** 60-day money-back guarantee as long as you don't drive more than 4,000 km. Bumper-to-bumper 3 years/60,000 km; powertrain 5 years/160,000 km; rust perforation 6 years/160,000 km. **Supplementary warranty:** A smart idea to protect you from frequent drivetrain failures. **Highway/city fuel economy:** *6.2L man.:* 7.7/12.9 L/100 km, 37/22 mpg. *Auto.:* 8.1/14.3 L/100 km, 35/20 mpg. *7.0L man.:* 8.2/14.2 L/100 km, 34/20 mpg. *Auto.:* 8.2/14.2 L/100 km, 34/20 mpg. *ZR1 man.:* 10.2/15.5 L/100 km, 28/18 mpg.

OWNER-REPORTED PROBLEMS: Harsh, delayed transmission shifts; active handling system and traction control constantly malfunction; car can only be driven in "reduced power mode":

> The service department has investigated the problem with the active handling system and the traction control system at least three times already. I have driven the car less than 1,350 miles [2,170 km]. From the time I purchased the vehicle it has been out of service for more than 18 days and has been in the shop for service 13 days.

Harsh squeaks and rattles caused by the car's structural deficiencies. The car was built as a convertible and, therefore, has too much body flex. Servicing the different sophisticated fuel injection systems isn't easy, even (especially) for GM mechanics. The headliner sags and blocks the rear-view mirror view; right rear axle suddenly snaps in half; chronic stalling and excessive steering vibration; and fuel tank will only take half a tankful of gasoline:

> My Corvette will only take a half-tank of gas before auto-shutoff is activated. To fill tank I have to turn nozzle upside down. This method causes fuel overflow and spillage on the ground.

SERVICE BULLETIN-REPORTED PROBLEMS: Persistent oil leaks over a period of seven years that affect most of GM's model lineup:

ENGINE—OIL LEAKS FROM REAR COVER

BULLETIN NO.: 05-06-01-034J   DATE: NOVEMBER 12, 2009

5.3L, 5.7L, 6.0L, 6.2L, 7.0L—ENGINE OIL LEAK AT REAR COVER ASSEMBLY AREA (ENGINE BLOCK POROSITY RTV REPAIR PROCEDURE)

2004–07 Buick Rainier; 2008–09 Buick LaCrosse Super; Allure Super (Canada Only); 2005–10 Cadillac CTS-V; 2007–10 Cadillac Escalade, Escalade ESV, Escalade EXT; 2003–09 Chevrolet TrailBlazer; 2003–10 Chevrolet Corvette; 2004–06 Chevrolet SSR; 2005–10 Chevrolet Silverado, Silverado SS; 2006–07 Chevrolet Monte Carlo SS; 2006–09 Chevrolet; TrailBlazer SS, Impala SS; 2007–10 Chevrolet Avalanche, Suburban, Tahoe; 2009–10 Chevrolet Colorado Pickup; 2010 Chevrolet Camaro; 2003–09 GMC Envoy; 2003–10 GMC Sierra; 2004–05 GMC Envoy XUV; 2010 GMC Yukon XL, Yukon Denali, Yukon XL Denali; 2009–10 GMC Canyon ; 2004–06 Pontiac GTO; 2005–08 Pontiac Grand Prix GXP; 2008–09 Pontiac G8 GT; 2009 Pontiac G8 GXP; 2005–09 Saab 9-7X 5.3i; 2008–09 Saab 9-7X Aero; 2003–10 Hummer H2; and the 2006–10 Hummer H3. All with 5.3L, 5.7L, 6.0L, 6.2L, 7.0L engines (all aluminum block)

CONDITION: Customers may comment on an engine oil leak.

CAUSE: It may be determined that the leak is coming from the rear cover gasket. This condition may be caused by engine block porosity on the sealing surface.

CTS   ★ ★ ★

RATING: Average. As Cadillac reinvents itself in a futile attempt to lure younger buyers, its cars are becoming more complex and less distinctive. **Strong points:** Roomier cabin than other cars in this class (the Sport Wagon's generous cargo space is especially noteworthy); a tasteful, well-appointed interior loaded with high-tech gadgetry; competent and secure handling; and available all-wheel drive. NHTSA has given five stars for side crashworthiness and four stars for front crash protection and rollover resistance. IIHS awarded its top rating of "Good" for frontal offset crashworthiness, side impact protection, and head-restraint effectiveness. **Weak points:** Not as agile as its rivals; sport suspensions may be hard on the kidneys; poor rear visibility; and an awkward driving position caused by uneven pedal depth and limited knee room due to the intrusion of the centre stack. Owners also complain of fit and finish deficiencies and frequent electronic malfunctions. Rear-seat access requires some acrobatics due to the low rear roof line, and the rear seatback could use additional bolstering. Also, the trunk's narrow opening adds to the difficulty of loading bulky items. **New for 2011:** A CTS coupe will be out in July.

KEY FACTS

CANADIAN PRICE (VERY NEGOTIABLE):
Base: $40,650, *3.6:* $48,780, *CTS-V:* $72,045 **U.S. PRICE:** *Base:* $36,465, *3.6:* $41,565, *CTS-V:* $67,720 **CANADIAN FREIGHT:** $1,420 **U.S. FREIGHT:** $825
POWERTRAIN (REAR-DRIVE/AWD)
Engines: 3.0L V6 (270 hp) • 3.6L V6 (304 hp) • 6.2L V8 (556 hp); Transmissions: 6-speed man. • 6-speed auto.
DIMENSIONS/CAPACITY (BASE CTS)
Passengers: 2/3; Wheelbase: 113 in.; H: 58/L: 192/W: 73 in.; Headroom F/R: 3.0/1.5 in.; Legroom F/R: 44.0/28.5 in.; Cargo volume: 14 cu. ft.; Fuel tank: 70L/premium; Tow limit: 1,000 lb.; Load capacity: 890 lb.; Turning circle: 38 ft.; Ground clearance: 5.0 in.; Weight: 3,940 lb.

OVERVIEW: *CTS Sedan and Coupe:* A 270 hp 3.0L V6 is the standard engine; the 304 hp 3.6L will be optional. *CTS Sport Wagon:* Slightly shorter than the CTS sedan, the CTS Sport Wagon provides 7.6 metres (25 feet) of cargo space accessible via a power-assisted liftgate. The Sport Wagon also carries a base 3.0L and optional 3.6L V6 and employs either a rear-drive or all-wheel-drive system, plus a suspension that can be adjusted from cushy to sporty (firm). *CTS-V Sedan and*

Coupe: This 556 hp "muscle" Cadillac returns with no significant changes. The Coupe version uses a smaller 3.6L V6. Standard safety features include anti-lock disc brakes, traction control, stability control, front-seat side airbags, full-length side curtain airbags, and GM's OnStar emergency communications system.

COST ANALYSIS: Go now for the upgraded, though cheaper, 2010 version, or wait until late winter to get a 2011 when applicable rebates will be sweetened. Think carefully about whether you want all-wheel drive: that option will cost you about $4,500 more with the base 3.0L engine or $2,600 when coupled to the 3.6L engine. **Best alternative:** Acura TL SH-AWD, BMW 3 Series, Hyundai Genesis, Infiniti G37, and Lincoln MKS and Town Car. **Options:** Neither the adaptive cruise control nor the advanced DVD navigation system is worth the extra money. **Rebates:** $4,000–$6,000 in sales incentives. **Depreciation:** Unbelievably fast. A 2004 base CTS that sold new for $39,000 is now worth a little over $8,500; a 2004 CTS-V that went for $70,000 new now sells for no more than $12,500. **Insurance cost:** Higher than average. **Parts supply/cost:** Parts are often back-ordered and electronic components are quite pricey. **Annual maintenance cost:** Higher than average. **Warranty:** 60-day money-back guarantee as long as you don't drive more than 4,000 km. Bumper-to-bumper 4 years/80,000 km; powertrain 5 years/160,000 km; rust perforation 6 years/160,000 km. **Supplementary warranty:** A good thing to have. **Highway/city fuel economy:** *3.0L:* 7.2/11.23 L/100 km, 39/25 mpg. *3.6L:* 6.9/11.4 L/100 km, 41/25 mpg. *3.6L AWD:* 7.9/13 L/100 km, 36/22 mpg. *CTS-V man.:* 10.5/14.9 L/100 km, 27/19 mpg. *CTS-V auto.:* 11/17.5 L/100 km, 28/16 mpg.

OWNER-REPORTED PROBLEMS: Sudden acceleration caused driver death because there was no brake override feature:

> The contact rented a 2010 Cadillac CTS. The contact stated that while driving 35 mph [56 km/h] the vehicle accelerated rapidly and crashed into a guard rail without the air bags deploying. The contact called the police because the driver was not responding inside of the vehicle. The EMT removed the driver from the vehicle and he was taken to the hospital. The driver died at the hospital due to blunt force trauma. The manufacturer recovered information from the black box and it revealed that the driver was pressing the brake pedal and accelerator pedal together. The contact feels the vehicle accelerated without the driver pressing on the accelerator pedal.

Engine and transmission failures, electrical system malfunctions, and fit and finish glitches. The CTS doesn't have a spare tire, jack, or lug wrench; the sunroof can implode; and there's excessive vibration and powertrain drone/boom when the car is underway at 64–121 km/h.

SERVICE BULLETIN-REPORTED PROBLEMS: Tires leak air or suddenly go flat; inoperative power liftgate; noisy fuel system on cold start; faulty propshaft bolts; and powertrain noise or vibration when cruising:

2008–10 Cadillac CTS with 6L50 Automatic Transmission

Phasing drone, boom, moan or vibration in seat, floor pan or door panel at 87–97 kph (54–60 mph) or at 64 kph (40 mph) in 6th gear or 1000–1300 RPM with torque converter clutch (TCC) engaged. Reprogram TCM and install washers.

ENCLAVE, TRAVERSE, ACADIA ★★★★

The Buick Enclave.

RATING: Above Average. These are practically identical seven- and eight-passenger crossover SUVs with the Traverse being the most recent addition. **Strong points:** All three vehicles have five-star front and side NHTSA crashworthiness scores, while rollover resistance earned them each four stars. Sales have been hard hit by high fuel costs and tighter credit, making 20 percent discounts not unusual with these models. Although they are fuel-thirsty SUVs, maintenance costs and mechanical/body failures aren't excessive. Saturn's discontinued Outlook has the same characteristics as the trio above and sells used at a 50-percent discount. **Weak points:** Side airbags sometimes fail to deploy; head restraints force your chin into your chest; transmission oil leaks and malfunctions; fuel pump flow module fails,

KEY FACTS

CANADIAN PRICE (VERY NEGOTIABLE):
Enclave: $41,595–$51,995; *Traverse:* $29,224–$39,985; *Acadia:* $37,800–$51,335 **U.S. PRICE:** *Enclave:* $35,515–$43,995; *Traverse:* $35,620–$53,560; *Acadia:* $31,740–$42,175 **CANADIAN FREIGHT:** $1,400 **U.S. FREIGHT:** $975
POWERTRAIN (FRONT-DRIVE/AWD)
Engine: 3.6L V6 (288 hp); Transmission: 6-speed auto.
DIMENSIONS/CAPACITY (ENCLAVE)
Passengers: 7/8; Wheelbase: 119 in.; H: 72.5/L: 201.5/W: 79 in., Cargo volume: 115.3 in. (behind 1st row); 67.5 in (behind 2nd row); 23.2 in (behind 3rd row); Fuel tank: 83L/regular; Tow limit: 4,500 lb.; Turning circle: 40.4 ft.; Ground clearance: 8.4 in.; Weight: 4,780–4,985 lb.

making the engine run rough or stall; inaccurate fuel gauges; a noisy suspension; and headlight failures. **New for 2011:** Chrome wheels and new colours.

OVERVIEW: These large SUVs are an endangered species and GM is likely to pull the plug at any time. Still, they are tough and versatile; prices are easily bargained down.

COST ANALYSIS: These are bargain buys mainly because prices have plummeted due to high fuel prices. Buy a 2010 for the best price/quality advantage. **Best alternatives:** The Ford Flex, Mazda CX-9, Hyundai Veracruz, and Honda Pilot. If you don't mind downsizing a notch, consider the Ford Edge, Hyundai Santa Fe, or Nissan XTerra. **Options:** Stay away from Firestone and Bridgestone; *tirerack. com* is your best contact for dependable and safe tires. **Depreciation:** Faster than average. **Insurance cost:** Much higher than average. **Parts supply/cost:** Parts aren't hard to find and are competitively priced. **Annual maintenance cost:** Average. **Warranty:** Bumper-to-bumper 4 years/80,000 km; powertrain 5 years/160,000 km; rust perforation 6 years/160,000 km. **Supplementary warranty:** Not needed. **Highway/city fuel economy:** *2WD:* 8.4/12.7 L/100 km, 34/22 mpg. *AWD:* 9.0/13.4 L/100 km, 31/21 mpg.

OWNER-REPORTED PROBLEMS: Airbag failed to deploy; sudden unintended acceleration; car continued accelerating after accelerator was released and brakes were inoperative; driver's shoe can become stuck to the carpeting, thereby engaging the accelerator; vehicle will not "hold" when stopped on an incline:

> Vehicle will continue to roll back when on an incline (whether slight or drastic of an incline) if the brakes are not applied. This has caused a threat to my life and others several times. When I am stopped on an incline, I have to "punch the gas" in order to avoid hitting the car behind me. This type of applied advancement has caused the wheels to turn out or "burn rubber."

It is impossible to read the speed due to faint backlighting and small numbers. Poorly designed middle and rear seats:

> The middle and rear seats in the vehicle have head restraints that tilt forward and are not adjustable or removable and make it extremely difficult (impossible) to install carseats or high-back boosters correctly and safely. The seat belts are also very difficult to reach/buckle for a passenger in a booster seat. They are very low in the seat.

SERVICE BULLETIN-REPORTED PROBLEMS: Tires leak air or suddenly go flat; delayed shifting:

TRANSMISSION HESITATION, DELAYED SHIFTING, SHIFTING AT WRONG TIME (REPROGRAM TCM)

2010 Buick Enclave; 2010 Chevrolet Equinox, Traverse; 2010 GMC Acadia, Terrain; 2010 Saturn Outlook; 2010 Buick LaCrosse; 2010 Chevrolet Malibu; 2010 Pontiac G6; 2010 Saturn Aura.

CONDITION: Some customers may comment on transmission downshift hesitation, delayed shifting and shifting at the wrong time.

CORRECTION: A revised transmission calibration has been developed to address these issues.

ESCALADE, TAHOE, YUKON ★★★

The Cadillac Escalade.

RATING: Average, but hurry: Dealers are dumping these SUVs as GM winds down their production in favour of smaller, more-car-like crossover SUVs. All three vehicles are practically identical, though the Escalade comes with a 6.2L V8 and a plusher interior and is more gadget-laden. **Strengths:** Strong acceleration; many powertrain configurations; standard stability control; a quiet interior and comfortable ride; good towing capability; parts aren't hard to find and are reasonably priced; and repairs can be done by independent garages. A hybrid version is available. NHTSA gave these SUVs five stars for frontal passenger protection and three stars for rollover resistance. **Weaknesses:** Extremely poor fuel economy; rapid depreciation; small third-row seat sits too low and doesn't fold into the floor; ponderous handling; long braking distances; and below average reliability. Specific problem areas include loss of brakes; faulty powertrain, suspension, and climate controls; and various body glitches. **New for 2011:** Nothing much.

KEY FACTS

CANADIAN PRICE (VERY NEGOTIABLE):
Escalade AWD: $84,645, *Escalade Hybrid:* $94,790, *Tahoe:* $49,290–$69,100; *Yukon:* $49,290–$72,535; *Hybrid:* $68,625–$80,300 **U.S. PRICE:** *Escalade AWD:* $65,045, *Escalade Hybrid:* $84,125; *Tahoe:* $37,280–$53,615; *Yukon:* $38,020–$46,665 **CANADIAN FREIGHT:** $1,400 **U.S. FREIGHT:** $975 **POWERTRAIN (FRONT-DRIVE/AWD)** Engines: 5.3L V8 (320 hp) • 6.2L V8 (403 hp) • 6.0L V8 (332 hp); Transmissions: 6-speed auto. • CVT **DIMENSIONS/CAPACITY** Passengers: *Escalade:* 3/3/2; *Tahoe:* 3/33; Wheelbase: *Escalade:* 116 in.; *Hybrid:* 202.5 in.; H: 74.3/L: 202.5/W: 79 in., Cargo volume: 16.9 cu. ft. (behind 3rd row); Fuel tank: 98L/regular; Tow limit: *Escalade:* 8,100 lb; *Hybrid:* 5,600 lb.; Payload: *Escalade:* 1,609 lb.; *Hybrid:* 1,484; Turning circle: 40.4 ft.; Ground clearance: 9.0 in.; Weight: *Escalade:* 5,691–5,943 lb.; *Hybrid:* 6,116 lb,

OVERVIEW: These three trucks are only masquerading as car-like SUVs and will not likely last another two years if fuel prices continue their upward ride.

COST ANALYSIS: Wait until the new year when prices will fall and you will get these large SUVs for almost a third off the original price. **Best alternatives:** The Chevrolet Traverse, Buick Enclave, GMC Acadia, Hyundai Veracruz, Honda Pilot, Toyota Highlander (only with the brake override feature), Ford Flex, and Mazda CX-9. **Options:** Don't accept factory Bridgestone or Firestone tires. Independent suppliers will sell you better tires for less money. Also, stay away from the $2,065 glitch-prone power-sliding sunroof. **Depreciation:** Incredibly fast. Good for used buyers, a kick-in-the-pants for owners selling after 2–5 years. Let's look at how much we lose with the top-of-the-line model of each brand: A 2007 Escalade ESV that sold new for $79,000 is now worth $35,000; the same model-year $61,075 Tahoe LTZ AWD sells for $23,000; and a 2007 GMC Yukon XL that sold new for $66,170 won't fetch more than $26,500. **Insurance cost:** Much higher than average. **Parts supply/cost:** Parts are easy to find and competitively priced. **Annual maintenance cost:** Average. **Warranty:** Bumper-to-bumper 4 years/80,000 km; powertrain 5 years/160,000 km; rust perforation 6 years/160,000 km. **Supplementary warranty:** Not needed. **Highway/city fuel economy:** *Escalade AWD:* 10.8/17.7 L/100 km, 26/16 mpg. Other models should produce similar figures. Hybrid figures are not available.

OWNER-REPORTED PROBLEMS: Chrome-plated door handles peel and cut fingers; as rear window was closing, passenger's finger was trapped in the weather stripping and was amputated. Owners also report serious electrical shorts and drive system malfunctions. Worst of all, the overall fit and finish of these top-of-the-line vehicles is deplorable.

SERVICE BULLETIN-REPORTED PROBLEMS: Oil leaks from the rear engine cover; tires leak air or suddenly go flat; airbag warning light comes on for no reason; tapping/clicking/ticking noise at the windshield area; and a remedy for hard third-row seat removal and installation:

SILVERADO 1500, 2500, SIERRA, HD ★★★

The GMC Sierra.

RATING: Average. Although *Lemon-Aid* rates Ford 1500 and Super Duty models as Above Average, GM's HD series is catching up quickly. Unfortunately, the Dodge Ram (with its I-6 Cummins) comes in a distant third—even with unbelievably steep discounts. True, GM's 1500 pickups limp along with a design dating to model-year 2007. All the more reason why GM should eliminate the duplication of its divisions and merge GMC with Chevrolet. Money saved should go into a major redesign of the 1500 series to match the improvements now seen with GM's Heavy Duty (HD) series. *Quo vadis,* Chrysler? Without R&D cash to build a competitive truck, Chrysler will never regain the truck market share it has lost to Ford, GM, and the Asian automakers. **Strong points:** *1500:* Good choice of engines and transmissions; standard electronic stability control; comfortable seating; lots of storage capability; good fuel economy. Since its 2008 redesign,

CANADIAN PRICE (VERY NEGOTIABLE): *1500 Regular Cab 4×2:* $26,260, *1500 Regular Cab 4×4:* $29,860, *1500 Extended Cab 4×2:* $29,485, *1500 Extended Cab 4×4:* $34,010, *1500 Crew Cab 4×2:* $31,845, *1500 Crew Cab 4×4:* $35,605, *1500 4×2 Hybrid:* $47,505, *1500 4×4 Hybrid:* $51,565, *2500 Regular Cab 4×2:* $32,122, *2500 Regular Cab 4×4:* $35,605, *2500 Extended Cab 4×2:* $35;060, *2500 Extended Cab 4×4:* $38,249, *2500 Crew Cab 4×2:* $36,756, *2500 Crew Cab 4×4:* $40,145, *3500 Extended Cab 4×2:* $36,712, *3500 Extended Cab 4×4:* $39,902, *3500 Crew Cab 4×2:* $38,409, *3500 Crew Cab 4×4:* $41,598 **U.S. PRICE:** *1500 WT 4×2:* $19,345, *1500 WT 4×4:* $24,090, *1500 LS 4×2:* $30,360, *1500 LS 4×4:* $33,510, *1500 LT 4×2:* $26,810, *1500 LT 4×4:* $33,510, *1500 XFE:* $33,225, *1500 4×2 LTZ:* $38,625, *1500 4×4 LTZ:* $41,775, *1500 4×2 Hybrid:* $36,335, *2500HD 4×2:* $25,460, *3500HD 4×2:* $28,970 **CANADIAN FREIGHT:** $1,400 **U.S. FREIGHT:** $950

POWERTRAIN (FRONT-DRIVE)

Engines: 4.3L V6 (195 hp) • 4.8L V8 (302 hp) • 5.3L V8 (315 hp), *Hybrid:* 6.0L V8 (332 hp) • 6.2L V8 (403 hp) • 6.6L V8 TD (397 hp); Transmissions: 4-speed auto. • 6-speed auto., *Hybrid:* CVT

DIMENSIONS/CAPACITY

Passengers: *1500:* 2/1, *2500:* 3/3; Wheelbase: *1500:* 144 in., *2500:* 133.6–167 in.; *1500:* H: 74/L: 230/W: 80 in., *2500:* H: 77/L: 240/W: 80 in.; Headroom F/R: *1500:* 6.5/6.0 in., *2500:* 6.0/5.0 in.; Legroom F/R: 41.5/29 in., *2500:* 40.5/27 in.; Fuel tank: 129L/regular; Tow limit: *Hybrid:* 6,100 lb., *1500:* 7,500 lb., *2500:* 13,600 lb., *HD Turbo Diesel:* 15,600 lb; Load capacity: *1500:* 1,570 lb., *2500:* 2,260 lb.; Turning circle: *1500:* 50 ft., *2500:* 55 ft.; Ground clearance: 9.5 in.; Weight: *1500:* 5,435 lb., *2500:* 6,920 lb.

the Silverado handles much better; offers a steadier, more-controllable ride (no more "Shakerado"); and has a more-refined, comfortable cabin. NHTSA gave the Silverado 1500 and Hybrid five stars for frontal crash protection and four stars for rollover resistance; the truck wasn't tested for side crash protection. IIHS has given the Silverado 1500 a "Good" rating for frontal offset protection and an "Acceptable" score for head-restraint effectiveness. 2500: These heavy-duty work trucks are built primarily to be load-carrying vehicles capable of working off-road, although this year's independent front end should improve handling and smooth out the ride. The standard engine is a powerful 360 hp 6.0L V8 backed up by a 397 hp 6.6L turbodiesel. The HD models' improvements this year help GM to catch up to Ford in handling and ride comfort. For example, the ability to control 10,000-pound-plus loads when descending with the new Exhaust Brake system gives GM a feature that Ford Super Duty trucks have used for some time. Hopefully, this new system will be glitch-free during its first year on the market. The same can be said for the new GM Duramax engine. GM's 2010 3500 HDs were outclassed when compared with Ford's 2010 Super Duty powerplant hooked to its new 6-speed transmission. Finally, while the GM Allison transmission has been around since the late-'40s, it hasn't performed as well as Ford's all-new TorqShift 6-speed found in the Super Duty models. Again, maybe this year's revised Allison tranny will enhance durability, make for smoother shifting, and remove the annoying downshift clunks GM truck owners have lived with for decades. **Weak points:** *1500:* Powertrain smoothness and reliability doesn't measure up to what the Dodge Ram, Ford-150 Series, Honda Ridgeline, and Nissan Titan can provide. The steering is over-assisted; there's excess body lean when cornering; climate controls aren't very user-friendly; and the servicing network is rather limited. GM Duramax-equipped pickups need diesel exhaust fluid (urea) refills every 8,000 kilometres (5,000 miles). This is more frequent than the oil change one usually does every 12,000 kilometres (7,500 miles). IIHS says the 1500's side crashworthiness merits a "Poor" rating. Seat pelvic/thorax and head curtain side air bags are available but aren't standard on the 2500 HD; Ford Super Duty trucks have them as a standard safety feature. It is not likely that GM's noise control will match Ford's Super duty. **New for 2011:** Chevrolet's 2011 Silverado and the practically identical GMC Sierra 1500 series will return relatively unchanged, but the 2500 and HD have gotten their share of upgrades and enhancements. Although the HD models are only slightly restyled, they have oodles of mechanical improvements. A new 6.6L Duramax turbo diesel delivers 397 horsepower and is touted as being more fuel efficient than before; towing capability is cranked up to 20,000 lb.; on the 3500s, there's a higher payload capacity up to 6,000 lb.; the 2500 payload limit is 3,100 lb.; a larger fuel tank allows 1,090 km (680 miles) between fill-ups with the 6.6L diesel; a new exhaust brake feature provides greater control on grades and reduces brake pad wear; and the standard four-wheel disc system has been revamped to deliver a smoother and quicker response. Snow plow capability is available for all 4×4 cab configurations and the frame has five-times more torsional stiffness and better vibration control. 2011s will also come with a stronger independent front suspension; improved upper and lower control arms; a revised front suspension to eliminate squeaks and clunks and improve the ride; a revised rear suspension to support greater loads while minimizing axle "hop"; and an improved power steering gear. And, to further enhance a quiet ride, engine, steering pump, and chassis noise has been reduced. For 2011, standard safety features include StabiliTrak electronic stability control system on all single-rear-wheel models; larger, four-wheel disc brakes with standard four-wheel ABS; a new high-strength steel tubular frame cross member that enhances safety and improves crashworthiness; trailer sway control on all single-rear-wheel models; and hill start assist also standard on single-rear-wheel models.

OVERVIEW: All V8s are flex-fuel capable, and the 4.8L and 5.3L engines have variable valve timing. Trucks with the 5.3L engine were also given a 6-speed automatic transmission and a revised rear axle ratio. All 1500 models have standard electronic stability control, seat-mounted side airbags, and side curtain airbags. All stereos also get a USB port. The 2010 Chevrolet Silverado 1500 didn't get a new turbodiesel V8 engine because GM is putting most of its money on changes to the HD lineup. Basically, this large pickup is a twin of the GMC Sierra and is offered in regular-, extended-, and crew-cab body styles. Regular cabs seat up to three passengers; extendeds and crews can carry six. There are three bed lengths: 5.8, 6.6, and 8.0 feet. Silverados offer two interiors: "pure pickup" and "luxury inspired." All V8s can run on ethanol-blended fuel. The 5.3 V8 saves fuel through Active Fuel Management cylinder deactivation. V6 and 4.8L V8 Silverados are coupled to a 4-speed automatic transmission. A 6-speed automatic is used with the 5.3L and 6.2L V8s. Rear-drive is standard and two four-wheel-drive systems are optional: a part-time setup that shouldn't be left engaged on dry pavement, and

GM's Autotrac, which can go anywhere. Both have a low-range gear for off-roading.

The Silverado 1500 Hybrid has a 6.0L V8 that pairs with an electric motor, producing 332 hp. It can run on one or both of its power sources depending on driving demands, and doesn't need to be plugged-in. The hybrid has a continuously variable automatic transmission (CVT) and a maximum towing capacity of 6,100 lb.

COST ANALYSIS: Buy the almost identical, but cheaper, 2010 base models. Get a 2011 HD if you need the additional power. **Best alternatives:** The Ford F-Series and Honda Ridgeline. **Options:** Consider the $600 Exterior Plus package, which includes a remote starter, fog lights, a garage door opener, and a locking tailgate with the EZ Lift feature. Also, consider getting adjustable gas and brake pedals if you need to put extra space between you and the steering-wheel-mounted airbag. **Rebates:** $4,000 in sales incentives on the 2010 HD models; about half as much on the 1500 series. As summer approaches, the rebates may almost double. **Depreciation:** Faster than average. **Insurance cost:** Much higher than average. **Parts supply/cost:** Parts aren't hard to find and are competitively priced by independent suppliers. **Annual maintenance cost:** Higher than average. **Warranty:** 60-day money-back guarantee as long as you don't drive more than 4,000 km. Bumper-to-bumper 4 years/80,000 km; powertrain 5 years/160,000 km; rust perforation 6 years/160,000 km. **Supplementary warranty:** Recommended. **Highway/city fuel economy:** *4.3L 2WD:* 10.0/14.1 L/100 km, 28/20 mpg. *4.3L 4WD:* 11.3/14.9 L/100 km, 24/19 mpg. *4.8L 2WD:* 10.6/14.7 L/100 km, 27/19 mpg. *4.8L 4WD:* 11.1/15.4 L/100 km, 25/18 mpg. *5.3L 2WD:* 10.1/14.5 L/100 km, 28/19 mpg. *5.3L 4WD:* 10.3/14.7 L/100 km, 27/19 mpg. *6.2L AWD:* 10.8/17.7 L/100 km, 26/16 mpg. *Hybrid 2WD:* 9.2/9.8 L/100 km, 31/29 mpg. *Hybrid 4WD:* 9.8/10.5 L/100 km, 29/27 mpg.

OWNER-REPORTED PROBLEMS: Powertrain, fuel system, suspension, and fit and finish deficiencies. Safety-related complaints include sun visors that don't block the sun's rays sufficiently; engine surging when the brakes are applied; a smaller spare tire that may cause the 4×4 feature to malfunction; and original equipment Goodyear tires that have a propensity to hydroplane on wet roads.

SERVICE BULLETIN-REPORTED PROBLEMS: Tires leak air or suddenly go flat; excessive interior wind noise; underbody clunk or pop type noise while turning or driving on uneven road surfaces (install body mount insulators on all affected 2004–10 large SUVs and trucks); and faulty propshaft bolts.

ASIAN VEHICLES

Hyundai Wins, Honda Loses

The past year turned out to be a mixed bag for the Asian automakers doing business in the U.S. market. Hyundai, Kia, and Subaru were the big winners, with all three posting not just market share gains, but absolute sales gains in a year in which the entire new car market shrank by about 25%. On the other side of the ledger, Toyota posted its first loss ever, though it managed to hold off surging Volkswagen to retain its crown as the world's biggest automaker only to be forced to stop sales and production of most of its lineup in late January due to faulty accelerator pedals and floor mats. Rival Honda saw its Prius-fighting Insight hybrid flounder.

www.motortrend.com/future/future_vehicles

Minivans, Maxi-troubles

Minivans had their day, but that day is gone. Hockey moms loved them; they don't anymore. Chrysler and Dodge, the progenitors of the class, still sell a lot of minivans; so do Honda and Toyota. For other brands, I suggest: If you're in it, get out. If you're not in it, stay out.

JOHN TEAHEN, JR.
COLUMNIST, *AUTOMOTIVE NEWS*

Doing More with Less

The math doesn't add up in the auto industry. Usually you get less quality and dependability, especially if you invest less money into production or cut supplier payouts. Examples are everywhere: Toyota since 1997, Honda since the 2008 redesigns, and Nissan's failure-plagued, revamped 2005 Quest minivan.

This year, following one of the worst world wide recessions in recent memory, the main difference between Asian vehicles (Japan and South Korea) and Detroit's is that the Asians are adding more vehicles in every marketing segment and downsizing those models that have outgrown their utility, while cash-strapped Chrysler, Ford, and GM are forced to carry over most vehicles with hardly any notable changes. They've also limited themselves to just a few new-vehicle launches, like the Jeep Grand Cherokee and Ford Explorer. Entirely new cars like the subcompact Mazda2 and Nissan Juke crossover will make their debut as Asian automakers strive to make vehicles safer on the road, cheaper to run, easier to handle, and more comfortable to drive. Ford has succeeded in doing "more with less" by shutting down its Mercury division and importing the European Fiesta, rather than having the Fiesta built in North America right away, to make the economies of scale work in Ford's favour. GM's rumoured intention to fold GMC into its Chevrolet division is another example of how less duplication can produce more profits.

Family sedan, luxury car, SUV, and minivan buyers will notice how the bigger vehicles have been given more power, more room, and a host of high-tech accoutrements that enhance both safety and convenience.

Starting at the top, Infiniti has an all-new 2011 M sports model that is even larger, more luxurious, and better-performing than the previous version. It carries a standard 330 hp 3.7L V6 (M37), a 420 hp 5.6L V8 (M56), or a 303 hp 3.5L V6 paired with a lithium-ion battery pack (M35 Hybrid). A second-generation Infiniti QX SUV based on the Patrol will be imported from Japan in the late fall of 2010.

Equus: A genus of mammals, including the horse, ass, etc. What's this Hyundai infatuation with horses? First, the ill-begotten, hoof-and-mouth diseased '80s-era Pony, and now a first-class equine entrant.

Even humble Hyundai is in the luxury car big leagues for 2011 with its the new Equus flagship sedan; it's jam-packed with safety and convenience gadgets that include a lane departure warning system that warns the driver through the seatbelt, in addition to a chime and warning light, when the car is veering out of its lane. There's also a sophisticated cruise control system, stability control, vehicle stability management and (count them) nine airbags for occupant collision protection. This rear-drive, full-sized luxury sedan is powered by a 4.6L V8 engine rated at 385 horsepower on premium fuel and 378 horsepower on regular unleaded. Indeed, Hyundai has come a long way since owning a little lemon grove populated by the Pony, Stellar, and Excel from the mid-'70s through the early-'90s.

The family sedan is the bread and butter car for automakers in North America. It is usually priced in the low-20s but can cost more than $30,000. Take a look at the most popular cars in this category and you will quickly see why GM and Chrysler's struggles are far from over. Almost every one of the top-10 sedans is an Asian model. There's the top-rate Nissan Altima, followed closely by the Hyundai Sonata, with the Volkswagen Jetta TDI, Toyota Camry, Subaru Legacy, Suzuki Kizashi, Honda Accord, Kia Optima, Volkswagen Jetta, and Ford Fusion finishing off the list.

To compete against these top-selling family sedans, Chrysler puts up its bottom-rung, poor-quality Avenger, Charger, and Sebring, while GM throws two relics and one unproven import into battle: the Impala, the Malibu, and its Daewoo-inspired Cobalt replacement, the Chevrolet Cruze. Going up against the Honda Civic, Toyota Corolla, and the new Mazda 3, the Cruze's boring exterior, cramped rear seating, flat seats, and unproven long-term reliability means the race is over before the starter's pistol has sounded. In effect, North American automakers are giving up this huge market to the Asians and Europeans in much the same way that the minivan market was lost to Honda, Mazda, and Toyota. At least Ford has the

Fusion capturing family sedan market share. But Chrysler and GM? They're doomed.

And the Asian competition keeps raising the bar in the largest segment of the automotive market. For example, Hyundai is adding a turbocharger to its re-engineered and restyled 2011 Sonata mid-sized sedan. The automaker claims that its turbocharged 2.0L engine will deliver 274 horsepower while returning up to 34 mpg—all on regular fuel. On the other hand, the Sonata's restyled exterior may take some getting used to. Says *Family Car Guide* columnist James Hamel (*www.familycarguide.com*):

> The exterior is dominated by deep slashes in the bodywork and a swooping rear roof-line that brings to mind a 1990's Chevy Caprice. While there are attractive aspects to specific pieces of the exterior design (nice tail-lights) the whole is such a conflicting mish-mash that it makes the 2011 Sonata look like a floundering fish gasping for air. White models suffer from this visual trait most especially.

Once the preferred runabout for many suburban families, minivan popularity has fallen off in recent years as buyers turn instead to more versatile three-row crossovers. Asian minivan manufacturers are fighting back, and minivans like the Honda Odyssey, Nissan Quest, and Toyota Sienna are returning with major restyling and engineering changes.

The 2011 Odyssey's changes have mostly to do with the restyled interior (pretty good) and a completely reworked exterior (pretty bad). Apparently, the same stylists who "uglified" this year's Sonata were also turned loose on the Odyssey. From the "lightning bolt" beltline under the side doors to the non-rectangular rear windshield, wraparound spoiler, Acura-like headlights, and doors that look like they're about to fall off, this year's restyling is a big disappointment. Fortunately, most of the engineering improvements were adopted with last year's model; so, if you also can't take the 2011's restyled exterior, buy a discounted second-series 2010 to keep the chrome and classic lines. Nissan's struggling Quest greets the 2011 model year in late winter with its own version of unconventional exterior styling similar to the Odyssey. Only Toyota's restyled Sienna actually looks like an improvement.

Toyota, for its part, has just brought out a third-gen Sienna that is more car-like in its handling and has improved fuel economy. And, hoping to put its safety woes behind it, Toyota has pledged to phase in a brake override feature to prevent its vehicles from suddenly accelerating with no brakes.

No market segment is safe from the Asian invasion (except, possibly, full-sized vans). In response to high fuel prices, Asian minicars are flooding the market with small, fuel-sipping small vehicles, and almost everyone is expanding their product lines to include more hybrids and "crossover" tall wagons. Also watch for better-performing and more-economical large pickups as well as high-performance models from Honda, Hyundai, Nissan, and Lexus that target Detroit's Camaro, Corvette, and Mustang.

Asian Quality

South Korean vehicles—once the laughing stock of car columnists and consumer advocates—have caught up to within a hair-breadth's distance of the Japanese competition in terms of quality and sales. Hyundai is finally putting better-quality parts in its Kia subsidiary's cars, SUVs, and minivans, although it seems to be too little, too late for many Kia models. Honda, like Toyota, has rested on its laurels since 2008.

2008 HONDA ODYSSEY 3.5 V6

All Technical Service Bulletins

NUMBER	DATE	TITLE
10-002	01/20/2010	Paint—Defect Warranty Claim Information
09-085	11/14/2009	Body—Front Door Glass Opens/Closes Slowly/Sticks
09-080	11/03/2009	Lighting—Water Inside Liftgate Tail Lamps
09-017	10/09/2009	Interior—Passenger Air Bag To Dash Gap
08-088	10/02/2009	Audio System—Revised Poor Reception Repair
09-047	09/16/2009	Engine Controls—MIL ON/Multiple DTCs Set
09-054	09/03/2009	Body—Power Locks Cycle Continuously While Driving
08-017	09/02/2009	Engine—Knocks Or Ticks At Idle
08-045	08/28/2009	Engine—Chirping Noise From Lower Timing Belt Area
08-051	08/26/2009	Navigation System—DVD Read Error/No Route Displayed
07-005	08/21/2009	Steering—Power Steering Pump Whines/Buzzes/Hums
09-053	07/14/2009	Engine, A/T Controls—A/T Judder At 20–45 MPH
09-046	06/26/2009	Body—Sliding Door Center Seal Torn/Worn
08-026	05/22/2009	Campaign—Can't Read Audio Display/Knobs Inop.
06-068	05/02/2009	Steering/Suspension—Vehicle Pulls Left/Right
09-001	04/24/2009	Navigation Radio—Various Malfunctions
07-045	03/05/2009	Brakes—Pedal Is Low/Feels Soft
06-001	03/04/2009	Audio/Navigation/RES—Warr. Exchange/Non-Warr. Repair
09-004	01/14/2009	Brakes—Park Brake Lamp ON With Park Brake OFF
08-078	11/12/2008	Electrical—B-CAN DTCs After Water Leaks To Interior
08-071	09/12/2008	Engine Controls—Engine Ping On Acceleration
08-055	08/01/2008	Body—Sliding Door Does Not Open All The Way
08-029	05/14/2008	Instruments—Outside Temp. Display Reads Too High
08-012	02/22/2008	Cell Phone—Revised HandsFreeLink Diagnostics
08-006	02/15/2008	Body—Power Sliding Door Buzzing Noises

The emerging BRIC (Brazil, Russia, India, and China) economies are also major players in both the production and the sale of new vehicles to Asian, European, and North American manufacturers. For example:

- Brazil is a big producer of ethanol and ethanol-fuelled vehicles, which it sells to its own burgeoning market and throughout the world. The country is also a major builder of conventional cars and car parts. The quality control of its vehicles has been average to above average.
- Russia's car industry is booming from both a production and a sales standpoint. Unfortunately, Russian cars are almost as badly built as what China spews out.
- Although struggling, India's Tata Motors is ramping up production at both the high and low ends of the auto market. Its March 2008 purchase of Jaguar and Land Rover from Ford (Ford took a $3 billion bath) reinforces the truism that cash and cachet will always trump common sense. Since the purchase, Tata has gone to the Indian government and asked for money. Tata's low-end $2,500 Nano car is remarkably cheap and practical, though basic to the extreme. It's scheduled to arrive in North America in early 2011 and sell for $7,000. The jury is still out as to the overall quality of Tata's Nano and recently acquired Jaguar and Land Rover models.
- Chinese car quality is non-existent; they make some of the least crashworthy and poorest quality vehicles one can find. Yet the Chinese market is larger and hotter than the flagging U.S. market by about a million more units annually. No wonder Ford, GM, and Chrysler spent some of their government loans in China to build joint factories. Presently, their merged sales are soaring and that more than compensates for the U.S. downturn.

Everybody knows the Japanese and South Koreans have a lock on reliable, fuel-sipping vehicles. Whether they're cars, minivans, sport-utilities, or pickups, and whether they're built in Japan, Canada, Mexico, or the United States, Asian cars give you much more performance and fuel economy for your money than if you were to buy the equivalent vehicle made by Chrysler, Ford, or General Motors—or by most European automakers, for that matter. Most of all, you can count on most Asian vehicles to be easy to repair and relatively slow to depreciate—both admirable qualities in a volatile auto market where models disappear and hapless owners may be left with irreparable, worthless pieces of junk in their driveways (hello, Jaguar, Land Rover, Saab, and Volvo). Undoubtedly, Asian automakers have a more-realistic mix of models that can withstand the vagaries of the marketplace as fuel prices rise and fall. They also know how to squeeze the most profit out of the cars they sell so well to emerging markets.

Nevertheless, Toyota's record number of safety-related recalls since last October and Honda's quality control decline have hurt both companies' sales: Honda reported a drop-off in June sales, down 14 percent among its Honda and Acura brands combined. The Honda division saw sales down 13 percent, and sales at the luxury Acura division dropped 21 percent. Meanwhile, Toyota Canada Inc. reported overall June sales down 13.8 percent from June 2009.

No matter how you cut it, the Detroit Three will be playing catch-up to Asian automakers for at least the next decade through mergers and joint projects, essentially giving truth to the age-old dictum "If you can't beat them, join them."

Acura

Acura, a division of Honda, sells seven cars under its nameplate: the Canada-exclusive CSX entry-level compact and its Type-S high-performance luxury sedan, the RL flagship luxury sedan, the TL near-luxury sedan, the TSX sport wagon, the MDX seven-passenger luxury SUV and RDX crossover wagons, and the ZDX luxury four-door sports coupe.

Let's not kid ourselves—most Acura products are basically fully loaded Hondas with a few additional features and unjustifiably high prices. Despite the fact that Acura and Honda dealers have abhorred real price competition for years, poor sales during the past year have forced them to give sizeable rebates and other sales incentives to customers. In their own right, Acuras are good buys. Maintenance costs are low, depreciation is generally slower than average, though there are some exceptions, and reliability and quality are much better than average. What few defects Acuras have are usually related to squeaks, rattles, minor trim glitches, and accessories such as the navigation, climate control, and sound systems.

CSX, TYPE-S ★★★★/★★

The Acura CSX.

RATING: *I-TECH:* Acura now calls its base CSX the I-TECH, and it's rated Above Average for an entry-level car that's sold only in Canada; *Type-S:* Average. Strictly for drivers desperate to pay extra cash for an Acura nameplate. **Strong points:** Called "a Civic in a tuxedo" by *Globe and Mail* car columnist Ted Laturnus, the CSX *is* a gussied-up Civic; however, it's also a well-balanced car that is both practical and fun to drive. It has more than enough power; handling is better than average; interior room is adequate, with lots of thoughtful storage areas; controls are a breeze to decipher and access; visibility is fairly good; outstanding workmanship and top-quality materials are evident everywhere (all automakers' Ontario plants are renowned for high quality control); its resale value is extraordinarily high; and low-cost leases are available. All CSX models use the same energy-absorbing frame structure that's found on the Civic, so crashworthiness ratings should match the Civic's five stars for frontal collisions, four stars for side impacts, and four stars for rollover resistance. **Weak points:** You are paying excess cash for a bit more cachet. Prices are firm, and freight charges are excessive. The 5-year/unlimited km corrosion perforation warranty is rather chintzy when compared with what is offered by less-prestigious automakers. **New for 2011:** Very little.

OVERVIEW: The CSX came on the scene as the 2006 model replacement for the discontinued entry-level EL, a successful Honda spin-off that was made in Canada for Canadians. The EL debuted in 1997 with the Acura 1.6 EL, and later came the 1.7 EL. Today's CSX I-TECH is essentially a restyled, more-powerful luxury version of the Honda Civic sedan.

The four-door CSX is sold in two trim levels: a base model and a Type-S version. Base models offer many useful features, like electronic stability control, anti-lock brakes, side and side curtain airbags, heated mirrors with integrated turn signals, steering-wheel audio controls, a CD/MP3 player, automatic climate control, cruise control, power windows, and a 60/40 split-folding rear seat. The Type-S model sells for $29,990 and comes with more-gimmicky features.

COST ANALYSIS: Get a discounted, identical 2010 model or wait until the redesigned 2012 models arrive. **Best alternatives:** Consider the Honda Civic Si ($1,500 cheaper), Hyundai Elantra (redesigned this year), Mazda3 Touring (manual transmission), Nissan Sentra, or Subaru Impreza. **Options:** Ditch the Bridgestone and Firestone tires for Michelin, Yokohama, or Pirelli. **Rebates:** Rebates are not likely; look for limited discounting. **Depreciation:** Very slow. In fact, a first-year

2006 CSX sold new for $25,400; today, the car is worth almost half its original value, or $12,500. Most Detroit-made cars lose half their value between the second and third year they're in use. **Insurance cost:** Higher than average. **Parts supply/cost:** Average. **Annual maintenance cost:** Less than average. **Warranty:** Bumper-to-bumper 5 years/100,000 km; rust perforation 5 years/unlimited km. **Supplementary warranty:** A waste of money. **City/highway fuel economy:** *I-TECH:* 8.7/6.4 L/100 km, 32/44 mpg. *Type-S:* 10.2/6.8 L/100 km, 28/42 mpg.

OWNER-REPORTED PROBLEMS: Most complaints are about premature front brake caliper and rotor wear causing the car to shudder or pull sharply to one side when braking. Other niggling glitches concern body panel gaps, too many squeaks and rattles, the black interior (which scuffs easily), and the climate control and electrical systems.

SERVICE BULLETIN-REPORTED PROBLEMS: Similar to problems outlined in the Honda Civic section.

Type-S

This is a $30,000 sportster for people who want that race-car feeling imparted by the peppy engine and close-ratio 6-speed manual transmission. Additional performance features include a speed-sensitive electric power-steering system, drive-by-wire throttle control, four-wheel disc ABS, vehicle stability assist with traction control, a sport suspension with stiffer springs, upgraded stabilizer bars (front and rear), and 17-inch tires.

The downside: Most of the high-performance and luxury features are available in the Civic Si for thousands less, and the Accord V6 is quite a bit more powerful and luxurious but much less high-strung (it uses regular fuel). The car's engine tends to hold its speed when downshifting; it is a little unstable when encountering strong side winds; the leather interior feels cheap; and fuel consumption is on the high side.

TL   ★★★★

RATING: Above Average. **Strong points:** Comes in front-drive and all-wheel-drive versions. Good fuel economy; plenty of power, delivered smoothly; comfortable ride; well constructed, with quality mechanical and body components; and impressive crashworthiness scores. **Weak points:** Imprecise steering and excessive road noise that are unacceptable for a luxury car of this caliber and expense; not as agile as the competition; suspension may be too firm for some; tight rear seating; buttons, buttons, everywhere. **New for 2011:** Nothing important.

OVERVIEW: The TL combines luxury and performance in a nicely styled front-drive, five-passenger sedan that uses the same chassis as the Accord and CL coupe. Two engines are offered and are mated to either a 5-speed Sequential SportShift automatic transmission or a 6-speed manual. A limited-slip differential provides impressive acceleration in a smooth and quiet manner. Handling is good, with firm suspension and relatively responsive steering. Bumps can be a bit jarring, but this is a small price to pay for the car's high-speed stability.

Interior accommodations are better than average all around; the cockpit layout is very user-friendly, although learning which buttons perform what tasks takes some practice. Visibility fore and aft is unobstructed.

KEY FACTS

CANADIAN PRICE (NEGOTIABLE): *Base:* $39,990, *TECH package:* $43,490 **U.S. PRICE:** *Base:* $35,105, *TECH package:* $38,835 **CANADIAN FREIGHT:** $1,895 **U.S. FREIGHT:** $880 **POWERTRAIN (FRONT-DRIVE/AWD)** Engines: 3.5L V6 (280 hp) • 3.7L V6 (305 hp); Transmissions: 5-speed auto. • 6-speed man.

DIMENSIONS/CAPACITY
Passengers: 2/3; Wheelbase: 109.2 in.; H: 57.1/L: 195.5/W: 74 in.; Headroom F/R: 3.5/3.5 in.; Legroom F/R: 42/27.5 in.; Cargo volume: 13.1 cu. ft.; Fuel tank: 50L/premium; Tow limit: 1,000 lb.; Load capacity: 850 lb.; Turning circle: 38.4 ft.; Weight: 3,699–3,948 lb.

Standard safety features include ABS, stability and traction control, front seat belt pretensioners, childproof door locks, three-point seat belts, head-protecting airbags, and a transmission/brake interlock. NHTSA awarded maximum five-star occupant protection in all categories. Head restraints are given a "Good" rating by IIHS.

COST ANALYSIS: Get the nearly-identical discounted 2010 model. **Best alternatives:** Consider the Hyundai Genesis or the cheaper Azera, Lexus ES (with brake override), Toyota Avalon (with brake override), and Nissan Maxima. **Options:** Don't waste your money on the satellite navigation system; it's confusing to calibrate and hard to see. Ditch the Bridgestone and Firestone tires, too. **Rebates:** $2,500 rebates; some discounting. **Depreciation:** Much slower than average. **Insurance cost:** Higher than average. **Parts supply/cost:** Easily found and moderately priced, especially most mechanical and electronic components, but with the exception of some body parts. **Annual maintenance cost:** Less than average. **Warranty:** Bumper-to-bumper 5 years/100,000 km; rust perforation 5 years/unlimited km. **Supplementary warranty:** Not needed. **City/highway fuel economy:** 3.5L: 11.6/7.5 L/100 km, 24/38 mpg. 3.7L: 12.3/8.1 L/100 km, 23/35 mpg.

OWNER-REPORTED PROBLEMS: Very few complaints, except for lagging, slipping transmission shifting that apparently dates back to the 2008 model:

> Transmission slipping in traffic with multiple close calls to accidents from behind. I am original owner and have kept perfect maintenance of auto. Transmission is failing on every shift between 1st, 2nd and 3rd gears when warm. Safety issue is when people from behind think I am accelerating yet I am stalled. The fix is $4000+.

Minor body fit and finish deficiencies, including sash and door squeaks, misaligned dash, and paint delamination/spotting.

SERVICE BULLETIN-REPORTED PROBLEMS: AC blower speed:

ERRATIC A/C BLOWER MOTOR SPEED

BULLETIN NO.: 09-057   DATE: JANUARY 9, 2010

2009–10 TL
SYMPTOM: The HVAC blower speed changes erratically and VSA DTCs 104 and/or 86 are stored.
PROBABLE CAUSE: The body ground G403 is faulty.
CORRECTIVE ACTION: Replace the body ground G403.

TSX ★★★

RATING: Average. This car is essentially the modified Accord sold in Europe. Buyers comparing the TSX with the Accord or TL will quickly discover that the TSX has less head and shoulder room up front and a more-cramped rear-seat area. **Strong points:** Great steering and handling; generously appointed; well-laid-out instruments and controls; improved navigation system controls; well built; good fuel economy; and good crashworthiness scores compiled by NHTSA and IIHS. A 5-year/100,000 km bumper-to-bumper warranty. **Weak points:** The 4-cylinder is underpowered and the V6 is overpriced. Premium fuel negates the small engine's fuel-sipping savings; the interior is a bit snug, especially in the rear; the low roofline hampers rear access; overly sensitive seat sensors may disable the airbag, even when an average-sized adult is seated; and the rear seats have insufficient thigh support. **New for 2011:** A new wagon based on the European Accord wagon.

OVERVIEW: Essentially a more-luxurious, sportier, smaller version of the Accord, the TSX is an entry-level sports car equipped with a base 201 hp 2.4L 4-cylinder engine and an optional 280 hp 3.5L V6

KEY FACTS

CANADIAN PRICE (NEGOTIABLE): *Base:* $32,990, *Premium:* $36,290, *TECH package:* $39,290, *V6:* $39,790, *V6 TECH package:* $42,790 **U.S. PRICE:** *Base:* $29,310, *TECH package:* $32,410, *V6:* $34,850, *V6 TECH package:* $37,950 **CANADIAN FREIGHT:** $1,895 **U.S. FREIGHT:** $860

POWERTRAIN (FRONT-DRIVE/AWD)

Engines: 2.4L 4-cyl. (201 hp) • 3.5L V6 (280 hp); Transmissions: 5-speed auto. • 6-speed man.

DIMENSIONS/CAPACITY

Passengers: 2/3; Wheelbase: 107 in.; H: 57/L: 186/W: 73 in.; Headroom F/R: 3.0/2.5 in.; Legroom F/R: 41/27.0 in.; Cargo volume: 13 cu. ft.; Fuel tank: 70L/premium; Tow limit: 1,000 lb.; Load capacity: 850 lb.; Turning circle: 36.7 ft.; Weight: 3,440 lb.

---

that competes in a luxury-sedan niche where V6 power is commonplace. It gets excellent gas mileage but runs on premium fuel only. The car is sportier than the TL, yet it isn't as harsh as the discontinued high-performance RSX. The 2010 models correct the vague steering and excessive cabin noise found with previous versions. Nevertheless, brake fade is still present after successive stops, manual shifts aren't as quick as with other cars in this class, and the V6 option doesn't give you sportier handling than the 4-banger.

Crash tests give five stars for driver and passenger crash protection in frontal collisions and side impacts and five stars for rollover resistance. Offset crash protection and head restraints are given a "Good" rating by IIHS.

COST ANALYSIS: Get a cheaper, almost-identical 2010 model. Acura is throwing in a cornucopia of standard safety, performance, and convenience features—like standard stability and traction control and head-protecting side airbags—to make this luxury sedan attractive to shoppers who don't feel size and V6 power are everything. Yet, when you consider the TSX's price is about $8,000 more than a 4-cylinder Honda Accord, you have to wonder whether the vehicle has a lot of cachet—or if its manufacturer has a lot of nerve. **Best alternatives:** Other cars worth considering, although they aren't as well made as the TSX, are the Audi A4, BMW 335i, Infiniti G37, Lexus IS 350, and Lincoln MKZ. The TSX is better styled than the Infiniti G37 or the Lexus IS. The BMW 3 Series and Mercedes C-Class look good but aren't as reliable as the TSX and will likely cost a bundle to maintain. The TSX's size and good looks outclass the TL by far, and the V6 puts it about where the former TL was in size and power. **Options:** Ditch the Bridgestone and Firestone original equipment tires for better-performing Michelin, Yokohama, or Pirelli. **Rebates:** $3,500 rebates, some discounting, and low finance rates. **Depreciation:** Much slower than average; a $35,900 2006 TSX is still worth almost half its original value. **Insurance cost:** Higher than average. **Parts supply/cost:** Easily found and moderately priced, especially most mechanical and electronic components. **Annual maintenance cost:** Less than average. **Warranty:** Bumper-to-bumper 5 years/100,000 km; rust perforation 5 years/unlimited km. **Supplementary warranty:** Not needed. **City/highway fuel economy:** *4-cylinder man.:* 10.5/7.0 L/100 km, 27/40 mpg. *4-cylinder auto.:* 9.6/6.5 L/100 km, 29/43 mpg. *6-cylinder auto.:* 11.3/7.4 L/100 km, 25/38 mpg.

OWNER-REPORTED PROBLEMS: Brakes (noisy brake pads and premature brake caliper and rotor wear); paint peeling and spotting; malfunctioning power accessories and entertainment systems; vehicle suddenly stalled while exiting a freeway. In a crash, seat belt did not restrain driver. Troublesome original equipment Michelin tires:

> Michelin Pilot HX MXM4 came installed on my 2010 Acura TSX. At 220 miles [355 km] tire developed a bubble, and at 280 miles [450 km] went flat. Tire was replaced at a cost of $208. There was a tear in the side wall. I had the car for less than 2 weeks, drove it extremely carefully (no hard braking, acceleration, and certainly did not hit any curbs or potholes). These tires are dangerous and if it was not for the on board tire pressure management I could have driven the vehicle with a flat tire and potentially crashed.

SERVICE BULLETIN-REPORTED PROBLEMS: Brake judder or squeal; fuel fill door is hard to open (2009–10 models); poor radio reception remedied by improved antenna adapters.

RL ★★★

RATING: Average. A Honda Legend to the rest of the world. **Strong points:** Acceptable acceleration that's smooth and quiet in all gear ranges; average steering and handling; loaded with goodies; above average reliability; top-quality body and mechanical components; all seats are well cushioned and give plenty of thigh support; good all-around visibility; impressive five-star ratings for front and side occupant protection and rollover resistance; IIHS rates rear, offset, and side occupant protection "Good"; and there's a comprehensive 5-year/100,000 km bumper-to-bumper warranty. **Weak points:** Bland styling; way overpriced and overweight; suspension may be overly firm for some; slow steering response; mediocre handling; interior feels cramped (the less-expensive TL is almost as roomy); dash console looks and feels disorganized; audio and navigation systems aren't easy to use; high fuel consumption; and problematic navigation system controls. **New for 2011:** Nothing significant.

KEY FACTS

CANADIAN PRICE (NEGOTIABLE): *Base:* $63,900, *Elite:* $69,500 **U.S. PRICE:** *Base:* $46,830 **CANADIAN FREIGHT:** $1,895 **U.S. FREIGHT:** $860
POWERTRAIN (AWD)
Engine: 3.7L V6 (300 hp); Transmission: 5-speed auto.
DIMENSIONS/CAPACITY
Passengers: 2/3; Wheelbase: 110.2 in.; H: 57.0/L: 195.7/W: 72.7 in.; Headroom F/R: 5.0/2.5 in.; Legroom F/R: 42.4/36.3 in.; Cargo volume: 13.2 cu. ft.; Fuel tank: 73.3L/premium; Tow limit: 1,000 lb.; Load capacity: 850 lb.; Turning circle: 36.1 ft.; Weight: 4,110 lb.

OVERVIEW: Acura's flagship luxury sedan uses the MDX's V6 hooked to a standard 5-speed automatic gearbox and all-wheel drive (stick shift isn't available). The RL is loaded with innovative high-tech safety and convenience features, like heated front seats, front and rear climate controls, a rear-seat trunk pass-through, xenon headlights (get used to oncoming drivers flashing their headlights at you), "smart" side airbags, front seat belt pretensioners, ABS, traction control, and an anti-skid system.

COST ANALYSIS: A prime candidate for cross-border shopping when you consider the RL's $17,000 markup in Canada. Be wary of the untested rear-drive platform and V8 on the 2011 model, slated to go on sale in late 2010. **Best alternatives:** BMW 535xi, Cadillac CTS Premium (3.6), Infiniti M35/M35x, and Mercedes-Benz E350. You may want to take a look at the TL sedan, as well. **Options:** Nothing. These cars come stuffed to the gills. **Rebates:** There are at least $10,000 worth of rebates and discounts you can use to bring the MSRP down to a more-rational level. **Depreciation:** Quicker than average, which is surprising for an Acura: a 2006 RL, bought for $69,500, now sells for $24,000...ouch! **Insurance cost:** Higher than average. **Parts supply/cost:** Most mechanical and electronic components are easily found and moderately priced. Body parts may be hard to come by, and they can be expensive. **Annual maintenance cost:** Less than average. **Warranty:** Bumper-to-bumper 5 years/100,000 km; rust perforation 5 years/unlimited km. **Supplementary warranty:** Not needed; the base warranty is fairly applied. **City/highway fuel economy:** 13.1/9.0 L/100 km, 31/22 mpg.

OWNER-REPORTED PROBLEMS: Electrical and audio system failures, accessories that malfunction, and fit and finish glitches.

MDX ★★★

Super Handling All-Wheel Drive (SH-AWD) and Active Damper System (the latter is available in the Elite edition); loaded with goodies; above average reliability; top-quality body and mechanical components; a five-star crashworthiness rating for front and side occupant protection and a four-star rating for rollover resistance; IIHS rates rear, offset, and side occupant protection "Good"; and there's a comprehensive 5-year/100,000 km bumper-to-bumper warranty. **Weak points:** Overpriced and overweight; acceleration and handling are acceptable but don't inspire confidence; the default suspension setting degrades emergency handling; the rear third seat is a tight fit; the dash console isn't user-friendly; audio and navigation systems are needlessly complicated; and high fuel consumption. **New for 2011:** Nothing important.

OVERVIEW: Introduced as a 2001 model, the MDX got its first complete redesign for the 2007 model year, making this mid-sized sport-utility more competitive. Acura's revamping has smoothed out the powertrain's functions, made the vehicle a bit more agile, and softened the suspension. On the other hand, the car loses its grip during avoidance manoeuvres and has a cramped interior when carrying a full passenger load, and the busy dashboard has tiny buttons everywhere.

> ## KEY FACTS
>
> **CANADIAN PRICE (NEGOTIABLE):** *Base:* $51,190, *TECH package:* $57,290, *Elite package:* $61,990 **U.S. PRICE:** *Base:* $42,230, *TECH package:* $45,905 **CANADIAN FREIGHT:** $1,895 **U.S. FREIGHT:** $860 **POWERTRAIN (AWD)** Engine: 3.7L V6 (300 hp); Transmission: 6-speed auto. **DIMENSIONS/CAPACITY** Passengers: 2/3/2; Wheelbase: 108.2 in.; H: 68.2/L: 191.6/W: 78.5 in.; Headroom F/R: 4.0/4.0 in.; Legroom F/R: 41/30 in.; Cargo volume: 42 cu. ft.; Fuel tank: 72.7L/premium; Tow limit: 5,000 lb.; Load capacity: 1,160 lb.; GVWR: 5,732 lb.; Turning circle: 40 ft.; Ground clearance: 5.0 in.; Weight: 4,561 lb.

COST ANALYSIS: Get a discounted, practically identical 2010 version. **Best alternatives:** The Lexus RX series, BMW X5, Infiniti FX35, Buick Enclave, Chevrolet Traverse, and GMC Acadia trio. Or, if you want to save lots of dough and have an SUV similar to the GM models mentioned previously, pick up a slightly used 2009 Saturn Outlook AWD. It sold new for $38,000, but now sells for less than $15,000 simply because the car was dropped for 2010. Would you like comparable Asian performance and reliability for about $11,000 less? Try a Honda Pilot (the MDX's cheaper cousin) for its additional passenger- and cargo-hauling capability, a Nissan Xterra, or a Toyota Highlander. The Volvo XC90 and Mercedes ML320, ML350, or ML550 have adequate cargo room with all the rows down, but they have neither comparable cargo room behind the second row nor a comparable level of quality control and dealer servicing. Furthermore, Ford's announcement that Volvo has been sold to Chinese interests obscures the future of Volvo sales and servicing in North America. **Options:** Forget the satellite navigation system. **Rebates:** Look for $3,000+ rebates on the 2010 models, and a similar amount in the late winter applicable to the early 2011 models. **Depreciation:** Much faster than average; a 2006 version is barely worth $20,000 (quite a comedown for a vehicle that sold originally for $51,600). **Insurance cost:** Higher than average. **Parts supply/cost:** Most mechanical and electronic components are easily found and moderately priced. Body parts may be hard to come by, and they can be expensive. **Annual maintenance cost:** Average. **Warranty:** Bumper-to-bumper 5 years/100,000 km; rust perforation 5 years/unlimited km.

Supplementary warranty: Not needed; the base warranty is fairly applied. **City/highway fuel economy:** 13.2/9.6 L/100 km, 21/29 mpg.

OWNER-REPORTED PROBLEMS: Noisy brake pads and premature brake wear; malfunctioning power accessories and entertainment systems; vehicle suddenly stalled while exiting a highway; dashboard display is unreadable in daylight; and in a crash, seat belt did not restrain driver. One complaint that the 2009 model's rear seat belts may be hazardous to children:

> The seat belt that hangs from the ceiling to the middle seat became wrapped around the child's neck. The child was unable to breathe properly. The child was seated in the rear driver's side seat.

SERVICE BULLETIN-REPORTED PROBLEMS: Poor audio reception.

RDX ★★★

RATING: Average. **Strong points:** Adequate power, though turbo lag (the delay between throttle application and acceleration) is a big minus. Handles like a tall sports car: tight and responsive, with excellent braking. Seating and driving positions work for occupants of all sizes. The nicely appointed interior is well laid-out, with plenty of small storage areas; the seats have good thigh and back support; above average reliability; top-quality mechanical components; a five-star crashworthiness rating for front and side occupant protection, and a four-star rating for rollover resistance; IIHS rates rear, offset, and side occupant protection "Good"; and there's a comprehensive 5-year/100,000 km bumper-to-bumper warranty. **Weak points:** The buzzy, fuel-thirsty 4-cylinder engine competes in a class where 6- and 8-cylinders are the norm; turbo lag; stiff-riding, with some jostling when passing over uneven terrain; more pavement noise than one would expect in a luxury car; the interior pillars look very unrefined, with some misaligned plastics; computerized audio, climate, and navigation systems have a high learning curve; no engine temperature gauge, and the turbo boost gauge is superfluous; and the small space-saver spare tire has no place in a car this expensive. The front-drive version is only sold in the States. **New for 2011:** Nothing significant.

OVERVIEW: Essentially a Honda CR-V clone, the RDX carries Honda's first turbocharged 4-cylinder engine, which makes it a pleasure to drive but a pain to fuel. The RDX takes over from the MDX as Acura's entry-level crossover SUV. Although its dimensions are similar to that of the Honda CR-V, the RDX uses a unique platform developed to handle the vehicle's advanced all-wheel-drive system and peppy turbocharged engine.

COST ANALYSIS: Get the practically identical 2010 model and compare prices in the States; there are sizeable reductions south of the border. The premium

KEY FACTS
CANADIAN PRICE (NEGOTIABLE): *Base:* $39,990, *TECH package:* $42,990 **U.S. PRICE:** *Base:* $32,620, *TECH package:* $35,720 **CANADIAN FREIGHT:** $1,895 **U.S. FREIGHT:** $860 **POWERTRAIN (AWD)** Engine: 2.3L 4 Turbo (240 hp); Transmission: 5-speed auto. **DIMENSIONS/CAPACITY** Passengers: 2/3; Wheelbase: 104.3 in.; H: 65.1/L: 182.4/W: 73.6 in.; Headroom F/R: 4.0/3.5 in.; Legroom F/R: 40.5/ 27.5 in.; Cargo volume: 27.8 cu. ft.; Fuel tank: 72.7L/premium; Tow limit: 1,500 lb.; Load capacity: 870 lb.; GVWR: 5,732 lb.; Turning circle: 41 ft.; Ground clearance: 6.2 in.; Weight: 3,941 lb.

for the RDX can be whittled down to about half as much through smart haggling. The extra dough gets you a more-powerful drivetrain, a more-refined interior, more tech gadgets, and different front-end styling. If these attributes don't turn you on, then save yourself the $4,000–$8,000 and get a CR-V. **Best alternatives:** Subaru Forester, Toyota RAV4 (only with brake override), BMW X3, Honda CR-V, Infiniti EX, and Mazda CX-7. **Rebates:** Look for $5,000+ rebates on the 2010s, and a similar amount in the summer of 2011 applicable to the early 2011 models. **Options:** The Bluetooth satellite navigation system should be compared with the less-expensive Garmin devices. The $4,000+ technology package—the 10-speaker audio system with satellite radio and the full computerized navigation package with backup camera—is a money-waster. **Rebates:** With a top price of $42,990, there are at least $5,000 worth of rebates and discounts that you can use to bring the suggested list price down to an acceptable level. **Depreciation:** Much faster than average: A first-year 2007 base model that sold for $41,000 now fetches $20,000. **Insurance cost:** Higher than average. **Parts supply/cost:** Except for turbo components, most mechanical and electronic components are easily found and moderately priced. Body parts may be hard to come by, and they can be expensive. **Annual maintenance cost:** Average. **Warranty:** Bumper-to-bumper 5 years/100,000 km; rust perforation 5 years/unlimited km. **Supplementary warranty:** Not needed. **City/highway fuel economy:** 11.7/8.7 L/100 km, 24/32 mpg.

OWNER-REPORTED PROBLEMS: Poor audio reception. Most of the problems reported by owners concern accessories, like the gauges, instruments, AC, and entertainment system, and electrical short circuits.

SERVICE BULLETIN-REPORTED PROBLEMS: N/A.

Honda

Honda's sales took a beating last year and the company's sales are still down about 14 percent through June of 2010. This means Honda and its dealers will have to add lots of rebates and sales incentives, like low-cost financing and cheap leases, to make room for next year's models. Buyers are well advised to tell Honda dealers to "stuff it" when asked to pay the manufacturer's suggested retail price (a 10 to 15 percent discount is suitable).

Honda's engineers have also tweaked the performance of its 2011 models to enhance fuel economy, safety, comfort, and convenience. In this way, Honda hopes to cover all its bases even though the game is continually changing and the small-car and performance fans are now more fickle.

One tweak that Honda hasn't admitted to doing, but which has caused an apparent decline in Honda quality over the past several years, is the "decontenting" of its product lineup. When one examines complaints of recent owners and matches them with confidential Honda service bulletins and NHTSA ODI owner safety complaints, it's obvious that quality content has been reduced to keep selling prices competitive. This is the same strategy that got Toyota in so much trouble, starting in 1997.

FIT ★★★★

RATING: Above Average. This four-door, five-passenger mini hatchback is surprisingly roomy and reasonably fuel-efficient, thanks to its small, 1.5L 4-cylinder engine mated to a 5-speed manual transmission. Slotted below the Civic, this little economy car is one of the better choices among the 2011 small cars. **Strong points:** Plenty of smooth, quiet power with either the manual or automatic transmission; handles and brakes like a sports car; good interior ergonomics; standard power accessories, ABS, and side curtain airbags; versatile interior; above average crashworthiness ratings; quality craftsmanship; and a good resale value. **Weak points:** A busy ride. If you thought the Ford Fusion head restraints were a "pain in the neck," read on:

KEY FACTS

CANADIAN PRICE (NEGOTIABLE): *DX:* $14,480, *LX:* $16,880, *Sport:* $18,780 **U.S. PRICE:** *Base:* $14,900, *Sport:* $16,410, *Sport Navi.:* $19,110 **CANADIAN FREIGHT:** $1,395 **U.S. FREIGHT:** $750 **POWERTRAIN (FRONT-DRIVE)** Engine: 1.5L 4-cyl. (109 hp); Transmissions: 5-speed man. • 5-speed auto. **DIMENSIONS/CAPACITY** Passengers: 2/3; Wheelbase: 97 in.; H: 60/L: 157/W: 66 in.; Headroom F/R: 5.5/3.5 in.; Legroom F/R: 40/26 in.; Cargo volume: 21 cu. ft.; Fuel tank: 41L/regular; Tow limit: No towing; Load capacity: 850 lb.; Turning circle: 34.3 ft.; Weight: 2,535 lb.

> The head rest pushes my head forward and strains my neck to the point that I either have to sit upright away from the seat or stretch my neck far out in pain. Either way it is not safe, whether in case of accident or generally for my health. With no cool-off period on new cars in California, I cannot return the car which at this point has 12 miles [19 km] on it, so I am forced to drive unsafely. I ran Google search for Honda head rest complaints and found out that customers have been complaining about Honda's new head rests for the same very reason since 2007 for most of their models—from Accord and Odyssey to Fit.
>
> What makes the matter worse is that you cannot reverse the headrest as there are grooves only on one of the two support poles. By making head restraint extremely uncomfortable to use, Honda is forcing its customers to drive unsafely, specifically without head restraint. I spoke to [the] service manager at my dealer and he told me that Honda does not have adjustable or reversible head restraints.
>
> He is also aware of the complaints from the customers. Solution should be easy to implement by making the head rest reversible for those like me with neck or back problems. I drove Hondas for 18 years and cannot believe that Honda has not responded to 3 years of continuous complaints.

Traction control and an anti-skid system are available, but only for the more-expensive models. Owner complaints include the following: The airbag failed to deploy; rear view is a bit narrow; some transmission seal leaks; weak AC; small gas tank; fuel sloshing noise heard under the front seats; no floormats; touchy, squeaky brakes; vehicle sways and wanders when encountering moderate side winds; jerky acceleration when driving in traffic; excess gear shifting over hilly terrain; some interior engine and road noise; bland exterior and interior styling; paint peeling and delamination; no centre armrest; dealers won't budge on prices; owners say fuel economy is overstated by about 30 percent; and reports that manual-transmission-equipped Fits are rare and seldom sell for their suggested retail price. **New for 2011:** Nothing important.

OVERVIEW: The 2011 Honda Fit is small on the outside, but big on the inside. It sips fuel and still performs well. Sure, its 1.5L engine isn't in the big leagues, but you will seldom realize you're driving a mini-compact. Hey, nine seconds to 100 km/h using a manual gearbox? That's outstanding, considering its competition (the Toyota Prius, seniors on walkers, and the Canadian Senate). The Fit beats most of its competitors and is no slouch with an automatic, either. Handling is easy and predictable, but the ride is somewhat choppy due to the car's small size. Innovative seats allow you to lift the rear seat's base up against the backrest to make room for bulky items, or the seat can be folded flat, which doubles the cargo space. You can even configure the seats to make a small bed.

NHTSA gives the Fit its top rating of five stars for occupant protection in a frontal collision; five stars for driver driver protection in a side impact; three stars for passenger protection in a side impact; and four stars for rollover prevention. Reliability should be above average, judging by European owner reviews of the Jazz.

COST ANALYSIS: Save money by buying a practically identical 2010 version. **Best alternatives:** Other good econocars this year are the Honda Civic, Hyundai Accent, Mazda3, and the Nissan Versa. Toyota's Yaris? It's a bit scary with its history of brake sensor failures. The Chevy Aveo, Dodge Caliber, and Mercedes Smart Car bring up the rear of the pack; cheap, but problematic. **Options:** Nothing worth the extra money. **Rebates:** Look for $1,500+ rebates on the 2010 models this year, and a similar amount in the late fall, applicable to the early 2011 models. Remember, sales have fallen below expectations, making dealers willing to discount. **Depreciation:** Slower than average. For example, a 2007 Fit that sold for $15,000 is still worth about $9,500. **Insurance cost:** Average. **Parts supply/cost:** No trouble finding parts at a fair price. **Annual maintenance cost:** Less than average. **Warranty:** Bumper-to-bumper 5 years/100,000 km; rust perforation 5 years/unlimited km. **Supplementary warranty:** Basic warranty is sufficient. **City/highway fuel economy:** *Man.:* 7.2/5.7 L/100 km, 39/50 mpg. *Auto.:* 7.1/5.5 L/100 km, 40/51 mpg. Interestingly, tests prove the automatic gearbox is more fuel-efficient than the manual transmission.

OWNER-REPORTED PROBLEMS: Painful head restraints; seat belts break and airbags fail to deploy; and the tire jack may bend sideways when lifting the car. Periodic brake failures; paint chipping and premature cosmetic rusting; insufficient legroom causes drivers to apply the brakes and accelerator at the same time; road debris easily destroys the AC condenser on earlier models—an expensive repair not covered under warranty—but discounts are given under a "goodwill" warranty; and the dashboard's elevated design obstructs forward visibility.

SERVICE BULLETIN-REPORTED PROBLEMS: Poor radio reception.

RATING: Above Average (psst...Honda, stop the quality slippage, we know what's going on). As Canada's most popular small car (although Mazda is closing the gap), the Honda Civic is one of the best-performing cars money can buy. It's a comfortable, refined, and Canadian-built vehicle that comes with most of the features that people want without having to pay for extras. **Strong points:** For the first time in decades, Honda's poor sales have forced the company to offer sizeable rebates and sales incentives. This means you should politely tell your Honda dealer that the list price isn't acceptable and that you want at least a 10 percent discount. The sales agent will hem and haw, but you will get that discount. These cars are noted for good acceleration; a smooth-shifting automatic transmission; great handling and good cornering control; responsive, direct steering; and a comfortable, firm ride. The two-tier instrument panel is nicely done and fits well into a friendly cabin environment that houses easily accessed instruments and controls. A tilt/telescoping steering wheel is standard, and interior space is more than adequate for most adults. Best of all, these cars generally have a good reliability rating and a strong resale value. **Weak points:** The coupe's steeply raked front windshield cuts forward visibility; long front roof pillars impede corner views; the expansive dash shelf and sloping nose make it tough to judge distance when parking, and rear visibility isn't impressive,

KEY FACTS

CANADIAN PRICE (NEGOTIABLE): *DX Coupe:* $16,190, *DX-G:* $18,880, *LX:* $20,780, *EX-L:* $22,980, *Si:* $25,880, *Hybrid Sedan:* $27,350 **U.S. PRICE:** *DX Coupe:* $15,455, *Sedan:* $15,655, *DX-VP:* $16,405, *LX:* $17,605, *LX-S:* $18.205, *EX:* $19,455, *EX Navi.:* 22,255; *EX-L:* $21,805, *EX-L Navi.:* $22,255, *Si Coupe:* $22,055, *Si Sedan:* $22,255, *Hybrid Sedan:* $23,800, *GX (Natural Gas):* $25,340 **CANADIAN FREIGHT:** $1,395 **U.S. FREIGHT:** $750

POWERTRAIN (FRONT-DRIVE)
Engines: 1.8L 4-cyl. (113 hp) • 1.8L 4-cyl. (140 hp) • 2.0L 4-cyl. (197 hp); Transmissions: 5-speed man. • 6-speed man. • 5-speed auto.

DIMENSIONS/CAPACITY
Passengers: 2/3; Wheelbase: 106.3 in.; H: 56.5/L: 176.7/W: 69 in.; Headroom F/R: 3.0/2.0 in.; Legroom F/R: 40.5/28 in.; Cargo volume: 12 cu. ft.; Fuel tank: 50L/regular; Tow limit: 1,500 lb.; Load capacity: 850 lb.; Turning circle: 39 ft.; Weight: 2,628 lb.

either; the suspension may be too firm for some; the coupe's interior noise is less isolated than in the sedan; the latest redesign has decreased overall passenger room slightly, although outward dimensions are larger; coupe's rear access takes some effort, and seating is a bit cramped; trunk hinges intrude into the cargo area; and some fit and finish problems, highlighted by interior rattles. **New for 2011:** A restyled exterior in early 2011.

OVERVIEW: The Civic is one of the most refined and competent subcompacts on the market today. Few larger and more-expensive cars can match its performance and roominess. Earlier improvements include offering more-powerful base engines on the Civic, Si, and Hybrid; additional standard safety features like front and side airbags and head-protecting side curtain airbags; improved brakes; electronic stability control on the sporty Si and Hybrid; sleeker styling; more interior room; and a more-rigid body to reduce rattles and vibrations.

COST ANALYSIS: A year-long slump in Honda sales has led to some price discounting as well as more-affordable leases and financing charges. Civics also retain higher resale values than most cars, taking the sting out of the excess loonies you may have originally paid. **Best alternatives:** Other cars worth considering that are cheaper are generally not as refined, like the Toyota Yaris. Instead, try the Hyundai Accent and Mazda3. **Options:** Try to get a free extra set of ignition keys written into the contract; Honda's anti-start, theft-protection keys may cost as much as $150 per set. Steer clear of the standard-issue radio and problematic Firestone or Bridgestone tires. **Rebates:** Mostly related to leasing and low-cost financing. **Depreciation:** What's that? A 2007 Civic Coupe that once sold for $17,200 is still worth almost $12,000. **Insurance cost:** Average. **Parts supply/cost:** Reasonably priced and easily found at dealers and independent suppliers. **Annual maintenance cost:** Much less than average. **Warranty:** Bumper-to-bumper 3 years/60,000 km; powertrain 5 years/100,000 km; rust perforation 6 years/ unlimited km. **Supplementary warranty:** Not needed. **City/highway fuel economy:** *1.8L (140 hp) man.:* 7.4/5.4 L/100 km, 38/52 mpg. *Auto.:* 8.2/5.7 L/ 100 km, 34/50 mpg. *2.0L man.:* 10.2/6.8 L/100 km, 28/42 mpg. *Hybrid:* 4.7/ 4.3 L/100 km, 60/66 mpg.

OWNER-REPORTED PROBLEMS: Honda engineers and designers have been asleep at the switch during the past few years. As a consequence, too many owners report serious safety-related failures and chronic performance glitches. For example, why does the pillar between the windshield and side window cause such an annoying blind spot, and does rear visibility have to be obstructed by the head restraints?

Other factory-related annoyances: Hard starts, won't crank, or suddenly stalls; engine oil leaks; car won't move in Drive; early automatic transmission replacement, transmission fluid leaks, and noisy engagement; stalling in Reverse or Drive; manual transmission grinds when shifting into Third gear; heater blower motor overheats or blows a fuse; malfunctioning alternator; wheel bearing, brake pedal booster, clutch pedal, or master cylinder noise; A-pillar or dash rattles;

sunroof rattling; windows bind or come out of run channels; faulty door lock cylinders; doors and trunk lid hard to close; inoperable fuel-door handle; and body and bumper paint peeling and cracking. Also oil leaks from the lower engine block crack; motor mounts failure; faulty main rear crankshaft seal; sluggish performance when it rains or when passing through a large puddle; transmission periodically wouldn't shift into Third or Fourth gear (torque converter replaced); premature wheel bearing replacement; excessive steering shimmy; and front strut leakage causes noise and difficult handling. Electrical system and fit and finish deficiencies include a poorly mounted driver's seat; inoperable door locks and power windows; a driver-side window that won't roll back up; sun visors that fall apart; an erratic fuel gauge, speedometer, and tachometer; an interior light that hums as it dims; lousy radio speakers; water leaks through the door bottoms, from the tail light into the trunk, and onto the driver-side footwell carpet; windows that often come off their tracks; AC condenser that is easily destroyed by road debris and doesn't cool properly, and condensate that drips from under the glove compartment (heating core needs to be replaced to fix the problem); dashboard buzzing; front and rear windshield creaking. Loose, rattling seat belt adjusters, door panels, and door latches.

And then there are the defects that threaten life and limb: Fire ignited in the seat belt wiring under the passenger seat; seat belts tighten up progressively when connected; child injured when he became entangled in an unfastened rear centre shoulder belt, which retracted, cutting off his air; seat belt doesn't always retract into the harness; seat belts failed to lock up in a sudden panic stop; many complaints of airbags failing to deploy in frontal collisions; Airbag warning light stays lit even though an adult passenger occupies the seat; inadvertent side airbag deployment; broken engine serpentine belt tensioner bolt; fractured front tie rod, causing complete steering loss; sudden acceleration or surging when AC or heater is engaged, or when the steering wheel is turned sharply; car veers sharply to the right when braking; brake and accelerator pedal are mounted too close together. Surging when brakes are applied; sudden acceleration:

> Sudden acceleration surge, to the point of having to completely hold the brake with both feet. At one point, after putting car into Neutral, the engine revved to 7000 rpm before owner could turn car off. The initial surging resulted in the owner's wife hitting her passenger mirror against another vehicle when the engine surged while in reverse.

Cruise control doesn't stay at its set speed; chronic stalling accompanied by steering-wheel lock-up. Engine momentarily maintains high rpm when decelerating. Fuel leakage into the engine compartment while vehicle was underway; car has to warm up a few minutes before brakes will work properly; vehicle rolls back when stopped on an incline with automatic transmission engaged; transmission surges forward when put into Reverse (blamed on transmission solenoid); automatic transmission will suddenly downshift in traffic; when accelerator pedal is tapped at less than 5 km/h, vehicle suddenly passes from Drive to Neutral to Reverse; transmission won't easily go into First gear; steering wheel wouldn't lock when parked; steering wheel shakes when turned sharply to the left or right; sometimes, the tire rubs on the fender; taller drivers' vision blocked by nonadjustable, windshield-mounted rear-view mirror; driver's sun visor keeps falling down, obstructing vision; loose driver's seat. Head restraint pushes head too far forward:

> I am writing to complain about the headrests in my car. I purchased a 2010 Honda Civic LX-S a week and a half ago. After driving it for about an hour, I noticed my neck and shoulders bothering me. My head is being forced downward by the headrests. This occurs in all headrest positions, but is worse when adjusted right behind my head. I have tilted the seat back as far as I safely can and still be able to drive. I am [a] 53 year old female, 5'3" tall, and wear bifocals. I am having difficulty focusing from tachometer to speedometer to road because I cannot [move] my head to use the right part of my glasses to see. I cannot tilt my head back at all because of the headrest. I also experienced a headache that evening as well due to eye strain. The NHSTA changed their headrest regulations in 2008. Test dummies for large males were used and then standards were put in place. After spending thousands of dollars on a new car, I am unable to safely drive it. I have to either remove, turn around, or jerry-rig a remedy for the headrest in order to drive and not suffer neck, back, shoulder and visual pain. The cost is my safety in an accident. Or, I can leave the headrest and drive with my posture in a horrid position. I cannot sit up straight, my head is forced downward so I cannot use my bifocals properly, and I cannot tilt the seat back any further and still see over the dashboard. There are complaints all over the internet, specifically for Honda Accords and Civics, as well as Nissans, Mercedes, Fords and other makes. I believe you need to reevaluate your recommendations for headrests or at least reissue new ones, indicating the range of the tilt. You recommended the minimum tilt needed for safety, but failed to issue instructions to car manufacturers for the outer edge of the tilt—where the tilt would harm drivers, especially short women.

Windshield cracked suddenly; difficult to see through bottom of windshield; with AC engaged at night, a film covers rear windshield (said to be caused by either an engine head gasket failure or "outgassing" from the interior's plastic trim). AC blamed for emitting toxic fumes:

> The HVAC (air conditioning/heating system/defroster) immediately started spewing toxic mold/mildew spores on a new vehicle test-driven at the dealer's. It occurs while driving, after running the air conditioning for a few minutes, turning the air conditioning off (while leaving the fan running) and waiting a few minutes. It then stinks for a few minutes and then disappears.

Trunk springs failed; exterior and interior lights dim to an unsafe level; rear running lights fail due to a faulty fuse box; heated side mirrors gradually lose their reflective ability; tire rims easily collect snow, ice, and dirt; and Dunlop and Firestone tires have tread separation. Electric shock when refueling:

> 1) When the fuel cap is removed there is [an] ESD discharge when the cap touches the body of the car. The ESD discharge can occur very close to the fuel inlet and where there are gasoline vapors. There is a potential for a fuel explosion or fire. The fuel cap

is attached to the fuel door so the max distance the cap can be moved from the fuel inlet is about 6 inches [15 cm]. 2) The ESD seems to build up very quickly (at least 1 mile [1.6 km] of driving). The problem occurs every time the car is refueled and has been present since the car was purchased. 3) The manufacturer was contacted and they indicated the issue was due to the buildup of ESD on the operator of the car. When the fuel cap is touched the ESD charge is then transferred to the cap which then discharges to the body of the car.

SERVICE BULLETIN-REPORTED PROBLEMS: Revised service bulletin to improve poor radio reception.

RATING: Not Recommended. **Strong points:** The Insight hybrid will save you a bit on fuel, and it costs less than the more-refined Toyota Prius. It also has a versatile hatchback design. **Weak points:** For the little bit of savings over a Prius, you'll have to contend with lethargic acceleration; Insight crawls up hills:

Car has small engine that needs assistance from electric motor. Electric motor helps the car during acceleration and climbing. The car should not charge the battery on climbs. As a result of this, extra load is added on the engine during climbs. With a 1300CC engine going up a grade, this could be very dangerous as you don't have enough power to climb at a certain rate other cars are capable of. If you visit *insightcentral.net* there are a lot of complaints about this. Honda needs to re-program the cars not to force charge during climbs. I understand that if the battery was very low or drained that force charging on climbs are a necessary evil. But my battery was 75% full!!!

The occasional brake failure (just like the Prius); a jumpy, jerky ride; a hard-to-access interior; cheap-looking plastics and carpeting; and cramped, poorly

KEY FACTS

CANADIAN PRICE (NEGOTIABLE): *LX:* $23,900, *EX:* $27,500 **U.S. PRICE:** *LX:* $19,800, *EX:* $21,300 **CANADIAN FREIGHT:** $1,395 **U.S. FREIGHT:** $750 **POWERTRAIN (FRONT-DRIVE)**
Engine: 1.3L 4-cyl. (98 hp); Transmission: CVT
DIMENSIONS/CAPACITY
Passengers: 2/3; Wheelbase: 100.3 in.; H: 56.1/L: 172.2/W: 66.6 in.; Headroom F/R: 5.0/1.5 in.; Legroom F/R: 40.5/26.5 in.; Cargo volume: 15.8 cu. ft.; Fuel tank: 50L/regular; Tow limit: N/R; Load capacity: 850 lb.; Turning circle: 36 ft.; Weight: 2,755 lb.

supported, knees-to-your-chin rear seats that are real head-bangers every time the car passes over uneven terrain. Get used to a raspy exhaust and moaning CVT gearbox when accelerating. Long-term reliability is unproven. **New for 2011:** Nothing noteworthy; no changes expected before 2014.

OVERVIEW: The Insight sells for $900 less than the Accord, and the car comes with multiple airbags, automatic climate control, power windows and locks, heated mirrors, CD audio with auxiliary jack, and anti-lock brakes. The EX gives you Bluetooth connectivity, a USB interface, paddle shifters, stability control, and a navigation system of doubtful utility.

COST ANALYSIS: This car has very little to offer except for some fuel savings and the cachet of buying a "green" car. But be wary of the hype: Your "green machine" uses toxic rare earth elements that kill Third World workers, and its electrical energy comes from coal-burning utilities. And the cost for a new battery pack is best left unsaid. **Best alternatives:** The Ford Escape Hybrid, Hyundai Accent, Mazda3, Nissan Sentra, or Suzuki SX4. **Options:** Steer clear of the standard-issue radio and problematic Firestone or Bridgestone tires. **Rebates:** $2,500 early in the new year. **Depreciation:** Quite rapid—a 2005 Insight that sold originally for $26,000 is now only worth $9,500. **Insurance cost:** Higher than average. **Parts supply/cost:** Electronic parts are expensive and hard to find. **Annual maintenance cost:** Average so far, but long-term costs are likely to be high. **Warranty:** Bumper-to-bumper 3 years/60,000 km; powertrain 5 years/100,000 km; rust perforation 6 years/unlimited km. **Supplementary warranty:** Not needed. **City/highway fuel economy:** *LX:* 4.8/4.5 L/100 km, 59/63 mpg. *EX:* 5.0/4.6 L/100 km, 56/61 mpg.

OWNER-REPORTED PROBLEMS: Airbags failed to deploy in a frontal collision. Sudden brake failures in Drive and Reverse (hybrids from all automakers have a history of sudden brake failures):

April 9, 2010 my husband and I were pulling into the garage of our home when our 2010 Honda Insight going about 2 miles per hour [3 km/h] would not stop when my husband put on the brake. The car crashed into the inside wall of our garage causing damage to the front end of the car, garage wall, and destroyed a sitting bench that was in front of the garage wall. As a passenger in the car, I saw my husband who was driving the car put the brake pedal all the way to the floor and the car would not stop! We had no control of the vehicle, and absolutely no brakes. After we crashed into the garage wall, he placed the car in Reverse and once again the brakes would not stop the car and we ended up in the road. The entire time my husband had the brake pedal to the floor and the car was not stopping. This was the first time we have encountered a problem with the brakes since we purchased our vehicle. We were extremely fortunate that there were no other cars in the road at the time or that we were going 50 mph [80 km/h] down a highway. There are two witnesses other than my husband and myself to this incident. The car was checked by a Honda dealership. Found no problems with the brakes. Blamed it on weather (45 degrees that day) or a thick floor mat could be the cause. Refused to say it was the brakes when my husband and I know it was for a fact it was the brakes or a computer glitch. I was in the car and watched what happened. It was not the floor mat or the weather!

SERVICE BULLETIN-REPORTED PROBLEMS: Tips on improving radio reception.

RATING: Recommended. **Strong points:** The 2011 CR-V has a slightly more-powerful, smoother-running 4-banger that gives more power than some competitors' similar small engines. Still, owners could use a bit more grunt for merging. Fuel economy and handling are fairly good—especially with standard electronic stability control (though Honda's ESC system does have some drawbacks)—but gas mileage is less than what Honda touts. The ride is firm but comfortable, with communicative steering, progressive brake pedal feel, and a 5-speed automatic transmission that performs flawlessly. The lift-up tailgate is much more convenient than the swing-out version used in previous years. More legroom than ever before, thanks to the roomy rear seats that recline and slide independently and fold down to create a flat cargo floor. **Weak points:** Strong sales make for few discounts, unlike Honda's other slow-selling models. No V6, and ABS is a standard feature only as part of the high-trim CR-V EX package. High-speed cornering is not recommended, due to excessive body lean and the cost of replacement tires. Its stopping distance is not the best in its class; the latest restyling has reduced cargo space and visibility; the temperature controls have to

KEY FACTS

CANADIAN PRICE (NEGOTIABLE): *LX:* $26,290, *LX 4WD:* $28,290, *EX:* $29,490, *EX 4WD:* $31,490, *EX-L 4WD:* $33,490, *EX-L Navi. 4WD:* $31,490 **U.S. PRICE:** *LX:* $21,545, *LX 4WD:* $22,795, *EX:* $23,845, *EX 4WD:* $25,095, *EX-L:* $26,495, *EX-L 4WD:* $27,745 **CANADIAN FREIGHT:** $1,400 **U.S. FREIGHT:** $750 **POWERTRAIN (FRONT-DRIVE/AWD)** Engine: 2.4L 4-cyl. (180 hp); Transmission: 5-speed auto. **DIMENSIONS/CAPACITY** Passengers: 2/3; Wheelbase: 103.1 in.; H: 66.1/L: 177.8/W: 71.6 in.; Headroom F/R: 4.0/4.0 in.; Legroom F/R: 40.1/ 29.0 in.; Cargo volume: 25.5 cu. ft.; Fuel tank: 50L/regular; Tow limit: 1,500 lb.; Load capacity: 850 lb.; Turning circle: 39 ft.; Ground clearance: 7.2 in.; Weight: 3,404 lb.

be reset each time (an analog dash would be more user-friendly); and Honda still needs to tweak the powertrain controls to correct a serious problem with hesitation right before acceleration that crops up from time to time in owner reports. The mirrors are skewed in a way that makes it difficult to park; the steering is still a bit stiff; the ride is bumpy at times; and annoying highway noises are omnipresent when at cruising speeds. **New for 2011:** A virtual rerun of the 2010 model; however, the 2.4L, 4-cylinder engine gets a 14 hp increase, bringing the total up to 180 hp.

OVERVIEW: One of Honda's few bestsellers during these hard economic times, the CR-V has distanced itself from the Toyota Sienna and enhanced the driving experience by making a driver-communicative SUV that is as reliable as it is cheap to service. This is a driver's car, with a peppy, fuel-saving 4-cylinder engine that has sufficient power for most occasions (okay, going uphill fully loaded isn't the 4-banger's forte) and sips gas. You always feel in control, contrary to the experience in many of the larger SUVs where the vehicle cocoons the driver into a quasi-somnolent state.

The 2009 redesign improvements made the CR-V equally manoeuvrable in tight quarters as on winding roads, and it doesn't get blown about as much in stiff crosswinds when cruising. The Real Time 4WD system works well on slippery roads, where the feature automatically engages the wheels for maximum traction. Another interesting high-tech improvement is the Grade Logic Control, which automatically downshifts or upshifts when driving up or down a hill. Also, Honda has reduced engine idle vibration and noise.

COST ANALYSIS: Buying a cheaper 2010 model will get you virtually the same equipment and give you the same overall performance as a more-expensive 2011 version. On the other hand, if you wait until mid-2011, you will get a discounted 2011 model and fewer factory-induced bugs (later versions work out the first six months of design and workmanship deficiencies). **Best alternatives:** The $27,790 CR-V remains one of the most reliable and easiest to drive small SUVs around. Its biggest competitor is the $26,500 Toyota RAV4. If you don't mind going downscale a bit, consider a Hyundai Tucson. **Options:** Get a free extra set of ignition keys written into the contract; Honda's anti-start, theft-protection keys may cost as much as $150 per set. Steer clear of the standard-issue radio and Continental, Firestone, or Bridgestone tires. **Rebates:** Not likely. **Depreciation:** Much slower than average. **Insurance cost:** Average. **Parts supply/cost:**

Reasonably priced and easily found at dealers and independent suppliers. **Annual maintenance cost:** Much less than average. **Warranty:** Bumper-to-bumper 3 years/60,000 km; powertrain 5 years/100,000 km; rust perforation 6 years/unlimited km. **Supplementary warranty:** Not needed. **City/highway fuel economy:** *Front-drive:* 9.8/7.1 L/100 km, 29/40 mpg. *AWD:* 10.1/7.5 L/100 km, 28/38 mpg. With this year's increased horsepower, expect a tad less fuel economy.

OWNER-REPORTED PROBLEMS: Owners have found safety-related failures that involve sudden unintended acceleration, electrical system shorts, premature brake wear, and the vehicle's design. Examples include airbags that fail to deploy, an AC condenser that's destroyed by road debris (a chronic failure on most of Honda's lineup), bent wheel studs that can easily snap, brake rotors that wear out prematurely, windshield washer nozzles that freeze up in cold weather, engine oil pan leaks, and a serious right rear blind spot:

> I have serious visibility problems when backing up and changing lanes in heavy traffic.... I backed into a sign pole in a parking lot in mid April, damaging the rear right corner of the vehicle. Two days ago, while I was very slowly and carefully backing out of a parking space, I came very close to a woman pushing a baby in a cart.

There's also a malfunctioning traction control:

> Traction control doesn't work well during winter. It doesn't work well too when the vehicle is parked on a parking that slopes up with about 6 inches [15 cm] of snow. I was in a hurry to go to work but I got towed the first time when my 2008 CRV was only 5 months old because it could not go forward when it was in the parking that slopes up even if I already plowed the snow. It could only reverse but didn't want to go forward.

Poor stability and rapid tread wear with Continental original-equipment tires:

> Continental OEM tire on Honda CRV causes vehicle to slide out of control on snow covered roads and constantly lose traction in rear. We have had numerous near accidents because of the poorly designed low rated tires. My wife is afraid of driving the CRV now. Two Honda dealers inspected vehicle for possible vehicle stability assist problem and both dealers confirmed that VSA was functioning properly. Dealer #2 stated that he had similar issues with other CRV owners because of the tires. Looking at tire reviews on line the Continental Contact 4×4 is rated as a very poor tire that wears out very quickly and with similar issues as I have stated. Even the authorized Continental dealer in my area says the tires are poor quality and has rarely seen them make 20,000 miles [32,187 km].

Omnipresent vibrations, rattles, noisy seatbelt retractors, and a "popping" sound:

> The 1st 2010 CR-V that we test drove had a random popping sound coming from behind the glove compartment when the AC was turned on. We asked the dealer for another car. This car seemed to be fine and we purchased it. After driving it about 100 miles [160 km] the popping noise started on this car too. When the AC is on I

get random popping noise behind the AC controls/glove compartment. Other times it will just pop when stopping. It might be something that's assembled incorrectly, and makes a popping noise as the plastic parts expand or contract when the A/C cycles on/off. I found several complaints that describe the exact same symptoms: *http://www.hondasuv.com/members/showthread.php?T=50417*; *http://www.hondasuv.com/members/showthread.php?p=435971*; *http://www.crvownersclub.com/forums/showthread.php?p=79026*

•

I unfortunately discovered a very annoying problem with the front passenger's seat belt retractor. Similar to the problem discussed in the Honda service bulletin 05-073, "A squeak or rattle is heard from the seat belt retractors while driving over bumps or rough roads." My problem comes from the front passenger seat and not the rear seats. I contacted the dealer I purchased the vehicle from, and they said the problem cannot be repaired. However, the service bulletin 05-073 states the issue was remedied by installing a rubber floor boot to insulate the retractors from the body.

SERVICE BULLETIN-REPORTED PROBLEMS: Tips on improving radio reception.

ACCORD, CROSSTOUR ★★★★

The Honda Accord.

RATING: *Accord:* Above Average. *Crosstour:* Above Average. The Accord is no longer the benchmark for dependability and performance in the family-sedan niche. In 1997, *Lemon-Aid* concluded that Toyota was "decontenting'" its vehicles, giving owners less quality to keep prices down. We subsequently lowered our rating for Toyota. Today, it appears that Honda has adopted the same strategy and is coasting on its past reputation for high-quality vehicles. We have lowered Honda's rating as well. **Strong points:** This is a driver's car, while its primary competitor, the Toyota Camry, is basically the Japanese version of your dad's Oldsmobile. One of the largest mid-sized cars on the market, the Accord provides excellent acceleration with all engines. It's roomy and well-equipped with user-friendly instruments and controls as well as a telescoping steering column. The car handles and rides well, thanks to large tires, a sturdy chassis, and standard stability control. NHTSA crashworthiness scores for front, side, and rollover protection were five, four, and five stars, respectively. The Accord was also given a "Good" rating by IIHS for head-restraint effectiveness, frontal offset, and side-impact protection. *Crosstour:* Responsive handling, a comfortable ride, and a car-like driving position. **Weak points:** Mediocre fuel economy with the V6, and some road noise intrusion into the cabin area. An astoundingly high number of performance and reliability defects on the 2009–10 models, with apparently biodegradable brakes topping the list. Annoying windshield dash reflection; distorted windshields; and creaks and rattles. Many owner reports of airbags that explode for no reason or fail to deploy, brake failures, and sudden unintended acceleration. *Crosstour:* Limited rear visibility, strut towers intrude into storage space, and the sloping rear end styling compromises the Crosstour's utility. For example: The current design provides 27.7 cubic feet (seats up) and 51.3 cubic feet (seats down) of storage space. A more-practical rear end design could raise those numbers considerably. **New for 2011:** Nothing earth-shattering: A mild facelift and new standard and optional features. Fuel economy is improved a bit on the 4-cylinder engine; SE model replaces the base LX model; alloy wheels, eight-way power driver's seat, Bluetooth connectivity, automatic headlamps, and security system are standard on all models. Six-CD stereo and USB audio interface are standard on all EX models and above.

OVERVIEW: A well-designed family car, the Accord was last revamped in 2008 and jumped leagues ahead of the competition by giving owners superior road performance and a roomy interior with loads of safety and convenience features thrown in. Too bad build quality and reliability deteriorated following that last redesign. Now, three model years later, Honda has made slight improvements to the revamped models and added the Crosstour, a versatile crossover utility vehicle with refined styling. The state of quality control is still an unknown.

KEY FACTS

CANADIAN PRICE (NEGOTIABLE): *Accord Coupe EX:* $27,790, *EX-L:* $30,090, *EX-L Navi.:* $32,090, *EX-L V6:* $34,890, *EX-L V6 Navi.:* $36,890; *Accord Crosstour EX-L:* $34,900, *EX-L 4WD:* $36,900, *EX-L 4WD Navi.:* $38,900 **U.S. PRICE:** *Accord Coupe LX-S: $22,555, EX:* $23,880, *EX-L:* $26,880, *EX-L Navi.:* $28,880, *EX-L V6:* $29,305, *EX-L V6 Navi.:* $31,305; *Accord Crosstour EX:* $29,670, *EX-L:* $32,570, *EX-L 4WD Navi.:* $34,770 **CANADIAN FREIGHT:** $1,395 **U.S. FREIGHT:** $750
POWERTRAIN (ACCORD FRONT-DRIVE)
Engines: 2.4L 4-cyl. (177 hp) • 2.4L 4-cyl. (190 hp) • 3.5L V6 (271 hp); Transmissions: 5-speed man. • 5-speed auto. • 6-speed man.
DIMENSIONS/CAPACITY (ACCORD SEDAN)
Passengers: 2/3; Wheelbase: 110.2 in.; H: 58.1/L: 194.0/W: 72.6 in.; Headroom F/R: 6.5/3.5 in.; Legroom F/R: 41.5/30 in.; Cargo volume: 14 cu. ft.; Fuel tank: 65L/regular; Tow limit: 1,500 lb.; Load capacity: 850 lb.; Turning circle: 37.7 ft.; Weight: 3,236–3,298 lb.
POWERTRAIN (CROSSTOUR FWD/4WD)
Engine: V6 (271 hp); Transmission: 5-speed auto.
DIMENSIONS/CAPACITY (CROSSTOUR SEDAN)
Passengers: 2/3; Wheelbase: 110.1 in.; H: 58.1/L: 196.8/W: 74.7 in.; Headroom F/R: 6.5/3.5 in.; Legroom F/R: 41.5/30 in.; Cargo volume: 25.7 cu. ft.; Fuel tank: 65L/regular; Tow limit: 1,500 lb.; Load capacity: 850 lb.; Turning circle: 40.2 ft.; Ground clearance: 8.1 in.; Weight: 3,852–4,070 lb.

If you want good fuel economy and performance with a conventional powertrain, choose one of the two 4-cylinder engines. The V6 is a bit of a gas hog and is needed only for highway travel with a full load. Ride comfort and responsive handling are assured by a suspension and steering set-up that enhances driver control. And what about space? Accord sedans are roomier than ever before, with interior dimensions and capacity that provide more interior space than you'll likely need.

Fast and nimble without a V6, this is the mid-sized sedan of choice for drivers who want maximum fuel economy and comfort along with lots of space for grocery hauling and occasional highway cruising. With the optional V6, the Accord is one of the most versatile mid-sized cars you can find. It offers something for everyone, and its high resale value means there's no way you can lose money buying one.

Accord Crosstour

The year-old Crosstour is billed as a "crossover utility vehicle," which is Honda-speak for a high-riding hatchback family station wagon equipped with four-wheel-drive capability. This five-seater Accord spin-off is equipped similarly to the Acura 2010 ZDX four-door sport coupe. There is a disappointing 25.7 cubic feet of cargo space (just double the size of the Accord's trunk) and 51.3 cubic feet with the rear seatbacks folded; this is less than the Toyota Venza, Nissan Murano, and Subaru Outback, which each have more than 60 cubic feet of cargo space. It is 300 to 500 pounds heavier than the Accord, depending on whether you choose the base or AWD model.

COST ANALYSIS: Get the latest 2011 model; the small upgrades are worth more than the expected small price increase. Furthermore, since the MSRP is quite soft, this year's price increase can likely be whittled down to nothing—*with* an extended warranty thrown in. Crosstour prices are expected to plummet due to its unique rear-end styling (hello, Pontiac Aztek?) and limited cargo space. **Best alternatives:** BMW 3 Series, Hyundai Elantra and Sonata, Mazda6, and Toyota Camry (only with the brake override feature); *Crosstour:* Nissan Murano, Subaru Outback, and Toyota Venza. **Options:** The V6 gives a smoother ride and has lots of reserve power for passing and merging, though the 4-banger will do for most driving needs. The DVD navigation with voice control found on the EX and V6 coupe is a bit gimmicky, but it's easier to use and understand than most of the competition's systems. **Rebates:** Not likely, except for some attractive leasing and financing deals. *Crosstour:* Look for $3,000–$5,000 sales incentives as Honda tries to jumpstart sales through incentives. **Depreciation:** Slower than average for all models. **Insurance cost:** Higher than average. **Parts supply/cost:** Good availability, and moderately priced. **Annual maintenance cost:** Less than average. **Warranty:** Bumper-to-bumper 3 years/60,000 km; powertrain 5 years/100,000 km; rust perforation 5 years/unlimited km. **Supplementary warranty:** Not needed. The less you deal with "headquarters," the better off you'll be. **City/highway fuel economy:** *2.4L 4-cylinder auto.:* 8.8/5.8 L/100 km, 39/42 mpg (with fuel-saving feature). *3.5L V6 6-speed man.:* 12.6/7.8 L/100 km, 36/22 mpg (with fuel-saving feature). *Auto.:* 11/6.7 L/100 km, 42/26 mpg (with fuel-saving feature). *Crosstour auto. 2WD:* 11.5/7.2 L/100 km, 25/39 mpg (with fuel-saving feature). *Auto. 4WD:* 12.3/8.0 L/100 km, 23/35 mpg (with fuel-saving feature).

OWNER-REPORTED PROBLEMS: Until the 2008 revamping, each Accord model year would usually have a few dozen reliability problems reported by owners to various government agencies and to *Lemon-Aid*; however, this is no longer the case. Honda's 2009 Accord has an incredible 194 consumer complaints logged by NHTSA alone, a number which is over four times the complaint average for most vehicles. The safety-related incidents mostly concern powertrain, brake, and body defects. Yet the 2010 models show barely a couple dozen complaints, leading one to conclude that either Honda fixed many of the factory-related glitches or the problems are still ticking away, waiting to fail when the 18-month mark is reached.

Here are some of the most-dangerous and most-frequent problems reported: Sudden unintended acceleration; spontaneous shattering of the sunroof; steering wheel locked up when making a left-hand turn; allegedly dangerous steering design:

> I went to purchase a 4-cylinder 2010 Honda Accord. I [noticed] that steering system was completely unacceptable and unsafe. I used to be a steering engineer hence know the system expectations. I did not buy the vehicle. Steering does not return to center. I drove my friend's car and it has the same issue. Someone can get really hurt. This is typically a safety to fuel economy tradeoff engineering choice. I do not work in auto industry anymore but wanted government to investigate this issue.

Chronic premature wearout of the front and rear brake pads (especially the rear pads). Loud and constant brake squealing (not a brake rotor/pad failure):

> Dealer has checked to be sure there has not been a re-design of pads—and there has not been. A check on *Consumer Reports* web site under the forum for Honda shows this is a widespread problem. Although most got at least 12 to 15 thousand miles [19,000–24,000 km], I live in hills which may explain part of the difference. Having to replace rear brake pads every 9,000 or 10,000 miles [14,500 or 16,000 km] is a safety problem.

A popping/knocking front suspension or steering rack noise; seatback digs into driver's back:

> The seats on the 2010 Honda Accord EX 4-cyl which I just purchased new are so constructed that after driving it I have had to consult my doctor and receive extensive treatment from a physical therapist!

Leaking fuel pump; engine cylinders shut down at the wrong time/speed:

> Car was also shutting the cylinders down at 30 mph [50 km/h], not the 55 mph [90 km/h] it was designed to do to save fuel. It was returned to us and 3 days later

started doing it again. Returned to dealer and was told it had the wrong plugs in it. They changed the plugs and returned the Accord to us. We drove the car about 90 miles [145 km], and it started, again.

Hole in AC condenser likely caused by road debris; metal creaking sound around the rear shelf deck likely due to broken spot welds in the rear shelf of the car; when the AC is activated, the headlights and interior lighting dim or flicker; and remote door locking and unlocking failures. Crosstour rear visibility obstructed:

2010 Honda Accord Crosstour design defect impedes proper rear view vision. The rear window of the vehicle has a heavy bar running horizontally in the middle of the window. The bar may have been required for the structure of the rear door, but it substantially blocked the rear vision for the driver.

SERVICE BULLETIN-REPORTED PROBLEMS: Inoperative keyless remote; poor radio reception remedy; and brake judder or squealing:

FRONT BRAKE JUDDER OR SQUEALING NOISES

BULLETIN NO.: 09-096   DATE: DECEMBER 24, 2009

FRONT BRAKES JUDDER AND/OR SQUEAL
2008–10 ACCORD
SYMPTOM: When the brakes are applied normally, the driver feels a juddering vibration through the steering wheel or brake pedal, and/or hears a squealing noise.
CORRECTIVE ACTION: Refinish the front brake discs, and install new brake pads with V-springs.

ODYSSEY ★★★★

RATING: Above Average. The Odyssey outclasses the Toyota Sienna in driving pleasure and is just a bit more reliable. In a Sienna, the driver is "driven"; in an Odyssey, the driver does the driving by being more actively involved in the overall performance of the vehicle. There have, however, been frequent reports of safety- and performance-related failures on previous-year Odysseys, and this is likely to be more of a problem as the redesigned model hits the showrooms. Of particular concern are airbag malfunctions, brake defects leading to sudden brake loss, and the frequent replacement of the brake calipers and rotors. **Strong points:** Plenty of power for high-speed merging; a spacious, versatile, and quiet interior; and numerous safety and convenience features. Plenty of mid-range torque means less shifting when the engine is under load. Car-like ride and handling; plenty of interior space; comfortable seats; second-row middle seats can be folded down as an armrest or removed completely, much like the middle-row captain's chairs, which can slide fore or aft, in unison or separately; second-row power windows; floor-stowable, 60/40 split third-row seats; easy back seat entry and exit; a convenient second driver-side door and a power tailgate; an extensive list

of standard equipment; most controls and displays are easy to reach and read. The Odyssey also has standard vehicle stability assist and traction control to prevent rollovers and enhance handling; side curtain airbags with rollover sensors for all rows; and adjustable brake and accelerator pedals. NHTSA gives the 2010 Odyssey five stars for front and side crashworthiness and four stars for rollover protection. IIHS says head restraints offer "Good" protection to occupants, and also gives a "Good" frontal and side protection rating. **Weak points:** Fuel consumption isn't as low as Honda promises, despite its innovative cylinder deactivation system. Unlike with the Sienna, all-wheel drive isn't available; middle-row seats don't fold flat like in other minivans, so they need to be stowed somewhere else; second-row head restraints block visibility; front-passenger legroom is marginal, owing to the restricted seat travel; you can't slide your legs comfortably under the dash; some passengers bump their shins on the glove box; it's difficult to calibrate the radio without taking your eyes off the road; some tire rumble, rattles, and body drumming at highway speeds; and rear-seat head restraints impede side and rear visibility. The storage well won't take any tire larger than a "space saver," meaning you'll carry your flat in the back. **New for 2011:** 2011s have been redesigned to incorporate the following changes: a restyled interior and wider/lower exterior, with the reworked front end taking its cue from the Accord Crosstour (frog-eye headlights are gone); a rear "lightning bolt" window line that dips down at the far rear side windows; more user-friendly instruments and controls; and a wider interior that permitted Honda to install a multi-configurable second-row bench seat that spreads the seats out and uses a total of five latch positions for child seats, as well as more-ample third-row seats. If you need extra cargo space, you can easily fold the third row seats, add the cargo, and bring the kids up into the second row. Additional comfort and infotainment features include an HDMI port; a wide screen to play one movie for all or play two separate video feeds simultaneously (copying Toyota's Sienna); a removable console with a hidden bin; and a small cooler in the central stack of the dash. Honda also boasts that not only has its 4-cylinder engine fuel economy improved on the 2011 model, but its 3.5L V6 will be more fuel-frugal than the Sienna's 4-banger, giving Odyssey owners 19 mpg in the city and a hard-to-believe 28 mpg on the highway. The brakes are larger, and independent rear suspension has been added.

OVERVIEW: The Odyssey has a lean look, but the interior is wide and long enough to accommodate most large objects. Sliding doors are offered as standard equipment, and if you buy the EX version, they will both be power-assisted. The Odyssey is powered by a competent V6, which includes variable cylinder deactivation to increase fuel economy. Gas consumption may be cut up to 10 percent by the engine's ability to automatically switch between 6-cylinder and 3-cylinder activation, depending on engine load.

COST ANALYSIS: Because sales have been slow over the past year, Honda dealers are discounting their 2010s by as much as 20 percent through lower transaction prices and attractive lease/loan programs; the upgraded 2011 is expected to cost about 10 percent less once the fall hoopla dies down. Make sure you have a specific delivery date spelled out in the contract, along with a protected price, in case there's a price increase while you're waiting for delivery. **Best alternatives:** If you want better handling and reliability, the closest competitor to the Odyssey is Toyota's Sienna minivan. One major difference between the two models is the seating. Toyota's are like La-Z Boy armchairs and are a chore to remove. Honda seats are more basic and are easier to install or remove. The Mazda5 and Chrysler's Caravan are acceptable choices for different reasons: This year's redesigned Mazda5 has less room but burns less fuel (without a high-tech engine add-on), and Chrysler's minivans aren't as reliable as the Odyssey or Mazda but offer better prices, lots of room for people and things, and plenty of convenience and safety features. The Kia Sedona minivan is also a decent choice. If you're looking for lots of towing "grunt" and plenty of usable space, rear-drive GM full-sized vans are fairly reliable vehicles that often carry sizeable discounts that will get larger as we get into 2011, or when fuel prices uptick. Try to resist the gimmicky video entertainment, DVD navigation system, and expensive leather seats. See if you can trade the original-equipment Firestone or Bridgestone tires for something better (check with *www.tirerack.com*). **Rebates:** Any patient haggler will get a few thousand dollars cut from the base price; your goal should be to get at least 10 percent taken off of the MSRP. Low-cost financing and leasing programs will also help bring down the transaction price. **Depreciation:** About average. A 2006 LX Odyssey that originally sold for $33,200 is now worth about $14,000. **Insurance cost:** Higher than average. **Annual maintenance cost:** Average. **Parts supply/**

cost: Moderately priced parts; availability is better than average because the Odyssey uses many generic Accord parts. CVT transmission and cylinder deactivation parts may be costly and may not available outside the Honda dealer network. **Warranty:** Bumper-to-bumper 3 years/60,000 km; powertrain 5 years/100,000 km; rust perforation 5 years/unlimited km. **Supplementary warranty:** Not needed. **City/highway fuel economy:** 13.3/8.5 L/100 km, 21/33 mpg. *EX-L & Touring:* 12.3/7.8 L/100 km, 23/36 mpg.

OWNER-REPORTED PROBLEMS: Airbags didn't deploy after a severe rear-ender; airbag cover warps; early engine failure:

> 2010 Honda Odyssey engine defect causes it to fail and cease operation while driving, having the driver lose the ability to fully control the vehicle. Defect is in the oil supply to the overhead camshaft causing it to seize and breaking the timing belt. Much upper end engine damage.

Engine surges to 6000 rpms in Neutral with both feet on the brakes; automatic transmission breakdowns; transmission slams into gear or suddenly locks in low gear while the vehicle is underway; steering pulls continually to the right; malfunction indicator lamp (MIL) comes on for no reason; windshield shattered on its own; excessive wind noise from the passenger and driver pillar area; poor paint job; third-row folding seat collapsed and broke a child's fingers; many complaints of road debris destroying the AC condenser; premature front brake wear and excessive brake grinding noise are common problems that afflict all Hondas, but the 2007–08 brake system is particularly vulnerable; sudden brake loss after the VSA light comes on (some dealers suggest unplugging the VSA); brake loss when backing out of a parking lot; brake pedal sinks to the floor; and a history of mushy braking:

> Have just bought a 2010 Honda Odyssey on October 16, 2009. On January 16, 2010, I was driving in New York City traffic stopped at a light behind several cars. Suddenly the car's engine started to race and lurched forward even with my foot on the brake. For several seconds the car kept lurching forward as I tried to step down on the brake even harder. As suddenly, the unintended acceleration stopped. I came within inches of crashing into the car in front of me. I have four passengers in the car who witnessed this event at the time.

•

> We noticed the brakes appeared to be soft and spongy. When I finally took it in for service, I was told it needed a new master cylinder (at 2,800 miles [4,500 km]), which they replaced. After I picked it up, I drove it a few miles and the brakes still felt soft and spongy, so I drove back to the dealership. The service manager then drove the car and told me, "That's the way the Odyssey brakes are."

SERVICE BULLETIN-REPORTED PROBLEMS: Front door glass opens/closes slowly and sticks, and remedy for poor radio reception.

KEY FACTS

CANADIAN PRICE (NEGOTIABLE): *LX:* $26,990, *SC:* $31,690, *EX 4WD:* $32,090 **U.S. PRICE:** *LX:* $20,525, *SC:* $24,320 **CANADIAN FREIGHT:** $1,395 **U.S. FREIGHT:** $750
POWERTRAIN (FRONT-DRIVE/AWD)
Engine: 2.4L 4-cyl. (166 hp); Transmission: 5-speed auto.
DIMENSIONS/CAPACITY
Passengers: 2/2; Wheelbase: 101.3 in.; H: 70.3/L: 169.9/W: 77.1 in.; Headroom F/R: 7.5/2.0 in.; Legroom F/R: 41/31 in.; Cargo volume: 74.5 cu. ft.; Fuel tank: 80L/regular; Tow limit: 1,500 lb.; Load capacity: 675 lb.; Turning circle: 36 ft.; Ground clearance: 7.0 in.; Weight: 3,527 lb.

RATING: Above Average. **Strong points:** Easy handling; standard electronic stability control and side curtain airbags; wide doorways make loading and unloading cargo a breeze; a spacious interior and washable floor; good fit and finish; all seats fold back to make a small bed; and versatile rear seats can fold to the side or be removed completely. NHTSA-tested crashworthiness is rated five stars for front and side occupant protection and three stars for rollover protection. IIHS says frontal offset protection, side-impact protection, and head restraint effectiveness are "Good." **Weak points:** The automatic transmission hobbles the 4-cylinder engine; a stiff, jerky ride; large roof pillars obstruct outward visibility; driving position is uncomfortable for some; the rear-hinged rear side doors don't open independently of the front doors; and excessive road noise. With both the Element and the Pilot, Honda maintains a death grip on dated boxy styling that screams out, "I am old!" **New for 2011:** An improved suspension, upgraded shock absorbers, and better brakes.

OVERVIEW: Based on the Honda Civic platform, the Element is a small, boxy SUV that is more of a cargo-hauler than a passenger-carrier. This doesn't take away the fact that the vehicle comes well-appointed and is powerful enough with its 4-banger and automatic transmission to accomplish most driving chores.

COST ANALYSIS: Element sales are now less than half what they were in 2008. Hungry dealers will haggle, so get the upgraded 2011 version in mid-2011 to snare the most sales incentives (about 10 percent) and get a better-quality second-series model. **Best alternatives:** Try to get your mind around a less-quirky-looking and more-versatile wagon or hatchback, like the Chevrolet HHR, Honda Fit, Hyundai Elantra, Kia Rondo or Soul, Mazda5, Nissan Versa, Suzuki SX4, or Toyota Matrix (only with the brake override feature). **Options:** Be wary of poorly performing Bridgestone and Firestone original-equipment tires. **Rebates:** Good leasing and low-finance deals; discounts of about 10 percent. **Depreciation:** Average; a 2006 that went for $24,000 new now sells for $12,500. **Insurance cost:** Average. **Annual maintenance cost:** Average. **Parts supply/cost:** Parts are easy to find and relatively inexpensive. **Warranty:** Bumper-to-bumper 3 years/60,000 km; powertrain 5 years/100,000 km; rust perforation 5 years/unlimited km. **Supplementary warranty:** Not necessary. **City/highway fuel economy:** *Front-drive:* 10.5/8.1 L/100 km, 27/35 mpg. *AWD:* 11.0/8.3 L/100 km, 26/34 mpg.

OWNER-REPORTED PROBLEMS: Reliability has proven to be much better than average. Nevertheless, you can expect problems with the premature wearout of key brake components (preceded by mushy braking), mysterious windshield cracks, and malfunctioning tire-pressure sensors.

SERVICE BULLETIN-REPORTED PROBLEMS: Repair for poor radio reception.

PILOT ★★★★

RATING: Above Average. The second-generation Pilot has grown into a large-sized people-carrier that offers a comfortable ride, first-class handling, and plenty of passenger space. **Strong points:** Adequate power for highway cruising; superb handling; a versatile interior; seating for up to eight; the third-row seat folds flat into sections to free up storage space; and there's a small storage area in the floor.

KEY FACTS

CANADIAN PRICE (NEGOTIABLE): *LX:* $36,820, *LX 4WD:* $39,820, *EX 4WD:* $42,720, *EX-L 4WD:* $45,020, *EX-L res 4WD:* $46,620, *Touring 4WD:* $50,420 **U.S. PRICE:** *LX:* $28,045, *LX 4WD:* $29,645, *EX:* $30,895, *EX 4WD:* $32,495, *EX-L:* $33,395, *EX-L 4WD:* $35,595, *Touring 4WD:* $38,795 **CANADIAN FREIGHT:** $1,395 **U.S. FREIGHT:** $750

POWERTRAIN (FRONT-DRIVE/AWD)

Engine: 3.5L V6 (250 hp); Transmission: 5-speed auto.

DIMENSIONS/CAPACITY

Passengers: 2/3/3; Wheelbase: 109.2 in.; H: 71.0/L: 190.9/W: 78.5 in.; Headroom: F/R1/R2: 40/39.8/38.2 in.; Legroom: F/R1/R2: 41.4/38.5/32.1 in.; Cargo volume: 18 cu. ft.; Fuel tank: 79.5L/ regular; Tow limit: 3,500–4,500 lb.; Load capacity: 1,320 lb.; Turning circle: 36.7 ft.; Ground clearance: 8.0 in.; Weight: 4,319 lb.

Chock full of safety and convenience features and earning good crashworthiness scores (a four-star overall rating, four stars for frontal and rollover protection, five stars for side protection, and "Good" head-restraint protection). Overall reliability has been excellent. The Pilot also has standard vehicle stability assist and traction control to prevent rollovers and enhance handling, side curtain airbags with rollover sensors for all rows, and adjustable brake and accelerator pedals. Fuel consumption can be improved by using the V6 engine's cylinder-shut-off system. The GPS and voice operation feature are easy to use—with a little practice. **Weak points:** Mediocre acceleration accompanied by some torque steer; so-so braking; and a boxy exterior. Unimpressive fuel economy—the much-heralded cylinder deactivation system doesn't save as much fuel as Honda fantasizes, and it makes the vehicle seriously underpowered. Suspension lacks the ability to effectively absorb bumps or shocks. Interior plastic materials and overall fit and finish aren't up to Honda's reputation for quality, and road noise is omnipresent. The centre console can be a little confusing to operate until you've studied it a little while. Honda also needs to make the radio and AC operation more user-friendly, with fewer buttons. **New for 2011:** Carried over practically unchanged; the rear entertainment system becomes standard equipment on Touring models.

OVERVIEW: It's the mouse that roars. The Pilot is truck-like on the outside, but it's a much tamer vehicle when you look closely. It combines car-like comfort and handling in a crossover package where ride comfort, utility, and passenger accommodations are foremost.

COST ANALYSIS: Dealers are willing to dicker over prices, leases, and financing due to Honda's poor sales during the past year. Unsold 2010 Pilots are also eligible for all kinds of automaker incentives that will drive down the 2011 model prices. Be prepared to walk away if salespeople won't haggle. **Best alternatives:** GM's heavily discounted Tahoe and Yukon SUVs are selling at bargain prices. **Options:** Nothing essential. **Rebates:** Look for $3,000–$5,000 discounts, attractive low financing rates, and special leasing prices. **Depreciation:** Slower than average. **Insurance cost:** Higher than average. **Annual maintenance cost:** Below average. **Parts supply/cost:** Average availability. Most parts are moderately priced, except for cylinder deactivation components, which may be costly because only Honda dealers sell them. **Warranty:** Bumper-to-bumper 3 years/60,000 km;

powertrain 5 years/100,000 km; rust perforation 5 years/unlimited km. **Supplementary warranty:** A waste of money. **City/highway fuel economy:** *Front-drive:* 12.7/8.7 L/100 km, 22/32 mpg. *AWD:* 13.1/9.1 L/100 km, 22/31 mpg.

OWNER-REPORTED PROBLEMS: Airbags failed to deploy; sudden unintended acceleration and brake failure; mushy brakes; headlights dip too low to be effective; hard-to-read speedometer; excessive side mirror vibrations; and poor wiring design:

> 2010 Honda Pilot Touring hit a bump in the road and the ABS and VSA sensor wires were severed causing both features to be disabled. The sensor wire goes from the middle of the undercarriage to each rear wheel and is totally unprotected. Also, the sensor and wire are one piece and should have a connector rather than one piece so it could be repaired. Additionally, the wire should be encased in a wire conduit (the flexible wire conduit that could be purchased from a parts store).

SERVICE BULLETIN-REPORTED PROBLEMS: Moonroof malfunctions; loose/broken third-row seatback cover; inoperative keyless remote; sun visor falls down; auxiliary power socket comes out of console; front suspension clicking on acceleration/braking; and a fix for poor radio reception.

RIDGELINE ★★★★★

RATING: Recommended. The mid-sized Ridgeline was first launched in Canada as a 2006 model and sold between $35,000 and $42,000; the 2010 model is expected to cost between $34,490 and $42,990. So, in spite of its added equipment over five model years, the pickup costs about the same as its original introductory price, plus it has the best estimated gas mileage in its class. **Strong points:** Some room for price haggling, mostly on financing and leasing deals. Good, quiet acceleration; a smooth-shifting automatic transmission; secure handling

KEY FACTS

CANADIAN PRICE (NEGOTIABLE): *DX:* $34,990, *VP:* $36,690, *EX-L:* $41,490, *EX-L Navi.:* $43,690 **U.S. PRICE:** *RT:* $28,900, *RTS:* $31,605, *RTL:* $34,480, *RTL Navi.:* $36,830 **CANADIAN FREIGHT:** $1,395 **U.S. FREIGHT:** $750

POWERTRAIN (FRONT-DRIVE/4WD)

Engines: 3.5L V6 (250 hp); Transmission: 5-speed auto.

DIMENSIONS/CAPACITY

Passengers: 2/3; Wheelbase: 122 in.; H: 70.3/L: 207/W: 69 in.; Headroom F/R: 6.5/4.5 in.; Legroom F/R: 42/28 in.; Fuel tank: 83.3L/regular; Tow limit: 5,000 lb.; Load capacity: 1,554 lb.; Turning circle: 42.6 ft.; Ground clearance: 7.5 in.; Weight: 4,504 lb.; GVWR: 6,050 lb.

and good cornering control; communicative, direct steering; a comfortable, supple ride; a friendly cabin environment where everything is easily accessed and storage spaces abound; a tailgate that opens either vertically or horizontally; an all-weather, lockable trunk beneath the cargo bed; and no intrusive wheel arch in the five-foot-long bed. Reliability and overall dependability are legendary, and crashworthiness is exemplary. **Weak points:** High sales price; bed is too small for some needs; not well-suited for off-roading; and unusual styling for a pickup. **New for 2011:** This year's redesign will ensure smoother acceleration, provide additional infotainment features, enhance the truck's load-carrying capability, and improve the instrument panel.

OVERVIEW: The Ridgeline mixes performance with convenience. It's an ideal truck for most jobs, as long as you keep it on the highway. Off-road, this unibody pickup offers only medium performance relative to its nearest body-on-frame competitors, the Toyota Tacoma and the Nissan Frontier. Its long wheelbase and independent rear suspension give the Ridgeline an impressive in-bed trunk and excellent road manners but make it difficult for the truck to traverse anything that's rougher than a stone road or has a breakover angle greater than 21 degrees. NHTSA crashworthiness ratings are outstanding: Front and side occupant protection is rated five stars, and rollover protection is given four stars. IIHS gives the 1996–2010 models its top score ("Good") for frontal and side occupation protection and qualifies head-restraint protection as "Good" for all 2009–10 models.

COST ANALYSIS: Go for the 2011 upgrades. Inasmuch as small and mid-sized pickups retain a higher resale value than most cars, this should take the sting out of the higher price you may have paid. **Best alternatives:** Other pickups worth considering are the Nissan Frontier, Toyota Tacoma (only with the brake override feature), Ford F-Series, and the GM Silverado and Sierra duo. **Options:** Firestone and Bridgestone original-equipment tires will not give you the best performance or durability; try to trade them for something better. **Rebates:** Look for $2,500–$4,000 rebates in the winter of 2011. **Depreciation:** Slower than average; a 2006 model is still worth more than half its original price. **Insurance cost:** Higher than average. **Parts supply/cost:** Mostly reasonably priced and easily found at dealers and independent suppliers. Body parts are a bit costly and harder to find. **Annual maintenance cost:** Laughably low. **Warranty:** Bumper-to-bumper 3 years/60,000 km; powertrain 5 years/100,000 km; rust perforation 6 years/unlimited km. **Supplementary warranty:** A waste of money. Less than 50 safety-related incidents have been reported to NHTSA federal investigators within the last four model years, while 200 complaints would be the average for most vehicles. **City/highway fuel economy:** 14.1/9.8 L/100 km, 20/29 mpg.

OWNER-REPORTED PROBLEMS: Vehicle went out of control without either the vehicle stability assist (VSA) or ABS activated; engine surges when coming to a stop; premature failure of the automatic transmission; brake and accelerator pedals are mounted too close together; many AC heater failures due to defective wiring or fan motor switch (one fire reported); centre sliding portion of the rear window exploded for no reason. Snow collects under the wipers while driving and freezes them to the cowl:

> The wipers shut off under the increased momentary load. The only way to get them to reset is to stop, turn the vehicle off and restart it. This is very difficult to do when you are completely blinded with slush looking forward.

Loose tailgate cables cause the tailgate to malfunction; side wall tread suddenly flew off the original-equipment Michelin LTX tires; and the heated seats heat up even when the switch is turned off.

SERVICE BULLETIN-REPORTED PROBLEMS: Steering column ticking and poor radio reception fix.

Hyundai

Americans like Hyundai; Canadians *love* Hyundai. Hyundai regularly beats Honda in Canadian sales, and its Kia subsidiary regularly bests Volkswagen. South of the border, both companies are doing well, but Hyundai is really on a tear in Canada with an extensive, reasonably priced lineup.

Hyundai and Kia are racking up impressive sales across Canada for three reasons: Their vehicles are relatively cheap when compared with the competition, their quality is almost equal to the best that comes from Japan, and owners can count on getting a comprehensive base warranty. Increased sales and positive quality surveys also indicate the company is on a much surer footing than it was in the late '70s, when Hyundai Canada was run by a ragtag gang of Toronto-based auto newbies who had their collective head up their collective exhaust pipes. They made money by dumping cheap but poor-quality Pony, Stellar, and Excel compacts into the market to compete against equally poor-quality American small cars. At that time, Hyundai got an important toe-hold in the North American market because Detroit iron was too expensive and not very fuel-efficient and fuel prices were going through the roof. However, when fuel became relatively cheap again, you couldn't give a Hyundai away.

Korean Quality?

Don't laugh. As predicted by *Lemon-Aid* a decade ago, Hyundai is now building cars and minivans that are as reliable and defect-free as the best that Japan offers—and selling them for much less. This quality turnaround has been accomplished through the use of better-made components and corporate espionage. In fact, Hyundai hired away a bevy of Toyota's top quality-control engineers in 2003—and got a satchel-full of Toyota's secret documents in the bargain. Following a cease-and-desist letter from Toyota in 2006, Hyundai returned the pilfered papers. Hyundai says it never looked at the secret reports stolen from Toyota (wink, wink; nudge, nudge), but insiders say the privileged information was a major factor in Hyundai's leapfrogging over the competition with better quality-control systems.

Hyundai and Kia are also copying the successful international marketing strategy that's been employed by Japanese automakers over the past four decades: Secure a solid beachhead in one car segment, and then branch out from there. Models that don't sell get dumped, like the Entourage minivan, Tiburon, and Azera. Hyundai is also sharing components with its Kia subsidiary to keep production costs down while raising quality. Owner surveys of these blended cars indicate that there has been an appreciable rise in quality since the reworked 2006 models arrived. Nevertheless, Kia still has a long ways to go to reach parity with Hyundai's impressive quality control.

If you still have doubts as to Hyundai's car quality, check out the most recent J.D. Power survey reports, or click on NHTSA's online consumer complaints database (*www.safercar.gov*). Here's all you would find on the 2009 entry-level Accent:

2009 HYUNDAI ACCENT L4 1.6L

All Technical Service Bulletins

NUMBER	DATE	TITLE
09-FL-016	10/07/2009	Engine Controls—Rough Idle/Multiple DTCs Set
09-SS-005	09/18/2009	M/T—Creaking Noise At Idle
09-BD-011	09/01/2009	Body—Sunroof Creaking/Ticking Noises
09-AT-013	07/01/2009	A/T—MIL ON/DTCs P0705/P0707/P0708/No Start In P/N
08-SS-004	08/01/2008	Steering/Suspension—Drift/Pull Diagnosis/Repair
08-ST-001	07/30/2008	Steering—Power Steering Pump Whine

That's it—six items, and they're all relatively minor in nature.

The South Koreans are investing heavily in North America as they troll for dealers recently dumped by bankrupt Chrysler and General Motors. They are bringing out an extensive lineup of fuel-efficient new cars, minivans, and SUVs, and are targeting increasingly upscale customers without forgetting their entry-level base. For example, Hyundai recently enhanced its luxury lineup with the 2009 Genesis luxury sedan and a Camaro/Mustang stalker, the 2010 Genesis Coupe. Waiting in the wings is the 2011 Equus, a $70,000, V8-powered rear-drive luxury sedan that is aimed at the BMW 5 Series and the Mercedes-Benz E-Class. The Equus was developed on the rear-drive Genesis sedan platform, but the wheelbase was stretched by 10.9 cm (4.3 in.). It's 29 cm (11.4 in.) longer than the 2010 Mercedes E-Class.

At the other end of the fuel economy spectrum, both Hyundai and Kia intend to launch several new fuel-frugal small cars in the near future and offer drivers fuel-saving options that include a hybrid Sonata, smaller engines, direct-injection gasoline engines, plug-in hybrids, and fuel cell technology. Hyundai calls the fuel economy initiative "Blue Drive": a fancy name for cheaper models with less content, less weight, and more miles per gallon. For example, Blue Edition models have a lower gear ratio and tires with less rolling resistance. Power windows and door locks, as well as other formerly standard amenities, will become optional, thereby trading convenience for cash savings.

ACCENT ★★★★★

best buy

RATING: Recommended, if you're using your Accent primarily as a fuel-sipping urban dweller consigned to occasional forays on the highway. Think of it as a more-refined and peppier Metro/Sprint from South Korea, built for light duty around town. **Strong points:** Reasonably priced and very well-appointed; good fuel economy; adequate engine and automatic transmission performance in most situations; easy handling; a comfortable and quiet ride; a fair amount of interior room; comfortable driving position with good visibility and height-adjustable, form-fitting bucket seats that provide plenty of support; an incredibly good reliability record, with few complaints relative to safety or quality control; and it's cheap on gas. A 5-year/100,000 km bumper-to-bumper warranty. Some impressive but conflicting crashworthiness scores (see the "Weak points"): NHTSA gives the Accent five stars for front-impact protection and four stars for side collision and rollover protection. **Weak points:** Automatic transmission hobbles horsepower;

KEY FACTS

CANADIAN PRICE (NEGOTIABLE):
Hatchback: $9,999, *Sedan:* $10,999
U.S. PRICE: *Hatchback:* $9,970, *Sedan:*
$13,645 **CANADIAN FREIGHT:** $1,595
U.S. FREIGHT: $750
POWERTRAIN (FRONT-DRIVE)
Engine: 1.6L 4-cyl. (110 hp);
Transmissions: 5-speed man. • 4-speed
auto.
DIMENSIONS/CAPACITY
Passengers: 2/3; Wheelbase: 98.4 in.;
H: 57.9/L: 159.3/W: 66.7 in.; Headroom
F/R: 4.5/2.0 in.; Legroom F/R: 40.5/
25.5 in.; Cargo volume: 12 cu. ft.; Fuel
tank: 45L/regular; Tow limit: N/A; Load
capacity: 850 lb.; Turning circle: 36 ft.;
Weight: 2,590 lb.

engine could use a bit more torque and noise-vibration dampening; ride is on the firm side; numb steering feel; and acrobatic rear-seat entry/exit with the hatchback. Frontal offset crash protection rated only "Acceptable" by IIHS, and head restraints and side crash protection were rated "Poor." **New for 2011:** Carried over practically unchanged; a redesign is expected next spring.

OVERVIEW: Accent lends its basic design to the Rio from Hyundai's Kia division, making this front-drive, entry-level sedan one of the cheapest feature-laden small cars sold in North America. Carrying a homegrown 1.6L 4-cylinder engine coupled to a 5-speed manual or 4-speed automatic transmission, the Accent offers bare-bones motoring without sacrificing basic amenities, including AC, a height-adjustable driver's seat with lumbar support, and split-folding rear seats.

COST ANALYSIS: The Accent is hot—and almost impossible to find. No surprise, when one sees the transaction price dipping below $10,000. Buy a practically identical 2009, and haggle down the price without giving up content. Remember, cheaper 2010s mean less equipment. **Best alternatives:** Honda Civic or Fit, Mazda3, Nissan Versa or Sentra, Suzuki SX4, and Toyota Yaris. **Options:** Not needed. **Rebates:** $1,000–$2,000 through low-cost financing, leasing deals, and discounting. **Depreciation:** Slower than average, now that fuel prices are rising. **Insurance cost:** Average. **Parts supply/cost:** Parts aren't hard to find, and they're reasonably priced. **Annual maintenance cost:** Average. **Warranty:** Bumper-to-bumper 5 years/100,000 km; rust perforation 5 years/unlimited km. **Supplementary warranty:** No longer needed, such is the improvement in quality control. **City/highway fuel economy:** *Man.:* 7.2/5.7 L/100 km, 39/50 mpg. *Auto.:* 7.6/5.5 L/100 km, 37/51 mpg.

OWNER-REPORTED PROBLEMS: Airbags failed to deploy; on the freeway, accelerator, brakes, and steering wheel suddenly locked up; car suddenly lost power and misfired when cruising on the highway; engine surging when stopped at a traffic light; delayed automatic transmission engagement; power-steering pump whine; turn signal malfunctions; key sticks in the ignition; and Kumho tire premature wear and blistering. One owner reports that the car's undercarriage cables attract groundhogs who love to snack on them, thereby disabling the tranny and key dash gauges:

> I put down moth balls and fox scent to ward the hogs off, but they love Accent wires; losing the transmission and speedometer can make driving a little dangerous.

SERVICE BULLETIN-REPORTED PROBLEMS: Rough running and creaking noise at idle; power steering whine; sunroof creaking, ticking; and a tendency to drift or pull to one side.

ELANTRA ★★★★

RATING: Above Average. **Strong points:** New 4-cylinder engine delivers adequate (not spectacular) power; smooth-shifting automatic transmission; good handling and a quiet, comfortable ride; electronic stability control comes with the SE trim; well-appointed and spacious interior; comfortable seats; seatback slides far enough back to easily accommodate six-foot-plus drivers; classy, quiet interior; and above-average crashworthiness scores. For example, NHTSA gives the car five stars for frontal crash protection and four stars for side and rollover protection. A good base warranty is standard. **Weak points:** Elantra is showing its age and is in serious need of a more-powerful engine and higher transmission gearing. Not a lot of grunt at low engine rpm; steering feels light; noisy brakes; soft suspension is "floaty," and it dips when passing over rough spots; excessive engine noise when accelerating; some wind noise; brakes are a bit grabby and take some skill to modulate; a narrow trunk opening and a small trunk pass-through; and trunk lid hinges cut available space. **New for 2011:** Not much new this year; next year is when major changes are expected.

KEY FACTS

CANADIAN PRICE (NEGOTIABLE): *L:* $14,999, *L auto.:* $16,199, *GL:* $17,399, *GL auto.:* $18,599, *GLS man.:* $19,799, *GLS auto.:* $20,999, *GLS Sport:* $22,049, *GLS Sport auto.:* $23,249 **U.S. PRICE:** *Base:* $14,145, *GLS auto.:* $16,895, *SE:* $17,845 **CANADIAN FREIGHT:** $1,495 **U.S. FREIGHT:** $750

POWERTRAIN (FRONT-DRIVE)
Engine: 2.0L 4-cyl. (138 hp); Transmissions: 5-speed man. • 4-speed auto.

DIMENSIONS/CAPACITY (TOURING)
Passengers: 2/3; Wheelbase: 106.3 in.; H: 58.3/L: 176.2.4/W: 69.5 in.; Headroom F/R: 2.5/2.0 in.; Legroom F/R: 43.5/35 in.; Cargo volume: 24.3 cu. ft.; Fuel tank: 53L/regular; Tow limit: 2,000 lb.; Load capacity: 850 lb.; Turning circle: 37 ft.; Weight: 2,723 lb.

OVERVIEW: Elantra's unique styling is hard to miss, with its bubbly exterior, fat rear end, unique nose, tall shape, large headlights, and high-mounted tail lights. One big advantage, though, is that the roomy interior pushes the car into the mid-size category. A wagon version, called the Touring, arrived in early 2009, but its extra little goodies don't seem worth the extra cash. A 138 hp 2.0L 4-cylinder powerplant hooked to a 4-speed automatic transmission supplies much-needed power, but there are other cars in this price range that offer more fuel-efficient powertrains. The ride and handling are quite good, owing mainly to the Elantra's long wheelbase and sophisticated suspension.

COST ANALYSIS: Get a discounted 2010 model or wait until next year's upgraded model. **Best alternatives:** The Honda Civic, Hyundai Accent, Mazda3, Suzuki SX4, and Toyota Corolla (only with brake override). **Options:** Electronic stability control is a must-have. Also, opt for the automatic transmission: It's quieter and shifts more smoothly than the manual, and fuel economy isn't much affected. **Rebates:** $2,000 rebates and low-cost financing, mainly because Hyundai doesn't want to lose traction in its sales momentum. **Depreciation:** Slower than average, which is surprising because it's not often that you see a 2007 model South Korean vehicle worth a bit more than half its $15,000 original price. **Insurance cost:** Average. **Parts supply/cost:** Parts are easy to find and reasonably priced, with heavy discounting by independents. **Annual maintenance cost:** Average. **Warranty:** Bumper-to-bumper 5 years/100,000 km; rust perforation 5 years/ unlimited km. **Supplementary warranty:** Not needed. **City/highway fuel economy:** *Man.:* 8.1/5.7 L/100 km, 35/50 mpg. *Auto.:* 7.8/5.8 L/100 km, 36/49 mpg. *Touring man.:* 8.9/6.4 L/100 km, 32/44 mpg. *Touring auto.:* 8.7/6.5 L/100 km, 32/43 mpg.

OWNER-REPORTED PROBLEMS: Airbags failed to deploy:

> My wife and I were involved in an accident. Another car ran the red light and hit us. My wife and I were injured and our car was totaled. None of the airbags went off on our brand new Hyundai Elantra. We were later told by Hyundai that passenger airbags don't always go off because of weight variations in some adults. My wife is 5'4" and her weight is normal for her height.

In another incident, both airbags deployed for no reason; cruise control speed suddenly sped up from 100 to 120 km/h; defective solenoids blamed for early transmission failures; car may roll away even with emergency brake applied; sudden steering lock-up; brakes freeze up when vehicle is driven through snow; cruise control suddenly resets itself to a higher speed; throttle sensor sticks when cruising; chronic stalling, believed to be a fuel-pump-related problem; Airbag light and tire-pressure monitoring system alert come on for no reason; and in-dash front panel squeaks.

SERVICE BULLETIN-REPORTED PROBLEMS: Automatic transmission malfunctions; harsh transmission shifts and defaults to "safe" mode (change the input or output speed sensor); front end noise; cellphone troubleshooting; anti-theft system self-activates; and sunroof creaking, ticking.

SONATA ★★★★

RATING: Above Average. The 2009 model's engine and interior refinements gave the Sonata all of the safety and performance features it needs to play in the big leagues against Japan's and Detroit's family sedans. **Strong points:** A credible alternative to most Detroit-bred family cars, and it's priced at thousands of dollars less. Well equipped and stylish; sizzling V6 power, and it burns only a bit more than the 4-banger does; good handling; comfortable ride; user-friendly controls and gauges; spacious trunk, and a conveniently low lift-in height; fairly quiet cabin that seats three comfortably in the back; and much-improved quality control. NHTSA awarded the Sonata four stars for front-impact occupant protection and five stars for rollover resistance and side-impact protection. IIHS gave the Sonata a "Good" rating for front offset protection, head-restraint effectiveness, and side-impact protection. Owners also get a comprehensive base warranty. **Weak points:** Prices have been boosted by a couple thousand dollars during the past few years; fuel economy could be better; the suspension is somewhat bouncy and noisy; lots of body lean under hard cornering; and the steering lacks feedback. **New for 2011:** A hybrid-powertrain-equipped 2011 model is expected to arrive at the end of 2010.

OVERVIEW: This is the mid-sized sedan that Hyundai should have built years ago. Sure, incremental engine and suspension improvements over the years made the

KEY FACTS

CANADIAN PRICE (NEGOTIABLE): *GL:* $22,649, *GL auto.:* $24,249, *GLS auto.:* $26,249, *Limited:* $28,999, *Limited Navi.:* $30,999 **U.S. PRICE:** *GLS auto.:* $19,195, *SE:* $22,595, *Limited:* $25,295 **CANADIAN FREIGHT:** $1,565 **U.S. FREIGHT:** $750

POWERTRAIN (FRONT-DRIVE)
Engines: 2.4L 4-cyl. (198 hp) • 2.0L 4-cyl. turbo (274 hp); Transmissions: 6-speed man. • 6-speed auto.

DIMENSIONS/CAPACITY
Passengers: 2/3; Wheelbase: 110 in.; H: 57.8/L: 189: 7/W: 72.2 in.; Headroom F/R: 3.0/3.0 in.; Legroom F/R: 41/29.5 in.; Cargo volume: 16.3 cu. ft.; Fuel tank: 67L/regular; Tow limit: 2,000 lb.; Load capacity: 860 lb.; Turning circle: 39 ft.; Weight: 3,168–3,322 lb.

Sonata a pleasant car to own, but it lacked the refinement of a Honda or Toyota. Soon, that will no longer be true.

Styled similarly to the Honda Accord, the redesigned Sonata meets or exceeds the engine performance standards of its competitors, although its fuel economy isn't as good. The Sonata rides on a double-wishbone front suspension and a multi-link rear suspension that is more softly sprung than usual, making the car a bit "bouncier" than its competitors.

Hyundai has again put the emphasis on safety, giving buyers a lot more safety features for their money than they get with competing models. For example, Sonatas include four-wheel ABS; stability and traction control; front and side curtain airbags; front and rear seat belt pretensioners; an integrated rear child safety seat; and a "smart" passenger-side airbag that won't deploy if the passenger weighs less than 30 kg (66 lb.). Well, at least that's the theory—in practice, owners report the airbag is often disabled no matter what the passenger's weight.

COST ANALYSIS: Wait for the upgraded late-2011 model. It will cost more, but market forces in the new year will push those prices down again, and Hyundai will have had time to work out the first six months' worth of production "bugs." **Best alternatives:** The Honda Accord, Nissan Sentra, Mazda5 or Mazda6, and Toyota Camry (with the brake override feature). **Options:** Choose the V6 engine for better performance and handling; you will lose only a bit of fuel economy. If you get the 4-banger, keep in mind that good fuel economy means putting up with a bit more engine noise. Be wary of the sunroof; it eats up a lot of headroom and has a history of leaking. **Rebates:** As you get into the new year, expect $3,000 rebates and zero percent financing or attractive leasing deals on all models. **Depreciation:** Average; similar to the Elantra. **Insurance cost:** Average. **Parts supply cost:** Easy to find and relatively inexpensive. **Annual maintenance cost:** Average. **Warranty:** Bumper-to-bumper 5 years/100,000 km; rust perforation 5 years/unlimited km. **Supplementary warranty:** Not needed. **City/highway fuel economy:** *Man.:* 9.7/6.2 L/100 km, 29/46 mpg. *auto.:* 9.5/6.2 L/100 km, 30/46 mpg. *V6 auto.:* 10.8/6.9 L/100 km, 26/41 mpg.

OWNER-REPORTED PROBLEMS: Sudden, unintended acceleration when passing other cars; same thing happens when shifting to Reverse; cruise control resets itself to a higher speed; passenger side airbag disabled when normal-sized adult occupies the seat; parked vehicle rolled downhill, even though transmission was left in Drive; manual transmission lunges forward when shifting from first to second gear; premature wearout of the rear brakes; and noisy shocks/struts.

SERVICE BULLETIN-REPORTED PROBLEMS: Automatic transmission malfunctions; transmission shifts harshly and drops into "safe" default mode; squeaking noise when turning steering wheel; water leaks onto the passenger-side front-seat floor; alarm system self-activates; and remedy for sunroof creaking, ticking.

GENESIS ★★★★

RATING: Above Average. The Genesis is an unexceptional car, without a price advantage and with similar features found on well-proven, better-performing competitors. **Strong points:** Acceptable acceleration, but the V6 and V8 engines produce less torque at higher rpm than the Chrysler 300 or Pontiac G8 does. First-class interior fit and finish; a quiet, vibration-free, and spacious cabin; and clear and easy-to-read gauges. Impressive crashworthiness rankings: NHTSA gave the sedan its top, five-star rating for front, side, and rollover occupant protection; IIHS frontal offset, side-impact, and head-restraint protection were rated "Good." **Weak points:** Unimpressive fuel economy; ho-hum styling; and excessive body roll in hard cornering. A "floaty" suspension makes for a wandering ride and imprecise steering (Infiniti M and BMW models have stiffer suspensions that produce a more-secure feeling). Hyundai mechanics say the suspension is tuned for a full load, so anything less makes the vehicle wander. Original-equipment Dunlop tires may be too sensitive to the crown in the road. Navigation and audio system controls are cumbersome. Hyundai recommends premium fuel for extra horsepower from the V8, but it's not worth the higher fuel cost for just eight more horses. Long-term reliability has yet to be determined; however, most of Hyundai's newly introduced vehicles have had fewer factory glitches than the competition. **New for 2011:** A slight restyling.

KEY FACTS

CANADIAN PRICE (NEGOTIABLE): *Coupe:* $24,495, *Sedan:* $38,999 **U.S. PRICE:** *Coupe:* $22,000, *Sedan:* $33,000
CANADIAN FREIGHT: *Coupe:* $1,565, *Sedan:* $1,760 **U.S. FREIGHT:** $750
POWERTRAIN (REAR-DRIVE)
Engines: 3.3 V6 (268 hp) • 3.8L V6 (290 hp) • 4.6L V8 (368 hp); Transmissions: 6-speed man. • 5-speed manumatic • 6-speed manumatic
DIMENSIONS/CAPACITY (SEDAN)
Passengers: 2/3; Wheelbase: 115 in.; H: 58.3/L: 195.9/W: 74.4 in.; Cargo volume: 15.9 cu. ft.; Fuel tank: 65L–73L/regular/premium; Tow limit: 5,000 lb.; Ground clearance: 5.2 in.; Turning circle: 36 ft.; Weight: 3,748 lb.
DIMENSIONS/CAPACITY (COUPE)
Passengers: 2/3; Wheelbase: 115.6 in.; H: 58.3/L: 195.6/W: 73.4 in.; Cargo volume: 15.9 cu. ft.; Fuel tank: 65L–73L/regular/premium; Tow limit: 5,000 lb.; Ground clearance: 5.2 in.; Turning circle: 36 ft.; Weight: 3,748 lb.

OVERVIEW: Hyundai's Genesis targets BMW and Mercedes-Benz big spenders with its own luxury rear-drive until the Equus gets its footing later this year. The smaller 2010 Genesis Coupe was launched a year after the sedan and targets the Chevrolet Camaro and Ford Mustang. It features two performance-focused engines: a 2.0L turbocharged 4-cylinder and a range-topping, all-aluminum 3.8L V6. The basic version comes standard with a 6-speed manual; shoppers looking for a 5-speed Shiftronic automatic with manual mode will pay a few thousand dollars more.

These luxury cars are loaded with high-tech safety gear that includes ABS, traction control, an anti-skid system, side curtain airbags, front side airbags, and rear side airbags. There's also a heated and cooled driver's seat, wireless cell phone link, a navigation system with a hard drive for storing digital music files, a rear-view camera, and front- and rear-obstacle detection. A knob in the centre console governs audio, navigation, and other functions.

COST ANALYSIS: The rear-drive 2011 Genesis sedan is a better buy than the coupe, thanks to its powertrain improvements. **Best alternatives:** *Sedan:* The BMW 3 Series, Cadillac CTS, Ford Taurus, Lincoln MKS, Mercedes-Benz E-Class, and Toyota Avalon (only with the brake override feature). *Coupe:* The Chevrolet Camaro, Ford Mustang, and—for sheer sportster thrills without the bills—Mazda MX-5. **Options:** Stay away from the overly complicated navigation system. **Rebates:** Look for $3,000–$5,000 rebates, deep discounting, and sweet financing deals when the competition heats up in early 2011. **Depreciation:** Varies from average to slower than average, depending on whether you buy the coupe or the sedan. For example, a 2010 base Genesis sedan that originally sold for $39,000 is now—barely a year later—worth about $31,000. The same year coupe does a lot better: original selling price was $24,500, value today is $21,000. **Insurance cost:** Higher than average. **Parts supply/cost:** Parts are likely to be expensive and in short supply until independent suppliers start stocking them. **Annual maintenance cost:** Should be average. **Warranty:** Bumper-to-bumper 5 years/100,000 km; rust perforation 5 years/unlimited km. **Supplementary warranty:** Not needed. **City/highway fuel economy:** *Coupe 2.0L man.:* 10.1/6.6 L/100 km, 28/43 mpg. *Coupe 2.0L auto.:* 10.4/6.6 L/100 km, 27/43 mpg. *Coupe 3.8L man.:* 12.0/7.6 L/100 km, 24/37 mpg. *Coupe 3.8L auto.:* 11.9/7.3 L/100 km, 24/39 mpg. *Sedan 3.8L:* 11.4/7.2 L/100 km, 25/39 mpg. *Sedan 4.6L:* 12.6/8.1 L/100 km, 22/35 mpg.

OWNER-REPORTED PROBLEMS: *Coupe:* Stalling upon acceleration:

> While trying to normally accelerate, the car virtually died. Acceleration flat spot. Somewhat similar to the old carbureted cars. Very infrequent, however, the other day losing acceleration almost caused a major accident.

Electronic stability control (ESC) locked driver's brakes when he was turning the vehicle; more ESC malfunctions and Bluetooth problems; early replacement of the automatic transmission; rear seat does not conform to regulations relative to the installation of child safety seats; misaligned hood allows for severe wind buffeting of the hood. *Sedan:* Small pebble damaged the AC condenser ($800); Bluetooth malfunctions.

SERVICE BULLETIN-REPORTED PROBLEMS: *Coupe:* Engine rpms slowly drop to idle; front bumper gaps; quarter panel creak, tick when passing over rough roads; sunroof sun shade slides open when car accelerates; and the anti-theft alarm self-activates. *Sedan:* No start in Park, Neutral; self-activating anti-theft alarm; brake lights flash for no reason; and troubleshooting tips to eliminate sunroof creaking, ticking.

TUCSON ★★★★★

RATING: Recommended. **Strong points:** Reasonably priced and well equipped; V6 engine provides smooth, sustained acceleration; sure-footed (thanks to the standard stability control) and smooth-riding; roomy and easily accessed cabin; and above average reliability. NHTSA gave it a five-star crashworthiness rating for front- and side-impact occupant protection and a four-star rating for rollover protection. IIHS rated side-impact protection as "Acceptable," and head restraints were designated "Good." **Weak points:** The 4-cylinder engine struggles with a full load, and the expected fuel economy doesn't materialize. Vehicle isn't as agile as others in its class. **New for 2011:** A better powertrain setup; the hybrid 2011 model will arrive in the spring of 2011.

OVERVIEW: The Tucson is Hyundai's compact crossover that was first introduced for the 2005 model year. It is smaller than the Santa Fe and built on the same Elantra-based platform as the Kia Sportage. The standard powerplant in all Tucsons is a 2.0L DOHC 4-cylinder engine. The optional all-wheel-drive system can send 99 percent of the power to the front wheels or split the traction between the front and rear wheels.

KEY FACTS

CANADIAN PRICE (NEGOTIABLE): *GL:* $20,999, *GL auto.:* $24,299, *GL AWD:* $26,699, *GLS:* $26,799, *Limited AWD:* $32,449, *Limited AWD Navi.:* $34,449 **U.S. PRICE:** *GLS:* $18,995, *Limited FWD:* $24,345 **CANADIAN FREIGHT:** $1,595 **U.S. FREIGHT:** $750 **POWERTRAIN (FRONT-DRIVE/AWD)** Engines: 2.0L 4-cyl. (165 hp) • 2.4L V6. (176 hp); Transmissions: 5-speed man. • 6-speed manumatic **DIMENSIONS/CAPACITY** Passengers: 2/3; Wheelbase: 103.5 in.; H: 68.1/L: 170.3/W: 70.7 in.; Headroom F/R: 5.0/4.0 in.; Legroom F/R: 41/29 in.; Cargo volume: 65.5 cu. ft.; Fuel tank: 58L/regular; Tow limit: 1,000 lb.; Load capacity: 860 lb.; Turning circle: 35.4 ft.; Ground clearance: 7.0 in.; Weight: 3,240 lb.

COST ANALYSIS: Buy the 2011 for a better-performing engine and transmission. **Best alternatives:** The Honda CR-V and Toyota RAV4. **Options:** Nothing important. **Rebates:** Expect $2,000 discounts, zero percent financing, and attractive leasing deals on all models. **Depreciation:** Less than average. A 2009 base Tucson originally sold for $21,000; today, it is worth $16,500. **Insurance cost:** Average. **Parts supply/cost:** Easy to find and relatively inexpensive. **Annual maintenance cost:** Less than average. **Warranty:** Bumper-to-bumper 5 years/100,000 km; rust perforation 5 years/ unlimited km. **Supplementary warranty:** Not needed. **City/highway fuel economy:** *2.4L man.:* 9.6/6.7 L/100 km, 29/42 mpg. *Auto:* 9.0/6.3 L/100 km, 31/45 mpg. *FWD:* 9.8/7.1 L/100 km, 29/40 mpg.

OWNER-REPORTED PROBLEMS: Firewall insulation caught fire; automatic transmission banks and jerks into gear:

Sudden downshifting with loud clunk and lurching of vehicle at 35 mph [55 km/h]. Felt as if I had been hit from behind by another vehicle. Instinctively hit the brakes and pulled over to check for exterior damage, and found none. Continued down the road and experienced unusual increases in rpms. When I arrived at my destination, the vehicle would not go in Reverse. Owned vehicle only 11 days. Incident occurred at 500 miles [800 km].

Transmission slams into gear with such force that the seatbelt tensioner locks up:

Car violently downshifts. To the point [where it] feels like someone slammed on the brakes. Actually slowed the car down enough that I pushed forward in the [driver's seat], and the seat belt tensioned up to keep me [from] going forward. This has happened several times. I have asked the dealer about this, and they said there is no defect, and that it is "normal" behaviour. But I have never been in a car that shifts this hard and this violently to make me worry about crashing.

Vehicle sways left and right while cruising; rear of the vehicle slides as if it were on ice; rear-tire lock-up; excessive vibrations at 100 km/h; windshield wipers malfunction; and windshield wiper fluid leaks out of the filler neck.

SERVICE BULLETIN-REPORTED PROBLEMS: Harsh, delayed shift diagnosis, and a faulty oil temperature sensor could lead to the automatic transmission sticking in Third gear and a lit Check Engine light.

RATING: Recommended. This SUV does almost everything right. **Strong points:** Acceptable acceleration with the base 2.7L V6, but the 3.3L gives you more power without much fuel wasted. Smooth-shifting automatic transmission; good steering response; fairly agile; comfortable, controlled ride; standard stability/traction control and full-body side curtain airbags; lots of interior room; and much-improved quality control. A spacious interior allows for an optional pair of flat-folding third-row seats. Owner complaints are rare. NHTSA and IIHS gave the Santa Fe their top ratings for offset and front- and side-impact protection. Rollover resistance got four stars, and head-restraint effectiveness was rated "Good." **Weak points:** Needs more zip, a better ride, and handling balance; fuel economy is disappointing; tall drivers may need more headroom. **New for 2011:** Carried over unchanged.

OVERVIEW: Redesigned in 2007, the Santa Fe is a competitively priced family SUV that offers impressive room, good build quality, and many standard safety and performance features that cost a lot more when bought with competing models. This mid-sized crossover comes with front-drive or with all-wheel drive that allows locking in a 50/50 front/rear power split.

KEY FACTS

CANADIAN PRICE (NEGOTIABLE): *2.4 GL:* $25,999, *2.4 GL auto.:* $25,999 *3.5 GL auto.:* $28,999, *3.5 GL AWD:* $30,999, *3.5 GL FWD Sport:* $31,299, *3.5 GL AWD Sport:* $33,299, *Limited:* $35,799, *Limited Navi.:* $37,599 **U.S. PRICE:** *GLS:* $21,695, *SE:* $25,995, *Limited:* $26,645 **CANADIAN FREIGHT:** $1,595 **U.S. FREIGHT:** $750

POWERTRAIN (FRONT-DRIVE/AWD)
Engines: 2.7L V6 (185 hp) • 3.3L V6 (242 hp); Transmissions: 5-speed man. • 4-speed auto. • 5-speed manumatic

DIMENSIONS/CAPACITY
Passengers: 2/3/2; Wheelbase: 107 in.; H: 58/L: 189: 72 in.; Headroom F/R1/R2: 3.0/4.5/0.0 in.; Legroom F/R1/R2: 41/27.5/26 in.; Cargo volume: 37.5 cu. ft.; Fuel tank: 75L/regular; Tow limit: 3,500 lb.; Load capacity: 1,120 lb.; Turning circle: 39 ft.; Ground clearance: 7.0 in.; Weight: 3,253 lb.

COST ANALYSIS: Don't waste your money on a 2011. Instead, buy an almost identical, discounted 2010 for thousands less. **Best alternatives:** Nissan Xterra; GM Terrain, Traverse, Acadia, or Enclave; Toyota RAV4 or Highlander (only with the brake override); or a used Saturn Outlook. **Rebates:** Expect $3,000 rebates, zero percent financing, and cheap leases on all models. **Depreciation:** Average. **Insurance cost:** Average. **Parts supply/cost:** Easy to find, and relatively inexpensive. **Annual maintenance cost:** Average. **Warranty:** Bumper-to-bumper 5 years/100,000 km; rust perforation 5 years/unlimited km. **Supplementary warranty:** Not needed. **City/highway fuel economy:** 2.4L *man.*: 10.7/7.5 L/100 km, 26/38 mpg. *Auto:* 10.2/7.2 L/100 km, 28/39 mpg. *3.5L FWD:* 10.1/7.6 L/100 km, 28/37 mpg. *3.5L AWD:* 10.5/7.7 L/100 km, 27/37 mpg.

OWNER-REPORTED PROBLEMS: Sudden acceleration accompanied by loss of braking; vehicle frequently shuts down when underway; a loud knock and transmission jerk whenever the vehicle is first started; when shifting, the jerkiness of the transmission feels like someone is hitting the rear end; passenger-side airbag is disabled when an average-sized passenger is seated; sudden brake failure, with pedal going to the floor; horn needs to be pounded in the right spot to activate; rear window exploded for no reason; excessive engine and steering vibration when underway; door lock failures; low-beam headlights don't give far enough illumination; steel belts may unravel on Bridgestone Dueler tires; and tire-pressure monitor system light comes on for no reason.

SERVICE BULLETIN-REPORTED PROBLEMS: Sunroof creaking, ticking; automatic transmission malfunctions; defaults to the "failsafe" mode; harsh transmission engagement; no start in Park or Neutral.

A/T—MIL ON/DTCS P0705/P0707/P0708/NO START IN P/N

BULLETIN NO.: 09-AT-013   DATE: JULY 2009

ALL EXCEPT VERACRUZ AND GENESIS

DESCRIPTION: An improperly adjusted or improperly operating range switch may result in the following conditions:

- Diagnostic trouble codes:
  - P0705—Range switch signal problem
  - P0707—Range switch—open circuit
  - P0708—Range switch—short circuit or multiple inputs
- Malfunction Indicator Light (MIL) illuminated
- Impossible engine start in "P" or "N"

This TSB provides information concerning the proper adjustment and diagnosis of the transaxle range switch.

The above service bulletin applies to Hyundai models going back to the 1999 model year.

VERACRUZ ★★★★

RATING: Above Average. **Strong points:** The powerful V6 and 6-speed automatic transmission perform flawlessly to deliver smooth acceleration and a comfortable ride. NHTSA and IIHS gave the Veracruz their top ratings for offset and front- and side-impact protection. Rollover resistance got four stars, and head-restraint effectiveness was rated "Acceptable." Backed by a comprehensive base warranty. **Weak points:** Some suspension noise, and not as agile as some of its rivals. **New for 2011:** Carried over unchanged; the Veracruz is likely to be dropped after its 2010 model year.

OVERVIEW: The seven-passenger Veracruz uses a stretched Santa Fe platform and offers all of the safety, performance, and convenience features you'll find on SUVs that cost $10,000 more.

COST ANALYSIS: Buy a discounted 2010, inasmuch as the 2011s are practically identical. **Best alternatives:** Competes mostly with other higher-end mid-sized crossovers, like the Honda Pilot, Nissan Murano, and Lexus RX series. **Options:** Stay away from original-equipment Bridgestone or Dunlop tires; Michelins are much better performers and are more durable. **Rebates:** Expect $4,000 rebates, low-interest financing, and sweet leasing deals. **Depreciation:** Faster than average. A 2007 Limited that sold originally for $46,000 is now worth barely $24,000. **Insurance cost:** Above average. **Parts supply/cost:** Not easy to find; moderately expensive powertrain components.

KEY FACTS

CANADIAN PRICE (NEGOTIABLE): *GL:* $32,999, *GLS:* $36,999, *Limited:* $43,299 **U.S. PRICE:** *GLS:* $28,145, *Limited:* $34,195 **CANADIAN FREIGHT:** $1,595 **U.S. FREIGHT:** $750

POWERTRAIN (FRONT-DRIVE/AWD)
Engine: 3.8L V6 (260 hp); Transmission: 6-speed auto.

DIMENSIONS/CAPACITY
Passengers: 2/3/2; Wheelbase: 110.4 in.; H: 68.9/L: 190.6/W: 76.6 in.; Headroom F/R1/R2: 3.0/4.0/1.0 in.; Legroom F/R1/R2: 39/29.5/25.5 in.; Cargo volume: 41.5 cu. ft.; Fuel tank: 78L/regular; Tow limit: 3,500 lb.; Load capacity: 1,160 lb.; Turning circle: 36.7 ft.; Ground clearance: 8.1 in.; Weight: 3,253 lb.

Annual maintenance cost: Higher than average. **Warranty:** Bumper-to-bumper 5 years/100,000 km; rust perforation 5 years/unlimited km. **Supplementary warranty:** Not needed. **City/highway fuel economy:** *FWD:* 12.7/8.5 L/100 km, 22/33 mpg. *AWD:* 13.2/8.9 L/100 km, 21/32 mpg.

OWNER-REPORTED PROBLEMS: Airbag warning light comes on for no reason; sudden unintended acceleration while vehicle was in Reverse. Vehicle sometimes accelerates normally and then suddenly drops into Neutral. Premature wearout of brake calipers and out-of-round rotors:

> Hyundai has brake and rotor issues and won't do anything about it.... The vehicle off the lot had rotor problems. Had them shaved, then replaced and they were worn out within a year... If you search Internet you will find brake issue with all vehicles from Hyundai...!

Rear hatch opens on its own; opened rear hatch may suddenly fall down; chronic stalling and no-starts likely caused by a poor-quality fuel pump; windshield wipers may suddenly fail when most needed; high- and low-beam headlights can't be adjusted separately, causing the high beams to shoot up way too high, and low beams are too low; and the key fob opens the rear liftgate when the Open Door key is punched.

SERVICE BULLETIN-REPORTED PROBLEMS: Troubleshooting tips for the Bluetooth feature and a fix for sunroof creaking, ticking.

Infiniti

Several decades ago, three Japanese companies decided they would spin off their vehicles and create "luxury" or "high-performance" brands; they were Mazda (Amati), Nissan (Infiniti), and Toyota (Lexus). Only Mazda failed in its attempt. Infiniti first brought us excellent driver-oriented Q-coded vehicles, then cut back to make them more-comfortably Toyota-like, and then returned to its performance roots.

Unlike Toyota's Lexus division, which started out with softly sprung vehicles akin to your dad's fully loaded Oldsmobile, Nissan's number one alter ego has historically stressed performance over comfort and opulence, and has offered buyers lots of high-performance features at what were initially very reasonable prices. But the company got greedy during the mid-'90s. Its Infiniti lineup became more mainstream and lost its price and performance edge, particularly after the company stripped out or downgraded the Q45's features, resurrected its embarrassingly incompetent G20, and dropped the J30 and J30t.

But Infiniti is fighting to get that performance edge back. There are now greater differences between Nissan and Infiniti vehicles, even though most models share the same platform. Infinitis usually add more-powerful engines, more gears, steering and suspensions tweaked for sportier driving, and more-luxurious interior appointments. These improvements have produced a new roster of sporty luxury vehicles: the Infiniti G, EX, FX, M, and QX. The 2011 model year is turning out to be one of the most important in Infiniti's now 21-year history—with the introduction of the all-new Infiniti M luxury sedan and Infiniti QX luxury SUV.

Although Infinitis are sold and serviced by a small dealer network across Canada, this limited support base doesn't compromise either the availability or quality of servicing. Furthermore, these cars are reasonably dependable, so there is less need for service. The only two drawbacks are that powertrain and body parts are sometimes in short supply and that adding on complicated high-tech features has made servicing a lot more complicated and costly than ever before.

G25, G37 ★★★★

The Infiniti G37.

RATING: Above Average. The G25 is the entry-level sedan fitted with a 218 hp 2.5L V6. In the States, it sells for $31,825, or $2,300 less than the G37. **Strong points:** A powerful, smooth, and responsive powertrain; predictable handling; and a firm but comfortable ride. The car is fairly agile, quiet, and comfortable. The convertible has five horses less than the coupe (325 hp) but lots more than you'll find with the equivalent BMW or Mercedes. Crashworthiness is impressive: NHTSA gives the G37 a five-star ranking for frontal, side, and rollover occupant protection, and IIHS gives it a "Good" rating for frontal offset and side crashworthiness. **Weak points:** The G series comes with a small rear seat and cargo area; towing is not advised; and IIHS rated head-restraint effectiveness as "Marginal." The convertible model has even less room and has yet to be crash tested. **New for 2011:** Coupe Sport gets new front styling; IPL high-performance tuning (348 hp); scratch shield paint protection and a new colour is added; Navigation Package is now standard.

KEY FACTS

CANADIAN PRICE (NEGOTIABLE): *Coupe:* $46,300, *G37x AWD Coupe:* $48,800, *Sport Coupe:* $48,800, *Sport Coupe M6:* $48,800, *Sedan:* $38,690, *AWD Sedan:* $42,550, *Convertible Sport:* $57,400, *Convertible Premier:* $60,700 **U.S. PRICE:** *Coupe:* $36,050, *G37x AWD Coupe:* $39,150, *Sport Coupe M6:* $40,400, *Sedan:* $33,250, *G37x AWD Sedan:* $36,050, *Sport Sedan M6:* $37,000, *Convertible:* $44,350, *Convertible Sport 6MT:* $46,950 **CANADIAN FREIGHT:** $1,825 **U.S. FREIGHT:** $865

POWERTRAIN (REAR-DRIVE/AWD)

Engines: 3.7L V6 (328 hp sedan; 330 hp coupe; 325 hp convertible) • 2.5L V6 (218 hp); Transmissions: 6-speed man. • 7-speed auto.

DIMENSIONS/CAPACITY

Passengers: 2/2; 2/3; Wheelbase: 112.2 in.; H: 54.7–55.3/L: 183.1/W: 71.8 in.; Headroom F/R: 2.5/1.5 in.; Legroom F/R: 41/27.5 in.; Cargo volume: 7.4–13.5 cu. ft.; Fuel tank: 76L/premium; Tow limit: 1,000 lb.; Load capacity: 900 lb.; Turning circle: 35.4 ft.; Ground clearance: 5.1 in.; Weight: 3,642–3,847 lb.

OVERVIEW: The G37 is a premium mid-sized car with SUV pretensions. It is sold as a two-door coupe, a four-door sedan, and a two-door convertible with a power-retractable hardtop. The G37 targets shoppers who would normally buy the Acura RDX or the BMW X3. Not for off-road, but definitely a comfortable, well-equipped, and versatile vehicle for most driving needs. It is priced in the same range as the Infiniti G series and is essentially a G35 wagon. The convertible model is priced right within striking range of BMW's 328i/335i Cabriolet and the new 2011 Lexus IS 250 or IS 350 C convertible. The Mercedes-Benz CLK350 AMG Edition Cabriolet has priced itself out of that market.

COST ANALYSIS: Get the 2010 G37 because it's practically identical to the costlier 2011 version. You can save about $11,000 by shopping in the States. **Best alternatives:** The Infiniti EX35 and the BMW 3 Series. **Options:** The limited-slip differential in the Sport package. **Rebates:** $5,000+ discounts, low-cost financing, and attractive leases; discounts will be sweetened in early 2011. **Depreciation:** Average. **Insurance cost:** Higher than average. **Parts supply/cost:** Expensive parts that can be easily found in the Maxima parts bin. **Annual maintenance cost:** Lower than average. **Warranty:** Bumper-to-bumper 4 years/100,000 km; powertrain 6 years/110,000 km; rust perforation 7 years/unlimited km. **Supplementary warranty:** Not needed. **City/highway fuel economy:** *Man.:* 12.4/7.9 L/100 km, 23/36 mpg. *Auto.:* 11.2/7.5 L/100 km, 25/38 mpg. *AWD:* 11.7/7.8 L/100 km, 24/36 mpg. *Convertible man.:* 12.9/8.4 L/100 km, 22/34. *Auto.:* 11.9/7.8 L/100 km, 24/36 mpg. *Coupe man.:* 12.4/7.9 L/100 km, 23/36 mpg; *Manumatic 7-speed:* 11.7/7.8 L/100 km, 25/38 mpg.

OWNER-REPORTED PROBLEMS: Engine surges when braking (confirmed by TSB #ITBO7-048), or is slow to brake:

> I own a two-month old Infiniti G37X. When braking at highway speed, the engine does not seem to slow down as fast as it should. I brought this to my Infiniti dealer this week. They conducted tests on it and found that it "performs as designed." However, they acknowledged that the transmission does not slow down when the brake is applied—that the engine is designed to "click down" from gear to gear. But when braking hard at a highway speed, the car does not slow down immediately because of this design.

Made a fairly hard brake for a red light—car slid a little to a stop, but continued accelerating at 2500 to 3500 rpms while I held both feet on the brake to keep it in place. It was like holding back a revved up jet—rpms would not come down even when I shifted car to Neutral.

Engine tapping, clicking sound at start-up requires the use of a costlier "factory" oil; transmission suddenly downshifted to 15 km/h from 100km/h:

A chip was changed. However, the failure occurred three more times. The dealer then stated that the fluid in the vehicle was too full and was the cause of the failure.

The manual transmission gears grind when shifting, causing a delayed shift, especially in Sixth gear; transmission was replaced under warranty. The anti-traction feature activated on its own and caused the wheels to lock on a rainy day; defective Bridgestone Pole Position tires; Tire Pressure light did not come on when tire went flat; premature brake replacement; the area between the gas pedal and centre console gets quite hot; audio system malfunctions; and poor fit and finish. Incidentally, this car is not as much a "chick magnet" as it is a rodent attractant:

Infiniti G37 has electrical wiring insulation made of soy-based polymer. Soy-based polymer is apparently biodegradable. The problem is that it is also attractive to rodents, who eat the wiring, creating electrical safety hazards. It also creates an economic stress on consumers and insurers who have to pay for repairs done to these automobiles, which Infiniti claims is not covered under any existing warranty.

SERVICE BULLETIN-REPORTED PROBLEMS: Automatic transmission shifter boot comes loose; drivebelt noise; and the warranty is extended for Campaign PO308 in relation to the radio seek function.

EX35 ★★★★

KEY FACTS

CANADIAN PRICE (NEGOTIABLE): *EX35 AWD:* $41,250 **U.S. PRICE:** *Base 3.7:* $33,800, *AWD:* $35,200, *Journey:* $36,000, *Journey AWD:* $37,400
CANADIAN FREIGHT: $1,825 **U.S. FREIGHT:** $865
POWERTRAIN (REAR-DRIVE/AWD)
Engine: 3.5L V6 (297 hp); Transmission: 7-speed auto.
DIMENSIONS/CAPACITY
Passengers: 2/3; Wheelbase: 110.2 in.; H: 61.9/L: 182.3/W: 71 in.; Headroom F/R: 3.0/3.0 in.; Legroom F/R: 42/26 in.; Cargo volume: 18.6 cu. ft.; Fuel tank: 76L/premium; Tow limit: N/A; Load capacity: 860 lb.; Turning circle: 36 ft.; Ground clearance: 5.5 in.; Weight: 3,757–3,979 lb.

RATING: Above Average. The EX and G series are entry-level Infinitis with the most to offer from a price and quality perspective—as long as you have short legs or never ride in the rear seat. **Strong points:** Drives like a car with power to spare, and the smooth, responsive automatic/manual transmission works flawlessly with the well-calibrated V6; overall, the car is much more agile, quiet, and comfortable than the G series. A classy, though small, interior. NHTSA gives the EX35 a five-star rating for side-impact occupant protection and four stars for frontal and rollover safety. IIHS gives it an all-around "Good" rating. **Weak points:** Not as sporty as Infiniti's sport sedans or some of BMW's crossovers; really a four-seater; limited cargo space; back seat occupants must keep a knee-to-chin posture when the front seats are pushed all the way back; taller drivers will want more headroom (especially with the sunroof-equipped Journey model); right-rear visibility is compromised by right-rear head restraint and side pillar; no towing; and fuel economy is unimpressive. **New for 2011:** A 7-speed automatic transmission; better instrument panel illumination; and revised 18- and 19-inch wheels.

OVERVIEW: Offering the room of a small station wagon, the EX35 is a small, upscale SUV wannabe that targets shoppers who would normally buy the Acura RDX or the BMW X3. Smaller than the Infiniti FX, it is priced in the same range as the Infiniti G series and is essentially a G35 wagon. Not for off-road, but definitely a comfortable, well-equipped, and versatile vehicle for most driving needs.

COST ANALYSIS: Buying a 2010 or a 2011 is really a coin-flip. EX sales have been sluggish, so if you opt for an improved 2011 and wait until the spring or summer of 2011 for prices to fall, you could do well. By then, the higher prices will have likely been cut through extra rebates and other sales incentives, making the upgraded 2011s not that much more expensive than the 2010 versions. The new 7-speed automatic may give a slight boost to fuel economy, but keep in mind that any new powertrain is a risky buy its first year on the market. Also, the larger 18-inch wheels may make for a bumpier ride and cut your gas mileage. On the other hand, getting old 17-inch wheels on a significantly discounted 2010 may be a good enough reason to buy last year's model now. **Best alternatives:** Acura RDX, BMW 3 Series or X3, Cadillac SRX, and Lincoln MKX. **Options:** The Navigation Package is overpriced and mostly fluff. **Rebates:** $4,000+ discounts, low-cost financing, and cheaper leases; discounts will become even more generous in early 2011 as the temperature drops and the competition heats up. **Depreciation:** Average. **Insurance cost:** Higher than average. **Parts supply/cost:** Expensive parts that can be easily found in the Maxima parts bin. **Annual maintenance cost:** Lower than average. **Warranty:** Bumper-to-bumper 4 years/100,000 km; powertrain 6 years/110,000 km; rust perforation 7 years/unlimited km. **Supplementary warranty:** Not needed. **City/highway fuel economy:** *EX 3.5L AWD and 5-speed auto.: 12.9/8.6 L/100 km, 22/33 mpg.*

OWNER-REPORTED PROBLEMS: Passenger-side front airbag may be disabled when a normal-sized adult is seated. The Adaptive Cruise Control feature no longer uses an audible warning system following recall repairs. Poor-quality body hardware; for example, the hitch will break if you tow anything at all. Says one owner:

> It will probably do damage even if you only use it for a bike rack. It is a very nicely built part which fits exactly as advertised, however, it mounts to the bumper supports which are made of a very flimsy sheet metal. As a result, continued up and down motion such as a bouncy bike rack or the routine undulations of a trailer captured by the ball mount will fatigue and break the metal that holds the bumper mounting supports to the car.

SERVICE BULLETIN-REPORTED PROBLEMS: Front brake judder; engine drivebelt noise; and a navigation system software update.

FX37, FX50 ★★★★

The Infiniti FX37.

RATING: Above Average. **Strong points:** Both engines have power to spare, delivered by a smooth and quiet drivetrain. Handling is precise and secure. Decent towing capacity and torque. NHTSA gives the vehicles five stars for frontal collision crashworthiness and three stars for rollover protection. **Weak points:** A tight cabin, limited rear visibility, and some reliability concerns. **New for 2011:** A new power liftgate.

KEY FACTS

CANADIAN PRICE (NEGOTIABLE): *FX35:* $52,300, *FX50:* $64,500 **U.S. PRICE:** *FX35:* $42,850, *AWD:* $44,300, *FX50:* $59,000 **CANADIAN FREIGHT:** $1,825 **U.S. FREIGHT:** $865 **POWERTRAIN (REAR-DRIVE/AWD)** Engine: 3.5L V6 (303 hp) • 5.0L V8 (390 hp); Transmission: 7-speed auto.

DIMENSIONS/CAPACITY
Passengers: 2/3; Wheelbase: 113.5 in.; H: 66.1/L: 191.2/W: 75.9 in.; Cargo volume: 24.7 cu. ft.; Fuel tank: 90L/premium; Tow limit: 3,500 lb.; Turning circle: 36.7 ft.; Ground clearance: 7.3 in.; Weight: 4,299 lb., 4,575 lb.

OVERVIEW: These are well-appointed, agile luxury crossover SUVs that drive and ride like sports sedans. The primary difference between the two vehicles is their engines, plus a few additional features.

COST ANALYSIS: It will be hard to haggle, due to the popularity of the FX series. These vehicles are good candidates for cross-border shopping, though; in the States, the price may be cut by $10,000 and the freight fee reduced by half. **Best alternatives:** BMW X6 xDrive. **Options:** Nothing is needed. **Rebates:** Look for discounts of about 10 percent as well as some very attractive leasing deals in the first quarter of 2011. **Depreciation:** Average. **Insurance cost:** Higher than average. **Parts supply/cost:** Expensive powertrain and body parts that aren't easily available. **Annual maintenance cost:** Higher than average. **Warranty:** Bumper-to-bumper 4 years/100,000 km; powertrain 6 years/110,000 km; rust perforation 7 years/unlimited km. **Supplementary warranty:** Not needed. **City/highway fuel economy:** *FX35:* 13.3/9.3 L/100 km, 21/30 mpg. *FX50:* 14.6/10.1 L/100 km, 19/28 mpg.

OWNER-REPORTED PROBLEMS: The early replacement of brake calipers and rotors; car lurches forward when started; electronic malfunctions stall the car; electrical shocks are felt when exiting the vehicle; and sound system malfunctions. Surprisingly, body hardware and fit and finish get top marks, unlike with the top-of-the-line QX56.

SERVICE BULLETIN-REPORTED PROBLEMS: *FX35:* Transfer case whine or vibrations; drivebelt noise; and door mirrors shake or vibrate. *FX50:* Transfer case whine or vibrations; drivebelt noise; door mirrors shake, vibrate; and navigation system software update.

M37, M56 ★★★★

RATING: Above Average. These vehicles are the high-performance successors to the discontinued Q45. The major difference between the M37 and M56 is engine size, plus additional performance and convenience gadgets. **Strong points:** Well appointed; superior acceleration and handling; easy entry and exit; head restraints lower into the seatback; and low depreciation. NHTSA gives both vehicles a four-star overall crashworthiness rating and five stars for side protection. **Weak points:** Some road noise, and the vehicles require premium fuel while delivering disappointing fuel economy. **New for 2011:** New M37 and M56 model designations, with rear-wheel drive or Infiniti's Intelligent All-Wheel Drive system. The M37

The Infiniti M37.

features a 330 hp 3.7L V6 engine with 27 more horses than the previous generation M35's 3.5L V6, while the M56 offers 95 additional horses with its all-new 420 hp 5.6L V8. Both engines feature Infiniti's advanced VVEL (Variable Valve Event & Lift) system, and all models are equipped with a standard 7-speed automatic transmission. A special Sport Touring Package, offered on rear-drive models, includes 4-Wheel Active Steer (4WAS), sport-tuned suspension, sport brakes, and 20-inch wheels and tires.

OVERVIEW: The M37 and M56 rear-drive/AWD luxury sedans ride on a four-wheel independent suspension and carry either a V6 or V8 engine. They share the QX's drivetrain but are set on a shorter wheelbase. Because of their lighter curb weight and their potent engines, these cars can do 0–100 km/h in less than six seconds. Forget about fuel economy, though.

New technologies include Infiniti Drive Mode Selector, a four-mode driver-selectable control of throttle and transmission mapping; Active Noise Control, which reduces engine noise, providing a quieter cabin; a blind spot warning and intervention (BSI) feature that helps the driver return the vehicle back toward the center of the lane of travel in the event of unintended drift; and Active Trace Control, which adjusts engine torque and the control of braking at each of the four wheels to help enhance cornering performance.

Other 2011 techno-gadgets (get ready for the acronyms) include an upgraded navigation system, a Bose Studio Surround premium audio system, Intelligent Cruise Control (Full-Speed Range), Lane Departure Warning (LDW) and Lane Departure Prevention (LDP) systems, Distance Control Assist (DCA), Intelligent Brake Assist (IBA) with Forward Collision Warning (FCW), and Front Pre-Crash Seat Belts.

KEY FACTS

CANADIAN PRICE (NEGOTIABLE): *M37:* $52,400, *M37x AWD:* $54,900, *M37 Sport:* $63,400, *M56:* $66.200, *M56x AWD:* $68,700, *M56 Sport:* $73,400 **U.S. PRICE:** *M37:* $46,250, *M37x AWD:* $48,400, *M56:* $57,550, *M56x AWD:* $60,050 **CANADIAN FREIGHT:** $1,890 **U.S. FREIGHT:** $865

POWERTRAIN (REAR-DRIVE/AWD)
Engines: 3.7L V6 (330 hp) • 5.6L V8 (420 hp); Transmission: 7-speed auto.

DIMENSIONS/CAPACITY
Passengers: 2/3; Wheelbase: 114.2 in.; H: 59.1/L: 194.7/W: 72.6 in.; Headroom F/R: 4.0/3.0 in.; Legroom F/R: 41/30 in.; Cargo volume: 14.9 cu. ft.; Fuel tank: 90L/premium; Tow limit: N/A; Load capacity: 860 lb.; Turning circle: 36.7 ft.; Weight: 3,858 lb., 4,012 lb.

COST ANALYSIS: The M37 is Infiniti's entry-level M model, while the M56 piles on the safety, performance, and convenience options to give shoppers more high-performance thrills and luxury. It comes packed with all the techno-goodies car companies stuff into their vehicles to impress shoppers who have money to burn. **Best alternatives:** Other cars you may wish to consider are the Acura RL V6, Audi A6, Cadillac DTS, and BMW 5 Series. **Options:** The limited-slip differential in the Sport Touring Package. **Rebates:** $4,500+ discounts, low-cost financing, and attractive leases; discounts will be sweetened in early 2011. **Depreciation:** Average. **Insurance cost:** Higher than average. **Parts supply/cost:** Expensive parts that aren't that hard to find. **Annual maintenance cost:** Lower than average. **Warranty:** Bumper-to-bumper 4 years/100,000 km; powertrain 6 years/110,000 km; rust perforation 7 years/unlimited km. **Supplementary warranty:** Not needed. **City/highway fuel economy:** *M37 rear-drive:* 11.4/7.6 L/100 km, 25/37 mpg. *AWD:* 12/8.3 L/100 km, 24/34 mpg. *Sport:* 11.4/7.6 L/100 km, 25/37 mpg. *M56:* 12.9/8.0 L/100 km, 22/35 mpg. *AWD:* 13.4/8.5 L/100 km, 21/33 mpg. *Sport:* 11.4/7.6 L/100 km, 22/35 mpg.

OWNER-REPORTED PROBLEMS: *M35:* Brake failures and the car tends to oversteer to the point where the driver can lose control. Since the 2007 model year, owners say there is a "rocks rattling in a can" sound coming from underneath the car. Other concerns include steering that pulls hard to one side and wanders (tramlining) at all speeds, making the vehicle almost impossible to control (some relief is gained by replacing the Goodyear Eagle RS-A tires with Michelin Primacy MXV4 tires or by changing the steering rack), and a variety of sound system malfunctions. *M45:* Sudden unintended acceleration.

SERVICE BULLETIN-REPORTED PROBLEMS: *M35:* Engine hesitation, stall from idle, inoperative door mirror actuator, and drivebelt noise. *M45:* Inoperative door mirror actuator and drivebelt noise.

QX56 ★★★

RATING: Average. The QX is now a gussied-up, overpriced Nissan Patrol, instead of the Armada clone it was previously. **Strong points:** It's more comfortable, more controllable, more efficient, and more powerful than earlier models. Increased V8 power; better road handling; an upgraded, smooth-shifting automatic transmission; and lots of towing capacity and torque make the QX a more-obedient Brontosaurus. The car has a plush interior and standard navigation system, plus more gadgets and convenience features than you will ever need (nine cup holders and four bottle holders). You'll also find plenty of interior room and predictable, responsive handling (thanks to the independent rear suspension). NHTSA gives the 2010 QX56 a five-star ranking for front-impact occupant protection. **Weak points:** Way overpriced—a poster child for cross-border shopping. Fuel economy is brutal, although not as bad as with previous models because of the 7-speed transmission. You also get a stiff, jarring ride. Steering-wheel-mounted controls are needlessly complex and the side fender vents look out of place—oh, and only the vent on the driver's side is functional. Talking about dysfunctional, why on Earth did Infiniti put the side-mirror adjusting switch next to the driver's knee instead of on the door panel, where it is usually found on other vehicles? NHTSA gives the QX a surprisingly paltry three stars for rollover safety, and the jury's still out over the car's long-term reliability; with all of its changes this year, factory-related defects will likely be on the rise. **New for 2011:** A V8 with 80 more horses; a 7-speed automatic transmission with Adaptive Shift Control; a stiffer platform that reduces body roll; and a revised four-wheel-drive system. Styling is more curvaceous, less Armada; the car is lighter by 161 pounds; fuel economy has been increased by 14 percent; and the second-row seating has additional legroom that now bests seating found in the Mercedes-Benz GL450, the QX's closest rival. Third-row seats are now power-adjustable to get out of the way when passengers are boarding, and they have a power-reclining feature for added comfort.

OVERVIEW: This is Infiniti's SUV luxury flagship, loaded with every conceivable safety, performance, and convenience feature one could ever imagine. Yet, someone forgot to design a decent-sized third-row rear seat that's large enough for most people.

Although the QX56 has been on the market in Canada since 2004 and has a loyal following, the car almost got axed this year due to rising fuel prices and the trend to downsized vehicles in each market niche. But, when Infiniti realized the average QX owner was estimated at 45 years old—seven years younger than the average age for luxury car owners in North America—the automaker had a change of heart. Instead of dumping the QX, Infiniti will use it as a "halo" car to draw in

> ## KEY FACTS
>
> **CANADIAN PRICE (NEGOTIABLE):** *Base:* $73,000 **U.S. PRICE:** *Base:* $56,700, *AWD:* $59,800 **CANADIAN FREIGHT:** $1,890 **U.S. FREIGHT:** $860
> **POWERTRAIN (AWD)**
> Engine: 5.6L V8 (400 hp); Transmission: 7-speed auto.
> **DIMENSIONS/CAPACITY**
> Passengers: 2/3/2; 2/3/3; Wheelbase: 121.1 in.; H: 62.6/L: 208.3/W: 79.9 in.; Cargo volume: 16.6 cu. ft.; Fuel tank: 98L/premium; Tow limit: 8,500 lb.; Load capacity: N/A; Turning circle: 41.6 ft.; Ground clearance: 9.2 in.; Weight: 5,850 lb.

new buyers to the company's other luxury offerings...at least for a year or two longer.

COST ANALYSIS: It will be hard to haggle, due to the popularity of the QX series. Thus, you have two recourses: Wait until spring of 2011 for prices to moderate by about $5,000, or buy the car in the States and save up to $14,000 U.S., if you include the reduced freight fees. **Best alternatives:** Nissan's Armada, or GM's Tahoe, Yukon, Denali, or Escalade. The GM vehicles all ride better, have greater curb appeal, and are quieter. The Mercedes GX and Audi Q7 are much better looking alternatives, but they aren't as reliable. **Options:** Nothing is needed. **Rebates:** Look for discounts of about 10 percent as well as some very attractive leasing deals in the second quarter of 2011. **Depreciation:** Faster than average. A new 2009 that sold for $70,000 now sells for $48,000. **Insurance cost:** Higher than average. **Parts supply/cost:** Expensive parts that aren't easily found with independent suppliers. **Annual maintenance cost:** Higher than average. **Warranty:** Bumper-to-bumper 4 years/100,000 km; powertrain 6 years/110,000 km; rust perforation 7 years/unlimited km. **Supplementary warranty:** A good idea for the powertrain. **City/highway fuel economy:** 15.7/10.3 L/100 km, 18/27 mpg.

OWNER-REPORTED PROBLEMS: Body hardware and fit and finish deficiencies create a plethora of rattles and clunks; some brake failures and frequent brake repairs; malfunctioning rear air-leveling suspension makes the rear bottom-out without any alert sent to the driver. It makes trailer-towing a white-knuckle experience. Excessive steering shake and shimmy when passing over small bumps in the road; power accessories often malfunction; and the sound system is glitch-prone.

SERVICE BULLETIN-REPORTED PROBLEMS: Infiniti will replace the drivetrain's front propeller shaft for free on all 2010 models under a special warranty extension (Campaign PC037); another warranty extension covers the free replacement of the Intelligent Cruise Control Sensor (Campaign PC028); engine drivebelt noise; driveshaft U-joint noise or vibration; and front end suspension popping, clunking.

Kia

Functionality, Fuel Economy, and Fresh Styling

Despite the poor sales felt by most automakers during the past 18 months, Hyundai and its Kia subsidiary have done quite well by covering practically all the market niches from small econocars to top-of-the-line luxury cars, SUVs, and minivans. While Hyundai goes upscale with high-tech and fuel-frugal models placed throughout its model lineup, Kia is putting its money into an expanded lineup of less-expensive fuel-efficient vehicles that carry more standard features and are freshly styled. Positive reports from buyers of Kia's recently redesigned cars, minivans, and SUVs have led industry analysts to conclude that Hyundai's product improvement efforts are paying off with some Kia models—principally, the Optima, Rondo, Borrago, and Sportage. On the other hand, models like the Soul, Sedona, and Sorento continue to anchor Kia's quality ratings, forcing Hyundai to add more quality content this year without raising prices significantly.

Sins of the Past

Kia has long suffered from a reputation for making primitive, low-quality vehicles that are risky buys. Nevertheless, that impression is slowly fading away. In fact, Kia has recently posted impressive sales gains because some of their vehicles are now better and Kia offers a more-comprehensive warranty. Plus, its low prices are hard to beat.

RIO, RIO5 ★★★

The Kia Rio.

RATING: Average. The Rio sedan and Rio5 hatchback combine good fuel economy and interior room with useful standard features. **Strong points:** The 1.6L engine is usually adequate for most chores, and handling is acceptable, with plenty of steering feedback and good brakes; the ride is also comfortable, though sometimes busy; and passenger and cargo room are better than average. NHTSA gave the Rio four stars for frontal, side, and rollover crash protection. IIHS rates the Rio's frontal offset protection as "Acceptable." **Weak points:** Slow acceleration with the automatic transmission; insufficient highway passing power; excessive engine noise at higher speeds; harsh ride when passing over small bumps; trunk lid hinges intrude into the trunk area; actual fuel consumption is much higher than what is promised; poor rear-corner visibility with the Rio5; and below-average

KEY FACTS

CANADIAN PRICE (NEGOTIABLE): *Rio EX:* $13,695, *Rio EX Convenience:* $15,795, *Rio5 EX:* $14,095, *Rio5 EX Convenience:* $16,395, *Rio5 Sport:* $18,695 **U.S. PRICE:** *Rio SX:* $11,695, *Rio LX:* $14,995, *Rio5 LX:* $13,895 **CANADIAN FREIGHT:** $1,455 **U.S. FREIGHT:** $695 **POWERTRAIN (FRONT-DRIVE)** Engine: 1.6L 4-cyl. (110 hp); Transmissions: 5-speed man. • 4-speed auto. **DIMENSIONS/CAPACITY (RIO)** Passengers: 2/3; Wheelbase: 98.5 in.; H: 57.9/L: 167/W: 66.8 in.; Headroom F/R: 4.5/2.0 in.; Legroom F/R: 40/25 in.; Cargo volume: *Rio:* 11.9 cu. ft., *Rio5:* 15.8 cu. ft.; Fuel tank: 45L/regular; Tow limit: Not recommended; Load capacity: 850 lb.; Turning circle: 32.3 ft.; Weight: 2,435–2,505 lb.

IIHS crashworthiness scores for side collisions and head-restraint effectiveness. **New for 2011:** Carried over relatively unchanged.

OVERVIEW: The base Rio sedan won't spoil you with electronic gadgets and lah-dee-da comfort and convenience features, but it's an adequately equipped, solid econocar. Available as a four-door sedan or as the five-door hatchback Rio5, it comes with a manual transmission, an optional 4-speed automatic, wind-up windows, and manual door locks. On the other hand, safety features that are extra-cost items on more-expensive cars—like front seat belt pretensioners, disc brakes on all four wheels, and six airbags (dual frontal, front-seat side-impact, and full-coverage side curtain)—are standard features.

COST ANALYSIS: The discounted 2010s are cheaper buys than the almost identical 2011 version. **Best alternatives:** The Honda Fit, Hyundai Accent, Nissan Versa, and Toyota Yaris (with the brake override feature) are more-refined small cars that offer better performance while also conserving fuel. **Options:** Nothing important. **Rebates:** Look for $1,500 rebates or discounts and low financing rates in early 2011. **Depreciation:** Slower than average. **Insurance cost:** Average. **Parts supply/cost:** Average costs; parts aren't hard to find. **Annual maintenance cost:** Less than average. **Warranty:** Bumper-to-bumper 5 years/100,000 km; powertrain 5 years/100,000 km; rust perforation 5 years/unlimited km. **Supplementary warranty:** A wise buy for the engine/tranny considering Kia's previous powertrain troubles. **City/highway fuel economy:** *Man.:* 7.1/5.8 L/100 km, 49/40 mpg. *Auto.:* 7.7/5.6 L/100 km, 50/38 mpg.

OWNER-REPORTED PROBLEMS: Sharing the Accent platform and using more Hyundai components has undoubtedly improved Kia's quality, judging by J.D. Power survey results and the lower number of owner complaints. The Rio and Rio5 have registered fewer owner complaints than the newer Kia Soul. Nevertheless, the following problems have been reported: automatic transmission malfunctions; tie-rod and balljoints broke away from the chassis while vehicle was turning; poor fit and finish; premature brake repairs; electrical shorts; airbags failed to deploy in a frontal collision; passenger-side airbag was disabled, even though an average-sized occupant was seated; sudden acceleration in Reverse, with loss of brakes; brakes locked up when applied; and the rear window shattered when the driver's door was closed.

SERVICE BULLETIN-REPORTED PROBLEMS: The stabilizer bar link upper mounting nut(s) (right and/or left) may have been insufficiently torqued on some 2010s, permitting some metal-to-metal movement and a squeaking noise; they will be tightened free of charge under Campaign SA034.

SOUL ★ ★

RATING: Below Average, mainly due to poor-quality materials and craftsmanship. **Strong points:** Inexpensive and well equipped with safety devices like ABS, stability control, six airbags, and active head restraints—features that are rare on entry-level small cars. User-friendly controls; plenty of interior room; comfortable seats; a competent engine (the 2.0L is a better choice for reserve power); a compliant suspension, without undue body roll or front-end plow; and fairly agile when cornering, with good steering feedback. The IIHS gives the 2010 Soul its top "Good" rating for frontal offset, side, roof strength, and head restraint occupant crash protection. I, for one, want a re-test by NHTSA. **Weak points:** Base engine could use more grunt at low engine rpm; automatic transmission needs a Fifth gear; shifting is noisy and rough; omnipresent rattles; and body glitches. Also, limited cargo room when compared to its rivals; poor-quality, easily broken, or prematurely worn interior items; excessive wind and road noise; a busy highway ride; fuel economy is seriously overstated; poor rearward visibility through the small rear windshield; and the car has not yet been crash tested by the NHTSA. **New for 2011:** Carried over unchanged.

OVERVIEW: Fairly well equipped; the only downside is that the equipment is generally of poor quality. Soul is a little four-door hatchback/wagon that combines safety with acceptable urban performance while keeping your fuel bills low. The best combination is the 2.0L engine hooked to a 5-speed manual transmission. If

KEY FACTS

CANADIAN PRICE (NEGOTIABLE): *1.6:* $15,795, *2.0 2U:* $18,295, *Auto.:* $19,495, *2.0 4U:* $20,295, *Auto.:* $21,495, *Retro:* $20,995, *Auto.:* $22,195, *Burner:* $21,295, *Auto.:* $22,495, *SX:* $21,895, *Auto.:* $23,095 **U.S. PRICE:** *1.6:* $13,300, *2.0 2U:* $15,195, *Auto.:* $16,195, *2.0 4U:* $17,195, *Auto.:* $18,195, *Sport:* $17,195, *Auto.:* $18,195 **CANADIAN FREIGHT:** $1,650 **U.S. FREIGHT:** $695 **POWERTRAIN (FRONT-DRIVE)** Engines: 1.6L 4-cyl. (122 hp) • 2.0L 4-cyl. (142 hp); Transmissions: 5-speed man. • 4-speed auto.

DIMENSIONS/CAPACITY Passengers: 2/3; Wheelbase: 100.4 in.; H: 63.4/L: 161.6/W: 70.3 in.; Cargo volume: 19.3 cu. ft.; Fuel tank: 48L/ regular; Tow limit: N/A; Turning circle: 34.4 ft.; Weight: 2,624–2,855 lb.

you get the 4-speed automatic shifter, understand that the engine will seem sluggish without a Fifth gear. Invest in the ABS and stability control by moving upscale to the Soul 2u. Forget the space-robbing sunroof.

COST ANALYSIS: A leftover 2010 is cheaper and is practically identical to this year's model. You could save a few thousand dollars by purchasing your Kia in the States, but it hardly seems worth the bother. Show your dealer the *Lemon-Aid* prices and ask for a similar price. **Best Alternatives:** Other contenders are the Honda Civic, Hyundai Elantra, Nissan Cube or Versa, Scion xB, and Toyota Yaris or Corolla (with the brake override feature). **Options:** Larger 18-inch wheels and the driver's seat height adjuster. **Rebates:** Look for $1,000 rebates and low financing rates in early 2011. **Depreciation:** Faster than average. A base 2010 Soul that retailed new for $15,500 is now worth only $11,000 used, and the 2010 model year isn't over yet. **Insurance cost:** Average. **Parts supply/cost:** Average costs; some parts delayed. **Annual maintenance cost:** Average. **Warranty:** Bumper-to-bumper 5 years/100,000 km; powertrain 5 years/100,000 km; rust perforation 5 years/unlimited km. **Supplementary warranty:** A wise buy for the engine/tranny, considering Kia's previous powertrain troubles. **City/ highway fuel economy:** 1.6L: 7.7/6.3 L/100 km, 37/45 mpg. 2.0L: 8.6/6.5 L/100 km, 33/43 mpg.

OWNER-REPORTED PROBLEMS: Airbags failed to deploy when vehicle hit a deer; brake pedal is too small; rear brake failure caused a rear-ender; automatic transmission slips and often sticks in gear or grinds when going into Second gear; fuel spews out when refueling; driver door fails to latch; steering column came off while car was underway; accident report questions the Soul's high crashworthiness score:

> We rear-ended a 2004 Expedition in our 2010 Kia Soul at 20 mph [32 km/h]. My wife sustained a "traumatic brain injury" as a result of the air bag wiring harness being cut in half (both sides) before the sensors were activated. I have photos of the wiring hardness cut in the accident and the car. My 29 year old wife will now spend the rest of her life disabled. This is a dangerous car. Kia states the airbags will not activate at 20 mph [32 km/h]. This is not a 5 star frontal impact design. The fuel shut off did not activate, "all safety features failed".

A plethora of fit and finish deficiencies:

My 2010 Kia Soul has such severe interior damage from the sub-standard material they used that the market value has depreciated far beyond the norm. Any metal, even plastic that touches the doors (seat belt buckle), pillars, center console, glove box, etc....becomes damaged. The material has no padding under it so there is no absorption and it is "honey comb" design which when scratched breaks the "honey comb" which has a light grey under it. My father bought the same car at the same time and he too has this problem. The car's showing this damage immediately. The dealership has no way of fixing it and the manufacturer is telling us to wait for their solution, many people have been waiting for over a year. Kia has put other 2010 Souls on the lot with completely different material so this should be the solution... chipping paint that has started to rust with 6000 miles [9,650 km] on it. We deserve consumer protection. Please check *www.kiasoulforum.com* for greater awareness of this very public issue. Also, rear view window so small and high it is a danger.

Door panels tend to scratch up with the slightest touch; chips in the glass and paint; and the engine design attracts pools of water.

SERVICE BULLETIN-REPORTED PROBLEMS: Drivebelt squealing noise remedy and the following warranty extension campaigns allowing for free repairs: rear wiper squeal noise repair (Campaign SA026); crash pad centre tray damper pad (Campaign SA027); manual transmission shifter skirt replacement (Campaign SA015); mood lamp control unit replacement (Campaign SA010); and audio system software update (Campaign SA009).

FORTE, FORTE KOUP   ★ ★ ★

The Kia Forte.

KEY FACTS

CANADIAN PRICE (NEGOTIABLE): *LX:* $15,795, *Auto.:* $16,995, *EX:* $19,295, *SX:* $21,095, *Auto.:* $22,295, *EX Koup:* $18,495, *Auto.:* $19,695, *SX Koup:* $21,495, *Auto.:* $22,695 **U.S. PRICE:** *LX:* $13,695, *Auto.:* $14,685, *EX:* $15,995, *Auto.:* $16,995, *SX:* $17,495, *Auto.:* $18,495, *EX Koup:* $16,595, *Auto.:* $17,595, *SX Koup:* $17,695, *Auto.:* $18,695 **CANADIAN FREIGHT:** $1,650 **U.S. FREIGHT:** $695

POWERTRAIN (FRONT-DRIVE)

Engines: 2.0L 4-cyl. (156 hp) • 2.4L 4-cyl. (173 hp); Transmissions: 5-speed man. • 6-speed man. • 4-speed auto. • 5-speed auto.

DIMENSIONS/CAPACITY

Passengers: 2/3; Wheelbase: 104.3 in.; H: 57.5/L: 176.3/W: 69.4 in.; Cargo volume: 12.6 cu. ft.; Fuel tank: 51.9L/ regular; Tow limit: N/A; Turning circle: 33.8 ft.; Ground clearance: 5.5 in.; Weight: 2,707–2,868 lb.

RATING: Average. Kia slew the poor-quality dragon; now, its newest compact sedan gets the engine and suspension refinements Kia's lineup lacked in the past. **Strong points:** Good acceleration; four-wheel disc brakes; exemplary fit and finish; nicely bolstered, comfortable front seats; lots of interior room up front; competent engines at high revs, with plenty of reserve power and a smoothly shifting automatic transmission; sure-footed and precise handling and a comfortable ride; standard Bluetooth and steering wheel controls with voice activation; heated side-view windows; fewer rattles and body glitches; a large dealer network with both Kia and Hyundai providing servicing; and a comprehensive base warranty. **Weak points:** Steering wheel tilts but doesn't telescope (EX trim excepted); rear seating is cramped for three; long-term reliability is unproven; the vehicle has not yet been crash tested; and prices are likely to stay firm as higher fuel costs add to the overall popularity of these new econocars. Overall quality is still so-so. **New for 2011:** Kia has rolled out a third body style: a five-door hatchback.

OVERVIEW: All three body styles have what it takes to satisfy the needs of the daily commuter as well as excite the most ardent high-performance fan. Two different 4-cylinder engines deliver more than enough power without wasting fuel. In fact, the SX features an upgraded 2.4L inline 4-banger that delivers 173 hp—more than the most powerful versions of the Toyota Corolla, or even the Mazda3. Handling is a breeze, thanks to the Forte's front-drive unibody frame and four-wheel independent suspension, which provide a smooth and sporty ride, with a minimum of noise, vibration, and harshness.

COST ANALYSIS: It's a little early to take a chance on this relatively new econocar. Already, we have seen some serious quality problems with the compact Soul as it enters its second year. Wait at least another year before getting a Forte. As for buying a Forte south of the border: Is saving $5,000 worth the trouble? **Best Alternatives:** The Ford Focus, Honda Civic, Hyundai Elantra, Mazda3, and Toyota Corolla (only with the brake override feature). **City/highway fuel economy:** 2.0L: 8.3/5.8 L/100 km, 34/49 mpg. 2.4L: 9.2/6.2 L/100 km, 31/46 mpg.

OWNER-REPORTED PROBLEMS: Steering locked suddenly as the vehicle stalled out; engine surging; sometimes it feels as if the gas pedal were stuck; and major paint defects.

SERVICE BULLETIN-REPORTED PROBLEMS: Hard starts; rough idle; pop noise on 2–3 manual shift; manual transmission 2–3 shift shock (Campaign SA022); sunroof noise (Campaign SA030); automatic transmission shift hesitation (Campaign SA020); replacement of the junction box relay (Campaign SA012); manual transmission inspection of the driveshaft housing seal (Campaign SA011); seatbelt buckle replacement (Campaign SC078); fuel filler cap replacement (Campaign SA023); and a fix for doors rattling as they are closed.

RONDO ★★★★

RATING: Above Average. **Strong points:** Competent engines; offers small-car dimensions with minivan utility; can carry seven passengers to the Mazda5's six; easy entry and exit; a comfortable and quiet ride; good fit and finish; and standard stability control and side curtain airbags. NHTSA gave the Rondo five stars for frontal and side crash protection. Rollover protection earned four stars. **Weak points:** Not as agile as its Mazda5 rival, and mediocre fuel economy with the V6. **New for 2011:** Nothing important; scheduled to be restyled in 2013.

OVERVIEW: Kia's Rondo is one of the best compact hatchbacks on the market; it's a pity that it's so often overlooked. Seating seven, it offers an impressive amount of room for its size, although third-row seating is for children only.

COST ANALYSIS: The Rondo and Mazda5 cost practically the same; however, Mazda dealers aren't quick to offer discounts, while Kia dealers try harder to close the deal. **Best alternative:** The Mazda5, especially with its 2011 upgrades; Nissan Cube; Honda Odyssey; and the Toyota Sienna (with the brake override

KEY FACTS

CANADIAN PRICE (NEGOTIABLE): *LX:* $19, 995, *EX 5-pass.:* $22,595, *7-pass.:* $23,545, *Premium:* $24,795, *EX V6 5-pass.:* $23,595, *EX V6 7-pass.:* $24,595, *EX V6 Luxury:* $26,795 **U.S. PRICE:** *Base 2.4L:* $17,495, *LX 2.4L:* $18,495, *LX 2.7L V6:* $19,495, *EX 2.4L:* $21,295, *EX 2.7 V6:* $22,295 **CANADIAN FREIGHT:** $1,650 **U.S. FREIGHT:** $695
POWERTRAIN (FRONT-DRIVE)
Engines: 2.4L 4-cyl. (175 hp) • 2.7L V6 (192 hp); Transmissions: 4-speed auto. • 5-speed auto.

DIMENSIONS/CAPACITY

Passengers: 2/3/2; Wheelbase: 106.3 in.; H: 65/L: 178.9/W: 71.7 in.; Headroom F/R1/R2: 6.0/5.0/0.0 in.; Legroom F/R1/R2: 40/28/23 in.; Cargo volume: 33 cu. ft.; Fuel tank: 60L/regular; Tow limit: 2,000 lb.; Load capacity: 825 lb.; Turning circle: 39 ft.; Ground clearance: 6.1 in.; Weight: 3,333 lb.

feature). **Options:** The V6 engine is essential if you intend to carry full loads. **Rebates:** Look for $3,000 rebates and low financing rates in early 2010. **Depreciation:** A bit faster than average. **Insurance cost:** Average. **Parts supply/cost:** Average. **Annual maintenance cost:** Average. **Warranty:** Bumper-to-bumper 5 years/100,000 km; powertrain 5 years/100,000 km; rust perforation 5 years/unlimited km. **Supplementary warranty:** A toss-up; extra powertrain coverage is all that is needed. **City/highway fuel economy:** 2.4L: 10.6/7.5 L/100 km, 27/38 mpg. 2.7L: 11.5/7.7 L/100 km, 25/37 mpg.

OWNER-REPORTED PROBLEMS: Owners complain mostly about climate control malfunctions and frequent brake component replacements (calipers and rotors); passenger airbag warning light stays on for no reason; severe vibration and shaking when cruising at 90 km/h; transmission stalling and grinding; fuel consumption is much higher than what's promised by Kia; and vibration and loud cabin roar if one of the windows is opened while the vehicle is underway.

MAGENTIS ★★★

RATING: Average. Consider buying a competitor with more refinement, a proven history of reliability, and good quality control. **Strong points:** Nicely appointed; good overall visibility; plenty of front headroom; firm, supportive front bucket seats with plenty of fore and aft travel; better-than-average fuel economy with regular fuel; nice ride quality and handling; spacious trunk; four-star front and side crashworthiness rating, and five stars awarded for rollover resistance; and servicing can be carried out by both Hyundai and Kia dealers. A 5-year/100,000 km all-inclusive warranty. **Weak points:** An underpowered 4-cylinder engine; only average V6 performance; mediocre braking; average rear headroom; considerable body lean when turning; excessive wind and tire noise; trunk has a small opening; stability and traction control are optional on base models and standard only on the higher-end versions; and fit and finish isn't up to Honda's or Toyota's standards. **New for 2011:** Nothing major; Kia is coasting on last year's redesign.

OVERVIEW: Kia's mid-sized sedan is essentially a rebadged Hyundai Sonata, sold also as the Optima in the States. All models include front side airbags, side curtain airbags, seat belt pretensioners, ABS, four-wheel disc brakes, and anti-whiplash head restraints that have received IIHS's top safety rating.

COST ANALYSIS: Save money with a 2009. Since the 2010s are carryovers from last year, hold out for major discounting and generous rebates to cut the retail price by at least 15 percent. **Best alternatives:** Consider the Chevrolet Malibu, Honda Accord, Hyundai Elantra, and Toyota Camry. **Options:** Save your money. **Rebates:** Look for $2,500 rebates or discounts and low financing rates early in 2010. **Depreciation:** Slower than average. **Insurance cost:** Average. **Parts supply/cost:** Average. **Annual maintenance cost:** Average. **Warranty:** Bumper-to-bumper 5 years/100,000 km; powertrain 5 years/100,000 km; rust perforation 5 years/unlimited km. **Supplementary warranty:** A wise buy for the engine and transmission. **City/highway fuel economy:** 2.4L man.: 9.4/6.2 L/100 km, 30/46 mpg. 2.4L auto.: 9.4/6.2 L/100 km, 30/46 mpg. 2.7L: 10.5/7.0 L/100 km, 27/40 mpg.

OWNER-REPORTED PROBLEMS: Sudden unintended acceleration; vehicle shut off in Drive and restarted; vehicle shot forward, causing a crash. Passenger-side airbag is disabled when passenger of any size is seated; seat belt harness's shoulder belts were nonfunctional in a collision; when downshifting, the engine surges at about 40 km/h; parked car will roll down an incline, despite being put in First gear; vehicle pulls to the right when underway; windows leak air; low-beam headlights don't illuminate far enough; and headlights dim when applying the brakes or when slowing down.

KEY FACTS

CANADIAN PRICE (NEGOTIABLE): *LX:* $21,995, *LX V6:* $24,295, *LX Premium:* $25,445, *SX:* $29,495, *SX V6:* $30,795 **U.S. PRICE:** *Optima:* $17,995 **CANADIAN FREIGHT:** $1,650 **U.S. FREIGHT** $695 **POWERTRAIN (FRONT-DRIVE)** Engines: 2.4L 4-cyl. (175 hp) • 2.7L V6 (190 hp); Transmissions: 5-speed man. • 5-speed auto. **DIMENSIONS/CAPACITY** Passengers: 2/3; Wheelbase: 107 in.; H: 58.2/L: 188.9/W: 71 in.; Legroom F/R: 39.7/38 in.; Cargo volume: 14.8 cu. ft.; Fuel tank: 62L/regular; Tow limit: *2.4L:* No towing, *2.7L:* 1,000–2,000 lb.; Turning circle: 35.4 ft.; Weight: 3,157 lb.

SEDONA ★★

KEY FACTS

CANADIAN PRICE (NEGOTIABLE): *LX:* $27,05, *LX Convenience:* $29,045, *EX:* $33,295, *EX Power:* $35,595, *EX Luxury:* $39,195, *EX Navigation:* $40,195
U.S. PRICE: *Base:* $22,195 **CANADIAN FREIGHT:** $1,650 **U.S. FREIGHT:** $695
POWERTRAIN (FRONT-DRIVE)
Engine: 3.8L V6 (250 hp); Transmission: 5-speed auto.
DIMENSIONS/CAPACITY
Passengers: 2/2/3; Wheelbase: 119 in.; H: 69./L: 202/W: 78 in.; Headroom F/R1/R2: 5.0/2.0/3.0 in.; Legroom F/R1/R2: 40/31/28 in.; Cargo volume: 65 cu. ft.; Fuel tank: 80L/regular; Tow limit: 3,500 lb.; Load capacity: 1,155 lb.; Turning circle: 43 ft.; Ground clearance: 5.0 in.; Weight: 4,802 lb.

RATING: Below Average. In theory, this should be the minivan everyone should buy. But, sadly, a good idea has been hobbled by poor execution; it isn't expected to last beyond the 2011 model year. **Strong points:** An entry-level Sedona will cost about $6,000 less than the equivalent Honda or Toyota minivan. The Sedona is well-appointed, and stability control is a standard feature. The engine supplies more than enough power in all gear ranges; the automatic transmission shifts smoothly and quietly; the ride is comfortable; and handling is very responsive. A low ground clearance adds stability and helps passengers access the interior. Important interior features include a low step-in; a convenient "walk-through" space between front seats; second-row seats that flip and fold for access to the third row; a split rear bench that folds into the floor (a Honda idea); well laid-out, user-friendly instruments and controls; lots of storage areas; active head restraints; and side curtain airbags for head protection in all three rows. There's also good visibility, minimal engine and road noise, excellent crashworthiness scores, good braking, traction control, stability control, and a comprehensive base warranty. **Weak points:** Reliability, reliability, and reliability. Both the Sedona and the discontinued Hyundai Entourage minivans are riddled with factory-related defects affecting primarily the powertrain, brakes, electronic system, suspension, and fit and finish. Fuel consumption is also much higher than what Kia and Transport Canada represent. **New for 2011:** Nothing important; a "dead van, walking."

OVERVIEW: Sedona leapfrogged over most of the competition when it was restyled and reengineered a few years ago. Only problem is they forgot to improve the quality along with the performance. The latest model refines all the previous changes and offers buyers a minivan that's similar in size to the Honda Odyssey and Toyota Sienna; full of standard safety, performance, and convenience goodies; and backed by a comprehensive warranty. But, on the other hand, who wants a minivan that will spend much of its time in the service bay?

COST ANALYSIS: Without a doubt, this is a cheaper minivan than the Japanese competition, but the money you save may be spent on expensive repairs later on. **Best alternatives:** Consider the Honda Odyssey, Mazda5, and Toyota Sienna. Chrysler's minivans are good second choices that will be cheaper and feature-loaded as well. Their only drawback will be the need for you to buy an extended warranty to protect yourself from tranny failures. **Options:** The $5,000 EX Luxury option is a waste of money on nonessentials. Stay away from the power-sliding doors; they open when they should close and close when they should open. **Rebates:** Look for $3,500 rebates, low financing rates, and attractive leases. **Depreciation:** Faster than average. **Insurance cost:** Average. **Parts supply/cost:** Average costs, but availability has been spotty. **Annual maintenance cost:** Higher than average. **Warranty:** Bumper-to-bumper 5 years/100,000 km; powertrain 5 years/100,000 km; rust perforation 5 years/unlimited km. **Supplementary warranty:** A wise buy, considering Kia's previous transmission troubles and the installation of a new set-up on the 2006s. **City/highway fuel economy:** 13.2/8.8 L/100 km, 22/33 mpg.

OWNER-REPORTED PROBLEMS: Right door handle broke off when opening the door; erratic opening and closing of the power-sliding door (a common failure with all minivans' power-assisted doors); the Sedona eats brakes and tires; front axle failure due to bearing and seal defect; vehicle rolled back while in Park. Suddenly accelerated to 145–161 km/h when passing another car; chronic stalling while underway or turning into an intersection; engine constantly misfires. Electrical malfunctions:

> With only 700 miles [1,127 km] on Sedona minivan I have had an air bag sensor go bad, a drivers side sliding door sensor go bad, a passenger side front door sensor go bad, the IP computer (fuse box inside vehicle near drivers side) burned up completely.

SPORTAGE ★★★★

RATING: Above Average. The Sportage has become a 4-cylinder "crossover" similar to the Tucson. Question: Why not simply buy a Tucson? **Strong points:** A lively 4-banger and a comfortable, quiet ride; dependable handling, thanks to the responsive steering and better-tuned suspension; and standard stability control and curtain airbags. The 4-cylinder is adequate for most chores and is a bit less buzzy this year. NHTSA gives the 2010 Sportage five stars for frontal and side

KEY FACTS

CANADIAN PRICE (NEGOTIABLE): *LX:* $21,745, *LX Convenience:* $23,945, *LX AWD:* $25,945, *LX V6:* $27,285, *LX V6 AWD:* $29,285, *LX V6 Luxury:* $30,985 **U.S. PRICE:** *Base:* $18,295, *LX:* $20,295, *EX:* $23,295 **CANADIAN FREIGHT:** $1,650 **U.S. FREIGHT:** $695
POWERTRAIN (FRONT-DRIVE/AWD)
Engine: 2.4L 4-cyl. (176 hp); Transmissions: 6-speed man. • 6-speed auto.
DIMENSIONS/CAPACITY
Passengers: 2/3; Wheelbase: 103.5 in.; H: 66.7/L: 171.3/W: 70.9 in.; Headroom F/R: 4.0/5.0 in.; Legroom F/R: 40/29 in.; Cargo volume: 31 cu. ft.; Fuel tank: 58L-65L/regular; Tow limit: 1,000–2,000 lb.; Load capacity: 860 lb.; Turning circle: 38 ft.; Ground clearance: 6.0 in.; Weight: 3,230–3,527 lb.

occupant crash protection; rollover protection was given three stars. "Acceptable" IIHS scores. The Sportage is reasonably priced and has a better reliability record than the Sorento does. **Weak points:** On paper, the powertrain setup and suspension system scream *performance*, but the Sportage on the road takes it down to a whisper. It's neither in the front nor the rear of the performance pack. Roadway feedback is barely noticeable, and the car exhibits excess body roll and pulling. One wishes Kia had chosen Hyundai's more-powerful, direct-injected 4-cylinder engine instead. Styled like a Pontiac Vibe with upscale Audi headlights and LED lighting; interior hard plastic garnishings cheapen the look; the firm leather seats look good, but are hard on the…"butt." **New for 2011:** All models will use Kia's 176 hp 2.4L engine coupled to a 6-speed tranny, which Kia claims is a more fuel-efficient and powerful setup than the 2.7L V6 and 5-speed team it replaces. Later in the year the high-performance Sportage SX will arrive with its 270 hp 2.0L turbocharged engine and lots of performance enhancements. The car's restyled exterior looks like a Pontiac Vibe from the side.

OVERVIEW: The Sportage has been around forever. Now—in its downsized configuration, resting on the Hyundai Tucson's frame, and with its use of Kia's ubiquitous 2.4L 4-cylinder engine—Sportage offers power, car-like handling, and better dependability. Standard equipment for the base LX version, which has a 4-cylinder engine hooked to a manual 5-speed transmission, includes power windows and door locks, cruise control, tilt steering, power side mirrors, and four-wheel disc brakes with ABS.

COST ANALYSIS: Wait a bit before opting for the 2011 and leave the power- and performance-challenged 2010 version alone. **Best alternatives:** The Ford Escape, Honda CR-V, Hyundai Tucson, Kia Rondo, Mazda Tribute, and Toyota RAV4. **Options:** The LX V6; the EX version is padded with nonessentials. Forget the rear spoiler. **Depreciation:** Average. **Insurance cost:** Average. **Parts supply/cost:** Average cost; some delays for parts. **Annual maintenance cost:** Average. **Warranty:** Bumper-to-bumper 5 years/100,000 km; powertrain 5 years/100,000 km; rust perforation 5 years/unlimited km. **Supplementary warranty:** Worth considering. **City/highway fuel economy (2010):** *2.0L man.:* 10.3/7.8 L/100 km, 27/36 mpg. *2.0L auto.:* 10.2/8.0 L/100 km, 28/35 mpg. *2.0L AWD:* 10.8/8.3 L/100 km, 25/33 mpg. *2.7L:* 11.5/8.5 L/100 km, 26/34 mpg. *2.7L AWD:* 11.7/8.8 L/100 km, 24/32 mpg. Owners report they get nowhere near these numbers.

OWNER-REPORTED PROBLEMS: *2010:* Passenger-side airbag often disables itself when passenger shuffles in the seat; a too-sensitive accelerator pedal causes car to lurch forward; vehicle continually pulls to the right; can be hard to steer; traction control feature causes the car to suddenly slow down, endangering following vehicles; car constantly stalls and is hard to start; brakes sometimes make a grinding sound and then fail; speedometer and clock are hard to read in daylight; tire-pressure sensor comes on for no reason; and the gas tank is vulnerable to road debris.

SORENTO ★★

RATING: Below Average. What, $39,000 for this? Poor reliability and future orphanhood make the Sorento's 2010 carryover model a poor buy. **Strong points:** Okay, it *is* well appointed and you get more SUV for fewer bucks, but what you do get may be all show and no go—and not very reliable, either. (Not really "strong points," eh?) The base engine will do what is required. You also have standard

KEY FACTS

CANADIAN PRICE (NEGOTIABLE): *2.4 LX:* $23,995, *Auto.:* $26,595, *2.4 LX AWD:* $28,495, *2.4 EX:* $29,795, *2.4 EX auto.:* $29,795, *2.4 EX AWD:* $31,695, *3.5 LX:* $29,095, *3.5 LX 7-seat:* $30,295, *3.5 LX AWD:* $20,995, *3.5 LX AWD 7-seat:* $32,195, *3.5 EX:* $31,795, *3.5 EX AWD:* $33,695, *3.5 EX AWD (with sunroof):* $34,995, *3.5 EX AWD Luxury:* $37,995, *3.5 EX AWD Luxury 7-seat:* $39,195 **U.S. PRICE:** *2.4 LX:* $22,395, *2.4 LX AWD:* $24,095, *3.5 LX:* $29,095, *3.5 LX AWD:* $20,995, *2.4 EX:* $24,795, *2.4 EX AWD:* $26,495, *3.5 EX V6:* $27,395, *3.5 EX V6 AWD:* $27,395 **CANADIAN FREIGHT:** $1,650 **U.S. FREIGHT:** $695

POWERTRAIN (REAR-DRIVE/4WD)
Engines: 2.4L 4-cyl. (175 hp) • 3.5L V6 (276 hp); Transmissions: 6-speed man. • 6-speed auto.

DIMENSIONS/CAPACITY
Passengers: 2/3; 2/3/2; Wheelbase: 106.3 in.; H: 68.7/L: 183.9/W: 74.2 in.; Cargo volume: 37 cu. ft.; Fuel tank: 80L/regular; Tow limit: 3,500 lb.; Load capacity: 999 lb.; Turning circle: 38 ft.; Ground clearance: 7.5 in.; Weight: 3,571–3,682 lb.

stability control and a fairly roomy interior with good fit and finish. At first glance, this is an off-roader's delight, with low-range gearing and good ground clearance, but there's always that pesky reliability thing. NHTSA gives four stars for front, side, and rollover protection. IIHS says frontal offset crashworthiness and head-restraint protection are "Good." **Weak points:** Your off-roading fun will end as soon as the tranny or brakes give out. (Did we mention reliability?) Fuel consumption is much higher than represented, and IIHS says side-impact crashworthiness is "Poor." **New for 2011:** A new unibody platform and an additional third-row seat. The new Sorento is also longer and wider than previous models.

OVERVIEW: The Sorento represents good value in theory, with its strong towing capacity and excellent safety ratings. However, it falls short on reliability, fuel economy, and ride quality.

COST ANALYSIS: The Sorento skipped the 2010 model year; make sure you know what you're buying. **Best alternatives:** The Honda CR-V, Hyundai Tucson, and Toyota RAV4. **Options:** The Sport package isn't worth its cost. **Rebates:** Look for $4,000 rebates and low financing and leasing rates in early 2011. **Depreciation:** Faster than average for an Asian make. **Insurance cost:** Average. **Annual maintenance cost:** Higher than average. **Warranty:** Bumper-to-bumper 5 years/100,000 km; powertrain 5 years/100,000 km; rust perforation 5 years/unlimited km. **Supplementary warranty:** A wise buy, considering Kia's previous transmission troubles. **City/highway fuel economy:** *2.4L man.:* 10.6/7.4 L/100 km, 27/38 mpg. *Auto.:* 9.7/6.9 L/100 km, 29/41 mpg. *2.4L AWD:* 9.9/7.4 L/100 km, 29/38 mpg. *V6 man.:* 10.3/7.7 L/100 km, 27/37 mpg. *V6 AWD:* 10.6/7.4 L/100 km, 25/36 mpg.

OWNER-REPORTED PROBLEMS: Same old story of the passenger-side airbags being disabled when an adult passenger is seated. Other concerns include engine fire; engine harmonic balancer failure; airbags failed to deploy; automatic transmission failures; transmission torque converter locks up; vehicle jerks, stutters, and stalls; driveline vibration; faulty wiring harness; early brake wearout; chrome bezel instrument panel creates a painful and annoying reflection; headlight illumination is too short; speedometer reads slower than the actual speed; and tire valves sometimes leak.

BORREGO ★★

RATING: Below Average. The Borrego lacks the refined ride comfort and handling found in other luxury three-row SUVs, due to its truck-like body-on-frame construction. **Strong points:** The V6 performs quite well in all driving situations and can handle heavy loads with ease. The V8 cranks up the towing capability to 7,500 lb., with plenty of power in reserve for serious stump pulling. There's also a smooth-shifting automatic transmission, a quiet interior, user-friendly controls, ample third-row seating, a standard trailer hitch and electric harness, and standard stability control. NHTSA gives the Borrego five stars for frontal and side occupant crash protection. Rollover protection was given four stars. Few owner complaints over reliability, so far. **Weak points:** A hard, jolting ride; poor emergency handling; head restraints are too close to the back of the head; lacks a power tailgate; and fuel consumption is much higher than represented. **New for 2011:** Nothing major; The Borrego is selling poorly and may not make it through the 2010 model year.

OVERVIEW: The Borrego is a truck. It's a nicely appointed truck, but a truck just the same. This means you can carry a family of seven in comfort, tow practically anything, go off-roading (within reason), and manoeuvre in small areas due to the Borrego's

KEY FACTS

CANADIAN PRICE (NEGOTIABLE): *LX V6:* $37,395, *EX V6:* $41,395, *LX V8:* $39,895, *EX V8:* $44,395 **U.S. PRICE:** *LX 3.8 V6:* $26,245, *LX 3.8 V6 AWD:* $28,295, *LX V8 AWD:* $30,995, *EX 3.8 V6:* $27,995, *EX 3.8 V6 AWD:* $27,995, *EX 4.6 V8:* $30,995, *EX V8:* $32,995, *EX V8 Limited:* $27,995 **CANADIAN FREIGHT:** $1,650 **U.S. FREIGHT:** $695

POWERTRAIN (REAR-DRIVE/4WD)
Engines: 3.8L V6 (276 hp) • 4.6L V8 (337 hp); Transmissions: 5-speed manumatic • 6-speed auto.

DIMENSIONS/CAPACITY
Passengers: 2/3/2; Wheelbase: 114 in.; H: 71/L: 192/W: 75 in.; Headroom F/R1/R2: 3.5/5.0/3.0 in.; Legroom F/R1/R2: 40.5/29/26 in.; Cargo volume: 41.5 cu. ft.; Fuel tank: 78L/regular; Tow limit: 5,000–7,500 lb.; Load capacity: 1,155 lb.; Turning circle: 38 ft.; Ground clearance: 7.5 in.; Weight: 4,735 lb.

tight (for its size) turning circle. For these and other truck-like attributes, the Borrego outshines the Ford Explorer. On the other hand, you won't find any styling breakthroughs (Kia thinks boxy is beautiful), the vehicle struggles in some off-road areas, and fuel economy is nonexistent.

COST ANALYSIS: Lots of deal-making is going on with this gas-guzzler as the price of fuel moves upward. **Best alternatives:** Nissan Pathfinder and Toyota 4Runner for truck-like attributes. Vehicles with more car-like qualities are the Chevy Traverse, Ford Flex, Honda Pilot, and Mazda CX-9. **Options:** Skid plate protection, if going off-road. Forego the heated leather seats, chrome wheels, and space-stealing sunroof. **Rebates:** Look for $4,000 rebates, low financing rates, and leasing deals in early 2011. **Depreciation:** Much faster than average: A $43,500, top-of-the-line 2009 Borrego EX V8 sells used for less than $30,000. **Insurance cost:** Much higher than average. **Parts supply/cost:** Moderately expensive and hard to find; expect long delays for parts. **Annual maintenance cost:** Expected to be much higher than average. **Warranty:** Bumper-to-bumper 5 years/100,000 km; powertrain 5 years/100,000 km; rust perforation 5 years/unlimited km. **Supplementary warranty:** A wise buy, considering Kia's previous transmission troubles and its 2009 revamping. **City/highway fuel economy:** *3.8L manumatic:* 12.7/9.4 L/100 km, 22/30 mpg. *3.8L AWD:* 13.0/9.4 L/100 km, 22/30 mpg. *4.6L:* 13.8/9.3 L/100 km, 20/30 mpg. *AWD:* 13.8/9.3 L/100 km, 20/29 mpg.

OWNER-REPORTED PROBLEMS: Vehicle sticks in Drive once underway; car suddenly accelerates when vehicle is in Drive; vehicle wanders along the road, requires constant steering correction; and the car constantly pulls to the right.

Lexus

The first Lexus, the LS 400, appeared in 1989 and didn't share any major components with previous Toyotas. Equipped with a V8 engine and noted for its outstanding engine performance, quietness, well-appointed interior, and impressive build quality, the car was an immediate success. Now the Lexus name has supplanted Cadillac as a term for luxury and quality, and it has been chosen as the most popular luxury car company in Germany. No one had heard of Lexus vehicles suffering from sudden unintended acceleration—yet.

Lexus's impeccable reputation for quality and safety has been hurt by the past year's news barrage of owner complaints, recalls, and mea culpas issued by Toyota's president who admits (rather reluctantly and with tears flowing) that "ahem, well, you know, yes, I've got it—the company lost its way."

Yep. Toyota/Lexus lost its way big time. Sales have been affected for both brands. They'll climb back, but buyers will no longer say "I'm gonna buy a Toyota or a

Lexus." Instead, they will look at vehicles offered in the luxury or family class and then make their choice. That's what Toyota/Lexus now faces.

Lexus is a luxury automaker on its own merits, even though many models have mostly been dressed-up Camrys. Unlike Acura and Infiniti, Lexus is seen by some as the epitome of luxury and comfort, with a small dab of performance thrown in. Lexus executives know that no matter how often car enthusiast magazines say that drivers want "road feel," "responsive handling," and "high-performance" thrills, the truth of the matter is that most drivers simply want cars that look good and that give them bragging rights for safety, performance, convenience, and comfort; they want to travel from point A to point B, without interruption, in cars that are more than fully equipped Civics or warmed-over Maximas. Lexus figures that hardcore high-performance aficionados can move up to its sportier IS models and the rest will stick with the Camry-based "Japanese Oldsmobile" ES series.

Although these imports do set advanced benchmarks for quality control in most cases, they don't demonstrate engineering perfection, as a recent spate of engine failures—including sludge buildup and automatic transmissions that hesitate and then surge when shifting—proves. And yes, cheaper luxury cars from Acura, Hyundai, Kia, Nissan, and Toyota give you almost as much comfort and reliability, but without as much cachet and resale value.

Speaking of resale values, don't believe the hype. Used Lexus models aren't impervious to some wallet-busting depreciation hits. Take for example a 2007 entry-level ES 350: new, it sold for almost $43,000; today you can get one for about $21,000. What? A three-year-old Lexus selling for less than half its original value? Welcome to the real world.

Technical service bulletins show that these cars have been affected mostly by powertrain and electrical malfunctions, faulty emissions-control components, computer module miscalibrations, and minor body fit and trim

You really wanna cry? A 2007 top-of-the-line hybrid RX 400h 4x4 hybrid that sold originally for $62,250 is now worth $27,000. Mama, get out the smelling salts!

glitches. Many owners haven't heard of these problems, because Lexus dealers have been particularly adept at fixing many of them before they become chronic.

Most of the 2011 Lexus models are carryovers from last year, so don't look for sweeping changes this year. There will be a slight restyling of the GS 350, 450h, and 460. And, of course, Toyota has sworn to phase in a standard brake override feature on all its models to combat sudden unintended acceleration. Hold the company to that promise and don't buy any Lexus that doesn't have that life-saving feature.

I don't know whether Toyota has fixed its sudden acceleration problem; however, I wouldn't buy any 2011 Toyota or Lexus model without the override feature. Only the RX series is certain to have it for 2011.

ES 350 ★★★

KEY FACTS

CANADIAN PRICE (NEGOTIABLE): *Base:* $41,950, *Navi.:* $45,800, *Premium:* $49,150, *Ultra Premium:* $52,000
U.S. PRICE: *Base:* $35,525 **CANADIAN FREIGHT:** $1,895 **U.S. FREIGHT:** $875
POWERTRAIN (FRONT-DRIVE)
Engine: 3.5L V6 (268 hp); Transmission: 6-speed auto.
DIMENSIONS/CAPACITY
Passengers: 2/3; Wheelbase: 109.3 in.; H: 57.1/L: 191.1/W: 71.7 in.; Headroom F/R: 2.5/1.5 in.; Legroom F/R: 42/28.5 in.; Cargo volume: 14.7 cu. ft.; Fuel tank: 70L/premium; Tow limit: N/A; Load capacity: 900 lb.; Turning circle: 38.7 ft.; Ground clearance: 4.0 in.; Weight: 3,580 lb.

RATING: Average; Not Recommended without the brake override feature. A near-luxury sedan that's really an all-dressed Camry clone. **Strong points:** Good acceleration; pleasantly quiet ride; and excellent quality control and warranty performance. Five-star NHTSA crashworthiness rating for frontal and side impacts, and four-star rollover protection. IIHS gave "Good" ratings for front- and side-impact protection. **Weak points:** Dangerous automatic transmission that hesitates and surges when shifting; primarily a four-seater, as three adults can't sit comfortably in the rear; headroom is inadequate for tall occupants; steering feel is muted; manual shifting system isn't very user-friendly and overall handling isn't as nimble as with its BMW or Mercedes rivals; trunk space is limited (low liftover, though); rear-corner visibility is hampered by the high rear end; and head restraints were rated "Marginal" by IIHS. **New for 2011:** Instead of requiring premium 91-octane fuel, Lexus has re-rated the car to use regular 87-octane gasoline. This drops horsepower and torque down to 268 hp from 272 and 248 pound-feet from last year's 254 pound-feet.

OVERVIEW: This entry-level Lexus front-drive carries a 268 hp V6 mated to an electronically controlled 6-speed automatic transmission that handles the 3.5L engine's horses effortlessly, without sacrificing fuel economy. All ES 350s feature dual front and side airbags, anti-lock brakes, double-piston front brake calipers, an optional Adaptive Variable Suspension, power-adjustable pedals with memory setting, 60/40 split-folding rear seats, a DVD navigation system, a 10-way power-adjustable driver's seat with memory, rain-sensing wipers, and one of the rarest features of all: a conventional spare tire.

COST ANALYSIS: A discounted leftover 2010 model will give you four extra horses, a slightly higher fuel bill, and no brake override feature in case of sudden unintended acceleration. Consider getting the usurious freight/PDI fee cut in half. **Best alternatives:** The all-dressed Camry, the Acura TL, the BMW 3 Series, and the Toyota Avalon. **Options:** Run like the wind if the dealer asks for another $7,000 for the "Emperor's New Clothes" Ultra Luxury Package. **Rebates:** Mostly low-cost financing. **Depreciation:** Much lower than average. **Insurance cost:** Much higher than average. **Parts supply/cost:** Good availability, and parts are moderately priced. **Annual maintenance cost:** Below average. **Warranty:** Bumper-to-bumper 4 years/80,000 km; powertrain 6 years/120,000 km; rust perforation 6 years/unlimited km. **Supplementary warranty:** May be needed to cover automatic transmission malfunctions. **City/highway fuel economy:** 2010: 10.9/7.2 L/100 km, 26/39 mpg.

OWNER-REPORTED PROBLEMS: Sudden, unintended acceleration; stuck accelerator; automatic transmission shifts erratically, suddenly accelerates, or slips and hesitates before going into gear; some minor transmission malfunctions; car lurches forward when the cruise control is re-engaged; brake failure; radio system glitches; fit and finish imperfections; tire side wall blew out after a low-speed impact with the curb when parking; tire monitor system malfunctions; engine ticking (replace camshaft housing or camshaft); Bluetooth cell phone voice distortion; rubbing noise from rear of vehicle; and an inoperative moonroof.

SERVICE BULLETIN-REPORTED PROBLEMS: Troubleshooting Bluetooth cell phone sound quality; windshield ticking; and silencing a rubbing noise coming from the rear of the vehicle.

IS 250, IS 350, IS F ★★★★

RATING: Above Average. **Strong points:** More standard safety, performance, and convenience features than with the IS 300; the car is wider, longer, and more solid-looking; a competent standard IS 350 3.5L engine; easy handling and effective braking; an upgraded interior; optional navigation screen is user-friendly and easily read; pleasant riding; low beltline provides a great view; and first-class workmanship. NHTSA crashworthiness figures are five stars for side-impact and rollover protection and four stars for front-impact protection. IIHS gives a "Good"

The Lexus IS 250.

KEY FACTS

CANADIAN PRICE (NEGOTIABLE): *IS 250:* $34,400, *Auto.:* $36,000, *AWD:* $40,550, *IS 250C:* $52100, *Auto.:* $53,700, *IS 350C:* $45,900, *Auto.:* $60,400, *IS F:* $68,000 **U.S. PRICE:** *IS 350:* $32,145, *IS 350C:* $41,060 **CANADIAN FREIGHT:** $1,895 **U.S. FREIGHT:** $875 **POWERTRAIN (REAR-DRIVE/AWD)** Engines: 2.5L V6 (204 hp) • 3.5L V6 (306 hp) • 5.0L V8 (416 hp); Transmissions: 6-speed man. • 6-speed auto.

DIMENSIONS/CAPACITY

Passengers: 2/3; Wheelbase: 107.5 in.; H: 55.7/L: 182.5/W: 70.9 in.; Headroom F/R: 2.0/2.0 in.; Legroom F/R: 41.5/ 25.5 in.; Cargo volume: 10.8 cu. ft.; Fuel tank: 65L/premium; Tow limit: 1,500 lb.; Load capacity: 825 lb.; Turning circle: 33.5 ft.; Ground clearance: 4.7–5.3 in.; Weight: 3,814 lb.

rating to frontal offset protection and an "Acceptable" score to head-restraint protection. *IS F:* Lots of tire-smoking power; high-performance handling; and a relatively quiet, high-quality interior. **Weak points:** The IS 250 feels rather sluggish when pushed. Handling on both the 250 and 350 models doesn't feel as sharp or responsive as with the BMW competition, owing in large part to an intrusive Vehicle Dynamics Integrated Management (VDIM) system that automatically eases up on the throttle during hard cornering. Emergency braking also isn't a confidence-builder. Cramped rear seating. The car requires premium fuel and has outrageously high freight charges. *IS F:* A bone-jarring, teeth-chattering ride; a too-firm suspension; no manual transmission option; and a tiny cabin. **New for 2011:** The addition of the IS 350 AWD; all sedans get new front styling and interior trims; Audi-like LED daytime running lights, new front and rear bumper treatments, new headlights and tail lights, standard 17-inch wheels, and optional 18-inch wheels. The IS F gets an upgraded suspension, new colours, and new gauges.

OVERVIEW: Targeting BMW's 3 Series, Lexus's entry-level IS 250 and IS 350 rear-drive sport-compact sedans come with either a 204 hp 2.5L V6 or a 306 hp 3.5L V6. The F version ups the ante considerably with its 416 hp 5.0L V8 powerplant, which is going into its third year on the market. Owner comments have been positive, and the car's residual value has been quite strong.

COST ANALYSIS: Best alternatives: Try the Acura TL, BMW 3 Series, and Infiniti G35. Audi's A4 would be a contender, were it not for its poor quality-control history. **Options:** Don't waste money on the sunroof, heated seats, or leather upholstery. **Rebates:** Expect $2,000–$3,000 discounts early in 2010, along with attractive financing and leasing deals. **Depreciation:** Much lower than average. **Insurance cost:** Higher than average. **Parts supply/cost:** Average availability, though parts may be quite expensive because of the lack of independent parts suppliers. **Annual maintenance cost:** Below average. **Warranty:** Bumper-to-bumper 4 years/80,000 km; powertrain 6 years/120,000 km; rust perforation 6 years/unlimited km. **Supplementary warranty:** Not necessary. **City/highway fuel economy:** *IS 250 man.*: 11.4/7.5 L/100 km, 25/38 mpg. *IS 250 auto.*: 9.8/6.8 L/100 km, 29/42 mpg. *IS 250 AWD*: 10.5/7.6 L/100 km, 27/37 mpg. *IS 350*: 10.9/7.8 L/100 km, 27/37 mpg. *IS 350C*: 11.5/7.9 L/100 km, 25/36 mpg. *IS F*: 13.0/8.5 L/100 km, 22/33 mpg.

OWNER-REPORTED PROBLEMS: Sudden unintended acceleration:

> On several occasions [...] the rpms increase randomly after the car has stopped and is stationary. The car inches forward and the driver has to apply more pressure on the brake pedal to make sure the car doesn't lurch forward and hit the car in front. The rpms go up almost 1000 rpms from idling. Happens in D and R. When turning on car putting the gear [in] R the car just lurches backwards unless the brake pedal is heavily [depressed]. This seems to be a software/ECM issue.

Many reports of premature brake wear, poor audio, and fit and finish imperfections. Poor instrument visibility:

> The visual displays on the center dashboard console indicating HVAC and audio information for the Lexus IS 250 C are so light as to be virtually invisible to the driver, particularly in bright sun and when the driver is wearing sunglasses.

Sunroof shattered while vehicle was underway; excessive window rattling when driving with the top down; loss of transmission fluid; and AC mildew odour (Lexus replaced vehicle).

SERVICE BULLETIN-REPORTED PROBLEMS: Engine runs rough, misfires; troubleshooting Bluetooth cell phone sound quality; windshield ticking; and rear brake squeal or squeak on the IS F models.

GS 350, GS 450H, GS 460 ★★★★

The Lexus GS 450h.

KEY FACTS

CANADIAN PRICE (NEGOTIABLE): *350:* $52,500, *350 Premium:* $58,450, *350 AWD:* $54,500, *350 AWD Premium:* $59,600, *350 AWD Ultra Premium:* $62,550, *460 Ultra Premium:* $71,000, *440h Hybrid:* $71,900 **U.S. PRICE:** *350:* $46,000, *GS 450h:* $57,950 **CANADIAN FREIGHT:** $1,895 **U.S. FREIGHT:** $875 **POWERTRAIN (REAR-DRIVE/AWD)** Engines: 3.5L V6 (303 hp) • 3.5L V6 Hybrid (340 hp) • 4.6L V8 (342 hp); Transmissions: 6-speed auto. • 8-speed auto. • CVT

DIMENSIONS/CAPACITY

Passengers: 2/3; Wheelbase: 112.2 in.; H: 56.1/L: 190/W: 71.7 in.; Headroom F/R: 2.0/2.0 in.; Legroom F/R: 41.5/ 28 in.; Cargo volume: 14.8 cu. ft.; Fuel tank: 70L/premium; Tow limit: N/A; Load capacity: 815 lb.; Turning circle: 37.1 ft.; Ground clearance: 5.0 in.; Weight: 3,685 lb.

RATING: Above Average. An exercise in passive driving—an abundance of electronic gadgetry cannot transform these luxury sedans into sports cars. **Strong points:** Good high-performance powertrain set-up; pleasantly quiet ride; acceptable handling and braking; average fuel economy, though premium fuel must be used; and exceptional quality control. **Weak points:** Primarily a four-seater with limited headroom for six-footers; the Audi A6 offers more rear legroom; middle-rear passengers, as usual in rear-drive sedans, get to ride the powertrain hump and thump the low roof with their heads; high window line impedes rear visibility; and some instruments are hidden by the steering wheel. No NHTSA crashworthiness data available. **New for 2011:** The addition of a brake override feature to the GS 350 and 460 range.

OVERVIEW: The GS 350 luxury sedan comes with a 303 hp 3.5L V6 engine hooked to a 6-speed automatic transmission with sequential manual shift. The GS 460 and the GS 450h gas-electric hybrid are powered by a 342 hp V8 and a 340 hp V6, respectively. The GS 450h can run on one or both of its power sources, uses a continuously variable automatic transmission (CVT), and doesn't need plug-in charging. Standard safety features include traction/anti-skid control, ABS, front knee airbags, front side airbags, side curtain airbags, a rear-view camera, and a Pre-Collision System designed to automatically cinch seat belts and apply the brakes if an unavoidable crash is detected. Other standard features include driver-adjustable shock absorbers (460 and 450h models), leather upholstery, and dual-zone climate controls, plus oodles of other safety, performance, and convenience features.

COST ANALYSIS: Since the 2011s are practically identical to last year's model, why not opt for a "leftover Lexus" and save thousands by dropping the selling price by 15 percent? **Best alternatives:** Granted, GS models are comfortable, polished luxury sedans, but sporty performers they are not. The Infiniti M, for example, allows for more driver input and is more satisfying to drive, owing mainly to smooth power delivery, crisper shifts, precise steering, more-predictable brakes, and a less-intrusive stability system. The Acura TL and BMW 5 Series are two other models you may consider. **Options:** Lexus has now packaged GS options so that it is almost impossible to get the essential without getting the frivolous or dangerous. Try to stay away from the in-dash navigator; it complicates the calibration of the sound system and climate controls. Other money-wasting options include a power sunshade, moonroof, the Mark Levinson stereo, XM radio, ventilated seats, spoiler, Intuitive Park Assist parking sensors, and rain-sensing wipers with Adaptive Front Lighting swivelling headlights. Be wary of the Dynamic Radar Cruise Control that reduces your speed when cars cut you off; if it malfunctions, as other systems have, you're toast. **Rebates:** By early winter, expect $3,000 rebates, zero percent financing, "giveaway" leasing terms, and discounting on the MSRP by about 10 percent. **Depreciation:** Slower than average. **Insurance cost:** Much higher than average. **Parts supply/cost:** Parts aren't easily found outside of the dealer network, and they're fairly pricey. **Annual maintenance cost:** Much less than average. **Warranty:** Bumper-to-bumper 4 years/80,000 km; powertrain 6 years/120,000 km; rust perforation 6 years/ unlimited km. **Supplementary warranty:** Not necessary. **City/highway fuel economy:** *GS 350:* 10.9/7.4 L/100 km, 26/38 mpg. *GS 350 AWD:* 11.6/8.0 L/ 100 km, 24/35 mpg. *GS 450h:* 8.7/7.8 L/100 km, 23/35 mpg. *GS 460:* 12.4/8.1 L/ 100 km, 32/36 mpg.

OWNER-REPORTED PROBLEMS: Car suddenly accelerated as it was being parked; vehicle wandering at highway speeds requires constant steering corrections; and brake failure.

SERVICE BULLETIN-REPORTED PROBLEMS: Front sway bar thumping; windshield ticking.

RX 350, RX 450H ★★★★ / ★★★

RATING: *RX 350:* Above Average. Lexus invented the luxury crossover segment with the RX series in 1998, and it has since been a perennial bestseller. *RX 450h:* Average. Some fuel savings, but at a heavy price. Its price will plummet as you get closer to the battery pack's replacement time. **Strong points:** Now in its third generation, the 2010 doesn't disappoint with its attractive styling, great safety ratings, lots of luxury in a spacious cabin, and a smooth, car-like ride. The RX received a "Top Safety Pick" award from IIHS. To earn that status, vehicles must

The Lexus RX 350.

KEY FACTS

CANADIAN PRICE (NEGOTIABLE): *RX 350:* $46,900, *Premium 1:* $50,350, *Premium 2:* $51,950, *RX 350 Touring:* $55,350, *RX 350 Sport:* $57,400, *Ultra Premium:* $62,700, *RX 450h:* $59,500, *Touring:* $62,900, *450h Ultra:* $72,000 **U.S. PRICE:** *RX 350:* $37,975, *RX 450h:* $43,235 **CANADIAN FREIGHT:** $1,895 **U.S. FREIGHT:** $875

POWERTRAIN (FRONT-DRIVE/AWD)
Engines: 3.5L V6 (275 hp) • 3.5L V6 Hybrid (295 hp); Transmissions: 6-speed auto. • CVT

DIMENSIONS/CAPACITY
Passengers: 2/3; Wheelbase: 107.9 in.; H: 66.3/L: 187.8/W: 74.2 in.; Headroom F/R: 3.5/4.0 in.; Legroom F/R: 40.5/29.0 in.; Cargo volume: 40 cu. ft.; Fuel tank: 70L/premium; Tow limit: 3,500 lb.; Load capacity: 925 lb.; Turning circle: 37.1 ft.; Ground clearance: 7.3 in.; Weight: 4,178 lb.

be ranked as "Good"—the institute's top crash rating—in front, side, and rear impacts and be equipped with electronic stability control. Improved braking response and feel; more back-seat legroom; and the backrest's recline lever is more-easily accessible. Also, the RX has excellent gas mileage for a luxury crossover. **Weak points:** High, firm prices; the car doesn't feel as agile as its competition (this year's 350 model has 400 more pounds); no third-seat option; expensive options packages; less steering feedback when compared to the RX 450h, although the latter version takes more effort to turn; modest cargo capacity; and excessive road noise. The hybrid's acceleration is slower, thanks to its 300 extra pounds this year, and its Remote Touch multifunction joystick and screen force you to take your eyes off the road. **New for 2011:** The new brake override feature and two new colours.

OVERVIEW: Exterior styling is slightly different in the latest RX. Suspension is independent all around, and the progressive electronic power-steering system is speed sensing for enhanced control. The front-drive and all-wheel-drive RX models come identically equipped. Rear cargo room has been increased slightly, and anti-lock brakes, stability control, traction control, and 10 airbags are standard.

COST ANALYSIS: Get the 2010 for the improvements, but take a good 7 percent off the list price. **Best alternatives:** The BMW 5 Series, Cadillac SRX, Hyundai Veracruz, and Lincoln MKX. **Options:** Stay away from the moonroof option. Not only is it nonessential and often failure-prone, but it also comes in packages that include other frivolous features. Be wary of the Adaptive Cruise Control; it may behave erratically. **Rebates:** Expect $2,000 rebates, zero percent financing, good leasing terms, and discounting on the MSRP by about 10 percent. Discounting and rebates will become more attractive in the summer of 2010. **Depreciation:** Slower than average. **Insurance cost:** Much higher than average. **Parts supply/ cost:** Parts are hard to find from independent sources; prices are on the high side. **Annual maintenance cost:** Less than average. **Warranty:** Bumper-to-bumper 4 years/80,000 km; powertrain 6 years/120,000 km; rust perforation 6 years/ unlimited km. **Supplementary warranty:** Not needed. **City/highway fuel economy:** *RX 350:* 11.6/8.2 L/100 km, 24/34 mpg. *RX 450h:* 6.6/7.2 L/100 km, 43/39 mpg.

OWNER-REPORTED PROBLEMS: Hybrid suddenly accelerated as it was being parked, brakes were ineffective, and the front tire exploded. Car surges forward when the brakes are applied. RX 450h brake failures are similar to those reported on the Prius:

> I wanted to alert you that other hybrid models that were manufactured with the same braking system as the Prius suffer the same issue. I have a 2010 Lexus 450h RX and its brakes disengage when I am driving on bumpy roads and over pot holes. I live in a northeastern city with many bumps and my brakes stop working often and as a result I have to slam them on much more quickly.

The 4×4 system doesn't perform as advertised:

> The RX450h is downright dangerous. The 4 wheel drive does not switch "on demand" as the advertising says. I live in snowy Massachusetts and do not need permanent 4 wheel drive, but it is essential when the roads are full of snow or ice. I was puzzled at first that the 4 wheel drive only actuated under 25 mph [40 km/h]. I tested it on sharp corners in the snow: the back slid out; and on faster, gradual corners: the car side slipped. Never did the 4 wheel drive switch on and correct the slide. I looked in the manual for the method to manually activate 4 wheel drive but couldn't find it. I contacted Lexus. They said that I should use the snow switch. This is a menu item which annoyingly much be switched on every time you drive. It didn't work as it only changes the gear and acceleration characteristics like any other winter/summer switch. They also said that it should work at high speeds when more power is needed. I tried that and found that at 60 mph [95 km/h] if I absolutely floored the accelerator on a steep hill the 4 wheel drive would switch on briefly.

Audio system problems and poor fit and finish are other owner grievances. Owners also report excessive dust/powder blows from the AC vents; driver's door rattles; engine ticking (replace camshaft housing and camshaft); fluid leaks from the transfer case; tire monitor system malfunctions; liftgate-area water leaks;

inoperative moonroof; the vehicle pulling to the right, and the original equipment Firestone Dueler H/L 400 tire having hairline splits along the sidewall.

SERVICE BULLETIN-REPORTED PROBLEMS: Wind noise from front side windows; windshield ticking noise; hybrid engine ticking and engine MIL light on; poor rear bumper cover fit; and power liftgate malfunctions.

Mazda

Back From the Brink

Mazda has grown up. Following its debut four decades ago as a marginal automaker selling cheap, hard-to-service, and small here-today-gone-tomorrow rustbuckets, it has left its unremarkable past behind. Granted, Mazda did snare the innovative Wankel rotary engine from GM (destined for the Vega and Astre) that had a reputation for being a small, powerful gas-guzzler. Mazda put the Wankel in its RX-7 series of roadsters (1978–2002) and its RX-8 sport cars (2004–2010). The engine is no longer used, partially due to higher fuel prices, but also due to the rotary engine's hard starting, frequent stalling, high emissions, excessive oil consumption, and expensive sojourns to the repair bay.

The 2011 Mazda2 is a nicely styled, pokey fuel miser that handles well but seems a bit overpriced in view of its cramped interior. Consider a Honda Fit instead.

Mazda almost went bankrupt in 1994. Then Ford stepped in to turn the company around through purchasing Mazda shares and putting out shared products. Mazda soon turned profitable through better management and a popular new array of small cars and trucks made in partnership with Ford. The company's sole minivan, the MPV, never got any traction and was taken off the market in 2006.

Mazda is going downstream this year with its brand-new $13,995 Mazda2, a four-door hatchback that uses a 100 hp 1.5L 4-cylinder engine with a standard five-speed manual transmission or optional four-speed automatic. It gets 7.2 L/100 km (39 mpg) in the city and 5.6 L/100 km (50 mpg) on the highway.

The Mazda3 does everything the Mazda2 doesn't. There's plenty of interior room, the car has power to spare, and the powertrain performs flawlessly. No wonder the "3" has constantly been on backorder for the performance crowd since its debut as a 2004 model. This peppy and fuel-efficient compact takes Mazda back to its compact-car roots and adds some performance thrills to its fuel-saving powertrain.

A bit more upstream, Mazda's mini-minivan, the Mazda5, is revamped this year and has more innovative features to attract the minivan crowd to a smaller conveyance. The Mazda6 returns with a hatchback and a wagon to accompany its sedan version. The Tribute (Ford's Escape SUV twin), the CX-7, and CX-9 have all weathered the recession relatively well, so they return with few changes.

After selling the B-Series compact pickup (the Ford Ranger's twin) in North America for almost 40 years, Mazda has dropped its once-popular vehicle. The fifth-generation (1998–2009) B-Series compact trucks saw a steady downward slide in sales, from 41,620 units in 1998 to only 1,319 units in 2008. 2010 is the truck's last model year; Ford's Ranger gets the axe in 2011, although a Thai-built version will be sold in other countries under the Ranger name. Another Mazda that won't be around for long is the RX-8 high-end sports car; insiders say 2011 will also be the last year for that model. The car has been a sales dud in North America (Mazda sold only 128 RX-8s in April of 2010 for a total of 428 year to date) and cannot meet more stringent EuroV emissions standards.

MAZDA3 ★★★★

Most everyone says the Mazda3 grill "grins" more than it has to.

RATING: Above Average; it would have been Recommended if it weren't for an upsurge in factory-related defects during the past year, as proven by confidential Mazda service bulletins. **Strong points:** Good powertrain set-up, with plenty of reserve power for passing and merging; easy, predictable handling; good steering feedback; small turning radius; rear multi-link suspension gives the car great

KEY FACTS

CANADIAN PRICE (NEGOTIABLE): *GX sedan:* 15,995, *Auto.:* $17,195, *GS sedan:* $19,395, *Auto.:* $20,595, *GT sedan:* $22,995, *Auto.:* $24,195, *GT Luxury sedan:* $25,185, *Auto.:* $26,385, *GX Sport:* $16,995, *Auto.:* $18,195, *GS Sport:* $20,895, *Auto.:* $22,095, *GT Sport:* $23,995, *Auto.:* $25,195, *GT Luxury Sport:* $26,185, *Auto.:* $27,385 **U. S. PRICE:** *SV 4d:* $15,345, *Sport:* $16,255, *Touring:* $17,925, *s Sport:* $19,195, *s Grand Touring:* $21,645 **CANADIAN FREIGHT:** $1,395 **U.S. FREIGHT:** $750

POWERTRAIN (FRONT-DRIVE)
Engines: 2.0L 4-cyl. (148 hp) • 2.5L 4-cyl. (167 hp) • 2.3L 4-cyl. Turbo (263 hp); Transmissions: 5-speed man. • 6-speed man. • 5-speed auto.

DIMENSIONS/CAPACITY (SEDAN)
Passengers: 2/3; Wheelbase: 104 in.; H: 58/L: 181/W: 69.1 in.; Headroom F/R: 5.5/2.0 in.; Legroom F/R: 41.5/27 in.; Cargo volume: 12 cu. ft.; Fuel tank: 55L/ regular; Tow limit: N/A; Load capacity: 850 lb.; Turning circle (hatchback): 34.2 ft.; Ground clearance: 6.1 in.; Weight: 3,065 lb.

stability at higher speeds; spacious, easy-to-load trunk; user-friendly instruments and controls; and better-than-average workmanship. NHTSA's front- and side-impact crashworthiness rating is five stars, and rollover resistance earned four stars. IIHS gives the Mazda3 its top score, "Good," for frontal offset, side, and head-restraint protection. **Weak points:** The Mazda3 has a history of automatic transmission malfunctions (but no more than with Honda or Toyota vehicles), prematurely worn-out brake rotors and pads, door lock failures, and fit and finish deficiencies. Some road noise intrudes into the cabin; a very small trunk; a high deck cuts rear visibility; limited rear footroom; and be wary of Mazda dealers overcharging for scheduled maintenance. **New for 2011:** Carried over mostly unchanged.

OVERVIEW: Going into its seventh year, the Mazda3 is an econobox with flair that pleases commuters and "tuners" alike. The car offers spirited acceleration and smooth, sporty shifting. Handling is enhanced with a highly rigid body structure, front and rear stabilizer bars, a multi-link rear suspension, and four-wheel disc brakes. Interior room is quite ample with the car's relatively long wheelbase, extra width, and straight sides, which maximize headroom, legroom, and shoulder room.

COST ANALYSIS: The cheaper and virtually identical 2010 version is recommended, but it may be hard to find as higher gas prices cause buyers to stampede toward anything that is cheap to buy and fuel. Hatchback models give you the most versatility. **Best alternatives:** The Honda Civic. **Options:** Don't accept the original Goodyear Eagle RS-A tires; go to *www. tirerack.com* to find some better tires for less money. The 5-speed automatic transmission with AC is a good start, although the 6-speed manual is lots more fun to drive. **Rebates:** Not likely. **Depreciation:** Much less than average. Consider this: A 2007 base Mazda3 that sold for $16,795 is still worth about $9,500. **Insurance cost:** Average. **Parts supply/cost:** Parts are easy to find. **Annual maintenance cost:** Less than average, so far. **Warranty:** Bumper-to-bumper 3 years/80,000 km; powertrain 5 years/100,000 km; rust perforation 5 years/ unlimited km. **Supplementary warranty:** Not needed. **City/highway fuel economy:** 2.0L: 8.1/5.9 L/100 km, 35/48 mpg. 2.3L: 11.5/8.0 L/100 km, 25/35 mpg. 2.5L: 10.1/6.9 L/100 km, 28/41 mpg.

OWNER-REPORTED PROBLEMS: Engine compartment fire; airbags failed to deploy; weak rims may fracture after hitting a small pothole; sudden unintended acceleration; stalling while cruising on the highway; delayed acceleration; manual transmission may go into Reverse when shifted into Fourth gear; car rolls away when parked on an incline; car tends to pull to one side; premature power-steering pump failures first seen as a stiffening of the steering, or the steering will suddenly lock. Goodyear Eagle RS-A 205/50 R17 tires provide little traction on ice or snow and may wear out prematurely. Goodyear refuses claims, saying there is no proof of "poor workmanship" on their part—the tires simply wear out quickly, especially the so-called "Mazda 3S" original equipment tires. Shameful!

> This car/tire combination provided extremely low traction on packed snow and ice. The dealership and Mazda have been unwilling to provide adequate tires so the car is no longer being driven when there is snow or ice on the roads.

Other concerns are mostly regarding transmission and brake deficiencies. The transmission can be hard to shift, especially from Third to Fourth gear or when gearing down; engine surges when downshifting or going into Neutral prior to stopping; complete brake failures; premature wearout of brake pads and rotors, accompanied by an annoying grinding sound and pulling to one side when the brakes are applied; brake rotors are easily grooved; whine in the steering system; body vibration and steering-wheel shimmy; rear glass window may explode in chilly weather:

> Morning: 16 degrees F. Approached my car in the morning and heard a crackling noise. I thought the sound was ice. I started the car and the rear defogger. As I sat in my driveway...approximately 30 seconds after turning on the defogger...the rear glass exploded with a loud noise. Glass was thrown into the rear passenger seats. The car is 4 months old and under warranty. I took the car to the dealer and they would not repair under warranty. I called Mazda and was told that this is due to outside influence (i.e. the same as if a tree branch fell on the car). He indicated that I should expect that this could happen in the cold weather. I cannot believe that I should expect that my rear window can explode in cold weather.

Rear-view mirror easily breaks away from the front windshield; excessive sunroof vibration and noise when driving with the sunroof open; driver's seat feels loose, rocks back and forth; front doors would not unlock with the key or from the inside.

SERVICE BULLETIN-REPORTED PROBLEMS: Excessive engine vibration; oil seepage from the inner CV joint boot; manual transmission may be noisy or hard to shift into Third or Fourth gear; the same transmission may go into "limp home" mode; steering wheel is off-centre; brake noise, judder, dragging; accessory charger sticks in the auxiliary power port; tips on avoiding floor mat/throttle interference; sunroof malfunctions; windshield flaws; front door window won't open completely; poor dash surface appearance; crack appears in centre of dash; liftgate to emblem gap; moisture, water droplets in tail lights; seat heater won't turn off;

creaking noise comes from the upper area of the C-pillar; seatback squeaking; more squeaking heard from under the driver's seat; leather seat squeaking; driver's seat chatter, seat lift may be inoperative; front seat clunks when the brakes are applied; unlocked front doors won't open from the inside or from the outside with a key; front door panel buzzing; front door glass rattling; rear-door lock freeze; map lamp and front seat head restraint rattles; and audio system malfunctions.

MAZDA5 ★★★

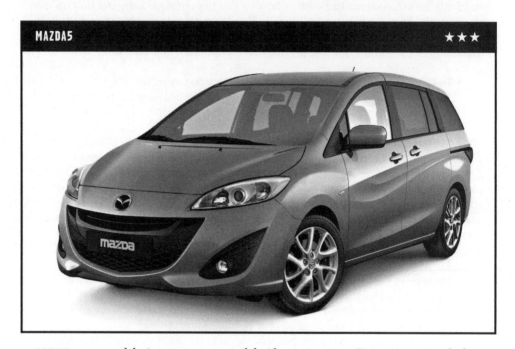

RATING: *2011 model:* Average. *2010 model:* Above Average. Every time Mazda has redesigned a model, factory- or supplier-induced problems have abounded. *Lemon-Aid* remembers all too clearly the glitches that followed the MPV and RX-8 redesigns. Buyers who don't need the extra seating or 14 additional horses should consider buying a heavily discounted 2010 version, or wait until next year when prices will fall and quality will improve.

The Mazda5 is basically a compact miniwagon that's based broadly on the Mazda3 and carries six passengers in three rows of seats. Used mostly for urban errands and light commuting, the "5" employs a peppy, though fuel-frugal, 2.3L 153 hp 4-cylinder engine hooked to a standard 5-speed manual transmission or a 5-speed automatic. So far, the engine has had few problems during the past four years the Mazda5 has run in Canada. **Strong points:** All the advantages of a small minivan, without the handling or fuel penalties; reasonably priced; decent fuel economy; adequate 2.3L engine; a comfortable ride; and relatively quiet interior (except for omnipresent road noise—a common trait with small wagons). NHTSA's front- and side-impact crashworthiness rating for the 2010 model is five stars, and rollover resistance scored four stars. **Weak points:** The small 4-cylinder engine doesn't have much torque ("grunt," or pulling power) for heavy loads or hill climbing, and towing isn't recommended. There isn't much room for passengers in the third-row seat. There's also a history of automatic transmission malfunctions (but no more than with Honda or Toyota vehicles), premature wear-out of brake rotors and pads, and fit and finish deficiencies. **New for 2011:** Mazda will likely put in the slightly more powerful 167 hp 2.5L 4-cylinder engine used by the Mazda3. Also, look for a major restyling along the lines of the Mazda3, with the same front end "grin" and prominent front fenders. The rear quarter panel and glass will go all the way rearward to cover the rearmost window pillars, creating a sleeker, sportier look. Occupancy is expected to go from six to seven passengers, thanks to a new second-row centre seat. Other improvements: wider, thicker seats; power-sliding side doors; a redesigned dash; and more cargo space (52.7 cubic feet with the rear seats folded flat).

OVERVIEW: The 2010 version is a relatively tall and narrow car, with a thick, obtrusive front A-pillar. Nevertheless, it handles well, despite some body roll and steering that's a bit vague. Drivers will find this vehicle a breeze to park, easy to manoeuvre, and fairly spacious inside. Two wide-opening sliding doors make for easy entry and exit.

COST ANALYSIS: Get the 2010 model with a discount of at least 15 percent. Wait a year for the 2011 to work out its redesign glitches. **Best alternatives:** The Honda Civic, Hyundai Tucson, and Toyota Matrix (only with the brake override feature). **Options:** Any good tires, instead of Bridgestone or Firestone. **Rebates:** Huge discounts on the 2010s due mainly to the 2011 launch hype. **Depreciation:** Much slower than average. **Insurance cost:** Average. **Parts supply/cost:** Easy to find. **Annual maintenance cost:** Less than average, so far. **Warranty:** Bumper-to-bumper 3 years/80,000 km; powertrain 5 years/100,000 km; rust perforation 5 years/unlimited km. **Supplementary warranty:** Not needed. **City/highway fuel economy:** *Man.:* 9.6/7.0 L/100 km, 29/40 mpg. *Auto.:* 9.9/7.2 L/100 km, 29/39 mpg.

OWNER-REPORTED PROBLEMS: Suspension, fuel system, and fit and finish are the most common problems reported. Also, owners report a few automatic transmission failures; transmission gear hunting and fluid leaks; power-steering malfunctions; electrical system shorts; and rapid brake and tire wear. Airbag warning light and Traction Stability Control (TSC) light come on for no reason:

Riding over a bump or rough road illuminates TSC light on dash. The light should go off on its own, but does not until car is turned off. All Mazda on-line forums acknowledge this is a known problem.

SERVICE BULLETIN-REPORTED PROBLEMS: Engine, body vibration at cruising speed; brake noise, judder, dragging; tips on avoiding floor mat/throttle interference; accessory charger sticks in the auxiliary power port; diagnosing windshield flaws; poor dash surface appearance; seatback squeaking; more squeaking heard from under the driver's seat; leather seat squeaking; driver's seat chatter/seat lift may be inoperative; front seat clunks when the brakes are applied; accessory charger sticks in the auxiliary power port; and the steering wheel may be off centre.

MAZDA6 ★★★

RATING: Average. A car enthusiast's family sedan, although not as refined or as sporty as Honda's Accord. The car stands out for its sharp styling, comfortable ride, and nimble handling. **Strong points:** Good powertrain set-up; very agile, with nice overall handling; responsive, precise steering; a tighter turning circle than with previous versions; all-independent suspension; impressive braking; comfortable seating; and acceptable workmanship. High prices are easily bargained down as the model year plays out. NHTSA gives its top five-star score to the Mazda6 for front, side, and rollover protection. Also, IIHS gives its top score, "Good," for frontal offset and side occupant protection. **Weak points:** Excessive road noise intrudes into the cabin; unusually low roofline restricts access into the cabin, and the V6 can cut your fuel economy by almost 20 percent. IIHS rates head-restraint effectiveness as "Marginal." Mazda has a history of automatic transmission and fit and finish deficiencies and scheduled maintenance overcharges. One major Mazda6 drawback may be its price—too high to lure customers away from the competition. **New for 2011:** Improved fuel economy, says Mazda—and would they kid you? Other changes are minimal: redesigned wheels, headlights, foglights, steering wheel, folding mirrors with embedded turn signals, cloth seats, and vinyl door armrests.

OVERVIEW: Blame it all on Nissan. They kicked off the family feud over mid-sized sedans by revamping their Altima to offer a sweet combination of high performance, a capacious interior, and clean, aerodynamic styling. Then Toyota reworked its Camry, and Honda responded with its seventh-generation Accord. And then it was Mazda's turn, so voilà! We have the Mazda6.

COST ANALYSIS: The 2009s underwent a major redesign, and the carried-over 2010s are almost identical to the 2011 version. **Best alternatives:** The Ford Fusion, Honda Accord, Hyundai Tucson, Nissan Altima, and Toyota Camry or Matrix (only with the brake override feature). **Options:** The V6 is a better-performing and more-reliable engine; be wary of the Bridgestone and Firestone tires. **Rebates:** $3,500 sales incentives and low-cost leases and financing are most likely. **Depreciation:** Faster than average. A 2007 top-of-the-line GT V6 that sold for $33,195 is now worth only $16,000. **Insurance cost:** Average. **Parts supply/cost:** Easy to find. **Annual maintenance cost:** Average. **Warranty:** Bumper-to-bumper 3 years/80,000 km; powertrain 5 years/100,000 km; rust perforation 5 years/ unlimited km. **Supplementary warranty:** Not needed. **City/highway fuel economy:** 2.5L man.: 10.4/6.9 L/100 km, 27/41 mpg. 2.5L auto.: 9.7/6.7 L/100 km, 29/42 mpg. 3.7L: 12.1/8.0 L/100 km, 23/35 mpg.

OWNER-REPORTED PROBLEMS: Some minor problems with the transmission and electrical and fuel systems. Other owners have reported that the automatic transmission "weep hole" leaks fluid, the engine makes a ticking sound at low rpms, and the remote door lock feature often malfunctions.

SERVICE BULLETIN-REPORTED PROBLEMS: Manual transmission may be noisy or hard to shift into Third or Fourth gear; brake noise, judder, dragging; tips on avoiding floor mat/throttle interference; steering wheel may be off centre; accessory charger sticks in the auxiliary power port; diagnosing windshield flaws; poor dash surface appearance; exposed dashboard foam; broken console lid latch; A-pillar water leaks (see bulletin on following page). Water leak from HVAC housing; water in tail lights; front facia "popped out" at fender; poor AC compressor performance; sunroof malfunctions; instrument cluster and door speaker rattling; seatback squeaking; more squeaking heard from under the driver's seat; leather seat squeaking; driver's seat chatter, seat lift may be inoperative; front seat head restraint rattles; front seat clunks when the brakes are applied; seats are noisy and shake when braking; poor Bluetooth phone reception; and the horn intermittently self-activates.

MAZDA SERVICE PROGRAM (M5P29)—WATER LEAK FROM LEFT SIDE A-PILLAR/COWL AREA

2010 Mazda6 vehicles.

DESCRIPTION: On certain 2010 Mazda6 vehicles, water may leak from the left side A-pillar/cowl area.

Plugging this water leak is an involved process that's fortunately covered under Campaign #M5P29. A similar problem on any other Mazda should be eligible for this free repair using this precedent.

MX-5   ★★★★★

RATING: Recommended. An exceptional, reasonably priced roadster. **Strong points:** Well-matched powertrain provides better-than-expected acceleration and top-end power at the 7000 rpm range; classic sports car handling; perfectly weighted steering with plenty of road feedback; a firm but comfortable suspension; impressive braking; mirrors are bigger and more effective than those found in most luxury sports cars; a user-friendly, manually operated top; engine is fairly quiet, and less road noise intrudes into the cabin; instruments and controls are easy to read and access; a slightly roomier interior; good fuel economy; no safety-related complaints, and few performance-related ones; and a high resale value. The 2005 earned five stars for rollover protection, four stars for frontal crashworthiness, and three stars for side-impact protection, but NHTSA hasn't crash tested the MX-5 since then. IIHS gave it an "Average" rating for head-restraint effectiveness. **Weak points:** All the things that make roadsters so much "fun": limited passenger and cargo room (still not much room for six-footers); difficult entry and exit; restricted rear visibility with the top up; and a can of tire sealant instead of a spare tire. **New for 2011:** Nothing important. Everything was redesigned or tweaked a year ago, including the exterior styling, interior trim and fittings, engine, suspension, and exhaust.

OVERVIEW: The MX-5 is a stubby, lightweight, rear-drive, two-seater convertible sports car that combines new technology with old British roadster styling reminiscent of the Triumph, the Austin-Healy, and the Lotus Elan. It comes in a variety of trim levels: The three convertibles are the Sport, Touring, and Grand Touring. The fourth model is the Touring (Power-Retractable) Hard Top. The lineup begins with the soft-top-only Sport; a removable hardtop is available as an option. All models come with a heated glass rear window.

It's amazing how well the MX-5 is put together, considering that it isn't particularly innovative and most parts are borrowed from Mazda's other models. For example, the engine is borrowed from the Mazda3 and Mazda6 and the suspension is taken from the RX-8. A 5-speed manual gearbox is standard fare, while the 6-speed automatic and 6-speed manual are optional. The MX-5 is shorter than most other sports cars; nevertheless, this is a fun car to drive, costing much less than other vehicles in its class.

COST ANALYSIS: Get a discounted 2010, if you can find one; it's identical to the costlier 2011. **Best alternatives:** The BMW Z cars, Chevrolet Camaro, Ford Mustang, Mercedes-Benz SLK, and Porsche Boxster. **Options:** The 6-speed manual transmission is a toss-up, since the 5-speed is so smooth. **Rebates:** Look for $2,000 discounts by year's end. **Depreciation:** Slower than average: A 2007 base Miata sold for $28,095; today, that same car is worth $16,500. **Insurance cost:** Higher than average. **Parts supply/cost:** Parts are easy to find, but they often cost more than average. **Annual maintenance cost:** Much less than average, particularly when compared to other roadsters. **Warranty:** Bumper-to-bumper 3 years/80,000 km; powertrain 5 years/100,000 km; rust perforation 5 years/unlimited km. **Supplementary warranty:** Not needed. **City/highway fuel economy:** *5-speed man.:* 9.2/7.1 L/100 km, 31/40 mpg. *6-speed man.:* 9.7/7.1 L/100 km, 29/40 mpg. *6-speed auto.:* 10.1/7.2 L/100 km, 28/39 mpg.

OWNER-REPORTED PROBLEMS: Some minor driveline, fuel system, and fit and finish complaints. Tall drivers note that their right leg is put in an awkward position that quickly causes severe cramping.

KEY FACTS

CANADIAN PRICE (FIRM): *GX:* $28,995, *GS:* $33,495, *GT:* $39,995 **U.S. PRICE:** *Sport:* $22,960, *Touring:* $25,300, *Grand Touring:* $26,560, *PRHT Touring:* $27,000, *PRHT Grand Touring:* $28,400 **CANADIAN FREIGHT:** $1,595 **U.S. FREIGHT:** $750

POWERTRAIN (REAR-DRIVE)
Engine: 2.0L 4-cyl. (167 hp); Transmissions: 5-speed man. • 6-speed man. • 6-speed auto.

DIMENSIONS/CAPACITY
Passengers: 2; Wheelbase: 91.7 in.; H: 49/L: 158.7/W: 67.7 in.; Headroom: 1.5 in.; Legroom: 40 in.; Cargo volume: 5.2 cu. ft.; Fuel tank: 48L/regular; Tow limit: N/A; Load capacity: 340 lb.; Turning circle: 30.8 ft.; Ground clearance: 4.6 in.; Weight: 2,458–2,632 lb.

SERVICE BULLETIN-REPORTED PROBLEMS: Excessive brake noise, judder, dragging; steering wheel is off centre; windshield flaws; poor dash surface appearance; inoperative remote keyless entry; accessory charger sticks in the auxiliary power port; seatback squeaking; front seat clunks when the brakes are applied; and leather seat squeaking.

CX-7, CX-9 ★★✩★★★

The Mazda CX-7.

RATING: *CX-7:* Below Average. *CX-9:* Average. **Strong points:** *CX-7:* Well-equipped; turbocharged engine has power to spare; excellent handling, with a relatively tight turning radius and responsive steering; plenty of cargo room; and good all-around visibility. *CX-9:* The only engine offered, a 273 hp 3.7L V6, delivers plenty of power with little noise or delay. Handling is better than average, ride is fairly smooth over irregular terrain, and there is plenty of headroom, legroom, and storage space. Instruments and controls are nicely laid out and not hard to master. **Weak points:** *CX-7:* Base engine is a so-so performer, and the turbocharged version is hampered by considerable "turbo lag," which increases the response time from the throttle to the engine. Both engines are also relatively noisy, with the 2.5L producing a coarse drone and the turbo powerplant emitting an annoying whine. Ride comfort is so-so and may be a bit too firm for some; irregular roadways give occupants a shaky ride; tall occupants may find headroom too limited; rear seating is a bit low and cramped; and interior garnishings seem a bit on the cheap side. Mediocre fuel economy; the turbo-equipped model requires premium fuel. *CX-9:* Third-row seating is mainly for children; rear visibility is limited; and gas consumption is relatively high. **New for 2011:** *CX-7:* This mid-sized SUV is mostly carried over unchanged, except for the debut of a new upscale 4-cylinder iTouring model. *CX-9:* Better fuel economy, promises Mazda (wink, wink, nudge, nudge); redesigned wheels.

OVERVIEW: *CX-7:* Essentially a small five-passenger front-drive and AWD SUV crossover, the CX-7 debuted as a 2007 model in Canada and has been one of Mazda's best-selling models ever since. Available safety features include ABS, traction control, anti-skid system, side curtain airbags, and front side airbags. *CX-9:* The seven-passenger CX-9 is not an extended CX-7. In fact, it shares its platform with the popular Ford Edge and adds a better interior in the process. Its Ford DNA makes the "9" a quieter-running and more agile performer than its smaller sibling.

COST ANALYSIS: There has been strong demand for these cars and that may be their saving grace, because the more CXs sold, the better servicing and supply should be. **Best alternatives:** The Chevrolet Equinox or Traverse, Ford Flex, GMC Acadia or Terrain, Honda Pilot, Hyundai Tucson or Santa Fe, Mazda CX-9, or the Toyota Highlander (only with the brake override feature). **Options:** Nothing extra is needed. **Rebates:** Look for $3,000 discounts by year's end. **Depreciation:** Faster than average: A 2007 base CX-7 than once sold for $31,995 now sells for $13,000. The CX-9? Not much better. The base model first sold for $39,595; now it's worth only $17,000. **Insurance cost:** Higher than average. **Parts supply/cost:** Parts are easy to find, but they often cost more than average. **Annual maintenance cost:** Average. **Warranty:** Bumper-to-bumper 3 years/80,000 km; powertrain 5 years/100,000 km; rust perforation 5 years/unlimited km. **Supplementary warranty:** Don't drive without one. **City/highway fuel economy:** *CX-7 2.5L:* 10.4/7.2 L/100 km, 27/39 mpg. *2.3L:* 12.2/8.7 L/100 km, 23/32 mpg. *CX-9 front-drive:* 13.4/9.1 L/100 km, 21/31 mpg. *AWD:* 14.0/9.6 L/100 km, 20/29 mpg.

OWNER-REPORTED PROBLEMS: *CX-7:* Drivers have reported minor engine problems in addition to fuel system, brake, and fit and finish deficiencies. Gauges on the instrument panel are hard to read at night and in bright sunlight; excessive condensation in the front headlights; repeated AC compressor failures; accelerator and brake pedals are mounted too close together; and persistent brake squeaking. *CX-9:* Also few complaints reported. Premature brake wear; heated seats continue to overheat, despite recall repairs; poor fit and finish; and audio system malfunctions.

KEY FACTS

CANADIAN PRICE (SOFT): *GX FWD:* $27,995, *GS AWD:* $32,295, *GT AWD:* $38,990, *CX-9 GS:* $37,995, *GS AWD:* $39,995, *GT:* $47,450. **U.S. PRICE:** *GX-7 i SV:* $21,700, *i Sport:* $22,490, *s Touring:* $25,950, *AWD:* $27,650, *s Grand Touring:* $31,335, *AWD:* $33,035, *CX-9 Sport:* $28,805, *AWD:* $30,205, *Touring:* $30,725, *AWD:* $32,125, *Grand Touring:* $32,815, *AWD:* $34,215 **CANADIAN FREIGHT:** $1,595 **U.S. FREIGHT:** $750 **POWERTRAIN (FRONT-DRIVE/AWD)** Engines: 2.5L 4-cyl. (161 hp) • 2.3L 4-cyl. (244 hp); *CX-9:* 3.7L V6 (273 hp); Transmissions: 5-speed auto. • 6-speed auto.; *CX-9:* 6-speed auto. **DIMENSIONS/CAPACITY (CX-7 AND CX-9)** Passengers: 2/3, 2/3/2; Wheelbase: 108.2 in., 113.2 in.; H: 52.7, 68.0/L: 184.3, 200.8/W: 73.7, 76.2 in.; Cargo volume: 29.9 cu. ft., 37.5 cu. ft.; Fuel tank: 69L, 76L/regular or premium; Tow limit: 2,000 lb., 3,500 lb.; Load capacity: 1,190 lb.; Turning circle: 37.4 ft.; Ground clearance: 8.1 in., 8.0 in.; Weight: 3,500–4,007 lb., 4,265–4,585 lb.

SERVICE BULLETIN-REPORTED PROBLEMS: Cold engine ping (CX-9 only); rear brake groan and front brake squeak when brakes are applied; and battery loses its charge because the seat warmer won't shut off.

Mitsubishi

Living on Borrowed Time

Mitsubishi has had a rocky road in Canada, particularly since 2003. This is mainly because of its practically nonexistent dealer network, maladministration, and the rise of many Japanese and South Korean makes that are more refined and better accepted by shoppers. The automaker's two redesigned models—the 2007 Endeavor and 2008 Lancer—were expected to showcase the company's engineering and styling prowess, but they floundered in the economic recession that hit in mid-2008.

RVR compact crossover

Mitsubishi has yet to recover from the recession. Nevertheless, the automaker is fighting back by bringing a new compact crossover called the RVR—an "old" new small car that has been running on European and Japanese roads for some time—to Canada this fall. It has a pleasing, simple style and a rigid, lightweight body. The RVR is just over a foot shorter than the Outlander and shares the Outlander's stance and packaging, while giving slightly better fuel economy.

Mitsubishi's 2011 RVR: a small crossover coming before year's end.

The RVR carries a 4-cylinder engine with either a 5-speed manual transmission or a Sportronic 6-speed CVT with paddle shifters. An energy-recycling regenerative braking system, eco-friendly technology such as drag-reducing electric steering, and improved aerodynamics all combine to keep the car in the "green zone." It also comes with many safety features, including Active Stability Control, Hill Start Assist, and anti-lock brakes, as well as a plethora of airbags.

Mitsubishi also sells the following models in Canada: the compact Lancer ($16,998–$23,598) and its variants, the Sportback ($24,098), Sportback Ralliart ($33,698), and Evolution ($41,998–$51,798); the mid-sized Galant ($23,998); and the Endeavor ($35,998), Endeavor 4×4 ($42,998), Outlander ($24,998), and Outlander 4×4 ($25,498–$34,498) sport-utilities.

Should You Buy a Mitsubishi?

It depends on the model. The Chrysler Colt, launched in Japan by Mitsubishi in 1962, was so well-received in foreign markets that Chrysler bought 15 percent of Mitsubishi in 1971 and started selling the popular line of compacts in North America through dual dealerships (Chrysler/Mitsubishi). The Colts were popular small cars that were both reliable and cheap. Then Mitsubishi started getting fancy in its lineup with more technologically advanced turbo and AWD designs and the addition of sporty cars to its lineup. This resulted in the decline of the cars' reliability (think of the powertrain-challenged 1989–98 Eagle Talon sports coupe, Eclipse, and Laser) and increased prices and servicing costs. Plus, many Chrysler mechanics were ill-equipped to service "foreign" vehicles they hadn't studied and had to wait for parts that were often back-ordered for weeks at a time. Chrysler and Mitsubishi reduced their shared models in 1997, and shortly thereafter parted ways. This has left Mitsubishi struggling with its small Canadian dealer network and little new product.

All things considered, Mitsubishis are acceptable, cheap buys—mechanically. However, when you buy the product, you also buy the management, and that part is rotten to the core. The purchase of any Mitsubishi product is particularly risky for Canadians because of the company's weak dealer network. Moreover, insiders say that after a quarter-century, the automaker is seriously considering leaving the North American market; the recession caused joblessness and weak consumer confidence, which decimated Mitsubishi's sales. In fact, North American car sales for July 2009 fell 56 percent to just over 3,000 units, and SUV sales dropped 20 percent to 1,500 units.

Will Mitsubishi pull out of North America? Yes—it's just a matter of time before the company follows truck-maker Isuzu and partially VW-owned Suzuki.

RATING: With the exception of the RVR (which is new to the market), all Mitsubishis are rated Average, with easily negotiated base prices. These cars are still fairly reliable; however, servicing continues to be a problem on models with complicated fuel-delivery systems or other high-tech features. Problems they all share include poor original equipment tire traction; sudden loss of brakes, and premature replacement of the brake pads and rotors; early clutch failures; and airbags that don't deploy when they should. NHTSA has given these vehicles mostly four- and five-star crash protection scores.

COST ANALYSIS: Although the Endeavor mid-sized SUV is the best of the lot, its maintenance is highly dealer-dependent. When Mitsubishi leaves town, repairs and parts will be hard to find. **Best alternatives:** The Honda Civic; Hyundai Accent, Elantra, or Tucson 4×4; Mazda3; Nissan Sentra; and Toyota Yaris or Matrix. **Options:** Electronic stability control is recommended, but stay away from any of the models equipped with cash-gobbling turbocharged engines. Turbo repairs will devour your wallet. **Rebates:** Look for $3,000 discounts on the small cars and $5,000 on the SUVs. The Eclipse Spyder sportster, on the other hand, will continue to sell at its full retail price. **Depreciation:** Average. **Insurance cost:** Above average for the SUVs and Spyder. **Parts supply/cost:** Not always easy to find. **Annual maintenance cost:** Average. **Warranty:** Bumper-to-bumper 3 years/80,000 km; powertrain 5 years/100,000 km; rust perforation 5 years/unlimited km. **Supplementary warranty:** A good idea, if the warranty is sold by an insured independent company.

Nissan

Nissan has risen from the dead so many times, it should star in a George A. Romero zombie flick. And it looks as if the automaker will do it again by surviving this recession with a few feathers plucked but carrying a lineup of models that covers almost every marketing niche, with a few (like the small Cube and Juke) that are hard to pin down.

A boxy-looking $17,398 (plus $1,325 freight) compact, the Cube carries a 122 hp 1.8L 4-cylinder engine hooked to a 6-speed manual transmission or an optional CVT; Europe gets the 1.5L diesel powerplant. The Cube was introduced in Asia in 1998 and has been sold since May 2009 in North America and Europe.

A compact, sporty crossover, the Juke is new for 2011. It carries a 1.6L 4-cylinder engine coupled to a 6-speed manual tranny; a CVT transmission shifts the AWD variants.

While many manufacturers continue to dial back on their product development activities, Nissan has ploughed ahead into the 2011 model year with the introduction of the all-new NV full-sized commercial van (Nissan's first entry into the commercial van market) and a redesigned Quest minivan.

Nissan is continuing its tenuous ties to Suzuki by allowing Suzuki to market the Nissan Frontier pickup as the Suzuki Equator. Nevertheless, industry insiders report that the Equator's poor sales and Suzuki's cozying up to Volkswagen—having sold the German automaker almost 20 percent of their company—may have soured relations with Nissan. The Equator isn't expected to stay around after 2011.

Quality slipping

Judging by the last three years of complaints registered by *Lemon-Aid* and government/private agencies, Nissan quality control has let its guard down, particularly when it comes to fuel, climate, electrical, AC, and audio systems, in addition to brake failure, reduced braking effectiveness, and fit and finish deficiencies. Furthermore, there have been a plethora of owner complaints relative to prematurely worn-out brakes and tires, bad seats and seat anchoring, and a symphony of unwanted sounds that cover the spectrum of audio oddities.

The Nissan NV full-sized van seriously threatens Detroit's monopoly of commercial vans and will likely knock the Mercedes Sprinter out of the ring.

VERSA ★★★

RATING: Average. **Strong points:** Good-quality interior appointments; tilt steering column; and standard side-impact and side curtain airbags. A 6-speed manual transmission is available, whereas most small cars offer only a 4- or 5-speed gearbox. IIHS gave the car its top, "Good," score for head-restraint, offset, and side crash protection. As *Canadian Driver* columnist Paul Williams put it, the Versa is the "jumbo shrimp" of micro cars. The car's larger wheelbase makes for a smooth ride and creates a lot more interior room than what is offered by other small cars in its class. A tall roofline makes for easy access. Visibility is first rate, and there's minimal road noise. The fuel tank dwarfs the mini-car field, where most tanks are 45L; standard 15-inch wheels are used, versus the competition's 14-inchers; and the Versa carries a 122 hp engine, while the other micro cars get by with 103–110 hp powerplants. The 1.8L 4-cylinder engine provides plenty of power, and handling is responsive and predictable, thanks to the tight, power-assisted steering and independent front suspension. **Weak points:** Engine lacks "grunt" at higher rpms and produces an annoying drone when pushed; the manual 6-speed is a bit clunky;

KEY FACTS

CANADIAN PRICE (NEGOTIABLE): *1.6 Sedan:* $12,698, *Auto.:* $13,698, *1.8 S Hatchback:* $14,198, *Auto.:* $15,198, *SL Hatchback:* $17,398, *Auto.:* $18,698 **U.S. PRICE:** *Versa Sedan:* $9,990, *Hatchback:* $13,552 **CANADIAN FREIGHT:** $1,325 **U.S. FREIGHT:** $750

POWERTRAIN (FRONT-DRIVE)
Engines: 1.6L 4-cyl. (107 hp) • 1.8L 4-cyl. (122 hp); Transmissions: 5-speed man. • 6-speed man. • CVT • 4-speed auto.

DIMENSIONS/CAPACITY
Passengers: 2/3; Wheelbase: 102.4 in.; H: 60.4/L: 169.1/W: 66.7 in.; Headroom F/R: 5.0/3.5 in.; Legroom F/R: 40/30 in.; Cargo volume: 17.8 cu. ft., 13.8 cu. ft.; Fuel tank: 50L/regular; Tow limit: N/A; Load capacity: 860 lb.; Turning circle: 37 ft.; Ground clearance: 5.0 in.; Weight: 2,538–2,758 lb.

the suspension is tuned more to the soft side; less-effective rear drum brakes; no stability control on some models; and owners say real-world fuel economy is about 20 percent less than what is represented. NHTSA awarded the Versa only two stars for overall occupant crash protection. **New for 2011:** Standard six-CD radio for Versa Sedan 1.8 S; anti-lock brake system (ABS) now standard on all models except Sedan 1.6 Base.

OVERVIEW: The Versa is Nissan's first "micro" car since the Micra was dropped in 1991 and the Sentra became the company's entry-level model. Targeting mainly the GM Aveo, Honda Fit, Hyundai Accent, and Toyota Yaris, the Versa is the largest of these small cars.

COST ANALYSIS: Get the 2010 hatchback coupled to a 6-speed manual transmission for the best overall performance and highest residual value. **Best alternatives:** Honda Fit and Hyundai Accent. Nevertheless, the Versa's relatively strong engine and large body make it stand out. **Options:** The 6-speed transmission is a much better performer than the CVT, and the hatchback has a better reliability record than the sedan. **Rebates:** Not likely. Expect a little discounting by early summer. **Depreciation:** Below average. **Insurance cost:** Average. **Parts supply/cost:** Parts aren't hard to find and are relatively inexpensive. **Annual maintenance cost:** Predicted to be much less than average. **Warranty:** Bumper-to-bumper 3 years/60,000 km; powertrain 5 years/100,000 km; rust perforation 5 years/unlimited km. **Supplementary warranty:** Not needed. **City/highway fuel economy:** *1.6L:* 7.7/5.8 L/100 km, 37/49 mpg. *Auto.:* 7.8/5.9 L/100 km, 36/48 mpg. *1.8L:* 7.9/6.3 L/100 km, 36/45 mpg. *Auto.:* 8.5/6.2 L/100 km, 33/46 mpg. *CVT:* 7.3/5.8 L/100 km, 39/49 mpg. Owners say their real gas consumption is much higher than these estimates.

OWNER-REPORTED PROBLEMS: Brake failures, reduced braking effectiveness, and many complaints of hard starting. Speedometer can't be read in daylight, and only the driver-side door can be unlocked from the outside. Owners also report problems with the fuel and climate systems, paint, and body integrity.

SERVICE BULLETIN-REPORTED PROBLEMS: Diagnosing CVT oil leaks; rear brake squealing; front axle clicking; front-seat creaking; drive belt noise troubleshooting tips; can't remove key from the ignition, even though vehicle is in Park and shut off; repair tips for a malfunctioning fuel gauge. There's also a voluntary service program (Campaign #PM053) involving the free replacement of the instrument panel cluster and a free correction for seatbacks that won't recline.

SENTRA ★★★

RATING: Average. **Strong points:** The 2.5L engine provides lots of power; occupants are treated to a quiet, comfortable, "floaty" ride; easy handling if not pushed hard; plenty of cabin space, and the rear seat cushion can be folded forward, permitting the split rear seatback to fold flat with the floor; a commodious trunk; the locking glove box could house a laptop; and good quality control, with few safety- or performance-related defects. NHTSA gives five-star crashworthiness scores for everything but rollover resistance, which earned four stars. **Weak points:** The 2.0L engine is underpowered; manual transmission shifter's location may be too high and forward for some drivers; some body lean when cornering under power, and the rear end tends to fishtail; lots of road wander; long braking distances, probably due to the use of rear drum brakes instead of the more-effective disc brakes; and the front side pillar obstructs the view of what lies ahead. Body integrity and paint head the list of fit and finish complaints. **New for 2011:** SE-R-style rear spoiler added to the Sentra 2.0 CVT, 2.0 S, and 2.0 SL; anti-lock brake system (ABS) and electronic brake-force distribution (EBD) are now standard on the Sentra 2.0; Vehicle Dynamic Control (VDC) and traction control system (TCS) are now standard on the Sentra 2.0, 2.0 S, and 2.0 SR.

KEY FACTS

CANADIAN PRICE (NEGOTIABLE): *2.0:* $15,198, *Auto.:* $16,498, *2.0 S:* $18,198, *Auto.:* $19,498, *2.0 SL:* $23,098, *2.0 SE-R:* $21,798, *2.0 SE-R Spec V:* $23,198 **U.S. PRICE:** *2.0:* $15,420, *2.0 S:* $17,160, *2.0 SR:* $17,160, *2.0 SL:* $18,560, *2.0 SE-R:* $19,580, *2.0 SE-R Spec V:* $20,080 **CANADIAN FREIGHT:** $1,325

U.S. FREIGHT: $750

POWERTRAIN (FRONT-DRIVE)
Engines: 2.0L 4-cyl. (140 hp) • 2.5L 4-cyl. (177 hp) • 2.5L 4-cyl. (200 hp); Transmissions: 6-speed man. • CVT

DIMENSIONS/CAPACITY
Passengers: 2/3; Wheelbase: 105.7 in.; H: 59.5/L: 179.8/W: 70.5 in.; Headroom F/R: 6.0/2.0 in.; Legroom F/R: 41/26.5 in.; Cargo volume: 13.1 cu. ft.; Fuel tank: 50L/regular/premium; Tow limit: 1,000 lb.; Load capacity: 850 lb.; Turning circle: 35.4 ft.; Ground clearance: 5.5 in.; Weight: 2,819–3,079 lb.

OVERVIEW: Unlike many bare-bones economy cars, entry-level Sentras offer dependable motoring with lots of safety, performance, and comfort. Besides making for a roomier interior, the large body produces a quieter, smoother ride. These entry-level small sedans come in three trim levels: a fuel-frugal base 140 hp 2.0L 4-cylinder engine and two 2.5L 4-bangers that produce 177 and 200 horses, respectively.

COST ANALYSIS: Get the practically identical and cheaper 2010. **Best alternatives:** Sentra's engine and body dimension improvements over the past few years have made it a good competitor for the Honda Civic, Hyundai Elantra, and Mazda3. **Options:** Choose the 177 hp 2.5L 4-cylinder for the best power and fuel economy combination. **Rebates:** Expect $1,500 rebates in early 2010. **Depreciation:** Average. **Insurance cost:** Average for the base models. **Parts supply/cost:** Inexpensive parts can be found practically anywhere. Suspension parts and parts needed for recall campaigns are often back ordered. **Annual maintenance cost:** Less than average. **Warranty:** Bumper-to-bumper 3 years/60,000 km; powertrain 5 years/100,000 km; rust perforation 5 years/unlimited km. **Supplementary warranty:** Not needed. **City/highway fuel economy:** 2.0L: 8.4/6.4 L/100 km, 34/44 mpg. 2.0L CVT: 7.5/5.8 L/100 km, 38/49 mpg. SE-R: 8.7/6.5 L/100 km, 32/43 mpg. Spec V: 9.8/7.0 L/100 km, 29/40 mpg. Note that many owners report getting about 30 percent less fuel economy than advertised.

OWNER-REPORTED PROBLEMS: Airbags failed to deploy; gas pedal is mounted too close to the brake pedal; sudden unintended acceleration; faulty computer module causes the vehicle to shut down; early replacement of Bridgestone Turanza EL400 tires. Premature wearout of rear tires due to factory misalignment of the rear suspension:

> Rear suspension was inspected and I was informed that it was out of alignment, and they could not bring it to within specs. The fix was a total rear suspension replacement.... I now have a front strut bearing gone and have been waiting 2 months for parts...with my front end alignment out because of this, and no word on part arrival.

Engine piston slap; blown engine head gasket; power-steering failure; unstable front seats; seat belts snap back so quickly that they can cause injury; sun visors are mounted on the wrong side (shorter visor should be on the driver's side); bottom of the windshield may be distorted; and tire-pressure indicator malfunctions. Other problem areas include fuel, climate, electrical, and audio systems, in addition to horrendous fit and finish deficiencies.

SERVICE BULLETIN-REPORTED PROBLEMS: A voluntary fix (Campaign #PM053) involving the free replacement of the instrument panel cluster and a fix for front-seat creaking. Loose front/rear door weatherstrip and drive belt noise diagnosis.

ALTIMA ★★★★

RATING: Above Average. **Strong points:** A powerful 4-cylinder engine that delivers good fuel economy, and an even better V6 that provides scintillating acceleration while sipping fuel; flawless automatic transmission shifting; good braking; well laid-out instruments and controls; and better-than-average interior room. The 2.5 S handles well and is relatively softly sprung, whereas the 3.5 SE corners better but delivers a stiffer, more-jittery ride. Quality problems have abated during the last two model years. NHTSA gave the two-door Altima five stars for side and rollover crash protection; four stars were awarded for front crashworthiness. The four-door version got five stars for front and side crash protection and four stars for rollover protection. IIHS scored frontal offset and side crash protection as "Good," and head restraints as "Acceptable." **Weak points:** Pricier 3.5 SE models come equipped with a firmer suspension and wider tires that degrade ride comfort. Electronic stability control isn't available with the base model. Limited rear headroom; snug rear seating for three adults; and the 3-year/60,000 km warranty is too short. *Hybrid:* Less fuel savings than advertised; a small trunk; and cycling between gasoline and electric power is a bit rough. **New for 2011:** Carried over without any significant changes.

KEY FACTS

CANADIAN PRICE: *2.5 S:* 23,798, *Auto.:* $25,098, *3.5 S:* $28,298, *3.5 SR:* $31,898, *Hybrid:* $33,398, *2.5 S Coupe:* $27,398, *Auto.:* $25,098 **U.S. PRICE:** *2.5 S:* $19,900, *Auto.:* $21,840, *2.5 S with SL Package:* $25,630, *3.5 SR:* $24,520, *Hybrid:* $26,780 **CANADIAN FREIGHT:** $1,395 **U.S. FREIGHT:** $750 **POWERTRAIN (FRONT-DRIVE)** Engines: 2.5L 4-cyl. (175 hp) • 2.5L 4-cyl. (198 hp) • 3.5L V6 (270 hp); Transmissions: 6-speed man. • CVT **DIMENSIONS/CAPACITY (2.5S)** Passengers: 2/3; Wheelbase: 109.3 in.; H: 57.9/L: 190.7/W: 70.7. in.; Headroom F/R: 4.5/2.0 in.; Legroom F/R: 41.5/29 in.; Cargo volume: 7.4–13.1 cu. ft.; Fuel tank: 76L/regular; Tow limit: 1,000 lb.; Load capacity: 900 lb.; Turning circle: 34.6 ft.; Ground clearance: 5.4 in.; Weight: 3,168–3,492 lb.

OVERVIEW: Nissan's front-drive, mid-sized sedan stakes out the territory occupied by the Honda Accord, Mazda6, and Toyota Camry. The car's base 4-cylinder engine is almost as powerful as the competition's V6 powerplants, and the optional 270 hp 3.5L V6 has few equals among cars in this price and size class. And, when you consider that the Altima is much lighter than most of its competitors, it's obvious why this car produces sizzling (and sometimes uncontrollable) acceleration with little fuel penalty. Four-wheel independent suspension strikes the right balance between a comfortable ride and sporty handling. The 3.5 S, 3.5 SE, and new-for-2010 SR models add even more performance and luxury enhancements.

COST ANALYSIS: No need to buy a 2011 model; a discounted 2010 equipped with the V6 engine is just as good—and cheaper, as well. **Best alternatives:** The Honda Accord, Hyundai Elantra or Sonata, Mazda6, and Toyota Camry (only with the brake override option). **Options:** Watch out for option loading after you agree to a reasonable base price. Canny Nissan sales agents pretend that some options *must* be purchased, or that some can't be bought without having others included. **Rebates:** $3,000 rebates or discounts and zero percent financing on fully loaded models. Attractive leasing deals are also common. **Depreciation:** Slower than average, especially the much-coveted V6-equipped models. For example, a 2006 SE-R high-performance model is still worth more than half its original $36,000 price. **Insurance cost:** Higher than average. **Parts supply/cost:** Slightly higher than average, but most parts are easily found. **Annual maintenance cost:** Average. **Warranty:** Bumper-to-bumper 3 years/60,000 km; powertrain 5 years/100,000 km; rust perforation 5 years/unlimited km. **Supplementary warranty:** Not needed. **City/highway fuel economy:** *2.5:* 8.8/6.2 L/100 km, 32/46 mpg. *CVT:* 8.7/6.0 L/100 km, 32/47 mpg. *Coupe:* 9.0/6.3 L/100 km, 31/45 mpg. *Auto.:* 8.9/6.2 L/100 km, 32/46 mpg. *3.5 sedan:* 10.2/7.2 L/100 km, 28/39 mpg. *Coupe:* 11.4/7.3 L/100 km, 25/39 mpg. *Auto.:* 10.2/7.3 L/100 km, 28/39 mpg. *Hybrid:* 5.6/5.9 L/100 km, 50/48 mpg.

OWNER-REPORTED PROBLEMS: Sudden unintended acceleration; passenger-side airbags may be disabled even though an average-sized adult is seated; airbags failed to deploy in a frontal collision; a fusible link failure may cause the vehicle to shut down completely; hybrid models also may suddenly lose all power:

> Hybrid suddenly lost all power (both electric and gasoline generated) while moving in traffic. I had to cut across 2 lanes through heavy traffic (while coasting) to get to the curb. After waiting and shutting the car down, I was able to restart it. I took it to the local dealer, which simply said the car "showed no codes" and, therefore, was unable to diagnose the problem or make repairs. I consider this a major safety problem.

Vehicle may jerk when accelerating; while cruising, vehicle suddenly veered to the right as the steering "froze"; transmission popped out of gear; in another transmission-related incident, the car couldn't accelerate adequately and the transmission was replaced, after it was back ordered for several weeks. Owners also report frequent AC, electrical, and fuel system failures. Fit and finish is still reportedly subpar. Hybrid owners complain that the cruise control locks out the regenerative braking system. This makes the brakes less effective, reduces fuel economy, and increases brake wear.

SERVICE BULLETIN-REPORTED PROBLEMS: Rough-running hybrid engine and hybrid coolant leaks; fuel gauge issues; engine drive belt noise diagnosis; side mirror windnoise; inoperative driver's seatback handle; faulty driver seat lumbar support; an inoperative driver-side seatback release lever; and the driver's seat moves side to side.

MAXIMA ★★★★

RATING: Above Average. **Strong points:** Competent powertrain performance, decent handling, and a comfortable ride. Last year's redesign didn't degrade quality, as evidenced by the small number of safety- and performance-related complaints reported to public and governmental agencies. The 2010 earned NHTSA's top 5-star crashworthiness rating. **Weak points:** Handling is a bit ponderous when compared with the competition; 18-inch tires produce high-speed tire whine; tall occupants may find rear seating a bit cramped; the latest redesign produced a shorter, though wider, car; small trunk opening limits what luggage you can carry; requires premium fuel; and many incidents of the SkyView roof suddenly shattering. **New for 2011:** Nothing important.

OVERVIEW: After its recent redesign, the front-drive, mid-sized Maxima soldiers on as Nissan's luxury flagship, a competent and roomy sedan that's a mini-step above the bestselling Altima. Its 290 hp 3.5L V6 is coupled to a continuously variable transmission, and the vehicle comes with an impressive array of

KEY FACTS

CANADIAN PRICE (NEGOTIABLE): *3.5 SV:* $39,450 **U.S. PRICE:** *3.5 S:* $30,690, *3.5 SV:* $33,410, *3.5 SV with Sport Package:* $35,440, *3.5 SV with Premium Package:* $36,640 **CANADIAN FREIGHT:** $1,425
U.S. FREIGHT: $750
POWERTRAIN (FRONT-DRIVE)
Engine: 3.5L V6 (290 hp); Transmission: CVT
DIMENSIONS/CAPACITY
Passengers: 2/3; Wheelbase: 109.3 in.; H: 57.8/L: 190.6/W: 73.2 in.; Headroom F/R: 4.0/2.0 in.; Legroom F/R: 42/ 30 in.; Cargo volume: 14.2 cu. ft.; Fuel tank: 70L/premium; Tow limit: 1,000 lb.; Load capacity: 900 lb.; Turning circle: 37.4 ft.; Ground clearance: 5.6 in.; Weight: 3,574 lb.

standard equipment and a host of performance and safety features, such as large front brakes with full brake assist, a power driver's seat, xenon headlights, and 18-inch wheels. Granted, you get plenty of horsepower, comfort, and gadgets, but unfortunately the car isn't backed up with all the technical refinements and quality components provided by its Honda and Toyota rivals.

COST ANALYSIS: The revamped 2009 and the 2010 are your best buys from quality and cost perspectives. **Best alternatives:** The Acura TSX, BMW 3 Series, and automatic-transmission-equipped versions of the Honda Accord V6, Lexus IS, 5-speed Mazda6 GT V6, and Toyota Camry V6 (only with the brake override option). **Options:** Traction control wouldn't be a bad idea if you are lead-footed; otherwise, keep things simple. **Rebates:** $3,500 discounts and low-interest financing and leasing in early 2011. **Depreciation:** Average. **Insurance cost:** Higher than average. **Parts supply/cost:** Moderate parts prices, and some powertrain parts may be back ordered. **Annual maintenance cost:** Average. **Warranty:** Bumper-to-bumper 3 years/60,000 km; powertrain 5 years/100,000 km; rust perforation 5 years/unlimited km. **Supplementary warranty:** Not needed. **City/highway fuel economy:** 10.9/7.7 L/100 km, 26/37 mpg.

OWNER-REPORTED PROBLEMS: Front airbags failed to deploy; passenger-side airbag is disabled when the seat is occupied; unstable driver's seat rocks back and forth; sometimes vehicle won't shift into Drive; when brakes are applied, engine surges; drivers report they must constantly fight the steering wheel to keep from veering to the left or right:

> This becomes a safety problem when on narrow four lane roads, you must constantly fight the steering wheel to keep the car on the road or keep from running into the car on your left. I...took the car to the dealer and was told that I would just have to get used to this because of the electronic steering is different from my previous cars. I was told there was no adjustment that could be made to correct this problem. I am 70 years old and have driven a few cars in my time and can tell you this car should not drive the way it does, it is just an accident waiting to happen. It feels as if the car is trying to drive itself without turning the steering wheel, there seems to be a problem with other vehicles with the electronic steering—IE: Toyota and Chevrolet and just wondering if they all have the same electronic steering components.

Electrical problems knock out the interior lights, door locks, and other controls; headlights may provide insufficient illumination; head restraints obstruct rear visibility, particularly when backing up; and the adjustable steering wheel may stick in its highest position.

SERVICE BULLETIN-REPORTED PROBLEMS: A front strut creaking, groaning, or rubbing noise can be corrected by installing upgraded coil springs. Engine drive belt noise diagnosis; the navigation system map may not match your vehicle's location; a fix for a chattering sunroof; driver's seat shifts slightly; can't turn ignition to the ON position; and a malfunctioning fuel gauge fix.

RATING: Above Average. More car than truck. **Strong points:** Standard features abound, with stability control, curtain airbags, active head restraints, and anti-lock brakes. The fuel-thrifty 2.5L 4-banger gets a bit noisy when pushed, but the fuel savings are worth it. The quiet-running CVT transmission smoothes out the power delivery. Handling is a pleasure. Well-crafted interior, comfortable front seating, and impressive braking. Interestingly, fit and finish elicits few complaints, whereas this has been a chronic problem with Nissan's other models. NHTSA gives the 2010 Rogue five stars for side crashworthiness and four stars for front-occupant crash protection and rollover resistance. IIHS gave its top, "Good," rating for frontal offset, side, and head-restraint protection. **Weak points:** Some of the standard features are fairly basic, and those that are in the premium packages should be standard; engine sounds like a diesel when accelerating, and it could use a bit more "grunt"; lacks cargo space and rear-seat versatility; and poor rearward visibility. **New for 2011:** More sizzle than steak. New front fascia and grille, front spoiler, rear spoiler, chrome license plate finisher, and door side guard moulding with chrome accent trim; front and rear tire deflectors, underbody cover, and lower rolling-resistance 17-inch tires; new centre cluster, meters, and drive computer; upgraded seat cloth (Rogue S models); mood lighting, rear heater ducts, outside temperature display, driver's seat manual lifter, and additional 12-volt power outlet (now two); driver's seatback pocket; cargo light and illuminated visor vanity mirror added (Rogue S models); one-touch auto-up power

KEY FACTS

CANADIAN PRICE (NEGOTIABLE): *S FWD:* 24,698, *S AWD:* $27,498, *SL FWD:* $27,298, *SL AWD:* $29,298 **U.S. PRICE:** *S FWD:* 20,460, *S AWD:* $21,710, *S Krome FWD:* $25,060, *S Krome AWD:* $25,310, *SL FWD:* $22,050, *SL AWD:* $23,300 **CANADIAN FREIGHT:** $1,500

U.S. FREIGHT: $750

POWERTRAIN (FRONT-DRIVE/AWD)
Engine: 2.5L 4-cyl. (170 hp);
Transmission: CVT

DIMENSIONS/CAPACITY
Passengers: 2/3; Wheelbase: 105.9 in.; H: 65.3/L: 182.9/W: 70.9 in.; Headroom F/R: 3.5/4.0 in.; Legroom F/R: 42/30 in.; Cargo volume: 28.9 cu. ft.; Fuel tank: 60L/regular; Tow limit: 1,500 lb.; Load capacity: 953 lb.; *AWD:* 1,026 lb.; Turning circle: 37.4 ft.; Ground clearance: 8.3 in.; Weight: 3,315–3,469 lb.

function added to Rogue S driver's window; a 4.3-inch colour display audio system with USB interface added to the Rogue SV; USB port in centre console on Rogue SV; 2-DIN audio system with an iPod connection added to the Rogue S; MP3/auxiliary/RDS and speed-sensitive volume control; and a rearview monitor added to the SV, as the SV model replaces the previous Rogue SL.

OVERVIEW: This compact SUV is based on the Sentra sedan and gives car-like handling and better fuel economy than the competition that's still wedded to truck platforms. Nevertheless, the Rogue's car DNA becomes all the more evident as the engine protests going through the upper reaches of the CVT when accelerating.

COST ANALYSIS: The 2009 model was redesigned, so paying more for an almost identical 2011 version doesn't make sense; instead opt for a cheaper, leftover 2010. Delay your purchase until early 2011 so as to take advantage of the inevitable discounts, rebates, and factory improvements. **Best alternatives:** The Buick Enclave, GMC Acadia, and Ford Escape/Mazda Tribute. **Options:** Consider getting the top-drawer Bose audio system, but stay away from the failure-prone, expensive, and back-ordered run-flat tires. **Rebates:** $2,500 by late 2010, in addition to low-cost financing and leasing. **Depreciation:** A bit slower than average: A first year base 2009 Rogue that sold for $23,798 now goes for about $17,000. **Insurance cost:** Higher than average. **Parts supply/cost:** Parts are easily found in the Sentra bin, and are reasonably priced. **Annual maintenance cost:** Average. **Warranty:** Bumper-to-bumper 3 years/60,000 km; powertrain 5 years/100,000 km; rust perforation 5 years/unlimited km. **Supplementary warranty:** Not needed. **City/highway fuel economy:** *Front-drive:* 9.2/7.3 L/100 km, 31/39 mpg. *AWD:* 9.6/7.8 L/100 km, 29/36 mpg.

OWNER-REPORTED PROBLEMS: While parking, vehicle suddenly accelerated into a brick wall; transmission, steering wheel, gear shifter, and brake failures (brakes may also suddenly lock up).

> Nissan Rogue transmission failure at 16,000 miles [25,750 km]. Transmission began to make strange noises under load from the front end. Dealer replaced transmission and claimed there is no current recall. A check on the internet indicates the problem is pervasive.

Tire-pressure monitoring systems are so sensitive that they often give false alerts, so drivers end up ignoring them. Steering wheel vibrations may numb your hands:

> I think it's absurd my vehicle has 2,100 miles [3,380 km] on it and I've never owned a car that does this. You have to move your hands off the wheel because they go numb. I was told drive faster or take a different route to work.

Driver-side door handle broke and it took over a month to get the part:

In the meantime, the only way to access my vehicle is by using the passenger side door and climb over the seats. If I were physically unable to climb over the seats, I would not be able to operate my vehicle. Fortunately, I am able, but if a person was not, they would either have to rent a vehicle or use some other means of transportation. I find this problem inexcusable. A simple door handle part must be sent from Japan to fix this problem.

SERVICE BULLETIN-REPORTED PROBLEMS: A grinding, knocking noise and vibration from the rear of the vehicle at low speed or when turning may be caused by a defective rear propeller shaft. Restraints may create a rubbing noise from the spiral cable; drive belt noise diagnosis; drivetrain rear end grinding/knocking on turns; a transmission rattle will be fixed free of charge under Campaign #P9249; and speedometer may be inaccurate.

MURANO ★★★★

RATING: Above Average. **Strong points:** Nicely equipped with a refined, responsive powertrain that includes a smooth V6 coupled to a quiet CVT transmission; sports-car-like performance; a plush, easily accessed, comfortable, and roomy interior; standard stability control; a comfortable ride, good fuel economy; no-surprise, responsive car-like handling; and better-than-average reliability. NHTSA gives the Murano five stars for side crash protection and four stars for frontal crashworthiness and rollover resistance. IIHS gives the Murano "Good," a perfect score, for frontal offset, side, and head-restraint protection. **Weak points:** Cargo space behind the second row is less than the competition's; limited rear visibility; and requires premium fuel. **New for 2011:** A minor restyling and the debut of the Cross Cabriolet.

OVERVIEW: The mid-sized Murano continues to be the car-based "ying" to the Pathfinder's truck-based "yang." Both vehicles embody strong, in-your-face styling and are loaded with many standard safety, performance, and convenience features.

KEY FACTS

CANADIAN PRICE (NEGOTIABLE): *S:* $38,298, *SL:* $39,998, *LE:* $47,998
U.S. PRICE: *S:* $28,340, *SL:* $30,460, *SL with Value Package:* $34,250, *LE:* $37,110 **CANADIAN FREIGHT:** $1,500
U.S. FREIGHT: $750
POWERTRAIN (FRONT-DRIVE/AWD)
Engine: 3.5L V6 (265 hp); Transmission: CVT
DIMENSIONS/CAPACITY
Passengers: 2/3; Wheelbase: 111.2 in.; H: 68.1/L: 188.5/W: 74.1 in.; Headroom F/R: 3.0/3.0 in.; Legroom F/R: 40.5/28 in.; Cargo volume: 31.6 cu. ft.; Fuel tank: 82L/premium; Tow limit: 3,500 lb.; Load capacity: 900 lb.; Turning circle: 39.4 ft.; Ground clearance: 6.5 in.; Weight: 4,034–4,153 lb.

COST ANALYSIS: The 2010 model isn't much different from the 2011 version and it's a lot cheaper. Delay your purchase until mid-2011 so as to take advantage of the inevitable discounts, rebates, and factory quality fixes. **Best alternatives:** The Buick Enclave, GMC Acadia, and Hyundai Santa Fe. **Options:** Don't buy the failure-prone, expensive, and back-ordered run-flat tires. **Rebates:** $3,500 rebate by early 2011. **Depreciation:** Average. **Insurance cost:** Higher than average. **Parts supply/cost:** Parts are sometimes hard to find and can be costly. **Annual maintenance cost:** Higher than average. **Warranty:** Bumper-to-bumper 3 years/60,000 km; powertrain 5 years/100,000 km; rust perforation 5 years/unlimited km. **Supplementary warranty:** Not needed. **City/highway fuel economy:** 11.8/8.7 L/100 km, 24/32 mpg.

OWNER-REPORTED PROBLEMS: Passenger-side airbag is disabled when a normal-sized occupant is seated. Nissan recalled the 2009s for this defect. Owners also report frequent brake replacements (calipers and rotors) and poor body fit and finish, including paint defects and water/air leaks. Other concerns: Airbag warning light comes on continually, even after multiple resets by the dealer; vehicle rolls down incline when stopped in traffic; Check Engine light comes on after each fill-up (cap must be carefully resealed); faulty transmission body causes the powertrain to vibrate when cruising; headlights may suddenly shut off; the Start/Stop ignition button can be accidently pressed, and this can suddenly shut down the vehicle when it's underway; tilt steering wheel may be unsafe in a crash:

> Unsafe design of tilt steering wheel adjustment lever (SWAL) that will cause a shattered left knee in a front or rear crash (FORC). The SWAL is positioned on the lower left side of the steering column so that the left knee will be shattered in a FORC. Other vehicles do not have this design flaw. Nissan maintains that the SWAL design has not resulted in problems and therefore nothing will be done.

Remote-controlled door locks operate erratically; inoperative sunroof; faulty sun visors suddenly flop down, completely blocking visibility; and excessive vibration (fixed by reducing tire pressure from 41 psi to 36 psi).

SERVICE BULLETIN-REPORTED PROBLEMS: A grinding, knocking noise and vibration from the rear of the vehicle at low speed or when turning may be caused by a defective rear propeller shaft. Drive belt noise diagnosis; front axle clicking noises on acceleration; and an inaccurate fuel gauge.

Nissan/Suzuki

FRONTIER/EQUATOR ★★★★★

The Nissan Frontier.

RATING: Recommended. **Strong points:** Well equipped; carries a powerful V6, with horsepower to spare; the 4-cylinder engine is acceptable for light chores; handling is quick and nimble; an accommodating interior; plenty of storage in the centre console; and outstanding reliability. NHTSA gives the Frontier and Equator four stars for frontal crash protection, five stars for side crashworthiness, and three stars for rollover resistance. **Weak points:** Ride is a bit stiff; stability control is optional; rear seatroom is tight in the Crew Cab; and you'll need to eat your Wheaties before attempting to lift the tailgate. **New for 2011:** LE King Cab and SV Crew Cab LWB 6MT models are no longer available; S Crew Cab SWB and PRO-4X Crew Cab SWB 6MT models added; vehicle immobilizer and bed rail caps standard on Frontier SV, PRO-4X, and SL; and LATCH child safety seat anchors added to King Cab rear seats. *Equator:* Carried over relatively unchanged; likely to be axed next year.

OVERVIEW: This year's Frontier continues to be joined by its Suzuki twin, the Equator. They are gutsy

KEY FACTS

CANADIAN PRICE (NEGOTIABLE): *King XE 4x2:* $24,098, *King SE 4x2:* $28,048, *King SE 4x4:* $30,048, *King PRO-4X:* $32,998, *Crew XE 4x2:* $31,848, *Crew SE:* $33,848, *Crew LE:* $41,098, *Crew PRO-4X:* $38,498, *Equator Crew Cab JX:* $35,000 **U.S. PRICE:** *King Cab:* $17,540, *Crew Cab:* $22,290 **CANADIAN FREIGHT:** $1,440 **U.S. FREIGHT:** $750

POWERTRAIN (REAR-DRIVE/4WD)
Engines: 2.5L 4-cyl. (152 hp) • 4.0L V6 (261 hp); Transmissions: 5-speed man. • 6-speed man. • 5-speed auto.

DIMENSIONS/CAPACITY
Passengers: 2/3; Wheelbase: 125.9 in.; H: 68.7/L: 205.5/W: 72.8 in.; Headroom F/R: 3.0/3.5 in.; Legroom F/R: 40/27 in.; Cargo volume: 60 cu. ft.; Fuel tank: 80L/ regular; Tow limit: 3,500–6,500 lb.; Load capacity: 967–1,452 lb.; Turning circle: 43.3 ft.; Ground clearance: 8.7 in.; Weight: 3,710–4,667 lb.

pickups that are compact in name only. The PRO-4X model offers serious off-road features seldom found among compact trucks, like a locking rear differential, Bilstein dampers, and skid plates.

COST ANALYSIS: For the same model year and an almost identical pickup, Suzuki dealers are hungrier to haggle than their well-fed Nissan counterparts. A cheaper 2010 Frontier/Equator will give most everything that's offered with the 2011 version. Delay your purchase until early 2011 so as to take advantage of the inevitable discounts, rebates, and manufacturing fixes. **Best alternatives:** The Mazda B-Series and Toyota Tacoma (only with the brake override feature). **Options:** Run away from the failure-prone, expensive, and back-ordered run-flat tires. **Rebates:** *Frontier:* $2,000 by early 2011; *Equator:* $3,500 during the same period. **Depreciation:** Average for Nissan; a nightmare for Suzuki owners. For example, a 2010 Equator JX 4×4 that sold for $35,000 new is now worth about $10,000 less, and the year is just barely half over. A similar Nissan Frontier will be worth a couple of thousand dollars more. **Insurance cost:** Higher than average. **Parts supply/cost:** Parts are everywhere, and they don't cost much, since many parts are shared with the Pathfinder, Xterra, and Titan. **Annual maintenance cost:** Average. **Warranty:** Bumper-to-bumper 3 years/60,000 km; powertrain 5 years/100,000 km; rust perforation 5 years/unlimited km. **Supplementary warranty:** Not needed. **Maintenance/repair costs:** Less than average. **City/highway fuel economy:** 2.5L man.: 10.7/8.7 L/100 km, 26/32 mpg. 2.5L auto.: 12.6/9.2 L/100 km, 22/31 mpg. 4.0L 4×2 auto.: 14.2/9.2 L/100 km, 20/31 mpg. 4.0L 4×4: 13.7/10.4 L/100 km, 21/27 mpg. 4.0L 4×4 auto.: 14.7/10.4 L/100 km, 19/27 mpg.

OWNER-REPORTED PROBLEMS: Faulty fuel-level sending unit sensor:

> I went online to *nissanhelp.com* after performing a search, I came across many others who have experienced the same problem. Apparently it has something to do with the fuel sending unit. A similar problem was found on the 2000–2004 Xterra models and a recall was performed when the vehicle would stop after not getting any fuel.

SERVICE BULLETIN-REPORTED PROBLEMS: Service Campaign #PC036 calls for the inspection and free replacement of the front propeller shaft or the u-joint (journal/journal bearings) on the 2010 four-wheel-drive Armada, Frontier, Pathfinder, Titan, and Xterra. Inoperative AC blower motor; engine timing chain buzzing or whining; front suspension noise.

Subaru

Subaru has come a long way since its first model, an ugly, underpowered (0–80 km/h in 37 seconds), $1,297 minicar import brought to the States in the late '60s by Malcolm Bricklin. Part genius and part flim-flam entrepreneur, Bricklin left Subaru in 1971; a few years later, he suckered New Brunswick Premier Richard Hatfield into investing and losing $4.5 million of the province's money in the Bricklin car company (1974–76), maker of the Bricklin SV 1, a gull-winged sports car.

In 1995, Subaru realized it was losing the battle with Honda and Toyota for buyers of its front-drive compact cars, so it bet the farm on building versatile and reasonably priced all-wheel-drive Outback and Forester models—and on Paul Hogan (a.k.a. Crocodile Dundee), an Australian actor *cum* Subaru pitchman. Sales soared, with most cars selling close to their MSRP and keeping much of their value come trade-in time.

Even in these hard economic times, when nine out of 10 automakers' models are in the cellar, buyers are clamouring for Subaru's all-wheel-drive Forester, Impreza, and Legacy. And the company doesn't intend to risk its success with any dramatic changes. Except for a slight freshening of the Impreza, the company's overall product lineup this year stands pat, with most of the redesigns and styling changes scheduled for 2012 and later.

Malcolm Bricklin was an extraordinary promoter who made this homely runt of a car (the Subaru 360) a cult classic, put Subaru on the map, and drove Premier Hatfield from office.

Only 2,854 Bricklins were built before the automaker went into receivership, owing New Brunswick $23 million.

Although all Subarus provide full-time AWD capability, studies show that most owners don't need the off-road prowess; only 5 percent will ever use their Subaru for off-roading. The other 95 percent just like knowing they have the option of going wherever they please, whenever they please—and they don't seem to care that an AWD burns about 2 percent more fuel. And, as one retired Quebec mechanic told me, "All-wheel drive simply means that you will get stuck deeper, further from home. It's no replacement for common sense."

FORESTER, IMPREZA, WRX, STI　　　★★★/★★★/★★

The Subaru Forester.

RATING: *Forester:* Above Average. *Impreza:* Average. *WRX and STI:* Below Average. **Strong points:** Impressive acceleration with the base 2.5L engine; however, the WRX, STI, and STI Limited models have even more powerful 305 hp engines. But with that power comes complexity—a complexity that requires good access to parts and service that are frequently lacking. Competent handling, without any torque steer; Forester passengers are spoiled by agile and secure handling, thanks to a tight turning circle; a roomy cabin; lots of storage space with the wagons; a nice control layout; and average quality control. Impressive NHTSA crash test results. *Forester and Impreza:* Five stars for front and side crash protection, and four stars for rollover resistance. The Forester also excelled in IIHS crash tests, getting the Institute's top, "Good," mark for frontal offset, side, and head-restraint protection and for roof strength. The Impreza WRX would likely post similar results. **Weak points:** Keep in mind, there is nothing remarkable about Subaru's lineup except for the inclusion of AWD in all models. If you don't need the AWD capability, you're wasting your money. Last year's extra height, greater ground clearance, and increased suspension travel create more body roll when cornering; AWD cuts fuel economy; the outdated 4-speed automatic transmission shifts roughly and wastes fuel; and the Outback Sport doesn't ride as comfortably or handle as well as other Imprezas. There's also problematic entry and exit, and the seats require additional lumbar bolstering and more height. WRX and STI require premium fuel. **New for 2011:** The WRX STI is joined by a four-door sedan, along with a major chassis upgrade and revamped styling. All Imprezas get larger rear head restraints. The Forester's 2.5L engine will be 10 percent more fuel efficient.

OVERVIEW: The Forester is a cross between a wagon and a sport-utility. Based on the shorter Impreza, it uses the Legacy Outback's 2.5L engine, or an optional

CANADIAN PRICE (FORESTER: FIRM; IMPREZA: NEGOTIABLE): *Forester 2.5X: $25,995, Forester Outdoor Package: $25,995, Forester PZEV: $28,095, Forester PZEV Outdoor Package: $28,095, Forester Touring Package: $28,695, Forester Sport-tech: $28,695, Forester Limited: $32,795, Forester Limited with Multimedia Option: $34,795, Forester XT Limited: $$28,095, Forester XT Limited with Multimedia Option: $37,295; Impreza 2.5i: $20,995, Auto.: $22,095, Impreza 2.5i Convenience: $21,995, Auto.: $23,095, Impreza 2.5i Sport: $24,695, Auto.: $25,795, Impreza 2.5i Limited: $26,695, Auto.: $27,795, Impreza Hatchback: $21,895, Auto.: $22,995, Impreza Hatchback Convenience: $22,895, Auto.: $23,995, Impreza Hatchback Sport: $25,595, Auto.: $26,695, Impreza Hatchback Limited: $27,595, Auto.: $28,695; WRX sedan: $32,495, WRX Limited: $35,495, STI: $39,995, STI with Sport-Tech Package: $45,995* **U.S. PRICE:** *Forester 2.5X: $20,295, Forester Premium: $22,795, Forester X Limited: $25,995, Forester XT Premium: $26,495, Forester XT Limited: $28,495, Impreza 2.5i: $17,495, Impreza Premium: $18,495, Impreza Outback Sport: $19,995, Impreza GT: $26,995, WRX sedan: $24,995, WRX Premium: $27,495, WRX Limited: $28,495, STI: $34,995* **CANADIAN FREIGHT:** $1,525 **U.S. FREIGHT:** $695

POWERTRAIN (AWD)
Engines: 2.5L 4-cyl. (170 hp) • 2.5L 4-cyl. Turbo (265 hp) • 2.5L 4-cyl. Turbo (305 hp); Transmissions: 5-speed man. • 6-speed man. • 4-speed auto.

DIMENSIONS/CAPACITY (FORESTER)
Passengers: 2/3; Wheelbase: 103 in.; H: 66/L: 180/W: 70 in.; Headroom F/R: 6.5/6.5 in.; Legroom F/R: 41/29.5 in.; Cargo volume: 35.5 cu. ft.; Fuel tank: 64L/regular/premium; Tow limit: 2,400 lb.; Load capacity: 900 lb.; Turning circle: 38 ft.; Ground clearance: 8.9 in.; Weight: 3,064–3,373 lb.

DIMENSIONS/CAPACITY (IMPREZA)
Passengers: 2/3; Wheelbase: 103.1 in.; H: 58/L: 173.8/W: 77.7 in.; Headroom F/R: 6.0/3.5 in.; Legroom F/R: 41.5/28 in.; Cargo volume: 11.2 cu. ft.; Fuel tank: 64L/regular/premium; Tow limit: Not recommended; Load capacity: 900 lb.; Turning circle: 37 ft.; Ground clearance: 6.1 in.; Weight: 3,064–3,384 lb.

turbocharged version of the same powerplant, coupled to a 5-speed manual transmission or an optional 4-speed automatic. Its road manners are more subdued, and its engine provides plenty of power and torque for off-roading.

Redesigned last year, the Forester now comes with a roomier rear seat; an upgraded interior; standard curtain airbags; more-responsive, precise steering with greater road feel; and a much-more-comfortable ride. Its two "boxer" 4-cylinder engines are both competitive in terms of power and fuel economy, despite being coupled to an outmoded 4-speed automatic transmission.

The Impreza is essentially a shorter Legacy with additional convenience features. It comes as a four-door sedan, a wagon, and an Outback Sport wagon, all powered by a 170 hp 2.5L flat-four engine or a 224 hp turbocharged 2.5L. The rally-inspired WRX models have a more-powerful turbocharged engine (a 305 hp 2.5L variant), lots of standard performance features, a sport suspension, an aluminum hood with functional scoop, and higher-quality instruments, controls, trim, and seats.

COST ANALYSIS: Be wary of Subaru's high-performance WRX and STI models. They require special parts and specialized mechanical know-how that may be hard to find in these troubled times. Instead, buy an upgraded 2010 Forester or Impreza and haggle for a 10 percent discount. Better yet, compare prices with dealers in the States; prices may be $10,000 less on some models bought south of the border. Remember, WRX versions are expensive, problematic Imprezas, but when they run right, they'll equal the sporty performance of most of the entry-level Audis and BMWs—cars that cost thousands of dollars more. **Best alternatives:** If you don't really need a 4×4, there are some front-drives worth considering: the Honda Civic, Hyundai Elantra or Sonata, Mazda6, and Toyota Corolla or Matrix (only with the brake override feature) **Rebates:** $1,500 rebates on the more-expensive models, and low-interest financing. **Options:** Larger tires to smooth out the ride. **Depreciation:** Slower than average, and faster than average. Foresters hold their value best: A 2007 Forester that originally sold for $27,000 is still worth a respectable $14,500. But WRX models lose their value quickly: A 2007 entry-level WRX that sold for $35,500 is now barely worth $16,000. **Insurance cost:** Higher than average. **Parts supply/cost:** Parts aren't easy to find, and they can be costly; expect delayed recall repairs. **Annual maintenance cost:** Higher than average. Mediocre, expensive servicing is hard to overcome because independent garages can't service Subaru AWD powertrains and turbochargers. **Warranty:** Bumper-to-bumper 3 years/60,000 km; powertrain 5 years/100,000 km; rust perforation 5 years/unlimited km. **Supplementary warranty:** Protect yourself with an extended powertrain warranty. **City/highway fuel economy:** *2.5L:* 10.6/7.5 L/100 km, 27/38 mpg. *Auto.:* 10.4/7.7 L/100 km, 27/37 mpg. *WRX:* 11.3/8.1 L/100 km, 25/35 mpg. *STI.:* 12.2/8.7 L/100 km, 23/33 mpg.

OWNER-REPORTED PROBLEMS: *Forester:* Sudden unintended acceleration occurred while the vehicle was cruising on the highway; owner brought his 2010 Forester to dealer to adjust the computer per a Subaru recall. The next day, the vehicle suddenly accelerated out of control. Driver's side outside rear-view mirror distorts images like a carnival funhouse:

> Me and a lot of other Subaru owners are stuck with a defective and unsafe mirror. I will give you a web site forum with other Subaru owners with the same complaint: *www. subaruforester.org/vbulletin/f88/2010-light-assembly-condensationn-mirror-67147.*

Rear tail lights fog up constantly:

> The service manager said there was a service bulletin issued on 12/17/2007. Due to a design change, the head lens and tail lens fog up...will not be covered under warranty and won't be fixed. The bulletin does not mention year 2010.

Gas fumes settle into the cabin when the car is parked overnight; chronic hard starting; the front passenger seatbelt storage spool will not release. *Impreza:* WRX models have had fewer owner complaints (mostly paint, trim, and body hardware) than the Impreza, which has been afflicted with similar fit and finish deficiencies, plus engine, exhaust, and fuel system complaints. Also, reports of sudden unintended acceleration:

While driving approximately 15 mph [24 km/h] on normal road conditions, there was sudden, aggressive, and forceful acceleration. The driver immediately depressed the brake pedal, but there was no response. The driver placed the gear shifter into Park, but the vehicle failed to slow down. The vehicle crashed into a brick wall. The failure occurred without warning. The police and ambulance were called to the scene and a police report was filed. The driver sustained severe back injuries. The vehicle was completely destroyed.

When accelerating, there's also a serious shift lag, then the vehicle surges ahead; defective engine had to be replaced; head restraints push head forward at an uncomfortable angle, causing neck strain and backache; and the moonroof system cavity allows debris and small animals to enter between the headliner and interior walls—the perfect place for fungi and mould to incubate. *STI:* Sudden engine failure due to a failed ringland with piston #4. It took two weeks to rebuild the engine to correct this defect, which is common to 2008–10 Impreza STIs.

SERVICE BULLETIN-REPORTED PROBLEMS: *Forester:* Long crank times; a metallic noise from the B- and C-pillar areas (middle and rear of the vehicle); and a front stabilizer bar rubbing noise. *Impreza:* The front stabilizer bar rubbing noise affects the Impreza, as well.

LEGACY, OUTBACK ★★★/★★

The Subaru Outback.

RATING: *Legacy:* Average. *Outback:* Below Average; the car's higher number of safety complaints (related almost entirely to hesitation and stalling) shows sloppy assembly and the use of subpar components. Both cars are distinguished by their standard full-time all-wheel-drive drivetrain. This AWD feature handles difficult terrain without the fuel penalty or clumsiness of many truck-based SUVs. Without

KEY FACTS

CANADIAN PRICE (NEGOTIABLE):
Legacy 2.5i: $23,995, *CVT:* $25,195,
Convenience: $26,395, *PZEV:* $27,095,
Sport: $27,995, *Auto.:* $29,195, *Limited:*
$31,995, *Limited with Multimedia*
Option: $34,295, *GT:* $38,595, *3.6R:*
$31,895, *3.6R Limited:* $34,695, *3.6R*
Limited with Multimedia Option: $36,995
U.S. PRICE: *Legacy 2.5i:* $20,995,
Limited: $25,295, *3.6R Limited:* $28,295
CANADIAN FREIGHT: $1,525 **U.S. FREIGHT:**
$695
POWERTRAIN (AWD)
Engines: 2.5L 4-cyl. (170 hp) • 2.5L
4-cyl. Turbo (265 hp) • 3.6L V6 (256 hp);
Transmissions: 5-speed man. • 6-speed
man. • 5-speed auto. • CVT
DIMENSIONS/CAPACITY (LEGACY)
Passengers: 2/3; Wheelbase: 108.2 in.;
H: 59.2/L: 186.4/W: 71.6 in.; Headroom
F/R: 6.0/3.0 in.; Legroom F/R: 43/30 in.;
Cargo volume: 15 cu. ft.; Fuel tank: 70L/
regular/premium; Tow limit: 1,000 lb.;
Load capacity: 850 lb.; Turning circle:
36.8 ft.; Ground clearance: 5.9 in.;
Weight: 3,273–3,522 lb.
DIMENSIONS/CAPACITY (OUTBACK)
Passengers: 2/3; Wheelbase: 107.8 in.;
H: 65.7/L: 188.1/W: 71.6 in.; Headroom
F/R: 4.0/6.0 in.; Legroom F/R: 39.5/
29 in.; Cargo volume: 36.5 cu. ft.; Fuel
tank: 70L/regular; Tow limit: 2,700 lb.;
Load capacity: 900 lb.; Turning circle:
39 ft.; Ground clearance: 8.6 in.; Weight:
3,540 lb.

it, the Outback would be just a raised wagon variant that's well equipped but outclassed by most of the import competition. **Strong points:** A refined and reliable AWD system; a well-balanced 6-cylinder engine; precise, responsive handling, and a comfortable ride; interior materials and fit and finish have been substantially upgraded; standard electronic stability control; the GT version handles best and has power to spare; and lots of cargo room. NHTSA gives the Legacy and Outback four stars for front and side protection and rollover resistance. IIHS gives it its top, "Good," rating for frontal offset, side, and rollover crash protection. **Weak points:** The base 2.5L engine is a sluggish performer, undoubtedly because of the car's heft. On the other hand, the more-powerful GT version is a fuel hog. Fuel economy, though improved for 2010, still trails rivals like the Toyota Camry, Chevrolet Malibu, and Ford Fusion. Another mixed blessing: The stability control feature (VDC) adds exponential complexity to a vehicle that is already complicated to repair. Other minuses: Crosswinds require constant steering correction; excessive engine and road noise; limited rear access; front seats need more padding; interior garnishes look and feel cheap; stereo dials are minuscule; entertainment system doesn't let you change playlists, albums, or artists unless the car is stopped; the Mazda6 and Ford Fusion offer more cargo space; the V6 engine requires premium fuel; and these cars are very dealer-dependent for parts and servicing. God help you if the dealer goes under, or you need parts when dealers are cutting back on inventory. **New for 2011:** Carried over without any significant changes.

OVERVIEW: A competent full-time 4×4 performer for drivers who want to move up in size, comfort, and features. Available as a four-door sedan or five-door wagon, the Legacy is cleanly and conventionally styled, with a hint of the Acura Legend in the rear end.

Legacy spec.B sedan

The spec.B mid-sized sedan comes equipped with a high-performance variant of the turbocharged 2.5L engine. It is mated to the same 6-speed manual transmission that is found in the WRX STI and comes with a Bilstein sport suspension. The spec.B also has a feature called SI-Drive (short for Subaru Intelligent Drive), which is a rotary dial that allows the driver to select one of three engine performance settings. Subaru's continuing to sell the spec.B in Canada is good news for enthusiasts who need a little more space and comfort with their AWD performance car than what is offered with the WRX.

COST ANALYSIS: Get a nearly identical leftover discounted 2010 model. **Best alternatives:** The Honda CR-V, Hyundai Tucson or Santa Fe, and Toyota RAV4 (only with the brake override feature). **Options:** Base models hooked to an automatic transmission are severely performance-challenged. Stay away from the Firestone and Bridgestone original-equipment tires. **Rebates:** $2,000 rebates and low-interest financing. **Depreciation:** Slower than average. **Insurance cost:** Average. **Parts supply/cost:** Parts aren't easily found, and they can be costly. **Annual maintenance cost:** Average. **Warranty:** Bumper-to-bumper 3 years/60,000 km; powertrain 5 years/100,000 km; rust perforation 5 years/ unlimited km. **Supplementary warranty:** A good idea. **City/highway fuel economy:** *Legacy 2.5:* 10.6/7.4 L/100 km, 27/38 mpg. *Auto.:* 9.2/6.5 L/100 km, 31/43 mpg. *GT:* 11.5/8.0 L/100 km, 25/35 mpg. *3.6R:* 11.8/8.2 L/100 km, 24/34 mpg. *Outback 2.5:* 10.6/7.4 L/100 km, 27/38 mpg. *Auto.:* 9.5/6.9 L/100 km, 30/41 mpg. *3.6:* 11.8/8.2 L/100 km, 24/34 mpg.

OWNER-REPORTED PROBLEMS: *Legacy:* Passenger-side airbags are still disabled when normal-sized passengers are seated (a problem for years); chronic stalling:

> While driving at a rate of speed between 13–35 mph [20–56 km/h] and down-shifting the car shuts off! I lose power-steering and my ABS brakes. It has happened while pulling into parking lots and also while going around corners. It seems to occur when the AC is on. Hot weather exaggerates the issue.

Long delay to get up to speed when accelerating; brake failures; steering shimmy and wobbles, and car sways from right to left (partially corrected by replacing the steering column dampening spring and force-balancing the tires); Airbag warning light comes on for no reason; head restraints still force driver's head into a painful and unsafe chin-to-chest position (worse for short drivers), a problem plaguing all Subarus for several years, and still present in spite of the 2010 head restraint redesign. Running lights do not illuminate high or far enough and headlights have a similar handicap. One owner suspects the lights are conforming to European rules rather than North American regulations. Owners have to pay $50 twice per year to have the federally mandated tire-pressure monitoring system reset when they change tires in the spring and fall. There is no customer reset for this federally mandated device. Driver-side floor mats "creep" toward the accelerator pedal. *Outback:* Almost four times the number of safety-related complaints registered for the 2010 Impreza. Sudden unintended acceleration:

> Sudden acceleration disabling the cruise control to slow down and then hitting the resume button caused the car to surge. The rpm increased from 2000 to 6000 rpm. This occurs whenever the set speed is 20 mph [32 km/h] greater than the current

speed. The dealer could not correct this, claiming that the full acceleration is by design.

Chronic hesitation, stalling (insiders say Subaru has a fix for this on the same year manual transmission-equipped models); steering shimmy, wobble, and vehicle wander; Airbag warning light comes on for no reason; passenger-side airbag may suddenly disable itself while vehicle is underway; and many reports of a severe water leak into the passenger compartment.

SERVICE BULLETIN-REPORTED PROBLEMS: Free replacement of cracked ABS electronic control unit cover (Campaign #WVP-26, issued June 2010); measured to reduce steering wheel vibration at highway speeds; water leaks from sunroof, through headliner and map light area; sunroof binds or stops halfway when opening; driver's seat rocking; and an inoperative driver's seat lumbar support.

Suzuki

The Suzuki Kazashi.

Suzuki, like Mitsubishi, is on its last legs in North America and is expected to follow Isuzu in quitting the North American market entirely. Sales have been dismal since 2003. The company has little product available, except for a three-year-old SX4 crossover (the Aerio's replacement) and a new Equator light-duty pickup, which is really a rebadged Nissan Frontier (see the Nissan/Suzuki section). Suzuki ditched its Swift, Vitara, and XL-7 models, and dealers are running for the hills. Says Bloomberg News, July 10, 2009 (*www.bloomberg.com*):

> Suzuki Motor Corp. and Mitsubishi Motors Corp., suffering from plunging U.S. sales and excess North American plant capacity, may have to quit the market after a quarter century. Suzuki, Japan's fourth-largest carmaker, reported a 78 percent drop in unit sales in June, pushing its first-half decline to 60 percent, the market's worst. Mitsubishi is down 51 percent this year, and is stuck in a slump that began in 2003. Both carmakers "should withdraw from the U.S.," said Yuuki Sakurai, chief executive of Tokyo-based Fukoku Capital Management Inc., which oversees about $10 billion in Tokyo.

All of this sounds hard to believe. After all, Suzuki has been making very good entry-level small cars and acceptable sport-utility vehicles for well over two decades—just the kinds of cars that should be hot sellers in a recession. But they aren't selling.

Suzuki proves that simply building good, cheap cars and SUVs isn't enough to succeed as an auto manufacturer in North America. You also have to have a large advertising budget and almost perfect timing in your launches and promotion. Suzuki never put much money into advertising, and it has had a revolving door of incompetent executives who have run the company into the ground. Most shoppers don't give the company a second thought, since many of its products were sold under GM's name. And many of those who do recognize the Suzuki badge blame the company for selling unreliable Daewoo entry-level compacts under its own name.

Most all of Suzuki's 2011 vehicles are 2010 carryovers, a fact that shows the company has given up on the North American market. The one new car, the Kizashi, is a $30,000 (plus $1,495 freight and PDI) sporty all-wheel-drive, mid-sized sedan that carries a 180 hp 2.4L four-cylinder engine coupled to a continuously variable transmission (CVT).

Death by Daewoo

GM has long had a manufacturing and retail partnership with Suzuki. In 2002, GM bought a controlling interest in the assets of bankrupt Korean automaker Daewoo and convinced Suzuki Canada to sell two of the Daewoo cars as the Suzuki Swift+ (Aveo) and Verona (Epica). Prior to that deal, Suzuki had made considerable progress in raising its own product quality scores to a level that rivaled other Japanese models.

Unfortunately, Suzuki's rebadged Daewoo cars gave Suzuki a black eye in 2005 when J.D. Power announced that Suzuki had finished last in its Initial Quality Study of 36 nameplates. One of the cars that contributed most to the poor quality rating was the Suzuki Forenza, sold in Canada as the Optra. Suzuki never recovered from the bad publicity and poor administration. And as we go into another period of high fuel costs, where a rising tide should raise all compact-car-sales boats, Suzuki and Mitsubishi will probably be left high and dry.

SX4	★★★★

RATING: Above Average. This roomy little car is a winner because of its better-than-average overall performance, low price, and versatile body styles that rival many wagons and hatchbacks. What's worrisome is the company's huge losses and rumours that it will soon quit the North American market, where it has lost millions of dollars over the past eight years. **Strong points:** All models are bargain-priced, and they deliver a lot of content. On the road, the SX4 performs fairly well. Its lightweight and relatively powerful engine gets it quickly up to cruising speed; handling is fairly nimble; the automatic transmission shifts smoothly; the ride quality is good; and brakes are adequate, though a bit soft. The tall roofline ensures plenty of headroom for all passengers, makes for easy passenger access, and enhances overall visibility. There's a surprising amount of

KEY FACTS

CANADIAN PRICE (SOFT): *Base sedan:* $17,695, *Auto.:* $18,795, *Sport:* $19,695, *Auto.:* $20,795, *Hatchback:* $17,695, *Hatchback JS:* $20,295, *AWD:* $21,595, *AWD Auto.:* $22,695, *JLX AWD:* $24,695 **U.S. PRICE:** *Base sedan:* $17,695, *Auto.:* $18,795, *Sport:* $19,695, *Auto.:* $20,795, *Hatchback:* $17,695, *Hatchback JS:* $20,295, *AWD:* $21,595, *AWD auto.:* $22,695, *JLX AWD:* $24,695 **CANADIAN FREIGHT:** $1,395 **U.S. FREIGHT:** $750 **POWERTRAIN (FRONT-DRIVE/AWD)** Engine: 2.0L 4-cyl. (150 hp); Transmissions: 6-speed man. • CVT **DIMENSIONS/CAPACITY (SEDAN)** Passengers: 2/3; Wheelbase: 98.4 in.; H: 60.8/L: 176.8/W: 69.1 in.; Headroom F/R: 4.5/3.5 in.; Legroom F/R: 40/25 in.; Cargo volume: 16 cu. ft.; Fuel tank: 50L/regular; Tow limit: No towing; Load capacity: 815 lb.; Turning circle: 34.8 ft.; Ground clearance: 6.3 in.; Weight: 2,748–3,930 lb.

occupant and cargo room, and legroom is on par with or better than most of its competition. Lots of glass all around, making the cabin appear much larger than it is. ABS and front and side curtain airbags are standard. NHTSA gives the car five stars for side-impact occupant protection and four stars for frontal and rollover crashworthiness. IIHS rates frontal offset and side-impact crashworthiness as "Good." **Weak points:** Excessive engine and road noise, and the ride is jarring when passing over small bumps; fuel economy is sharply reduced with the AWD, but not so much with the automatic transmission; and stability control is optional. IIHS rates head-restraint protection as "Marginal." **New for 2011:** Carried over mostly unchanged.

OVERVIEW: "The cure for the common Corolla," says *Car and Driver* magazine. Available in both front-drive and all-wheel-drive trims, the SX4 crossover is a fun-to-drive, inexpensive small SUV-like hatchback with interior features and performance qualities that make it a great alternative to the top-ranked small cars. Practical dimensions, combined with a lengthy list of features and sporty dynamics, make the SX4 a good choice for anyone who's put off by the higher-priced competition. Reliability hasn't been a major issue, but a limited servicing network, less-than-average fuel economy with the AWD, and a cheap-looking plastic-wrapped cabin has turned many buyers away.

COST ANALYSIS: Get the practically identical 2010 model if it's offered with a 20 percent discount/rebate. **Best alternatives:** The Honda Fit or Civic, Mazda3, Nissan Versa or Rogue, and Toyota Yaris or Matrix (with the brake override feature) are affordable alternatives that have more-established reputations. **Options:** Stay away from the Firestone and Bridgestone original-equipment tires. The Garmin GPS option looks like a real bargain. **Rebates:** $2,000 rebates and low-interest financing. **Depreciation:** Higher than average. A 2007 base SX4 that sold originally for $16,000 is now worth only $7,500. Few Japanese cars lose their value that quickly. **Insurance cost:** Average. **Parts supply/cost:** Parts aren't easily found, and can be costly. **Annual maintenance cost:** Average. **Warranty:** Bumper-to-bumper 3 years/60,000 km; powertrain 5 years/100,000 km; rust perforation 5 years/unlimited km. **Supplementary warranty:** It's a good idea to get an extended powertrain warranty. **City/highway fuel economy:** *Base sedan:* 9.0/6.0 L/100 km, 31/47 mpg. *CVT:* 8.0/6.1 L/100 km, 35/46 mpg. *SP sedan:* 9.1/6.2 L/100 km, 31/46 mpg. *Sport sedan CVT:* 8.9/6.7 L/100 km, 32/42. *Hatchback:* 9.1/6.3 L/100 km, 31/45 mpg. *Hatchback CVT:* 8.2/6.4 L/100 km, 34/44 mpg. *JX:* 9.3/6.6 L/100 km, 30/42 mpg. *JX CVT:* 8.9/6.9 L/100 km, 31/41 mpg.

OWNER-REPORTED PROBLEMS: What is most surprising is that Suzuki doesn't generate a lot of consumer complaints, yet its vehicles are decidedly cheaper than most in the small car category. Owner complaints mostly target the fuel system and fit and finish. Some other concerns: When brakes are applied, vehicle may suddenly accelerate on its own; the Airbag warning light comes on randomly; tire-pressure monitoring system malfunctions and gives alert for no reason; fuel smell in the cabin; hard starting; condensation builds up in the AC and drips onto the floor when the car is shut down; rainwater cascades down from the roof and stains the upholstery whenever the door is opened; and paint is easily chipped, and the unprotected metal is quick to rust.

SERVICE BULLETIN-REPORTED PROBLEMS: Paint discoloured under wrap guard.

Toyota

Toyota: "Oh! What a Feeling" (of Disappointment)

I had recommended Toyota models since the early '70s, when the company first came to Canada. Yes, Toyotas were reliable and cheap (though rust-prone), and the automaker kept its head down during the rust wars. Still, I never fully trusted the company.

All this came to a head almost a decade ago when Toyota and its dealers used the Toyota Access program to, in my opinion, keep retail prices artificially high in Canada. *Lemon-Aid* made a formal complaint to Ottawa, alleging Toyota price-fixing, and the next thing we knew, Toyota settled and agreed to give $2 million to a Canadian charity— without admitting guilt. Slick, eh?

So fast forward to Toyota's sudden acceleration woes during this past year. The company admitted nothing, and Toyota's President, Mr. Toyoda, cried as he testified before the U.S. Congress early in the year as Toyota recalled almost its entire lineup to change floor carpets and throttles.

But there was no admission of guilt, no recognition of 2002 and 2003 Camry service bulletins where Toyota clearly states that their Camrys will suddenly accelerate due to defective computer modules.

ENGINE CONTROLS—LIGHT THROTTLE SURGING CONDITION

BULLETIN NO.: EG008-03   DATE: MAY 16, 2003

2003 Camry

INTRODUCTION

Some 2003 model year Camry vehicles equipped with the 1MZ-FE engine may exhibit a surging during light throttle input at speeds between 38–42 mph with lock-up (LU) "ON." The Engine Control Module (ECM) (SAE term: Powertrain Control Module/PCM) calibration has been revised to correct this condition

WARRANTY INFORMATION

This repair is covered under the Toyota Federal Emissions Warranty. This warranty is in effect for 96 months or 80,000 miles [129,000 km], whichever occurs first, from the vehicle's in-service date. *Warranty application is limited to correction of a problem based upon a customer's specific complaint.

And get this: Apple Inc. co-founder Steve Wozniak repeatedly called Toyota over the course of several months to report brake failures with his Prius. Toyota officials ignored him. However, when he mentioned the problem in an aside during an Apple press conference, all hell broke loose. The company fixed his car and recalled thousands of others. Is that what it takes to give Toyota a conscience?

The U.S. government fined Toyota $16 million for dragging its feet in ordering recalls. In the meantime, the public says electronic component failures are the real culprit and Toyota just ignores the clamour. Toyota says the problem isn't electronic-based; this contention is backed up by the Washington-based National Highway Traffic and Safety Administration. But, just in case Toyota and the government are wrong, Toyota says it will phase in a standard brake override (of the accelerator) feature in upcoming models (European vehicles have had them as a standard feature for years).

My recommendation: Don't trust Toyota. No brake override feature, no sale.

This year, Toyota is carrying over most of its lineup with little or nothing changed, except for the phasing in of the brake override feature. The other big exception is the 2011 Sienna minivan. It has been extensively redesigned for the first time since 2005; when those models came out, *Lemon-Aid* decided that the factory-related defects and poor-quality components embedded in the redesign were so pervasive that we could not recommend the 2005s, and we lowered our ratings on subsequent models.

With the redesigned 2011s, will Toyota continue with the same cost-cutting, "decontenting" practices that doomed its 2005 model and caused a dramatic erosion of Toyota safety and quality on subsequent models? It's highly likely that they will, since lower-quality content isn't easily seen in the showroom. That's why smart shoppers will let the first year of the Sienna's redesign go by before spending $30,000+ on hype and hope.

Toyota's Quality Myth

Toyota's image as a builder of quality vehicles was legendary. Then, in the late '90s, that reputation took a battering when angry owners refused to pay $6,000–$9,000 to repair the sludged-up engines used on most of Toyota's lineup. The company eventually relented and quietly settled most claims (see *www.oilgelsettlement.com*).

More recently, Toyota has stonewalled owners over dangerously defective drivetrains that possibly affect all of its 1999–2009 lineup. A look at NHTSA's safety complaint database shows a ton of complaints alleging the vehicles have a "lag and lurch" problem when accelerating, decelerating, or turning.

> Difficulty shifting my 2004 Camry from Park to Reverse, then upon shifting into Drive the car accelerated uncontrollably, would not stop, collided with a mobile home, airbags did not deploy, resulting in the death of one passenger and injury of driver.

•

> My 2002 Lexus ES 300's transmission gets confused when shifting into and out of the lower gears, then spends too long trying to figure out what gear to be in. This causes dangerous delays in acceleration, the effect is the same as a momentary engine stall. We have had this happen on several occasions, freeway ramp entrances are certainly the most dangerous place that this has occurred. Dealer acknowledges that there have been complaints about the shifting delays but they say no fix is available. This is our third ES 300, the previous models used a cable between the gas pedal and the throttle, this new one uses what is called "fly by wire," a position sensor on the accelerator that a computer is supposed to use to figure out what to tell the engine and transmission. It isn't working very well. If not rectified, this problem will certainly lead to a crash someday—then we'll get to see how good the safety equipment is.

Yes, it does appear that Toyota has been relying on its reputation, while Honda, Kia, Mazda, and Hyundai have continued to improve their overall quality.

A perusal of *Lemon-Aid* readers' letters and emails, as well as NHTSA reports, shows that recent-model Toyotas have been plagued by engineering mistakes that put occupants' lives in jeopardy. These include Corollas that wander all over the road, Prius hybrids that temporarily lose the ability to brake, and Tundra trucks with rear ends that bounce uncontrollably over even the smoothest roadways. Other safety failures include engine and transmission malfunctions; fuel spewing out of cracked gas tanks; sudden unintended acceleration; gauge lights that can't be seen in daylight; and electrical system glitches that can transform a power door into a guillotine. This year's *Lemon-Aid* has lowered the ratings on a number of Toyota's most popular models to reflect these dangers and to warn buyers of the potential for harm.

TOYOTA SAFETY COMPLAINTS BY YEAR

Model	2010	2009	2008
Avalon	20	33	83
Camry	258	381	205
Corolla	581	691	112
Highlander	33	25	108
Matrix	7	5	32
Prius	1,707	270	707
RAV4	70	111	115
Sequoia	5	0	27
Sienna	39	23	92
Tacoma	38	152	132
Tundra	46	21	145
Venza	17	61	–
Yaris	9	25	41

The huge number of Prius safety-related complaints is a real shocker.

A quick glance at NHTSA's 2010 safety defects complaint log shows that the Camry, Corolla, and Prius are "runaway" bestsellers—runaway in the sense that you may find yourself an unwilling hostage in a car careening out of control with a stuck accelerator, no brakes, and limited steering. This chart shows the data from *www. safercar.gov.*

When running properly, Toyotas do hold up very well over the years, are especially forgiving of owner neglect, and cost very little to service at independent garages. But the kicker for most buyers is how little most Toyotas depreciate; it's not unusual to see a five-year-old Camry or Avalon selling for over half its original selling price—a value reached by most Detroit Three vehicles after only their third year of ownership. But this is not the case with Toyota hybrids, which depreciate quite rapidly as word gets out that their fuel economy is not all that impressive when one considers that a $3,000 (U.S.) battery pack replacement can buy a lot of gas.

YARIS ★★★★

RATING: Above Average. The Yaris feels about right as the classic commuter car, where functionality trumps style and driving pleasure. Not a sporty performer by any stretch. **Strong points:** Roomy, economical, and versatile, with a wee bit of styling flash. Plenty of usable power; accelerates a bit faster than the Honda Fit or Hyundai Accent; excellent fuel economy; lots of interior space up front; and an incredible array of storage areas, including a huge trunk and standard 60/40 split-folding rear seats. Well-designed instruments and controls; comfortable, high front seating; easy rear access; and excellent visibility fore and aft. Yaris passes

over uneven terrain with less jarring movements than do other minicompacts and is quite nimble when cornering. Surprisingly quiet for an economy car. NHTSA gives the Yaris four stars for frontal, side, and rollover crash protection; liftback versions get five stars for front and side protection. IIHS rates frontal offset and side crashworthiness protection as "Good." **Weak points:** Higher priced than most of the competition, and not overly generous with standard features (get used to roll-down windows and manual locks). Says the *Chicago Sun-Times*, "The Yaris five-door is basically a hood, hatch and four doors attached to a metal skeleton supported by four wheels." Interior ergonomics are not the best, with its cramped rear seating; its tall profile and light weight make the car vulnerable to side-wind buffeting; the base tires provide poor traction in wet conditions; excessive torque steer (sudden pulling to one side when accelerating); some wind noise from the base of the windshield; and the steering wheel is mounted too far away for some drivers. IIHS rates head-restraint protection as "Marginal." **New for 2011:** Nothing significant.

KEY FACTS

CANADIAN PRICE (NEGOTIABLE): *Sedan:* $14,750, *CE:* $13,620, *LE:* $14,920, *RS:* $19,555 **U.S. PRICE:** *Sedan:* $12,605
CANADIAN FREIGHT: $1,280 **U.S. FREIGHT:** $785
POWERTRAIN (FRONT-DRIVE)
Engine: 1.5L 4-cyl. (106 hp); Transmissions: 5-speed man. • 4-speed auto.
DIMENSIONS/CAPACITY
Passengers: 2/3; Wheelbase: 100.4 in.; H: 57.5/L: 169.3/W: 66.7 in.; Headroom F/R: 3.5/1.5 in.; Legroom F/R: 40.5/27 in.; Cargo volume: 13.7 cu. ft.; Fuel tank: 42L/regular; Tow limit: 700 lb.; Load capacity: 845 lb.; Turning circle: 30.8 ft.; Ground clearance: 5.5 in.; Weight: 2,315–2,355 lb.

OVERVIEW: This entry-level five-passenger econocar gives decent fuel economy without sacrificing performance. It's essentially a spin-off of Toyota's popular Echo hatchback, a Canada-only hatch built specifically for the Canadian market, whose demise is deeply lamented.

Positioned just below the Corolla, the Yaris costs about $2,000 less, but manages to offer about the same amount of passenger space, thanks to a tall roof, low floor height, and upright seating position. The Yaris has a more-modern look than the Echo it replaced, and its interior improvements—like large windows, additional legroom, and high-quality trim and seats—give it the allure of a much-more-expensive car.

COST ANALYSIS: Get the 2011 model (only if it has the standard brake override feature installed). 2010 models are cheaper, but lack this important safety feature. **Best alternatives:** The Honda Fit is worth the extra money—it's got more room and is a lot more fun to drive. The Honda Civic, Hyundai Accent, Nissan Versa, Suzuki Aerio, and Mazda3 are worthwhile candidates also. **Options:** Consider snow tires and better-quality 14-inch tires for improved traction in inclement weather. Beware of option loading, where you have to buy a host of overpriced, nonessential, impractical features in order to get the one or two amenities you require. **Rebates:** 2009 models get $1,500–$2,000 rebates. **Depreciation:** Much slower than average. **Insurance cost:** Below average. **Parts supply/cost:** Easily found and reasonably priced. **Annual maintenance cost:** Costs over the long term are predicted to be low. **Warranty:** Bumper-to-bumper 3 years/60,000 km; powertrain 5 years/100,000 km; rust perforation 5 years/unlimited km. **Supplementary warranty:** Not needed. **City/highway fuel:** *Man.:* 6.9/5.5 L/100 km, 41/51 mpg. *Auto.:* 7.0/5.7 L/100 km, 40/50 mpg.

OWNER COMPLAINTS: You won't believe this, but the 2010 Yaris has only 10 safety complaints sent by owners to the NHTSA so far this year. That's about 1,690 fewer than the 2010 Prius. What problems are we looking at? Passenger-side airbag is disabled when an average-sized passenger is seated, requiring that the warning light be constantly reset; airbags did not deploy in a high-speed frontal collision; engine surges while vehicle is idling; transmission failures; steering wheel is not centred; when going over a patch of rough road, the car's ABS/tracking system alarm sounded and the car surged violently to the left then right, making the driver lose control; vehicle wanders all over the road, requiring constant steering corrections; driver-side window spontaneously shattered; ignition sticks in the starter position; ignition key tumbler and surrounding metal cylinder overheat; daytime running lights are too bright.

SERVICE BULLETIN-REPORTED PROBLEMS: Malfunction indicator lamp comes on due to faulty automatic transmission signals; front-seat squeaking; AC blower is inoperative or noisy; inoperative satellite radio; and a paint stain in the trunk area.

COROLLA ★★

RATING: Below Average. The Corolla has dropped two notches in *Lemon-Aid*'s rating due to its large number of safety-related complaints, which is 10 times the average amount one would expect. **Strong points:** Pleasant ride and good braking; good interior ergonomics and crashworthiness scores; and a high resale value. **Weak points:** Loose steering and a bouncy suspension. It's hard to keep the vehicle moving in a straight line without keeping your eyes glued to the road and both hands tightly gripping on the steering wheel. Sound like fun? Average acceleration requires constant shifting to keep in the pack; automatic-transmission-equipped versions are even slower still; clumsy emergency handling; lots of high-speed wind and road noise; limited front legroom; head restraints block rear visibility; and some reports of airbags deploying inadvertently or failing to deploy. Side and side curtain airbags are optional on the CE but standard on the LE and Sport. Stability control is also optional. IIHS rates head-restraint protection as "Poor." Overall reliability is average to below average. **New for 2011:** Nothing significant.

KEY FACTS

CANADIAN PRICE (NEGOTIABLE): *CE:* $15,460, *S:* $20,285, *LE:* $21,165, *XRS:* $22,550 **U.S. PRICE:** *Base:* $15,450, *S:* $16,520, *LE:* $16,850, *XRS:* $18,960
CANADIAN FREIGHT: $1,320 **U.S. FREIGHT:** $760
POWERTRAIN (FRONT-DRIVE)
Engines: 1.8L 4-cyl. (132 hp) • 2.4L 4-cyl. (158 hp); Transmissions: 5-speed man. • 4-speed auto. • 5-speed auto.
DIMENSIONS/CAPACITY
Passengers: 2/3; Wheelbase: 102.4 in.; H: 57.7/L: 178.7/W: 69.3 in.; Headroom F/R: 4.0/2.0 in.; Legroom F/R: 41/28 in.; Cargo volume: 12.3 cu. ft.; Fuel tank: 50L/regular; Tow limit: 1,500 lb.; Load capacity: 825 lb.; Turning circle: 37.1 ft.; Ground clearance: 5.8 in., *XRS:* 5.3 in.; Weight: 2,722 lb.

OVERVIEW: A step up from the Yaris, the Corolla has long been Toyota's conservative standard-bearer in the compact sedan class. Over the years, however, the car has grown in size and price, to the point where it can now be considered a small family sedan. All Corollas ride on a front-drive platform with independent suspension on all wheels. There are three variants: the value-leader CE, and the more-upscale LE and S models. Power is supplied by a torquey 132 hp 1.8L twin-cam 4-cylinder, teamed with a standard 5-speed manual gearbox or optional 4- or 5-speed automatics.

COST ANALYSIS: Selling prices are firming up as the market turns to smaller cars. **Best alternatives:** Other small cars that are good investments include the Honda Civic, Hyundai Elantra, and Mazda3 or Mazda6. **Options:** The built-in rear child seat is a sound buy. For better steering response and additional high-speed stability, order the optional 185/65R14 tires that come with the LE. **Rebates:** $1,500 rebates, low-interest financing, and modest discounting early in 2011. **Depreciation:** Much slower than average. **Insurance cost:** Average. **Parts supply/cost:** Parts are easily found and reasonably priced. **Annual maintenance cost:** Lower than average. **Warranty:** Bumper-to-bumper 3 years/60,000 km; powertrain 5 years/100,000 km; rust perforation 5 years/ unlimited km. **Supplementary warranty:** Not needed. **City/highway fuel economy:** *1.8L man.:* 7.5/5.6 L/100 km, 38/50 mpg. *2.4L auto.:* 9.5/6.7 L/100 km, 30/42 mpg.

OWNER-REPORTED PROBLEMS: Yikes! Almost 600 complaints against the 2010 Corolla, while the Yaris only has 10. Owners report a major steering defect that makes the Corolla unsafe to drive. Steering tends to allow the vehicle to wander all over the road; car cannot track a straight line on a flat road (alignments and a new steering rack don't help):

> It is very difficult to keep the vehicle within the lane. If it deviates (which is normal) and a correction is made, the car over-reacts and the vehicle veers to the other side of the lane. Another correction puts the vehicle back to the other side. So the vehicle moves side to side.

Steering may lock up without warning:

> While driving at 60 mph [96 km/h], the steering became very hard and difficult to turn. He would have to pull on the steering wheel when the failure occurred to keep the vehicle centered in its lane. The steering wheel would not re-center itself when making a turn during the failure.

Sudden acceleration accompanied by total brake failure:

> While driving 50 mph [80 km/h] the vehicle suddenly accelerated. As the vehicle is accelerating the contact is trying to slow the vehicle down by applying the brakes. At this time the brakes are malfunctioning and increasing in speed. The contact was unable to slow the vehicle down and crashed into another vehicle.

Driver cannot open the rear window with the other windows closed, as it produces a dramatic vibration and shaking inside the vehicle; car can be parked on a small hill with the parking brake applied and still roll away; harsh downshift when stopping; the vehicle stalls in the rain; side airbag's plastic housing pops off; bolts holding the door come loose; inner and outer tie rods bent; instrument-panel rattling; windshield back glass ticking; front-seat squeaking, and the front power seat grinds and groans.

SERVICE BULLETIN-REPORTED PROBLEMS: Engine rattle/knock on startup:

ENGINE RATTLE/KNOCK ON COLD START UP

BULLETIN NO.: TSB-0087-09   DATE: MARCH 13, 2009

Immediately following a cold soak startup some 2009–10 model year Corolla and Matrix vehicles may exhibit a brief knock/rattle noise from the engine compartment for approximately one second. Follow the repair procedure below to address this condition.

PREVIOUS PART NUMBER	CURRENT PART NUMBER	PART NAME	QTY
13050-0T010	13050-0T011	Gear Assembly, Camshaft Timing	1
11213-37020	Same	Gasket, Cylinder Head Cover	1
11159-37010	Same	Gasket, Camshaft Bearing Cap Oil Hole	2
13552-0T020	Same	Gasket, Timing Chain Tensioner	1

Steering wheel feels off-centre; premature front brake pad wear:

PREMATURE FRONT BRAKE PAD WEAR

BULLETIN NO.: TSB-0392-09   DATE: DECEMBER 3, 2009

Some 2009–10 model year Corolla vehicles may exhibit premature pad wear. Use the following replacement pads to address this condition.

PREVIOUS PART NUMBER	CURRENT PART NUMBER	PART NAME	QTY
04465-02240 (NAP) 04465-02220 (JPP)	04465-12630	Pad, Kit Disc Brake, Front	1
04945-12100 (NAP)	Same	Shim, Anti-Squeal, Front	1
04945-02150 (JPP)	Same		1
N/A	08887-80609	Disc Brake Caliper Grease (50 g Tube)	1

Loose lower B-pillar moulding; water dripping from headliner near the A-pillar (front of the cabin); inoperative satellite radio; front-seat squeak; clunk, pop noise when turning; and a stinky AC:

A/C—INTERMITTENT ODORS

BULLETIN NO.: TSB-0384-09   DATE: NOVEMBER 19, 2009

Some 2009–10 Corolla vehicles may exhibit an intermittent HVAC system odor. A newly designed evaporator sub-assembly has been made available to decrease the potential for HVAC odor.

CAMRY, CAMRY HYBRID ★★

The Toyota Camry.

KEY FACTS

CANADIAN PRICE (NEGOTIABLE): *LE:* $24,900, *SE:* $26,205, *Auto.:* $27,600, *LE V6:* $28,345, *XLE:* $30,925, *SE V6:* $31,555, *XLE V6:* $36,040, *Hybrid:* $30,900 **U.S. PRICE:** *Base: $19,720, LE:* $21,175, *Auto.:* $22,225, *SE:* $22,490, *auto.:* $23,490, *LE V6:* $24,890, X*LE:* $26,250, *SE V6:* $26,165, X*LE V6:* $29,370, *Hybrid:* $26,575 **CANADIAN FREIGHT:** $1,420 **U.S. FREIGHT:** $750 **POWERTRAIN (FRONT-DRIVE)** Engines: 2.4L 4-cyl. Hybrid (187 hp) • 2.5L 4-cyl. (169 or 179 hp) • 3.5L V6 (268 hp); Transmissions: 6-speed man. • 6-speed auto. • CVT **DIMENSIONS/CAPACITY** Passengers: 2/3; Wheelbase: 109.3 in.; H: *Camry:* 57.9, *Hybrid:* 57.5/L: 189.2/ W: 71.7 in.; Headroom F/R: 5.0/2.0 in.; Legroom F/R: 42/29 in.; Cargo volume: *Camry:* 15 cu. ft., *Hybrid:* 10.6 cu. ft.; Fuel tank: *Camry:* 70L, *Hybrid:* 65L/regular/ premium; Tow limit: *Camry:* 1,000 lb., *Hybrid:* Not advised; Load capacity: 900 lb.; Turning circle: 36.1 ft.; Ground clearance: *Camry:* 5.3 in., *Hybrid:* 5.9 in.; Weight: *Camry:* 3,307 lb., *Hybrid:* 3,638 lb.

RATING: Below Average. The Camry is another example of one of Toyota's "good cars gone bad." **Strong points:** Last year's redesign corrected most of the Camry's performance gaps; a retuned SE trim level delivers sporty handling; the base 4-cylinder is a competent, responsive performer; surprisingly, the 3.5L V6 powertrain set-up delivers fuel economy figures that are almost as good as the base 4-banger; there's a nice array of new standard safety and convenience features that include a telescoping steering column, side airbags, and stability control; pleasant ride; quiet interior; well laid-out instruments and controls; nicely padded dash and door panels; lots of interior passenger and storage space; and a high resale value. IIHS rates the Camry's frontal offset and side protection as "Good." **Weak points:** Reported safety-related failures (six times the average number of reported complaints) are particularly worrisome because they have been mentioned year after year, and can be especially lethal to older drivers with slower reflexes. Indeed, probably few Camry drivers are NASCAR proficient and therefore don't have the necessary driving skills to confront sudden engine surging or delayed transmission engagement when accelerating, merging, passing, or turning. NHTSA gives the Camry and its Hybrid variant only three stars for overall crashworthiness; IIHS rates head-restraint effectiveness as only "Marginal." Hybrid fuel economy is overstated by almost 30 percent, say *Consumer Reports* and almost everyone else. **New for 2011:** A slight restyling until the 2012 redesign.

OVERVIEW: The Camry is available only as a four-door sedan based on the Avalon platform. Power is supplied by a peppy 169 hp 2.5L 4-cylinder engine (179 hp with the SE), a 187 hp 2.4L gas-electric hybrid 4-cylinder, or a 268 hp 3.5L V6. The base engine can be coupled to a 6-speed manual or a 6-speed automatic, and the V6 uses a 6-speed automatic. Hybrids come with a continuously variable transmission (CVT). There are many standard features available, like side airbags, side curtain airbags, a driver's knee airbag, and anti-lock four-wheel disc brakes, on all Camrys; stability and traction control can be found on the higher-end models and the Hybrid (traction/anti-skid control). Rear seats have shoulder belts for the middle passenger; low-beam lights are quite bright; and the headlights switch on and off automatically as conditions change.

COST ANALYSIS: Buy a cheaper, almost identical 2010 model. **Best alternatives:** The Honda Accord, Hyundai Sonata and Elantra, Mazda5 and Mazda6, and Nissan Sentra. **Options:** Stay away from the optional moonroof; it robs you of much-needed headroom and exposes you to deafening wind roar, rattling, and leaks. Original equipment Firestone and Bridgestone tires should be shunned in favour of better-performing tires recommended by *thetirerack.com*:

> The car has Bridgestone Turanza EL 400–02 tires, which had 689 miles [1,109 km/h] on them. The rear driver side tire failed at 60 mph [96 km/h] when the tread split. After reading all the similar complaints by other Toyota car owners, I believe these tires are dangerous. After a very ugly discussion with the dealership, the one tire was replaced, but Toyota would not replace the remaining three.

Rebates: $2,000 rebates, plus low-interest financing and very attractive leasing deals in the early winter of 2011. **Depreciation:** Lower than average; in Canada, the ongoing safety complaints targeting Camrys have not affected the car's resale value. **Insurance cost:** Higher than average. **Parts supply/cost:** Owners report long service waits for their Hybrids. Parts are generally moderately priced. **Annual maintenance cost:** Average. **Warranty:** Bumper-to-bumper 3 years/60,000 km; powertrain 5 years/100,000 km; rust perforation 5 years/ unlimited km. **Supplementary warranty:** Not needed. **City/highway fuel economy:** *Hybrid:* Supposedly averages 5.7 L/100 km and 50 mpg for city and highway driving combined, but many owners say their vehicle's real-world fuel consumption is much more. *2.5L SE man.:* 9.5/6.1 L/100 km, 30/46 mpg. *2.4L auto.:* 9.0/6.1 L/100 km, 31/46 mpg. *3.5L V6:* 10.7/7.0 L/100 km, 26/40 mpg.

OWNER-REPORTED PROBLEMS: Almost 300 safety-related failures have been reported to the NHTSA for the 2010 Camry. This is about six times the average number of complaints most cars would generate during their first year on the market. As seen with other Toyota models (like the 2010 Prius, which has received 1,700 complaints), sudden unintended acceleration without any brakes is the top reported problem for Camrys, with an added twist: They still speed out of control after having recall work done, or the recall repair creates another safety hazard:

Although I was mashing down on the brakes as hard as I could, the vehicle moved forward (producing skid marks) and hit the truck in front of me. My Camry pushed into the truck's trailer hitch, bending the rebar in the front of my car, which pushed up the radiator, etc. There was a witness who was standing next to the drive-in window because the restaurant had messed up his order. He reported to the officer that came to the scene that he heard the Camry's engine start revving, and when he looked to see why, he could see that I was trying to get the car to stop. Obviously, the Toyota Camry recall work is not effective.

•

Recall repair on my 2008 Toyota Camry resulted in them filing down the bottom and left lower side of my accelerator pedal. As a result, when wearing leather shoes my foot has slipped off the accelerated pedal system several times. The dealer insists that there is nothing further that can be done.

An airline pilot and Camry owner blames electronic computer module programming that overrides driver input—a problem that can also cause major aircraft crashes:

I was driving my 2010 Camry in the Great Smokey Mountains descending a mountain road. I tested downshifting at several speeds into various gears to determine if it was possible to slow down the car under runaway accelerator conditions. I had wrongly assumed that bad drivers had failed to use the controls of the car to slow down and stop such vehicles. The computer refused to accept my command to downshift into 1st gear at speeds above 25 mph [40 km/h]. I did not try higher speeds into 2nd. Clearly the product manager and program engineers at Toyota do not understand that saving the transmission or engine from stress could lead to destruction of that same car and [its] occupants in their foolish decision to limit driver command and control. A fault in the computer could lead to entire failure of the transmission shift commands and engineer control system (ECU). This same flawed thinking has led to many Airbus aircraft fatal crashes. The flight control computer feels it is more intelligent [than] the stupid captain at the controls so it will not allow a flight control input it does not agree with. When the sensors are defective, or the flight envelope requires emergency actions, etc., tough luck. Now, I realize that Toyota has followed the same flawed thinking. I am an instrument rated pilot and I believe the operator should have total control of the vehicle. No command interlocks to prevent emergency operations should be tolerated. How can I trust this vehicle now that I know it will kill due to programming errors even if I try to regain control in a normal manner?

Other safety problems reported: Airbags fail to deploy when they should; when accelerating from a stop, the vehicle hesitates, sometimes to a count of three, before suddenly accelerating; and when decelerating, the vehicle speeds up, as if the cruise control were engaged:

The consumer noticed when driving at highway speeds, when he removed his foot from the accelerator pedal he expected the vehicle to naturally slow down with no braking necessary. However, the vehicle did not respond immediately. The vehicle acted as though the cruise control was engaged. When the engine did respond, there was a 2 to 5 second search pattern engaged with a sweep low rpm to high rpm while it tried to find a performance solution and set point.

The close placement of the brake and accelerator pedals also causes unwanted acceleration due to driver error; however, this cannot explain the large number of incidences of sudden acceleration reported. Frequent failures of the engine cam head, which is often back ordered; electronic power steering operates erratically and is sometimes unresponsive:

Starting at speeds around 55–60 mph [88–96 km/h], the steering wheel wobbles half an inch to an inch, although I've only [driven] it off the dealer's lot within the last month. This wobble causes the vehicle to sway back and forth within my lane, which could cause a serious accident if another vehicle was close enough to mine.

Steering constantly pulls the car to the left, into oncoming traffic, no matter how many alignments you get; car caught on fire after being plugged into a block heater; the centre console below the gear shift becomes extremely hot; Hybrid's lower beam lights are inadequate for lighting the highway; driver-seat lumbar support may be painful for some drivers; rear window exploded spontaneously while vehicle was stopped in traffic:

Two areas of glass failure were noted, roughly following the radius of the glass on either side in a vertical pattern as it bends to meet the rear pillars. The window remained intact (albeit shattered) long enough to record it on my iPhone, clearly showing two areas of failure with gaps of 0.25–1.5 inches between the center (flatter) portion of the glass and the left and right sides where it bends to meet the rear pillars. The [window] fell into the car as soon as I resumed movement on the street. The sound was like that of a gunshot.

Passenger-side window fell out; front windshield distortion looks like little bubbles are embedded in the glass; rear window-defrosting wires don't clear the upper top of the windshield; and a number of Hybrid AC failures have also been reported. Owners of the 2010 Camry say it's a "rat-hotel":

While driving 40 mph [64 km/h], the driver noticed a rat crawled from under the passenger seat into the glove compartment and into the air conditioner. The [sight] of the rat almost caused the driver to crash. The contact was able to get the rat out of the vehicle. Two days later the contact took the vehicle to the dealer to repair the back seat and the seat belt that the rat has chewed through and also clean the air conditioner.

SERVICE BULLETIN-REPORTED PROBLEMS: A Toyota secret warranty (Campaign # (LSC) 90K) will cover the cost to replace the VVT-I oil hose in some V6-equipped Camrys. When the oil hose fails, it will cause unusual engine noise and make the engine run hot. This campaign will expire March 31, 2013.

Remedy for brake pulsation, vibration:

BRAKES—VIBRATION/PULSATION WHEN BRAKING

BULLETIN NO.: TSB-0169-09   DATE: JUNE 4, 2009

Some 2007–10 Camry vehicles may exhibit a vibration or pulsation condition when braking. New front brake pads are available to address customer concerns. Follow the repair procedure below.

PREVIOUS PART NUMBER	CURRENT PART NUMBER	PART NAME	QTY
04465-06100	04465-33470	Pad, Kit Disc Brake, Front	1
04466-06060 04466-33160	04466-06090	Pad, Kit Disc Brake, Rear	As Needed
04945-06130	Same	Shim Kit, Anti Squeal, Front	*

*Visually inspect the shims for heat discoloration. If discolored, replace the shims.

OP CODE	DESCRIPTION	TIME	OFP	T1	T2
BR9003	Machine Front Discs and Replace Pads (Both Sides). Inspect and Replace the Rear Brake Pads if required (per repair instructions below).	3.5	43512-33130 (rotor)	9B	13

Cloudy, foggy clock face; dust or powder is blown through the air vents:

A/C—DUST/POWDER BLOWS FROM DASH VENTS

BULLETIN NO.: TSB-0075-08   DATE: MAY 27, 2008

Some Avalon (2006–09) and Camry and Camry HV (2007–10) vehicles may exhibit a condition where dust or powder appears visible around the HVAC vents. A newly designed evaporator is available to help reduce this concern.

Satellite radio inoperative; heavy static on Bluetooth calls; sunroof pops when it is opened; loose sun visor mounts; intermittent AC odours; rattle, front-seat squeaking; buzz noise from the driver's side of the dash:

RATTLE/BUZZ FROM DRIVER'S SIDE OF DASH

BULLETIN: TSB-0229-09   DATE: JULY 27, 2009

BRAKE BOOSTER RATTLE/BUZZ NOISE

2005–10 Avalon

2007–10 Camry

2008–09 Highlander

2006–09 RAV4

2004–10 Sienna

Some Toyota vehicles may emit a rattle or buzz type noise from the driver's instrument panel area. The noise can be duplicated when lightly accelerating and then decelerating, or when depressing the brake pedal with the shift lever in Park and then releasing the brake pedal. An updated vacuum check valve is now available to reduce this noise.

Knocking noise from the roof area:

KNOCKING NOISE FROM THE ROOF AREA

BULLETIN NO.: TSB-0090-10   DATE: MARCH 12, 2010

Some 2007–10 model year North American built Camry and Camry HV vehicles may exhibit a knocking noise from the roof structure of the vehicle. This may be caused by a separation of the NVH dampening bonds between the roof sheet metal and the roof reinforcement. Use the following procedure to correct this condition.

Water leaks onto the headliner/footwell area; engine ticking noise; front-seat squeaking; power-seat grinding, groaning; moonroof makes a knocking noise; radio noise; excessive dust from vents; console door won't open; transmission control module (TCM) updates for shift improvement; torque converter shudder on light acceleration; and paint is stained under the Rapguard protective wrap.

PRIUS ★

bad buy

KEY FACTS

CANADIAN PRICE (NEGOTIABLE): *Base:* $27,800, *Premium Package auto.:* $30,045, *Premium with Solar Panel Option:* $31,635, *Touring Package:* $31,865, *Technology Package:* $37,395 **U.S. PRICE:** *Prius II:* $22,800, *Prius III:* $23,800, *Prius IV:* $26,600, *Prius V:* $28,070 **CANADIAN FREIGHT:** $1,420 **U.S. FREIGHT:** $750 **POWERTRAIN (FRONT-DRIVE)** Engine: 1.8L 4-cyl. (134 hp); Transmission: CVT **DIMENSIONS/CAPACITY** Passengers: 2/3; Wheelbase: 106.3 in.; H: 58.3/L: 175.6/W: 68.7 in.; Headroom F/R: 4.0/2.0 in.; Legroom F/R: 40.5/30 in.; Cargo volume: 15.7 cu. ft.; Fuel tank: 45L/regular; Tow limit: No towing; Load capacity: 810 lb.; Turning circle: 34.2 ft.; Ground clearance: 5.5 in.; Weight: 3,042 lb.

RATING: Not Recommended. One of the most dangerous cars on the road, even after its many recall corrections. Sudden acceleration, no brakes or weak brakes, and a cruise control that doesn't turn off are scary enough. But what about a steering column that becomes unhinged? Bottom line: Don't buy a Prius. **Strong points:** Good fuel economy and acceleration in most situations and little cabin noise. NHTSA gave Prius a five-star rating for side crash protection, and four stars for front-impact protection and rollover resistance. IIHS gave its top, "Good," rating for frontal offset, side, and head-restraint protection. **Weak points:** The car is too darn dangerous to drive. It's also pricey; Honda's Insight sells for almost $4,000 less ($27,800 versus $23,900). Poorer performance in cold weather; battery pack will eventually cost about $3,000 (U.S.) to replace; fuel economy may be 20 percent less than advertised; 50 percent depreciation after three years; higher-than-average insurance premiums; dealer-dependent servicing means higher servicing costs; rear seating is cramped for three adults; sales and servicing may not be available outside of large urban areas; and the CVT cannot be easily repaired by independent agencies. Owners say the Prius is slow-steering, has lots of body roll when cornering, and is stall-prone. Braking isn't very precise or responsive, and the car is very unstable when hit by crosswinds. Highway rescuers are wary of the car's 500-volt electrical system, and are taking special courses to prevent electrocution and avoid toxic battery components. Reliability is subpar and its performance is summed up quite well by Ontario-based car columnist and editor of *Straight-Six.Com* John LeBlanc, who calls the Prius "the worst car of the last decade." **New for 2011:** Carried over mostly unchanged.

OVERVIEW: This third-generation Prius contains a 1.8L DOHC 16-valve 4-cylinder engine. It may sound hard to believe, but the bigger engine doesn't have to work as hard. So at highway speeds, the lower rpms save about 1.3 km/L (3 mpg). The gasoline engine delivers a total of 98 hp, and when combined with the hybrid system, you get 134 hp—24 more horses than with last year's model. The Prius is now approaching the Camry in size, and its powerplant is more sophisticated, powerful, and efficient than what you get with similar vehicles in the marketplace. Interestingly, because the car relies primarily on electrical energy, fuel economy is better in the city than on the highway—the opposite of what one finds with gasoline-powered vehicles.

An electric motor is the main power source, and it uses an innovative and fairly reliable CVT for smooth and efficient shifting (these transmissions have been troublesome when used on Detroit cars, like the Saturn Vue). The motor is used mainly for acceleration, with the gasoline engine kicking in when needed to provide power. Braking automatically shuts off the engine, as the electric motor acts as a generator to replenish the environmentally unfriendly NiMH battery pack. The Solar Panel option uses solar energy to keep the vehicle cool when it's parked.

COST ANALYSIS: Don't buy this vehicle, ever. Even the promised phased-in brake override feature is not enough to protect you from brake failures and a faulty cruise control (see *www.safecar.gov*). **Best alternatives:** The Honda Civic, Fit, or Insight; Hyundai Accent; and the Nissan Versa. In a Prius versus Insight match-up, the Prius gets better fuel economy but is more expensive; the Insight, despite its fewer horses, is more fun to drive, though it's not as fast as the Prius. On the other hand, the Insight won't abduct you at high speed, or send you head-on into a guardrail with no brakes. **Options:** Stability control and the 17-inch wheels will make for quicker steering response and better road feedback. **Rebates:** The Prius's popularity rises and falls in tandem with fuel prices and safety defect horror stories, so $1,500 (maximum) rebates will quickly come and go. **Depreciation:** Unbelievably fast. A 2004 Prius that sold for $29,990 is now worth about $8,000; a similar Honda Accord EX, which originally sold originally for $24,800, is now worth $13,500. **Insurance cost:** Higher than average. **Parts supply/cost:** Parts aren't easily found, and they can be costly. **Annual maintenance cost:** Average, so far. **Warranty:** Bumper-to-bumper 3 years/60,000 km; powertrain 5 years/100,000 km; hybrid-related components (battery, battery-control module, inverter with converter) 8 years/unlimited km; major emissions components 8 years/130,000 km; rust perforation 5 years/unlimited km. **Supplementary warranty:** Not needed. **City/highway fuel economy:** 3.7/4.0 L/100 km, 76/71 mpg.

OWNER-REPORTED PROBLEMS: Almost 1,800 complaints posted for the 2010 model; 50 reports would be average. Almost all of the complaints concern sudden acceleration, loss of brakes, and cruise control failures. Sudden acceleration and loss of braking occurs right after passing over uneven terrain. The car is also extremely vulnerable to side winds, and light steering doesn't help much, causing the vehicle to wander all over the road and require constant steering corrections. There is poor braking at both low and high speeds, and often the car accelerates when the brakes are applied:

> While driving 5 mph [8 km/h] into a parking space, the brakes did not work when the pedal was depressed. On two separate occasions, the vehicle struck a garage door and the contact rear-ended another vehicle due to the brake failure.

Car lurches forward when brakes are applied; many reports of loss of braking even after having the recalled ECU replaced:

> Since Toyota updated the software for the recall, I still experience the same problem multiple times, and it is not only [happening] during slow and steady application

of brakes, also [happening] when I use the brake in more sudden fashion even at moderate speed (30–40 mph [48–64 km/h]). I brought my Prius back to the Toyota service center again in May 2010 to recheck the ABS ECU software and they said they software is the latest updated version, and my braking system is meeting [the manufacturer's] specification.

Cruise control doesn't disengage quickly enough:

I have to press the brake harder than any prior vehicles I have owned to kill the cruise control and if I release the brake before the cruise control is released then the car lurches forward. This is a safety issue with this vehicle and I called Toyota and they said that there is no safety issue and would not speak to me further about it without going to the dealer. The dealer had already told me that it is operating normally and that this is how the 2010 new Prius model year operates. I have a 2006 Prius as well and the cruise disengages normally. Many other people have experienced this issue and have documented their experiences on the forum *priuschat.com*. They have even fixed the problem themselves by moving the cruise control disengagement closer to the top of the brake pedal.

The steering column may fall out of its mount:

My wife and 2 daughters were driving on Interstate 90/94 when the entire steering column slowly dropped. I double checked the lever underneath to adjust it, but that was tight. I could see wires and bolts where the column had been dropped several inches. I lifted the column up and thought it would lock in or click back in place. When I did this, the entire column collapsed in my lap. An alarm sounded and I had no control of the steering while going 110 kph.

Inaccurate fuel readings; traction control engages when it shouldn't; airbags failed to deploy; headlights go on and off intermittently; portions of the hybrid screen cluster are blotted out by what appear to be smudges on the inside of the split screen; musty AC smell; headlights shut off one at a time without warning; brake rotors have cracks perpendicular to the rotation; and the rear-seat seatbelts are hard to latch because the female part recedes down into the seat.

SERVICE BULLETIN-REPORTED PROBLEMS: Rear brake squeaking:

REAR BRAKE SQUEAK

BULLETIN NO.: TSB-0098-10   DATE: APRIL 8, 2010

Some 2010 Prius vehicles may experience rear brake squeak when backing up or moving forward during the first few brake applications when the brakes are cold. An updated rear brake shim kit is available to reduce the likelihood of this condition occurring.

Coolant leak from hybrid inverter drain plug (see bulletin on following page). Loose brake pedal pad; front-seat squeak; poor FM radio reception (radio with updated tuning has been developed to improve the reception); satellite radio inoperative; heavy static on Bluetooth; and a cargo net trim panel gap.

HYBRID—COOLANT LEAK FROM INVERTER DRAIN PLUG

BULLETIN NO.: TSB-0352-09   DATE: OCTOBER 6, 2009

COOLANT LEAK FROM TRANSAXLE DRAIN PLUG

Some 2010 model year Prius vehicles may exhibit a condition where coolant is leaking from the transaxle coolant drain plug. Use the repair procedure below to address this condition.

AVALON ★★★★

RATING: Above Average (with the brake override feature). The Avalon is a "geezer teaser" that can turn deadly through delayed shifts and engine surging. **Strong points:** Good powertrain performance—when it's working right—and acceptable handling and ride; a roomy, limousine-like interior with reclining backrests and plenty of storage space; large doors make for easy front- and rear-seat access; comfortable seats; a quiet interior; exceptional reliability when compared with some of Toyota's other models; and a good resale value. NHTSA gives the car five stars for front and side crash protection and four stars for rollover resistance. IIHS rates frontal offset and side crashworthiness as "Good." **Weak points:** Rear-corner blind spots; mushy brake pedal; a "floaty" suspension and ultra-light steering degrades handling; and it's a bit fuel-thirsty. **New for 2011:** Nothing new; the 2012 model will have all the changes.

KEY FACTS

CANADIAN PRICE (NEGOTIABLE): *Base:* $37,755 **U.S. PRICE:** *Base:* $32,445, *Limited:* $35,685 **CANADIAN FREIGHT:** $1,420 **U.S. FREIGHT:** $750

POWERTRAIN (FRONT-DRIVE)
Engine: 3.5L V6 (268 hp); Transmission: 6-speed auto.

DIMENSIONS/CAPACITY
Passengers: 2/3; Wheelbase: 111 in.; H: 59/L: 197.6/W: 72.8 in.; Cargo volume: 14.4 cu. ft.; Fuel tank: 70L/regular; Headroom F/R: 3.0/2.5 in.; Legroom F/R: 41/31 in.; Tow limit: Not recommended; Load capacity: 875 lb.; Turning circle: 36.9 ft.; Ground clearance: 5.3 in.; Weight: 3,567 lb.

OVERVIEW: This five-passenger near-luxury four-door offers more value and reliability than do other cars in its class that cost thousands of dollars more. A front-engine, front-drive, mid-sized sedan based on a stretched Camry platform, the Avalon is similar in size to the Ford Taurus and bigger than the rear-drive Cressida it replaced. Yet, despite its generous interior space, the car has a relatively small profile.

COST ANALYSIS: Buy a 2011 model only if it has the brake override feature. **Best alternatives:** The Honda Accord V6, Hyundai Genesis, Mazda6, and Nissan Altima. **Options:** The engine-immobilizing anti-theft system and dealer-installed towing package are worthwhile items. Stay away from the navigation control system; it's a pain to program. Sonar cruise control doesn't let other drivers know you may suddenly slow down. **Rebates:** $3,000+ on the 2010s, plus low-interest financing. **Depreciation:** Average. **Insurance cost:** Higher than average. **Parts supply/cost:** Parts are relatively inexpensive and easily found. If the Avalon is discontinued, parts still won't be a problem because so many were sold and the model hasn't changed much over the years. **Annual maintenance cost:** Less than average. **Warranty:** Bumper-to-bumper 3 years/60,000 km; powertrain 5 years/100,000 km; rust perforation 5 years/unlimited km. **Supplementary warranty:** Not needed. **City/highway fuel economy:** 10.7/7.0 L/100 km, 27/40 mpg.

OWNER-REPORTED PROBLEMS: Phew, when it comes to safety-related defects logged by NHTSA on the 2010 Avalon, what a relief that there are only 20 incidents reported (50 complaints would be the average). Here are some of the failures reported: "lag and lurch" when accelerating; with cruise control engaged, applying the brake slows the car, but as soon as the foot is taken off the brake, the car surges back to its former speed; "chin-to-chest" head restraints; vehicle rolls backward down an incline as the driver's foot eases off the brake; electrical shorts shut down dash lights:

> We have had all the lights on our dash go out for a period of 10 seconds or so on 2 different occasions while we were applying the brakes and making a turn. The dash lights on all our gauges go out and come back on [their] own.

Practically all of the owner complaints not related to safety concern poor fit and finish and water leaking into the headliner/footwell area. Other concerns include engine ticking noise; transmission control module (TCM) updates needed to improve shifting; rear windshield ticking noise; and a front power-seat grinding, groaning noise.

SERVICE BULLETIN-REPORTED PROBLEMS: Satellite radio inoperative; navigation door won't close; inoperative high beam DRL lights; rattles, buzz from driver's side of the dash; and a front-seat squeak.

SIENNA ★★

RATING: Below Average. No brake override yet, serious safety complaints involving injuries to children and adults, and an unproven redesigned model all add up to a failing grade for this year's Sienna. There has been a resurgence of safety-related defects since the 2004 model was redesigned. That said, the Sienna's 2011 redesign is worrisome because reworked Siennas have been glitch-prone in the past, at least for the year or two following their redesign—hence, the Below Average designation for this year's revamped version. **Strong points:** Nicely restyled; smooth 3.5L V6 powertrain (most of the time); optional full-time AWD; standard stability control; three-row side curtain airbags; a comfortable, stable ride; plenty of standard safety, performance, and convenience features; a fourth door; a tight turning circle; a good amount of passenger and cargo room; and acceptable reliability. NHTSA gives the Sienna four stars for overall crashworthiness. IIHS gives its top, "Good," rating for frontal offset, side, and head restraint crashworthiness. **Weak points:** Recommended options are bundled with costly gadgets; an unusually large number of body rattles and safety-related complaints. The 2011s still aren't as versatile as Chrysler's vans, the over-priced (go cross-

KEY FACTS

CANADIAN PRICE (NEGOTIABLE): *Base:* $27,900, *CE:* $28,900, *LE:* $32,500, *LE AWD:* $35,350, *Sport:* $36,600, *XLE:* $38,700, *Limited:* $48,150, *Auto.:* $49,100 **U.S. PRICE:** *Base:* $24,460, *LE:* $25,545, *SE:* $30,750, *XLE:* $32,375, *Limited:* $38,700 **CANADIAN FREIGHT:** $1,490 **U.S. FREIGHT:** $825
POWERTRAIN (FRONT-DRIVE/AWD)
Engines: 2.7L 4-cyl. (187 hp) • 3.5L V6 (266 hp); Transmission: 6-speed auto.
DIMENSIONS/CAPACITY
Passengers: 2/3/2; 2/3/3; Wheelbase: 119.3 in.; H: 69.5/L: 200.2/W: 78.2 in.; Headroom F/R1/R2: 3.5/4.0/2.5 in.; Legroom F/R1/R2: 40.5/31.5/2.5 in.; Cargo volume: 39.1 cu. ft.; Fuel tank: 79L/regular; Tow limit: 3,500 lb.; Load capacity: 1,120 lb.; Turning circle: 36.7 ft.; Ground clearance: 6.2 in.; Weight: 4,189–4,735 lb.

border) Limited version is "all sizzle, but little steak," and the second-row seats don't stow inside the vehicle; which has long been a popular feature with Chrysler vans. How's this for "spin control": Toyota says slimmer seats and controls add to the feeling of "roominess." No matter how they spin it, the interior looks less luxurious than before. Be wary of the fast-wearing and expensive-to-replace run-flat tires.

New for 2011: All 2011s get a wider track to improve handling and stability, a more-aerodynamic body, standard 17-inch alloy wheels, and projector beam headlamps. This year, we'll also see all-new styling, a redesigned interior that offers more room, more-comfortable seats, and easier interior access. The 2011s have more features and sportier handling. For example, there's a new base 4-cylinder and a new SE (Sport Edition) model with a stiffer suspension, 19-inch tires, and sporty styling add-ons. Overall length has been reduced a bit (0.8 inches), width has increased by the same amount, and height has increased by 1.8 inches. The wheelbase is unchanged. This redesign makes for a more-spacious cabin that is longer by 1.5 inches and wider up front by 1.2 inches.

New interior features include second-row captain's chairs that fold up, easier-to-access third-row seats that can be removed from the van without tools, easy-clean seat fabric, and climate controls for third-row passengers. Interestingly, Limited models offer second-row La-Z-Boy-type recliners and a split-screen that permits rear passengers to watch two different videos on the same screen using the Sienna's DVD player and a portable DVD player. The Sienna's sliding side door openings are two inches wider, making for easier third-row access, and some models are equipped with power sliding rear doors and a power rear hatch—two features known more for their malfunctions than their utility:

> While loading my kids at a parking lot, we opened the rear hatch with the remote control, it opened completely and when one of the kids was putting his stuff in the back the hatch started to close to the point in which it wouldn't stop. My wife and I had to hold the hatch to not let it continue closing with my kid in the way. The hatch continued to push down and [press] my kid. After a few seconds of pulling the hatch up, finally it came back and opened again, just to then close again by itself with no apparent reason.

> •

> Couple of months after I got the car, there were several incidents [in which] me and family members were hit on our heads and shoulders by self closing liftgate [and we] didn't know what the cause was. After researching about this problem, Toyota had recalled Sienna in the past about this same problem for older models for faulty strut used for power liftgates.

OVERVIEW: Toyota's redesigned, third-generation Sienna has become more car-like than ever in its highway handling and comfort, while offering a larger, restyled interior. It is sold in a broad range of models, and stands out as the only van with an all-wheel-drive option (not recommended). It's available with either a 4- or 6-cylinder engine and as a seven- or eight-passenger carrier.

Toyota built the Sienna for comfort and convenience. If you want more performance and driver interaction, get a Honda Odyssey. Sienna's V6 turns in respectable acceleration times, and the handling is also more car-like this year, but not as agile as with the Odyssey. However, the spacious interior accommodates up to eight passengers. All models come with standard four-wheel disc brakes, and all-wheel drive is available.

COST ANALYSIS: Toyota is keeping 2011 prices near last year's levels, making this year's model a better buy from a price perspective. As far as quality is concerned, it would be wise to delay your purchase a year or more to give Toyota time to "debug" the reworked Sienna and take advantage of more-generous summer and fall 2011 sales incentives. **Best alternatives:** The Honda Odyssey or the redesigned Mazda5 (a mini-minivan). The Odyssey's interior is more space-efficient and practical, and the van is scheduled for its own redesign next year. Chrysler's minivans bring up the rear of the pack due primarily to their automatic transmission failures and shaky financial footing. Why not Nissan's Quest? Its serious powertrain and fit and finish deficiencies over the past five years preclude its purchase until we see if the upcoming redesign removes or exacerbates present design flaws. **Options:** Power windows and door locks, rear heater, and AC unit. Be wary of the power-sliding door. As with all minivans offering this feature, these doors can injure children and pose unnecessary risks to other occupants. Go for Michelin or Pirelli original-equipment tires. Don't buy Bridgestone or Dunlop run-flats. **Rebates:** *2010:* $3,000—dealers need room for the more-popular, revamped 2011s. *2011:* $1,500 in the new year. **Depreciation:** Faster than average and expected to lose much more value as the revamped 2011s cannibalize sales. For example, a 2007 CE seven-passenger Sienna that sold for $31,200 now sells for $14,000. **Insurance cost:** Higher than average. **Parts supply/cost:** Excellent supply of reasonably priced parts taken from the Camry's parts bin, but run-flat tire replacements are expensive and hard to find. **Annual maintenance cost:** Less than average. **Warranty:** Bumper-to-bumper 3 years/60,000 km; powertrain 5 years/100,000 km; rust perforation 5 years/unlimited km. **Supplementary warranty:** An extended warranty isn't necessary. **City/highway fuel economy:** 2.7L: 10.4/7.5 L/100 km, 27/38 mpg. 3.5L: 11.5/8.1 L/100 km, 25/35 mpg. *AWD:* 12.8/9.0 L/100 km, 22/31 mpg.

OWNER-REPORTED PROBLEMS: In a nutshell, recent Siennas continue to suddenly accelerate, have cruise controls that won't turn off, lose braking capability, and employ dangerous power-sliding side doors:

> At around 5 pm on a clear Monday evening I went to turn left into a parking spot. I stepped on the gas and nothing happened, I let up a bit and stepped again and my 2010 Toyota Sienna shot forward. I slammed on the brake halfway into the parking spot and ran into the tree in front of the van. I looked down and could see the outline

of the gas pedal so my foot was definitely on the brake. I was very shaken up. The van's bumper and hood are damaged and the tree lost some bark. I had it towed to the Toyota dealership and Toyota is having it investigated. It has been there for a month now.

In another reported incident, a driver accelerated to pass another car, and his Sienna suddenly accelerated out of control, while the brakes were useless:

The cruise control stuck while accelerating and would not disengage by pressing the brake pedal or by pulling the cruise control lever (located on the steering column) towards the driver.

Not only does sudden acceleration endanger your life, but the subsequent crash can imprison you within the vehicle:

Uncontrolled acceleration where depressing the brake pedal was "soft" and did not have any effect in stopping the vehicle. I was pulling into my garage and as I neared the point where I wanted to stop, I pressed on the brake pedal. This had no effect and the vehicle continued to accelerate. The vehicle proceeded through the other end of the garage. There is a drop from the floor of the garage to the ground on the back side of the garage. When the heavy front end of the 2010 Toyota Sienna went through the garage wall, it dropped to the ground and the vehicle was balanced like on a teeter-totter with 1 rear wheel in the air instead of on the garage floor. This position stopped the vehicle from continuing to move forward. I was unable to get out because the doors were locked and did not release when I tried to open the door. I called the local security force who came to my assistance. With the security force pulling on the door from the outside, I was able to get out through the rear passenger door.

Brakes can take a couple of seconds before they engage; the slightest touch of the gear shifter causes a shift into Neutral; passenger-side sliding doors are still failure-prone after a decade of complaints:

My 17 month old's head got jammed between the right rear wheel and the right rear door panel while the electric door slid open. Even though my wife pulled on the door handle the door kept sliding open. My baby's head was crushed between the tire and door panel. This is a very unsafe design as my wife tried to stop the door from sliding back and the door kept moving.

Airbags fail to deploy, multiple warning lights come on, and the vehicle cannot be shifted; engine ticking; more ticking from the windshield/back glass; and transfer-case fluid leaks. Sunroof may spontaneously explode; rear tires quickly wear out (suspect a faulty rear member bar); and second-row seats are unstable, injuring several children when the seats moved.

SERVICE BULLETIN-REPORTED PROBLEMS: Rattle, buzz from driver's side of the dash; squeaky seat; inoperative second-row Ottoman seat; and the sliding door rattles while driving:

RAV4   ★★★★

RATING: Above Average. **Strong points:** Base models offer a nice array of standard safety, performance, and convenience features, including electronic stability control and standard brake override; 4-cylinder acceleration from a stop is acceptable with a full load; excellent V6 powertrain performance; precise handling and a comfortable ride are big improvements over earlier, more firmly sprung models; RAV4 seats five, but an optional third-row bench on Base and Limited models increases capacity to seven; comfortable seats; a quiet interior; cabin gauges and controls are easy to access and read; exceptional reliability; and good fuel economy with the 4-cylinder engine (the V6 is almost as fuel-frugal). NHTSA gives the RAV4 five stars for front and side crashworthiness and four stars for rollover protection. IIHS says head-restraint protection and frontal offset and side crashworthiness are "Good." **Weak points:** Transmission is hesitant to shift to a lower gear when under load, and sometimes produces jerky low-speed shifts; some noseplow and body lean when cornering under power; and some road and wind noise. Resale value is only average, which is good news only for smart used-car shoppers. **New for 2011:** Except for the phasing in of the brake override feature and more options, this year's model is mostly a carryover of the 2010 version.

KEY FACTS

CANADIAN PRICE (NEGOTIABLE): *Base: $24,595, Base 4WD: $27,230, Base 4WD V6: $29,845, Sport: $28,345, Sport V6: $30,100, Sport 4WD: $30,540, Sport 4WD V6: $32,295, Limited: $30,185, Limited V6: $32,440, Limited 4WD: $32,385 Limited 4WD V6: $34,640*

U.S. PRICE: *Base: $21,675, Base 4WD: $23,075, Base 4WD V6: N/A, Sport: $23,375, Sport V6: $25,305, Sport 4WD: $24,775, Limited: $24,665, Limited V6: $27,985, Limited 4WD: $26,055, Limited 4WD V6: $27,985* **CANADIAN FREIGHT:** $1,490

U.S. FREIGHT: $825

POWERTRAIN (FRONT-DRIVE/AWD)

Engines: 2.5L 4-cyl. (179 hp) • 3.5L V6 (269 hp); Transmissions: 4-speed auto. • 5-speed auto.

DIMENSIONS/CAPACITY

Passengers: 2/3; 2/3/2; Wheelbase: 104.7 in.; H: 71.5/L: 181.9/W: 71.5 in.; Cargo volume: 35.9 cu. ft.; Fuel tank: 70L/regular; Headroom F/R: 6.55/4.0 in.; Legroom F/R: 41.5/29 in.; Tow limit: 1,500–3,500 lb.; Load capacity: 825 lb.; Turning circle: 37.4 ft.; Ground clearance: 7.5 in.; Weight: 3,360–3,686 lb.

OVERVIEW: This SUV crossover combines a car-type unibody platform with elevated seating and optional all-wheel drive (AWD). Although classed as a compact SUV, the RAV4 is large enough to carry a kid-sized third-row bench seat, giving it seven-passenger capacity. A powerful V6 makes this downsized SUV one of the fastest crossovers on the market. The electronic brake override system was phased in during production of 2010 RAV4s and is slated to be included on all 2011 RAV4s. This fact alone raises *Lemon-Aid's* rating of the 2011 model.

COST ANALYSIS: If you can find a discounted 2010 with the brake override feature, buy it. **Best alternatives:** The Honda CR-V, Hyundai Tucson, or Nissan X-Trail. **Options:** The engine-immobilizing anti-theft system and dealer-installed towing package are worthwhile items. The Sport model has an option that uses run-flat tires and dispenses with the tailgate-mounted spare tire. Stick with the regular tire; it's cheaper and less problematic. **Rebates:** $2,000+ on the 2010s and $1,000 on the 2011s, plus low-interest financing and leasing. **Depreciation:** Average; a 2007 Base 4WD that sold for $29,300 is now worth about half as much. **Insurance cost:** Higher than average. **Parts supply/cost:** Parts are relatively inexpensive and easily found. **Annual maintenance cost:** Less than average. **Warranty:** Bumper-to-bumper 3 years/60,000 km; powertrain 5 years/100,000 km; rust perforation 5 years/unlimited km. **Supplementary warranty:** A waste of money. **City/highway fuel economy:** *2.5L: 9.4/6.9 L/100 km, 30/41 mpg. 2.5L AWD: 9.7/7.2 L/100 km, 29/39 mpg. 3.5L: 10.7/7.4 L/100 km, 26/38 mpg. 3.5L AWD: 11.7/7.7 L/100 km, 25/37 mpg.*

OWNER-REPORTED PROBLEMS: The 2010 model has received 71 safety-related complaints logged by NHTSA, which is only slightly higher than the average of 50 complaints per model year for most vehicles. Safety complaints are mostly about sudden acceleration (even after recall repair was done) and loss of braking. Other reports: Fire erupted in the engine compartment; original-equipment Yokohama tires may blow out their side walls; spare-tire cover becomes loose (elastic deteriorates) and blows off; defroster system is weak; and one report says the RAV4's air circulation system may endanger occupants' health:

> The car always starts and stays on recirculate. Knowing the hazards and recommendations for safety levels of the toxic gases that accumulate in a closed car

(such as *http://www.snopes.com/medical/toxins/benzene.asp*), Toyota's current air system is proving hazardous to everything's health! This terrible feature can not be turned off. Toyota's automatic system for air control is not responsive to conditions but instead encourages passengers to remain captive with recirculating toxic gases and is in fact detrimental to everyone's health.

Practically all of the non-safety-related owner complaints relate to poor fit and finish and audio system malfunctions. Owners also deride the flimsy glove box lid, loose sun visor, constantly flickering traction control light, sticking ignition key, uncomfortable head restraints, squeaks and rattles from the dashboard and rear-seat area, and wide rear roof pillars that obstruct visibility. Mice may enter the vehicle at will through the clean-air filter—dealer suggested the owner buy a mouse trap:

> Check Engine light indicated. The car was taken to the dealer, where the dealer mentioned, "Evidence of rodent/small animal has chewed wiring harness at connector completely through." The car will need wiring harness.

SERVICE BULLETIN-REPORTED PROBLEMS: Automatic transmission whine can be eliminated by replacing the poorer quality left front driveshaft damper, say TSB #0192-10, published July 15, 2010. Rough idle:

BULLETIN NO.: TSB-0046-10	ROUGH IDLE/MIL ON/EVAP SYSTEM DTCS SET	DATE: JANUARY 28, 2010

INTRODUCTION: Some 2006–10 model year RAV4 vehicles may exhibit one or more of the following conditions due to fuel in the EVAP system:

- MIL "ON" with the following DTCs stored: P043E, P043F, P2401, P2401, and P2419
- Intermittent rough idle when at operating temperature. Follow the repair procedure in this bulletin to address this condition.

OP CODE	DESCRIPTION	ENGINE	TIME	OFP	T1	T2
EG9028	R & R Fuel Tank & Charcoal Canister	2AR-FE 2AZ-FE	2.4	77001-4218# 77001-0R010	08	13
		2GR-FE	2.3			
Combo A	R &R Canister Filter Assembly	–	0.1			

Satellite radio inoperative; loose sun visor mount; squeaking front seat; no crank, no start:

	INTERMITTENT NO CRANK/NO START	
BULLETIN NO.: TSB-0348-09		DATE: SEPTEMBER 30, 2009

2008–09 Highlander
2009–10 Matrix
2006–10 RAV4

Some Highlander, Matrix, and RAV4 vehicles may intermittently exhibit a "no crank" condition. The engine can usually be started after moving the shift lever to the Neutral position or by cycling the shift lever in and out of the Park position. A revised neutral start switch assembly is available to address this condition.

OP CODE	DESCRIPTION	MODEL	TIME	OFP	T1	T2
832131	R & R Park/Neutral Position Switch Assembly	Highlander	0.9	84540-42010	17	99
		Matrix	0.5			
		RAV4	0.7			

VENZA ★★★

RATING: Average. This combination of a small SUV and a wagon has proven itself to be relatively problem-free and a good highway performer. **Strong points:** Powerful and efficient engines; a roomy interior; a pleasant driving demeanour; a comfy ride; innovative interior storage areas; an automatic headlight dimmer; easy entry and exit; foldable rear seats, a large cargo area and rear hatch opening; a low rear loading height; and standard stability and traction control. NHTSA gave the Venza a five-star rating for front and side crashworthiness, while rollover protection garnered four stars. IIHS rated the vehicle as "Good" for frontal offset, side, and head-restraint protection. **Weak points:** Not an exciting drive; no third-row seat; radio station indicator washes out in sunlight; high-intensity discharge headlights are annoying to other drivers, are often stolen, and are expensive to replace. Resale value is lower than one would expect for a Toyota SUV. **New for 2011:** Standard brake override feature to be phased in.

OVERVIEW: Toyota's Venza is a five-passenger wagon sold in two trim levels that match the two available engines. Going into its second year, the car offers the styling and comfort of a passenger car with the flexibility of a small SUV. A perfect alternative for Toyota customers who need more vehicle than what the Camry offers but not as much as the Highlander.

COST ANALYSIS: Most of the 2010s have been sold; expect to pay almost full list price for a 2011. **Best alternatives:** The Ford Edge, Nissan Murano, and Toyota Highlander. **Options:** Stay away from the panoramic roof option and back up camera; both are expensive gadgets of doubtful utility. **Rebates:** $1,000 on the 2011s later in the new year, plus low-interest financing throughout 2011. **Depreciation:** Moderate; a first-year, 2009 entry-level Venza that sold for $28,270 is now worth about $22,500. **Insurance cost:** Average. **Parts supply/cost:** Parts are average-priced and easily found. **Annual maintenance cost:** Less than average. **Warranty:** Bumper-to-bumper 3 years/60,000 km; powertrain 5 years/100,000 km; rust perforation 5 years/unlimited km. **Supplementary warranty:** Not needed. **City/highway fuel economy:** 2.7L: 10.0/6.8 L/100 km, 28/42 mpg. *AWD:* 10.2/7.1 L/100 km, 28/40mpg. *3.5L:* 11.0/7.6 L/100 km, 26/37 mpg. *AWD:* 11.5/7.9 L/100 km, 25/36 mpg.

KEY FACTS

CANADIAN PRICE (NEGOTIABLE): *Base front-drive:* $29,160, *AWD:* $30,610, *V6:* $30,650, *AWD:* $32,100 **U.S. PRICE:** *Base front-drive:* $26,275, *V6 front-drive:* $28,100, *AWD:* $27,725, *V6 AWD:* $29,550 **CANADIAN FREIGHT:** $1,490 **U.S. FREIGHT:** $785 **POWERTRAIN (FRONT-DRIVE/AWD)** Engines: 2.7L 4-cyl. (182 hp) • 3.5L V6 (268 hp); Transmission: 6-speed auto. **DIMENSIONS/CAPACITY** Passengers: 2/3; Wheelbase: 109.3 in.; H: 63.4/L: 189/W: 75 in.; Cargo volume: 30.7 cu. ft.; Fuel tank: 67L/regular; Headroom F/R: N/A; Legroom F/R: N/A; Tow limit: 2,500–3,500 lb.; Load capacity: 875 lb.; Turning circle: 39.1 ft.; Ground clearance: 8.1 in.; Weight: 3,760–4,045 lb.

OWNER-REPORTED PROBLEMS: Very few safety-related complaints filed against the 2010 Venza. Here is a sample of those incidents that were posted: sudden unintended acceleration; intermittent engine surging:

> I have a 2010 FWD Venza with 2000 miles [3,200 kilometres]. This past weekend we had four separate instances of the unexpected engine revving. After taking foot off gas and applying brake lightly, preparing for a full brake...the engine "revved" for approximately 1–2 second. Oddly, no acceleration occurred in the vehicle.

Transmission would not go into Reverse; the Hill-Start Assist feature doesn't prevent the car from rolling back when stopped on a hill in traffic:

> I feel Toyota should immediately send out a safety notice requiring all employees be briefed about the Hill-Start Assist feature, how it doesn't activate automatically, and how to activate the feature when stopped on an uphill slope.

Brakes don't immediately brake when slow and steady pressure is applied; sometimes, after the brakes are applied, the car won't accelerate; automatic rear hatch slams shut; seatbelt began strangling three-year old and child had to be cut free; sunroof exploded for no reason; and the radio overheated up to 145 degrees.

SERVICE BULLETIN-REPORTED PROBLEMS: False security alarm activation; wind noise from the front door area; rattle from the centre of the instrument panel only requires a simple adjustment; steering column popping when turning; squeaking front seat; rear-end suspension squawk:

| BULLETIN NO.: TSB-0082-10 | REAR-END SUSPENSION SQUAWK NOISE | DATE: FEBRUARY 26, 2010 |

INTRODUCTION: Some 2009–10 Venza vehicles may exhibit a "squawk/groan" noise from the rear suspension when traveling over bumps, accelerating from a stop, and/or during slow rolling stops. The abnormal noise may be caused by rear coil spring contact with the lower strut seat due to a displaced or damaged rear coil spring lower insulator. An updated rear coil spring lower insulator is available for this condition.

PREVIOUS PART NUMBER	CURRENT PART NUMBER	PART NAME	QTY
48258-0T010	48258-0T020	Insulator, Rear Coil Spring, Lower	2
Same	90080-17217	Nut, Rear Support to Rear Shock Absorber	2

OP CODE	DESCRIPTION	TIME	OFP	T1	T2
482151	Rear Coil Spring (One Side)	1.3	48258-0T010	91	57
Combo A	Opposite Side	0.6			
Combo D	Toe-In	0.2			

HIGHLANDER ★★★★

RATING: Above Average, only if a no-cost brake override system is included. **Strong points:** Powerful engines and a smooth, refined powertrain; the Hybrid can propel itself on electric power alone; a quiet interior enhances the comfortable ride; responsive handling; roomy second-row seating is fairly versatile. NHTSA gives the vehicle five stars for frontal and side crashworthiness and four stars for rollover resistance. IIHS rates the vehicle as "Good" for frontal offset, side, and head-restraint protection. **Weak points:** Steering is somewhat vague, there's a high step-in, and the vehicle isn't very agile. The third-row seat is a bit tight and doesn't fold in a 50/50 split. No news as to when the brake override feature will be phased in. **New for 2011:** Minor styling revisions.

OVERVIEW: A crossover alternative to a minivan, this competent, refined, family-friendly SUV puts function ahead of style and provides cargo and passenger

versatility along with a high level of component and workmanship quality. V6-equipped models best represent the Highlander's attributes, as the Hybrid models' higher prices will take years to offset in fuel savings. Nevertheless, the Hybrid is the only gas-electric seven-seat crossover for sale in the U.S.

COST ANALYSIS: Look for an identical 2010 model discounted by about 15 percent. **Best alternatives:** From the Detroit SUV side: the Ford Flex, Buick Enclave, GMC Acadia, or Chevrolet Traverse. A good Asian SUV is the Honda Pilot. The Honda Odyssey is the only suitable Asian minivan choice. **Options:** Say yes to the engine-immobilizing anti-theft system; no to the failure-prone and costly-to-maintain tire-pressure monitoring system. **Rebates:** $2,000+ on the 2010s, plus low-interest financing and leasing. **Depreciation:** Faster than average; a base 2007 V6 AWD version that sold originally for $38,470 can now be picked up for $17,500. **Insurance cost:** Higher than average. **Parts supply/cost:** Parts are relatively inexpensive and easily found. **Annual maintenance cost:** Average. **Warranty:** Bumper-to-bumper 3 years/60,000 km; powertrain 5 years/100,000 km; rust perforation 5 years/unlimited km. **Supplementary warranty:** Not needed. **City/highway fuel economy:** 10.4/7.3

KEY FACTS

CANADIAN PRICE (NEGOTIABLE): *Base:* $33,250, *V6:* $37,870, *Sport V6:* $42,810, *Limited V6:* $46,510, *Hybrid:* $43,025, *Hybrid Limited:* $55,075 **U.S. PRICE:** *Base:* $25,855, *V6:* $29,200, *Sport V6:* $30,050, *Sport 4WD:* $31,500, *Limited:* $33,220, *Limited 4WD:* $34,670, *Hybrid:* $34,900, *Hybrid Limited:* $41,220 **CANADIAN FREIGHT:** $1,490 **U.S. FREIGHT:** $825 **POWERTRAIN (FRONT-DRIVE/AWD)** Engines: 2.7L 4-cyl. (187 hp) • 3.3L V6 (270 hp) • 3.5L V6 (270 hp); Transmissions: 5-speed auto. • 6-speed auto. • CVT **DIMENSIONS/CAPACITY** Passengers: 2/3/2, *Hybrid:* 2/3; Wheelbase: 110 in.; H: 69.3/L: 188.4/W: 75.2 in.; Cargo volume: 10.3 cu. ft.; Fuel tank: 72.5L/regular; Headroom F/R1/R2: 3.5/5.0/0.0 in.; Legroom F/R1/R2: 41.5/32/23.5 in.; Tow limit: 3,500–5,000 lb.; Load capacity: 1,200 lb.; Turning circle: 38.7 ft.; Ground clearance: 8.1 in.; Weight: 4,050–4,641 lb.

L/100 km, 27/39, mpg. *V6:* 12.3/8.8 L/100 km, 23/32 mpg. *Hybrid:* 7.4/8.0 L/100 km, 38/35 mpg.

OWNER-REPORTED PROBLEMS: NHTSA's safety-defect log sheet shows very few complaints were registered against the 2009 or 2010 Highlander. 2010 model owners reported the following: sudden unintended acceleration *after* the recall fix; steering veered to the left and right while brakes went out; owners report that there is a long delay from the time the brakes are applied and when the braking actually occurs:

> This occurs consistently, especially at low speeds like when parking or stopping at a stop sign. I would guess that this is the same issue that the Prius has. This could be a real safety issue—especially for pedestrians since the car takes more distance to stop due to this gap. My wife actually experiences a small surge prior to the gap in braking. I just did a quick web search and saw dozens of similar complaints from other Highlander Hybrid owners.

Headlights and brake lights come on after they are shut off; windshield distortion:

> This is likely caused by the plastic film pressed between the glass. This defect causes visual distortion and is incredibly distractive while driving and causes eye strain.

The tire-pressure monitoring system has to be reset by the dealer when the tires are changed ($135 twice a year).

SERVICE BULLETIN-REPORTED PROBLEMS: False security alarm activation; distorted radio sub-woofer (an updated JBL amplifier will correct the problem); inoperative satellite radio; popping noise from front window; and a squeaky front seat.

TACOMA ★★★

RATING: Above Average. This cheap and reliable light-duty truck would have been rated higher if it weren't for owner reports of Toyota's infamous decade-old lag and lurch transmission and sudden acceleration problems spilling over to the 2010s. **Strong points:** Well-chosen powertrain and steering set-up; ideal for off-road work with the optional suspension; good acceleration; standard electronic stability control; very responsive handling over smooth roads; a well-garnished, roomy interior; plenty of storage space; and good reliability. Given five stars by NHTSA for frontal crashworthiness and four stars for rollover resistance. IIHS rates front, side, and head-restraint protection as "Good." **Weak points:** The ride can be jolting and lead to loss of steering control, and the driving position seems low when compared with the competition. Delayed transmission engagement is still present. Depreciation during the first three years takes a big bite out of the Tacoma's resale value. **New for 2011:** A brake override system, slightly revised styling, and more standard features; a redesign is scheduled next year.

OVERVIEW: Toyota's entry-level pickup isn't as utilitarian as its predecessors or some of its competition, but has sufficient power and is relatively inexpensive if not too gussied up. If you decide to go for the optional off-road suspension, you will quickly notice the firmer ride and increased road feedback.

KEY FACTS

CANADIAN PRICE (NEGOTIABLE): *Access Cab 4x2: $21,355, Auto.: $22,355, 4x4: $25,999, 4x4 V6: $28,320, 4x4 auto.: $29,340, Double Cab V6: $32,615, Double Cab auto.: $31,845* **U.S. PRICE:** *Access Cab 4x2: $19,655, Auto.: $20,555, 4x4: $24,390, 4x4 V6: $25,045, 4x4 auto.: $25,925, Double Cab V6: $26,145, Double Cab auto.: $27,025* **CANADIAN FREIGHT:** $1,490 **U.S. FREIGHT:** $825 **POWERTRAIN (REAR-DRIVE/AWD)** Engines: 2.7L 4-cyl. (159 hp) • 4.0L V6 (236 hp); Transmissions: 5-speed man. • 6-speed man. • 4-speed auto. • 5-speed auto.

DIMENSIONS/CAPACITY
Passengers: 2/2; Wheelbase: 127.8 in.; H: 65.7/L: 208.1/W: 72.2 in.; Fuel tank: 80L/regular; Headroom F/R: 4.0/3.0 in.; Legroom F/R: 42.5/28 in.; Tow limit: 3,500–6,500 lb.; Load capacity: 1,100 lb.; Turning circle: 44.6 ft.; Ground clearance: 8.1 in.; Weight: 3,560 lb.

COST ANALYSIS: Look for an identical 2010 model discounted by about 15 percent. **Best alternatives:** The 2010 Mazda B-Series and this year's Nissan Frontier. **Options:** The stiffer suspension for off-roading, an engine-immobilizing anti-theft system, and the dealer-installed towing package are all worthwhile items. **Rebates:** $1,500+ on the 2010s, plus low-interest financing and leasing. **Depreciation:** Faster than average for both front-drives and four-wheel drives; a 2007 Access Cab front-drive that sold originally for $22,635 now fetches barely $9,500. An entry-level 2007 4WD V6 that sold for $29,660 is now worth $14,500. **Insurance cost:** Average. **Parts supply/cost:** Inexpensive and easily found. **Annual maintenance cost:** Average. **Warranty:** Bumper-to-bumper 3 years/60,000 km; powertrain 5 years/100,000 km; rust perforation 5 years/unlimited km. **Supplementary warranty:** Not needed. **City/highway fuel economy:** *2.7L:* 10.5/7.8 L/100 km, 27/36 mpg. *Auto.:* 11.0/7.9 L/100 km, 26/36 mpg. *AWD:* 12.0/9.1 L/100 km, 24/31 mpg. *4.0L 4×4:* 14.7/10.8 L/100 km, 19/26 mpg. *Auto.:* 13.4/9.9 L/100 km, 21/29 mpg.

OWNER-REPORTED PROBLEMS: Fewer safety-related incidents reported with the 2010 Tacoma than what one would normally find with most vehicles. 2010 model owners report the following: Truck accelerated on its own as driver waited for pedestrians to clear the crosswalk; the throttle stuck when passing another vehicle; when brakes were applied, vehicle suddenly accelerated; when cruise control was disengaged, then re-engaged, the vehicle accelerated up to 130 km/h; premature automatic transmission failures; an automatic transmission shift lag and lurch, especially when coming out of a turn; vehicle veers to the left when accelerating (not because of the tires or alignment); the truck bounces and hops over uneven pavement (a problem owners have been reporting for years):

> While driving at 70 kph [110 km/h], the vehicle will lose control and bounce extremely hard when...there is an uneven pavement and when hauling a heavy load.

SERVICE BULLETIN-REPORTED PROBLEMS: Improved low speed Second to First downshift (use a revised electronic control module); manual transmission clutch slips in all gears:

BULLETIN NO.: TSB-0385-09	CLUTCH SLIPPING IN ALL GEARS	DATE: NOVEMBER 23, 2009

2007–10 FJ Cruiser
2005–10 Tacoma
INTRODUCTION: Some customers of manual transmission equipped V6 FJ Cruiser and Tacoma vehicles may experience a slipping feeling in all forward gears and reverse. The center section of the clutch disk may have separated from the friction material section of the clutch disk. Installation of a new clutch disk and clutch cover pressure plate is required to repair the vehicle. Follow the repair procedure in this bulletin to address customer concerns.

Jolting, bouncy rear suspension ride with a heavy load:

BULLETIN NO.: TSB-0305-08	HARSH REAR SUSPENSION RIDE WITH HEAVY LOAD	DATE: SEPTEMBER 30, 2008

2005–10 Tacoma
INTRODUCTION: Some customers of Tacoma 4×4 or Pre Runner vehicles with Access or Double cabs may experience a harsh ride from the rear suspension while carrying heavy cargo in the bed and driving over bumps or uneven road surfaces. Updated rear spring assemblies and front and rear shocks are available to improve this condition. Customers should be advised that vehicle ride characteristics in an unloaded condition may exhibit an increase in rear suspension firmness.

AC blower motor ticking, squeaking, or squealing; rattle noise from the glove box area or from the front seat; an inoperative satellite radio; poor defroster performance (a newly designed defroster air nozzle is available); and water drips from dome lamp area of headliner:

WATER CONDENSATION DRIPPING FROM HEADLINER

2005–10 Tacoma

INTRODUCTION: Some double cab customers may complain about water dripping from the dome lamp area in the headliner.

OP CODE	VWC	DESCRIPTION	TIME	OFP	T1	T2
743201	S	Roof Headlining Assembly (Double Cab)	2.9	63310-AD030##	66	63

TUNDRA ★

bad buy

RATING: Not Recommended. It's an excellent concept that's been poorly executed. The Tundra's lag and lurch transmission/throttle problem and dangerous rear-end bounce make the truck a risky highway traveller. **Strong points:** Strong powertrain performance; a roomy interior with plenty of storage space; large doors make for easy front- and rear-seat access; comfortable seats; and a quiet interior. **Weak points:** Engines are fuel-thirsty due to the Tundra's excess weight, and handling is degraded by excessive rear-end bounce; rear axle shaft bearing growling; low-range gearing is for the most slippery roads (only the GM and Dodge pickups use a 4×4 system that can be left engaged on all surfaces); powertrain lag and lurch is hazardous to all; there's no factory-integrated trailer-braking system; steering needs to be retuned to dial in more road feedback and quicker response; the interior design looks early Paleolithic—not as stylish as Ford and Chrysler, nor as upscale as GM's Silverado and Sierra; and passengers may find headroom a bit tight. **New for 2011:** A brake override system, more V6 power (34 more horses), trailer-sway control, improved head restraints, ashtrays are no longer standard, and the cigarette lighter has been replaced by a 12-volt power outlet.

KEY FACTS

CANADIAN PRICE (NEGOTIABLE): *4.6 Regular Cab 4×2:* $25,310, *4.6 Regular Cab 4×4:* $28,795, *5.7 Regular Cab 4×2:* $28,975, *5.7 Regular Cab 4×4:* $29,895, *4.6 Double Cab SR5 4×2:* $32,040, *4.6 Double Cab SR5 4×4:* $36,105, *5.7 Double Cab SR5 4×2:* $36,015, *5.7 Double Cab SR5 4×4:* $37,205, *5.7 Double Cab Limited 4×4:* $48,275, *CrewMax SR5 4×2:* $37,630, *CrewMax SR5 4×4:* $41,745, *CrewMax Platinum:* $52,020 **U.S. PRICE:** Prices start at $24,910 for the 2WD V6 regular-cab and top out at $43,430 for the 4WD Limited CrewMax with the 5.7L V8. This represents an increase of $425–$480.

CANADIAN FREIGHT: $1,490 **U.S. FREIGHT:** $975

POWERTRAIN (REAR-DRIVE/AWD)
Engines: 4.0L V6 (270 hp) • 4.6L V8 (310 hp) • 5.7L V8 (381 hp); Transmission: 6-speed auto.

DIMENSIONS/CAPACITY
Passengers: 2/1; 2/3; 3/3 Wheelbase: 145.7 in.; H: 75.6/L: 228.71/W: 79.9 in.; Fuel tank: 100L/regular; Headroom F/R: 5.5/3.5 in.; Legroom F/R: 42.5/28.5 in.; Tow limit: 8,100–10,800 lb.; Load capacity: 1,755–1,900 lb.; Turning circle: 44 ft.; Ground clearance: 10 in.; Weight: 4,830–5,480 lb.

For 2011, there are fewer body and engine variations and slight price increases. This means you can no longer get a 2011 Tundra 4×4 regular-cab with the 4.6L V8. In fact, all 2011 Tundra 4×4 regular-cab models come with the 5.7L V8. They start at $30,105 (U.S.—all of the following prices are also in U.S. dollars) with the 6-foot bed and hit $30,435 with the 8.1-foot bed.

Double Cabs are Tundra's most popular models. Their 2011 prices have gone up by $685–$1,030, but those prices aren't expected to hold as fuel prices rise and big-truck enthusiasm wanes later this year. Base prices for 4×2 Tundra Double Cabs range from $27,250 with the 4.0L V6 and 6.5-foot bed to $37,835 in Limited trim with the 5.7 V8 6.5-foot bed. 4×4 2011 Tundra Double Cabs begin at $30,445 with the 4.6L V8 and the 6.5-foot bed and range to $40,895 in Limited trim with the 5.7 V8 and 6.5-foot bed

OVERVIEW: A heavy full-sized truck that has more glitches than goodies, this year's freshened Tundra has an improved V6 that's stronger and more fuel-efficient than the engine it replaces. Thanks, Toyota. Now get off your butt and fix the Tundra's hazardous powertrain and "shake, rattle, and roll" suspension.

COST ANALYSIS: Go for the 2011 model with all its refinements. Consider waiting until mid-2011 for Toyota to iron out its suspension bounce/vibration, growling noise, and transmission lag problems, and for prices to drift downward. **Best alternatives:** Ford's F-Series pickups, or GM's Sierra or Silverado. **Options:** The engine-immobilizing anti-theft system is worthwhile. Stay away from the Bridgestone and Firestone tires and make sure the spare tire is the same make and size as your regular tire:

I purchased a 2010 Toyota Tundra in Aug. at nearly 3K miles [4800 km], both the front tires—Bridgestone Dueler H/T P275 65R18 114T M+S—has to be replaced due to extreme cupping. Now at close to 8500 total miles [13,700 km], front tires are cupping again. Dealer tells me to "keep driving." There's nothing they can do.

•

The contact owns a 2010 Toyota Tundra. While having the vehicle serviced for unrelated issues, the contact noticed that the spare tire was a different tire and wheel size than the stock ones that came with the vehicle. The contact stated that according to the owners manual, the vehicle would be unsafe to drive with a different tire or wheel size installed.

And remember, the TRD package gives a ride that may be too stiff for some. **Rebates:** $4,000+ on the leftover 2010s, plus low-interest financing and various leasing deals. **Depreciation:** Much faster than average; a 2007 base 4×2 Access Cab that once sold for $22,635 is now worth a bit over $9,000. **Insurance cost:** Higher than average. **Parts supply/cost:** Parts are moderately expensive and sometimes hard to find. **Annual maintenance cost:** Average. **Warranty:** Bumper-to-bumper 3 years/60,000 km; powertrain 5 years/100,000 km; rust perforation 5 years/unlimited km. **Supplementary warranty:** Yes, on the powertrain. **City/highway fuel economy:** *4.6L 4×2:* 14.0/9.9 L/100 km, 20/29 mpg. *4×4:* 14.9/10.5 L/100 km, 18/26 mpg. *5.7L 4×2:* 15.3/10.9 L/100 km, 19/27 mpg. *4×4:* 16.8/11.8 L/100 km, 17/24 mpg.

OWNER-REPORTED PROBLEMS: Sudden, unintended acceleration; stuck accelerator; vehicle speeds up when coming to a stop; rear wheel came off the vehicle because the lug nuts weren't tightened sufficiently at the factory. Engine lag and lurch when accelerating; engine knocking caused by a piston striking the cylinder wall of the 5.7L V8 engine; engine suddenly self-destructed; repeated failure of the transmission and transfer case; vehicle will stall in any gear. Owners complain the truck is a "Shake-undra" with excessive bed bounce when going over smooth roadways:

> I was travelling at about 65 mph [105 km/h] and moved to the number 4 lane, same thing—bed bounce was violent for about 2 miles [3 kilometres]. This is very dangerous because it felt like I had very limited control of the truck while bouncing.

•

> On highway this truck shakes uncontrollably. It feels like it is bending in the middle between a cabin and a bed. While driving everyone in the truck keeps bouncing off the seat at times. If this was disclosed as "normal" as a dealer says I would have never bought this truck.

TCM updates needed to improve shifting; brake pedal slowly goes to the floor when applied with sustained pressure; fuel rail split causing gasoline to leak onto the engine; water leaks into the headliner/footwell area; engine ticking noise; heat/AC/ventilation system is a "rodent lair" (the inside air may be laced with rodent feces; rodents are attracted by the ready-made cubbyholes throughout the vehicle and enjoy snacking on the soya-based electrical wiring coverings); inoperative instrument lighting for the power-mirror control (must turn on dome light to see); rear windshield ticking noise; front power-seat grinding, groaning noise; lots of owner complaints relate to poor fit and finish; blue paint is easily scratched and looks bad; and sudden Bridgestone Dueler tire side wall blowout. CrewMax windshields are particularly vulnerable to stress cracks.

SERVICE BULLETIN-REPORTED PROBLEMS: A front end grinding noise:

FRONT-END GRINDING NOISE IN 4WD					

BULLETIN NO.: TSB-0338-09   DATE: SEPTEMBER 16, 2009

Some 2008–10 model year Sequoia and 2007–10 model year Tundra vehicles may exhibit a grinding noise from the front of the vehicle while in 4WD. An updated differential support bolt is available to address this condition. Follow the repair procedure in this bulletin to inspect and replace the differential support bolt.

OP CODE	DESCRIPTION	TIME	OFP	T1	T2
TC9012	R & R Differential Support Bolt and Apply Sealant	1.2	90105-A0181	91	12

Front driveshaft ticking; snow ingestion into air cleaner box; squeaky front seat; inoperative satellite radio; and heavy phone static with Bluetooth calls.

EUROPEAN VEHICLES

Estimated cost for the Tata-*cum*-Jaguar anti-assassin Jaguar XJ sports car—about $400,000 (CDN). In Canada, a new 2010 Jaguar XJ SuperSport sells for $130,500; a used 2010 costs about $30,000 less.

Tata Sells Anti-terrorist Jaguar XJ

Tata Motors, Jaguar's India-based owner, has unveiled the Sentinel, its armoured luxury limousine based on a converted Jaguar XJ. The car comes with a 5.0L V8 engine, coupled to a six-speed automatic gearbox, has a top speed of 195 km/h and will do 0–100 km/h in 9.7 seconds. More powerful brakes were lifted from the super-charged V8 XJ and the suspension and steering have been retuned to handle the extra weight. The three-ton steel- and Kevlar-plated limo is built in Birmingham, England and is guaranteed to withstand repeated hits from a range of firearms including a .44 Magnum hand gun, AK47 assault rifle and even an armour-piercing 7.62 NATO round. It is also grenade-proof, [offering] blast protection from 15 kg of TNT.

THE GUARDIAN
AUGUST 25, 2010

Europe Recovers

The two-year-old worldwide economic recession may end up reinvigorating the European auto industry after all. After losing billions of dollars in sales; getting government handouts from France, Germany, Italy, and Spain; and wallowing in red ink, European automakers are returning to profitability thanks to cost-cutting and the surge in demand for German luxury vehicles. Audi, BMW, and Mercedes-Benz have had substantial sales increases in addition to double-digit sales gains by Indian-owned Jaguar and Land Rover. Apparently, rich buyers in North America and China are fueling a flight to luxury.

The market for the Smart car in North America is imploding, with sales down 41 percent from 2008 to 2009 and down a further 60 percent YTD in 2010. Why? Simple: The Smart is significantly overpriced for the U.S. and Canadian markets, especially when you can buy a base Hyundai Accent for $9,999.

Now, we come to Porsche, Volkswagen, and Audi: three powerhouses of German engineering and creative design that have strongly rebounded from the recession. Volkswagen has done particularly well because, while fuel prices remain high, it offers the most fuel-saving and high-performing vehicles of any European automaker; its North American marketing presence is relatively intact, with minimal dealer attrition; and the company is well positioned to ride the upcoming diesel craze to fatter future profits as hybrids and electric-car sales falter. On the other hand, increased small-car competition from the Japanese and South Koreans, who have been importing more-refined econocars and cheaper crossovers, will probably erode VW and Mercedes small-car and SUV sales. Already, the Mercedes Smart Car is rumoured to be in its last year, and VW has purchased a substantial interest in Suzuki—just in case.

European automakers hard-hit by poor sales a year ago have tried to achieve sustainability by going to two extremes: focusing on entry-level econocars and on luxury high-performance vehicles. The key to this strategy is making joint production deals with competitors, no matter the quality of the product they produce. Fiat, for example, will replace many of Chrysler's cars and trucks with its own problem-plagued lineup, and Ford will bring most of its European small product lineup to North America, reliving its dismal Cortina, Fiesta, and XR4Ti past. *Lemon-Aid* predicts Chrysler will lose millions with its Fiat affiliation and Ford will simply break even until Fiesta production starts on this side of the Atlantic.

Be Wary of European "Orphans"

Orphans are those vehicles that have been sold by their parent builder, or, as in Volvo's case, sold twice to different automobile manufacturers. Usually, when this occurs, the purchased companies dwindle into bankruptcy after a year or two. It happened with American Motors, Bricklin, Chrysler, and Delorean, and will likely happen to Jaguar, Land Rover, Saab, and Volvo.

There are many problems with buying orphan models First, there's the high cost of servicing, due to increased costs for parts that become rarer and rarer. Second, it's incredibly difficult to find mechanics who can spot the likely causes of some common failures; there isn't a large pool of them who work on those vehicles all the time, and those who can work on them don't have current service bulletins to guide them. There's also an absence of secret ("goodwill") warranties to pay for work outside of the warranty period, because the automaker will have dropped the warranty extensions along with the models. Finally, these unwanted cars suffer from a plummeting resale value.

Tata-owned Jaguar and Land Rover are two orphan car companies that are making some money for a change, thanks to better sales in India and Asia. Sales volumes rose 58 percent through June of 2010 for the two luxury brands, helping Tata post a consolidated net profit of $422 million (U.S.) in the three-month period leading up to June; this is after suffering a net loss in the same period a year ago. Sales of the two prestige brands were severely hit by the global economic slowdown after Tata Motors bought the automakers from Ford for $2.5 billion dollars in 2008.

GM has sold Saab to Spyker, a tiny Dutch company that builds $1 million luxury high-performance cars. The small automaker has never made a profit and will likely go bankrupt by year's end when it tries to cash in its GM stock, given as part of the sale.

Volvo is also on shaky ground now that it has been sold to Geely, a Chinese truck manufacturer that has limited experience in automobile manufacturing and marketing and no experience in North America. The 13-year-old company will face the formidable task of integrating the Swedish and Chinese corporate cultures, with a little Ford thrown into the mix. Its greatest challenge, though will be to make a profit from what has been a perennial money pit for Ford. Even in selling off the dying brand to Geely, Ford lost money; originally purchased for $6.45 billion in 1999, Volvo sold for a measly $1.5 billion (U.S.). Having lost its quality edge after the Ford purchase over a decade ago, Volvo models will likely show a further decline in quality, plus poor parts supply and spotty servicing support...just before the company closes its doors.

Luxury Lemons

European vehicles are generally a driver's delight and a frugal consumer's nightmare. They're noted for having a high level of performance combined with a full array of standard comfort and convenience features. They're fun to drive, well-appointed, and attractively styled. On the other hand, you can forget the myth about all European luxury vehicles holding their value; most don't. They're also unreliable, overpriced, and a pain in the butt to service.

This last point is important to remember because, in hard economic times such as these, cash-strapped dealers do not invest in a large parts inventory or mechanic training to adequately service what they sell. For them, the present is chaotic and the future is unknown and threatening, so you should buy a model that's been sold for years in relatively large quantities and has parts that are available from independent suppliers. If you insist on buying a European make, be sure you know where it can be serviced by independent mechanics if the dealership's service falters or servicing costs are too high. Interestingly, in my travels across Canada, independent Volkswagen and Volvo garages seem to be fairly well distributed,

DEPRECIATION: A EUROPEAN LUXURY CAR NIGHTMARE

MODEL	NEW 2006	NEW 2008	USED 2006	USED 2008
Audi A3 2.0T	$32,950	$32,300	$13,000	$21,000
Audi A6 Quattro	$62,510	$63,600	$21,500	$36,500
BMW 323i	$35,200	$35,900	$12,000	$24,000
BMW 525i, 528i	$58,600	$59,900	$20,500	$38,500
BMW X3	$44,900	$45,300	$17,500	$27,000
BMW X5	$59,500	$61,900	$22,000	$35,500
Jaguar S-Type	$64,295	$62,000	$15,000	$28,500
Jaguar XJ	$88,500	$85,000	$19,000	$36,000
Mercedes B-Class	$30,950	$29,900	$12,000	$18,500
Mercedes E-Class	$74,300	$65,800	$20,000	$35,000
Mercedes ML350	$55,750	$59,900	$22,000	$35,000
Land Rover LR3	$53,900	$44.900	$18,000	$26,000
Land Rover Range Rover	$99,900	$100,900	$29,000	$44,000
Porsche Boxster	$64,100	$58,100	$25,500	$40,000
Porsche Cayenne	$60,100	$55,200	$23,500	$34,500
VW Passat AWD	$44,990	$44,675	$16,500	$20,500
Volvo S80	$54,995	$54,995	$18,500	$33,000
Volvo XC70 AWD	$47,121	$46,495	$18,000	$30,500

The low residual values get worse as time goes by. Also, notice how original sales prices declined over the three years studied as well.

while BMW, Jaguar, Mercedes, and Saab repairers are found mostly in the larger cities, if at all.

So what's wrong with European cars? First, they can't compare to cheaper Asian competitors in terms of performance and durability. Who wants a Mercedes when offered a Lexus? Why get a dealer-dependent VW Jetta when you can have more fun with a Mazda3 Sport (even with a stupid grin on its front grille)? Second, when times get tough, European automakers get out of town; Asians, on the other hand, tough it out. Remember ARO, Dacia, Fiat, Peugeot, Renault, Skoda, and Yugo? And, finally, European vehicles aren't that dependable and tend to be poorly serviced, with maintenance bills that rival the cost of a week in Cannes. Shoppers understandably balk at these outrageously high prices, and European automakers respond by adding nonessential, problem-prone gadgets that drive up costs even more. In effect, they are selling the sizzle because the steak is *pourri*.

On his website, The Truth About Cars (*www.thetruthaboutcars.com*), British independent automotive journalist Robert Farago writes:

> Once upon a time, a company called Mercedes-Benz built luxury cars. Not elk aversive city runabouts. [An allusion to the Smart Car.] Not German taxis. Not teeny tiny hairdressers' playthings. And definitely not off-roaders…. In the process, the Mercedes

brand lost its reputation for quality and exclusivity. In fact, the brand has become so devalued that Mercedes themselves abandoned it, reviving the Nazi-friendly Maybach marque for its top-of-the-range limo. Now that Mercedes has morphed with Chrysler, the company is busy proving that the average of something good and something bad is something mediocre.

You won't read this kind of straight reporting from the cowering North American motoring press, as they fawn over any new techno-gadget-laden vehicle hailing from England, Germany, or Sweden. It's easy for them; they get their cars and press junkets for free.

Lemon-Aid readers who own pricey European imports invariably tell me of powertrains that stall, transmissions that jump out of gear, nightmarish electrical glitches that run the gamut from annoying to life-threatening, and computer malfunctions that are difficult to diagnose and hard to fix. Other problems noted by owners include premature brake wear, excessive brake noise, AC failures, faulty computer modules leading to erratic shifting, poor driveability, hard starts, and loss of power. Interestingly, although Ladas were low-quality Soviet imports, their deficiencies pale in comparison to what I've seen coming out of today's European luxury corral. Plus, servicing diesels will get costlier and more complicated in 2011, now that your diesel's urea tank has to be refilled regularly—only by the dealer. Yikes!

Service, *Nicht Gut*

Have you visited a European automaker's dealership lately? Although poor servicing is usually more acute with vehicles that are new on the market, it has long been the Achilles' heel of European importers. Owners give European dealerships low ratings for mishandling complaints, for inadequately training their service representatives, and for hiring an insufficient number of mechanics—not to mention for the abrasive, arrogant attitude typified by some automakers and dealers who bully customers because they have a virtual monopoly on sales and servicing in their regions. Look at their dealer networks and you'll see that most European automakers are crowded in Ontario and on the West Coast, leaving their customers in eastern Canada or the Prairies to fend for themselves. This means finding someone to do competent repairs is about as easy as getting Bloc Québécois leader Gilles Duceppe to vote Liberal.

"Risky" European Automakers

Lemon-Aid cannot recommend vehicles from the following five European automakers because the risks associated with buying them are too great: Jaguar, Land Rover, Saab, Smart, and Volvo. We believe these manufacturers may not remain solvent following the present automotive recession. If the companies do survive, buyers risk owning vehicles with plummeting resale values that cannot be serviced due to a shortage of skilled mechanics or underfunded parts inventories. Most of these companies have been disowned by their parent manufacturers and sold for barely a third of their value to Indian, Dutch, and Chinese interests. Their former owners couldn't support the cost of ownership, and neither can you.

Audi

Saddled in the early '80s with a reputation for making poor-quality cars that would suddenly accelerate out of control, Audi fought back for two decades and staged a spectacular comeback with well-built, moderately priced front-drive and AWD Quattro sedans and wagons. Through an expanded lineup of sedans, coupes, and Cabriolets during the last decade, Audi has gained a reputation for making sure-footed all-wheel-drive luxury cars that are loaded with lots of high-tech bells and whistles—and they look drop-dead gorgeous. But there's an ugly side to Audi ownership, too.

The TT Quattro Coupe combines smooth, chrome-free styling with flawless highway performance. Audi has also tweaked the TT's exterior design and improved the two-door's drivetrains for the 2011 model year. Still, drivers question the new Audis' ability to last: Will their durability measure up to their good looks and impressive performance?

Audi's quality control, servicing, and warranty support remain problematic and are not expected to get much better as the company rebounds from the recession. It's no secret that most Audis' reliability declines quickly after a few years of use, causing many owners to walk away when their lease or warranty expires. As used Audis pile up in dealer inventories, resale values take a beating, even among the models that have a relatively clean record. Take, for example, the 2006 TT Quattro Coupe that originally sold for $56,000; it's now worth barely $22,000 after four years of use—a boon for used car buyers, a bust for owners. The fact that Audi powertrains are only covered under warranty up to 4 years/80,000 km is far from reassuring, since engines and transmissions have traditionally been Audi's weakest components and many other automakers cover their vehicles up to 5 years/100,000 km. This is confirmed by surveys published by *Consumer Reports* that show serious powertrain problems with the entire Audi lineup, including the recently launched Q7 SUV and the entry-level A3. The A7, set to debut in 2011, is rated Not Recommended until it proves its worth.

A3	★ ★ ★

RATING: Average. **Strong points:** The car's a superb highway performer, thanks to its powerful and smooth-running engines and transmissions. Handling is crisp, steering is accurate, and cornering is accomplished with minimal body roll. Lots of safety, performance, and convenience features. Audi rates the A3 as capable of carrying five passengers; however, the three back-seat passengers had better be

friends. IIHS rates the A3 as "Good" for head-restraint protection and in protecting occupants in frontal offset and side crashes. **Weak points:** Fairly expensive for an entry-level Audi; on top of that, depreciation will likely be much faster than average, which doubles your losses. Also, a freight fee that nudges $2,000 should be made a felony. Premium gas is required, and insurance premiums are higher than average. Numerous factory-related problems affecting primarily the electrical system, powertrain, brakes, and accessories. Fit and finish is not up to luxury-car standards, either. No NHTSA crashworthiness data. **New for 2011:** Minor exterior changes and slight tweaks inside the cabin.

OVERVIEW: Based on the redesigned Volkswagen Golf, the A3 is Audi's entry-level, compact, four-door hatchback. It's a well-appointed, generously powered vehicle that arrived in the summer of 2005. The A3 comes in Standard and Premium trim levels, with a choice of two engines: 2.0 T versions have a 200 hp 2.0L turbocharged 4-cylinder engine, available with a 6-speed manual or 6-speed automatic transmission, and the 2.0 TDI has a 140 hp 4-cylinder turbodiesel with the automatic only. All A3s are available in front-drive, and Audi's Quattro all-wheel drive is available on automatic transmission 2.0 Ts. Standard safety features include ABS, traction control, an anti-skid system, front side airbags, rear side airbags, and side curtain airbags.

KEY FACTS

CANADIAN PRICE (NEGOTIABLE): *2.0 TFSI:* $32,300, *Premium:* $35,000, *Quattro:* $36,900, *Quattro Premium:* $39,950, *TDI:* $35,300, *TDI Premium:* $38,000
U.S. PRICE: *2.0 TFSI:* $27,270, *Premium:* $28,750, *Premium Quattro:* $30,850, *Premium Plus:* $29,270, *Premium Plus auto.:* $30,750, *Premium Plus Quattro:* $32,850, *TDI Premium:* $30,250
CANADIAN FREIGHT: $1,995 **U.S. FREIGHT:** $875
POWERTRAIN (FRONT-DRIVE/AWD)
Engines: 2.0L 4-cyl. Turbo (200 hp) • 2.0L 4-cyl. Diesel (140 hp); Transmission: 6-speed man. • 6-speed auto.
DIMENSIONS/CAPACITY
Passengers: 2/3; Wheelbase: 101.5 in.; H: 56/L: 168.7/W: 77 in.; Headroom F/R: 4.5/2.0 in.; Legroom F/R: 42.5/25.5 in.; Cargo volume: 19.5 cu. ft.; Fuel tank: 55L/premium/diesel; Tow limit: Not recommended; Load capacity: 990 lb.; Turning circle: 35 ft.; Ground clearance: 4.0 in.; Weight: 3,305 lb.

COST ANALYSIS: This four-door hatchback is smaller and less costly than Audi's A4 compacts, and is just as much fun to drive. Since these cars are mostly carryovers from the 2010s, look for a discounted previous model year. **Best alternatives:** Acura TSX, BMW 3 Series, and a fully loaded VW Jetta TDI. **Rebates:** Not likely, though prices will probably soften in late winter. **Depreciation:** Faster than average. A $40,000 2006 A3 is now worth only $14,000. Audi values nosedive when the base warranty expires. **Insurance cost:** Higher than average. **Parts supply/cost:** Pure hell! Owners report months-long waits for fuel system and other powertrain components to arrive to fix an all-too-common lag and lurch condition. The present recession is making the problem of limited part supplies and high parts costs untenable—sufficient reason not to buy an Audi this year. Independent suppliers scratch their heads when you ask about Audi parts. **Annual maintenance cost:** Predicted to be much higher than average. **Warranty:** Bumper-to-bumper 4 years/80,000 km; rust perforation 10 years/ unlimited km. **Supplementary warranty:** Don't leave the dealership without getting at least five-year coverage for the powertrain. **Highway/city fuel economy:** *2.0 front-drive man.:* 6.7/10.4 L/100 km, 42/27 mpg. *2.0 front-drive auto.:* 6.9/9.4 L/100 km, 41/30 mpg. *2.0 AWD:* 7.5/9.6 L/100 km, 38/29 mpg.

OWNER-REPORTED PROBLEMS: Sudden loss of diesel power when accelerating; the same failure occurs with other 2010 models:

> The contact owns a 2010 Audi A3 Quattro. While driving at approximately 75 mph [120 km/h], the engine shut off completely. There were no warning lights before or after the failure; the contact had to coast to the side of the road. He attempted to restart the vehicle but it would not respond. The vehicle was towed to the dealership but the dealer had not diagnosed the problem at the time of the complaint. The failure mileage was 215 miles [345 kilometres].

Transmission engages and then disengages when accelerating away from a stoplight or when parking:

> We thought it may have been just bad gas. It seems the problem is getting worse and more frequent as of late. Reading forums and articles online, it seems to be the symptoms of the transmission which is a DSG/S-tronic transmission.

Blinking headlights and interior lights when the brakes are applied. Premature brake replacements (rotors and calipers). Complaints that aren't safety-related include: engine, transmission, climate control, fuel and electrical system failures, as well as fit and finish deficiencies.

SERVICE BULLETIN-REPORTED PROBLEMS: Electrical harness damage from animal bites; instrument displays dim or darken; higher than normal oil consumption; free O_2 sensor replacement or ECM update (Campaign 23F5); various sunroof issues are addressed; and interior lighting flickers.

The Audi A4.

RATING: Below Average. The recession has made Audi quality and servicing problems worse. You cannot lose almost one-half of your sales in a one-year period and still pay the best mechanics, keep a costly parts inventory, and repair factory glitches through "goodwill" programs. On the positive side, so many of these vehicles have been sold for so long that sustained digging will usually find you the part and a mechanic who can service the vehicle competently. But back-ordered parts? I see no solution before a couple of years of restructuring. **Strong points:** Loaded with safety, performance, and convenience features. The base 2.0L engine provides gobs of low-end torque and accelerates as well with the automatic transmission as it does with the manual. The turbocharger works well, with no turbo delay or torque steer. The manual gearbox, Tiptronic automatic transmission, and CVT all work flawlessly. Comfortable ride; exceptional handling, though not as sporty as Acura's TSX; impressive braking performance (when the brakes are working properly); and lots of cargo room in the wagon. NHTSA gave both the A4 and the S4 a four-star crashworthiness score for front, side, and rollover protection; IIHS posted similarly impressive scores, giving a "Good" rating to frontal offset, side, and head-restraint protection. **Weak points:** Not as fast as its rivals; the ride is stiff at low speeds, and a bit firm at other times; some body roll and brake dive under extreme conditions; braking can be a bit twitchy; some tire drumming and engine noise; and limited rear seatroom, where the front seatbacks continually press against rear occupants' knees. Overpriced, with an outrageously high $2,000 freight charge and depreciation that is a wallet-buster. Another expense to consider is the car's high maintenance cost, especially because of its overall poor reliability. **New for 2011:** *A4:* Tiptronic transmissions

KEY FACTS

CANADIAN PRICE (NEGOTIABLE): *2.0 TFSI: $38,300, Quattro: $38,700, Quattro Premium: $43,600, S4 3.0 TFSI Quattro: $52,500, S4 Quattro 7-speed: $54,100* **U.S. PRICE:** *2.0 TFSI: $31,950, Quattro Premium: $32,850, Quattro Premium 8-speed: $34,140, Premium Plus: $35,400, Quattro Premium Plus: $36,250, Quattro Premium 8-speed: $37,540, Quattro Premium: $32,850, Quattro Prestige: $41,450, Quattro Prestige 8-speed: $42,740; S4 Premium Plus Quattro: $46,600, S4 Premium Plus Quattro 7-speed: $48,000, S4 Prestige Quattro: $52,900, S4 Prestige Quattro 7-speed: $54,300* **CANADIAN FREIGHT:** $1,995 **U.S. FREIGHT:** $875 **POWERTRAIN (FRONT-DRIVE/AWD)** Engines: 2.0L 4-cyl. (211 hp) • 3.0L SC V6 (333 hp) • 3.2L V6 (265 hp); Transmissions: 6-speed man. • 8-speed auto. • 7-speed auto. • CVT **DIMENSIONS/CAPACITY (A4 SEDAN)** Passengers: 2/3; Wheelbase: 110.5 in.; H: 56.2/L: 169.5/W: 71.8 in.; Headroom F/R: 3.5/2.5 in.; Legroom F/R: 41.5/ 24.5 in.; Cargo volume: 16.9 cu. ft.; Fuel tank: 62L/premium; Tow limit: Not recommended; Load capacity: 1,060 lb.; Turning circle: 37.4 ft.; Ground clearance: 4.2 in.; Weight: 3,750 lb.

have been upgraded to 8-speeds. *S4:* HD radio is now integrated into the optional navigation system and an 8-speed transmission replaces the old 6-speed. Upscale models get a reverse camera and parking sensors, while the Premium Plus versions gets an auto-dimming mirror (ho-hum).

OVERVIEW: This is Audi's bread-and-butter model, probably because it comes in so many variations, including sedans, Avant wagons, and convertibles; the lineup also includes high-performance models that are sold under the S4 and RS 4 labels. The A4 bills itself as Audi's family sport sedan and targets the BMW 3 Series and Volvo S40/S60 customer by featuring a roomy interior, an 8-speed automatic transmission, all-wheel drive, independent suspension, low-speed traction enhancement, automatic climate control, and more airbags than you can imagine.

The 2011 Audi A4 lineup also includes a restyled, upgraded supercharged S4 sedan model, along with four-door sedans and Avant wagons. The Cabriolet convertible is redesigned and is sold as part of Audi's A5 lineup. Sedans and wagons continue to offer Audi's Quattro all-wheel drive, and some versions of the sedan are available as front-drives. Sedans and Avants come as the 2.0 T and feature a turbocharged 211 hp 2.0L 4-cylinder engine. A continuously variable automatic transmission is standard on front-drive 2.0 Ts. The S4 is powered by a powerful 333 hp 3.0L supercharged V6 mated to either a 6-speed manual or an 8-speed automatic. This new drivetrain has impressive torque that kicks in at just 2500 rpm and remains constant through 4850 rpm, making the car especially responsive in everyday driving. The S4 has 18-inch wheels and unique exterior and interior features. Available safety features include ABS, traction control, an anti-skid system, front side airbags, rear side airbags, and side curtain airbags. Other features include a navigation system; Audi Drive Select, which allows the driver to customize steering and suspension settings; a blind-spot alert; keyless entry and engine start; a wireless cell phone link; and a rear-view camera.

COST ANALYSIS: The A4 and A5 are dressed-up VW Passats, so don't be mesmerized by the Audi badge. Go for a discounted, practically identical 2010, but only if you won't miss the 8-speed automatic transmission. Better yet, buy this model used, and get your servicing from an independent agency with a reputation for performing competent repairs. **Best alternatives:** If you like the S4 Quattro tire-burner, also consider the BMW M3 convertible or 5 Series and the Porsche 911 Carrera. A4 alternatives are the Acura TL or TSX, Audi TT Coupe, BMW 3 Series, Cadillac CTS, Infiniti G37, Lexus ES 350 or IS series, and Subaru Legacy GT. **Options:** An automatic transmission and all-wheel drive. Think twice about getting the power moonroof if you're a tall driver. **Rebates:** $3,000–$6,000 rebates, and a variety of dealer incentive plans and low-interest financing programs. **Depreciation:** Incredibly fast; a 2008 A4 that sold for $35,000 is now worth $23,000, a 2008 S4 that once cost $74,400 now barely fetches $44,000, and the top-of-the-line RS4 Quattro that sold new for $94,200 is worth only $58,000 used. **Insurance cost:** Higher than average. **Parts supply/cost:** Often back ordered and expensive. Forget about saving money by getting parts from independent suppliers; they carry few Audi parts. **Annual maintenance cost:** Higher than average, but not exorbitant. **Warranty:** Bumper-to-bumper 4 years/80,000 km; rust perforation 10 years/unlimited km. **Supplementary warranty:** Don't leave the dealership without it. **Highway/city fuel economy:** 2.0 front-drive man.: 6.5/9.0 L/100 km, 43/31 mpg. 2.0 front-drive auto.: 7.4/10.1 L/100 km, 43/30mpg. 2.0 Quattro man.: 7.4/10.1 L/100 km, 38/28 mpg. 2.0 Quattro auto.: 7.4/10.1 L/100 km, 38/28mpg. S4: 8.1/12.2 L/100 km, 35/23 mpg. S4 auto.: 7.9/12.1 L/100 km, 36/23 mpg. Remember, AWD models trade fuel economy for better traction.

OWNER-REPORTED PROBLEMS: An acceleration lag and engine surge; vehicle lunges every time the Tiptronic transmission is downshifted; CVT allows the vehicle to roll down an incline when stopped; secondary radiator is easily damaged from road debris; and sudden waterpump failure. Quality control is far from acceptable. The following problems have all taken these cars out of service for extended periods in the past: airbag fails to deploy; excessive steering shake due to a faulty lower control arm; engine, fuel-system, and powertrain component failures; defective brakes; electrical shorts; and abysmal fit and finish. The electrical system is the car's weakest link, and it has plagued Audi's entire lineup for the past decade. Normally, this wouldn't be catastrophic; however, as the cars become more electronically complex and competent mechanics are fired as dealerships open and close, you're looking at a greater chance of poor-quality servicing, long waits for service, and unacceptably high maintenance and repair costs.

SERVICE BULLETIN-REPORTED PROBLEMS: Electrical harness damage from animal bites; various sunroof issues are addressed; and interior lighting flickers.

A6, S6, R8 ★★★

RATING: Average. The A6 would have been rated higher if its resale value were higher. **Strong points:** A potent base engine that produces incredible acceleration times; superb steering and handling; comfortable seating; plenty of passenger and cargo room (it beats out both BMW and Mercedes in this area); easy front and rear access; and very good build quality. The Avant wagon performs

The Audi A6.

like a sport-utility, with side airbags, high-intensity discharge (HID) xenon headlights, and excellent outward visibility. IIHS considers offset crash protection and head-restraint effectiveness to be "Good." **Weak points:** The V8 is a bit "growly" when pushed; no real-world performance or reliability data on the V10 yet; firm suspension can make for a jittery ride; radio and navigation controls aren't easily accessed and are counterintuitive; some tire thumping and highway wind noise; the wagon's two-place rear seat is rather small; no NHTSA crashworthiness ratings; limited availability of the most popular models; a chintzy powertrain warranty; and servicing can be problematic. And, if high servicing costs aren't enough, at the end of four years you may find your Audi is worth only a third of its value. **New for 2011:** *A6:* Redesigned with borrowed A7 parts.

OVERVIEW: Audi's A6 3.2 is essentially a larger, fully-equipped A4, and the S models are high-performance, feature-laden variants. The A6 is a comfortable, spacious front-drive luxury vehicle that comes as a sedan or wagon and offers standard dual front side airbags and head-protecting side curtain airbags; torso side airbags are optional. Also standard are ABS, an anti-skid system, and xenon headlights (thieves love 'em). There's even a multi-tasking joystick control for all the entertainment, navigation, and climate-control functions. It's similar in function to BMW's iDrive system, which has been roundly criticized as being both confusing and dangerously distracting. The A6 sedan comes with a base 255 hp 3.2L V6 or an optional 350 hp 4.2L V8. Both engines are mated to a 6-speed automatic transmission with manual-shift capability; Audi's Quattro all-wheel drive is also available.

The 2011 Audi R8 is an all-wheel-drive, two-seat coupe with a mid-mounted engine. The entry-level 4.2 has a 420 hp 4.2L V8 engine, but the 5.2L has a 525 hp V10. Both models are available with an 8-speed Tiptronic automatic transmission or Audi's R tronic automated manual. As with other Audis, depreciation is a value-killer. A 2008 top-of-the-line R8 (its debut year) that sold new for $139,000 is now worth about $111,000—$28,000 less—in not quite two years.

COST ANALYSIS: Best alternatives: Other vehicles worth taking a look at are the Acura TL, BMW 5 Series, and Lexus GS. **Options:** Think twice about getting the power moonroof if you're a tall driver. **Rebates:** $7,000 rebates and low-interest financing. **Depreciation:** Lightspeed fast; a 2006 A6 Quattro which sold new for $62,510 sells used for barely one third that price. **Insurance cost:** Higher than average. **Parts supply/cost:** Very dealer-dependent and expensive. Independent suppliers carry few Audi parts. **Annual maintenance cost:** Low during the warranty period, and then it climbs steadily. **Warranty:** Bumper-to-bumper 4 years/80,000 km; powertrain 4 years/80,000 km; rust perforation 10 years/unlimited km. **Supplementary warranty:** A prerequisite to Audi ownership, and it guarantees a good resale price. **Highway/city fuel economy:** 3.2: 7.4/11.4 L/100 km, 35/23 mpg. 3.0: 8.0/12.0 L/100 km, 35/24 mpg. 4.2 *Quattro*: 8.8/13.1 L/100 km, 32/22 mpg. S6 5.2: 10.4/15.2 L/100 km, 27/19 mpg.

OWNER-REPORTED PROBLEMS: Airbags fail to deploy; front seat fails to stay anchored in a rear-ender; severe hesitation on acceleration; vehicle loses power or stalls when making right turns; premature transmission failure; transmission slips from automatic to manual mode without warning; chronic hesitation at low speeds; faulty gas-tank sensors transmit the wrong measurement of remaining fuel; distorted front windshield; and early wearout of original equipment Continental tires.

SERVICE BULLETIN-REPORTED PROBLEMS: Excessive vibration on hard turns; delayed acceleration; electrical harness damage from animal bites; higher than normal oil consumption; brake moans in turns or when accelerating; inoperative daytime running lights; various sunroof issues are addressed; water in foglamps; and interior lighting flickers.

KEY FACTS

CANADIAN PRICE (NEGOTIABLE): *A6 3.2 FSI:* $52,900, *3.0 TFSI Quattro:* $62,700, *3.0 TFSI Quattro Premium:* $66,900, *A6 4.2 FSI Quattro:* $75,900, *S6 5.2 FSI Quattro:* $99,500, *R8 4.2 FSI Quattro:* $141,000, *R8 5.2 FSI Quattro:* $173,000 **U.S. PRICE:** *A6 3.2 FSI:* $45,200, *3.2 FSI Premium Plus:* $46,900, *3.0 TFSI Quattro Premium:* $50,200, *3.0 TFSI Quattro Premium Plus:* $51,600, *3.0 TFSI Quattro Prestige:* $53,400, *4.2 FSI Quattro:* $59,150, *S6 5.2 FSI Quattro:* $76,100, *R8 4.2L Quattro:* $114,200, *R8 4.2L Spyder Quattro:* $144,000, *R8 5.2L Spyder Quattro:* $161,000, *R8 Spyder Quattro auto.:* $170,000 **CANADIAN FREIGHT:** $1,995 **U.S. FREIGHT:** $875 **POWERTRAIN (FRONT-DRIVE/AWD)** Engines: 3.2L V6 (265 hp) • 3.0L V6 (300 hp) • 4.2L V8 (350 hp) • 5.2L V10 (435 hp); Transmissions: 8-speed auto. • 6-speed man. and R tronic • CVT **DIMENSIONS/CAPACITY** Passengers: 2/3; Wheelbase: 111.9 in.; H: 57.5/L: 193.5/W: 73 in.; Headroom F/R: 3.0/3.0 in.; Legroom F/R: 42/27.5 in.; Cargo volume: 19.2 cu. ft.; Fuel tank: 80.1L/premium; Tow limit: 2,000 lb.; Load capacity: 1,100 lb.; Turning circle: 40 ft.; R8: 38.7 ft.; Ground clearance: *A6:* 5.0 in.; *S6:* 4.3 in.; *R8:* 4.5 in.; Weight: 3,836 lb.

TT COUPE ★★★★

KEY FACTS

CANADIAN PRICE (FIRM): *2.0 TFSI Quattro Coupe: $49,350, TTS: $57,600, TFSI Quattro Cabriolet: $52,350, TTS Quattro Cabriolet: $61,900;* **U.S. PRICE:** *2.0 TFSI Premium: $37,800, TFSI Premium Plus: $39,800, TFSI Prestige: $42,580* **CANADIAN FREIGHT:** $1,995 **U.S. FREIGHT:** $825
POWERTRAIN (FRONT-DRIVE/AWD)
Engines: 2.0L 4-cyl. (211 hp) • 2.0L 4-cyl. Turbo (265 hp); Transmissions: 6-speed man. • 6-speed manumatic
DIMENSIONS/CAPACITY
Passengers: 2/2; Wheelbase: 97.2 in.; H: 53.2/L: 165.2/W: 72.5 in.; Headroom F/R: 3.5/N/A in.; Legroom F/R: 41/N/A in.; Cargo volume: 13.1 cu. ft.; Fuel tank: 62L/premium; Tow limit: No towing; Load capacity: 770 lb.; Turning circle: 36 ft.; Ground clearance: 4.4 in.; Weight: 2,965 lb.

RATING: Above Average, but be prepared for a surprisingly low resale value. **Strong points:** Impressive acceleration with the base 200 hp powerplant; all-wheel drive available; good handling and road holding; very well appointed and tastefully designed interior; comfortable, supportive seats; plenty of passenger and cargo space (especially with the rear seatbacks folded); standard ABS; "smart" dual front airbags; standard stability control; and a predicted high resale value. **Weak points:** Base engine lacks low-end torque; excess weight limits handling; poor rear and side visibility; ride may be too firm for some; confusing interior controls; a useless back seat; difficult rear-seat access; lots of engine and road noise; and limited availability. No crashworthiness data available. **New for 2011:** A refreshed exterior design and 11 more horses for the base engine; Audi has decided to completely eliminate the TT's 3.2L V6 engine option.

TT Coupes carry two variation of the same 2.0L, 4-cylinder engine: a 211 hp 2.0L 4-banger and a 265 hp turbocharged variant of the same engine. On the safety front, all of the 2011 models will have self-supporting run-flat tires; a tire pressure warning system; full-sized dual-stage front airbags, triggered in two stages; and side (head/thorax) and knee airbags. There's also a connection for playing and charging your iPod located in the glove box, which you can control via the radio or the multi-function steering wheel. A Bluetooth mobile telephone feature allows for hands-free operation with voice-controlled capabilities.

OVERVIEW: These cars, like most Audis, don't hold their value well. Used bargains abound, if you are a savvy Audi mechanic or have access to a competent independent repairer. The TT Coupe Quattro debuted in the spring of 1999 as a $49,000 sporty front-drive hatchback with 2+2 seating, set on the same platform used by the A4 and the VW Golf, Jetta, and New Beetle. The TT's engines are coupled to a manual 6-speed front-drive gearbox. Shorter and more firmly sprung than the A4, the TT's engines are turbocharged, though only the optional engine comes with standard AWD. A spoiler and anti-skid system are also standard.

More beautifully styled and with better handling than most sporty cars, the TT comes with lots of high-tech standard features that include four-wheel disc brakes, airbags everywhere, stability and traction control, a power top (Quattro), a heated-glass rear window, and a power-retractable glass windbreak between the roll bars (convertible). An alarm system employs a pulse radar system to catch prying hands invading the cockpit area.

COST ANALYSIS: Go for an almost identical discounted 2010, priced thousands of dollars cheaper. It carries the 3.2L engine, which is a better performer than the 4-cylinder powerplants. **Best alternatives:** The BMW Z Series, Hyundai Genesis Coupe, Infiniti G37 Coupe, or Mazda Miata. **Options:** Think twice about getting the power moonroof if you're a tall driver. **Rebates:** $4,000 rebates and low-interest financing. **Depreciation:** Surprisingly fast, but slower than other Audi models, like the A5 and A6. **Insurance cost:** Higher than average. **Parts supply/cost:** Very dealer-dependent and expensive. Independent suppliers carry few Audi parts. **Annual maintenance cost:** Low during the warranty period, and then it climbs steadily. **Warranty:** Bumper-to-bumper 4 years/80,000 km; powertrain 4 years/80,000 km; rust perforation 10 years/unlimited km. **Supplementary warranty:** A prerequisite to Audi ownership, and it guarantees a good resale price. **Highway/city fuel economy:** 2.0: 7.0/9.5 L/100 km, 40/30 mpg.

OWNER-REPORTED PROBLEMS: No safety-related incidents reported.

SERVICE BULLETIN-REPORTED PROBLEMS: Electrical harness damage from animal bites; instrument displays dim or darken; higher than normal oil consumption; instrument panel rattle; and interior lighting flickers.

BMW

BMW had a close call. Long the European sales leader through thick and thin economic times, the latest recession has sent the automaker reeling. Sales of cars and trucks (X3, X5, and X6) were down almost 30 percent, and the automaker had

BMW's X3 (above) is larger and better performing for 2011.

to use rebates, generous leasing programs, and discounts to move its vehicles. Sales in 2010 are quite robust, though, and the company is moving ahead with its debut of the all new X1 in early 2011 and redesigned 5 Series and X3. Insiders say the M5 and M6 will skip this model year.

BMW continues to make well-built, well-appointed cars with excellent handling and superior driving comfort. No matter if fuel prices rise or fall, BMW has a product that will be appropriate for the times. Entry-level shoppers have the 1 and 3 Series; families with more disposable income may opt for the 5 and 6 Series; and for those who have the cash to buy loads of cachet, there's always the flagship 7 Series. Sport-utility fans also have four vehicles to choose from: the just-arrived X1 (a "baby SUV"), the compact X3, and the larger X5 and X6.

BMWs have excellent road manners and shout out "I got mine!" Unfortunately, there's barely a whisper to warn you of chronic brake, fuel system, and powertrain problems that can be quite expensive to troubleshoot and repair. Shhhh… There's also the incredibly complicated centre-console-mounted iDrive feature that some have renamed the "iDie" controller. Lately, BMW has made the iDrive more user-friendly, but the system still takes some getting used to.

Other BMW minuses: limited interior room (except in the high-end models), some quality-control deficiencies (notably the electrical system, brake pads, and fit and finish), and its vehicles can be difficult and expensive to service. A good website that lists BMW problems and fixes is *www.roadfly.com*.

Other than cachet, there are many acceptable reasons for buying a BMW, including fair overall reliability; impressive, high-performance road handling; and a low rate of depreciation. Keep in mind, though, that there are plenty of other cars that cost less, offer more interior room, are more reliable, and perform better.

So, if you're buying a BMW, remember that this is not the year to try out new fuel, electrical, or powertrain systems. Stick with the cars that have had the fewest changes, and if that means buying a leftover 2010, then so be it; you will likely save on the retail price, as well. Remember, though, that the entry-level versions of these little status symbols are more show than go, and just a few options can blow your budget. Adding to that, the larger, better-performing high-end models are much more expensive and don't give you the same standard features as many Japanese and South Korean imports do. Also, be prepared to endure long servicing waits and body and trim glitches, as well as brake, electrical, powertrain, and accessory problems.

RATING: Above Average. **Strong points:** Better handling than earlier models; more rear legroom and storage capability; distinctive styling; slow depreciation. IIHS rates the Mini as "Good" for offset crash protection and head-restraint effectiveness; side crashworthiness was given an "Average" score. NHTSA says this little tyke merits a four-star rating for its frontal collision crashworthiness and five stars for side occupant protection and resistance to rollovers. Owner reliability complaints have been few, and there's a 4-year/80,000 km all-inclusive base warranty. **Weak points:** A high freight/PDI fee; mediocre fuel economy, considering the powertrain components; a kidney-pounding ride; and limited front and rear visibility. Stability and traction control are standard only with the upscale models. **New for 2011:** Engine refinements and updated steering software to reduce "torque steer" (the car pulling to one side as it accelerates). The steering software may be retrofitted for 2008–10 models—for a price. The 1.6L 4-cylinder now produces 121 horsepower, while the turbocharged S puts out 181 horses. Cooper S buyers will get engines with an overboost function that temporarily boosts torque output. S models will get AWD for the first time. 2011s will also get new front and rear bumpers, larger foglights, and updated taillights.

OVERVIEW: This eye-catching classic British-*cum*-German car is a good highway performer, although the Mini's off-road prowess remains limited due to its low ground clearance (among other things). The 2011 S model gets AWD, which does improve handling. Overall, this is a city car that's only to be used for short commutes and the occasional trip to see the folks.

COST ANALYSIS: Okay, so the Mini's no longer cheap, nor is it as fast as the competition—but stylish, it remains, with its uniquely hunkered-down cute look. It has more interior space than the Austin did (weren't we all smaller

KEY FACTS

CANADIAN PRICE (FIRM): *Cooper:* $24,900, *Cooper S:* $29,900, *Cooper Convertible:* $29,950, *Cooper S Convertible:* $36,350, *Clubman:* $26,500, *S Clubman:* $31,500, *Cooper JCW:* $36,600, *JCW Convertible:* $42,500, *JCW Clubman:* $38,400 **U.S. PRICE:** *Cooper:* $19,500, *Cooper S:* $23,000, *Cooper Convertible:* $24,950, *Cooper S Convertible:* $27,850, *Clubman:* $21,150, *S Clubman:* $24,750, *JCW Cooper:* $29,500, *JCW Clubman:* $31,700, *JCW Convertible:* $34,700 **CANADIAN FREIGHT:** $1,395 **U.S. FREIGHT:** $725

POWERTRAIN (FRONT-DRIVE)

Engines: 1.6L 4-cyl. (121 hp) • 1.6L 4-cyl. Turbo (172 hp) • 1.6L 4-cyl. Turbo (208 hp); Transmissions: 6-speed man. • 6-speed auto.

DIMENSIONS/CAPACITY

Passengers: 2/2; Wheelbase: 97.1 in.; H: 55.3/L: 145.6/W: 66.2 in.; Headroom F/R: 3.5/2.0 in.; Legroom F/R: 41.5/22.0 in.; Cargo volume: 5.6 cu. ft.; Fuel tank: 50L/premium; Tow limit: No towing; Load capacity: 815 lb.; Turning circle: 35.1 ft.; Ground clearance: 4.8 in.; Weight: 2,535 lb.

back then?), there are 50/50 split-folding seats for additional storage space, and the fully independent suspension carries a body that we're told is much more rigid than what's offered by the competition. Plus, it's almost as cheap to drive a Mini as it is to walk. **Best alternatives:** The Mazda Miata and Porsche Boxster. The Ford Mustang convertible is the perfect muscle car to contrast with the Mini's less-is-more ethos. The Mustang possesses style in droves and offers an exciting driving experience (especially with the 2011's "boosted" V6)—just with higher fuel consumption and more weight. Or you could consider a classic roadster, such as the Mazda Miata. Though it comes as a two-seater only, it's perhaps the closest to the Mini Cooper's lightweight joy, its controls and responses a seeming extension of the driver's wishes. Plus, unlike the Mini, the Miata will spend more time on the road than in the shop. For the high-performance crowd, the John Cooper Works (JCW) editions offer more driving thrills. **Highway/city fuel economy:** *1.6L man.:* 5.3/7.1 L/100 km, 53/40 mpg. *1.6L auto.:* 5.7/7.9 L/100 km, 50/36 mpg. *S man.:* 5.7/7.8 L/100 km, 50/38 mpg. *S auto.:* 6.2/8.7 L/100 km, 46/32 mpg. *Cooper JCW:* 5.7/7.8 L/100 km, 50/36 mpg.

OWNER-REPORTED PROBLEMS: Fire ignited in the dash area; airbags failed to deploy; front end is too low to accommodate a curb without rupturing the radiator hose; complete clutch failure; sunroof suddenly shattered; windshield stress cracks; AC whistling, squeaking, and rear hatch/door window rattling; speedometer needle vibration; and inoperative interior lights. See *www.mini.ca* and *www.mini2.com/forum* for a good overview of ownership pros and cons. Overall reliability has been average with the non-turbo and below average with the Cooper S.

SERVICE BULLETIN-REPORTED PROBLEMS: Intermittently, the transmission warning light is displayed; rear seat backrest squeak; roof area rattling; rear end knocking on bumps; and troubleshooting tips for various electrical malfunctions.

RATING: Average. *M3:* Not Recommended; the transmission hesitation on acceleration or deceleration can get you killed. Many competitors deliver more interior room and standard features for less money. Smart BMW buyers will stick with the simple, large-volume, entry-level models until the recession blows over. **Strong points:** Very well appointed; cockpit amenities include a standard tilt/ telescope steering wheel, optional power-memory seats, power lumbar adjustments, an in-dash CD player, steering-wheel audio and cruise controls, standard traction and stability control, and rear side-impact airbags. Good acceleration (highlighted by the M3's incredibly fast performance); the 6-cylinder engines and the transmissions are the essence of harmonious cooperation, even when coupled to an automatic transmission—there's not actually that much difference between the manual and the automatic from a performance perspective. Light and precise gear shifting with easy clutch and shift action; competent and predictable handling on dry surfaces; no-surprise suspension and steering make for crisp high-speed and emergency handling; lots of road feedback, which enhances rear-end stability; smooth, efficient braking that produces short stopping distances; and top-notch quality control. NHTSA gives its top crashworthiness score—five stars—for front and side protection; rollover resistance received four stars. **Weak points:** Seriously overpriced; depreciation is only slightly slower than with Audi's lineup; a somewhat harsh ride (the M3 is harsher than most); insufficient front headroom and seat lumbar support for tall occupants; limited rear-seat room and cargo area; tricky entry and exit, even on sedans; confusing navigation system controls; excessive tire noise, especially with the M3; and premium fuel required. **New for 2011:** The 2011 BMW 3 Series sedans and wagons will be carried over relatively unchanged. The coupes and convertibles will be slightly restyled (a blunter front end, rear butt lift, and rear LED lighting); the 335i swaps its twin-turbo motor for one with just one turbo; and the new Sport-level 335is coupe and convertible will debut, both powered by 320 hp 3.0L turbocharged 6-cylinder engines.

KEY FACTS

CANADIAN PRICE (NEGOTIABLE): *323i Sedan:* $34,900, *328i Sedan:* $41,400, *328i Convertible:* $56,800, *328i xDrive Sedan:* $44,000, *328i xDrive Touring:* $45,600, *3281 Coupe:* $43,800, *328i xDrive Coupe:* $46,300, *335i Sedan:* $51,300, *335i Coupe:* $52,900, *335i Convertible:* $68,400, *335i xDrive Coupe:* $53,600, *335i xDrive Sedan:* $52,000, *335d Sedan:* $49,900, *M3 Sedan:* $69,900, *M3 Coupe:* $71,300 **U.S. PRICE:** *328i Coupe:* $36,200, *Convertible:* $45,000, *Sedan:* $33,150, *Sports Wagon:* $35,700, *xDrive:* $38,100, *325i Convertible:* $51,200, *xDrive Sedan:* $35,150, *xDrive Sports Wagon:* $37,700, *335i Coupe:* $42,650, *335is Convertible:* $58,200, *335i Sedan:* $40,600, *335i xDrive Sedan:* $42,500, *335i xDrive Coupe:* $44,550, *335d Sedan:* $43,950, *M3 Sedan:* $55,400, *M3 Coupe:* $58,400, *M3 Convertible:* $67,050 **CANADIAN FREIGHT:** $1,995 **U.S. FREIGHT:** $825 **POWERTRAIN (REAR-DRIVE/AWD)** Engines: 3.0L 6-cyl. (230 hp) • 3.0L 6-cyl. Turbo (300 hp) • 3.0L 6-cyl. Diesel (265 hp) • 4.0L V8 (414 hp); Transmissions: 6-speed man. • 6-speed auto. • 7-speed auto. **DIMENSIONS/CAPACITY** Passengers: 2/3; Wheelbase: 109 in.; H: 56/L: 178/W: 72 in.; Headroom F/R: 3.5/2.5 in.; Legroom F/R: 40.5/27.5 in.; Cargo volume: 11 cu. ft.; Fuel tank: 63L/ premium; Tow limit: No towing; Load capacity: 1,060 lb.; Turning circle: 19.4 ft.; Weight: 3,485 lb.

The 3 Series model lineup, offering the entry-level 328, mid-line 335, and high-performance M3, remains practically unchanged; the 328i should continue to be available with rear-wheel drive or with BMW's xDrive AWD hooked to a 230 hp 3.0L 6-cylinder engine. All of the other models will remain powered by a turbocharged 300 hp version of the 3.0L 6-cylinder. The rear-drive 335d will return with its 265 hp 3.0L 6-cylinder turbodiesel powerplant. M3 models return with last year's 414 hp 4.0L V8.

All BMW 3 Series gasoline engines should remain available with a 6-speed manual transmission. A 6-speed automatic will most likely remain available on the 328i and 335i, and continues to be standard on the 335d. The M3 will return with its 7-speed automatic, which it will share with the 335is.

OVERVIEW: With BMW's recent mechanical upgrades, styling changes, and increased exterior and interior dimensions, the 3 Series has come to resemble its more-expensive big brothers, with super-smooth powertrain performance and enhanced handling.

All BMW 3 Series gasoline engines should remain available with a 6-speed manual transmission. Most-likely remaining available on the 328i and 335i, and standard on the 335d, is a 6-speed automatic. The M3 will return with its 7-speed automatic.

COST ANALYSIS: Buy the cheaper 2010s, which embody the 2009 upgrades, yet are practically identical to the costlier 2011 models. Be wary of the diesel power option; the system is relatively new and much more complicated to service and repair than earlier versions. **Best alternatives:** Other cars worth considering are the Hyundai Genesis Coupe or Sedan and the Lexus IS series. **Options:** If you buy a convertible, invest $1,500 in the rollover protection system that pops up from behind the rear seat. The optional Sport suspension does enhance handling and steering, but it also produces an overly harsh, jiggly ride on rough pavement. Wider tires compromise traction in snow. Stay away from the Turanza run-flats and Bridgestone tires:

Bridgestone tire exhibits unsafe characteristics in wet weather, with noticeable drift and hydroplaning in any amount of standing water, even as little as 1/16 inch [1.5 mm]. In heavy rains, even with no standing water present, the tire seems incapable of dispersing water as quickly as it falls, again leading to vehicle instability. From a ride quality point of view the tire is also unsatisfactory in that it flat spots every morning, especially in cool weather but even in warmer weather as well, leading to vibrations in the initial miles of any drive. It is also especially harsh over roadway expansion joints, and is so loud on concrete pavements that it poses a safety hazard due to driver fatigue induced by the continuous noise. I also understand that there may be an issue regarding the rating as an "all season tire" with many owners reporting that this tire is virtually useless in any kind of snow conditions.

Rebates: Not likely. Dealers will push generous leases and low-interest financing. **Depreciation:** The entry-level models keep their value fairly well, but as you get into the pricier BMWs, the depreciation is mind-spinning. For example, a 2007 BMW 323i that once sold for $35,600 is still worth about $20,000, but a 2007 7 Series that sold for $108,400 is now worth only $38,000. Ouch! **Insurance cost:** Higher than average. **Parts supply/cost:** Parts are less expensive than those for other cars in this class. Unfortunately, they aren't easily found outside of the dealer network, where they're often back-ordered. That said, parts and repairs are far easier to find than with Audi, Jaguar, Mini, Porsche, and Saab. **Annual maintenance cost:** Average—until the warranty runs out Then your mechanic starts sharing your paycheque. **Warranty:** Bumper-to-bumper 4 years/80,000 km; rust perforation 6 years/unlimited km. **Supplementary warranty:** Not needed. **Highway/city fuel economy:** *323i:* 6.9/11.1 L/100 km, 41/25 mpg. *Auto.:* 6.7/11.2 L/100 km, 42/25 mph. *328i:* 7.0/10.9 L/100 km, 40/26 mpg. *Auto.:* 6.9/11.3 L/100 km, 41/25 mpg. *328i xDrive:* 7.6/12.2 L/100 km, 37/23 mpg. *Auto.:* 7.8/11.9 L/100 km, 36/24 mpg. *335i:* 7.9/11.9 L/100 km, 36/24 mpg. *Auto.:* 7.6/11.9 L/|100 km, 37/24 mpg. *335i xDrive:* 7.9/12.2 L/100 km, 36/23 mpg. *Auto.:* 7.9/12.2 L/100 km, 36/23 mpg. *335d:* 5.4/9.0 L/100 km, 52/31 mpg. *M3:* 9.7/15.3 L/100 km, 29/18 mpg. *M3 Cabrio:* 10.1/15.7 L/100 km, 28/18 mpg.

OWNER-REPORTED PROBLEMS: Fire originated in the fog light socket (see *www.bmwfire.com*); engines, brakes, electrical system (telematics), and some body trim and accessories are the most failure-prone components; engine overheating is a serious problem, and it's most common on past models; premature tire wear, and noisy run-flat tires—owners forced to pay for tire failures. *325i:* Excessive hesitation on acceleration:

When the driver demands a sudden increase in acceleration, the car hesitates anywhere from 1.5 to 3 seconds. This is a dangerous condition when someone is making a left turn in traffic, or getting onto a highway, or passing on a 2 lane country road, etc. Other cars traveling at 60 mph [96.5 km/h] are moving at 88 ft./sec. [27 m/s]. The amount of leeway this car needs is much too excessive.

Bridgestone tire-tread separation and side wall buckling:

Bridgestone Potenza RE050A runflat tires. The tires buckled on the side wall after less than 8,000 miles [12,870 km]. Out of curiosity I checked the Bimmerfest (*www.bimmerfest.com/forums/showthread.php?t=146728*) forum and discovered this is a widespread problem among BMW owners.

328: Airbag failed to deploy; premature tire failure (bubbles in the tread); sudden acceleration; when accelerating, engine cuts out and then surges forward (suspected failure of the throttle assembly); severe engine vibrations after a cold start as Check Engine light comes on; sunroof spontaneously shattered; there's a rear-quarter blind spot with the convertibles; and the front passenger head restraint won't go down far enough to protect short passengers. *330i:* Side airbag deployed when vehicle hit a pothole; vehicle overheats in low gears; and vehicle slips out of Second gear when accelerating. *335i:* Sunroof suddenly exploded; faulty fuel injectors; and engine stalling and loss of power fixed by replacing the fuel pump—now exhaust is booming, fuel economy has dropped, and there's considerable "turbo lag" when accelerating. Many other cases of loss of power on the highway or the high-pressure fuel pump failing, with some owners having to replace the pump four times:

> My high pressure fuel pump (HPFP) failed in my 2010 BMW 335i while on an onramp to get onto the highway. When I accelerated I felt a chugging sensation from the car followed by a gong. The [gong] was alerting me that my car had went into "limp mode" and would not allow me to accelerate any further than I had already... BMW has had this issue ever since introducing the N54 engine in various models in 2006 or so and has yet to have resolved the issue.

335d: After a short downpour, engine started sputtering. Dealer and BMW said there was water in the fuel and held the car owner responsible for the full cost of the repairs. *M3:* Tail light socket overheats, blowing the bulb and shorting other lights: costs $600 to rewire. Vehicle loses power due to faulty fuel pumps; transmission hesitates when accelerating in Second gear (see *www.roadfly.com*):

> There are times, however, when the car is decelerating but not coming to a full stop (when taking a turn at an intersection, for example), that the transmission will begin its automated downshifts but then become incredibly unresponsive. In these cases, if I press on the accelerator before coming to a full stop, I'll notice a significant lag before the engine actually revs up.

SERVICE BULLETIN-REPORTED PROBLEMS: Loss of power may be caused by an insufficient oil supply to the inlet VANOS adjustment unit; steering column rubbing noises; and repair tips for retractable hardtop leaks.

The BMW X3.

RATING: *X3 and X6:* Average; overpriced vehicles that depreciate quickly. *X5:* Below Average. The X5 is quick to depreciate and has a spotty reliability record.

X3: A small crossover SUV for the upscale crowd that wants a compact five-seater SUV that behaves like a sports sedan. The 2011 version is slightly larger than the 2004–10 model and will get same upgrades as the 3 Series sedan. For example, the 35i xDrive will carry a base 240 hp 3.0L powerplant or a 300 hp turbocharged 3.0L inline-six. Engines will mate to an 8-speed automatic transmission, increasing fuel economy and low-end torque. The suspension has also been updated so that models equipped with the Electronic Damping Control (EDC) will get shock absorbers that can be adjusted to road conditions and driving style.

X3 buyers will find the car has gained a half-inch in height, 3.36 inches in length, and 1.1 inches in width. Ground clearance increases by half an inch, and the 110.6-inch wheelbase is 0.6 inches longer. The second-row seats have much more leg and elbow room than the previous model. Also, the vehicle's cargo capacity is an estimated 56.6 cubic feet—the largest in its class. **Strong points:** Responsive handling; precise, predictable steering; abundant cargo space; good cabin access; and a quiet, nicely appointed interior. **Weak points:** This little SUV wannabe responds to a need no one has expressed. Way overpriced; options are a minefield of inflated charges; mind-spinning depreciation; a stiff and choppy ride that is a bit better than the previous X3; a somewhat narrow interior; and not very reliable, with powertrain deficiencies, serious fit and finish problems, audio system malfunctions, power equipment failures, and electrical system glitches.

X3

CANADIAN PRICE (SOFT): *28i:* $39,800, *30i:* $45,900, *35i:* $47,000 (est.) **U.S. PRICE:** *30i:* $38,850, *35i:* $39,000 (est.) **CANADIAN FREIGHT:** $1,995 **U.S. FREIGHT:** $875

POWERTRAIN (REAR-DRIVE/AWD)

Engines: 3.0L 6-cyl. (240 hp) • 3.0L 6-cyl. (300 hp) Transmission: 8-speed auto.

DIMENSIONS/CAPACITY

Passengers: 2/3; Wheelbase: 110.6 in.; H: 67/L: 182.8/W: 74 in.; Headroom F/R: 4.0/3.0 in.; Legroom F/R: 41.5/27.5 in.; Cargo volume: 56.6 cu. ft.; Fuel tank: 67L/premium; Tow limit: 3.500 lb.; Load capacity: 1,005 lb.; Turning circle: 38.4 ft.; Ground clearance: 8.5 in.; Weight: 4,067 lb.

X5

CANADIAN PRICE (NEGOTIABLE): *30i xDrive:* $58,800, *35d xDrive:* $62,800, *48i xDrive:* $72,100, *X5M:* $97,900 **U.S. PRICE:** *35i xDrive:* $46,675, *35i xDrive Premium:* $52,475, *35i xDrive Sport Activity:* $54,975, *35d xDrive:* $52,175, *50i xDrive:* $59,275, *X5 M:* $86,375 **CANADIAN FREIGHT:** $1,995 **U.S. FREIGHT:** $875

POWERTRAIN (REAR-DRIVE/AWD)

Engines: 3.0L Turbo. 6-cyl. (300 hp) • 4.4L V8 Turbo. V8 (400 hp); Transmissions: 6-speed auto • 8-speed auto.

DIMENSIONS/CAPACITY

Passengers: 2/3/2; Wheelbase: 115.4 in.; H: 69.9/L: 191/W: 76.1 in.; Headroom F/R: 3.5/2.5 in.; Legroom F/R: 40/27.5 in.; Cargo volume: 21.8 cu. ft.; Fuel tank: 93L/premium; Tow limit: 6,000 lb.; Load capacity: 1,350 lb.; Turning circle: 42 ft.; Ground clearance: 8.3 in.; Weight: 5,025 lb.

X6

CANADIAN PRICE (NEGOTIABLE): *351 xDrive:* $65,600, *501 xDrive:* $80,900, *X6M:* $99,900, *Active Hybrid:* $99,900 **U.S. PRICE:** *351 xDrive:* $65,600, *501 xDrive:* $80,900, *X6M:* $99,900, *Active Hybrid:* $99,900 **CANADIAN FREIGHT:** $1,995 **U.S. FREIGHT:** $875

POWERTRAIN (REAR-DRIVE/AWD)

Engines: 3.0L 6-cyl. (300 hp) • 4.4L 8-cyl. (400 hp) • 4.4L 8-cyl. (555 hp) • 4.4L 8-cyl. Hybrid (480 hp); Transmission: 8-speed auto.

DIMENSIONS/CAPACITY

Passengers: 2/2; Wheelbase: 116 in.; H: 67/L: 192/W: 78 in.; Headroom F/R: 3.5/2.5 in.; Legroom F/R: 40/27.5 in.; Fuel tank: 85L/premium; Tow limit: No towing; Load capacity: 1,190 lb.; Turning circle: 42 ft.; Ground clearance: 8.5 in.; Weight: 4,895–5,687 lb.

X5: This mid-sized seven-seater, BMW's first crossover SUV, has been on the market since 1999. For 2011, the X5 gets slight restyling (trim, bumpers, fenders, headlamps, fog lights, LED tail lights, etc.) and a new 35i xDrive equipped with a 3.0L inline-six, and a new 4.4L V8 with the new 50i xDrive. **Strong points:** The X5 engines deliver plenty of power, and there's a turbocharged diesel option; smooth, responsive power delivery; secure handling; good steering feedback; comfortable first- and second-row seating; and a well-appointed interior. Suspension improvements have smoothed out the ride. **Weak points:** The X5 has long-standing quality control issues with the fuel system, brakes, powertrain, electrical components, climate control, body integrity, and fit and finish. The complicated shifter and iDrive controls can be hard to master without a lot of patience and frustration; and the third-row seats are a bit cramped.

X6: An X5 spin-off, the X6 gives you many of the X5 advantages and disadvantages, but in a larger box. 2011 versions have one turbo less and still unleash 300 horses. Moreover, all models get the 8-speed automatic transmission and an "energy regeneration" system (don't ask). **Strong points:** On the market only four years, the X6 is billed as BMW's "sports activity" coupe because it's loaded with high-performance features. It carries a standard turbocharged 3.0L 6-cylinder engine or a powerful optional 4.4L V8, seats only four, and is a bit taller than most coupes. The AWD system can vary the torque from side to side to minimize under-steer. **Weak points:** Relatively new on the market, so servicing and parts availability may be problematic.

OVERVIEW: Here is where BMW took on the Asian automakers and came out second best. Despite BMW's recent sophisticated (and complicated) engineering, mechanical upgrades, styling changes, and increased exterior and interior dimensions, the X3, X5, and X6 SUVs are not very impressive from either a performance or a comfort/convenience perspective. Despite tax credits and superior gas mileage figures, BMW is reportedly having a tough time selling its new diesel-equipped X5 35d xDrive. Last year's X6 35i xDrive and 50i xDrive gasoline engines are rated at 15/21 mpg and 13/18 mpg, respectively. As for the 6-speed transmissions now replaced by 8-speeds, BMW says fuel economy is increased by seven percent and 0–60 mph times are shaved by one- to two-tenths of one percent. Big deal, eh?

COST ANALYSIS: Buy an almost identical, cheaper 2010, or wait for the X5's second-series models in mid-2011. The X3 is a better buy as a 2011, but give the car a year or so to shake off its redesign bugs. The X6? A big, brash, and beautiful barge—for potentates and *poseurs*. **Best alternatives:** Acura RDX and Honda CR-V. Other worthy contenders: the GM Acadia, Enclave, Escalade, Terrain, or Traverse, and the Lexus RX Series. **Rebates:** $4,000–$7,000 discounts along with low-rate financing and generous leasing terms. **Depreciation:** Faster than a speeding bullet. A 2006 X3 that once sold for $45,000 is now worth $19,000—a loss of $26,000. Hold on, it gets worse: a 2006 X5 sold for $59,500 new, yet its used value is now only $23,000—a loss of almost $37,000. The X5 that sold new for almost $15,000 more than the X3 winds up being worth only $4,000 more after 4 years. Does this make sense to you? Incidentally, the 2008 X6 (its debut year) sold new for $64,000 may eventually take the crown for "treasure turning to trash." Its value two years later: $39,000—a loss of $25,000. **Insurance cost:** Higher than average. **Parts supply/cost:** Moderately expensive; often on dealer back-order, and they aren't easily found outside of the dealer network. **Annual maintenance cost:** Average until the warranty runs out, and then your mechanic gets to know you real well. **Warranty:** Bumper-to-bumper 4 years/80,000 km; rust perforation 6 years/unlimited km. **Supplementary warranty:** A wise decision. **Highway/city fuel economy:** *X3 28i:* 8.3/12.2 L/100 km, 34/23 mpg. *X3 30i:* 8.2/12.5 L/100 km, 34/23 mpg. *X5 30i:* 9.3/13.6 L/100 km, 30/21 mpg. *Diesel:* 7.5/10.7 L/100 km, 38/26 mpg. *X5 48i:* 10.2/15.6 L/100 km, 28/18 mpg. *X5 M:* 11.9/17.2 L/100 km, 24/16mpg. *X6 35i:* 10.0/14.4 L/100 km, 28/20mpg. *X6 50i:* 11.0/17.1 L/100 km, 26/17 mpg. *X6 M:* 11.9/17.2 L/100 km, 24/16 mpg. *X6 Hybrid:* 10.3/12.6 L/100 km, 27/22 mpg.

OWNER-REPORTED PROBLEMS: Parts are scarce outside of major metropolitan areas, and independent mechanics who can service these vehicles are rare. Servicing deficiencies are accentuated by a weak dealer network and unreliable suppliers. *X3:* One safety complaint: The car caught fire while parked. What few general complaints there are target the fit and finish, power equipment, audio system, fuel system, and transmission as most in need of special attention. *X5:* Two safety-related complaints have been logged by NHTSA for the 2010 model: chronic stalling (see *http://www.xoutpost.com/bmw-sav-forums/X5-E70-forum/68822-engine-warning-battery-failure-same-time.html*), and the driver's seatbelt shoulder strap isn't adjustable for the driver's height, making it cross at the neck of short-statured drivers. Owners also report problems with the powertrain, electrical system, climate controls, brakes, audio system, body integrity, and fit and finish. During the X5's first decade in North America, it earned an unenviable reputation for its poor quality and unreliable performance. Insiders say that the quality problems surged because the X5 was a totally new kind of BMW, rushed to production with many components that were not compatible with the new vehicle's structure and hadn't been proven under real driving conditions. *X6:* One safety-related complaint, of stalling caused by a faulty fuel pump.

SERVICE BULLETIN-REPORTED PROBLEMS: *X3:* Reduced engine power; water leaking from the panoramic sunroof; steering column rub, scrape noise; and interference, noise from the radio speakers. *X5:* Airbag warning light comes on; reduced engine power; engine oil leak on the right-hand side of the engine crankcase; diesel engine oil leaks; can't engage Drive or Reverse; automatic transmission gears cannot be engaged, or transmission clunks when the vehicle is started; driveability concerns; jolt, delay when accelerating from a stop; various electrical and driveability concerns; more electrical problems outlined; inoperative navigation system; intermittent engine valve lash adjuster noise; brakes squeak or squeal when applied; rear suspension cracking, banging noise; front end clicking, popping noise; luggage compartment and front door rattling; loose seat thigh support cover; front seat noise troubleshooting tips; front seatback and head restraint noise; intermittent passenger seat squeaking; interference, noise from the radio speakers; variable radio reception; steering clicking noise; sunroof wind noise and water leaks; sunroof rear panel won't close; sunroof loses initialization; AC blows warm air; motion sensor triggers false alarms; brake light bulb failure; lighting switch on too early or too late; cracked door mirrors; inoperative windows one-touch feature; glove box malfunctions; discoloured aluminum surface on running boards; and washer fluid leaks onto cabin floor. *X6:* Fuel pump fuel level sensor repair and a fix for a rough-running engine following cold starts.

Jaguar

Not Recommended. Period.

The only places where Jaguars have sold well this year are India, the home base of the automaker's new owner, and Asia, where buyers still mistakenly believe they're quality luxury cars. They'll learn soon enough why Westerners and Europeans see

Jaguar as a doddering old uncle who's had multiple hip replacements, suffers from Alzheimer's, has been thrown out of his American rest home, and is now in intensive care somewhere in India. There, the uncle has found rich benefactors who remember how great he was and are paying for his life-support. Unfortunately, they'll soon realize that Jaguar is too far gone to be anything but an Asian niche-car invalid.

Jaguar is proof positive that the British can't build quality cars and Ford can't build British cars. Granted, Jaguar once excelled in smart styling, ride, handling, and comfort, but all of that is now available from the Japanese and South Koreans for much less money.

An unreasonably high retail price, subpar quality, and fears that Jaguar is still one step away from bankruptcy have led to an abnormally high rate of depreciation. A 2006 XKR convertible, similar to the one pictured above, that cost $117,350 new is now worth $37,000. No wonder prudent shoppers prefer to lease rather than purchase their Jags.

When Ford bought Jaguar in 1999, it transformed the company's luxury cars into a hodgepodge of Taurus/Sable and Lincoln parts thrown together with a Jaguar badge. No wonder Taurus-sourced powertrain, electronic, and body problems persist—problems such as sudden, unintended acceleration; automatic transmission and brake failures; shimmying; and excessive cabin noise when driving with the rear windows open.

High-end Jaguars have excess weight that makes it necessary to install lots of complicated and difficult-to-troubleshoot devices, as well as larger engines encased in aluminum bodies, in order to make them decent highway performers. Entry-level Jags have a different problem: convincing buyers that the X-Types are more than gussied-up Ford-Tata-Nanos.

Mercedes-Benz

Small and Luxurious

Daimler AG, Mercedes' governing company, expects to make a healthy profit after three years of dwindling sales. The automaker is predicting a $7.8 billion (U.S.) profit by the end of 2010—mostly generated by strong sales of the lucrative E-Class and S-Class models, a drop in costly sales incentives, and a surprisingly sharp rebound in the demand from Chinese and U.S. car buyers.

The company has pulled off this turnaround by increasing sales of smaller and less-expensive cars in the United States, while selling fewer—but larger and more expensive—models in Europe. This means we'll soon see new subcompacts, electric vehicles, crossovers, and a return to 4-cylinder engines that haven't been offered in years. Most of these front-drive minicars will be based on Daimler's new A/B platform.

Is it "Moose-Proof"?

An all-new C-Class arrives in 2011, followed by three models spun off from the popular B-Class subcompact in 2012 and 2013. Mercedes is intentionally taking its time in introducing these three small-car derivatives, mindful, no doubt, of the nightmarish press criticism that followed its first "mini-Benz" A-car press presentation in 1997.

Then, the A-Class overturned in a test run called the "moose test," a performance exercise used in Sweden for decades that calls for the driver to suddenly change lanes while going 70–80 km/h (45–50 mph), as though trying to avoid hitting a moose. What was most galling to the shocked Daimler dignitaries was that the Trabant—a much older, widely mocked car from Eastern Germany—passed the test with flying colours.

Minicar performance fears aside, Mercedes' poor quality reputation lingers on. In a 2007 *Consumer Reports* survey of 36 leading automobile brands, Mercedes-Benz ranked dead last in predicted reliability. In *CR*'s April 2010 Auto Guide edition, Mercedes' 2004–08 models have more "Poor Reliability" black spots than Walt Disney's *101 Dalmatians*. Even so, *Consumer Reports*' April edition recommends the C-Class, GLK-Class, M-Class, S-Class, and SLK-Class models. Overall, the company's lineup gets an "Average" rating, except for the R-Class, which underperforms in almost every category.

Way before *Consumer Reports* got involved, everyone (except for some clueless buyers) knew that Mercedes' 1998 M-Class sport-utilities were abysmally bad. You couldn't have made a worse vehicle, judging by the unending stream of desperate-sounding service bulletins sent by the head office to dealers after the vehicles' official launch. Two bulletins stand out in my mind. One was an authorization for dry-cleaning payouts to dealers whose customers' clothing had been stained by the dye from the burgundy-coloured leather seats. The other was a lengthy scientific explanation (which the Germans compose so well) as to why drivers were "tasered" by static electricity when entering or exiting their vehicles.

Car columnists have always known that Mercedes has made some bad cars and SUVs, but it took business reporters (not auto beat writers) from the gutsy *Wall Street Journal* to spill the beans. In a February 2, 2002, article titled "An Engineering Icon Slips," the *WSJ* cited several confidential industry-initiated surveys that showed that Mercedes' quality and customer satisfaction had fallen dramatically since 1999—to a level below that of GM's Opel, a brand that had one of the worst reputations for poor quality in Europe.

Industry insiders give different reasons for why Mercedes-Benz quality isn't world class. They say quality control has been diluted by the more than doubling of M-B's product lineup since 1997. Helpful, too, were the company's aggressive PR campaigns and the Teutonic mindset that tended to blame the driver rather than the product—both spectacularly successful in keeping the quality myth alive in the media until the *Wall Street Journal* broke its story. Neither mindset nor PR worked to mitigate owners' displeasure over M-B's engine sludge stonewalling, though. It cost Mercedes $32 million (U.S.) to settle with owners of 1998–2001 models after the company denied that there was a factory-related problem.

Although Mercedes sales are on the upswing, its vehicles' residual values have fallen dramatically. At the top end, a 2006 65 AMG that cost $227,900 new is now worth $44,000—less than 20 percent of its original value. Even the entry-level B-Class models feel the depreciation bite; a 2007 B-Class 200 that originally sold for $31,400 is now worth only $14,500, and a 2007 E-Class E320 BlueTEC sedan (once priced at $67,801) can now be bought for $27,000.

B-CLASS ★★

RATING: Below Average. First launched as a 2006 model, this car is sold mainly in Canada and Europe. It's Mercedes' second-smallest car, following the Smart, and is feature-laden, with four-wheel disc brakes, side airbags, and stability control. Fuel economy isn't all that impressive, and the retail price could be trimmed by at least $3,000, putting the car in BMW Mini or VW GTI territory. Furthermore, the "B" has an unusually large turning circle, which cuts its urban usefulness; seats are unusually firm; and the interior is everyday ho-hum. Shoppers would be wise to consider the equivalent Mazda or other Japanese or European compacts. **New for 2011:** Carried over relatively unchanged. The 2013 coupe, crossover, and sedan versions will arrive in mid-2012.

OVERVIEW: M-B's latest entry into the North American premium-compact-car

KEY FACTS

CANADIAN PRICE (NEGOTIABLE): *B200:* $29,900, *Turbo:* $32,400 **CANADIAN FREIGHT:** $1,995
POWERTRAIN (FRONT-DRIVE)
Engines: 2.0L 4-cyl. (134 hp) • 2.0L Turbo 4-cyl. (193 hp); Transmissions: 5-speed man. • 6-speed man. • CVT
DIMENSIONS/CAPACITY
Passengers: 2/3; Wheelbase: 109.4 in.; H: 63.1/L: 168.2/W: 69.6 in.; Legroom F/R: 43.0/25.5 in.; Cargo volume: 19.1 cu. ft.; Fuel tank: 54L/premium; Tow limit: No towing; Turning circle: 39.2 ft.; Weight: 2,854 lb.

market, the B-Class complements the C-Class lineup in the same way that the A3 and A4 models draw less demanding Audi shoppers and the 1-Series and 3-Series bring BMW cars within reach of buyers with fewer dollars to spare. There's also the B's small outside, big inside versatility, and respectable fuel economy. Still, without the Mercedes cachet, this is an ordinary, middle-of-the-pack, overpriced subcompact.

COST ANALYSIS: Take a pass on this year's models until prices come down by mid-2011, or pick up a practically identical 2010 model. **Best alternatives:** Take a look at the BMW 1 Series, Kia Rondo, Mazda5, or Toyota Matrix (with the brake override feature). **Options:** Seriously consider whether you really need the turbo option instead of the standard powertrain setup. They both drive similarly, but the turbo will use more gas and may be costlier to fix or maintain in the future. **Depreciation:** Faster than average; a $30,000 2008 B-Class 200 is now barely worth $18,500. **Insurance cost:** Higher than average. **Parts supply/cost:** Limited availability, and parts are expensive. **Annual maintenance cost:** Average. **Warranty:** Bumper-to-bumper 4 years/80,000 km; powertrain 5 years/120,000 km; rust perforation 5 years/120,000 km. **Supplementary warranty:** Not needed. **Highway/city fuel economy** *Man.:* 6.7/9.2 L/100 km, 42/30 mpg. *CVT:* 7.2/9.2 L/100 km, 39/30 mpg. *Turbo and 6-speed man.:* 6.9/10.2 L/100 km, 40/28 mpg. *Turbo with CVT:* 7.4/9.5 L/100 km, 38/30 mpg.

OWNER-REPORTED PROBLEMS: Mostly fit and finish and premature brake wear gripes.

C-CLASS ★★★

RATING: Average. These little entry-level cars lack the sparkling V6 power, simplicity, and popular pricing found with the Japanese luxury competition; save up for an E-Class or a Hyundai Genesis. **Strong points:** Plenty of high-tech safety features; adequate, though not outstanding, powertrain matchup; available AWD; a comfortable ride; easy handling; excellent braking; and an innovative anti-theft system. 2009 C-Class models earned NHTSA's top five-star rating for side crashworthiness, and four stars were given out for front and rollover protection. IIHS crash tests gave top marks ("Good") for frontal offset, side, and head-restraint protection. Average reliability. **Weak points:** The light steering requires constant correction; a choppy ride with the sport suspension; complicated controls; limited rear-seat and cargo room; tight entry and exit; some tire thumping; and some engine and wind noise. Also, the cars are noted for their weak resale value. Very dealer-dependent for parts and servicing. **New for 2011:** A slightly restyled sedan

and a new coupe, based on the sedan, arrive in 2011. Some refinements to the drivetrain are expected, but there will likely be no changes to the powertrain. Expect the 2011 models to carry over the 2010 model's 225 hp 3.0L V6 and 268 hp 3.5-L V6 as well as the AMG's 451 hp V8.

OVERVIEW: Four models continue in this lineup. The C300 Luxury and C300 Sport have a 228 hp 3.0L V6; the C350 Sport offers a 268 hp 3.5L V6; and the C63 AMG carries a 451 hp 6.2L V8. The C300 Sport is available with a manual or automatic transmission; all other C-Class cars use a 7-speed automatic. The C300 is also available with Mercedes' 4MATIC all-wheel drive. All C300 models can run on ethanol-blended E85 fuel. Sport models have a sport suspension and unique interior and exterior styling. Available safety features include ABS, traction control, anti-skid system, front and rear side airbags, and curtain side airbags. Newly standard are front hip-protecting side airbags. Newly available are keyless entry/engine start and a rearview camera. Also available on rear-drive Sport models is a Dynamic Handling Package, which includes active suspension, specific 18-inch wheels, and steering-wheel shift paddles on cars with an automatic transmission.

KEY FACTS

CANADIAN PRICE (NEGOTIABLE): *C250:* $35,900, *C250 4MATIC:* $39,900, *C300:* $41,600, *300 4MATIC 7-speed:* $44,900, *C350:* $48,600, *350 4MATIC:* $50,600, *C63 AMG:* $63,900 **U.S. PRICE:** *C300 Luxury Sedan:* $35,900, *Sport Sedan:* $33,990, *C350 Sport Sedan:* $39,990 **CANADIAN FREIGHT:** $1,490 **U.S. FREIGHT:** $875

POWERTRAIN (REAR-DRIVE/AWD)

Engines: 3.0L V6 (225 hp) • 3.5L V6 (268 hp) • 6.2L V8 (451 hp); Transmissions: 6-speed man. • 7-speed auto.

DIMENSIONS/CAPACITY

Passengers: 2/3; Wheelbase: 108.7 in.; H: 56.9/L: 182/W: 70.0 in.; Headroom F/R: 2.5/1.5 in.; Legroom F/R: 42/26 in.; Cargo volume: 12.4 cu. ft.; Fuel tank: 62L/premium; Tow limit: Not recommended; Load capacity: 835 lb.; Turning circle: 35.3 ft.; Ground clearance: 4.2 in.; Weight: 3,565 lb.

COST ANALYSIS: Take a pass on this year's models until prices come down by mid-2011, or better yet, get a discounted (by at least 15 percent) practically identical 2010 version. **Best alternatives:** Take a look at the Audi TT, BMW 3 Series, or a Hyundai Genesis Coupe. **Options:** The Bose sound system is a good investment. **Rebates:** $4,000–$5,000 rebates, generous leasing deals, and low-interest financing. **Depreciation:** Faster than average; a $37,000 2006 C-Class Coupe is now barely worth $14,500. **Insurance cost:** Higher than average. **Parts supply/cost:** Limited availability, and parts are expensive. **Annual maintenance cost:** Average. **Warranty:** Bumper-to-bumper 4 years/80,000 km; powertrain 5 years/120,000 km; rust perforation 5 years/120,000 km. **Supplementary warranty:** Not needed. **Highway/city fuel economy:** *3.0L:* 7.7/11.7 L/100 km, 37/24 mpg. *Auto.:* 7.8/11.7 L/100 km, 36/24 mpg. *4MATIC:* 8.0/12.0 L/100 km, 35/24 mpg. *3.5L:* 8.0/12.2 L/100 km, 35/23 mpg. *AMG:* 10.4/17.2 L/100 km, 27/16 mpg.

OWNER-REPORTED PROBLEMS: Transmission; fuel, electrical, and climate control systems; brakes; body hardware and paint; power system; audio devices; and fit and finish deficiencies.

SERVICE BULLETIN-REPORTED PROBLEMS: Oil leaks at back of engine; hard 1–2 shift; 2–3 upshift slip during cold acceleration; harsh engagement from Park to Drive; steering gear leakage; engine squeaking noise from the belt drive; front suspension noise; front seat backrest noise; front seat noise when sitting down; knocking noise from the glove box area; inoperative seat heater (omigod!); four-way lumbar support fails; and the exterior lights stay on intermittently.

E-CLASS ★★★

RATING: Average. The E-Class is your father's Oldsmobile—if the Oldsmobile were German. Redesigned only a few times during the past decade, these family sedans, wagons, and convertibles manage to hold five people in relative comfort while performing acceptably well, though the redesigned 2010s don't ride or steer as well as the previous iteration (decontenting?). **Strong points:** Solid acceleration in the higher gear ranges; well-appointed with many new safety, performance, and convenience features; good engine and transmission combo; 4MATIC all-wheel drive operates flawlessly; easy handling; good braking; acceptable ride; roomy interior; lots of cargo room (with the 4MATIC wagon); innovative anti-theft system; and acceptable quality control. NHTSA awarded the 2009 model four stars for driver and passenger frontal crash protection; rollover resistance and side protection rated five stars; IIHS designated the same model year "Good" for offset crashworthiness and head-restraint effectiveness; side-impact protection was rated "Acceptable." **Weak points:** The car feels much slower than it actually is due to lack of low-end torque, and handling is not quite as crisp as with the BMW 5 Series; numb steering; complicated electronic control centre and navigation system controls are a pain to use; overly firm seats; a surprisingly small trunk; and tall drivers may be bothered by the knee bolsters. **New for 2011:** This is mostly a carryover year, except that the E-Class lineup gets a turbodiesel E350 BlueTEC sedan (can you spell "urea fill-up"?), as well as the new C-Class-based E350 convertible and E550 station wagon entries.

OVERVIEW: Mercedes' E-Class cars have improved incrementally over the years, but they have also suffered from some content-cutting and poor quality control relative to the automatic transmission, brakes, fuel pump, and electronics. This year, we rate the E-Class as Average again, and shoppers are cautioned to be wary of the latest diesel-equipped models, which require costly periodic urea fill-ups.

What have we got against urea-guzzling cleaner diesels? Simple: They make it easy for dealers to scam diesel owners.

Consumer Reports recently took its own diesel-powered Mercedes-Benz GL320 BlueTEC to a dealer because a warning light indicated that the SUV was low on AdBlue urea. The fill-up cost $316.99! The GL needed 7.5 gallons, which accounted for $241.50 of the total bill ($32.20/gallon). Labour (twisting a cap and pouring) and tax accounted for the remaining $75.49.

It took *CR* about 26,660 kilometres (16,565 miles) to run low on AdBlue, which means they'll be spending $1,457.80 on the stuff over 160,935 kilometres

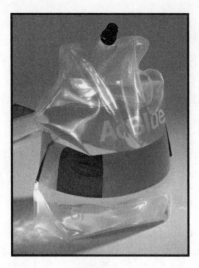

(100,000 miles); BMW covers this cost for its diesel-powered vehicles up to 80,470 kilometres (50,000 miles).

Besides adding to the retail cost, the new diesels haven't had the quality or servicing support of gasoline-powered engines. Plus, cautious dealers who are hunkering down during the present economic recession aren't likely to hire specialized mechanics or invest in expensive diesel inventory or diagnostic machines until the present fragile economy strengthens.

The gasoline-powered E350 has a 268 hp 3.5L V6 engine, the E550 has a 382 hp 5.5L V8, the E63 has a 518 hp 6.2L V8, and the E350 BlueTEC has a 210 hp 3.0L turbodiesel V6. A 7-speed automatic transmission is standard, and all coupe, sedan, and convertible models are rear-drives; the E350 and E550 sedans, though, offer 4MATIC AWD. Station wagons come only with AWD coupled to a V6 gasoline engine.

COST ANALYSIS: Again, diesel buyers be wary—diesels have been radically changed since 2007 and are much harder to have serviced competently. Performance enthusiasts will want to check out the E500's supercharged V8. All others should look for a heavily discounted 2010 sedan or wagon. **Best alternatives:** The Hyundai Genesis sedan or high-performance coupe. They both have lower price tags, fantastic interiors, rear-drive power delivery, and nearly 400 hp V8s. The sedan costs $39,000, while a fully-loaded coupe retails for a thousand dollars less. Other choices include the Acura RL, BMW 5 Series, Infiniti M35x, and Lexus GS AWD. Why no Volvo S80? Ask Geely, its newly minted owner. **Options:** Nothing is needed. **Rebates:** $5,000+ rebates/discounts, generous leasing deals, and low-interest rate financing. **Depreciation:** Faster than average. Forget those myths about Mercedes' high resale values: A $74,300 2006 E350 is now worth $20,000—less than a third of its original price. A 2005 version of the same car is worth $6,000 less ($14,000). **Insurance cost:** Higher than average. **Parts supply/ cost:** Hard to find outside the dealer network, and they can be expensive at times (body and electronic parts, especially). **Annual maintenance cost:** More than average. **Warranty:** Bumper-to-bumper 4 years/80,000 km; powertrain 5 years/120,000 km; rust perforation 5 years/120,000 km. **Supplementar y warranty:** Not needed. **Highway/city fuel economy:** E350: 8.3/12.7 L/ 100 km, 34/22 mpg. E550: 8.6/13.8 L/100 km, 33/20 mpg. E63: 10.2/16.5 L/100 km, 28/17 mpg.

OWNER-REPORTED PROBLEMS: Inadvertent airbag deployment; engine surged as vehicle was being parked and car sped out of control; automatic transmission malfunctions; transmission defaults into Second gear after each start cycle; turn signal and cruise control levers are mounted too close together; inoperative climate control; premature replacement of brake rotor and pads; body hardware and fit and finish deficiencies; impossible to drive comfortably with the window open; wind ear pressure can be intolerable; early tire blowouts with original equipment tires; power equipment and audio system breakdowns; and the Check Engine light may come on for no reason.

SERVICE BULLETIN-REPORTED PROBLEMS: Apparently, the 2010 redesign of the E-Class has contributed to a serious decline in the vehicles' quality and reliability: another reason why it's always a good idea to check public complaints and performance stats with an automaker's internal service bulletins. This year's bulletins show the following deficiencies: automatic converter "hard" lock-up when shifting from First to Second gear; transmission may have slippage when making the same shifts after a cold startup; various emissions and driveability concerns; inoperative seat heater; engine drive belt squeaking; rear brakes squealing; oil loss at the rear caps (cover plugs) of the engine camshaft; lumbar supports fail; the vehicle drops at the rear axle after standing for a long time; internal steering rack leakage; detached water deflector below windshield; loose or sagging underfloor panelling; and auxiliary water pump failure.

Volkswagen

VW's China Bet Pays Off

China loves Volkswagen.

VW entered the Chinese market over three decades ago, and now that country's superheated auto market has given Volkswagen AG, Europe's largest car manufacturer, its biggest quarterly profit in two years. The cars that doubled VW's profit in China for the second quarter of 2010 were the VW Jetta and its luxury-division Audi A6.

The downside for VW is that China's economy is showing signs of slowing down and its European success has been mitigated by the winding down of the "cash for clunkers" stimulus programs. Auto analysts also believe that the high-flying value of the euro and the declining worth of the Japanese yen will leave VW and other European-based automakers in a weak position compared to Japanese importers.

So, VW is standing pat with its present lineup and is bringing back its 2011 models—except for the reworked Jetta and retired New Beetle—unchanged. Incidentally, the new New Beetle may return as a 2012 model patterned after the Mini Cooper's performance and set on the Jetta platform.

VW's old New Beetle: gone and best left forgotten.

VW's revamped 2011 Jetta has a restyled interior and exterior. Its new wheelbase and extended length make the Jetta significantly bigger than its predecessor, resulting in more cabin space and greater comfort. On the other hand, it carries a wimpy 115 hp 2.0L base engine, instead of the 2010's 170 hp 2.5L, and reliability is expected to go down as the years add up.

VW has also bought a major interest in Suzuki, allowing the German automaker to diversify and venture into the small car and compact SUV markets.

How did VW increase market share during a recession? It was a combination of diesel popularity, less exposure to the slumping American market than other automakers, the right mix of vehicles that respond well to up-and-down fuel prices, and a solid international footing. Volkswagen is well-established internationally, with profitable operations in Latin America; an expanding presence in China, Russia, and India; and a dominant role in Western Europe, where it also markets its Seat and Skoda brands.

VW's small, fuel-efficient cars and diesel improvements have touched a nerve with Canadian shoppers in much the same way as the company's first Beetle captured the imagination and support of consumers in the mid-'60s. Building on that support, Volkswagen began delivery last year of its clean-diesel car, rated at 7 L/100 km (34 mpg)—a figure that beats most cars, except hybrids and the Smart Fortwo.

As with most European cars, Volkswagens are practical drivers' cars that offer excellent handling and great fuel economy, without sacrificing interior comfort. But overall reliability isn't very good (particularly after the fifth year of ownership), and servicing is often better and much cheaper at independent garages, which have grown increasingly popular as owners flee more expensive VW dealerships. Unfortunately, parts are fairly expensive, and both dealers and independent garages have trouble finding them due to chaotic parts distribution following dealer and supplier closures last year.

Diesel Savings Illusory?

Keep in mind that, unless you travel more than 30,000 km a year, diesel cost savings may be illusory. Granted, there are usually fewer things that go wrong with diesel engines, and their fuel economy is high, but gasoline-powered Asian compacts are much more reliable, their parts are cheaper and more easily found, and they're almost as fuel frugal. And here's the danger with diesels for the 2010 model year: They have been completely reworked to be as emissions-free as possible. Mechanics aren't yet familiar with them. Backup parts are still "in the pipeline," supposedly, and dealers aren't rushing to buy replacement parts until they can sell their old stock. Therefore, wise shoppers will steer clear of VW's diesel-equipped vehicles at least until the 2012 model year, when we can hope that servicing know-how and parts distribution will have improved.

Don't Buy a VW This Year

After telling you why you shouldn't buy a diesel-equipped VW this year, I will now tell you why you shouldn't buy a Volkswagen at all. Every year I peruse thousands of U.S. government automobile owner reports of safety-related incidents. In looking at the 2010 models—yes, vehicles not even a year old—I am astounded to see the large number of VWs that have automatic transmissions that lag and lurch or suddenly drop into Neutral until the car is stopped and restarted. This deadly defect apparently affects VW's entire lineup and has done so for a number of years.

Let me be clear: *Lemon-Aid* will not recommend any 2010–11 model year VW equipped with the DSG transmission until there are assurances that the source of the transmission failures has been fixed at the factory level. Keep in mind that Volkswagen's 2010 predicted reliability rating from J.D. Power is still below average (*www.jdpower.com/autos/volkswagen/2010*). Poor servicing exacerbates the reliability problems and has long been a source of irritation among owners. They complain that service managers tell them "abnormal is normal" and that the cars are "working as they should," despite serious powertrain problems, electrical system malfunctions, and early brake replacements.

GOLF, JETTA, CC ★★★/★/★★★

The Volkswagen Golf.

RATING: *Golf:* Average; carried over mostly unchanged. *Jetta:* Not Recommended during the first year of its 2011 redesign, especially when equipped with the wimpy 115 hp 2.0L four cylinder engine. *CC:* Average. All models are Not Recommended with the DSG automated manual transmission, nor with the diesel engine. **Strong points:** The Golf and CC are good all-around front-drive performers when coupled to a manual shifter; the turbocharged 200 hp 2.0L 4-cylinder engine delivers high-performance thrills without much

KEY FACTS

CANADIAN PRICE (NEGOTIABLE): *City Golf:* $15,300, *Trendline:* $20,475, *Trendline Tiptronic:* $21,875, *Sportline:* $23,900, *Comfortline Tiptronic:* $24,275, *2.0 TDI:* $25,275, *2.5 Sportline Tiptronic:* $25,300, *2.5 Highline:* $26,475, *2.0 TDI Comfortline DSG:* $26,675, *2.5 Highline Tiptronic:* $27,875, *2.0 TDI Highline:* $28,775, *2.0 TDI Highline DSG:* $30,175, *Jetta 2.5 Trendline:* $22,175, *Jetta TDI Trendline:* $24,475, *Jetta 2.5 Comfortline:* $24,875, *Jetta TDI Comfortline:* $27,175, *Jetta 2.0 Highline:* $29,075, *Jetta TDI Highline:* $30,875, *Jetta Wolfsburg:* $27,275 **U.S. PRICE:** *Golf two-door:* $17,620, *Golf four-door:* $19,335, *Golf two-door TDI:* $22,354, *Golf four-door TDI:* $22,959, *Jetta S:* $17,735, *Jetta S Tiptronic:* $18,835, *Jetta SE:* $20,550, *Jetta SE Tiptronic:* $21,650, *Jetta SEL:* $23,455, *Jetta TDI:* $22,830, *Jetta TDI Tiptronic:* $23,930, *Jetta Limited:* $18,295, *Jetta Limited Tiptronic:* $19,395, *CC Sport:* $27,760, *CC Sport auto.:* $28,860, *CC Luxury:* $33,080, *CC VR6 Sport:* $39,310, *CC VR6 4MOTION:* $40,420 **CANADIAN FREIGHT:** $1,490 **U.S. FREIGHT:** $800 **POWERTRAIN (FRONT-DRIVE)** Engines: 2.0L 4-cyl. (115 hp) • 2.0L TDI 4-cyl. (140 hp) • 2.0L Turbo 4-cyl. (200 hp) • 2.5L 5-cyl. (170 hp); Transmissions: 5-speed man. • 6-speed man. • 6-speed auto. **DIMENSIONS/CAPACITY (JETTA)** Passengers: 2/3; Wheelbase: 104.4 in.; H: 57.2/L: 182.2/W: 70 in.; Cargo volume: 15.5 cu. ft.; Fuel tank: 55L/regular; Tow limit: 2,000 lb.; Turning circle: 35.8 ft.; Ground clearance: 5.5 in.; Weight: 3,082 lb.

of a fuel penalty. The 2.5L 5-cylinder engine is well suited for city driving and most leisurely highway cruising, thanks mainly to the car's light weight and handling prowess. Excellent braking; a comfortable ride; plenty of front legroom and cargo room; standard tilt/telescope steering column; a low load floor; and good fuel economy. Good crashworthiness scores from both NHTSA and IIHS for the 2010 Golf and Jetta, though the Jetta wasn't tested for side crashworthiness. The redesigned 2011 Jetta has yet to be tested. The Golf scored five stars for side crash protection and four stars for frontal collision and rollover protection from NHTSA; both the 2010 Golf and the 2010 Jetta got a "Good" rating for head restraint effectiveness, frontal offset, and side crash protection from IIHS. **Weak points:** The base Jetta's 115 hp 4-cylinder engine is the runt of the litter and doesn't perform well with an automatic transmission. It also fails to meet the driving expectations of most Jetta buyers who want both good fuel economy and an engine with plenty of low-end torque and cruising power. Diesel-engine-equipped models with cruise control can't handle small hills very well, and often slow down by 10–15 km/h. Excessive engine and road noise; difficult entry and exit; limited rear legroom due to the extra-long front seat tracks; restricted rear visibility; and folding rear seats don't lie flat. ESC (electronic stability control) is optional in Canada on the Golf hatch, standard on the Canadian wagon, and standard on all VWs in the States. Make sure your insurance company knows, because ESC could lower your insurance premiums. A high number of safety-related complaints have been logged by NHTSA on the 2010 models. Many incidents have been reported of airbags deploying for no reason, injuring or killing occupants. Maintenance costs increase dramatically after the fifth year of ownership. **New for 2011:** Except for the redesigned Jetta and the City Golf's standard electronic stability control (along with electronic differential lock and anti-slip feature), VW's lineup is mostly carried over unchanged. *2011 Jetta:* Drivers get a reduced price along with reduced engine power; the car has been restyled inside and out; and it is longer and has more interior room (especially rear legroom), thanks to its extended wheelbase. Volkswagen's best-selling car returns as a four-door sedan. A sporty GLI will arrive in the winter of 2011. Entry-level Jetta S models have a 115 hp 2.0L 4-cylinder engine. The SE and SEL uses the same 170 hp 2.5L 5-cylinder engine from the previous generation Jetta. The TDI continues with its 140 hp 2.0L turbodiesel 4-cylinder. Interestingly, the GLI will keep its 200 hp turbocharged 2.0L 4-cylinder—the same engine that, in the Audi TTS, produces 265 horses. A 5-speed manual transmission is standard on the S, SE, and SEL. A 6-speed manual is standard on the TDI and GLI. Optional on the S, SE, and SEL is a 6-speed automatic. The GLI and TDI offer a 6-speed dual-clutch automated manual that behaves much like an automatic…when it's not falling into Neutral or simply falling apart.

OVERVIEW: "Practical and fun to drive" pretty well sums up why these VWs continue to be so popular. Yet they offer much more, including lots of front interior room, plenty of power, responsive handling, and great fuel economy. Too bad overall reliability is so horrendous just after the base warranty expires.

Again, we raise the caveat that this first-year new diesel design will likely have higher servicing costs and parts availability problems; for this reason alone, buyers should delay their purchases until the 2012 model year. That said, in spite of *Lemon-Aid's* criticism of how much you really save, other analysts say diesel is the best alternative to paying high fuel prices at the moment. *Autoweek* magazine concluded, "For comfort, quiet, and highway handling, our drivers found the TDI had significant advantages over every other car in the test. It would have been our choice, in other words, for an easy daytrip on the interstates, regardless of fuel economy. And we topped the hybrids by driving with just a little attention to fuel economy, not making it an obsession."

COST ANALYSIS: Before opting for the cheapest 2011 Jetta with its four-cylinder 115-hp engine, take it for a test drive and see if the reduced power is acceptable. Also, be wary of last-minute "administration" or "processing" fees; they're scams. **Best alternatives:** Other cars worth considering are the Honda Civic or Accord, Mazda6, Nissan Sentra, and Toyota Corolla or Matrix (only if the brake override feature is included). **Options:** Stay away from the electric sunroof; it costs a bundle to repair and offers not much more than the well-designed manual sunroof. On top of that, you lose too much headroom. **Rebates:** $2,000 rebates on non-diesels, low-interest financing, and attractive leases. **Depreciation:** About average, especially with the Jetta. However, as you approach the end of the four-year warranty, the value drops precipitously, even with the popular Jetta. For example, a 2006 Jetta Wagon that first sold for $27,780 is now barely worth $12,500. **Insurance cost:** Higher than average. **Parts supply/cost:** Not hard to find, but parts can be more expensive than for most other cars in this class. Diesel parts may be harder to find and much more expensive. **Annual maintenance cost:** Less than average while under warranty. After that, repair costs start to climb dramatically. **Warranty:** Bumper-to-bumper 4 years/80,000 km; powertrain 5 years/100,000 km; rust perforation 12 years/unlimited km. **Supplementary warranty:** A good idea. **Highway/city fuel economy:** *Golf*

City 2.0L: 7.0/9.8 L/100 km, 40/28 mpg. *Golf 2.5L:* 7.0/10.4 L/100 km, 40/27 mpg. *Auto.:* 6.9/9.2 L/100 km, 41/31 mpg. *TDI:* 4.7/6.7 L/100 km, 60/42 mpg. *Auto.:* 4.6/6.7 L/100 km, 61/42 mpg. Jetta fuel economy should be similar.

OWNER-REPORTED PROBLEMS: Less than a dozen safety-related incidents reported. Still, those that were mentioned could have been life-threatening: *CC:* Scattered reports of stalling, hard starts, and premature brake replacements. *Golf:* Diesel-powered Golf suddenly lost power on the highway as diesel fuel started spraying all over the car; the source of the problem was a leaking fuel line at the injector for the number 2 cylinder. Chronic stalling with diesel and gasoline engines; 20 engine roller lifters had to be replaced; cruise control malfunctions; various electrical shorts cause the Check Engine and Tire Pressure warning lights to come on for no reason; sunroof suddenly exploded; rearview mirror can't be adjust completely; and the glove compartment door jams whenever the car manual is wedged inside. *Jetta:* Reports of both sudden unintended acceleration and chronic stalling:

> The clutch response is somehow different than any other car and after adding the "diesel turbo lag," it makes for a dangerous first acceleration. To my salesman's surprise, I did not stall the car when I drove it off the lot. However, I have since stalled it several times in traffic. When the clutch stalls, driver must completely turn off ignition and turn it back on before attempting to clutch-drive again. This is a known issue among 2010 manual TDI owners and one frequently discussed because it is very dangerous. Some owners on "TDI Club" list server are changing out their own clutches to stay alive.

Cruise control is not disabled when depressing the brake pedal; automatic DSG transmission is still putting occupants' lives in danger:

> I have a new 2010 VW Jetta SE. Current mileage is less than 1300 miles [2,090 kilometres]. Car has an automatic-DSG transmission. In mid May of 2010 I began having severe problems with the transmission locking into 3, 4 gears while in Drive especially when entering traffic from a start. This creates a severe power reduction from a start and can be life [threatening], and cause involvement in broad side accident while entering the flow of traffic. Transmission also jolts and bolts when driving, and when placing in Reverse or Drive from a start. The car has shifted in Neutral once while driving. I have had at least 15 occurrences since May 12th. When the situation happens I have to pull off the road and stop and wait for a safe condition to pull out in Third (locked) gear.

> •

> I have a 2010 US Version Volkswagen Jetta TDI with the DSG transmission. The car has around 4500 miles [7,245 kilometres] on the odometer and this problem has been with the car since day #1. The problem is manifested as a lurching, and erratic shifting of the transmission in gears 1 to 2 as well as from a stop. Even through I drive with a soft touch, I can rarely get a smooth start-off because of the unpredictable shifting of the transmission. Especially noticeable in stop and go driving.

While attempting to start the vehicle, the steering wheel locked; vehicle was idling on an incline with the brakes depressed and it started rolling backwards, even though brakes were continuously applied; premature replacement of the rear brakes; design of the roof sends excess rainwater to the front windshield and the wipers push large amounts of water into the driver's viewing range; wipers slow down as engine speed decreases; inoperative wiper motor; delayed horn response; bubbling in the sidewall of Continental original equipment tires; and heated seats can catch on fire and give occupants much more than a "hot-foot," as one owner so succinctly wrote to government investigators:

> My heated seats caught fire and burnt my ass...

SERVICE BULLETIN-REPORTED PROBLEMS: *Golf:* Noise from the front door lock area. *Golf and Jetta:* Headlights dim at idle; exhaust system rattles. *Jetta:* Fuel door switch falls into driver's door panel.

EOS ★★★

RATING: Average, as long as you stay away from the unpredictable, failure-prone DSG automated manual transmission. **Strong points:** A more-than-adequate 200 hp 4-cylinder engine; the car is agile, handles well, and provides a comfortable, taut ride; effective, smooth, and easy-to-modulate braking; standard traction and stability control; instruments and controls are intuitive and easily accessed; supportive front seats with plenty of headroom and legroom; rear seats are a bit firmer; acceptable cargo area. Pockets on side doors are handy for storage. IIHS gives Eos its top, "Good," rating for frontal offset and side crashworthiness and head restraint effectiveness. **Weak points:** The triumph of style over practicality; limited interior access, rear legroom, and headroom; and excessive cabin engine noise. The Eos gets none of the Jetta's 2011 upgrades; NHTSA hasn't crash-tested the Eos; and owners give it a below average reliability score. **New for 2011:** A light restyling.

KEY FACTS

CANADIAN PRICE (NEGOTIABLE):
Trendline: $36,575, *Comfortline:*
$43,375 **U.S. PRICE:** *Komfort:* $32,390,
Lux: $35,950 **CANADIAN FREIGHT:** $1,335
U.S. FREIGHT: $800
POWERTRAIN (FRONT-DRIVE)
Engines: 2.0L Turbo 4-cyl (200 hp);
Transmissions: 6-speed man. • 6-speed
auto.
DIMENSIONS/CAPACITY
Passengers: 2/2; Wheelbase: 101.5 in.;
H: 56.8/L: 173.6/W: 70.5 in.; Legroom
F/R: 41.3/33.3 in.; Cargo volume: 6.4 cu.
ft.; Fuel tank: 55L/premium; Tow limit:
Not recommended; Turning circle:
35.8 ft.; Ground clearance: 5.5 in.;
Weight: 3,474 lb.

OVERVIEW: The Jetta-based Eos is a four-seater convertible equipped with a retractable roof and powered by a 200 hp 2.0L turbocharged 4-cylinder engine coupled to either a standard 6-speed manual or an optional 6-speed automatic transmission. The Eos comes with standard head-protecting side curtain airbags. It also handles well, if you can put up with all of the road- and wind-noise intrusion into the cabin when the top is closed; it's practically unbearable when the top is open. Incidentally, the latest research shows that convertibles driven with the top down contribute to premature hearing loss (SORRY, WHAT WAS THAT? I CAN'T HEAR YOU!).

COST ANALYSIS: Look for a cheaper, leftover 2010 model, and seek a 10 percent discount. We've had reports that some VW dealers are asking for $300–$400 for "administration" or "processing" fees; don't pay them. **Best alternatives:** The BMW 3 Series Cabriolet, Mazda's Miata, the Mercedes-Benz CLK-Class Cabriolet, and Mitsubishi Eclipse Spyder. Of that grouping, the Miata and Spyder are your best bets from a cost/quality standpoint. **Rebates:** Rebates and discounts are quite modest ($1,000–$2,000). **Depreciation:** Fairly steep for a convertible; a 2007 Eos that sold for $36,900 is now worth only $20,000. **Insurance cost:** Higher than average. **Parts supply/cost:** Parts aren't hard to find, since they're taken from the Golf/Jetta parts bin, but they can be costly. **Annual maintenance cost:** Average during the first three years. After this, expect repair costs to climb rapidly. **Warranty:** Bumper-to-bumper 4 years/80,000 km; powertrain 5 years/100,000 km; rust perforation 12 years/unlimited km. **Highway/city fuel economy:** 6.6/10 L/100 km, 43/28 mpg. *Auto.:* 6.6/9.2 L/100 km, 43/31 mpg.

OWNER-REPORTED PROBLEMS: The Eos uses most of the same components that VW has put into its popular Golf and Jetta, so servicing and parts availability may be less of a problem than with other models (except for roof components and body panels). Nevertheless, short-term reliability reports are negative, reflecting similar deficiencies as noted by Jetta owners. Owners of two- and three-year-old models reports serious problems with the body integrity and hardware, power equipment, and audio system, not to mention a deadly "lag and lurch" problem:

> I was making a right turn when the car switched into Neutral causing the car behind me to hit the brakes so as not to hit me. My car then switched into Drive and lurched forward causing me to hit the brakes so as not to hit the car in front of me. This is the third time since I leased the car that it has shifted into Neutral and then into Drive.

•

A valve that measures the temperature of the clutch malfunctioned. As a "safety" precaution the transmission will not change gears if the clutch temperature is too high. This valve malfunctioned while I was on the freeway. The car operated as though I put it in Neutral and revved the engine. Once out of oncoming traffic, it took me three tries to restart my car. I proceeded to exit the freeway and get to a safer destination. While doing so, this malfunction occurred two more times. Upon taking my car to the dealer to be repaired I was initially told that the engine switch malfunctioned. [It was] only upon demanding to speak with the head mechanic and being asked to fully describe the situation that the true problem was discovered. It was made clear to me that this is a common problem with this model.

SERVICE BULLETIN-REPORTED PROBLEMS: Headlights dim at idle; exhaust system rattles.

PASSAT CC ★

bad buy

RATING: Not Recommended until Volkswagen improves quality and recalls vehicles that slip out of gear, lurch, and lag. The car may be dropped by year's end. **Strong points:** Well-appointed and holds its value fairly well. Impressive acceleration with the turbocharged engine. Great performance with the manual gearbox; smooth and quiet shifting with the automatic gearbox. The 4MOTION full-time all-wheel drive shifts effortlessly into gear; refined road manners; sophisticated, user-friendly all-wheel drive; no turbo lag; better-than-average emergency handling; impressive with the AWD system; quick and predictable steering; handling outclasses most of the competition's; and the suspension is both firm and comfortable. Quiet-running; plenty of passenger and cargo room; impressive interior fit and finish; and exceptional driving comfort. Good crashworthiness scores from both NHTSA and IIHS. NHTSA gave it five stars for side crash protection and four stars for frontal collision and rollover protection. IIHS gave the vehicle a "Good" rating for head restraint effectiveness and frontal offset and side crash protection. **Weak points:** Both engines hesitate when accelerating; excessive brake fade after successive stops; rear-corner blind spots,

KEY FACTS

CANADIAN PRICE (NEGOTIABLE): *CC Sportline:* $33,075, *CC Highline:* $38,875, *CC VR6 4MOTION:* $40,420 **U.S. PRICE:** *CC Sport:* $27,760, *CC Luxury:* $33,080, *CC VR6 Sport:* $39,310, *CC V6 4MOTION:* $45,875 **CANADIAN FREIGHT:** $1,365 **U.S. FREIGHT:** $800 **POWERTRAIN (FRONT-DRIVE/AWD)** Engines: 2.0L 4-cyl. (200 hp) • 3.6L V6 (280 hp); Transmissions: 6-speed man. • 6-speed manumatic.

DIMENSIONS/CAPACITY Passengers: 2/3; Wheelbase: 106.6 in.; H: 55.9/L: 188.8/W: 73 in.; Headroom F/R: 4.0/3.0 in.; Legroom F/R: 43/29 in.; Cargo volume: 14.2 cu. ft.; Fuel tank: 70L/premium; Tow limit: 2,000 lb.; Load capacity: 975 lb.; Turning circle: 38 ft.; Ground clearance: 4.5 in.; Weight: 3,853 lb.

and rear head restraints impede rear visibility; many safety and performance complaints (faulty airbags and transmissions, distorted windshields, and chronic stalling); plus, these models are expensive to purchase and give poor fuel economy. **New for 2011:** The CC is the only model now that the sedan and wagon versions have been axed to make room for a bevy of redesigned 2012 Passats.

OVERVIEW: The Passat is an attractive mid-sized car that rides on the same platform as the Audi A4. It has a more-stylish design than the Golf or Jetta, but it still provides a comfortable, roomy interior and gives good all-around performance for highway and city driving. The car's large wheelbase and squat appearance give it a massive, solid feeling, while its aerodynamic styling makes it look sleek and clean. Base 2.0T Passats come with a turbocharged 200 hp 4-cylinder engine and front-drive, while the 3.6L models use a 280 hp V6 harnessed to a front-drive or 4MOTION all-wheel-drive powertrain. Passats come fully loaded with anti-lock four-wheel disc brakes, traction and anti-skid control, front side and side curtain airbags, tinted glass, front and rear stabilizer bars, and full instrumentation. In addition to the standard 6-speed manual transmission found on 4-cylinder models, an optional problem-prone 6-speed Direct Shift Gearbox (DSG) automated manual transmission is available.

COST ANALYSIS: Get an identical 2010 wagon with a sizeable discount (at least 15 percent) and tell the dealer to take a hike if you are asked to pay a $300–$400 "administration" or "processing" fee. **Best alternatives:** The BMW 3 Series, Honda Accord, Hyundai Genesis, and Toyota Camry (with the brake override feature). **Options:** The AWD will give you the extra sure-footedness and traction when you want it. This is not so with the adaptive cruise control; it frequently malfunctions. **Rebates:** $3,000–$5,000. **Depreciation:** Faster than average. How'd you like to lose almost half the car's value after barely three years? That's what would happen if you bought a 2007 Passat sedan, which originally sold for $29,970. **Insurance cost:** Higher than average. These cars are a favourite among thieves—whether for stealing radios, wheels, VW badges, or entire cars. **Parts supply/cost:** Parts are getting harder to find as dealers and suppliers close their doors. **Annual maintenance cost:** Higher than average. **Warranty:** Bumper-to-bumper 4 years/80,000 km; powertrain 5 years/100,000 km; rust perforation 12 years/unlimited km. **Supplementary warranty:** A must-have. Maintenance costs are higher than average once the warranty expires. **Highway/city fuel economy:** *2.0L:* 6.6/10.0 L/100 km, 43/28 mpg. *Auto.:* 6.6/9.6 L/100 km, 43/29 mpg. *3.6L:* 8.3/12.7 L/100 km, 34/22 mpg.

OWNER-REPORTED PROBLEMS: The transmission lines are positioned in such a way that the cooling fan motor can cut the lines, causing catastrophic transmission failure. Chronic stalling; transmission defaults into Neutral and won't go into gear unless the car is restarted; transmission shudders as it shifts into gear:

> I purchased a 2010 VW Passat wagon with DSG in Dec. '09. Since the beginning I noticed a strange quivering/shutter as it gears down from 2nd to 1st gear. I took it in at 1500 miles [2,415 kilometres] and a service coordinator told me it was "normal". It progressively got worse and became a vibrating clunk when gearing down. It also started lurching forward when stopped as I took my foot off the brake.

Delayed steering response; blinding glare from the shiny plate around the shifter and the silver part of the dashboard that reflects into the side mirror:

> Third problem is the night glare in the rearview and sideview mirror from the headbeams of the other car behind my car. If the rearview mirror is in a dimmed position, [then] a dashboard reflection is showing in it. And if you need to look at the sideview mirror, the headbeams light [is] shooting the extremely bright light straight into your eyes. This dark and bright contrast gets you blinded & disoriented.

SERVICE BULLETIN-REPORTED PROBLEMS: Brake pedal pulsation, vibration; poor heater output; unpleasant odours from air vents; an inoperative seatback recliner; and exhaust system rattles.

TIGUAN ★★★

RATING: Average. **Strong points:** Well equipped with an upscale interior ambiance, roomy, easy handling, and provides a comfortable ride. The small turbocharged engine is an impressive performer, without exacting much of a fuel penalty. Excellent crash scores from both NHTSA and IIHS: five stars for frontal

KEY FACTS

CANADIAN PRICE (NEGOTIABLE):
Trendline: $33,830, *Comfortline:*
$39,530, *Highline:* $40,055 **U.S. PRICE:**
S: $23,200, *S 4MOTION:* $26,250,
Wolfsburg: $27,750, *Wolfsburg*
4MOTION: $29,700, *SEL:* $31,550, *SEL*
4MOTION: $33,500 **CANADIAN FREIGHT:**
$1,580 **U.S. FREIGHT:** $800
POWERTRAIN (FRONT-DRIVE/AWD)
Engine: 2.0L 4-cyl. Turbo (200 hp);
Transmissions: 6-speed man. • 6-speed
auto.
DIMENSIONS/CAPACITY
Passengers: 2/3; Wheelbase: 102.5 in.;
H: 66.0/L: 174.3/W: 71.2 in.; Headroom
F/R: 5.0/1.5 in.; Legroom F/R: 42/28 in.;
Cargo volume: 23.8 cu. ft.; Fuel tank:
70L/premium; Tow limit: 2,200 lb.; Load
capacity: 1,110 lb.; Turning circle:
39.4 ft.; Ground clearance: 6.9 in.;
Weight: 3,432 lb.

and side crash protection and four stars for rollover protection from NHTSA, and a "Good" rating for frontal offset and side crash protection and head restraint effectiveness from IIHS. **Weak points:** Pricey compared to the competition (did you see that $1,580 freight charge?); limited cargo space; side airbags for rear passengers are optional; and the 998 kg (2,200 lb.) towing limit is about 590 kg (1,300 lb.) less than V6-powered rivals. **New for 2011:** A minor facelift.

OVERVIEW: Based on the Golf platform, the Tiguan has been a sales success story mainly because it is well-positioned between moderately priced small SUVs like the Honda CR-V and more upscale offerings like the Acura RDX.

COST ANALYSIS: Most of the 2010s have been sold, so you will have to pay full price for a 2011 version. Watch out for VW dealers who tack on phony "administration" or "processing" fees. **Best alternatives:** A Honda CR-V or a Hyundai Tucson. **Options:** Be careful of option packages— they are pricey and full of non-essential features. Consider getting a good anti-theft system from an independent agency (who usually offer a better selection and cheaper prices). Think twice about the AWD option; it will drive up your fuel consumption and only ensure that you get stuck deeper, farther from home. **Rebates:** No more than $1,000–$2,000; VW knows it has a winner. **Depreciation:** Faster than average; a 2008 Highline AWD that once sold for $38,375 is now worth $24,000. **Insurance cost:** Average. **Parts supply/cost:** Parts are no problem inasmuch as many are available from the Rabbit inventory. **Annual maintenance cost:** Predicted to be average. **Warranty:** Bumper-to-bumper 4 years/80,000 km; powertrain 5 years/100,000 km; rust perforation 12 years/unlimited km. **Supplementary warranty:** Always a good idea with cars that are relatively new to the market. **Highway/city fuel economy:** 7.6/11.2 L/100 km, 37/25 mpg. *Auto.:* 8.1/11.4 L/100 km, 35/25 mpg. *AWD:* 8.3/11.6 L/100 km, 34/24 mpg.

OWNER-REPORTED PROBLEMS: The fuel line "quick-connect" fittings in the engine compartment (passenger-side firewall area) disconnected while one vehicle was underway; it stopped dead with the engine covered with fuel. Driveshaft bolts stripped because they were improperly torqued at the factory; AWD axle came loose while driving; sudden unintended acceleration when braking:

I was traveling west bound on a typical south Florida day, very hot and humid clear day. Just then a pick-up truck [pulled] out very fast in front of me. I slammed on my brakes with plenty of time to stop, but just before I came to a complete stop, the engine roared and I hit the truck very hard. At first I thought my foot slipped off the brake to the gas, but no way, I broke my foot because I hit the brake so hard.

SERVICE BULLETIN-REPORTED PROBLEMS: Exhaust system rattles; headlights dim at idle; and noise from the front door lock area.

Appendix I
MINI-REVIEWS AND PREVIEWS

Some of the vehicles rated in this section may not be available before early next year, or are relatively new to the market. Others may have been sold in small numbers, just dropped from production, or lack sufficient owner feedback to make a more detailed analysis.

2010–12 Models

These are volatile times, with the price of cars and trucks fluctuating dramatically and fuel costs staying stuck on HIGH. You don't want the economic burden of buying an unproven car that's on the market for the first time or has been radically changed this model year. Nor should you invest in a vehicle that doesn't have a positive reliability history, merely because it looks nice or is cheap. And you certainly don't want to overpay for a car or truck simply to be the first in your town with something "different." The uniqueness will pass; the repairs will remain constant.

Consider these tips:

1. If you really want to save money, try to buy a vehicle that's presently being used by one of your family members. Although you may risk a family squabble somewhere down the road, you'll likely get a good buy for next to nothing, you'll have a good idea of how it was driven and maintained, and you can use the same repair facilities that have been repairing your family's vehicles for years. Don't worry if a vehicle is almost 10 years old—that's becoming the norm for Canadian ownership, particularly the farther west you go.
2. Get a fuel-efficient car. Be wary of diesel-equipped or hybrid cars that may require more-expensive dealer servicing that could wipe out any fuel consumption savings. Don't trust hybrid fuel economy hype—sometimes it can be off by 40 percent. Also, don't buy a "lemon" simply because it's touted as being fuel-efficient; a failure-prone Chrysler Sebring may cost you more to repair than to fuel, and a 4-cylinder pickup like GM's Canyon and Colorado—though cheap to run—can make highway merging a white-knuckle affair.
3. Use *www.insurancehotline.com* to find out which cars are the cheapest to insure. Remember, having an additional licensed driver in the family places your policy in a higher risk category, with accompanying higher premiums. Not giving that extra driver permission to use the car has little bearing on your rates—you'll still pay more.
4. Used is always a better buy than new—there's little depreciation or upfront costs, and the cars have been pre-dented, pre-stained, and pre-rusted.

5. If you do buy used, buy privately. Other bargains are high-mileage vehicles sold by major rental agencies that offer simply worded money-back guarantees and reasonably priced extended warranties. Franchised new-car dealers can also give you a good deal if they include all of the car's repair history. Keep the vehicle for at least 10 years and then resell it privately.

6. Delay buying a new car until early 2011, when automaker and dealer clearance rebates bring down new prices and lots of inexpensive trade-ins reduce used prices. Also, refuse all preparation charges, wear and tear insurance, and "administration" or "processing" fees. It's uncanny how automakers and dealers create problems and then sell you the solution. For example, extended warranties are bought because the car industry rejects so many valid claims. Now, wear and tear insurance, selling for about $700, is used to "protect" those who lease their car and are afraid of the dealer's chargeback for accelerated wear and tear.

7. Buy an entry-level Asian model or Asian/American co-venture from dealer stock for better price leverage.

8. Stay away from most American front-drives—more-frequent failures and costlier repairs are a given.

9. Be wary of all European models. Even the venerable *Consumer Reports* now agrees with *Lemon-Aid*: European makes are way overpriced, depreciation is head-spinning, parts and servicing can be a problem, and poor quality control will drive you to "speak in tongues"—like French, German, Indian, etc.

10. Don't buy "nostalgia" cars; they aren't as good as the memories they invoke. This includes the resurrected Chevrolet Camaro and Ford Thunderbird.

11. Buy in the States, or use American lower prices as leverage with Canadian dealers. It's easy to find fully loaded trucks, sports cars, and luxury vehicles for up to $20,000 less than what you would pay in Canada. Look in Part Three of this guide and compare costs between the two countries.

Acura

ZDX

RATING: Below Average. An under-sized, tech-laden luxury crossover that targets the BMW X6 and punishes its passengers. **Price:** $55,990, or $59,590 with the Technology Package (soft)—about $10,000 less than the aforementioned BMW. In the States, you would pay $45,495 and $56,045, respectively. Another alternative is to opt for the Lexus RX 350, which also costs 10 grand less than the ZDX. Better yet, buy an MDX for a few thousand dollars less and get handling that's just as sharp, plus more seating and cargo room. **Strong points:** An MDX spin-off four-door, mid-sized luxury SUV that has sporty, coupe-like styling and combines sporty motoring with AWD functionality. Its powerful 300 hp 3.7L V6, hooked to Honda's smooth 6-speed automatic transmission, delivers lots of power in a smooth and efficient manner. Interior garnishings are sumptuous. Reliability has been average, although the car is only going into its second year on the market. **Weak points:** The car's coupe styling has several serious drawbacks—rear seat access takes both planning and acrobatics, the rear seats are cramped, and headroom is limited. Rear and side visibility are also seriously impaired by the low roof and small, narrow windows. And the ZDX doesn't even provide the utility expected of an SUV. More bad news: Depreciation will take a $10,000 bite out of your wallet as soon as the ZDX is driven off the dealer's lot. **Crashworthiness:** NHTSA gives the ZDX five stars for frontal and side occupant protection and four stars for rollover resistance.

Audi

Q5

RATING: Below Average. Audi's history of factory-related glitches and its "lag and lurch" powertrain are immediate turn-offs. 2011 sees the addition of a base 2.0 T, powered by a 211 hp turbocharged 2.0L 4-cylinder engine used by the Audi A4. Sales of the smaller models and 3.2 Standard upgrade have been quite good. **Price:** *2.0 TFSI Premium:* $41,200 (firm); *2.0 TFSI Premium Plus:* $45,300 (firm); *3.2 FSI Standard:* $45,500 (firm); *3.2 FSI Premium:* $49,900 (soft). The Q7's smaller brother debuted three years ago as a stylish five-passenger luxury crossover compact full of high-tech gadgetry, with everything ready to go awry. Most notable is the car's adaptive suspension that allows for firm, sporty handling, if so desired. The Q5 power comes by way of a 3.2L 270 hp V6 and the latest rear-biased version of AWD. **Strong points:** Stylish, luxury appointments; good acceleration; excellent handling; and full of nifty safety, performance, and convenience goodies. **Weak points:** Overpriced; limited rear seat room and cargo space; and, in the best German tradition, controls are needlessly complicated. Servicing is highly dependent upon a weak dealer network; parts are problematic; and servicing quality will depend on how well mechanics get to know this vehicle that's relatively new to the market and sold in small volume. Unlike the Q7, there is no diesel option. Owners report hard and delayed upshifts and downshifts between First and Second gear; sometimes, when coming to a stop, the transmission downshifts just as the engine suddenly surges; and excessive wind noise. **Crashworthiness:** NHTSA awarded five stars for front and side crashworthiness and four stars for rollover protection. IIHS gave its top, "Good," rating for frontal offset and side protection. Head restraint effectiveness is also rated "Good."

Q7

RATING: Not Recommended. These are complicated five- or seven-passenger machines that are new to the market and made from bits and pieces of VW's other models. 2011s get new gasoline and diesel powertrains that use an 8-speed automatic transmission. The downside to this powertrain changeover is that the V6-powered 3.6 Premium and V8-powered 4.2 Prestige have been discontinued, which can impact negatively on servicing and drive their resale price down. **Price:** *3.0 TFSI:* $53,900 (firm); *3.0 TFSI Premium:* $59,000 (soft); *3.0 TFSI Sport:* $69,200 (soft); *3.0 TDI:* $58,900 (soft); *3.0 TDI Premium:* $64,000 (soft). **Strong**

points: A more-refined powertrain: The new 3.0T Premium and 3.0T Prestige are powered by a supercharged 3.0L V6 engine, putting out 272 and 333 horses, respectively. The 3.0 TDI Premium carries a 225 hp 3.0L turbodiesel V6. Maximum towing capacity is 6,600 pounds. Q7s also handle well and are full of the latest techno safety, performance, and convenience features. **Weak points:** The Q7 is a VW Touareg/Porsche Cayenne combo with an Audi badge and new powertrains that have yet to be tested. Off-road prowess is not as great as the Touareg's or Cayenne's; fuel economy is not impressive; ride quality is ho-hum; rear visibility is limited; and the third-row entry/exit is problematic. Furthermore, early owner feedback indicates that this large crossover AWD wagon has a host of factory-related defects affecting its fuel and electrical systems, powertrain components, and fit and finish—exactly the problems owners find with Porsche and VW models. Poor servicing and recurring factory glitches are to be expected. **Crashworthiness:** NHTSA gives the Q7 five stars for front and side crash protection and four stars for rollover resistance. IIHS gives its top, "Good," score for frontal offset, side, and head-restraint protection.

BMW

1 Series

RATING: Below Average. A joy to drive—most of the time. For some, less of a joy to look at. BMW's entry-level car comes as the 128i and 135i, and as either a two-door coupe or convertible with a power-folding soft top. These vehicles come with a 3.0L inline 6-cylinder that's shared with the 3-Series: The 128i has 230 hp, while the 135i is turbocharged and has 300 hp. All models carry a 6-speed manual transmission, though the 128i offers an optional 6-speed automatic. This year, the top-end 135i offers an optional 7-speed automated manual transmission; in the past, this has been a problematic transmission. **Price:** $33,800 for the 128i Coupe; $41,000 for the 128i Convertible; $42,800 for the 135i Coupe; and $48,300 for the 135i Convertible. **Strong points:** Excellent acceleration, steering and handling; good outward visibility (coupes); average depreciation. **Weak points:** Styling is unique. Or, in *L.A. Times* car columnist Dan Neil's words:

> The new 1 Series BMW is ugly. Seriously ugly. Ugly with X-wings locked in attack formation... The 1 Series looks like it needs a jowl lift to repair its prolapsed cheeks. Or perhaps a truss. With the downward bowed accent lines running along its flanks, this car looks like it has suffered a high-speed hernia.

Harsh riding—you feel every bump in the road; poor outward visibility with the convertible top up; fuel consumption is a big let down. Owners also report chronic fuel pump failures covered by a 10-year secret warranty:

> As I pulled out into the road, the Engine light came on and the car had reduced power. The car (with only 5500 miles [8,850 km] or so) was shaking violently when going

under 10 miles [16 km] an hour. The RPMs fluctuated at idle to where the car almost stalled several times. I drove the 15 or so miles [24 km] home with my flashers on as the car was having trouble. The above is a description of a HPFP failure on the N54 engine. I would say many, many people get a bad fuel pump. BMW has covered the part for 10 years/120K miles [193,100 km], but it will fail again. There is no fix at this point. Just a new pump that eventually gives way. I know people who are on their 4th pump. Just do a Google search on "BMW HPFP" and see what comes up. The 135I, 335I, 535I [and] Z4 35I all have the N54 engine, and they all suffer from this defect. Loss of power really concerns me, what if I was going 65 mph [105 km/h] on a highway when the pump decided to fail? I brought the car into the dealership, and explained the long cranks and loss of power etc...and they explained BMW has to approve all fuel pump swaps. Got a call 2 days later to say they will replace the pump. In addition to the new pump, I will be getting a software update as well.

ABS malfunctions; early ignition coil, clutch plate, and DTC traction failures; run-flat tire alerts come on for no reason; cramped interior is awkward to get in and out of; and few storage spaces. **Crashworthiness:** No crashworthiness data available.

Fiat

500

RATING: Not Recommended during its first year on the market. Fiat's got some nerve. After walking out on its U.S. and Canadian owners in 1984 and leaving them high and dry with worthless warranties and rust-cankered vehicles, Fiat's announced a triumphant return to North America as Chrysler's saviour. Okay, I admit I have a grudge against Fiat due to their lack of integrity and their quality-challenged products. When Fiat pulled out of North America, I was in the trenches as president of the Automobile Protection Association and remember only too well the many Fiat owners who were stunned that their rusty, unreliable, and unwanted pieces of crap would never be fixed. The CAW, UAW, Ontario provincial government, and Canadian federal government should be ashamed of ever signing onto Chrysler's giveaway to Fiat, with government grants "greasing the skids." Now, Mexican workers are getting their salaries underwritten by our unions and governments. **Price:** $19,500 (estimated) for the base model. **Strong points:** Adequate acceleration, fuel frugal; good steering, handling, and outward visibility. The switch to a new platform for the North American imports is predicted to boost the 500's crashworthiness, reduce cabin noise and vibration, and lower the car's overall weight. **Weak points:** Quality! The May 2009 J.D. Power quality survey put Fiat at the bottom—28th of 28—in U.K. satisfaction rankings. Lexus, Skoda, Honda, Toyota, and Jaguar filled out the top five spots, while Citroen, Kia, Chevrolet, Mitsubishi, and Fiat rounded out the bottom five. Seating is only for four; parts availability and mechanic competency will be built up slowly; and a wimpy 100 hp engine for a vehicle that is priced a couple of thousand dollars more than the Honda Civic or Fit. Other minuses include a small interior, a harsh ride, and wind buffeting. **Crashworthiness:** Neither NHTSA nor IIHS has tested the 500. European crash-test results don't apply because the North American version will ride on an all-new platform shared with the Panda utility vehicle and the Lancia Ypsilon hatchback.

Ford

Fiesta

RATING: Not Recommended during its first year on the North American market. The Fiesta is a front-drive subcompact manufactured and marketed throughout the world since 1976. In early 2009, it became the second most popular car ever sold in Britain. Its return to Canada and the U.S. in the fall of 2010 makes it the first Fiesta model to be sold in North America since 1980. Essentially, Ford plans to import the little car from Europe until it can transfer production to Canada and the United States. The Fiesta has what it takes to be a fine small car; the only caveat is that Ford has never imported a European-derived vehicle that went on to become a success in North America. Poor quality, performance, and servicing have afflicted most of these imports and sent them packing back to Europe. Will the Fiesta repeat history? Don't be the first to find out. Alternatives include the Honda Fit, Hyundai Accent, Kia Rio, Nissan Versa, and Mazda2. **Price:** *Sedan:* $12,999; *Hatchback:* $16,799 (are you listening, Fiat?). **Strong points:** Available as a five-door hatchback or sedan, the 120 hp 1.6L 4-cylinder minicar was named "Car of the Year" in the February 2009 issue of Britain's *What?* magazine. The car accelerates well with the manual gearbox and has good steering, handling, and fuel economy (estimated at 6.8 L/100 km in the city and 5.1 L/100 km on the highway). There is also just adequate space in the front of this five-seater for the driver and passenger. A manual 5-speed transmission is standard and a 6-speed automated manual is optional. Little noise intrudes into the cabin. Available safety features include ABS, traction control, anti-skid system, curtain-side airbags, front-side airbags, and a driver knee airbag. A tilt and telescopic steering wheel, height-adjustable driver seat, and capless fuel filler also come with the car. **Weak points:** The automatic transmission cuts gas mileage by almost 15 percent and rear passenger space is cramped; even Honda's Fit has more storage space than the Fiesta five-door hatchback. Seats could use a bit more lumbar and thigh bolstering. **Crashworthiness:** Despite its small size, the 2011 Ford Fiesta earned four stars for overall crashworthiness from NHTSA. IIHS gave it top marks in frontal offset, side, and rear impact occupant protection, as well as protection from excessive roof intrusion into the cabin.

Econoline, E-Series

RATING: Average. These gas-guzzling full-sized vans quickly lose their value, making them a better deal used. Going into 2011, the E-Series and the Transit will be the only vans in the Ford lineup in North America. **Price:** *Commercial van:* $31,299; *Passenger van:* $36,399 (very soft). **Strong points:** Parts are plentiful and repairs aren't dealer-dependent. **Weak points:** Vulnerable to side winds; rapid brake wear; poor-quality original equipment tires; electrical system shorts; excessive steering wander or free play (2008–10); broken exhaust manifold studs (2009 and 2010 models); oil leaks into coolant; and excessive turbocharger carbon deposits causing surging, power loss, or black/white smoke (6.0L engines). Harsh automatic transmission shifts, improper gear selection, erratic converter clutch operation, or improper shift feel. Automatic transmission converter clutch lockup, causing hesitation and/or lack of power during shift (2005–10 models). **Crashworthiness:** NHTSA gives the van three stars for rollover protection.

Edge, MKX

RATING: Above Average. A five-passenger wagon/SUV crossover based on the same platform as the Fusion sedan, the Edge comes in either all-wheel drive (without low-range gearing) or front-drive. The only engine available is a 265 hp V6 hooked to a 6-speed automatic transmission. Standard features include ABS, traction/anti-skid control, and front-side and side-curtain airbags. **Price:** $30,499–$40,699 (negotiable). **Strong points:** The vehicle accelerates nicely, though there is some hesitation when downshifting. Although softly sprung, handling is better than average for a crossover. Good passenger and cargo room combined with a comfortable ride. **Weak points:** Mediocre fuel economy, lots of engine noise, and spongy-feeling brakes. Parts are a bit scarce and repairs are highly dealer-dependent. Optional equipment you don't need to buy: Ford's Vista Roof (a glass roof with a sliding glass sunroof over the front seats), a navigation system, a DVD entertainment system, leather upholstery, and larger wheels. Lincoln's MKX is a more luxury-laden spin-off. **Crashworthiness:** NHTSA gives the Edge and MKX five stars for front and side protection and four stars for rollover protection. IIHS rated the Edge "Good" in front offset, side, and rear crashworthiness.

Expedition

RATING: Average. These gas-guzzling full-sized SUVs quickly lose their value and, like Ford vans, are a better deal bought used. Going into 2011, Expeditions come with standard Trailer Sway Control that works with Ford's AdvanceTrac and Roll Stability Control to enhance safety while towing. Also new this year is an SOS Post-Crash Alert System, which activates the horn and emergency flashers should the airbags deploy. And, like the rest of Ford's lineup, Sync with available voice-activated navigation system, HD Radio, and Sirius Travel Link offers Expedition customers more choices in information and entertainment with driver-friendly access. The Expedition comes with a 310 hp V8 and truck-based chassis. Extended-length versions have more cargo space and seating for up to nine passengers. The Ford Expedition competes effectively with Chevrolet's Tahoe and Suburban. **Price:** *XLT:* $45,999 (soft); *Limited:* $58,349 (soft); *King Ranch:* $61,899 (very soft). **Strong points:** The Expedition has adequate passing/merging power and can tow up to 9,200 pounds. Occupants have a comfortable ride, and interior appointments are exceptional. Most large SUVs have heavy third row seats that must be manually removed for more cargo space; however, the Expedition has second- and third-row seats that automatically fold flat into the floor. Both seat rows offer plenty of room, and the seats are nicely bolstered. Repairs aren't dealer-dependent and parts can be easily found at discount suppliers. **Weak points:** A sometimes sluggish, noisy V8 and ponderous handling that's outclassed by GM's Tahoe and Yukon. Rapid depreciation: The $61,899 2010 King Ranch model is now worth about $40,000. NHTSA safety-related logs mention rapid brake wear; poor-quality original-equipment tires; harsh automatic transmission shifts; water leaks from the rear window; chin-to-chest head restraints; and poor headlights. 2009–10 Expedition and Navigator vehicles may exhibit a low-frequency knocking noise from the engine at hot idle. The noise is predominately heard from the right front wheelwell area and/or the right hand engine cam cover. This noise is likely generated from the right hand variable camshaft timing (VCT) phaser assembly. **Crashworthiness:** NHTSA gives the Expedition five stars for frontal and side crash protection. Three stars were awarded for AWD rollover resistance, but only two stars were given for front-drive rollover resistance. IIHS hasn't crash-tested the Expedition.

Flex

RATING: Above Average. This boxy front-drive, four-door wagon shares many components with Ford's Edge and Taurus X crossover SUVs. The Flex seats either six or seven passengers in its three rows of seats. Power comes from a 3.5L 262 hp V6 mated to a 6-speed automatic transmission; all-wheel drive is available. Safety features include ABS, traction control, an anti-skid system, front side airbags, and curtain side airbags. Some of the Flex's other features include a rear-view camera, power liftgate, voice-activated navigation system with real-time traffic and weather updates, four-panel glass roof, and refrigerated centre console. Another available feature is Ford's Sync, which is a voice-activated system that controls some cell phone and MP3 player functions. Other vehicles worth considering: The Chevrolet Traverse, GMC Acadia, Honda Pilot, Hyundai Santa Fe, Mazda CX-9, and Toyota Highlander (only if equipped with the brake override feature). **Price:** $32,699–$46,599 (soft). **Strong points:** Acceptable acceleration and handling; a roomy interior; third-row seating is a pleasure; entry/exit is made easy with the wide doors and low step-up; the cabin is generally quiet; and the soft, compliant suspension gives a comfortable ride for seven with car-like handling. Good overall visibility. **Weak points:** Pricey; loses value quickly; and is a gas-burner. The Flex is new to the market, so servicing is very dealer-dependent. Steering is a bit too light; excessive nose dive upon hard braking; a moderate amount of engine noise when accelerating; an inoperative power liftgate; reports of driveshaft seal leaks; a harsh, uneven idle; poor radio reception; doors make a popping sound when opened; power locks cycle on their own; airbags fail to deploy in a head-on collision; sudden brake failure; and chronic stalling:

> 2009 Ford Flex engine dies while driving without any warning. The problem is intermittent but certainly present in numerous 2009 Ford Flex vehicles. Follow this

Crashworthiness: NHTSA gave the Flex five stars for front and side protection and four stars for rollover resistance.

Taurus

RATING: Average. Be wary of buying this revised Taurus before it's been road-tested for at least a year. The front-drive 2010 version returned last year considerably improved, with a restyled exterior and interior, new features, and Ford's high-performance Taurus SHO (which had been MIA since 1999). All-wheel drive is offered on the SEL and Limited models, which use the same 3.5L 263 hp V6 engine hooked to a 6-speed automatic transmission. The SHO (super high-output) returns with an EcoBoost turbocharged 3.5L 365 hp V6 engine, 6-speed automatic transmission, and AWD. SHO models have performance-oriented steering, suspension tuning, brakes, and 20-inch summer performance tires. **Price:** $29,999–$48,199 (a bit firm). **Strong points:** Excellent overall reliability. Good acceleration and steering/handling with the SHO version; the base Taurus does reasonably well. A quiet interior and a comfortable ride. **Weak points:** Automatic transmission performance degraded by frequent gear-hunting (non-SHO); limited rear seat headroom; and the SHO ride can be uncomfortably firm. Electrical and suspension glitches reported, and roof pillars obstruct rearward vision. **Crashworthiness:** NHTSA gives the 2011 Taurus four stars for overall crash protection. IIHS has awarded the car its top, "Good," rating for front offset, side, and rear collision occupant protection.

Transit Connect

RATING: Below Average. It also wouldn't hurt for smart shoppers to wait until the front-drive Transit Connect van has been road-tested in the real world for at least another year to better judge overall reliability and servicing support. This year's Transit Connect lineup expands with a new trim level and versions that are capable of running on batteries, compressed natural gas (CNG), or liquid petroleum gas (LPG). Although the Transit Connect is new to North America, other countries have been driving this Focus-inspired compact van since 2002. Sold worldwide, it can seat two, four, or five passengers. It has minivan-like sliding rear side doors and two rear "barn doors," similar to a commercial van. Powered by a puny 2.0L 136 hp 4-cylinder engine and a rather primitive, fuel-thirsty 4-speed automatic transmission, the Transit is longer, wider, and heavier than a Focus. Ford says the Transit Connect has more than 135 cubic feet of total cargo capacity and a payload of up to 1,600 pounds. Just don't be in a hurry to get anywhere. Transit Connect Battery Electric Vehicle (BEV) versions are powered by a 74 hp electric motor and a 28-kilowatt-hour battery pack. Ford claims a range of 128 kilometres (80 miles), a top speed of 120 km/h (75 mph), and a charge time of 6–8 hours on a 240 volt circuit. Transit Connect models powered by CNG and

LPG are available to fleet customers only. This vehicle is aimed at the small-business commercial market and fits between the compact Chevrolet HHR and the recently dropped humongous and problematic Dodge Sprinter (now sold exclusively by Mercedes-Benz). **Price:** $26,799–$27,299 (soft). **Strong points:** An easily accessed, capacious rolling box with traction control; an anti-skid system; a vehicle tracking device; and an Internet connection. Handling is fairly good. Fuel economy is only acceptable. **Weak points:** Lethargic acceleration caused by a sluggish, uncertain transmission (a deal-breaker, for sure); very vulnerable to side winds; cheap interior materials; tall head restraints and closed rear quarter panels limit visibility; drivetrain pedals are too close to each other for such a wide interior and the pads are unusually small; you get a buggy navigation feature; and there's a symphony of engine and road noise that transform the interior into a Jamaican steel drum. Owners can expect problems with premature brake wear and powertrain glitches due to the Transit's heft. Internal service bulletins target various water leaks; excessive steering play, noise; rear brake thumping or knocking; rear cargo door rattles; wiper blade interference; a blower motor that won't turn off, or has one speed that's inoperative; and offensive odours produced by the rubber cargo mats. **Crashworthiness:** Good; NHTSA gives it five stars for protection from frontal- or side-impact injury, while IIHS has yet to test the van.

General Motors

DTS

RATING: Above Average. It's essentially your father's old, comfortable, roomy, bouncy, and ponderous Oldsmobile. **Price:** $55,535–$74,675 (very soft). **Strong points:** Good reliability, parts are plentiful, and repairs aren't dealer-dependent. **Weak points:** There have been reports of airbags failing to deploy, loss of braking, and the head restraints literally being a pain in the neck (try before you buy):

> Head rest is too far forward for his wife to drive the vehicle... The consumer stated when his wife adjusted the seat for driving, the head rest forced her head down. The consumer stated all that needed to be done, was to have the two head rest supports bent down backwards a little to solve the problem.

Other owner complaints concern electrical shorts, premature brake wear, and subpar fit and finish. **Crashworthiness:** Good; four- and five-star protection ratings across the board.

STS

RATING: Average. A rear-drive/AWD Seville replacement, the STS is attractively styled and has plenty of power and performance—all available for a premium price. **Price:** Carrying a price tag of $61,085 (soft) for the 3.6L 255 hp V6 with a 5-speed automatic transmission and $72,535 (soft) for the 4.6L 320 hp V8 AWD with a 6-speed automatic, these cars are for the well-heeled who haven't yet given up on American cars for getting their thrills. **Strong points:** Cadillac's switch to rear-drive enhances the STS's balance, handling, overall performance, and reliability. The torquey V6 with 302 horses is impressive and almost eclipses the V8's 320 hp advantage. Think: The V6 has just 18 fewer ponies than the optional 4.6L V8, and the V6 will likely cost some $11,000 less. Eleven grand for 18 horsepower? Plus, you get to use regular fuel. Standard features include StabiliTrak stability control, a Bose sound system with CD player, leather seats, Keyless Access with a push-button ignition start, Adaptive Remote Start, and Panic Brake Assist. STS has lots of potential as Cadillac fights a volatile market where price, fuel economy, reliability, and cachet rule. So far, the car appears to be doing well. The STS has had few safety-related complaints posted with NHTSA. Those posted concern the failure of the side airbags to deploy, the car's poor traction in the snow, sudden rear differential lock-up (also a CTS complaint), chronic stalling, and incomplete speedometer readings. **Weak points:** Way overpriced. Steering feels a bit vague and over-assisted. Plastic trim pieces have no place in a Cadillac. Sporty front seats may be too firm for some, while rear seats could use more lateral support and a longer seat bottom. Rear legroom and foot space is tight. Interior fit and finish is subpar. Setting memory functions for the driver's seat, mirrors, radio, and climate control can be confounding, and the blind spot warning icon is washed out by sunlight. Trunk volume is unusually small and restricts what can be carried. The predicted reliability rating provided by J.D. Power and Associates is just slightly above average. NHTSA's safety complaint log notes one entry that says the LED tail lights are distracting, due to their low refresh rates. Internal service bulletins cover drivetrain chatter and rear axle clunks; lack of Forward or Reverse gear; an automatic transmission grinding sound; upshift, downshift clunks; key sticking in the ignition; airbag warning light stays lit; clicking or ticking heard after a cold startup; side window chipping; and tires that slowly go flat. **Crashworthiness:** NHTSA gave the STS four stars for frontal and side protection and five stars for rollover resistance.

SRX

RATING: Below Average. During the first year following the 2010 redesign, the SRX will likely be more glitch-prone than ever. Base models are front-drive, while Luxury versions include all-wheel drive; both are powered by a 3.0L 265 hp V6 hooked to a 6-speed automatic transmission, with a maximum towing capacity of 3,500 pounds. Available safety features include ABS, traction control, anti-skid system, side curtain airbags, and front side airbags. Optional safety features include steering-linked headlights and adjustable pedals. Alternative vehicles are the Lexus RX or Acura RDX. **Price:** $41,575 for the base FWD; $47,175 for the entry-level AWD. Prices are negotiable, but they are firming up due to solid sales. **Strong points:** Good handling and a quiet interior. **Weak points:** Overpriced; quickly loses resale value; insufficient rear passenger room; poor fit and finish; costly, dealer-dependent servicing; and suspension may be too firm for some. Slow acceleration; the AWD model is slower to accelerate than the rear-drive, and the transmission often hesitates before downshifting. Owners report the following safety related glitches, no doubt related to the SRX's redesign: chronic stalling, where the vehicle then proceeds to roll downhill; electrical malfunctions that knock out instruments and gauges as the car automatically switches to Neutral; automatic transmission sticks in low gear (vehicle has to be brought to a stop and restarted); hood release is located too close to driver's left foot; brakes grind as pressure is slowly lifted off the brake pedal; hard to get a spare tire:

> Cadillac refuses to allow me to order a new 2010 SRX with a spare tire. The car comes standard with a can of fix-a-flat type solution to fix your tire. However if the fix-a-flat solution cannot fix the hole, you are stranded on the highway until you can buy a new tire. The only way to get a spare tire on a new SRX is if it is a fleet purchase (e.g. rental car companies). It is impossible to believe that a car manufacturer can refuse to offer a spare tire as an option on a new car. This is totally a safety issue and should be illegal. Please help me with this bizarre and almost unbelievable situation.

Crashworthiness: NHTSA has given its five-star rating for front and side crash protection; rollover resistance received four stars.

Aveo

RATING: Below Average. **Price:** $14,150–$16,850 (soft). **Strong points:** Parts are plentiful and repairs aren't dealer-dependent. **Weak points:** Depreciation is so rapid that a 2009 model that sold for $13,970 is now worth only $8,000. Worse is the car's poor reliability; almost every component has come up short. So, without adequate quality control and providing only mediocre highway performance, this Daewoo/Chevrolet is no bargain, despite its low price. Specific component failures include the powertrain and the fuel and electrical systems, and the vehicle has atrocious fit and finish. **Crashworthiness:** Better-than-average occupant protection.

Cruze

RATING: Not Recommended during its first year on the market. Remember, the Daewoo-engineered Cruze is brought to you by the same quality-challenged company that made the unimpressive Aveo (with Chevrolet), the Reno and Forenza (with Suzuki), and the gone-but-not-lamented Pontiac LeMans (all on its own). Ah, the memories. Chevrolet's Cruze started production in July 2010, replacing the Chevrolet Cobalt and Pontiac's G5. The Ohio-built front-drive 2011 Cruze is powered by a 1.8L 138 hp 4-cylinder engine; a supposedly more frugal 1.4L 138 hp turbocharged four is also available. Either engine can be hooked to a 6-speed manual or a 6-speed optional automatic transmission. Some good alternative models are the Ford Focus or Fiesta, Honda Civic or Fit, Hyundai Accent, Mazda2 (after it has been on the market a while), or VW Jetta (with a manual transmission). Why not a Toyota Corolla? Too many reported safety- and performance-related deficiencies. **Price:** *LS manual 6-speed: $14,995; LT automatic 6-speed: $19,495; LTZ automatic 6-speed: $24,780—*making the Ford Focus and

Honda Civic more-credible alternatives. **Strong points:** A peppy, smooth, and efficient turbocharged engine; good steering and handling; a large trunk; quiet cabin; good ride quality; and comfortable front seats. According to the U.S. Environmental Protection Agency, highway/city fuel economy for the base and turbocharged engines are as follows: *1.8L manual:* 36/26 mpg; *Auto.:* 35/22 mpg; *1.4L turbo auto.:* 36/24 mpg. **Weak points:** Expect lots of first-year factory-related defects; fuel economy is not extraordinary; cramped rear seating with seat cushions set too low; limited storage area. **Crashworthiness:** Yet to be tested.

Equinox, Terrain

RATING: Above Average. Stay away from 2009 or earlier models; they perform poorly and tend to fall apart after three years. The redesigned 2010 Equinox was restyled and given more-powerful engines in addition to some other new features. With any luck, reliability has been improved as well. With seating for five, this four-door crossover SUV offers a choice of two engines: a base 2.4L 182 hp 4-cylinder and an optional 3.0L 264 hp V6. Both variants are teamed with a smooth-performing 6-speed automatic transmission, and front-drive and all-wheel drive are available with all models. The Honda CR-V, Hyundai Tucson, Subaru Forester, and Toyota RAV4 are worthy alternatives. **Price:** *Chevrolet Equinox:* $25,995–$34,995; *GMC Terrain:* $27,465–$35,755 (firm). **Strong points:** Most of the important safety devices are standard (traction control, an anti-skid system, front side airbags, and side curtain airbags). Other handy features include remote engine start, a navigation system, a wireless cell phone link, DVD entertainment, a hard drive for storing digital audio files, a rear-view camera, and a power liftgate. GMC's MultiFlex rear seat can be moved 20 cm (8 in.) fore and aft to better accommodate people and cargo. GMC's Terrain shares its basic design and powertrain with the Chevrolet Equinox. Besides a plethora of airbags, the Terrain also comes with ABS, traction control, and an anti-skid system. A rear-view camera is standard on all Terrain models. Thrilling acceleration with the V6 and manual transmission; the 4-cylinder engine and automatic gearbox are acceptable and fairly quiet; acceptable handling and braking combined with a comfortable ride. Plenty of passenger and cargo room; a quiet interior; well-laid out controls; very comfortable seating; and a smooth-performing, fuel-sipping manual drivetrain. **Weak points:** V6 fuel economy is below average, but is a fair trade-off for the extra power; the 4-cylinder engine comes up short when passing other vehicles or merging into traffic; some delayed downshifting with the V6, and handling is better with the Honda competition; tall head restraints cut rear visibility; the dash buttons all look the same; cheap-looking, easily scratched, and hard-to-keep-clean door panels and dash materials:

> The lower body molding detached from the front wheel opening, and then to the rear wheel opening. Driver's leg was cut as a consequence because the corners of the doors became extremely sharp.

I failed to check where the fuel fill door was located. It is on the righthand side of the vehicle which is the wrong side. It creates a safety hazard when getting fuel (getting out into station traffic, walking between cars, and being a longer distance from the driver's door when most people leave their keys in the car when fueling). The front doors are located so that I bump my head (I have cut my head) unless the seat is back as far as possible. GM has no retrofit to move fuel fill door or unit to put seats back to give more head room.

Overall reliability has been below average, with premature brake caliper and rotor replacements being the top issue. The suspension, electrical, and fuel systems have also been failure-prone, and fit and finish continue to get low marks. Some reports that the Check Engine light often comes on due to bad sensors. **Crashworthiness:** NHTSA gives the Equinox and its Terrain twin five stars for rollover resistance and frontal and side occupant protection.

Express, Savana

RATING: Recommended. These full-sized, rear-drive vans have been around forever. **Price:** *Express:* $31,460; *Savana:* $31,460 (soft). **Strong points:** An easily accessed, capacious van. With fuel prices going higher, they're turning into "blue-light specials" and are discounted by up to 30 percent. Both vans are perfect recession buys because any independent garage can repair them, and most of their reliability issues aren't expensive to correct. **Weak points:** Fuel-thirsty, mediocre handling, and water leaks. **Crashworthiness:** NHTSA gives the Express 1500 cargo van five stars for frontal protection; the 1500 passenger van gets five stars for frontal protection and three stars for rollover resistance. The 2500 and 3500 12-passenger vans and the 3500 15-passenger van earned three stars each for rollover resistance. But, as *Lemon-Aid* has reported before, 15-passenger vans can be killers due to their high propensity to roll over.

HHR

RATING: Below Average. The HHR (Heritage High Roof) is a mini version of GM's 1949 Suburban, but it's equipped with many of the latest safety, performance, and convenience features. This five-passenger crossover compact wagon uses GM's Cobalt/Pursuit platform and a 4-cylinder engine. HHR's entry-level LS and 1LT models use a 2.2L 155 hp 4-cylinder engine, while a 2.4L 172 hp 4-cylinder is optional with the 1LT and standard with the 2LT. The high-performance, turbocharged SS has a 2.0L 250–260 hp 4-cylinder engine. It's not offered with the panel model. A 5-speed manual transmission is standard and a 4-speed automatic is optional. **Price:** $20,395–$30,955 (soft). The HHR targets Chrysler's PT Cruiser ($24,495) with a price that's $4,000 less than the base Cruiser, though prices are heavily discounted on both models. GM's also going after commercial fleet sales with its similarly priced two-seat panel-truck version that comes with windowless side panels and rear cargo doors in place of the HHR's conventional rear doors. **Strong points:** Small-statured drivers moving from a minivan or SUV will appreciate the HHR's high seating position. There's also adequate rear legroom and storage space. Additionally, the vehicle's interior is easily accessed through wide-opening doors and easy-entry seats. On the road, the HHR handles quite well. Steering is accurate and responsive. **Weak points:** The HHR is clearly underpowered without the turbocharged engine option; the better-performing 2.4L powerplant makes passing and merging almost acceptable. GM recommends premium fuel for the 2.4L and turbocharged engines. Expect a bouncy ride; tire thump, engine buzz, and turbo whine; mushy brakes; thinly padded seats; and front seatbacks that are too upright for some. Panels have no rear seating. Drivers over 6 feet tall will likely find their heads grazing the headliner, especially if a sunroof is installed. The under-floor storage bins are too shallow. Thick pillars block the view fore and aft, especially on the windowless side panels. Forward view is impeded by the low roof design. Owners report electrical, suspension, and brake system failures in addition to a slap-dash fit and finish. These deficiencies are due partly to the HHR's use of failure-prone Cobalt-derived components. Alternative vehicles worth considering are the Chrysler PT Cruiser and the Honda Element. **Crashworthiness:** NHTSA gives the HHR five stars for frontal- and side-impact occupant protection; rollover protection scored four stars.

Orlando

RATING: Not Recommended during its first year on the market, particularly in view of GM's less-than-stellar history of bringing poor-quality European imports into Canada (I know, Ford and Chrysler did it, too) and then abandoning them and their owners. Whether you call the Orlando a crossover SUV or a minivan, the truth is that Chevrolet is all set to build an Opel-inspired seven-seat people mover; it will combine reasonable fuel economy with a minivan passenger load in much the same way as the Mazda5, Kia Rondo, and my old favourite, the long-gone, greatly lamented Nissan Axxess. Tagged as the Orlando, the 2012 Chevy variant will have bolder styling, but its basic layout and underpinnings will closely mirror the Opel Zafira, Chevrolet Cruze, and GM Volt. In GM's lineup, it will fit beneath the Chevy Traverse (a mid-sized crossover that shares GM's Lambda platform with the Buick Enclave), GMC Acadia, and Chevrolet Equinox and Terrain. **Price:** $22,000 (estimated). **Strong points:** Thanks to its European DNA, the Orlando will likely ride and handle well and be reasonably fuel-efficient. Its wheelbase will be about 3 inches longer than the Cruze's, and it will have wider front and rear tracks than the Cruze, giving buyers a larger interior. **Weak points:** Minivans equipped with small, fuel-saving engines do less for less. Merging and hill-climbing with a full load will be patience-building exercises. Reliability will probably also be below average during the Orlando's first year on the market. **Crashworthiness:** No crashworthiness data yet available.

Spark

RATING: Not Recommended during its first year on the market, especially because it's a Daewoo tadpole that's best used only in the city. The Spark is a front-drive four-door hatchback that's smaller than Chevy's Aveo subcompact. Since it's built by Daewoo, think of it as Aveo's smaller brother. Yikes! This minicar has been kicking around the world for many years since it replaced the Daewoo Matiz.

Price: $12,500 (estimated). **Strong points:** Light, direct steering is useful in the city; you can count on almost 50 mpg, no matter which engine you choose. **Weak points:** Accept the fact that this is a four-passenger urban econocar and you won't be disappointed. Five TV's *Fifth Gear* in Britain clocked the acceleration time for 0–100 km/h (0–62 mph) with the 1.0L and 1.2L engines. The results? 15.5 and 12.1 seconds, respectively, so bring along a good book. Some may find steering too light for highway driving; gear shifts are a bit clunky; a harsh ride when going over uneven terrain; and refinement isn't what the Spark is best known for. **Crashworthiness:** The Spark (called the Matiz in South Korea) received the maximum five stars in South Korea's KNCAP's frontal crash test, offset frontal crash test, and side crash test. It earned a four-star rating from the European New Car Assessment Program (Euro NCAP) in November 2009.

Honda

CR-Z Hybrid

RATING: Not Recommended during its first year on the market. Honda's other two hybrid models (the Insight and Civic Hybrid) are struggling, and one gets the impression that the CR-Z is targeting the wrong demographic. But if fuel prices in Canada break $1.50 a litre, all bets are off. The car is a sporty ("sporty" by hybrid standards, I suppose) two-passenger hybrid coupe equipped with a manual shifter; however, it doesn't come with the rev-happy performance we enjoyed with earlier sporty Honda models, like the little CRX. A spin-off from Honda's "born again" Insight, a car that was axed in 2006 and resurrected as a 2010 model, the CR-Z has a shorter wheelbase, shorter length, and wider front and rear tracks than its cousin. Nevertheless, the Insight DNA is found everywhere in this little coupe. It's equipped with a 122 hp 1.5L 4-cylinder engine and uses the same hybrid system as the Insight, which only manages to produce 98 horses with its 1.3L 4-banger. A 6-speed manual transmission is standard, and a continuously variable transmission (CVT) with steering wheel paddle shifters is optional. Drivers can dial in the car's highway performance electronically by choosing Sport, Normal, or Economy mode. As with the Insight, an electric motor is used to augment the gasoline engine. **Price:** $23,490 ($24,290 with the CVT), and $19,200 in the U.S. **Strong points:** Fuel-efficient: EPA mileage figures will be 36 mpg in the city and 38 mpg on the highway. With the manual gearbox, predicted mileage falls to 31 mpg in the city and—thanks to the CVT—37 mpg on the highway. **Weak points:** Factory glitches are more common during the first year of a new model's debut or of an existing model's redesign. The CR-Z fuel economy numbers aren't all that impressive if one considers that the 1990 Honda CRX HF got 47 miles to the gallon on the highway. Stylistically, this is not a pretty car. Its extremely short rear end and long front overhang are somewhat jarring, and the rear tail lights and liftgate window are Insight derivatives. The wheels need to be upsized to fill in the wheelwells. So much for the clean CRX lines from another era. **Crashworthiness:** No NHTSA or IIHS crash-test data is available yet.

Honda's other hybrids

Honda may drop both the Civic Hybrid and the Insight from its lineup in Canada, according to a report by *Monvolant*, a Quebec news source (*monvolant.cyberpresse. ca*). The two hybrids will be eliminated from the product plan—likely in response to rotten Canadian sales. This would then leave the new CR-Z as the only hybrid in Honda Canada's lineup.

When the Insight was re-launched with the 2010 model ($23,900 for the LX and $27,500 for the EX), Honda Canada projected sales of 10,000 units. But negative press reviews, a high retail price, and an improved Toyota Prius hammered Honda hybrid sales so badly that just 748 Insights were sold through the second quarter of 2010. Worse still, there were only 643 Civic Hybrids ($26,350) sold in Canada during the same period. Honda says it plans to keep both models "for the present" and encourages buyers to have faith in its hybrids and not listen to rumours that the cars will soon be gone. Yeah, like we had faith in the Insight just before the first time it was yanked off the market?

Toyota's Prius isn't doing all that well, either. With just 2,272 third-gen Prius models sold in Canada during the second quarter, the vehicle is far off its initial sales target. Analysts suggest that buyers are turning away from hybrids because they are too expensive in Canada, our country lacks a lot of large urbanized cities (Toronto, Vancouver, and Montreal being the major exceptions), and we have a colder climate that sabotages hybrid fuel economy. Hybrid batteries depend on a chemical reaction to both release energy to the electric drive motor and accept charge during regenerative braking. This reaction is severely hampered when the battery is cold, so the engine runs longer and more frequently. Also, the need to heat the cabin in cold weather requires that the engine operate for longer periods.

Jaguar and Land Rover

RATING: Not Recommended. Jaguar, like Volvo, has had one too many owners. Jaguar and Land Rover are owned and built by India's Tata Motors, who purchased the companies in March of 2008. The $2.3 billion (CDN) purchase price is about a third what Ford originally paid for the luxury brands. Nevertheless, Tata's "bargain" contributed to the company's first loss in eight years of $520 million (up to March 2009). Jaguar and Land Rover's unit share of the loss was $504 million. Since then, both companies have earned a total of over $400 million in profits—mostly from increased sales to China and Europe.

Jaguar

Jaguar's tattered image, resulting from poor quality, got a boost in this year's J.D. Power vehicle dependability survey, which gave the company high marks for quality control. For a brand that's dependably undependable, this was unexpected good news, inasmuch as quality snafus had plagued the first XF cars off the assembly line and sullied what should have been a triumphant comeback. Except for the redesigned XJ, Jaguar's 2011 models return to Canada relatively unchanged.

XF: A boring sedan with an underwhelming exterior. Ask yourself, is a fairly old, underpowered V8 preferable to a current V6 with power to spare? This will be a pivotal year that will decide whether Jaguar and Land Rover stay in business. If the company fails, forget about service and resale value. The XF is a smaller Jaguar that debuted in early 2008 and embodies a blunt-nose and swept-back-roofline style that is now incorporated into the XJ. A high-performance XFR model has been added. Base versions reprise the 4.2L 300 hp V8, while Premium models use a 5.0L 385 hp V8. Supercharged versions crank up the horsepower to 510. All use a 6-speed automatic transmission with a rotary knob for gear selection. **Price:** $61,800 for the entry-level Luxury model (a price that's very negotiable, considering the car depreciates $17,000 when it leaves the showroom) and $68,300 for the Premium. **Strong points:** The car has power to spare and a well-appointed cabin. **Weak points:** Front and rear room is limited; steering is too light; and reliability is still subpar, with the powertrain, electrical, and suspension systems causing the most grief. **Crashworthiness:** Crashworthiness hasn't been ascertained.

XJ: Jaguar's full-sized flagship sedan, the Premium XJ, was launched in June 2009. It has none of the classic Jaguar looks, nor has it been as glitch-ridden as the XF. The 2011 XJ went on sale in May 2010, boasting an all-aluminum body and a coupe-like restyling (complete with a glass panoramic roof) that gives the car a more-spacious and less-conservative look. The XJL replaces the Vanden Plas. Trim levels include the base XJ, a mid-level Supercharged, and a top-line Supersport, all using different variations of the 5.0L V8 engine. The base XJ and XJL have 385 hp, while the XJ Supercharged and XJL Supercharged have 470 hp. The XJ Supersport and XJL Supersport produce 510 hp and must be specially ordered. For more rear leg room, the XJ8L, Vanden Plas, and Vanden Plas Supercharged models are 5 inches longer than the XJ8 and supercharged XJR versions. **Price:** $88,000 for the base model (very soft) and $130,500 for the XJ Supersport. **Strong points:** XJs are powerful cars that have an "I've got money to burn" cachet that is inescapable. Lots of power to spare with the standard powertrain, and a well-appointed cabin. **Weak points:** The car's too dealer-dependent, loses value quicker than Air Canada, and will be left high and dry if the company goes under or is sold to another suitor (sigh!). Plus, the car is a gas-guzzler and has limited storage space. (Allo, Jeeves!) The best alternative is the fully equipped Acura RL, with its front-drive V6. You get a great ride, plenty of power, and lots of luxurious appointments. **Crashworthiness:** Crashworthiness hasn't been ascertained.

Land Rover

Land Rover sells four SUV models in Canada, all which return for 2011 with minimal changes. Although the 2011 LR2 returns unchanged, the 2010 LR3 was restyled and re-engineered and continues as the LR4, with a new 5.0L 375 hp V8 engine, a more-luxurious interior, and better handling. According to J.D. Powers' latest owner survey, Land Rover's 2010 models scored below average in the ranking of models for overall reliability. This isn't surprising to *Lemon-Aid*; Land

Rover has been a perennial bottom-feeder in quality surveys for the past several decades. Industry watchers say the company's poor reputation is the result of electronic glitches that followed the replacement of Land Rover's BMW-sourced engines with Jaguar engines during the 2006 model year. For example, the 2006 Range Rover adopted the Jaguar engine but retained the original BMW electrical architecture—a sure-fire recipe for trouble and a constantly lit Check Engine light.

LR2: This five-passenger SUV has all-wheel drive without a low-range gear for off-roading. The sole powertrain teams a 3.2L 230 hp 6-cylinder engine with a 6-speed automatic transmission. First launched as the Freelander, the car had so many failure-prone components that Land Rover "fixed" the name and changed it to the LR3, and then the LR2 in 2006. This year, the LR2 gets a slight facelift, a new instrument cluster, and upgraded leather upholstery (let me see: In India, cows are sacred, but Jaguar—now an Indian company—uses cows for leather seats... makes sense to me). **Price:** $44,950, but can be beaten down by 15 to 20 percent. **Strong points:** A comfortable but firm ride and good handling. **Weak points:** Overpriced for what you get; unable to maintain a reasonable resale value; little steering feedback; and brakes are hard to modulate. Unreliable, with a host of brake, electrical system, and powertrain problems. **Crashworthiness:** Not tested.

LR4: Cheaper than the original version introduced in 2005, this is an updated version of the previous LR3. It's a mid-sized, luxo-4×4 SUV that can seat up to seven people with the optional third row. The LR4 is equipped with an all-new 5.0L 375 hp V8, replacing the LR3's 4.4L 300 hp V8. The interior has also been updated with a new navigation system, Bluetooth wireless connectivity, and an iPod hook-up with the satellite radio. **Price:** $59,990.

Range Rover: The Range Rover flagship gets new styling and upgraded engines for 2010. The HSE has a new 5.0L 375 hp V8, and the top-of-the-line Supercharged model has a supercharged 5.0L 510 hp V8 hooked to a 6-speed automatic with manual shift gate as its lone transmission. **Price:** *Base:* $93,830; *Range Rover Sport:* $73,200; *Supercharged version:* $87,400. All of these prices can be negotiated down by 15 to 20 percent. **Strong points:** It's well-appointed and provides a comfortable ride. **Weak points:** On the minus side, the car is a way overpriced gas-guzzler that depreciates enormously the minute it leaves the showroom. Handling is mediocre, brakes are just acceptable, and quality control is atrocious. **Crashworthiness:** Not tested.

Mercedes-Benz

ML 350

RATING: Not Recommended. Consider this: The 2010 Mercedes-Benz M-Class ranked 8th out of 15 luxury midsize SUVs in the *U.S. News and World Report's* analysis of 64 published reviews and test drives—including a check of reliability and safety data. **Price:** $58,900 (ML350 BlueTEC)–$97,500 (ML63). Imagine spending that amount of money for an SUV that only places in the middle of the pack. By the way, these same two models can be found in the States for $50,490 and $92,590, respectively. **Strong points:** A luxurious interior; the ride is comfortable and quiet; handling is responsive and fairly predictable. Good off-road performance, despite the lack of a low-range gear. **Weak points:** 2011s are carried over practically unchanged and are way overpriced; incredibly poor quality control; the V6 is a competent but fuel-thirsty powerplant; the 7-speed shifter is poorly calibrated, leading to rough, jerky shifting; confusing controls (love those Germans: "Our customers aren't smart enough for our cars"); and the electronic column shifter can be mistakenly knocked into Neutral. **Crashworthiness:** NHTSA gives the M-Class five stars for front and side crash protection and four stars for rollover resistance, while the IIHS ranked the 2010 and 2011 M-Class "Good" for frontal offset, side, and head restraint protection.

Smart

RATING: Below Average; this subcompact is highly dealer-dependent and seriously outclassed by the Ford Focus and Fiesta, Honda Fit, Hyundai Accent, Mazda2, and Nissan Versa. As things stand right now in the States, the Smart is an automotive orphan placed in the American-based Penske Child Care Centre. An all-electric Smart, expected in late 2010, will cost $35,000 (U.S.)—almost $10,000 less than the GM Volt gas/electric car. **Price**: *Fortwo Coupe:* $14,990; *Passion:* $18,250; *BRABUS:* $21,900; *BRABUS Cabriolet:* $21,250. **Strong points:** Once the car gets up to highway speeds (which may seem like it takes forever), it manages to keep up with traffic; fuel-frugal; highly practical for city driving and parking; good short-term reliability reports; slow depreciation; distinctive styling; its engine bay isn't as crammed as many small cars' often are; responsive steering and transmission performance; and the ride is almost comfortable, thanks to well-bolstered seats, a longer wheelbase, and a wide track. Standard stability control, side airbags, and ABS. Sold in most of Canada's roughly 45 Mercedes-Benz dealerships, with a 4-year/80,000 km all-inclusive warranty. **Weak points:** You pay a maxi price for a mini vehicle that's less refined than cheaper Honda, Hyundai, Kia, Nissan, Suzuki, or Toyota minicars; dealer-dependent servicing (trips must be planned carefully for servicing accessibility); slow acceleration from a stop; the automated manual shifter is annoyingly slow and rough; and you must use premium fuel. **Crashworthiness:** NHTSA gives the 2010 Smart four stars for frontal collision occupant protection, five stars for side protection, and three stars for rollover resistance. It also received "Good" ratings for front offset, side, and rear crash protection in IIHS tests.

Mazda

Mazda2

RATING: Not Recommended during its first year on the market. This subcompact five-seater (really, it's a four-seater) only comes as a four-door hatchback equipped with a 100 hp 1.5L 4-cylinder engine. The engine can be paired to either a 4-speed automatic transmission or a 5-speed manual gearbox. A success in Europe where it was known as the Demio, the Mazda2—like the Honda Fit (Jazz)—has proven itself in other countries. **Price**: *GX:* $13,995; *GS:* $18,195; *Yozora (night sky):* $19,280. **Strong points:** Roomier in the rear than the Ford Fiesta and costs less. Highway/city fuel economy is quite good: *Man.:* 5.6 /7.2 L/100 km, 50/39 mpg; *Auto.:* 5.8 /7.3 L/100 km, 49/39 mpg. Highway and city driving is a breeze due to the car's superb handling and comfortable ride. Mazda's new vehicle launches have produced fewer first-year factory defects than Detroit-based and some Japanese and South Korean automakers like Nissan, Toyota, Daewoo/GM, and Kia. The 2008 Mazda2 garnered the highest rating of five stars for adult protection, a class-leading four stars for child protection, and a respectable two stars for pedestrian protection from the EuroNCAP ADAC-administered crash testing. Standard safety features include electronic stability control and curtain airbags. **Weak points:** Slow when carrying a full load; interior is rather Spartan when compared with the competition. **Crashworthiness:** No crash-test data on the American model, yet.

Nissan

Cube

RATING: Above Average. This is the five-passenger front-drive's third year on the Canadian market, and so far it has proven to be a reliable, though odd-looking, small car. The Cube is essentially a box on wheels that has plenty of room, but no personality. It is ugly stylistically and induces a feeling of instant claustrophobia. No changes are expected for 2011 to this 1.8L 122 hp 4-cylinder-powered people-mover. **Price:** *Cube S:* $17,398; *Auto.:* $18,698; *SL:* $20,898; *Krom Edition:* $23,098. **Strong points:** The small number of complaints posted by NHTSA is surprising considering Nissan's history of churning out new and redesigned models before they have been "debugged." The 2005 Quest minivan leaps to mind as an example. In a comparison with the Kia Soul, the Cube is a better buy. Although the Kia is cheaper, neither the ride nor the handling can touch the Nissan. Then add in the fact that the Cube has been proven in other countries (it's in its third generation) and offers a high level of reliability/quality. Finally, Kia's reliability on some models is mediocre on a good day, and first-year Kias are notoriously glitch-prone. As for the initial cash savings with the Soul, they will be wiped out by the Kia's higher rate of depreciation. For example, a 2010 Soul that once sold for $15,500 is now worth about $10,500; the same model-oyear Cube that sold originally for $17,398 has a resale value of almost $14,500. **Weak points:** Esthetically, can you live with a car that stirs up strong feelings of like and dislike? Also, it's difficult to adjust the sideview mirrors while driving because they are mounted so low, and the instrument panel dims when the windshield wipers are activated. Some safety-related incidents recorded by NHTSA involve poor quality headlight lenses:

> The head light lenses on our new Nissan Cube were hazed over on both sides of the car. I took it back to the dealer and they were replaced at no cost. The issue is that the replacement head lights are worse than the ones replaced.

Crashworthiness: Ratings have been quite positive. NHTSA gave the Cube five stars for side crash protection and four stars for frontal crashworthiness and rollover resistance. IIHS awarded the Cube "Good" marks in frontal offset, side, and rear occupant protection.

Juke

RATING: Not Recommended during the Juke's first year on the market. An all-new 2011 model, this funky-looking small wagon crossover makes no attempt to blend into the crowd; it also makes no attempt to provide an outstanding driving experience or offer good fuel economy, unlike the Mini Cooper. No, the Juke takes a cheap shot and targets young consumers who want a well-performing car with a unique look that will be a conversation starter and an attention-getter. *Car and Driver* believes the car's unique styling resembles a frog. Others say it looks like a crocodile. Esthetics aside, many reviewers feel this little econobox that shares the Versa and Cube's B-platform offers a lot of features at a reasonable cost. This front-drive, five-door compact crossover uses a direct-injection, turbocharged 188 hp 1.6L 4-cylinder engine coupled to a 6-speed manual or hooked to an optional CVT automatic transmission. All-wheel drives use only an automatic shifter that splits engine power 50/50 between the front and rear wheels or the left and right sides. **Price:** *SV FWD:* $19,998; *Auto.:* $21,298; *SV AWD auto.:* $23,098; *SL FWD:* $23,548; *SL FWD auto.:* $24,848; *SL AWD auto.:* $26,648. **Strong points:** A reasonable front-drive price, without much difference in pricing between Canada and the States; excellent acceleration (hitting 62 km/h in 7.5 seconds—over a second quicker than the Honda CR-V); agile, with steering that is quick and sensitive; a comfortable ride; decent seating in front and back, complemented by reasonable storage space; a well-appointed interior; and a dashboard that changes colours (cool, or contrived?). **Weak points:** Styling is weird (*autoblog.com* says it has a "Baby Predator" front end), and traction is quickly lost in fast starts or on wet highways. A recommended optional "integrated control" system can render the car less unstable by uniformly setting the throttle, transmission, and steering response settings to Normal, Sport, or Eco modes. The U.S. EPA says gas consumption figures for the manual-equipped Juke are 24 mpg in the city and 31 mpg on the highway. Auto reviewers say spirited driving will lower the figure to about 21 mpg. Rear seatroom is decidedly on the skimpy side, meaning anyone over six feet will feel cramped. Reliability will be a problem during the first year, judging by the quality problems seen with Nissan's other first-year vehicles. **Crashworthiness:** An unknown, inasmuch as neither the NHTSA nor the IIHS has crash-tested the car.

Leaf

RATING: Not Recommended buy during its first year on the Canadian market, which is expected to start in January 2012. Nissan's first all-electric car (no, it doesn't have a tailpipe). **Price:** No Canadian price has been given out, but the car sells for $33,600 in the States, minus a $7,500 federal rebate. If it sells for the same price in Canada, the Leaf will likely cost about $5,600 more than the $28,000 Prius and $7,400 less than the $41,000 Chevrolet Volt. Incidentally, the list price doesn't include freight and preparation charges for any of the above cars. **Strong points:** Good acceleration in city traffic; comfortable seats, with an interior about the size of a Toyota Prius; quiet running; great navigation feature that computes how far you can travel on a map of where you are. **Weak points:** Lethargic steering, excessive leaning when cornering, and a few *ahem* electrical problems (BZZT! Cue the shorts, sparking, smoke, and flames!). The Leaf is advertised as being able to travel up to 160 kilometres without stopping to recharge—a process the automaker tells us would normally take "only" eight hours on a 220-volt circuit (wink, wink; nudge, nudge). But, just after reassuring us with the above claims, Nissan then adds this caveat (i.e., don't believe what we just said): "Battery capacity decreases with time and use. Actual range will vary depending upon driving/charging habits, speed, conditions, weather, temperature, and battery age." Age, weather, temperature, speed? Yikes!

NV

RATING: Not Recommended during its first year on the market. The all-new 2011 NV (Nissan Van) represents the automaker's first attempt at breaking into the lucrative full-sized commercial van market monopolized by Ford and General Motors. Built in Canton, Mississippi, the NVs are found in three formats, similar to what we see with the two Detroit-based automakers: the NV 1500, 2500, and 3500. There are two engines available: a 4.0L V6 and a 5.6L V8, both coupled to a 5-speed automatic transmission. Standard features include 17-inch steel wheels, fold-down passenger seatback, flat cargo floor, wide-coverage cargo area lighting system, water-repellent fabric on main seating surfaces, multifunction front layout and storage, multiple power outlets, cargo area side metal inner panels, multiple weld-nut attachment points for shelving and rack systems, recessed tie-down rings, sliding passenger-side door, and wide-opening front and rear doors. **Price:** Not available; Nissan now plans to sell these vans as 2012 models, sometime early next year. **Strong points:** These vans combine convenience and utility, as well as roominess and comfort; a truck-like driving position; plenty of headroom and legroom; no engine "dog house" that intrudes into the cab due to the set-back engine placement; wide front doors for easy entry and exit; bucket seating; availability of an optional taller roof; rear drive simplicity and durability; large armrests; and the 2500 and 3500 versions can be ordered with a high roof that includes a large overhead console. Lots of storage space; the under seat drawer, for example, fits small tools, stationery, or first aid kits, while the deep door pockets fit flashlights, legal-sized binders, and clipboards. There's a full-length cargo area inner panel to protect the outer walls from dents and dings from the inside, and there are multiple weld-nut attachment points for shelving and racks—again, requiring no sheet metal drilling. In addition, the NV's nearly vertical sidewalls maximize the usable cargo space, accommodating common aftermarket storage systems, as well as a bulkhead behind the driver. You'll also find a range of cargo area tie-down rings and ample cargo area lighting. From the seats forward, the NV looks, acts, and feels like a pickup. You don't have to take apart the interior to access the engine and you don't have to worry about tucking your work boots into a cramped footwell. The U.S. EPA says gas consumption figures should average 21 mpg on a good day. **Weak points:** Since it is so new to the market, factory-related defects will likely be a problem and servicing will be slow due to back-ordered parts and the mechanics' lack of familiarity with this new model. **Crashworthiness:** No crashworthiness data yet.

370Z, GT-R

RATING: Recommended. Nissan does have a couple of sports cars that are worth considering, although they have yet to be crash-tested. The 370Z is available as a $40,498 coupe or a $46,998 roadster. Is either model worth the price? Yes, both are excellent alternatives to the Chevrolet Corvette, which costs much more. The Nissan GT-R ($98,900) is the first AWD sports car to be fitted with an independent rear axle and is powered by a 485 hp twin-turbo V6.

Porsche

Now owned by Volkswagen, Porsche has also just come off one of its worst years ever. There are five Porsches to choose from: the entry-level Boxster, the 911, the Cayenne, the Cayman, and the newest addition, the Panamera.

RATING: *Boxster:* Below Average; *911, Cayenne, Cayman, and Panamera:* Not Recommended. Of these five cars, the 911, Cayenne, and Cayman owe their low rating to their high frequency of repair scores and greater need for dealer servicing. The Panamera is too new to the market to recommend. **Price:** *Boxster:* $59,600–$72,900; *911:* $96,700–$117,301; *Cayenne:* $56,700–$152,200; *Cayman:* $65,300–$77,500; *Panamera:* $115,100–$137,550. Shop in the States and you will see savings of up to $40,000 (CDN). Porsche was forced to cut its Canadian prices by almost 10 percent when the Canadian dollar increased value in September 2007. Now that the dollar is stronger once again, look for further price cuts. Adroit haggling should get you 20 percent off the suggested retail price. **Strong points:**

A legendary racing cachet and excellent road manners. **Weak points:** Outrageously overpriced and a source of worry regarding service, repairs, theft, depreciation, high insurance costs, and premature wear and tear from cold and snow. Recent consumer complaints show that even the entry-level Boxster hasn't escaped the typical Porsche factory-induced defects affecting the engine, transmission, electrical system, brakes, and fit and finish. On the 911 and Cayenne, the powertrain, climate system, suspension, and fit and finish should be your main concerns. Making the reliability failings hurt more is the company's attitude that its cars are perfect, and what problems do occur are caused mainly by "driver abuse." Much to most owners' surprise and contrary to what Porsche dealers will tell you, Porsches *do* depreciate quickly. For example, a 2009 Boxster that originally sold for $58,400 is now worth about $45,000. All of the other Porsche models also lose much of their value during the first few years they are on the road. **Crashworthiness:** Not tested.

Saab

RATING: Not Recommended. This includes the 9-3, 9-5, and 9-7X AWD. Saab prices for Canada are almost unobtainable; dealers are in turmoil and tell me they don't know what awaits them; parts can be hard to find—they could be anywhere between Sweden, the States, and Oshawa; and depreciation is cataclysmic. All three models suffer from an abundance of defective components that imperil the cars' reliability and your own financial solvency. Be especially wary of powertrain, electrical, and fuel system breakdowns; brake failures; and poor fit and finish. **Crashworthiness:** NHTSA has given the 9-3 four stars for frontal crashworthiness and rollover resistance; side crash protection was awarded five stars. The 9-5 and 9-7X AWD remain untested by NHTSA. IIHS rated the 9-3's frontal offset, side, and rear crash protection as "Good." The 9-5's frontal offset crash protection was given a "Good" rating and side impact protection scored "Average." Head restraints were rated "Average." The 9-7X models got the worst scores among the Saabs tested by the IIHS; frontal offset protection was given an "Average," side crashworthiness was judged to be "Marginal," and restraints were rated "Poor."

Suzuki

Kizashi

RATING: Below Average. This mid-sized front-drive is "more sizzle than steak" and offers nothing exceptional for a $30,000 Suzuki. With Suzuki's precarious financial underpinnings, now is not the time to take a chance on a new design that's only been on the market since March 2010 and is built by a small company struggling to survive. What'll be new for 2011? A sporty "S" model with enhanced steering, and a specially tuned suspension and chassis for sportier performance. Buyers also get a different front bumper, revised grille, side skirts, chrome trim, rear spoiler, and alloy wheels. This front-drive, five-door compact crossover comes with a 180 hp

2.4L 4-cylinder engine coupled to a 6-speed manual. The all-wheel-drive SX version carries the same engine hooked to a continuously variable transmission (CVT). Highway/city fuel economy is 6.8/9.3 L/100 km, 42/30 mpg. **Price:** *S FWD:* $27,000; *Sport FWD:* $28,500; *SX AWD:* $29,995. Some good alternatives: the Acura TSX ($33,000) or the Subaru Legacy (*2.5i Sedan:* $24,000; *Sedan Sport:* $28,000). **Strong points:** The Kizashi is a relatively well-equipped family sedan with standard electronic stability control. Handling is better than average, especially with the Sport model's precise steering. The trunk has a useful pass-through to the folded rear seats. A perusal of NHTSA owner-safety complaints and Suzuki's internal service bulletins shows no evidence of any quality problems. **Weak points:** Insufficient power, a firm ride, and a narrow interior that's invaded by engine noise (especially with the Sport version). And speaking of the "sportier" Sport model, since when do a spoiler and five more horses (185) make a sports car? Furthermore, the 6-speed manual's long throws are annoying and the "gentle" gearing favours fuel economy more that a sporty driving experience. The sunroof cuts into headroom, and rear seating is cramped. The 18-inch tires rumble on some road surfaces. **Crashworthiness:** NHTSA gives the car its top, five-star rating for front and side crashworthiness; four stars were awarded for rollover resistance. IIHS rated head restraints as "Good" and roof crashworthiness (a new category) as "Acceptable."

Toyota

FJ Cruiser

RATING: Recommended. The Cruiser takes its inspiration from the Toyota FJ40 Land Cruiser, built between 1956 and 1983. **Price:** $31,900–$37,500. Its prices are negotiable. It is powered by a competent 4.0L 239 hp V6 that can be used for either two- or four-wheel drive. A 5-speed automatic transmission comes with both versions, and a 6-speed manual gearbox is available with the all-wheel drive. **Strong points:** The Cruiser competes especially well off-road against the 2010 Ford Escape, Honda Element, Jeep Liberty or Wrangler, and Nissan Xterra. Although the FJ's turning circle is about 1.5 m (5 ft.), larger than those of similar-sized SUVs, off-roading should be a breeze if done carefully, thanks to standard electronic stability control, short overhangs, and better-than-average ground clearance. **Weak points:** The rear side doors are taken from the Honda Element, which means rear and side visibility are severely limited. There is also some side-wind vulnerability, and annoying wind noises are generated by the large side mirrors. Although touted as a five-passenger conveyance, a normal-sized fifth passenger in the back seat won't be comfortable. Plus, the rear seats are hard to access, forcing front occupants to unbuckle every time a rear occupant gets in or out. Front-seat headrests may be uncomfortably positioned for short occupants. Another minus is that premium fuel must be used. **Crashworthiness:** Interestingly, NHTSA crashworthiness scores for front and side impacts are five stars; however, rollover protection merits only three stars. This is disappointing and is almost never seen with vehicles that are equipped with electronic stability control.

Volkswagen

The "new" New Beetle

RATING: Not Recommended. Remember when Coca-Cola came out with their new Coca-Cola and buyers rebelled, forcing the bottler to retreat back to a "new" new Coca-Cola renamed "Classic"? That's what will likely happen with what VW calls its "new" New Beetle. For 2011, Volkswagen has taken the familiar Beetle design and literally flattened it to increase cabin and cargo space and add 3.5 inches to the car's length. We'll also see a more upright windshield, a wider track, and a reduced front overhang this year. **Price:** *Hatchback:* $24,175; *Convertible:* $29,175. **Strong points:** Competent 5-cylinder engine; easy handling; a sure-footed and comfortable, though firm, ride; impressive braking; standard traction and stability control; most instruments and controls are user-friendly; comfortable and supportive front seats with plenty of headroom and legroom up front; cargo area that can be expanded by folding down the seats; upgraded head-protecting airbags and front head restraints. **Weak points:** The noisy 2.5L engine doesn't excite; serious safety defects reported by owners; diesel engine fuel economy is good, but not as good as VW claims; easily buffeted by crosswinds; large head restraints and large front roof pillars obstruct front visibility; limited rear legroom and headroom; and skimpy interior storage and trunk space. The car's below average reliability will probably worsen as the "new" New Beetle works out its "new" redesign kinks. **Crashworthiness:** NHTSA gives the 2010 models five stars for side occupant crash protection and four stars for frontal and rollover protection. Interestingly, rear-seat passengers would not do as well in a side collision: The five-star side rating for front-seat passengers drops to only three stars for rear-seat occupants. Something to think about. IIHS gives the 2010 New Beetle a "Good" rating for frontal offset crash protection and head restraint effectiveness, but cites side crashworthiness as "Poor."

Routan

RATING: Not Recommended. A Chrysler minivan cousin with a German accent, the Routan is a seven-seat spin-off of the RT platform used by the Chrysler Town & Country and Dodge Grand Caravan. 2010 was its last model year in Canada. It was manufactured in Windsor, Ontario, alongside Chrysler's minivans and featured revised styling and firmer suspension tuning. **Price:** $28,075–$50,575 (very soft). **Strong points:** A tauter suspension and an interior that's plusher than what Chrysler offers. The 251-hp 4.0L V6 is a good performer and the van provides a comfortable ride. The cabin is also relatively quiet. **Weak points:** On the Canadian market for only two model years (2009 and 2010). Depreciation? A 2009 top-of-the-line $50,000 Execline is now worth about $30,000. If you are offered a Routan at a ridiculously low price, run—don't walk—away; it has all of the Caravan's problems without the warranty or servicing backup. Some of the more common safety complaints concern transmission failures, which means the transmission locks up in traffic; a poorly designed backup camera; unsafe child safety seat positioning; a power sliding door that can crush a child's hand; and unsafe power-assisted rear seats. **Crashworthiness:** NHTSA gives the Routan five stars for front and side crashworthiness and four stars for rollover resistance.

Touareg 2

RATING: Not Recommended; wait for the cheaper and more fuel-efficient second-series 2011 model. **Price:** $45,300–$61,800 (very soft). A redesigned 2011 Touareg is expected in late 2010. Early reports say it will shed some weight for better fuel economy, cost about $5,000 to $10,000 less than the Touareg 2, offer third-row seating, and make available an optional gas/electric hybrid powertrain. **Strong points:** Volkswagen's second-generation, mid-sized 2010 Touareg comes with lots of style, a plush and comfortable cabin, and some of the most impressive off-road capabilities in its class. **Weak points:** For those benefits, you pay an outrageously high price to get an SUV that doesn't offer third-row seating, has a pitifully poor reliability record, and has sky-high maintenance costs. As a quintessential lemon, its problem areas include the powertrain, fuel, and electrical systems; brakes; and fit and finish. **Crashworthiness:** NHTSA gives the Touareg five stars for front and side crashworthiness and four stars for rollover resistance.

Volvo

Volvo has always distinguished itself from the rest of the automotive pack through its much-vaunted standard safety features, crashworthiness, and engineering that emphasized function over style. But unfortunately, these noteworthy features were eclipsed by bland styling, ponderous highway performance, inconsistent quality control that compromised long-term reliability and drove up ownership costs, and chancy servicing by a small dealer network.

Asian automakers have successfully encroached on Volvo territory by bringing out new products in smaller packages: cars that are as safe and comfortable as Volvos to drive, with greater reliability and servicing support thrown in. Granted, several years ago Volvo met the Asian competition by dramatically restyling its cars and cranking up their performance capabilities by several notches. It dumped its boxy station wagons and rediscovered rounded edges, all-wheel drive, and high-performance powertrains and handling. The automaker's curvy AWD XC models were the latest examples of a mindset change that might have turned the company around.

But all this was too little, too late.

Now, after Ford's purchase of the automaker over a decade ago, and after having suffered through Ford's "benign neglect," Volvo has new owners from China who bought the company in early 2010 for 30 cents on the dollar. Sadly, the new owners are relatively inexperienced in manufacturing and marketing vehicles in North America, so don't expect much of a turn-around for the once proud and innovative Swedish automaker.

Volvo's Swedish lineage was diluted by Ford's ownership of the company, and the Chinese takeover will annihilate what's left of the Volvo legacy. Innovation and product improvements will be starved from underfunding, and quality control will continue to decline because the Beijing mindset will be to "move the metal" and worry about quality after gaining market share (also called TQSD: Toyota Quality Decline Syndrome). Furthermore, additional performance features have priced most Volvos out of the reach of the average car buyer and made the cars almost impossible to service by the average mechanic. And when a defective part is found, its replacement may be back ordered for weeks—if it can be found at all.

And add in the increased complexity of those 2011 models that have been redesigned (like the S60) or restyled (like the C70 and C30). The S60 has been restyled and given 43 more horses with its new 3.0L turbocharged 6-cylinder engine hooked to a 6-speed automatic transmission. It also has a new standard safety feature called the Pedestrian Detection with Full Auto Brake. It uses sensors to detect pedestrians who might step in front of the vehicle. If this happens, the system can apply full braking force at speeds up to 35 km/h. Imagine what fun the Chinese will have tinkering with this feature, and the excitement drivers will feel when their car suddenly comes to a screeching stop for what may be a non-existent person.

Recession-ravaged dealers have lost confidence in Volvo and don't have the money to invest in a well-stocked parts inventory. Also, loyal Volvo customers have lost confidence in a brand they once believed in; they don't want to buy a car that can't be service and can't be sold.

In the meantime, Volvo dealers are closing their doors, mechanics have turned off the lights, and Volvo owners have fewer places that will service their cars or honour their warranties.

Bottom line: Don't buy any Volvo until we see where the company's headed.

Some Final Precautions

Here's how to check out a new or used vehicle without a lot of hassle. But if you are deceived by a seller despite your best efforts, don't despair. As discussed in Part Two, Canadian federal and provincial laws dish out harsh penalties to new- and used-car dealers who hide or embellish important facts. Ontario's *Consumer Protection Act* (*www.e-laws.gov.on.ca/html/statutes/english/elaws_statutes_02c30_e.htm*), for example, lets consumers cancel a contract within one year of entering into an agreement if a seller makes a false, misleading, deceptive, or unconscionable representation. This includes using exaggeration, innuendo, or ambiguity about a material fact, or failing to state a material fact, if such use or failure deceives or tends to deceive.

Just keep in mind the following points:

- Dealers are *presumed* to know the history, quality, and true performance of what they sell.
- Even details like a vehicle's fuel economy can lead to a contract's cancellation if the dealer gave a higher-than-accurate figure. In *Sidney v. 1011067 Ontario Inc. (c.o.b. Southside Motors)* 15, the plaintiff was awarded $11,424.51 plus prejudgment interest. The plaintiff claimed the defendant advised him that the vehicle had a fuel efficiency of 800–900 km per tank of fuel when, in fact, the maximum efficiency was only 500 km per tank.

A Check-Up Checklist

Now, let's assume you're dealing with an honest seller and have chosen a vehicle that's priced right and seems to meet your needs. Take some time to assess its interior, its exterior, and its highway performance with the checklist below. If you're buying from a dealer, ask to take the vehicle home overnight in order to drive it over the same roads you use in your daily activities. Of course, if you're buying privately, it's doubtful that you'll get the vehicle for an overnight test—you may have to rent a similar one from a dealer or rental agency.

Safety Check

1. Is the vehicle equipped with electronic stability control and full-torso side airbags, and has it earned a high crashworthiness ranking? Remember, a study by the Insurance Institute for Highway Safety found side airbags that include head protection cut a driver's risk of death almost in half for driver's side collisions. Another study of theirs concluded that electronic stability control reduces the risk of fatal single-vehicle crashes by more than half.
2. Is outward visibility good in all directions?
3. Are there large blind spots, like ones created by side pillars, impeding vision?
4. Are the mirrors large enough for good side and rear views? Do they block your view or vibrate?
5. Are all instrument displays clearly visible (not washed out in sunlight)? Is there daytime or nighttime dash glare on the windshield? Are the controls easy to reach?
6. Are the handbrake and hood release easy to reach and use? Will the handbrake hold the vehicle on a hill?
7. Does the front seat have sufficient rearward travel to put you at a safe distance from the airbag's deployment (about 30 cm/12 in.) and still allow you to reach the brake and accelerator pedals? Are the brake and accelerator pedals adjustable? Are they spaced far enough apart?
8. Are the head restraints adjustable or non-adjustable? (The latter is better if you often forget to set them.) Do they push your chin into your chest?
9. Are the head restraints designed to permit rear visibility? (Some are annoyingly obtrusive.)
10. Are there rear three-point shoulder belts, similar to those on the front seats?
11. Is the seat belt latch plate easy to find and reach?

12. Does the seat belt fit comfortably across your chest, release easily, retract smoothly, and use pretensioners for maximum effectiveness?
13. Are there user-friendly child-seat anchor locations?
14. Does the automatic side sliding door latch securely, and does it immediately stop when encountering an object as it opens or closes?
15. Do the rear windows roll only halfway down? When they are down, are your ears assailed by booming wind noise? Does it cause the vehicle to vibrate excessively?

Exterior Check

Rust

Cosmetic rusting (rear hatch, exhaust system, front hood, door jamb) isn't unusual on new cars that have been on the dealer's lot for some time. Minor rusting is acceptable and can even help push the price way down, as long as the chassis and other major structural members aren't affected.

Knock gently on the front fenders, door bottoms, rear wheelwells, and rear doors—places where rust usually occurs first. Even if these areas have been repaired with plastic, lead, metal plates, or fibreglass, once rusting starts, it's difficult to stop. Use a small magnet to check which body panels have been repaired with non-metallic body fillers.

Use a flashlight to check for exhaust system and suspension component rust-out. Make sure the catalytic converter is present. In the past, many drivers removed this pollution-control device in the mistaken belief that it would improve fuel economy. The police can fine you for not having the converter, and you'll be forced to buy one (for $400+) in order to certify your vehicle.

Tires

Be wary of tire brands that have poor durability records; NHTSA's *www.safercar.org* will show you tire complaints and recalls, while *www.tirerack.com* will give you grass-roots owner experiences. Stay away from the Firestone/Bridgestone tires sold with many new vehicles; their poor reliability histories nearly guarantee future problems. Look at tire wear for clues that the vehicle is out of alignment, needs suspension repairs, or has serious chassis problems. Getting an alignment and new shocks and springs is part of routine maintenance, and it's relatively inexpensive to do with aftermarket parts. However, if your vehicle is an AWD or the MacPherson struts have to be replaced, you're looking at a $1,000 repair bill.

Accident damage

Most new cars have some shipping damage. In British Columbia, all accidents involving more than $2,000 in repairs must be reported to subsequent buyers.

Here are some tips on what you can do to avoid buying a damaged new or used vehicle. First, ask the following questions about the vehicle's accident history:

- Has it ever been in an accident? Was there a claim for transport damage when the vehicle was shipped from the factory? Can you show me the PDI (pre-delivery inspection) sheet? Do you have a vehicle history file?
- What was the damage and who fixed it?
- Is there any warranty outstanding? Can I have a copy of the work order?
- Has the vehicle's certificate of title been labelled "salvage"? ("Salvage" means that an expert has determined that the cost to properly repair the vehicle is more than its value. This usually happens after the vehicle has been in a serious accident.)

If the vehicle has been in an accident, you should either walk away from the sale or have the vehicle checked by a qualified auto body expert. Remember, not all salvage vehicles are bad—properly repaired ones can be a safe and sound investment if the price is low enough.

What to look for

1. If the vehicle has been repainted recently, check the quality of the job by inspecting the engine and trunk compartments and the inside door panels. Do it on a clear day so that you'll see any waves in the paint.
2. Check the paint—do all of the vehicle's panels match?
3. Inspect the paint for tiny bubbles. They may identify a poor priming job or premature rust.
4. Is there paint overspray or primer in the door jambs, wheelwells, or engine compartment? These are signs that the vehicle has had body repairs.
5. Check the gaps between body panels—are they equal? Unequal gaps may indicate improper panel alignment or a bent frame.
6. Do the doors, hood, and rear hatch open and shut properly?
7. Have the bumpers been damaged or recently repaired? Check the bumper support struts for corrosion damage.
8. Test the shock absorbers by pushing hard on a corner of the vehicle. If it bounces around like a ship at sea, the shocks need replacing.
9. Look for signs of premature rust or displacement from a collision on the muffler and exhaust pipe.
10. Make sure there's a readily accessible spare tire as well as a jack and tools for changing a flat. Also look for premature rusting in the side wheelwells, and for water in the rear hatch channel.
11. Look at how the vehicle sits. If one side or end is higher than the other, it could mean that the suspension is defective.
12. Ask the seller to turn on the headlights (low and high beams), turn signals, parking lights, and emergency blinking lights, and to blow the horn. From the rear, check that the brake lights, backup lights, turn indicators, tail lights, and licence plate light all work.

Interior Check

New vehicles often have a few hundred kilometres on the clock; used vehicles should have 20,000 km per model year. Thus, a three-year-old vehicle would ordinarily have been driven about 60,000 kilometres. The number of kilometres on the odometer isn't as important as how well the vehicle was driven and maintained. Still, high-mileage vehicles depreciate rapidly because most people consider them to be risky buys. On new cars, a few thousand kilometres showing may indicate the car was used as a demonstrator or sold and then taken back. Be suspicious. With used cars, subtract from your offer about $200 for each additional 10,000 kilometres above the average the car shows. Confirm the odometer figure by checking the vehicle's maintenance records.

The condition of the interior will often give you an idea of how the vehicle was used and maintained. For example, sagging rear seats plus a front passenger seat in pristine condition indicate that your minivan may have been used as a minibus. Delivery vans will have the paint on the driver's doorsill rubbed down to the metal, while the passenger doorsill will look like new.

What to look for

1. Watch for excessive wear of the seats, dash, accelerator, brake pedal, armrests, and roof lining.
2. Check the dash and roof lining for radio or cellular phone mounting holes (as used in police cruisers, taxis, and delivery vans). Is the radio tuned to local stations? If the radio is tuned for out of town stations, it could be an out-of-province car with a checkered history. Ask for more documentation as to previous ownership.
3. Turn the steering wheel. Listen for unusual noises and watch for excessive play (more than 2.5 cm/1 in.).
4. Test the emergency brake with the vehicle parked on a hill.
5. Inspect the seat belts. Is the webbing in good condition? Do the belts retract easily?
6. Make sure that door latches and locks are in good working order. If rear doors have no handles or locks, or if they've just been installed, your minivan may have been used to transport prisoners.
7. Can the seats be moved into all of the positions intended by the manufacturer? Look under them to make sure that the runners are functioning as they should.
8. Can headrests be adjusted easily?
9. Peel back the rugs and check the metal floor for signs of rust or dampness.

Road Test

1. Start the vehicle and listen for unusual noises. Shift automatics into Park and manuals into Neutral with the handbrake engaged. Open the hood to check for fluid leaks. Do this test with the engine running and then repeat it 10 minutes after the engine has been shut down, following the completion of the test drive.

2. With the motor running, check out all controls, including the windshield wipers, heater and defroster, and radio.
3. If the engine stalls or races at idle, a simple adjustment may fix the trouble. But loud clanks or low oil pressure could mean potentially expensive repairs.
4. Check all ventilation systems. Do the rear side windows roll down? Are there excessive air leaks around the door handles?
5. While in Neutral, push down on the accelerator abruptly while paying attention to the colour of the exhaust smoke. Black exhaust smoke may require only a minor engine adjustment; blue smoke may signal the need for major engine repairs.
6. Shift an automatic into Drive with the motor still idling. The vehicle should creep forward slowly without stalling or speeding. Listen for unusual noises when the transmission is engaged. Manual transmissions should engage as soon as the clutch is released. Slipping or stalling could require a new clutch. While driving, make absolutely sure that a four-wheel drive can be engaged without unusual noises or hesitation.
7. Shift an automatic transmission into Drive. While the motor is idling, apply the emergency brake. If the motor isn't racing and the brake is in good condition, the vehicle should stop.
8. Accelerate to 50 km/h while slowly moving through all the gears. Listen for transmission noises. Step lightly on the brakes. The response should be immediate and equal for all wheels.
9. In a deserted parking lot, test the vehicle's steering and suspension by driving in figure eights at low speeds.
10. Make sure the road is clear of traffic and pedestrians. While driving at 30 km/h, take both hands off the steering wheel to see whether the vehicle veers from one side to the other. If it does, the alignment or suspension could be defective, or the vehicle could have been in an accident.
11. Test the suspension by driving over some rough terrain.
12. Stop at the foot of a small hill and then see if the vehicle can climb it without difficulty. Stop on a hill and see if the transmission holds the car in place without you giving it gas (a "hill-holder" feature).
13. On an expressway, it should take no longer than 20 seconds for most cars and minivans to accelerate from a standing start to 100 km/h.
14. Drive through a tunnel with the windows open. Try to detect any unusual motor, exhaust, or suspension sounds.
15. After the test drive, verify the performance of the automatic transmission by shifting from Drive to Neutral to Reverse. Listen for clunking sounds during transmission engagement.

Many of these tests will undoubtedly turn up some defects, which may be major or minor (new vehicles have an average of a half-dozen major and minor defects). Ask an independent mechanic for an estimate, and try to convince the seller to pay part of the repair bill if you buy the vehicle. Keep in mind that many 3- to 5-year-old vehicles with 60,000–100,000 km on their odometers run the risk of having an engine timing belt or timing chain failure that can cause several thousand dollars' worth of repairs. If the timing belt or chain hasn't been replaced, plan to do it and deduct about $300 from the purchase price for the repair.

It's important to eliminate as many duds as possible through your own cursory check, since you'll later invest two hours and about $100 for a thorough mechanical inspection. Garages approved by the Automobile Protection Association (APA) or members of the Canadian Automobile Association (CAA) usually do a good job. CAA inspections run from $100 to $150 for non-members. Remember, if you get a bum steer from an independent testing agency, you can get the inspection fee refunded and hold the garage responsible for your subsequent repairs and consequential damages, like towing, missed work, or a ruined vacation.

Appendix II
TWENTY GAS-SAVING TIPS

Before we tell you how you can cut your fuel costs, let's first explain why government fuel economy figures are always much better than the gas mileage you can count on.

Drivers are rightfully complaining that their real-world gas mileage is about 15 percent less than the "official" estimates given by Transport Canada and the U.S. Environmental Protection Agency (EPA). These figures are regularly included in published and online car guides, are posted on the window stickers of nearly every vehicle sold, and are showcased in automakers' advertising. Few people know that fuel economy tests are carried out primarily by the automakers under optimal conditions. The government retests 10–15 percent of the vehicles to keep the manufacturers honest, but motorists still complain their cars burn more fuel than advertised.

Ethanol: A "Rat-Hole"

Ethanol fuel is another "smart" government idea that has turned out to be a rat-hole down which Canadian and American taxpayers have poured billions of dollars. Several years ago, *Lemon-Aid* warned readers that ethanol would not save fuel and most certainly wouldn't make for a greener planet. Now we have confirmation that we were right in an article filed by Canwest News Service on October 2, 2009; it quotes a confidential memo sent to Natural Resources

Minister Lisa Raitt by her deputy minister that says E85 fuel (85 percent ethanol and 15 percent ordinary gasoline) will do no good. In fact, Canwest concludes that E85 will bring no actual reductions in total greenhouse gas emissions, but will cost Canadian taxpayers $2.2 billion in federal subsidies, plus more from provinces—especially Ontario.

E85 has other drawbacks: You will pay more at the pump, despite huge subsidies given out to fuel companies by Ottawa; it burns 30 percent more fuel in cold weather; it's highly corrosive and requires rust-resistant tankers, storage tanks, pumps, and auto components; and in all of Canada, there are only four gas stations where you can buy E85. That means the estimated 300,000 E85 flex-fuel vehicles on the road today will likely never get near a filling station that can refuel their vehicle with the right product.

In the meantime, Canada's auto industry and its dealers are tuning FFVs to run on gasoline because they know widespread ethanol use will never happen and they don't want customers complaining that their cars' engines run poorly with gasoline.

Okay, now that we know ethanol and ethanol-fuelled vehicles aren't what they pretend to be, here are 20 real ways to cut your fuel consumption and save money:

1. **Buy a small 4-cylinder vehicle that has good crashworthiness and reliability ratings**—Generally, a vehicle with a minimum of 100 horses will get you around town and will be suitable for light commuting duties. I criticize VW for only offering 115 horses with the 2011 Jetta because I know Jetta buyers want more performance. Still, buying a low-horsepower car will cut your fuel bills by one-third to one-half if you are downsizing from a V8 or a 6-cylinder engine—assuming that you will not load up the vehicle with fuel-burning accessories. Air conditioning and other electrical accessories will put a greater load on a vehicle's engine, and thus reduce its fuel economy.

2. **Stay away from hybrids and diesels**—You have to do a lot of driving to make a diesel or hybrid pay off. If you do go for a diesel, stay away from the ones made by Ford and GM and go with the Chrysler Cummins, but get extra powertrain protection. All three Detroit automakers have chronic diesel-injector problems on their trucks and SUVs, covered by secret repair warranties. And the situation won't get better. GM stopped its truck production for four months in 2010 to install more-complicated urea-injecting emissions components on its diesel-equipped trucks. Hybrids are expensive, aren't as frugal as they pretend to be, keep you a captive customer, can be costly to service, and may be life-threatening. For example, only 60 volts across the chest can injure or kill, and a hybrid's NiMH battery can produce 270 volts. Furthermore, in a car accident with a hybrid, if the NiMH battery cable is damaged, heavy sparking can start a fire, toxic chemicals may be released, and the EMT rescuers must put on heavy rubber gloves before touching the car to extract passengers and get the car ready for towing. Getting this important NiMH battery information about hybrids from car

dealers can be very difficult. There is also an economic angle: If your NiMH battery has an eight-year warranty, its replacement cost could almost equal the cost of the gasoline you saved. Interestingly, Nissan is thinking of selling separate battery pack leases for its Leaf electric car in order to strengthen the car's residual value as it nears the eight-year mark.

3. **Order a manual-transmission-equipped vehicle**—With rare exceptions, manual transmissions save fuel. How much depends on factors including the vehicle's size, the owner's driving style, and traffic conditions. Another benefit to manual transmissions is that they make you a more alert driver because you have to be constantly aware of traffic conditions in order to gear down to a stop or shift to accelerate. Interestingly, only 12 percent of the vehicles on North American highways use manual transmissions. In Europe, it's just the opposite—over 90 percent of drivers choose a manual gearbox.

4. **Get an automatic transmission with more gears**—If you choose an automatic, remember that a 5-speed tranny saves you more fuel than a 4-speed. Some high-end cars actually have 7-speed transmissions, and 8-speeds are being considered.

5. **Don't buy a 4×4 vehicle**—You will burn more fuel whether or not the 4×4 feature is engaged, because of its extra weight and gearing.

6. **Be wary of the cruise control**—It's a good idea to hold a steady speed on flat terrain, but if you're driving in a hilly area, the cruise control can actually make your gas mileage worse. In hilly conditions, if traffic permits, it's better to let the vehicle slow down a little on the uphill sections and then gain the speed back on the downhill side. If you use the cruise control in these conditions, it will floor the accelerator if necessary to keep your speed constant while going uphill.

7. **Use the AC sparingly**—Don't turn on the air conditioner as your first response to heat. Start your drive by slowly accelerating with the windows open to exhaust the hot air out of the rear windows, and then put on the AC if needed. This tactic will also enable the air conditioning to work faster and more efficiently when it is turned on. Having the AC off and the windows open will not save gas, however. Furthermore, driving any vehicle with a window or sunroof open will likely produce a painful roar in the cabin and cause excessive vibration in the steering.

8. **Keep your vehicle aerodynamic**—Resist the urge to attach accessories like roof racks, spoilers, and cargo carriers that hamper a vehicle's aerodynamics. Incidentally, pickup truck drivers won't save fuel by lowering the tailgate when driving on the highway. With the gate closed, air flows across the top of the bed and does not get caught by the tailgate. The airflow patterns are less efficient with the tailgate open or removed.

9. **Use the Internet to find cheap gas**—Websites like *www.GasBuddy.com* will show you which stations are selling cheaper fuel, sometimes up to 10 cents less than the average price. The Internet can also be helpful in calculating your real-world gas mileage and savings—*www.sciencemadesimple.net/fuel_economy.php* is an easy-to-use site to try.

10. **Use regular-grade fuel**—Unless the engine "knocks," using a higher-octane fuel than what is recommended by the manufacturer is foolish. Using

premium fuel when the engine doesn't require it will not cause it to get better fuel consumption, and it may damage your emissions-control system. Some high-mileage vehicles, however, may need high-octane fuel if they "ping" (spark knocking) heavily on regular gas. Light knocking on acceleration is not a problem, but if the knocking continues at a constant speed, or if it's very loud, move up to a higher-octane fuel until it stops. Persistent, heavy knocking reduces an engine's efficiency and can damage it in extreme cases.

11. **Shop by price, not brand**—Gas is gas, and many different brands buy from the same refineries. Buy gasoline during the coolest time of day—early morning or late evening is best. During these times, gasoline is densest. Keep in mind that gas pumps measure volumes of gasoline, not densities of fuel concentration. It is also a smart idea to use credit cards that give cardholders cash rebates based on a percentage of their purchases.

12. **Coddle your throttle**—New vehicles don't usually attain their top mileage until they're broken in, which occurs at about 5,000–8,000 km of fairly gentle driving. Avoid the prolonged warming-up of the engine on cold mornings—30–45 seconds is plenty of time. Also, don't start and stop the engine needlessly. Idling your engine for one minute consumes the amount of gas equivalent to the gas used when you start the engine. Avoid revving the engine, especially just before you switch the engine off; this wastes fuel needlessly and washes oil down from the inside cylinder walls, leading to the loss of oil pressure and premature wear. Lead-footed acceleration, heavy braking, and high-speed driving all increase gas consumption. The EPA estimates that jackrabbit starts and sudden stops can reduce fuel economy by as much as a third.

13. **Drive economically**—Driving at 110 km/h instead of 90 km/h will lower your car's fuel economy by 17 percent. Driving at fast rates in low gears can consume up to 45 percent more fuel than necessary. Don't worry about whether windows are open or closed—tests carried out by *Consumer Reports* and others find it doesn't make any difference. Use only your right foot for both accelerating and braking. That way you can't accidentally ride the brake and use excessive gas.

14. **Get regular tune-ups, and change the oil and air filter frequently**—Don't let the Car Care Council and other trade groups convince you that more frequent tune-ups or adjustments will increase gas mileage. Once again, test findings show that the payoff is small—simply follow the instructions in the owner's manual. Malfunctioning emissions components, however, can burn lots of fuel. Have them "scope-checked" periodically by an independent garage, which will usually charge less than the dealer. Keep the brakes properly adjusted, since dragging brakes increases resistance. Check your gas cap—one out of every five vehicles on the road has a gas cap that is either damaged, loose, or missing altogether, which allows gas in your tank to vaporize.

15. **Be tire-smart**—Inflate all tires to their maximum limits, and don't believe all the extended tire durability and fuel-saving claims made by sellers of nitrogen gas used in tire inflation. Each tire should be periodically spun, balanced, and checked for unevenness. Remove the spare tire; instead, keep a cell phone

handy and join CAA. Changing a tire beside the road puts your life at risk, and it's a pain in the butt.

16. **Fight excess weight**—Remove excess weight from the trunk or the inside of the car, including extra tires, minivan back seats, and unnecessary heavy parts. Don't drive with a full fuel tank. Remember, carrying an extra 45 kg (100 lb.) in the trunk of your car may cut your car's fuel economy by 1–2 percent. An empty roof rack may cut fuel economy by 10 percent; fully loaded, it can reduce gas mileage by 18 percent. The further you run with the tank closer to empty, the further you run in a lighter car, thereby increasing the fuel mileage. Ideally, you never want to fill your tank more than a quarter- or half-tank full.

17. **Stay away from gas-saving gadgets**—They don't work, and they may cancel the manufacturer's warranty. Instead, park your car in the shade to reduce fuel evaporation, and buy a good windshield shade to keep the interior cool. Parking in your garage will help your car stay warm in winter and cool in summer, and you won't have to depend as much on your gas-guzzling air conditioning when you drive.

18. **Carpool**—Carpools reduce travel monotony and gas expenses—all riders chip in to help you buy. Conversation helps to keep the driver alert. Pooling also reduces traffic congestion.

19. **Consolidate trips**—Combine several short errands into one trip, and combine private errands with business trips as a tax write-off.

20. **Fill up in the States**—Plan your trips to the States to include a fill-up on your return leg. Fuel costs a heck of a lot less there than it does in Canada.

Appendix III

INTERNET INFO

Recent surveys show that close to 80 percent of car buyers get reliability and pricing information from the Internet before visiting a dealer or private seller. This trend has resulted in easier access to confidential price margins, secret warranties, and lower prices—if you know where to look.

Getting the Lowest Price

If you want a low price and abhor dealership visits and haggling, search out a reliable new- or used-car broker. For years, *Lemon-Aid* has recommended Dealfinder, an Ottawa-based auto broker that helps clients across Canada. Go to *www.dealfinder.com* for all of the particulars. Ottawa-based Bob Prest, a small broker who believes in big discounts, has helped many people find great deals:

> To: Bob Prest <dealfinder@magma.ca>, August 30, 2010.
>
> Thank you so much! We picked up our new RAV4 today and are happy with the process. The salesman we had talked to previously took care of the details and we were pleased that he was not cut out of the transaction. Yet I know from past experience that we could never have negotiated such a good price... Thanks to Phil as well. His book was a big help.

For those readers who feel comfortable negotiating all of the transaction details with the dealer themselves, here's what to do: First, compare a new vehicle's "discounted" MSRP prices published on the automaker's website with invoices downloaded from the Automobile Protection Association (*www.apa.ca*), the Canadian Automobile Association (CAA, *www.caa.ca*), and a host of other agencies. Second, check the prices you find against the ones listed in this book. Third, pay particular attention to the prices charged in the States by accessing the automaker's U.S. website—just type the company name into Google and add "USA." For example, "GM USA" will take you directly to the automaker's American website, whereas "GM Canada" gives you the Canadian headquarters, models, and prices. If you find the U.S. price is substantially lower than what Canadian dealers charge, take your U.S. printout to the Canadian dealers and ask them to come closer to the American price. There is no reason why you should pay more in Canada. And this includes freight and pre-delivery inspection fees.

Confidential Reliability Info

Unearthing reliability information from independent sources on the Internet takes a bit more patience. You should first wade through the thousands of consumer complaints logged in the NHTSA database at *www.safercar.org*. Next, use the NHTSA and ALLDATA service bulletin databases to confirm a specific problem's existence, find out if it's caused by a manufacturing defect, and learn how to correct it. Augment this information with tips found on car forums and protest/information sites. *Lemon-Aid* does this for you in its guides, but you can stay current about your vehicle's problems or research a particular failure in greater depth on your own by using the above search methods.

Automobile companies have helpful—though self-serving—websites, most of which feature detailed sections on their vehicles' histories and research and development, as well as all sorts of information of interest to auto enthusiasts and bargain hunters. For example, you can generally find out the amount of the freight fee before you even get to the dealership; sales agents generally prefer to hit you with this charge at the end of the transaction when your guard is down. Manufacturers can easily be accessed through a search engine like Google or by typing the automaker's name into your Internet browser's address bar followed by ".*com*" or ".*ca*". Or for extra fun and a more balanced presentation, type the vehicle model or manufacturer's name into a search engine, followed by "lemon," "problems," or "lawsuits."

Consumer Protection

Automobile Consumer Coalition (*www.carhelpcanada.com*)
Founded by former director of the Toronto Automobile Protection Association Mohamed Bouchama, the ACC's Car Help Canada website provides many of the same services as does the APA; however, the ACC is especially effective in Ontario and Alberta and uses a network of honest garages and dealers to help members get honest and fair prices for vehicles and repairs. The ACC has been particularly successful in getting new legislation enacted in Ontario and obtaining refunds for its members.

Automobile Protection Association (*www.apa.ca*)
A motherlode of honest, independent, and current car-buying information, the non-profit APA has been protecting Canadian motorists for over 40 years from its offices in Toronto and Montreal. This dynamic consumer group fights for safer vehicles for consumers and has exposed many scams associated with new-vehicle sales, leasing, and repairs. For a small fee, it will send you the invoice price for most new vehicles and help you out if you get a bad car or dealer. The APA also has a useful free online guide for digging out court judgments.

BBC TV's *Top Gear* (*www.topgear.com*)
Britain's automotive equivalent to CBC TV's *Marketplace*, *Top Gear* showcases the best and blows the whistle on the worst European-sold vehicles, auto products, and industry practices. Now that many new cars are being imported from Europe, it's prudent to find out how well they have performed in other countries. *Which?* and *What?* are two British-based product review magazines that also give out useful performance and reliability information on most cars sold in Europe. *Which?* is published by the non-profit British Consumers Association—much like

Consumer Reports' relationship with Consumers Union. All three magazines want you to subscribe before giving you detailed reviews. However, if you go to their online press releases, you will usually be able to get the info you need relating to their test findings.

Canadian Driver (*www.canadiandriver.com*)
This website simply gets better and better. It's an exceptionally well-structured and current Canadian website for new- and used-vehicle reviews, MSRPs, and consumer reports. Other car magazine websites:

- *Automotive News (www.autonews.com)*
- *Autonet.ca (www.autonet.ca)*
- *Car and Driver (www.caranddriver.com)*
- *Motor Trend (www.motortrend.com)*
- *Road & Track (www.roadandtrack.com)*
- *World of Wheels (www.wheels.ca)*

Canadian Legal Information Institute (*www.canlii.org*)
Be your own legal "eagle" and save big bucks. Use this site to find court judgments from every province and territory all the way up to the Supreme Court of Canada.

CBC TV's *Marketplace* (*www.cbc.ca/marketplace*)
Marketplace has been the CBC's premier national consumer show for almost forever. Staffers are dedicated to searching out scammers, airbag dangers, misleading advertising, and unsafe, poor-quality products. Search the archives for auto info, or contact the show's producers to suggest program ideas.

Class Actions in Canada (*www.classproceedings.ca*)
After successfully kicking Ford's rear end over its front-end thick film ignition (TFI) troubles and getting a million-dollar out-of-court settlement, this powerhouse Ontario-based law firm got a similar settlement from GM as compensation for a decade of defective V6 intake manifold gasket failures. Estimated damages were well over a billion dollars. The firm has also worked with others to force Liberty Mutual and other insurers to refund money paid by policy holders who were forced to accept accident repairs with used, reconditioned parts instead of new, original-equipment parts.

Class Actions in the U.S. (*www.lawyersandsettlements.com*)
This is a useful site if you want to use a company's class action woes in U.S. jurisdictions as leverage in settling your own Canadian claim out of court. If you decide to go the Canadian class action route, most of the legal legwork will have been done for you. The site is easy and free to search. Just type in the make of the vehicle you're investigating and read the results.

Competition Bureau Canada (*www.competitionbureau.gc.ca*)
The Competition Bureau is responsible for the administration and enforcement of the *Competition Act*, the *Consumer Packaging and Labelling Act*, the *Textile Labelling*

Act, and the *Precious Metals Marking Act*. Its role is to promote and maintain fair competition so that Canadians can benefit from lower prices, increased product choices, and quality services.

Most auto-related complaints submitted to the Bureau concern price-fixing and misleading advertising. After *Lemon-Aid*, the APA, and Mohamed Bouchama from the ACC submitted formal complaints to Ottawa against Toyota's Access pricing program a few years ago, the automaker settled the case for $2.3 million. The Bureau agreed to drop its inquiry into charges that the automaker rigged new car prices.

Almost 28 years earlier, an APA complaint forced GM to pay a $20,000 fine for lying in newspaper ads, touting the Vauxhall Firenza's triumphant cross-Canada "reliability run." The cars constantly broke down, and one auto journalist brought along for the ride spilled the beans to Ottawa probers. GM took the car off the market shortly thereafter.

Consumer Affairs (*www.consumeraffairs.com/automotive/manufacturers.htm*)
Expecting some namby-pamby consumer affairs site? You won't find that here. It's a "seller beware" kind of website, where you'll find the scandals before they hit the mainstream press.

***Consumer Reports* and Consumers Union** (*www.consumerreports.org/cro/cars.htm*)
It costs $5.95 (U.S.) a month to subscribe online, but *CR's* database is chock full of comparison tests and in-depth stories on products and services. The group's $29.95 New Car Price service is similar to what the APA offers, except for one caveat: *Consumer Reports* charges more than double the $14 U.S. it charges American subscribers for the service. As a former Consumers Union board member, I find this practice both insulting to the magazine's loyal Canadian fans and totally unjustified when you consider that the Canadian dollar is almost at parity with the American greenback.

***Protégez-Vous* (Protect Yourself)** (*www.protegez-vous.qc.ca*)
Quebec's French-language monthly consumer protection magazine and website is a hard-hitting critic of the auto industry. *Protégez-Vous* has supported the APA in testing dealer honesty and ratings of new and used cars in Quebec and throughout Canada. The magazine publishes dozens of test-drive results as well as articles relating to a broad range of products and services sold in Canada.

Supreme Court of Canada (*scc.lexum.umontreal.ca/en/index.html*)
It's not enough to have a solid claim against a company or the government. Supporting your position with a Supreme Court decision also helps. Three pro-consumer judgments rendered in February 2002 are particularly useful:

- *Bannon v. Thunder Bay (City)*: An injured resident missed the deadline to file a claim against Thunder Bay; however, the Supreme Court maintained that extenuating factors, such as being under the effects of medication, extended her time to file. A good case to remember next time your vehicle is damaged by a pothole or you are injured by a municipality's negligence.

- *R. v. Guignard:* This judgment says you can protest as long as you speak or write the truth and you don't disturb the peace or harass customers or workers.
- *Whiten v. Pilot Insurance Co.:* The insured's home burned down, and the insurance company refused to pay the claim. The jury was outraged and ordered the company to pay the $345,000 claim, plus $320,000 for legal costs and $1 million in punitive damages, making it the largest punitive damage award in Canadian history. The Supreme Court maintained the jury's decision, calling Pilot "the insurer from hell." This judgment scares the dickens out of insurers, who fear that they might face huge punitive damage awards if they don't pay promptly.

Auto Safety

Center for Auto Safety (*www.autosafety.org*)
A Ralph Nader–founded agency that provides free online info on model-specific safety- and performance-related defects.

Crashtest.com (*www.crashtest.com*)
This website has crash-test information from around the world. You can find additional crashworthiness data for cars just recently coming on to the North American market that have been sold for many years in Asia, Europe, or Australia. The Honda Fit (Jazz), Mercedes Smart, Magna's Opel lineup, and Ford's upcoming European Fiesta and Focus imports are just a few examples.

Insurance Institute for Highway Safety (*www.iihs.org*)
A dazzling site that's long on crash photos and graphs that show which vehicles are the most crashworthy in side and offset collisions and which head restraints work best.

SafetyForum (*www.safetyforum.com*)
The 'Forum contains comprehensive news archives and links to useful sites, plus names of court-recognized experts on everything from unsafe Chrysler minivan latches to dangerous van conversions.

Transport Canada (*www.tc.gc.ca/eng/roadsafety/safevehicles-defectinvestigations-index-76.htm*)
A ho-hum site that's in no way as informative as the NHTSA or IIHS sites. You can access recalls for 1970–2010 models, but owner complaints aren't listed, defect investigations aren't disclosed, and service bulletin summaries aren't provided. A list of used vehicles admissible for import is available at *www.tc.gc.ca/roadsafety/safevehicles/importation/usa/vafus/list2/menu.htm* or by calling the Registrar of Imported Vehicles (RIV) at 1-888-848-8240.

U.S. National Highway Traffic Safety Administration (*www.safercar.gov*)
This site has a comprehensive free database covering owner complaints, recall campaigns, crashworthiness and rollover ratings, defect investigations, service bulletin summaries, and safety research papers.

Mediation/Protest

GM Inside News (*www.gminsidenews.com/forums*)
This forum is a good place to start to get a general, dispassionate feel for GM's new-car performance and technical problems.

Links to other sites include:

- GM Piston Slap (*www.pistonslap.com*): Some GM motors appear to have problems...
- GM Truck Lemon Center (*agmlemon.freeservers.com*)

Roadfly's Car Forums and Automotive Chat Rooms (*www.roadfly.org/forums*)
Another site that's no butt-kisser. Here you'll learn about BMW fan fires, upgrades, and performance comparisons. It also contains message boards for Bentley, Cadillac, Chevy, Jaguar, Lotus, Porsche, Mercedes-Benz, and others.

MyVWLemon.com (*www.myvwlemon.com*)
Lots of venting, but enough interesting and entertaining discussions to be worthwhile.

Information/Services

Alberta Government's Vehicle Cost Calculator (*www.agric.gov.ab.ca/app24/ costcalculators/vehicle/getvechimpls.jsp*)
Your tax dollars at work... This handy calculator allows you to estimate and compare the ownership and operating costs for any business or non-business vehicles. Eleven types of vehicles can be compared and the ownership cost can be calculated by modifying the input values. Alternatively, you may select the same model if you wish to compare one vehicle but with variations in purchase price, options, fuel type (diesel or gas), interest rates, or length of ownership.

ALLDATA Service Bulletins (*www.alldata.com/recalls/index.html*)
Free summaries of automotive recalls and technical service bulletins are listed by year, make, model, and engine option. You can access your vehicle's full bulletins online by paying a $26.95 (U.S.) subscription fee.

The Auto Channel (*www.theautochannel.com*)
This website gives you useful, comprehensive information on choosing a new or used vehicle, filing a claim for compensation, or linking up with other owners.

Auto Extremist (*www.autoextremist.com*)
Rantings and ravings from a Detroit insider.

Automobile News Groups
These Usenet news groups are compilations of email raves and gripes that cover all makes and models. They fall into four distinct areas: *rec.autos.makers.ford* (or you can substitute any automaker's name at the end); *rec.autos.tech*; *rec.autos. driving*; and *rec.autos.misc*. The easiest way to find these groups, if you don't have a news server, is to type the address into the Groups tab of the Google search engine.

Canadian Automobile Association (*www.caa.ca*)
The Canadian Automobile Association (CAA) performs a similar service to what the Alberta government offers. They track rising repair and maintenance costs as different vehicles age. Toronto-based DesRosiers Automotive Consultants says, by year five, the average annual repair cost of a vehicle is about $800; after seven years, expect to pay up to $1,100 annually.

CANADIAN AUTOMOBILE ASSOCIATION'S PREDICTED ANNUAL REPAIR COSTS

	2010 CHEVROLET COBALT LT	2010 DODGE GRAND CARAVAN	2010 TOYOTA PRIUS PREMIUM
Depreciation: Depreciation is heavily weighted for first four years of ownership. If you keep the car longer, cost per kilometre is reduced dramatically	0.20	0.32	0.24
Fuel: Based on $1.02/litre	0.08	0.11	0.04
Maintenance/Repairs/Tires	0.05	0.05	0.04
Licence/Registration: Based on $200/ year	0.01	0.01	0.01
Cost to finance: Based on 6.25% interest rate and a 10% down payment on a four-year loan	0.04	0.05	0.06
Cost of government (13% HST)	0.04	0.05	0.05
Insurance: Based on typical insurance coverage with no young drivers	0.06	0.10	0.11
Total ownership cost/km over first four years	0.47	0.69	0.54
Total annual ownership cost: Based on driving 18,000 km/year	**$8,539.94**	**$13,833.85**	**$10,877.69**

Figures in this chart are dollars per kilometre. Most surprising are the total amounts spent each year and the high cost of the Toyota Prius Hybrid, a vehicle billed as a "money saver." Apparently, what the hybrid gives in fuel savings, it more than takes back in depreciation.

Kelley Blue Book and Edmunds (*www.kbb.com; www.edmunds.com*)
Prices and technical info are American-oriented, but you'll find good reviews of almost every vehicle sold in North America—plus there's an informative readers' forum.

Online Metric Conversions (*www.sciencemadesimple.net/conversions.html*)
A great place to instantly convert gallons to litres, miles to kilometres, etc.

Phil Bailey's Auto World (*www.baileycar.com*)
Phil Bailey owns his own garage and specializes in the diagnosis and repair of foreign cars, particularly British ones. He's been advising Montreal motorists for years on local radio shows and has an exceptionally well-written and informative website.

Straight-Six.com (*www.straight-six.com*)
Okay, for you high-performance aficionados, here's a website that doesn't idolize NASCAR, Earnhardt, or the Porsche Cayenne SUV (they call it the "Ca-Yawn").

Women's Garage (*www.womensgarage.com*)
Three Canadian mechanics with a combined 100 years' experience set up this site to take the mystery out of maintaining and repairing vehicles. Don't be deterred by the site's title—men will learn more than they'll care to admit.

Finally, here are a number of other websites that may be helpful:

- *forum.freeadvice.com*
- *www.lexusownersclub.com*
- *www.benzworld.org/forums*
- *www.bmwboard.com*
- *www.bmwnation.com*
- *www.carforums.com/forums*
- *www.consumeraffairs.com/automotive/ford_transmissions.htm*
- *www.datatown.com/chrysler*
- *www.epa.gov/otaq/consumer/warr95fs.txt*
- *www.flamingfords.info*
- *www.ford-trucks.com/forums*
- *www.hotbimmer.net*
- *www.ptcruiserlinks.com*
- *www.troublebenz.com/my_opinion/actions/links.htm*
- *www.vehicle-injuries.com*

CROSS-BORDER SHOPPING

Every time the loonie goes up in value, thousands of Canadians buy their new or used car across the border in the United States, where vehicles are 10 to 25 percent cheaper. For example, the Canadian dollar traded at par with the U.S. dollar in July 2008, and that year Canadian shoppers imported a record 240,000 vehicles from the United States into Canada. Imports slowed to a trickle in the first quarter of 2009 when the dollar dropped well below 90 cents (U.S.) (then, only 18,800 vehicles were imported). But, now with the Canadian dollar's value once again flying high, Canadian buyers are again flocking to dealer showrooms in the States. And, when you consider that most Canadians live within an hour's drive of the border, it's clear that getting a cross-border bargain is easier than ever.

Furthermore, dealers on both sides of the border are hungry for sales and aren't likely to knuckle under automaker pressure to refuse warranty repairs or service on cars purchased in the States, as they attempted to do a few years ago. Also, Transport Canada has made it easier to import new and used cars from the States, and businesses on both sides of the border have sprung up to facilitate purchases for Canadians.

Shopping Tips

Reported savings range from around 10 percent for subcompact and compact vehicles, compact SUVs, and small vans to over 25 percent in the luxury vehicle segment. Most manufacturers honour the warranty, and many dealers and independent garages will modify cars to Canadian standards, including speedometer and odometer labels, child tether anchorage, daytime running lights, French airbag labels, and anti-theft immobilization devices. Some will complete the import paperwork for you. Again, whether it's worthwhile importing a car from the U.S. is a personal decision. Keep in mind that there may be a few extra costs to consider. For instance, if the vehicle was not made in North America, you have to pay duty to bring it into Canada. Normally, the duty for cars is 6.2 percent of the value of the vehicle. There are also excise taxes on vehicles weighing more than 2,007 kg (4,425 lb). A listing of Canadian border crossing spots where you can bring in a just-purchased new or used car can be found at *www.ucanimport. com/Border_Crossing_Info.aspx*.

Consumer groups like Montreal-based Cars Without Borders and the Automobile Protection Association (*www.apa.ca*) say buying a car in the States as part of your vacation trip and driving it back to Canada or using an auto broker is a sure money-saver and easy to do. Canadian dealers say it's unpatriotic and not fair to dealers, and that U.S. cars have softer paint and weaker batteries.

Canadian independent new- and used-car dealers aren't buying that argument; they are some of the biggest buyers of used cars in the States. For example, Advantage Trading Ltd. in Burnaby, B.C. (one of the largest importers on the West Coast) says they can get U.S. cars so cheaply that they can offer discounts to Canadians and still make a handsome profit. The only downside is that there is a shortage of some popular makes and models.

If you do decide to import a vehicle on your own, Transport Canada suggests you use the Registrar of Imported Vehicles' comprehensive and easy-to-follow checklist of things you must do (*www.riv.ca/ImportingAVehicle.aspx*). It covers:

- What to do before importing a vehicle
- What to do at the border
- What to do after the vehicle enters Canada
- What RIV fees will be applied
- Who to contact for vehicle import questions, including contact information for the Canada Border Services Agency (CBSA)

This list is all you need to import almost any car and get big savings. There are also independent resources listed at *www.riv.ca/HelpfulLinks.aspx* and *www. importcartocanada.info/category/faq*. The latter site goes into even greater detail by answering these questions:

- Why buy a vehicle in the U.S. and import it into Canada?
- What are the differences between Canadian and U.S. vehicle MSRP prices?
- Why are vehicle prices so much higher in Canada than in the U.S.?
- What vehicles can be imported into Canada?
- How long does it take to import a vehicle into Canada from the U.S.?
- What should I watch out for when purchasing a vehicle to import into Canada?
- What types of modifications are needed to import a vehicle into Canada?
- What kinds of documents do I need to import a vehicle into Canada?
- Do I have to pay tax when I import a vehicle into Canada from the U.S.?
- Do I have to pay duty when I import a vehicle into Canada from the U.S.?
- Is there anyone that can import the vehicle into Canada for me?
- Can I drive my U.S. vehicle into Canada without notifying U.S. Customs?
- Where can I cross the border to import a vehicle into Canada?
- What do I do at the border?
- What should I do when I arrive at home in Canada with my new vehicle?
- What happens if my vehicle fails federal inspection?
- What is a recall clearance letter?
- Can I import a vehicle into Canada that is over 15 years old?
- How do I import a vehicle into Canada from a country other than the U.S.?
- Which vehicle manufacturers honour warranties on vehicles imported into Canada?

Where to Go

AutoCanada Income Fund (*www.autocan.ca*) specializes in cross-border shopping through 22 dealerships located across Canada, offering thousands of vehicles for sale. Currently, AutoCanada sells all makes of new and used vehicles through the following dealers:

Alberta

- Capital Chrysler Jeep Dodge, Edmonton
- Crosstown Chrysler Jeep Dodge, Edmonton
- Grande Prairie Chrysler Jeep Dodge, Grande Prairie
- Grande Prairie Hyundai, Grande Prairie
- Grande Prairie Mitsubishi, Grande Prairie
- Grande Prairie Nissan, Grande Prairie
- Grande Prairie Subaru, Grande Prairie
- Ponoka Chrysler Jeep Dodge, Ponoka
- Sherwood Park Hyundai, Sherwood Park

British Columbia

- Maple Ridge Chrysler Jeep Dodge, Maple Ridge
- Maple Ridge Volkswagen, Maple Ridge
- Northland Chrysler Jeep Dodge, Prince George
- Northland Hyundai, Prince George
- Northland Nissan, Prince George
- Okanagan Chrysler Jeep Dodge, Kelowna
- Victoria Hyundai, Victoria

Manitoba

- Thompson Chrysler Jeep Dodge, Thompson

New Brunswick

- Moncton Chrysler Jeep Dodge, Moncton

Nova Scotia

- Dartmouth Chrysler Jeep Dodge, Dartmouth

Ontario

- Cambridge Hyundai, Cambridge
- Colombo Chrysler Jeep Dodge, Woodbridge
- Doner Infiniti, Newmarket
- Doner Nissan, Newmarket

We leave the last word to Cars Without Borders (*www.carswithoutborders.com*):

> If you are shopping for a car, tires, car parts—do yourself a favor and check out the US pricing. In most cases there is an advantage and many times a LARGE benefit. At CarsWithoutBorders we are trying to help consumers to level the playing field. Companies are scaring Canadians into buying at home at higher prices but they know several hundred thousand cars are imported from the USA every year, so it is something that is doable and worthwhile.

SECRET WARRANTIES AND CONFIDENTIAL SERVICE BULLETINS

Many 2010–11 models appear in confidential documents that show which cars, trucks, vans, and SUVs have major failings that are covered by secret warranties or special service bulletins. In this section, we provide examples of the latest secret warranties and service bulletin alerts that cover major failures affecting a large number of vehicles. Remember to bring a copy of the appropriate bulletin to the dealer to use as leverage in getting free extended warranty repairs for what the automaker admits is a factory-related problem.

AUTOMAKER CONTACT INFORMATION

Chrysler Canada, Inc.	1-800-465-2001	Kia Canada, Inc.	1-877-542-2886
	1-800-387-9983	Land Rover Group Canada, Inc.	1-800-346-3493
	(Quebec)	Mazda Canada, Inc.	1-800-263-4680
Ford Motor Company of Canada, Ltd.	1-800-565-3673	Mercedes-Benz Canada, Inc.	1-800-387-0100
General Motors of Canada, Ltd.	1-800-263-3777	Nissan Canada, Inc.	1-800-387-0122
	(English)	Porsche Cars Canada, Ltd.	1-800-545-8039
	1-800-263-7854	Subaru Canada, Inc.	1-800-894-4212
	(French)	Suzuki Canada, Inc.	905-889-2677
	1-800-263-3830		ext 2254
	(TTY)	Toyota Canada, Inc.	1-888-869-6828
Honda Canada, Inc.	1-888-946-6329		(Toyota)
	(Honda)		1-800-265-3987
	1-888-922-8729		(Lexus)
	(Acura)	Volkswagen Canada, Inc.	1-800-822-8987
Hyundai Auto Canada	1-800-461-8242		(Volkswagen)
	(English)		1-800-822-2834
	1-800-461-5695		(Audi)
	(French)	Volvo Cars Canada, Ltd.	1-800-663-8255
Jaguar Canada, Inc.	1-800-668-6257		

Chrysler

AUTOMATIC TRANSMISSION SHIFT LEVER INTERLOCK SPRING

BULLETIN NO.: K16   DATE: AUGUST 2010

2007–08 Dodge Avenger, Chrysler Sebring Convertible and Sedan

SUBJECT: The transmission gear shift lever interlock spring retainer hook on about 278,000 of the above vehicles may break. A broken interlock spring retainer hook will result in the inability to move the gear shift lever out of the "PARK" position.

REPAIR: The transmission gear shift lever interlock spring retainer hook must be inspected. Hooks that do not pass the inspection criteria must have a steel reinforcement clip installed.

Ford

FUEL INJECTOR REPLACEMENT

BULLETIN NO.: 09B08   DATE: AUGUST 24, 2009

2008–09 F-250 through F-550 Vehicles Equipped with a 6.4L Diesel Engine

PROGRAM TERMS: This dealer bulletin is being republished with an expiration date of August 21, 2010, to further encourage dealers and customers to have this service performed as soon as possible. Over time, some fuel injectors may develop leaks that can lead to engine damage.

REASON FOR THIS PROGRAM: In some of the affected vehicles, fuel injector o-rings can prematurely wear. As a result, fuel may leak into the crankcase causing the oil level to rise. High oil levels can cause drivability concerns and ultimately lead to engine damage.

General Motors

TEMPORARY REDUCTION IN POWER BRAKE ASSIST IN EXTREME COLD WEATHER

BULLETIN NO.: 09051A   DATE: AUGUST 25, 2010

2009 Buick Enclave; 2009 Chevrolet Traverse; 2009 GMC Acadia; 2009 Saturn Outlook

THIS PROGRAM IS IN EFFECT UNTIL June 20, 2011.

CONDITION: Certain model year Buick Enclave, Chevrolet Traverse, GMC Acadia, and Saturn Outlook vehicles that are operated in temperatures of –5° to –49°F (–21° to –45°C) may have a condition in which the power brake assist may be temporarily reduced. In these extreme cold temperatures, the opening of one or both of the power brake booster vacuum check valves may be delayed, resulting in reduced power brake assist. As the valve(s) warm, which could take more than 1 minute, the valve operation returns to normal and full power brake assist returns.

EXTENDED CATALYTIC CONVERTER WARRANTY COVERAGE

BULLETIN NO.: 08300   DATE: JUNE 11, 2009

2006–07 Pontiac Solstice; 2007 Saturn Sky, Equipped with 2.4L Engine

CONDITION: Some customers of 2006–07 model year Pontiac Solstice vehicles, and 2007 model year Saturn Sky vehicles, equipped with a 2.4L engine (LE5), may comment on illumination of the malfunction indicator lamp (MAL) and/or lack of engine power. This may be caused by failure of the catalytic converter.

SPECIAL COVERAGE ADJUSTMENT: This special coverage covers the condition described above for a period of 10 years or 120,000 miles (193,000 km), whichever occurs first, from the date the vehicle was originally placed in service, regardless of ownership. Dealers/retailers are to replace the catalytic converter. The repairs will be made at no charge to the customer. Customers should not be charged for performing a system check when it is determined that the catalytic converter is not the cause of the customer complaint. Labor code T5722 is provided to submit claims for such system checks.

POWER STEERING ASSIST

BULLETIN NO.: 10183   DATE: JULY 20, 2010

2005–06 Chevrolet Malibu, Malibu Maxx; 2008 Chevrolet Malibu, Malibu Maxx; 2005–06 Pontiac G6; 2008 Pontiac G6; 2008 Saturn Aura

CONDITION: Some customers of 2005–06 model year Chevrolet Malibu, Malibu Maxx, Pontiac G6 vehicles, and 2008 model year Chevrolet Malibu, Malibu Maxx, Pontiac G6, and Saturn Aura vehicles equipped with electrical power steering may experience a loss of power steering assist caused by electrical input signals within the steering column assembly. If the power steering assist is lost, a chime will be heard and the Driver Information Center will display a "Power Steering" warning message. On some vehicles, the Service Vehicle Soon light will also illuminate. The vehicle can still be steered in a safe manner but will require greater driver effort at low vehicle speeds or when stopped.

SPECIAL COVERAGE ADJUSTMENT: This special coverage covers the condition described above for a period of 10 years or 100,000 miles (160,000 km), whichever occurs first, from the date the vehicle was originally placed in service, regardless of ownership. On 2005 & 2006 model year vehicles, dealers/retailers are to replace the steering column. On 2008 model year vehicles, dealers/retailers are to replace the power steering motor control module. The repairs will be made at no charge to the customer.

FUEL ODOUR OR SPOTTING ON GROUND—REPLACE FUEL PUMP MODULE

BULLETIN NO.: 09275A
DATE: MARCH 3, 2010

2006 Chevrolet Cobalt; 2006 Pontiac G4; 2006 Saturn Ion; 2007 Chevrolet Cobalt; 2007 Pontiac G5; 2007 Saturn Ion

CONDITION: Some 2006 model year Chevrolet Cobalt, Pontiac G4, and Saturn Ion vehicles originally sold or currently registered in Alabama, Arkansas, California, Florida, Georgia, Hawaii, Louisiana, Mississippi, North Carolina, New Mexico, Oklahoma, South Carolina, Tennessee, and Texas, and some 2007 model year Chevrolet Cobalt, Pontiac G5, and Saturn Ion vehicles originally sold or currently registered in Alabama, Arkansas, Georgia, Hawaii, Louisiana, Mississippi, North Carolina, New Mexico, Oklahoma, South Carolina, and Tennessee may have a condition in which the plastic supply or return port on the modular reservoir assembly (MRA) may crack. If either of these ports develop a crack, fuel will leak from the area. The customer may notice a fuel odor while the vehicle is being driven or after it is parked. If the crack becomes large enough, fuel may be observed dripping onto the ground and vehicle performance may be affected.

SPECIAL COVERAGE ADJUSTMENT: This special coverage covers the condition described above for a period of 10 years or 120,000 miles (193,000 km), whichever occurs first, from the date the vehicle was originally placed in service, regardless of ownership. Dealers are to replace the fuel pump module. The repairs will be made at no charge to the customer.

Honda

ENGINE BLOCK

BULLETIN NO.: 10-048
DATE: AUGUST 17, 2010

BACKGROUND: On some 2006–08 and early production 2009 Civics, the engine (cylinder) block may experience engine coolant leaks, resulting in overheating. To increase customer confidence, American Honda is extending the warranty to 8 years from the original date of purchase, with no mileage limit.

PAINT PEELING ON DARK BLUE 2003–05 ODYSSEYS

BULLETIN NO.: 08-031
DATE: MAY 21, 2008

BACKGROUND: American Honda is extending the warranty for Alabama-produced 2003–05 Odysseys with dark blue (midnight blue pearl, B-518P) paint. On potentially affected vehicles, the exterior paint may peel off the horizontal (flat) surfaces and in recessed areas around the glass or the sliding doors. Because of this possible problem, the following areas of exterior paint are now covered for 7 years, with no mileage limit:

- Roof (including under the top edge of the tailgate, under the top edge of the sliding glass doors, and the top panel of the sliding doors)
- Hood
- Top half of the quarter panels
- Top half of the fenders

NOTE: All other painted areas are covered by the normal warranty of 3 years or 36,000 miles [57,900 kilometres], whichever occurs first

MODEL INDEX

MODEL INDEX